Purchasing and Supply Management

With 50 Supply Chain Cases

The McGraw-Hill /Irwin Series Operations and Decision Sciences

OPERATIONS MANAGEMENT

Bowersox, Closs, and Cooper,
Supply Chain Logistics Management,
First Edition

Burt, Dobler, and Starling,
Purchasing and Supply Management,
Seventh Edition

Chase and Jacobs,
Operations Management for Competitive Advantage,
Eleventh Edition

Davis and Heineke,
Operations Management: Integrating Manufacturing and Services,
Fifth Edition

Davis and Heineke,
Managing Services,
First Edition

Finch,
OperationsNow,
Second Edition

Flaherty,
Global Operations Management,
First Edition

Fitzsimmons and Fitzsimmons,
Service Management,
Fourth Edition

Gehrlein,
Operations Management Cases,
First Edition

Gray and Larson,
Project Management,
Second Edition

Harrison and Samson,
Technology Management,
First Edition

Hill,
Manufacturing Strategy: Text & Cases,
Third Edition

Hopp and Spearman,
Factory Physics,
Second Edition

Jacobs and Whybark,
Why ERP?,
First Edition

Knod and Schonberger,
Operations Management,
Seventh Edition

Lambert and Stock,
Strategic Logistics Management,
Third Edition

Melnyk and Swink,
Value-Driven Operations Management,
First Edition

Moses, Seshadri, and Yakir,
HOM Operations Management Software,
First Edition

Nahmias,
Production and Operations Analysis,
Fifth Edition

Nicholas,
Competitive Manufacturing Management,
First Edition

Olson,
Introduction to Information Systems Project Management,
Second Edition

Pinto and Parente,
SimProject: A Project Management Simulation for Classroom Instruction,
First Edition

Schroeder,
Operations Management: Contemporary Concepts and Cases,
Second Edition

Seppanen, Kumar, and Chandra,
Process Analysis and Improvement,
First Edition

Simchi-Levi, Kaminsky, and Simchi-Levi,
Designing and Managing the Supply Chain,
Second Edition

Stevenson,
Operations Management,
Eighth Edition

Vollmann, Berry, Whybark, and Jacobs,
Manufacturing Planning & Control Systems,
Fifth Edition

BUSINESS STATISTICS

Aczel and Sounderpandian,
Complete Business Statistics,
Fifth Edition

ALEKS Corporation,
ALEKS for Business Statistics,
First Edition

Alwan,
Statistical Process Analysis,
First Edition

Bowerman and O'Connell,
Business Statistics in Practice,
Third Edition

Bowerman, O'Connell, and Orris,
Essentials of Business Statistics,
First Edition

Bryant and Smith,
Practical Data Analysis: Case Studies in Business Statistics, Volumes I, II, and III

Cooper and Schindler,
Business Research Methods,
Eighth Edition

Delurgio,
Forecasting Principles and Applications,
First Edition

Doane,
LearningStats CD Rom,
First Edition, 1.2

Doane, Mathieson, and Tracy,
Visual Statistics,
Second Edition, 2.0

Gitlow, Oppenheim, Oppenheim, and Levine,
Quality Management,
Third Edition

Lind, Marchal, and Wathen,
Basic Statistics for Business and Economics,
Fifth Edition

Lind, Marchal, and Wathen,
Statistical Techniques in Business and Economics,
Twelfth Edition

Merchant, Goffinet, and Koehler,
Basic Statistics Using Excel for Office XP,
Third Edition

Kutner, Nachtsheim, Neter and Li,
Applied Linear Statistical Models,
Fifth Edition

Kutner, Nachtsheim, and Neter,
Applied Linear Regression Models,
Fourth Edition

Sahai and Khurshid,
Pocket Dictionary of Statistics,
First Edition

Siegel,
Practical Business Statistics,
Fifth Edition

Wilson, Keating, and John Galt Solutions, Inc.,
Business Forecasting,
Fourth Edition

Zagorsky,
Business Information,
First Edition

QUANTITATIVE METHODS AND MANAGEMENT SCIENCE

Hillier and Hillier,
Introduction to Management Science,
Second Edition

Purchasing and Supply Management

With 50 Supply Chain Cases

Thirteenth Edition

Michiel R. Leenders, D.B.A., PMAC Fellow

Leenders Purchasing Management Association of Canada Chair, Professor of Purchasing Management Emeritus Richard Ivey School of Business The University of Western Ontario

P. Fraser Johnson, Ph.D.

Associate Professor, Operations Management, Richard Ivey School of Business The University of Western Ontario

Anna E. Flynn, Ph.D., C.P.M.

Vice President Institute for Supply Management (formerly NAPM)

Harold E. Fearon, Ph.D., C.P.M.

The National Association of Purchasing Management Professor Emeritus and Founder and Director Emeritus Center for Advanced Purchasing Studies Arizona State University

Boston Burr Ridge, IL Dubuque, IA Madison, WI New York San Francisco St. Louis
Bangkok Bogotá Caracas Kuala Lumpur Lisbon London Madrid Mexico City
Milan Montreal New Delhi Santiago Seoul Singapore Sydney Taipei Toronto

The McGraw·Hill Companies

PURCHASING & SUPPLY MANAGEMENT: WITH 50 SUPPLY CHAIN CASES
Published by McGraw-Hill/Irwin, a business unit of The McGraw-Hill Companies, Inc., 1221 Avenue of the Americas, New York, NY, 10020.

This book is printed on acid-free paper.

2 3 4 5 6 7 8 9 0 DOC/DOC 0 9 8 7 6

ISBN-13: 978-0-07-287379-5
ISBN-10: 0-07-287379-5

Editorial director: *Brent Gordon*
Executive editor: *Richard T. Hercher, Jr.*
Editorial assistant: *Lee Stone*
Senior marketing manager: *Douglas Reiner*
Senior media producer: *Victor Chiu*
Project manager: *Harvey Yep*
Senior production supervisor: *Sesha Bolisetty*
Design coordinator: *Cara David*
Senior media project manager: *Susan Lombardi*
Developer, Media technology: *Brian Nacik*
Cover design: *Cara David*
Typeface: *10/12 Times New Roman*
Compositor: *International Typesetting and Composition*
Printer: *R. R. Donnelley*

Library of Congress Cataloging-in-Publication Data

Purchasing and supply management : with 50 supply chain cases / Michiel R. Leenders . . .
[et al.].— 13th ed.
p. cm.
Includes bibliographical references and indexes.
ISBN 0-07-287379-5 (alk. paper)
1. Industrial procurement. 2. Materials management. I. Leenders, Michiel R.
HD39.5.L43 2006
658.7′2—dc22 2004065550

www.mhhe.com

Brief Contents

Table of Contents

Chapter 3
Supply Processes 58

Chapter 4
Information Systems and Technology 90

Chapter 5
Quality, Specification, and Service 115

Chapter 8
Price 197

Chapter 9
Cost Management, Discounts, and Negotiation 234

Chapter 10
Supplier Selection 255

Chapter 14
Global Supply 370

Chapter 15
Public Supply Management 398

About the Authors

Michiel R. Leenders is the Leenders Purchasing Management Association of Canada Chair and Professor Emeritus at the Richard Ivey School of Business at the University of Western Ontario. He received a degree in mining engineering from the University of Alberta, an MBA from the University of Western Ontario, and his doctorate from the Harvard Business School. Mike has written a large number of articles in a variety of magazines and journals. His texts have been translated into ten different languages and include: *Value-Driven Purchasing: The Key Steps in the Acquisition Process* (with Anna E. Flynn), published by Irwin Professional Publishing; *Reverse Marketing, The New Buyer–Supplier Relationship* (with David Blenkhorn), published by the Free Press; *Improving Purchasing Effectiveness through Supplier Development,* published by the Harvard Division of Research; and *Learning with Cases, Writing Cases, and Teaching with Cases* with James A. Erskine and Louise Mauffette-Leenders, published by the Richard Ivey School of Business. He also has co-authored nine editions of *Purchasing and Supply Management,* published by McGraw-Hill/Irwin. Mike has taught and consulted extensively both in Canada and internationally. He was the educational advisor to the Purchasing Management Association of Canada from 1961 to 1994. He received PMAC's Fellowship Award in 1975, the PMAC Chair in 1993, the Financial Post Leaders in Management Education Award in 1997, and the Hans Ovelgönne Purchasing Research Award in 2001. He is the director of the Ivey Purchasing Managers Index and a director of the ING Bank of Canada.

P. Fraser Johnson is a graduate of the Honors Business Administration Program at the Richard Ivey School of Business at the University of Western Ontario. Following graduation, Fraser worked in the automotive parts industry, where he held a number of senior management positions in both finance and operations. He returned to the Richard Ivey School of Business in 1991, where he earned an MBA and a PhD, specializing in Supply and Operations Management. After receiving his doctorate, Fraser joined the Faculty of Commerce at the University of British Columbia, where he taught supply chain management, logistics, transportation, and operations. He returned to the Richard Ivey School of Business in 1998, where he is currently an associate professor, teaching operations management, purchasing and supply management, and logistics, and has won several teaching awards. Fraser is an active researcher in the area of purchasing and supply management. He is the author of a significant number of articles that have been published in a wide variety of magazines and journals, and also has authored many teaching cases. In recognition of his ongoing research, Fraser was awarded the National Association of Purchasing Management Senior Research Fellowship in June 1999. Fraser has taught and consulted in both Canada and the United States. He has delivered a number of management seminars and has actively worked with the Purchasing Management Association of Canada in developing material for the PMAC Accreditation Program.

Anna E. Flynn, vice president and Institute for Supply Management (formerly NAPM) associate professor, provides subject matter and instructional design expertise to the educational product development team at the ISM and teaches supply management seminars and courses. Anna was senior lecturer and director of the undergraduate program in Supply Chain Management (SCM) at Arizona State University from January 1993 to May 2000. She developed corporate relationships with recruiters, acted as the academic and career advisor to undergraduates, and taught Purchasing and Supply Management and Research and Negotiation. The SCM program consistently received the highest ratings from students in the College of Business for teaching, as well as academic and career advising, areas for which Anna was directly responsible. For three consecutive years, Anna was one of 11 out of 2,000 faculty awarded a Faculty Appreciation Award. Recipients were singled out by graduating seniors as having had the greatest impact on their lives during their time at ASU. Anna is co-author of the NAPM Supply Management Knowledge Series Volume IV, *The Supply Management Leadership Process* (2000); is co-author of *Value-Driven Purchasing: Managing the Key Steps in the Acquisition Process* (1995); and has worked on three earlier editions of *Purchasing and Supply Management.* She earned a bachelor's degree in international studies from the University of Notre Dame and an MBA and a PhD, both from Arizona State University.

Harold E. Fearon is the National Association of Purchasing Management Professor Emeritus and former Chairman, Purchasing, Transportation and Operations Department, Arizona State University. Hal was the founder of the Center for Advanced Purchasing Studies (CAPS) and its director for the first nine years. He is now a member of the CAPS Board of Trustees. He is a graduate of Indiana University (BS with distinction and MBA) and Michigan State University (PhD in Business Administration). He is founding editor, and continues to serve as editor emeritus, of *The Journal of Supply Chain Management,* the scholarly quarterly in the purchasing/materials management area, and has published more than 450 articles in business and academic journals. Hal is also co-editor-in-chief of the fifth edition of *The Purchasing Handbook,* published by McGraw-Hill. Hal has authored and co-authored a significant number of texts, including *Purchasing Research in American Industry,* published by the American Management Association; five editions of *Fundamentals of Production/Operations Management,* published by West Publishing Company; and seven editions of *Purchasing and Supply Management,* published by McGraw-Hill/Irwin. Hal has been active as a lecturer and consultant both in North America and internationally. He received the President's Award from the National Association of Purchasing Management in 1991 and the J. Shipman Gold Medal Award, NAPM's highest honor, in 1992. In 2000 he was presented the Hans Ovelgönne Purchasing Research Award by the International Federation of Purchasing and Materials Management in recognition of his worldwide contributions to the profession.

Preface

Purchasing and supply management has become increasingly visible in a world where supply is a major determinant of corporate survival and success. Supply chain performance influences not only operational and financial risks but also reputational risk. Extending the supply chain globally into developing countries places new responsibilities on supplier and supply, not only to monitor environmental, social, political, and security concerns but also to influence them. Thus, the job of the supply manager of today goes way beyond the scope of supply chain efficiency and value for money spent to search for competitive advantage in the supply chain. Cost containment and improvement represent one challenge, the other is revenue enhancement. Not only must the supply group contribute directly to both the balance sheet and the income statement, it also must enhance the performance of other members of the corporate team. Superior internal relationship and knowledge management needs to be matched on the exterior in the supply network to assure the future operational and strategic needs of the organization will be met by future markets. The joy of purchasing and supply management lives in the magnitude of its challenges and the opportunities to achieve magnificent contributions.

For more than 70 years, this text and its predecessors have championed the purchasing and supply management cause. Based on the conviction that supply and suppliers have to contribute effectively to organizational goals and strategies, this and previous editions have focused on how to make that mission a reality.

Thus, the examples in the text and over 50 supply chain cases afford the chance to apply the latest research and theoretical developments in the field to real-life issues, opportunities, decisions, and problems faced by practitioners. Continuing advances in MIS and technology provide new ways to improve supply efficiency and effectiveness. New security, environmental, and transparency requirements and the search for meaningful supply metrics have further complicated the challenges faced by supply managers all over the world.

New chapters on insourcing and outsourcing, cost management, and negotiation and supplier relations have increased the number of chapters. However, all chapters have been shortened so that this edition has fewer pages in total than the previous one.

Since the sixth edition of this text over 25 years ago, Harold E. Fearon has been an author of this text. As the founder of the supply chain group at Arizona State University, the first editor of the *International Journal of Supply Chain Management,* and the conceptualizer and first director of CAPS, Hal Fearon has been one of the true trailblazers of our field for decades. In this edition, Hal decided to forgo the role of an active author, although his advice and past contributions are still evident throughout this text.

A book with text and cases depends on many to contribute through their research and writing to expand the body of knowledge of the field. Thus, to our academic colleagues our thanks for pushing out the theoretical boundaries of supply management. To many practitioners, we wish to extend our gratitude for proving what works and what does not and providing their stories in the cases in this text. Also, many case writers contributed their efforts as about half of all the cases in this edition are new.

Case contributors in alphabetical order included Saud Abbasi, Kersi Antia, Collin Ashton, Louis Beaubien, Larry Berglund, Kathryn Brohman, Daniel Campbell, Maxime Charlebois, Yasheng Chen, Jorge Colazo, Nancy Dai, Joerg Dietz, Dev K. Dutta, Tony Francolini, Mobina Hassan, Niki Healey, Margot Huddart, Basil Kalymon, Marshall King, Ari Kobetz, David Koltermann, Kristina Krupka, Manish Kumar, Matthew D. Lynall, Louise Mauffette-Leenders, Leane Morfopoulos, Elizabeth O'Neil, Peruvemba Sundaram Ravi, Suhaib Riaz, Frank Tang, Tim Tattersall, Michelle Theobalds, Rob Turner, Sarah Tremblay, Mike Wade, and Asad Wali.

We have had valuable feedback from many students, colleagues, and adopters over the last several editions of the book, which have helped in revising the book. While not all suggestions were incorporated into this new edition, we wish to thank everyone for their time and consideration in forming suggestions, which were greatly appreciated. We would like to thank, in particular, Patrick Penfield of Syracuse University, O. Karl Mann of Tennessee Technological University, Udayan Nandkeolyar of The University of Toledo, and Timothy S. Vaughan of University of Wisconsin–Eau Claire for their thoughtful comments and suggestions on this 13th edition.

The production side of any text is more complicated than most authors care to admit. The original manuscript preparation largely fell to Elaine Carson, who was obviously not scared off during the previous editions. At McGraw Hill/Irwin, Dick Hercher, Lee Stone, and many others contributed to turn our efforts into a presentable text.

We also thank Mary Fisher-Smith for her valuable comments about public supply.

Kathleen Little, C.P.M., ably indexed this text and many previous editions.

The support of Dean Carol Stephenson and our colleagues at the Richard Ivey School of Business has been most welcome.

The assistance of the Purchasing Management Association of Canada and the Institute for Supply Management in supporting the continuous improvement of supply education is also very much appreciated.

Michiel R. Leenders

P. Fraser Johnson

Anna E. Flynn

Harold E. Fearon

Chapter One

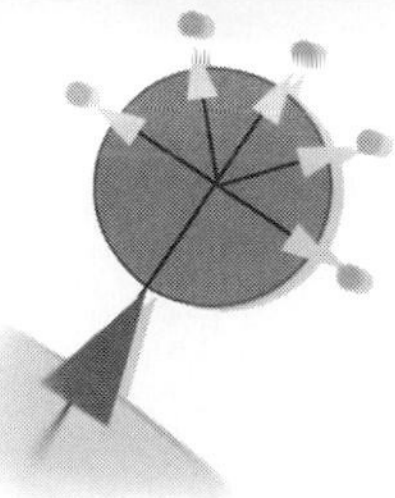

Purchasing and Supply Management

Chapter Outline

Key Questions for the Supply Manager

Should we

- Rethink how supply can contribute more effectively to organizational goals and strategies?
- Try to find out what the organization's total spend with suppliers really is?
- Calculate the effect on our organization's ROA at various purchasing savings levels?

How can we

- Get others to recognize the profit-leverage effect of purchasing/supply management?
- Determine appropriate salary levels for our purchasing personnel?
- Show how supply can affect our firm's competitive position?

Every organization on earth needs suppliers. No organization can survive without suppliers. Every organization also needs customers. Therefore, as shown in Figure 1–1 all organizations exist between suppliers and customers. The primary emphasis in this text is on the supplier side of the organization. The purchasing and supply function has primary responsibility for this side of each organization while marketing has the primary responsibility on the other side.

For more than 70 years, this text and its predecessors have presented the supply function and suppliers as critical to an organization's success, competitive advantage, and customer satisfaction. Whereas in the 1930s this was a novel idea, over the past few decades there has been growing interest at the executive level in the supply chain management and its impact on strategic goals and objectives.

FIGURE 1–1 **The Supplier–Customer Perspective of Supply**

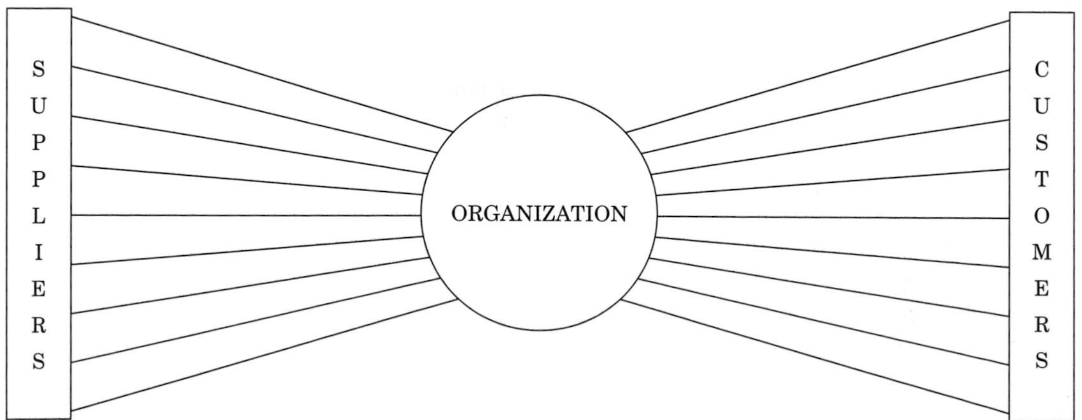

To increase long-term shareholder value, the company must increase revenue, decrease costs, or both. Supply's contribution should not be perceived as only focused on cost. Supply can and should also be concerned with revenue enhancement. What can supply and suppliers do to help the organization increase revenues or decrease costs? should be a standard question for any supply manager.

The supply function continues to evolve as technology and the worldwide competitive environment require innovative approaches. The traditionally held view that multiple sourcing increases supply security has been challenged by a trend toward single sourcing. Results from closer supplier relations and cooperation with suppliers question the wisdom of the traditional arm's-length dealings between purchaser and supplier. Negotiation is receiving increasing emphasis as opposed to competitive bidding, and longer-term contracts are replacing short-term buying techniques. E-commerce tools permit faster and lower-cost solutions, not only on the transaction side of supply but also in management decision support. All of these trends are a logical outcome of increased managerial concern with value and increasing procurement aggressiveness in developing suppliers to meet specific supply objectives of quality, quantity, delivery, price, service, and continuous improvement.

Effective purchasing and supply management contributes significantly to organizational success. This text explores the nature of this contribution and the management requirements for effective and efficient performance. The acquisition of materials, services, and equipment—of the right qualities, in the right quantities, at the right prices, at the right time, and on a continuing basis—long has occupied the attention of managers in both the public and private sectors. Today, the emphasis is on the total supply management process in the context of organizational goals and management of supply chains. The rapidly changing supply scene, with cycles of abundance and shortages, varying prices, lead times, and availability, provides a continuing challenge to those organizations wishing to obtain a maximum contribution from this area. Furthermore, environmental, security, and financial regulatory requirements have added considerable complexity to the task of ensuring that supply and suppliers provide competitive advantage.

PURCHASING AND SUPPLY MANAGEMENT

Although interest in the performance of the purchasing/supply function has been a phenomenon primarily of the 20th century, it was recognized as an independent and important function by many of the nation's railroad organizations well before 1900.

Yet, traditionally most firms regarded the purchasing function primarily as a clerical activity. However, during World War I and World War II, the success of a firm was not dependent on what it could sell, since the market was almost unlimited. Instead, the ability to obtain from suppliers the raw materials, supplies, and services needed to keep the factories and mines operating was the key determinant of organizational success. Consequently, attention was given to the organization, policies, and procedures of the supply function, and it emerged as a recognized managerial activity. During the 1950s and 1960s, supply management continued to gain stature as the number of people trained and competent to make sound supply decisions increased. Many companies elevated the chief purchasing officer to top management status, with titles such as vice president of purchasing, director of materials, or vice president of purchasing and supply.

As the decade of the 70s opened, organizations faced two vexing problems: an international shortage of almost all the basic raw materials needed to support operations and a rate of price increases far above the norm since the end of World War II. The Middle East oil embargo during the summer of 1973 intensified both the shortages and the price escalation. These developments put the spotlight directly on supply, for their performance in obtaining needed items from suppliers at realistic prices spelled the difference between success and failure. This emphasized again the crucial role played by supply and suppliers. As the decade of the 1990s unfolded, it became clear that organizations must have an efficient and effective supply function if they are to compete successfully with both domestic and international firms. In the early 21st century, the question is to what extent technology applications will change supply management, operationally as well as strategically.

In large supply organizations, supply professionals often are divided into two categories: the tacticians who need strong computer and information systems skills and the strategic thinkers who possess strong analytical and planning skills. The extent to which the structure, processes, and people in a specific organization will match these trends varies from organization to organization, and from industry to industry.

The future will see a gradual shift from predominantly defensive strategies, resulting from the need to change in order to remain competitive, to aggressive strategies, in which firms take an imaginative approach to achieving supply objectives to satisfy short-term *and* long-term organizational goals.[1] The focus on strategy now includes an emphasis on process and knowledge management. This text discusses what organizations should do today to remain competitive as well as what strategic, integrated purchasing and supply management will focus on tomorrow.

Growing management interest through necessity and improved insight into the opportunities in the supply area has resulted in a variety of organizational concepts. Terms such as *purchasing, procurement, materiel, materials management, logistics, sourcing, supply management,* and *supply chain management* are used almost interchangeably. No agreement exists on the definition of each of these terms, and managers in public and private institutions may have identical responsibilities but substantially different titles. The following definitions may be helpful in sorting out the more common understanding of the various terms.

Definitions

Some academics and practitioners limit the term *purchasing* to the process of buying: learning of the need, locating and selecting a supplier, negotiating price and other pertinent terms, and following up to ensure delivery and payment. This is not the perspective taken in this text. *Purchasing, supply management,* and *procurement* are used interchangeably to refer to the integration of related functions to provide effective and efficient materials and services to the organization. Thus, purchasing or supply management is not only concerned with the standard steps in the procurement process: (1) the recognition of need, (2) the translation of that need into a commercially equivalent description, (3) the search for potential suppliers, (4) the selection of a suitable source, (5) the agreement on order or contract details, (6) the delivery of the products or services, and (7) the payment of suppliers. Further responsibilities of purchasing may include receiving, inspection, storage,

[1] Michiel R. Leenders and David L. Blenkhorn, *Reverse Marketing: The New Buyer-Supplier Relationship* (New York: The Free Press, 1988), p. 2.

materials handling, scheduling, in- and outbound traffic, and disposal. Purchasing also may have responsibility for other components of the supply chain, such as the organization's customers and their customers and their suppliers' suppliers. This extension represents the term *supply chain management,* where the focus is on minimizing costs and times across the supply chain to the benefit of the final customer in the chain. The idea that competition may change from the firm level to the supply chain level has been advanced as the next stage of competitive evolution.

Lean purchasing or *lean supply management* refers primarily to a manufacturing context and the implementation of just-in-time (JIT) tools and techniques to ensure every step in the supply process adds value, that inventories are kept at a minimum level, and that distances and delays between process steps are kept as short as possible. Instant communication of job status is essential and shared.

The large number of physical moves associated with any purchasing or supply chain activity has focused attention on the role of logistics. According to the Council of Logistics Management, logistics is "that part of the supply chain that plans, implements, and controls the efficient, effective flow and storage of goods, services, and related information from the point of origin to the point of consumption in order to meet customers' requirements."[2] This definition includes inbound, outbound, internal, and external movements. Logistics is not confined to manufacturing organizations. It is relevant to service organizations and to both private- and public-sector firms.

The term *integrated logistics* is used by logistics proponents as equivalent to our definition of purchasing and supply management. Whether an organization chooses to separate logistics from supply management or not, clearly both functions are essential to a well-functioning, fully integrated supply system.

The attraction of the logistics concept is that it looks at the material flow process as a complete system, from initial need for materials to delivery of finished product or service to the customer. It attempts to provide the communication, coordination, and control needed to avoid the potential conflicts between the physical distribution and the materials management functions.

Supply and Logistics

Supply influences a number of logistics-related activities, such as how much to buy and inbound transportation. With an increased emphasis on controlling materials flows, the supply function must be concerned with decisions beyond supplier selection and price. As a result, some companies combine purchasing and logistics into a single organization.

Such was the case at Texas Instruments (TI) in 1999. TI had separate warehousing facilities for incoming and outgoing products all over the world. Benchmarking with companies like Wal-Mart revealed better options, including outsourcing, and the plan became to reduce all distribution centers to four: one in Utrecht (the Netherlands), one near Dallas, one in Singapore, and one near Tokyo. The decision was also made to have all centers part of the worldwide procurement and logistics organization whereas, formerly, some of the regional warehouses had reported to local managers outside the logistics function. The last move in this consolidation occurred in Japan at the end of 1999. TI used to own its own trucks, but it was also decided that this function should be outsourced. Mr. K. Bala, senior vice president

[2] Council of Logistics Management (CLM), "Definition of Logistics," http://www.clml.org, March 2001.

at TI, summed up the transformation of TI's logistics activities: "We moved from a situation where inbound and outbound transportation was handled separately from procurement. The warehouses were in local control. We have combined our logistics activities to create one seamless process, with control of our logistics service providers supervised by purchasing."[3]

Supply-chain management is a systems approach to managing the entire flow of information, materials, and services from raw materials suppliers through factories and warehouses to the end customer. The Institute for Supply Management (ISM) glossary defines *supply chain management* as "The design and management of seamless, value-added processes across organizational boundaries to meet the real needs of the end customer. The development and integration of people and technological resources are critical to successful supply chain integration."[4]

The term *value chain* has been used to trace a product or service through its various moves and transformations, identifying the costs added at each successive stage.

Some academics and practitioners believe the term *chain* does not properly convey what really happens in a supply or value chain and they prefer to use the term *supply network* or *supply web*.

The use of the concepts of purchasing, procurement, supply, and supply chain management will vary from organization to organization. It will depend on (1) their stage of development and/or sophistication, (2) the industry in which they operate, and (3) their competitive position.

The relative importance of the supply area compared to the other prime functions of the organization will be a major determinant of the management attention it will receive. How to assess the materials and services needs of a particular organization in context is one of the purposes of this book. Over 50 cases are provided to provide insight into a variety of situations and to give practice in resolving managerial problems.

THE SIZE OF AN ORGANIZATION'S SPEND AND FINANCIAL SIGNIFICANCE

The amount of money organizations spend with suppliers is staggering. Collectively, private and public organizations in North America spend about 1.5 times the GDPs of the United States, Canada, and Mexico combined, totaling at least $18 trillion U.S. Dollars spent with suppliers as a percentage of total revenue are a good indicator of supply's financial impact. In almost all manufacturing organizations, the supply area represents by far the largest single category of spend, ranging from 50 to 85 percent of revenue. Wages, by comparison, typically amount to about 10 to 20 percent.

According to Dave Nelson, former vice president of purchasing at Honda of America, "One of the reasons that Honda recognizes the importance of the purchasing function is that 80 percent of the cost of a car is purchased cost. So how goes purchasing is how goes Honda."[5] When an automobile producer sells a new car to a dealer for $18,000, it already

[3] Michiel R. Leenders and P. Fraser Johnson, *Major Changes in Supply Chain Responsibilities* (Tempe, AZ: Center for Advanced Purchasing Studies, 2001).

[4] Institute for Supply Management, "Glossary of Key Purchasing and Supply Terms," http://www.ism.ws

[5] Cherish Karoway, "The Power of Influence: Do We Have It?" *Purchasing Today*, January 1998, p. 32.

has spent more than $10,800 (about 60 percent) to buy the steel, tires, glass, paint, fabric, aluminum, copper, and electronic components necessary to build that car.

Obviously, the percentage of revenue that is paid out to suppliers varies from industry to industry and organization to organization. The increasing use of outsourcing over the last decade has increased the percentage of spend significantly. While in service organizations that are highly labor intensive this percentage might be close to 30 percent, the average for manufacturing firms is close to 65 percent.

The financial impact of the corporate spend is often illustrated by the profit-leverage effect and the return-on-assets effect.

Profit-Leverage Effect

The profit-leverage effect of supply savings is measured by the increase in profit obtained by a decrease in purchase spend. For example, for an organization with revenue of $100,000,000, purchases of $60,000,000, and profit of $8,000,000 before tax, a 10 percent reduction in purchase spend would result in an increase in profit of 75 percent, giving a leverage of 7.5. To achieve a $6,000,000 increase in profit by increasing sales, assuming the same percentage hold, might well require an increase of $75 million in sales, or 75 percent! Which of these two options—an increase in sales of 75 percent or a decrease in purchase spend of 10 percent—is more likely to be achieved?

This is not to suggest that it would be easy to reduce overall purchase costs by 10 percent. In a firm that has given major attention to the supply function over the years, it would be difficult, and perhaps impossible, to do. But, in a firm that has neglected supply, it would be a realistic objective. Because of the profit-leverage effect of supply, large savings are possible relative to the effort that would be needed to increase sales by the much-larger percentage necessary to generate the same effect on the Profit and Loss (P&L) statement. Since, in many firms, sales already has received much more attention, supply may be the last untapped "profit producer."

Return-on-Assets Effect

Financial experts are increasingly interested in return on assets (ROA) as a measure of corporate performance. Figure 1–2 shows the standard ROA model, using the same ratio of figures as in the previous example, and assuming that inventory accounts for 30 percent of total assets. If purchase costs were reduced by 10 percent, that would cause an extra benefit of a 10 percent reduction in the inventory asset base. The numbers in the boxes show the initial figures used in arriving at the 16 percent ROA performance.

The numbers below each box are the figures resulting from a 10 percent overall purchase price reduction, and the end product is a new ROA of 28.9 percent or about an 80 percent increase in return on assets.

Reduction in Inventory Investment

Charles Dehelly, senior executive vice president at Thomson Multimedia, headquartered in Paris, France, said: "One of my great challenges is to get purchasers interested in the company's balance sheet." Mr. Dehelly was pushing for reductions in inventory investment, not only by lowering purchase price, as shown in the example in Figure 1–2, but also by getting suppliers to take over inventory responsibility and ownership, thereby, removing asset dollars

FIGURE 1–2
Return-on-Assets Factors

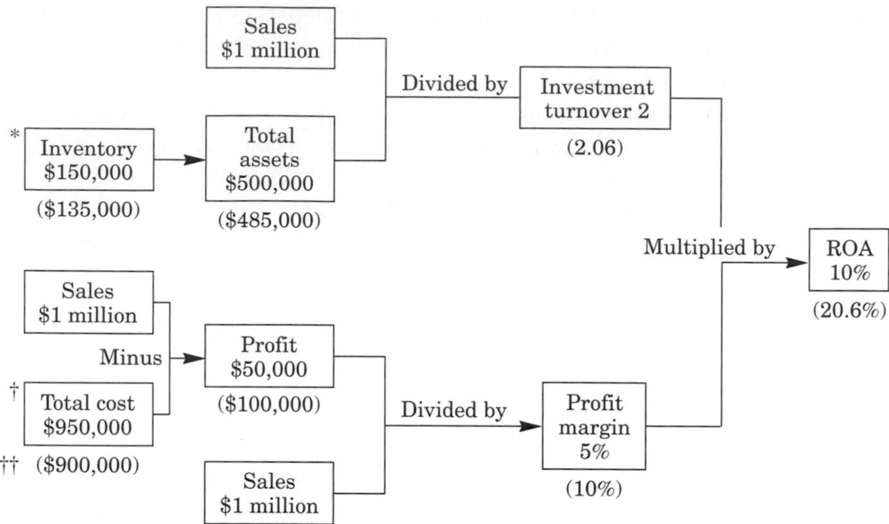

*Inventory is approximately 30 percent of total assets.
†Purchases account for half of total sales, or $500,000.
††Figures in parentheses assume a 10 percent reduction in purchase costs.

in the ROA calculations, but also taking on the risk of obsolescence and inventory carrying and disposal costs. Since accountants value inventory items at the purchaser at purchased cost, including transportation, but inventory at the supplier at manufacturing cost, the same items stored at the supplier typically have a lower inventory investment and carrying cost.

Thus, it is a prime responsibility of supply to manage the supply process with the lowest reasonable levels of inventory attainable. Inventory turnover and level are two major measures of supply chain performance.

Evidently, the financial impact of supply is on both the balance sheet and the income statement, the two key indicators of corporate financial health used by managers, analysts, financial institutions, and investors. While the financial impact of the supply spend is obviously significant, it is by no means the only impact of supply on an organization's ability to compete and be successful.

SUPPLY CONTRIBUTION

Although supply's financial impact is major, supply contributes to organizational goals and strategies in a variety of other ways. The three major perspectives on supply are shown in Figure 1–3:

1. Operational versus strategic.
2. Direct and indirect.
3. Negative, neutral, and positive.

FIGURE 1–3
Purchasing's Operational and Strategic Contributions

Source: Michiel R. Leenders and Anna E. Flynn, *Value-Driven Purchasing: Managing the Key Steps in the Acquisition Process* (Burr Ridge, IL: Richard D. Irwin, 1995), p. 7.

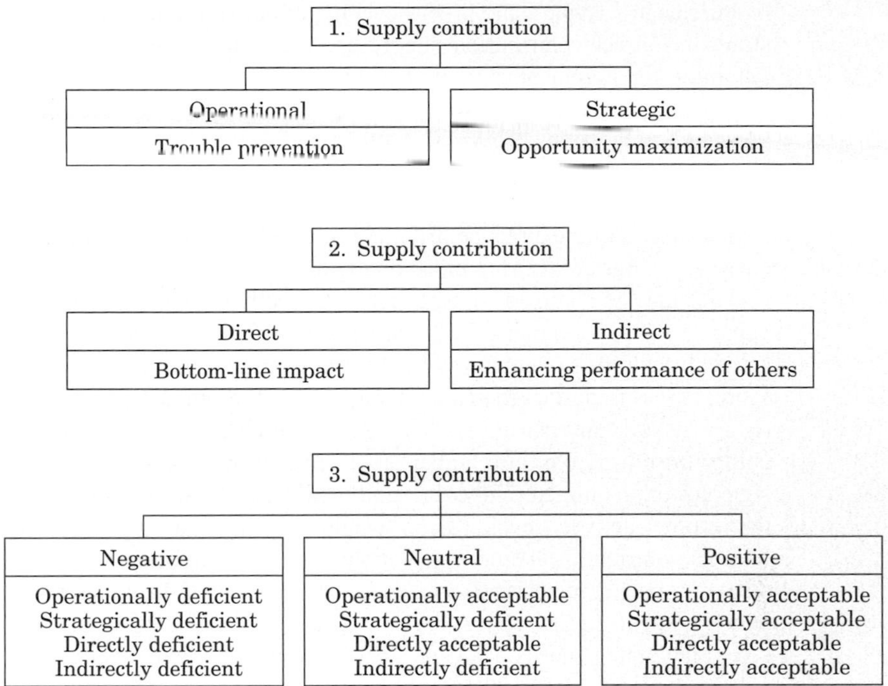

The Operational versus Strategic Contribution of Supply

First, supply can be viewed in two contexts: operational, which is characterized as *trouble avoidance,* and strategic, which is characterized as *opportunistic*.

The operational context is the most familiar. Many people inside the organization are inconvenienced to varying degrees when supply does not meet minimum expectations. Improper quality, wrong quantities, and late delivery may make life miserable for the ultimate user of the product or service. This is so basic and apparent that "no complaints" is assumed to be an indicator of good supply performance. The difficulty is that many users never expect anything more and hence may not receive anything more.

The operational side of supply concerns itself with the transactional, day-to-day operations traditionally associated with purchasing. The operational side can be streamlined and organized in ways designed to routinize and automate many of the transactions, thus freeing up time for the supply manager to focus on the strategic contribution.

The strategic side of supply is future oriented and searches for opportunities to provide competitive advantage. Whereas on the operational side the focus is on executing current tasks as designed, the strategic side focuses on new and better solutions to organizational and supply challenges. (Chapter 20 discusses the strategic side in detail.)

The Direct and Indirect Contribution of Supply

The second perspective is that of supply's potential direct or indirect contribution to organizational objectives.

Purchasing savings, the profit-leverage effect, and the return-on-assets effect demonstrate the direct contribution supply can make to the company's financial statements. Although the argument that purchasing savings flow directly to the bottom line appears self-evident, experience shows that savings do not always get that far. Budget heads when presented with savings may choose to spend this unexpected windfall on other requirements. To combat this phenomenon, some supply organizations have hired financial controllers to assure that purchasing savings do reach the bottom line.

The appeal of the direct contribution of supply is that both inventory reduction and purchasing savings are measurable and tangible evidence of supply contribution.

The supply function also contributes indirectly by enhancing the performance of other departments or individuals in the organization. This perspective puts supply on the management team of the organization. Just as in sports, the team's objective is to win. Who scores is less important than the total team's performance. For example, better quality may reduce rework, lower warranty costs, increase customer satisfaction, and/or increase the ability to sell more or at a higher price. Ideas from suppliers may result in improved design, lower manufacturing costs, and/or a faster idea-to-design-to-product-completion-to-customer-delivery cycle. Each would improve the organization's competitiveness. Indirect contributions come from supply's role as an information source; its effect on efficiency, competitive position, risk, and company image; the management training provided by assignments in the supply area; and its role in developing management strategy and social policy. The benefits of the indirect contribution may outweigh the direct contribution, but measuring the indirect benefits is difficult since it involves many "soft" or intangible contributions that are difficult to quantify.

Information Source

The contacts of the supply function in the marketplace provide a useful source of information for various functions within the organization. Primary examples include information about prices, availability of goods, new sources of supply, new products, and new technology, all of interest to many other parts of the organization. New marketing techniques and distribution systems used by suppliers may be of interest to the marketing group. News about major investments, mergers, acquisition candidates, international political and economic developments, pending bankruptcies, major promotions and appointments, and current and potential customers may be relevant to marketing, finance, research, and top management. Supply's unique position vis-à-vis the marketplace should provide a comprehensive listening post.

Effect on Efficiency

The efficiency with which supply processes are performed will show up in other operating results. While the firm's accounting system may not be sophisticated enough to identify poor efficiency as having been caused by poor purchase decisions, that could be the case. If supply selects a supplier who fails to deliver raw materials or parts that measure up to the agreed-on quality standards, this may result in a higher scrap rate or costly rework, requiring excessive direct labor expenditures. If the supplier does not meet the agreed-on delivery schedule, this may require a costly rescheduling of production, decreasing overall production efficiency, or, in the worst case, a shutdown of the production line—and fixed costs continue even though there is no output. Many supply managers refer to user departments as internal customers or clients and focus on improving the efficiency and effectiveness of the function with a goal of providing outstanding internal customer service.

Effect on Competitive Position/Customer Satisfaction

A firm cannot be competitive unless it can deliver end products or services to its customers when they are wanted, of the quality desired, and at a price the customer feels is fair. If supply doesn't do its job, the firm will not have the required materials or services when needed, of desired quality, and at a price that will keep end-product costs competitive and under control.

The ability of the supply organization to secure requirements of better quality, faster at a better price than competitors, will not only improve the organization's competitive position, but also improve customer satisfaction. The same can be said for greater flexibility to adjust to customers' changing needs. Thus, a demonstrably better-performing supply organization is a major asset on any corporate team.

A major chemical producer was able to develop a significantly lower-cost option for a key raw material that proved to be environmentally superior as well as better quality. By selling its better end product at somewhat lower prices, the chemical producer was able to double its market share, significantly improving its financial health and competitive position as well as the satisfaction of its customers.

Effect on Organizational Risk

Risk management is becoming an ever-increasing concern. The supply function clearly impacts the risk level for the organization in terms of operational, financial, and reputation risk. Supply disruptions in terms of energy, service, or direct or indirect requirements can impact the ability of the organization to operate as planned and as expected by its customers, creating operational risks.

Given that commodity and financial markets establish prices that may go up or down beyond the control of the individual purchaser, and that long-term supply agreements require price provisions, the supply area may represent a significant level of financial risk. Furthermore, unethical or questionable supply practices and suppliers may expose the organization to significant reputation risk.

Effect on Image

The actions of supply personnel influence directly the public relations and image of a company. If actual and potential suppliers are not treated in a businesslike manner, they will form a poor opinion of the entire organization and will communicate this to other firms. This poor image will adversely affect the purchaser's ability to get new business and to find new and better suppliers. Public confidence can be boosted by evidence of sound and ethical policies and fair implementation of them.

The large spend of any organization draws attention in terms of supplier chosen, the process used to choose suppliers, the ethics surrounding the supply process, and conformance to regulatory requirements. Are the suppliers chosen "clean" in terms of child labor, environmental behavior, and reputation? Is the acquisition process transparent and legally, ethically, strategically, and operationally defensible as sound practice? Do supply's actions take fully into account environmental, financial, and other regulatory requirements such as national security?

Maintaining a proper corporate image is the responsibility of every team member and supply is no exception.

Training Ground

The supply area also is an excellent training ground for new managers. The needs of the organization may be quickly grasped. Exposure to the pressure of decision making under uncertainty with potentially serious consequences allows for evaluation of the individual's ability and willingness to make sound decisions and assume responsibility. Contacts with many people at various levels and a variety of functions may assist the individual in learning about how the organization works. Many organizations find it useful to include the supply area as part of a formal job rotation system for high-potential employees.

Examples of senior corporate executives with significant supply experience include Thomas T. Stallkamp, vice chairman and CEO of MSX International, Inc., and former Chrysler president; Raymond C. Stark, vice president, Six Sigma and Productivity at Honeywell; and G. Richard Wagoner, president of General Motors' North American Operations.

Management Strategy and Social Policy

Supply also can be used as a tool of management strategy and social policy. Does management wish to introduce and stimulate competition? Does it favor geographical representation, minority interest, and environmental and social concerns? For example, are domestic sources preferred? Will resources be spent on assisting minority suppliers? As part of an overall organization strategy, the supply function can contribute a great deal. Assurance of supply of vital materials or services in a time of general shortages can be a major competitive advantage. Similarly, access to a better-quality or a lower-priced product or service may represent a substantial gain. These strategic positions in the marketplace may be gained through active exploration of international and domestic markets, technology, innovative management systems, and the imaginative use of corporate resources. Vertical integration and its companion decisions of make or buy (insource or outsource) are ever-present considerations in the management of supply.

The potential contribution of supply to strategy is obvious. Achievement depends on both top executive awareness of this potential and the ability to marshall corporate resources to this end. At the same time, it is the responsibility of those charged with the management of the supply function to seek strategic opportunities in the environment and to draw top executive attention to them. This requires a thorough familiarity with organizational objectives, strategy, and long-term plans and the ability to influence these in the light of new information. Chapter 20 discusses both potential supply contributions to business strategy *and* the major strategy areas within the supply function.

Progressive managers have recognized the potential contributions of the supply management area and have taken the necessary steps to ensure results. One important step in successful organizations has been the elevation to top executive status of the supply manager. Although titles are not always consistent with status and value in an organization, they still make a statement within and outside of most organizations. Currently, the most common title of the chief purchasing officer is vice president, followed by director and manager.

The elevation of the chief purchasing officer to executive status, coupled with high-caliber staff and the appropriate authority and responsibility, has resulted in an exciting and fruitful realization of the potential of the supply function in many companies.

DECISION MAKING IN THE SUPPLY MANAGEMENT CONTEXT

One of the appealing aspects of the supply function to its practitioners is the variety and nature of the decisions encountered. Should we make or buy? Should we inventory materials and how much? What price shall we pay? Where shall we place this order? What should the order size be? When will we require this material? Which alternative looks best as an approach to this problem? Which transportation mode and carrier should we use? Should we make a long- or a short-term contract? Should we cancel? How do we dispose of surplus material? Who will form the negotiation team and what should its strategy be? How do we protect ourselves for the future? Shall we change operating systems? Should we use reverse auctions? What should our e-commerce strategy be? Should we wait or act now? In view of the trade-offs, what is the best decision? What stance do we take regarding our customers who wish to supply us? Do we standardize? Is systems contracting worthwhile here? Should we use one supplier or multiple suppliers? Decisions such as these will have a major impact on the organization and its final customers. What makes these decisions exciting is that they almost always are made in a context of uncertainty and, therefore, entail risk.

Advances in management knowledge in recent years have substantially enlarged the number of ways in which supply decisions can be analyzed. The basic supplier selection decision is a classical decision tree model as shown in Figure 1–4. This is a choice between alternatives under uncertainty. In this example, the uncertainty relates to our own demand: We are not sure if it will be high, medium, or low. The outcome is concerned with both price and ability to supply. Does the decision maker wish to trade a higher price against

FIGURE 1–4
Simplified One-Stage Decision Tree Showing a Supplier Selection Decision

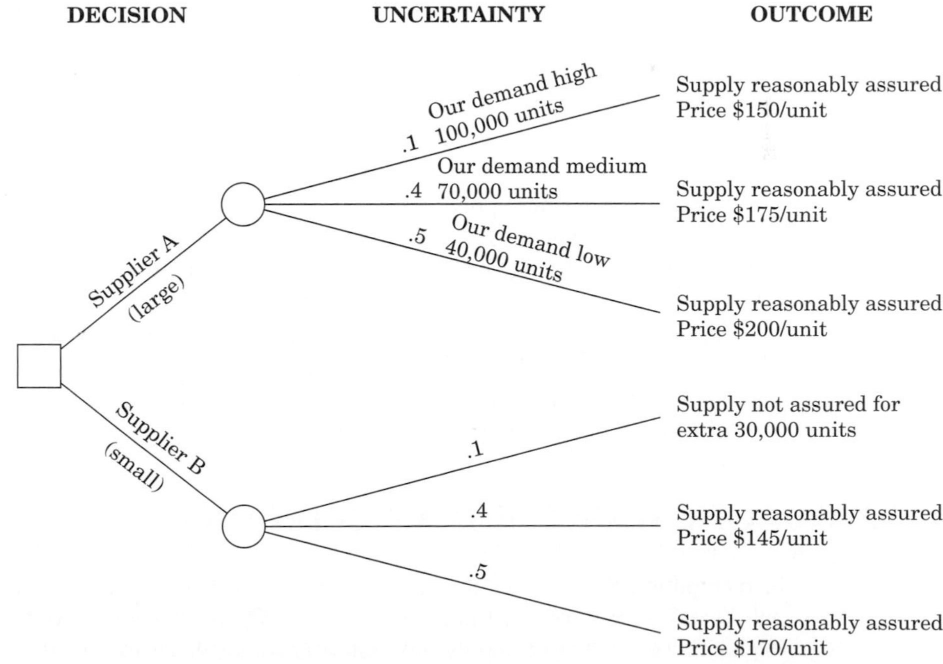

supply assurance under all circumstances? That it is difficult to quantify all consequences reinforces the need for sound judgment in key decisions. It also means that the decision maker's perception of the risk involved may in itself be a key variable. Thus, the opportunity is provided to blend managerial judgment, gained through experience and training, with the appropriate decision concepts and techniques.

THE DIFFERENCES BETWEEN COMMERCIAL AND CONSUMER ACQUISITION

Supply is a difficult function to understand because almost everyone is familiar with another version, that of personal buying. For this reason, it is easy for one to presume a familiarity or expertise with the acquisition function. A consumer point of view is characterized by a shopping basket philosophy. It assumes a retail type of marketing environment where there are many suppliers of relatively common items. Every customer buys on a current-need basis and also is the final consumer of the product or service acquired. Some price variation may occur from supplier to supplier, depending on what marketing strategy the supplier chooses to follow. The consumer has the freedom to choose the nature, quantity, and quality of items required and to choose the appropriate supplier. With some exceptions, the individual consumer has no power to influence the price, the method of marketing, or the manufacturer chosen by the supplier's management. The individual consumer's total business is a very small portion of the supplier's total sales.

Commercial supply management presents a different picture. The needs of most organizations are often specialized and the volumes of purchase tend to be large. The number of potential sources may be small, and there may be few customers in the total market. Many buying organizations are larger than their suppliers and may play a variety of roles with respect to their sources. Because large sums of money are involved, suppliers have a large stake in an individual customer and will resort to extreme measures to secure the wanted business. In such an environment, the right to award or withhold business represents real power. Special expertise is required to ensure proper satisfaction of corporate needs on the one hand and the appropriate systems and procedures on the other to ensure a continually effective and acceptable supply performance.

Suppliers spend large sums annually to find ways and means of persuading their customers to buy. Purchasing strength must be pitted against this marketing strength to ensure that the buying organization's needs now and in the future are adequately met. The supply function should be staffed with people who can deal on an equal basis with this marketing force. It is not sufficient in this environment to be only reactionary to outside pressures from suppliers. Foresight and a long-range planning outlook are vital so that future needs can be recognized and met on a planned basis.

SUPPLY QUALIFICATIONS AND ASSOCIATIONS

In recognition that the talent in supply has to match the challenges of the profession, public and private organizations as well as supply associations have taken the initiative to ensure well-qualified supply professionals are available to staff the function.

Education

Although there are no universal educational requirements for entry-level supply jobs, most large organizations require a college degree in business administration or management. Several major educational institutions, such as Arizona State University, Bowling Green State University, George Washington University, Miami University, Michigan State University, and Western Michigan University, now offer an undergraduate degree major in Purchasing/Materials/Supply/Supply Chain/Logistics Management as part of the bachelor in business administration degree. In addition, many schools offer certificate programs or some courses in purchasing, for either full- or part-time students. A number of schools, including Arizona State, Michigan State, and Howard University, also offer a specialization in supply chain management as part of a master of business administration degree program.

In Canada the Richard Ivey School of Business has offered for over 50 years a purchasing and supply course as part of its undergraduate and graduate degree offerings. Other universities such as HEC, Laval, York Queens, and Victoria have followed suit and academic interest in supply chain management is at an all-time high.

While, obviously, a university degree is not a guarantee of individual performance and success, the supply professional with one or more degrees is perceived on an educational par with professionals in other disciplines such as engineering, accounting, marketing, IT, HR, or finance. That perception is important in the role that supply professionals are invited to play on the organizational team.

Training Programs

Most larger firms now provide continuing education/training for their purchasing professionals. This training is organized on a formal, in-house seminar basis in which a given individual may participate in a variety of training sessions each year, or the firm may use a planned combination of seminars/courses offered by universities, associations, or private training organizations. This supply training then is supplemented by various general management courses and seminars.

Salary Levels

Obviously, salary levels for supply personnel vary widely dependent on duties and responsibilities, experience, educational qualifications, and type of organization. Professional magazines, such as *Purchasing* in the United States, survey salary levels annually for a variety of positions and report their findings in a special issue. Thus, salary levels can range from about $30,000 for entry-level positions without a university degree, without bonus, to over $1,000,000 for a senior vice president in a large organization with a considerable bonus in addition. It is obvious from these surveys that university graduates and those with technical degrees, like engineering, and advanced degrees, like an MBA, tend to receive significantly better compensation.

Professional Associations

As any profession matures, its professional associations emerge as focal points for efforts to advance professional practice and conduct. In the United States, the major professional association is the Institute for Supply Management (ISM), founded in 1915 as the National Association of Purchasing Agents. The ISM is an educational and research association with over 40,000 members, who belong to ISM through its more than 180 affiliated organizations in the United States.

In addition to regional and national conferences, ISM sponsors seminars for purchasing people. It publishes a variety of books and monographs and the leading scholarly journal in the field, *International Journal of Supply Chain Management,* which it began in 1965. Since the early 1930s, ISM has conducted the monthly "ISM Report on Business," which is one of the best-recognized current barometers of business activity in the manufacturing sector. In 1998, the association initiated the Nonmanufacturing ISM Report on Business. The survey results normally appear the second business day of each month on the front page of *The Wall Street Journal.* In January 2001, ISM and Forrester Research initiated the Report on e-Business, which is released every three months. Additionally, ISM and its Canadian counterpart, PMAC, work with colleges and universities to encourage and support the teaching of purchasing and supply management and related subjects and provide financial grants to support doctoral student research.

In 1974 the National Association of Purchasing Management initiated the Certified Purchasing Manager (C.P.M.) program, which tests purchasing people. On successful completion of the program, it certifies by award of the C.P.M. designation that the recipient has met the established knowledge, education, and experience standards.

In 1986 the Center for Advanced Purchasing Studies (CAPS) was established as a national affiliation agreement between ISM and the College of Business at Arizona State University. The Center has three major goals to be accomplished through its research program: (1) to improve purchasing effectiveness and efficiency, (2) to improve overall purchasing capability, and (3) to increase the competitiveness of U.S. companies in a global economy. CAPS conducts industrywide purchasing benchmarking studies; publishes a quarterly best practices publication called *Practix*; runs the annual Purchasing Executives' Roundtables in the United States, Europe, and Asia; and conducts and publishes focused purchasing research in areas of interest to industry.

In Canada, the professional association is the Purchasing Management Association of Canada (PMAC), formed in 1919. Its membership of over 7,000 is organized in 10 provincial and territorial institutes from coast to coast. Its primary objective is education, and in addition to sponsoring national conferences and publishing a magazine, it offers an accreditation program leading to the C.P.P. (Certified Professional Purchaser) designation. PMAC's accreditation program was started in 1963.

The Ivey Purchasing Managers Index (Ivey PMI) jointly sponsored by PMAC and the Richard Ivey School of Business, is the Canadian equivalent of ISM's Report on Business, but covers the complete Canadian economy.

In addition to ISM and PMAC, there are other professional purchasing associations, such as the National Institute of Governmental Purchasing (NIGP), the National Association of State Purchasing Officials (NASPO), the National Association of Educational Buyers (NAEB), and the American Society for Health Care Materials Management.

Several of these associations offer their own certification programs. Most industrialized countries have their own professional purchasing associations, for example, Institute of Purchasing and Supply Management (Australia), Chartered Institute of Purchasing and Supply (Great Britain), Indian Institute of Materials Management, and Japan Materials Management Association. These national associations are loosely organized into the

International Federation of Purchasing and Materials Management (IFPMM), which has as its objective the fostering of cooperation, education, and research in purchasing on a worldwide basis among the more than 40 member national associations representing over 200,000 supply professionals.

CHALLENGES FACING PURCHASING AND SUPPLY MANAGEMENT OVER THE NEXT DECADE

There are at least five major challenges facing the supply profession over the next decade: technology, supply chain management, measurement, growth and influence, and effective contribution to corporate success.

Technology

One of the most exciting and challenging developments to affect supply management in recent years is the advent of electronic business-to-business (B2B) commerce. New technology offers exciting opportunities to improve effectiveness and efficiency of supply management. The rapidity of technological change represents a significant challenge, however, in terms of assessment and implementation.

Supply Chain Management

The success of firms like Wal-Mart and Dell in exploiting supply chain opportunities has helped popularize the whole field of supply chain management. Nevertheless, significant challenges remain: while the giant firms in automotive, electronics, and retailing can force the various members of the supply chain to do their bidding, smaller companies do not have that luxury. Thus, each organization has to determine for itself how far it can extend its sphere of influence within the supply chain and how to respond to supply chain initiatives by others. Clearly, opportunities to reduce inventories, shorten lead times and distances, plan operations better, remove uncertainties, and squeeze waste out of the supply chain are still abundant. Thus, the search for extra value in the supply chain will continue for a considerable period of time.

Measurement

There is significant interest in better measurement of supply not only to provide senior management with better information regarding supply's contribution, but also to be able to assess the benefits of various supply experiments. No one set of measurements is likely to suffice for all supply organizations. Therefore, finding the set of measures most appropriate for a particular organization's circumstances is part of the measurement challenge.

Growth and Influence

Growth and influence in terms of the role of supply and its responsibilities inside an organization can be represented in four areas as identified in a recent CAPS study.[6] In the first place, supply can grow in the percentage of the organization's total spend for which it is meaningfully involved. Thus, categories of spend traditionally not involving purchasing

[6] Michiel R. Leenders and P. Fraser Johnson, *Major Changes in Supply Chain Responsibilities* (Tempe, AZ: Center for Advanced Purchasing Studies, 2001).

such as real estate, insurance, energy, benefit programs, part-time help, relocation services, consulting, marketing spend with advertising and media agencies, travel and facilities management, IT, and telecommunications and logistics have become part of procurement's responsibility in more progressive corporations.

Second, the growth of supply responsibilities can be seen in the span of supply chain activities under purchasing or supply leadership. Recent additions include accounts payable, legal, training and recruiting, programs and customer bid support, and involvement with new business development.

Third, growth can occur in the type of involvement of supply in what is acquired and supply chain responsibilities. Clearly, on the lowest level, there is no supply involvement at all. The next step up is a transactionary or documentary role. Next, professional involvement implies that supply personnel have the opportunity to exercise their expertise in important acquisition process stages. At the highest level, meaningful involvement, a term first coined by Dr. Ian Stuart at the University of Victoria, represents true team member status for supply at the executive table. Thus, in any major decision taken in the organization, the question "What are the supply implications of this decision?" is as natural and standard as "What are the financial implications of this decision?"

Fourth, supply can grow by its involvement in corporate activities from which it might have been previously excluded. While involvement in make-or-buy decisions, economic forecasts, countertrade, in- and outsourcing, and supplier conferences might be expected, other activities such as strategic planning, mergers and acquisitions, visionary task forces, and initial project planning might be good examples of broader corporate strategic integration.

Each of these four areas of opportunity for growth allows for supply to spread its wings and influence creation in organization and increase the value of its contributions.

Effective Contribution to Corporate Success

Ultimately, supply's measure of its contribution needs to be seen in the success of the organization as a whole. Contributing operationally and strategically, directly and indirectly, and in a positive mode, the challenge for supply is to be an effective team member. Meaningful involvement of supply can be demonstrated by the recognition accorded supply by all members of the organization.

How happy are other corporate team members to have supply on their team? Do they see supply's role as critical to the team's success? Thus, to gain not only senior management recognition but also the proper appreciation of peer managers in other functions is a continuing challenge for both supply professionals and academics.

THE ORGANIZATION OF THIS TEXT

The first four chapters of this text cover the introduction to the field, how supply is organized, standard acquisition process, and information systems and technology as applied to supply. Then the next five chapters deal with the standard supply concerns of quality and service; quantity and inventory; delivery and transportation; and price, cost, and negotiation. All of these first nine chapters are prerequisites to supplier selection, followed by disposal and law and ethics.

The following five chapters deal with metrics, global and public supply, and two major specialty categories of acquisition: capital goods and services. The last three chapters are all focused on major strategic issues: make or buy, insourcing, outsourcing, supplier relations, and strategic supply.

Conclusion

If the chief executive officer and all members of the management team can say, "Because of the kinds of suppliers we have and the way we relate to them, we can outperform our competition and provide greater customer satisfaction," then the supply function is contributing to its full potential.

This is the ambitious goal of this text: to provide insights for those who wish to understand the supply function better, whether or not they are or will be employed in supply directly.

Questions for Review and Discussion

1. What is the profit-leverage effect of supply? Is it the same in all organizations?
2. "Purchasing is not profit making; instead, it is profit taking since it spends organizational resources." Do you agree?
3. What kinds of decisions does a typical supply manager make?
4. "In the long term, the success of any organization depends on its ability to create and maintain a customer." Do you agree? What does this have to do with purchasing and supply management?
5. Is purchasing a profession? If not, why not? If yes, how will the profession, and the people practicing it, change over the next decade?
6. Differentiate between purchasing, procurement, materials management, logistics, supply management, and supply chain management.
7. In what ways might e-commerce influence the role of supply managers in their own organizations? In managing supply chains or networks?
8. In the petroleum and coal products industry, the total purchase/sales ratio is 80 percent, while in the food industry it is about 60 percent. Explain what these numbers mean. Of what significance is this number for a supply manager in a company in each of these industries?
9. How does supply management affect return on assets (ROA)? In what specific ways could you improve ROA through supply management?

References

Ballou, Ronald H. *Business Logistics/Supply Chain Management.* 5th ed. Upper Saddle River, NJ: Pearson Prentice Hall, 2004.

Burt, David N.; D. W. Dobler; and Stephen L. Starling. *World Class Supply Management.* 7th ed. New York: McGraw-Hill Irwin, 2003.

Chopra, Sunil, and P. Meindl. *Supply Chain Management.* 2nd ed. Upper Saddle River, NJ: Pearson Prentice Hall, 2004.

Handfield, R. B., and E. L. Nichols Jr. *Introduction to Supply Chain Management.* Upper Saddle River, NJ: Prentice Hall, 1998.

Hughes, Jon; Mark Ralf; and Bill Michells. *Transform Your Supply Chain.* London: Thomson, 1998.

Leenders, M. R., and A. E. Flynn. *Value-Driven Purchasing: Managing the Key Steps in the Acquisition Process.* Burr Ridge, IL: Irwin Professional Publishing, 1995.

Monczka, R.M., and R.J. Trent. *Purchasing and Sourcing Strategy: Trends and Implications.* Tempe, AZ: Centre for Advanced Purchasing Studies, 1995.

Monczka, R. M.; R. J. Trent; and R. Handfield. *Purchasing and Supply Management.* 2nd ed. Mason, OH: South-Western, 2002.

Neef, Dale. *e-Procurement*. Upper Saddle River, NJ: Prentice Hall, 2001.

Nelson, Dave; Patricia E. Moody; and Jonathan Stegner. *The Purchasing Machine*. New York: The Free Press, 2001.

Rozemeijer, Frank. *Creating Corporate Advantage in Purchasing*. Eindhoven, The Netherlands: Technische Universiteit Eindhoven, 2000.

Addresses

CAPS Research
2055 East Centennial Circle
P.O. Box 22160
Tempe, Arizona 85285-2160
http://www.capsresearch.org

Institute for Supply Management
2055 East Centennial Circle
P.O. Box 22160
Tempe, Arizona 85285-2160
http://www.ism.ws

NAEB: National Associaton of Educational Buyers Inc.
450 Wireless Boulevard
Hauppauge, NY 11788
http://www.naeb.org/index.html

PMAC: Purchasing Management Association of Canada
2 Carlton Street, Suite 1414
Toronto, Ontario M5B 1J3
Canada
http://www.pmac.ca

CIPS: Chartered Institute of Purchasing and Supply
Easton House
Easton on the Hill
Stamford, Lincolnshire, PE9 3NZ
United Kingdom
http://www.cips.org

IFPMM: International Federation of Purchasing and Materials Management
http://www.ifpmm.org

Case 1–1

Custom Equipment

It was July 2, and Matt Roberts had just been given his first assignment, the "Wire Management Program" (WMP), by the purchasing manager of Atlanta-based Custom Equipment Inc. The purpose of the WMP was to reduce the supplier base for the company's wire and cable requirements. As a newly hired purchasing agent, Matt wondered how to proceed.

CUSTOM EQUIPMENT

Custom Equipment Inc. (CE) was a relatively new division of Custom Equipment Global, a multinational electrical engineering and technology company. CE generated sales of $66 million in the past year, and had forecast growth of 25 percent for each of the upcoming four years.

CE's products were divided into assembly line equipment and press automation equipment. Assembly line products included units such as framers, in which a vehicle frame was fed onto a line and welded in specified areas. Press automation products were units built to move vehicle frames, doors, and hoods between machines already installed within the customer's assembly process. The machines were built in Atlanta, tested, approved, disassembled into sections, shipped to the customer's facility, and then re-assembled.

All machines at Custom Equipment were hand-built. Most units were unique due to the requirements of the manufacturer and the intended purpose of the machines. Each machine was comprised of steel, mechanical, electrical, and hydraulic parts. Wires and cables were purchased in lengths and installed throughout the unit. With automotive design changes occurring annually, CE was constantly reconditioning previous builds or bidding on new lines. CE prided itself on customer satisfaction. In the automotive industry, a key factor was on-time delivery of equipment required to begin production.

CE'S PURCHASING DEPARTMENT

The purchasing department at CE was composed of six purchasing agents and one manager. Responsibilities were divided into commodity groups. These groups consisted of electrical, mechanical, hydraulic/pneumatic, robots/weldguns, affiliate-produced parts/fabricated components, and steel/other metals. Matt was hired recently to replace two retiring purchasing agents.

MATT ROBERTS

Matt held an undergraduate business degree from a well-known business school. Upon graduation, Matt had worked for a year as an inventory analyst for a multinational manufacturing organization. He had applied to CE after visiting its display booth at a local manufacturing trade show. Matt was eager to make an early contribution at CE and he believed that the WMP presented an excellent opportunity.

WIRE MANAGEMENT PROGRAM (WMP)

Matt's manager had recently initiated the WMP believing that CE could improve value for all of its wire and cable requirements from volume leverage. Rationalizing the supplier base would also save time currently spent processing multiple supplier invoices. A stronger relationship could be fostered with the chosen supplier, which could help increase the priority of CE orders and open further opportunities for cost savings. Also, transportation costs could be reduced because all items would be arriving from a single source. Finally, sourcing from a single supplier would allow the purchasing agent to focus on issues involving higher dollar values.

Matt's manager had given him the impression that the WMP should be implemented before the end of October.

MANUFACTURING COMPONENTS

Last year CE's total component purchases totaled $32 million. CE had a total supplier base of 3,000 companies, of which less than 5 percent were regular suppliers. The first reason for having such a large number of suppliers was that newly hired purchasing agents usually had previously established relationships with certain suppliers. The second reason was that some suppliers specialized in certain products.

When CE was awarded a job, it needed to be thoroughly designed and tested within the engineering department's computer-aided design (CAD) system. Part of this process consisted of determining every component that would be required to complete the job. Required components, which were divided into hydraulic, mechanical, and electrical categories, were entered into a bill of materials (ingredient list). The bill of materials created a demand for specific parts within Custom Equipment's computer system. Purchasing agents identified requisitions related to their commodity group and satisfied them by creating purchase orders. There was usually some variation between actual requirements and initial expectations. When components were over-ordered, they needed to be returned to the supplier or held in inventory until a need arose. Returning products was usually time-consuming and obviously did not add any value. Keeping over-ordered material tied up company funds. When needed items were under-ordered or forgotten, they would need to be ordered immediately. Recently, many items were labeled as "rush," causing pressure on the purchasing agents to help resolve the problem through expediting.

Each assembly line and press automation product was divided into cells. Cells consisted of numerous components. Ninety-eight percent of component orders were job-specific. Some jobs were comprised of more than 10 separate cells, which entailed many engineers entering materials required for their designated cell. Certain parts were common across cells, but the entry time varied. A significant problem was that there could be numerous orders each day for 10 feet of the same wire, creating unnecessary ordering and processing costs, since each line on the purchase order had to be entered, received, and processed individually. This was often the cause of administrative problems and headaches, because a purchase order for electrical items could contain more than 100 items.

When a project-related item was received, it was kept in an unlocked receiving area until it was needed for the job. Custom Equipment's carrying costs amounted to 15 percent per annum. There were some incidences of workers "borrowing" items required for their jobs, which had not been ordered or which had not yet arrived. This created shrinkage problems, with no direct accountability. Also, in a pinch, the receiving area might issue parts from another job to one with a more urgent requirement; however, approval had to be obtained from the project manager.

The bottom line was that material availability was important because each job cell built on the previously completed cell. Missing components could significantly delay the production of later cells.

WIRES AND CABLES

Wires and cables were considered commodity products within the electrical industry. Wires were fabricated from copper rods rolled into a desired thickness and then covered with a protective coating. Cables were made by combining two or more copper wires, separated by insulation, and using an outer covering or jacket. Wire differed from cable primarily in the number of conductors, jacketing, insulation, and resistance to external factors.

Occasionally, situations arose in which a product was specified by the end-user. In these instances, CE engineers were forced to use the specified product, which might only be available through nonstandard vendors. Specified products occurred more often with motor cables than with wires.

Although current supply processes were generally accepted, Matt felt that the WMP gave him an ideal opportunity to analyze what changes would be possible. He knew, however, that buy-in from key users would be required before implementing any significant changes.

ELECTRICAL COMPONENT SUPPLIERS

Custom Equipment's wire and cable requirements for any one job were typically purchased from three to six different electrical suppliers. The suppliers' product lines contained significant overlap, which led to the desire of reducing the base to a single source. The amount of wire and cable purchased last year was approximately $700,000. Wire and cable purchases were predicted to increase at the same rate as corporate sales.

Matt asked some shop floor employees about CE's current six suppliers. The employees volunteered both positive and negative comments regarding the various suppliers. Matt considered these comments as "unofficial" past-performance reviews. However, he got the impression that some employees seemed to prefer certain suppliers because of friendships outside of work or because of similar nationalities. He was hesitant to consider all comments given due to these potential biases. He was also skeptical about some of the comments of the purchasing agents for similar reasons.

Matt discovered that the receiving manager had been keeping some records of suppliers' delivery performance for the last 30 months because of CE's ISO 9001 certification requirements. Criteria such as delivery, product returns, and overall supplier service were tracked and kept within the records of the receiving department. With these records, in conjunction with his conversations with the receiving manager, Matt believed he could develop an objective assessment of the suppliers' past performance. There had been no significant quality problems with any of CE's current suppliers according to the receiving manager. He believed that the vendors possessed relatively uniform quality.

THE NEXT STEP

Matt's boss had created the Wire Management Program to seek benefits from reducing the number of wire and cable suppliers. Matt's initial thought was that a single supplier could provide the best prices for CE's annual requirements. He realized that there were arguments both in favor and against using this approach. He would have to analyze the capabilities and managerial abilities of each company in order to reach a decision.

Matt began to think about possible methods to reduce the total number of wire and cable suppliers. CE had established strong relationships with some of the suppliers, and he therefore wanted to give all interested companies an opportunity to present their case. Whatever he chose, he would need to justify his recommendation to his manager and CE's engineers and other employees.

Case 1–2

Roger Gray

Late in the afternoon of August 23, Roger Gray, purchasing manager at Anderson Plastics, watched as his boss angrily left the room. It was the second time in a week that Roger had been blamed when the plant had run out of raw materials, and he wondered how he should address the materials management problems at the California plant.

ANDERSON PLASTICS INC.

Anderson Plastics Inc. was a large multinational supplier of plastic compounds, which constituted the raw material for a number of different plastic materials, such as polypropylenes, polyethylenes, styrenes, and nylons. These compounds were used to manufacture a variety of products, such as automotive bumpers and dashboards, helmets, packing material, and hard-shell suitcases.

The company had pursued a growth strategy, mainly through acquisitions, during the last decade. Currently, Anderson Plastics operated 13 manufacturing plants in North America, Europe, Latin America, and the Asia-Pacific region with a combined sales volume of about $1 billion. The company employed approximately 2,200 people worldwide.

ANDERSON PLASTICS

The California manufacturing plant was 110,000 sq. ft. in size and sat on about 14 acres of industrial land with access to a rail siding. A total of 74 people worked at the plant.

During the last decades, Anderson and its customers had moved to just-in-time systems (JIT), which required Anderson to work closely with customers to schedule delivery of raw materials. The result had been a trend toward lower supply chain inventories. However, this also increased the risk of stockouts, which could result in expensive downtime for Anderson's customers.

PURCHASING & MATERIALS MANAGEMENT

Until two years ago, purchasing at Anderson Plastics had been a noncentralized function, where each department was responsible for ordering its own raw materials. Because of materials management problems, such as excess inventory for some products while experiencing frequent stockouts of others, management decided to make a change. Therefore, Roger Gray, a production supervisor at the plant with 16 years' experience, was moved over to take control of a newly created centralized purchasing function for the plant.

The materials management system in place at Anderson Plastics had not yet been properly integrated with other parts of the Anderson Plastics organization or its suppliers. Roger had found the materials management system to be unreliable, frequently contributing to stockouts. While it was good at processing regular shipments, it could not handle unexpected requirements adequately. In addition, a parallel "handwritten" system was in effect, which required Gray to spend two to three hours a day filling out forms. In his first year, Gray developed a series of spreadsheet applications to automate some of the repetitive and error-prone tasks.

As the plant expanded, the number of products that Roger had to keep track of rose from 250 to 550. Even with his new spreadsheet applications, it became increasingly difficult for Roger to manage inventory levels accurately.

Roger was severely criticized when a stockout occurred, even though he believed that most of the time it was not his fault. Often, the materials management system was a couple of days behind real time and so it didn't reflect current inventory levels. At other times, transportation problems, especially the chronic unreliability of the U.S. rail system, caused shipments to be delayed. The plant only had a 10-silo capacity for raw materials and also used rail cars full of material as temporary warehouses when necessary. Roger felt that inventory levels were high, but he had never been criticized for carrying "too-much" inventory.

THE TWO RECENT INCIDENTS

Both of this week's stockouts were typical. The first had occurred because production had not informed Roger that a prime customer had suddenly ordered twice its usual requirement a week earlier and had failed to record the quantities withdrawn from inventory properly. Thus, Roger's record showed a significant amount of inventory still on hand.

Today's incident had involved a shipment by rail from Texas that should have arrived four days ago but which had been mysteriously delayed in transit. The supplier had shipped on the proper date and was not at fault.

Case 1–3

Cottrill Inc.

On November 12th, Judy Stevens, purchasing supervisor at the Cottrill Inc. plant in Columbus, Ohio, was reviewing a proposal from Saxton Wireless. Judy was dissatisfied with Cottrill's paging service from its current supplier and had been approached by Saxton about switching service providers. She knew that the sales representative at Saxton was expecting a reply later that day and needed to finalize her decision.

COTTRILL INC.

Cottrill was established in the mid-1800s and was the one of the largest corn refining operations in North America. The company operated six wet-milling plants, four in the United States and two in Canada. Cottrill was an industry leader and maintained this position by continuously developing new products, technologies, and manufacturing processes.

The Columbus plant had been operating for over 20 years and employed more than 100 people. It produced high-fructose corn syrup, starch, and glucose, which were used as supply inputs for a variety of industries including baked goods, beverages, confections, corrugating and paper, and processed foods. Cottrill competed primarily in the business-to-business segment and recognized that customers demanded both reliability and consistency.

THE PURCHASING DEPARTMENT

Cottrill's purchasing department had to ensure that the plant ran efficiently and was responsible for replenishing a variety of supplies at the plant, ranging from chemicals to communications equipment. A current initiative for Cottrill, and particularly for the purchasing department, was reducing the level of working capital. This had been a focus in the purchasing department for over two years, and the departmental target was an annual decrease of $300,000.

Judy Stevens was the purchasing supervisor at the Columbus plant and had one employee reporting to her. In general, the purchasing department had a large degree of autonomy as most decisions did not have to be cleared by Judy's boss, the plant controller.

THE PAGING SYSTEM

The majority of Cottrill's products were manufactured through a continuous flow process. Therefore, downtime at the Columbus plant was extremely costly and was estimated at $200,000 per hour. In an attempt to minimize plant downtime, management implemented an automated software program and an electronic pager system 12 years ago. The software program, called ProductionMessaging, monitored Cottrill's equipment. If an unusual condition, such as heat failure, was detected, this system automatically sent out a warning message to a pager. Pagers were grouped by process so that in the event of a malfunction, only the appropriate technicians and supervisors were notified. The plant had a total of 20 pagers, and this number included a variety of different models.

Usually one warning was experienced per week. Depending on the message sent by the system, pages could report a machine malfunction or simply inform staff about potentially anomalous machine operating statistics.

THE CURRENT SYSTEM

Cottrill initially approached Tallant, a large international wireless company, 12 years ago because they offered the only paging service that could be used in conjunction with the ProductionMessaging software system. The current contract with Tallant was open-ended and required 30 days' notice if Cottrill wished to terminate the contract. Tallant did not provide Cottrill with a designated service representative. Instead, if a problem occurred, someone would call a 1-800 number and then wait on hold until his or her call was taken to speak with a customer service representative. This process could become an issue if Cottrill was placed on hold during a plant emergency for an extended period of time.

Several recent events had caused Judy to become dissatisfied with the current arrangement with Tallant. In June, Judy contacted Tallant with a routine request to replace a broken pager. Judy was dissatisfied with Tallant's service, feeling that she spent too much time on the phone arranging the order and it took Tallant over a month to send out the replacement pager.

Judy contacted Tallant again in September to replace another pager. She was informed that Tallant no longer carried this model and that the option of renting the pager hardware would be discontinued in the near future. Judy ordered a comparable product, valued at approximately $150, but felt a little unsettled by the new information. Cottrill's budget was tight and she preferred renting this equipment instead of purchasing for cash flow reasons. Although annoyed with the disappointing level of service from Tallant, Judy was consumed with more pressing issues at Cottrill and brushed off both incidents.

THE SAXTON PROPOSAL

In late October, a Saxton sales representative, Natalie Hopkins, contacted Judy to present a proposal outlining the benefits to Cottrill of switching to Saxton's services. Saxton offered a simpler fee structure and also a lower overall cost than Tallant (see Exhibit 1). Additionally, by switching to Saxton, Judy would be able to directly access Natalie by e-mail or by phone if any service issues arose.

Although Saxton was a large wireless services company, it did not have the established reputation in the area of in-plant wireless messaging systems, nor did it have the local service history that Tallant did. Judy wondered about Saxton's current customers and was unclear whether Saxton had the necessary experience to handle the technological requirements of Cotrill's account. Tallant also required notice upon termination of the agreement, and Judy recognized that the paging service timeframes could overlap due to this constraint, effectively forcing Cottrill to pay for paging services from both companies during the transition. Additionally, if Cottrill did switch suppliers, all of the existing pager numbers would need to be changed and plant staff would need to be informed of the switch.

Since the initial meeting had gone well, both Judy and Natalie had agreed to move forward with the process and schedule a trial of Saxton's hardware. This test was

EXHIBIT 1 Per-Unit Comparison of Service Terms for Tallant and Saxton

	Tallant	Saxton
Monthly fee for airtime (per pager)	$16.95	$13.95
Monthly fee for phone number (per pager)	$1.95	None
Monthly fee for equipment rental (per pager)	$11.90	None
Yearly maintenance fee (per pager)	$60.00	None
Service provided (no additional cost)	1-800 # help line	Direct sales representative

necessary to confirm that Saxton's pagers would be compatible with the relevant applications in the ProductionMessaging software. After Judy spoke with Cottrill's systems group, a trial was scheduled for the first week in November.

Judy was not able to be present for the trial, but her contact in the systems group advised her of the events. Unfortunately, the pagers did not immediately function with the ProductionMessaging software. However, after several attempts to solve the functionality issue, Cottrill's systems group resolved the snags in the hardware and reworked the connection after completing some reprogramming. It appeared that the problem was under control, but Judy was worried about how easily the Saxton system could be implemented. Also, she was unsure about how the systems group perceived the functionality problems and if this would be an issue going forward.

DECISION CRITERIA

Judy often used a structured set of criteria to approach purchasing decisions at Cottrill. Although she had the final decision-making authority with this issue, she recognized that the systems group would have to support this switch. The systems group was primarily concerned with functionality, and providing that the Saxton product could perform to the similar level of functionality of Tallant, they would not have any objections to switching suppliers.

Judy wondered which criteria were most important to the decision of supplier selection and how these issues should be ranked. Judy knew that before a recommendation could be made, she would have to apply her evaluation framework and proposed criteria to the alternatives.

It was Monday morning, and Judy had taken some time to think about the issues of the Saxton hardware testing that had taken place the previous Friday. She had expected the trial to be executed without incident and wondered if the decision to switch suppliers was as simple as she had initially thought. Judy wanted to be certain that she had considered all of the implications involved with switching suppliers before making a decision. She knew that the change to Saxton was an option but recognized that Cottrill could also remain with Tallant, and was now wondering if there were any other alternatives. However, Judy understood that it had been nearly a week since the Saxton sales representative had presented her proposal and she was expecting Judy's response by the end of the day.

Chapter Two

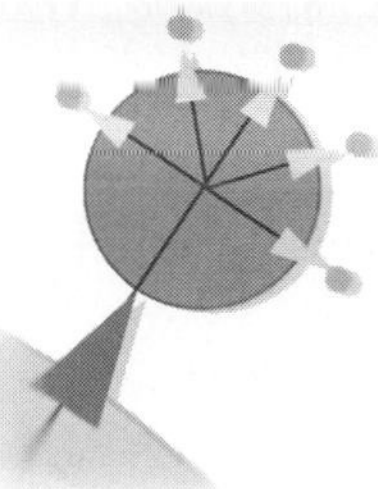

Supply Organization

Chapter Outline

Key Questions for the Supply Manager

Should we

- Separate sourcing and commodity management responsibilities?
- Use cross-functional sourcing teams to make better supply decisions?
- Move towards greater centralization?

How can we

- Fit supply's organization structure better with the structure of the corporate organization?
- Gain the maximum benefits from our organization structure?
- Structure and manage teams for effectiveness and efficiency?

Every organization in both the public and private sector is in varying degrees dependent on materials and services supplied by other organizations. No organization is self-sufficient. Even the smallest office needs space, heat, light, power, communication and office equipment, furniture, stationery, and miscellaneous supplies to carry on its activities. Purchasing and supply management is, therefore, one of the key business processes in every organization. Almost every company has a separate supply function as part of its organizational structure. One important management challenge is ensuring effective use of the resources and capabilities of the supply organization and the supply chain or network to maximize supply's contribution to organizational objectives.

Managing the balance between the competitive environment, corporate strategy, and organizational structure is an ongoing process for every company. Senior management selects strategies designed to address competitive challenges and adopts an appropriate corporate organizational structure to complement the company's strategy. The structure of supply has to be congruent with this organizationwide structure. The challenge for the chief purchasing officer (CPO) is to manage the supply organization to deliver the maximum benefits within the predefined structure. For example, a chief executive might decide that a decentralized organizational structure is appropriate in order to allow flexibility in responding to customer requirements. The supply organization also would be decentralized to the various business units to fit the corporate organizational model.

The organizational structure of the supply function influences how supply executes its responsibilities, how it works with other areas of the firm, and the skills and capabilities needed by supply personnel. Regardless of the structure adopted, work must be assigned to ensure the efficient and effective delivery of goods and services to the organization. This requires managing personnel and delegating responsibilities. Managing the people in the supply organization to their full potential is a significant challenge.

In this chapter, three questions are addressed: (1) What are the objectives of supply? (2) How might supply be organized to achieve these objectives effectively and efficiently? (3) What are the activities and responsibilities of supply management?

OBJECTIVES OF SUPPLY MANAGEMENT

The standard statement of the objectives of the supply function is that it should obtain the *right materials* (meeting quality requirements), in the *right quantity,* for delivery at the *right time* and *right place,* from the *right source* (a supplier who is reliable and will meet its commitments in a timely fashion), with the *right service* (both before and after the sale), and at the *right price* in the short and long term. The supply decision maker might be likened to a juggler, attempting to keep several balls in the air at the same time, for he or she must achieve these seven *rights* simultaneously. It is not acceptable to buy at the lowest price if the goods delivered are unsatisfactory from a quality/performance standpoint, or if they arrive two weeks behind schedule. On the other hand, the *right* price may be higher than normal if the item in question is an emergency requirement where adherence to normal lead time would result in a higher total cost of ownership. The *right price* is one aspect of lowest total cost of ownership. The supply decision maker attempts to balance the often-conflicting objectives and makes trade-offs to obtain the optimum mix of these seven rights. Obtaining this balance with an eye to both the short term and the long term requires supply managers to have both a tactical and strategic perspective.

A more encompassing statement of the overall goals of supply would include the following nine goals:

1. *Improve the organization's competitive position.* As a strategic player, the activities of supply management must be focused on contributing to overall organizational strategy, goals, and objectives. Supply managers must identify and exploit opportunities in the supply chain to contribute to revenue enhancement, asset management, and cost reduction. Supply can secure the lowest total cost source of supply, provide access to new technologies, and design flexible delivery arrangements, fast response times, access to high-quality products or services, and product design and engineering assistance. Companies that are successful in the long run must constantly look for opportunities in the supply chain to provide a superior value proposition for their customers, and supply represents a key area for such opportunities. Strategic supply is concerned with the long-term survival and prosperity of the organization. It focuses on bottom-line impact, the income statement, and the balance sheet. Chapter 20 discusses the potential contributions of purchasing and supply management to the overall strategy of the organization and specific internal supply strategies for strengthening the organization's competitive position.

2. *Provide an uninterrupted flow of materials, supplies, and services required to operate the organization.* Stockouts or late deliveries of materials, components, and services can be extremely costly in terms of lost production, lower revenues and profits, and diminished customer goodwill. For example, (1) an automobile producer cannot complete the car without the purchased tires, (2) an airline cannot keep its planes flying on schedule without purchased fuel, (3) a hospital cannot perform surgery without purchased surgical tools, and (4) an office cannot be used without purchased maintenance services.

3. *Keep inventory investment and loss at a minimum.* One way to ensure an uninterrupted material flow is to hold large inventories. But inventory assets require use of capital that cannot be invested elsewhere, and the cost of carrying inventory may be 20 to 50 percent of

its value per year. For example, if purchasing can support operations with an inventory investment of $10 million instead of $20 million, at an annual inventory carrying cost of 30 percent, the $10 million reduction in inventory represents a savings of $3 million in addition to freeing $10 million in working capital.

4. *Maintain and improve quality.* A certain quality level is required for each material or service input; otherwise the end product or service will not meet expectations or will result in higher-than-acceptable costs. The cost to correct a substandard quality input could be huge. For example, a spring assembled into the braking system of a diesel locomotive costs less than $5.00. However, if the spring turns out to be defective when the locomotive is in service, the replacement cost is in the thousands of dollars, caused by the teardown required to replace the spring, the lost revenue to the railroad because the locomotive is not in service, and the possible loss of locomotive reorders. Continuous improvement in supplier quality is directly linked to an organization's ability to compete effectively on a worldwide basis.

5. *Find or develop best-in-class suppliers.* The success of supply depends on its ability to link supply base decisions to organization strategy and its skill in locating or developing suppliers, analyzing supplier capabilities, selecting the appropriate supplier, and then working with that supplier to obtain continuous improvements. Only if the final selection results in suppliers who are both responsive and responsible will the firm obtain the items and services it needs.

6. *Standardize, where possible, the items bought and the processes used to procure them.* Standardization refers to the process of agreeing on a common specification or process. Specifications and processes may be standardized across an organization, an industry, a nation, or the world. Supply should constantly strive to standardize its capital equipment, materials, MRO, and services purchases wherever and whenever possible. For materials, standardization often leads to lower risk in the marketplace, lower prices through volume purchase agreements, and lower inventory and tracking costs while maintaining service levels. In the case of capital equipment, standardization results in reduction in MRO inventories and reduced costs for training staff on equipment operation and maintenance. In the case of services, standardization leads to supply base reduction, lower operating costs, more consistent service levels, and lower prices. Supply management process standardization also can result in shortened cycle time, lower transaction costs, and greater opportunities to share knowledge across functional and organizational boundaries. Because standardization touches on multiple stakeholders, it usually requires cross-functional and sometimes cross-organizational teamwork.

7. *Purchase required items and services at lowest total cost of ownership.* Purchased goods and services in the typical organization represent the largest share of that organization's total costs. Consequently, the profit-leverage effect discussed in Chapter 1 can be significant. Price is the most convenient method to compare competing proposals from suppliers. However, supply's responsibility is to obtain the needed goods and services at the lowest total cost of ownership, which necessitates consideration of other factors—such as quality levels, after-sales service, warranty costs, inventory and spare parts requirements, downtime, and so forth—that in the long term might have a greater cost impact on the organization than the original purchase price.

8. *Achieve harmonious, productive internal relationships.* Supply managers cannot effectively accomplish their goals and objectives without effective cooperation with the

appropriate individuals in other functions. Therefore, it is useful to examine relationships between supply and key internal business partners.

Supply and design engineering. Close to 70 percent of the value of any given requirement is established during the first few phases of the standard acquisition process: recognition and description of need. Therefore, close cooperation between design engineering and supply to assure proper specifications is essential. The design must be driven by final customer requirements for value and satisfaction, and be designed for manufacturability and procurability. It is obvious that such close liaison also needs proper involvement of marketing, operations, and finance/accounting to recognize these opportunities and constraints. It is during the design phase that all of these varied interests need to be appropriately incorporated, something that is unlikely to happen unless the various functional experts can represent their points of view well and are able to work effectively as a team. Too frequently, the failure to include supply considerations properly at the design stages results in inadequate product or service performance, costly delays, rework, and end user dissatisfaction.

Supply and operations. In most organizations, close supply–operations coordination is essential to operational excellence. In manufacturing companies especially, the total task of integrated logistics, meeting end-customer demands on the one side and using the supply networks on the other, while managing material and information flow, equipment, people, and space effectively represents an incredible challenge. Meeting quality, delivery, quantity, cost, flexibility, and continuity objectives profitably and competitively requires strategic as well as tactical skills of both operations and supply managers.

Supply and marketing/sales. Since supply and marketing are mirror images of each other, with negotiation and customer service in common, there are benefits from greater integration of the two functions. Although research indicates that supply is not typically included in marketing planning, supply and marketing often serve on new-product development teams in organizations. Supply can offer information on current and future market conditions and negotiation expertise, and marketing can keep supply up to date on marketing campaigns, special promotions, and sales forecasts and involve supply in meetings with end customers to help supply better understand customer needs. In many organizations, there is an effort to use a strategic sourcing process for spend categories such as advertising and media. This effort requires close cooperation of supply and marketing.

Supply and accounting/finance. Supply and accounting/finance interact in the areas of accounts payable, planning, and budgeting. Lack of horizontal goal alignment often leads to behavior in one area that conflicts with behavior in the other area. For example, finance/accounting may adopt a payment policy that is at odds with the payment terms of the contract. From the finance perspective, holding onto cash as long as possible is a good way to contribute to the organization's financial goals. From the supply perspective, building sound, mutually beneficial relationships with key suppliers contributes to financial performance. Supply managers often argue that accounting focuses too much on short-term gains from holding cash rather than the longer-term benefits of a strong buyer–supplier relationship that is influenced by paying according to contractual payment terms. Improved communication between supply and accounting/finance and greater goal congruence can help to alleviate some of the problems. Supply can help finance by providing funds flow forecasts, focusing on inventory minimization, and providing market information.

9. *Accomplish supply objectives at the lowest possible operating costs.* It takes resources to operate supply: salaries, communications expense, supplies, travel costs, computer costs, and accompanying overhead. The objectives of supply should be achieved as efficiently and economically as possible. Process inefficiencies represent waste and lead to excessive operating costs and unnecessarily high total cost of ownership. Supply managers should be continually alert to improvements possible in purchasing and supply processes, methods, procedures, and techniques. For example, opportunities to reduce transaction costs include e-procurement systems that automate the process from requisition to payment and purchasing cards and e-catalogs for small-value purchases. Companies with efficient supply processes can create competitive advantage through reduced costs, improved flexibility, faster time to market, and greater compliance, while allowing supply personnel to concentrate on value-added activities.

The objectives of supply must ultimately contribute to the attainment of short- and long-term organizational strategy, goals, and objectives. The process and function can be organized in a number of different ways to maximize supply's contribution effectively and efficiently.

ORGANIZATIONAL STRUCTURES FOR SUPPLY MANAGEMENT

Small and Medium-Sized Organizations

In practice it has been proven that assigning the supply function to supply professionals, properly trained and charged with the appropriate responsibilities and authorities, contributes more efficiently and effectively to organizational goals and strategies than assigning supply responsibilities to those for whom supply is a secondary responsibility. Nevertheless, in single business unit organizations, particularly small enterprises, it is not unusual to see supply responsibilities shared by a variety of individuals who have no supply expertise and purchase their own requirements from local retailers or wholesalers. As the size of the business unit increases, the idea of assigning a professional the responsibility of supply emerges and a separate function is created.

The size and activities of the supply function in a single business unit organization will depend on a number of factors, such as the size of the company and the nature of its business. Figure 2–1 provides an example of a supply organization in a typical medium-sized, single business unit enterprise. Obviously in small companies where the supply staff consists of only one or two individuals, the staff is expected to be flexible in terms of their capabilities and skills. Specialization will occur as the organization gets larger and the company can afford to hire additional supply personnel.

Specialization within the Supply Function

If the supply organization is to contribute well to organizational goals and objectives, it needs to be staffed by professionals with clearly defined responsibilities. Specialization

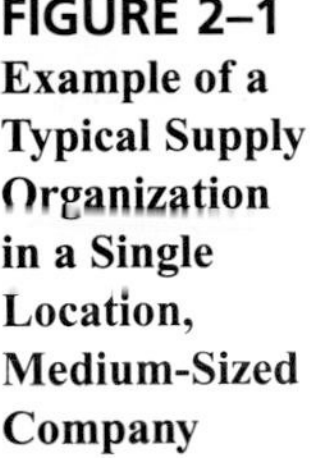

FIGURE 2–1
Example of a Typical Supply Organization in a Single Location, Medium-Sized Company

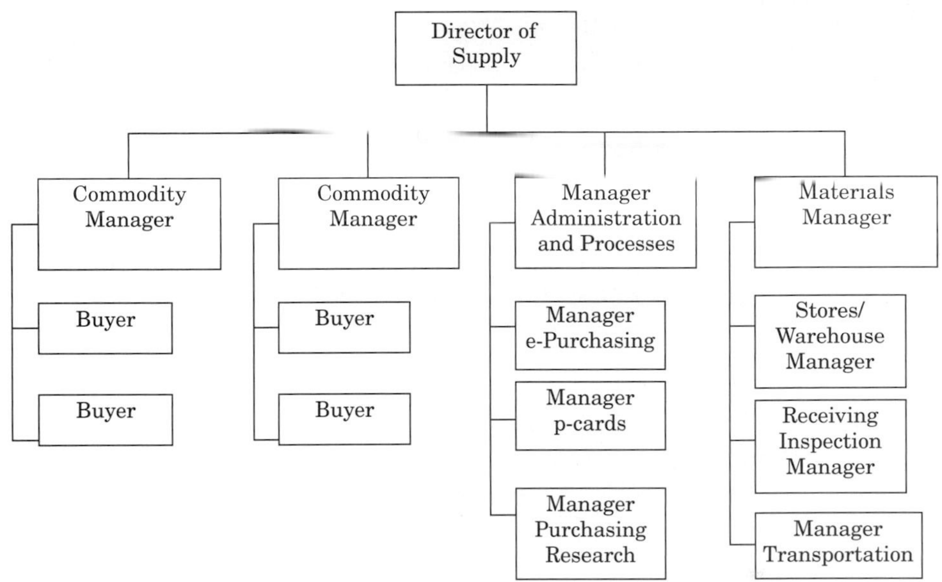

within the supply department allows staff to develop expertise in particular areas and may require the creation of specialized groups within the supply organizational structure. Most large supply organizations consist of four general areas of specialization: sourcing and commodity management, materials management, administration, and supply research.

Sourcing and Commodity Management

These personnel develop commodity strategies, identify potential suppliers, analyze supplier capabilities, select suppliers, and determine prices, terms, and conditions of supplier agreements; they create contracts and purchase orders. This activity is normally further specialized by type of commodity to be purchased, such as raw materials (which may be further specialized); fuels; capital equipment; office equipment and supplies; and maintenance, repair, and operating (MRO) supplies. Figure 2–2 presents a job description for a commodity specialist at Deere & Company.

A variation of commodity management is project buying, where the specialization of buying and negotiation is based on specific end products or projects, requiring the buyer to be intimately familiar with all aspects of the project from beginning to end. Project buying might be used in the supply organization of a large general contractor, where the purchasing for each job is part of a self-contained, temporary organization. At the completion of the project, the buyer then would be reassigned to another project. The United States Defense Acquisition University trains special project managers who are responsible for the proper acquisition and development of new military equipment initiatives. Such projects may last as long as 20 years.

Materials Management

This group manages the contract after it is signed, directs the flow of materials and services from the supplier, and keeps track of the supplier's delivery and quality commitments, so as to avoid any disruptive surprises. If problems develop, the materials management group

FIGURE 2–2
Commodity Specialist Job Description for Deere & Company

JOHN DEERE

Job Title: Commodity Specialist
Department: Supply Management
Job Function: Locate sources for and procure materials, products, supplies or services to support the assigned commodity requirements of the enterprise. Manage the relationships with suppliers.

Primary Duties:

1. Manage source selection and development through a team process including the evaluation of cost, quality, and manufacturing systems.
2. Develop and manage internal and external supplier/customer relationships, including strategic alliances where appropriate.
3. Lead and/or participate on simultaneous engineering teams; facilitate the integration of suppliers into the product delivery process (PDP).
4. Evaluate the cost effectiveness of designs, procure tooling, and qualify processes to assure the product meets specifications.
5. Make recommendations for design change and/or influence design through personal or supplier involvement.
6. Develop and execute supply management strategies to manage cost, quality, and continuous improvement.
7. Develop material control and logistics objectives.
8. Act as a primary communications link between tactical and strategic purchasing functions and business units; participate in team activities.

pressures and assists the supplier to resolve them. Materials management activities are frequently handled at the local plant or office level and involve regular communication with suppliers concerning requirements, such as order quantities and delivery dates. Figure 2–3 presents a job description for a supply management planner.

Administration

This group handles the physical preparation and routing of the formal purchase documents, manages the department budget, keeps the necessary data required to operate the department, and prepares reports needed by top management and supply. These personnel will likely manage operation of information systems, including e-procurement systems, B2B e-commerce, and EDI.

FIGURE 2–3
Supply Management Planner Job Description for Deere & Company

JOHN DEERE

Job Title: Supply Management Planner
Department: Supply Management
Job Function: To expedite, schedule, and/or analyze requirements for purchased materials in accordance with established requirements and inventory control criteria. May interact with suppliers to establish procedural agreements, obtain delivery commitments, and resolve quality problems.

Primary Duties:

1. Manages specific supplier performance and feedback along with managing day-to-day business plan and relationships with supplier.
2. Plans and/or executes inventory goals by product/supplier and plans/develops delivery system to meet material control objectives (i.e., JIT delivery, P.O.U.D., EDI).
3. Schedules material based on requirements and expedites deliveries that are delinquent or expected to be delinquent. Tracks and resolves problems with inbound shipments.
4. Interprets systems output to determine items requiring follow-up to suppliers on materials ordered to assure on-time delivery.
5. Is involved with the day-to-day problem resolution/corrective action with suppliers: to scrap, return, reclaim, or replace rejected material. Is responsible for bringing products within specifications.
6. Acts as the primary communications link between tactical and strategic purchasing functions and business unit; participates in supply management team activities.
7. Costs and implements current part revisions, including tooling, as part of the decision processing activity. Also reads and reacts to engineering decisions.
8. Conducts price/economic order quantity analysis and compares multiple quotes, including piece price, freight, duty, performance systems, and supplier rating. Also investigates invoice price errors.

Supply Research

Supply researchers work on special projects relating to the collection, classification, and analysis of data needed to make better purchasing decisions. Activities include studies on use of alternate materials, long-range demand, price and supply forecasts, and analysis of what it should cost an efficient supplier to produce and deliver a product or service.

This group is also responsible for performing benchmarking studies. For example, the global purchasing processes and systems group at Cable and Wireless plc, in the United Kingdom, benchmarks its purchasing processes to identify opportunities to improve its supply systems.[1]

Large Organizations

In large companies the centralization–decentralization issue is of key importance for the supply structure. The overall corporate structure sets the framework for the supply structure. Structural options can be viewed as a continuum ranging from centralized at one extreme to decentralized at the other. Centralization refers to where spending decisions are made, not where the purchasing and supply staff are located geographically. Therefore, the degree of centralization is reflected by the amount of spend managed or controlled by corporate supply. Three common organizational models are

1. Centralized, where the authority and responsibility for most supply-related functions are assigned to a central organization.
2. Hybrid, where authority and responsibility are shared between a central supply organization and business units, divisions, or operating plants. Hybrid structures may lean more heavily toward centralized or decentralized depending on how decision-making authority is divided. One type of hybrid supply structure is a "center-led" organization in which strategic direction is centralized and execution is decentralized.
3. Decentralized, where the authority and responsibility for supply-related functions are dispersed throughout the organization.

CAPS Research conducts Purchasing Performance Benchmarking Studies for a wide range of industries. One of the benchmarks is whether the participating companies use a centralized, decentralized, or hybrid structure. To read about the type of structure common in different industries, visit the CAPS Web site at http://www.capsresearch.org.

Centralized Supply Structure

Table 2–1 summarizes the advantages and disadvantages of a centralized supply structure.[2]

Decentralized Supply Structure

Table 2–2 summarizes the advantages and disadvantages of a decentralized supply structure.

Hybrid Supply Structure

In an organization with multiple business units, different divisions or business units often sell different products or services requiring a different mix of purchased items. Often the division or business unit is operated as a profit center where the division manager is given total responsibility for running the division, acts as president of an independent firm, and is

[1] Michiel R. Leenders and P. Fraser Johnson, *Major Changes in Supply Chain Responsibilities* (Tempe, AZ: Center for Advanced Purchasing Studies, 2001).

[2] Michiel R. Leenders and P. Fraser Johnson, *Major Structural Changes in Supply Organizations* (Tempe, AZ: Center for Advanced Purchasing Studies, 2000).

TABLE 2–1
Potential Advantages and Disadvantages of Centralization

Advantages	Disadvantages
• Strategic focus	• Lack of business unit focus
• Greater buying specialization	• Narrow specialization and job boredom
	• Cost of central unit highly visible
• Ability to pay for talent	• Corporate staff appears excessive
• Consolidation of requirements—*clout*	• Tendency to minimize legitimate differences in requirements
• Coordination and control of policies and procedures	• Lack of recognition of unique business unit needs
• Effective planning and research	• Focus on corporate requirements, not on business unit strategic requirements
	• Most knowledge sharing one-way
• Common suppliers	• Even common suppliers behave differently in geographic and market segments
• Proximity to major organizational decision makers	• Distance from users
• Critical mass	• Tendency to create organizational silos
• Firm brand recognition and stature	• Customer segments require adaptability to unique situations
• Reporting line—*power*	• Top management not able to spend time on suppliers
• Cost of purchasing low	• High visibility of purchasing operating costs

TABLE 2–2
Potential Advantages and Disadvantages of Decentralization

Advantages	Disadvantages
• Easier coordination/communication with operating department	• More difficult to communicate among business units
• Speed of response	• Encourages users not to plan ahead
	• Operational versus strategic focus
• Effective use of local sources	• Too much focus on local sources—ignores better supply opportunities
	• No critical mass in organization for visibility/effectiveness—"whole person syndrome"
	• Lacks clout
• Business unit autonomy	• Suboptimization
	• Business unit preferences not congruent with corporate preferences
	• Small differences get magnified
• Reporting line simplicity	• Reporting at low level in organization
• Undivided authority and responsibility	• Limits functional advancement opportunities
• Suits purchasing personnel preference	• Ignores larger organization considerations
• Broad job definition	• Limited expertise for requirements
• Geographical, cultural, political, environmental, social, language, currency appropriateness	• Lack of standardization
• Hide the cost of supply	• Cost of supply relatively high

FIGURE 2–4 Potential Advantages of the Hybrid Structure

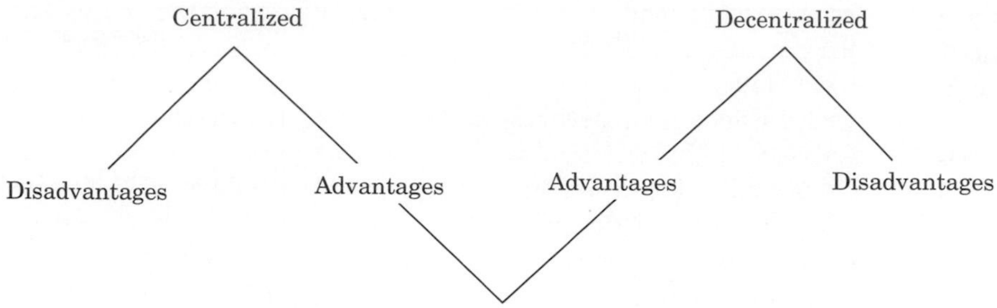

judged by profits made by the division. Since purchases are the largest single controllable cost of running the division and have a direct effect on its efficiency and competitive position, the profit-center manager may insist on having direct authority over purchasing. This has led firms to adopt decentralized-centralized purchasing, or a hybrid organizational structure, in which the supply function is partially centralized at the corporate or head office and partially decentralized to the business units.

Often the corporate supply organization works with the business unit supply departments in those tasks that are more effectively handled on a corporate basis: (1) establishment of policies, procedures, controls, and systems; (2) recruiting and training of personnel; (3) coordination of the purchase of common-use items in which more "clout" is needed, (4) auditing of supply performance, and (5) developement of corporatewide supply strategies. Therefore, hybrid organizational structures attempt to capture the benefits of both centralized and decentralized structures by creating an organizational structure that is neither completely centralized nor decentralized. (See Figure 2–4.)

Structure affects processes, procedures, systems, and relationships. Whether supply is centralized, decentralized, or a hybrid, supply personnel must focus on maximizing the advantages of the structure and minimizing the disadvantages. Supply managers can develop and implement strategies to overcome the obstacles and fully exploit the opportunities of organizational and supply structure.

Structure for Direct and Indirect Spend

Direct spend includes any goods that go into the end product; indirect spend is comprised of the goods and services that are needed to run the organization. Indirect spend includes purchases such as professional services, utilities, travel, employee benefits, and office supplies. In many organizations, the locus of control over direct spend is in a highly centralized supply group. This makes sense because anything that ultimately touches the final customer is worthy of expertise.

Indirect spend, on the other hand, is often outside the loop of a structured sourcing process and purchasing authority and responsibility is often left in the hands of the internal user. For example, a marketing manager needing to hire temporary labor would conduct the purchasing process in his or her own way. This highly decentralized approach leads to a fragmented spend for temporary labor including multiple suppliers, multiple rates, and varying contract terms and conditions. This is partly due to the belief that these types of purchases require a level of knowledge and expertise not found in a typical purchasing department.

The increasing focus on strategic cost management has led many senior managers to turn their attention to indirect spend to realize cost savings, reductions, or avoidances. To better manage indirect spend, some organizations will pull indirect spend categories into the purchasing process. Others expect supply managers to convince internal users that there is value in following a structured sourcing process. In some cases, supply provides analysis and recommendations, but the budget owner makes the purchasing decision. Cross-functional teams consisting of internal users (often across business units) and buyers or commodity managers may be given responsibility for the category. Sourcing, evaluating, and selecting suppliers for indirect spend will be discussed in greater detail in Chapter 10. Any purchase dollars that are not managed through a structured sourcing process may represent a target for cost savings, reduction, or avoidance.

Managing Organizational Change in Supply

Firms frequently make major changes to their purchasing organizational structure. CAPS conducted a study in 2000, in part to answer two questions: (1) Why are there so many structural changes in supply organizations at large companies? (2) If the hybrid organizational structure is theoretically so attractive, then why do so many large firms not use this structure and/or move out of it?[3] First, the researchers found that organizational structure change was the result of a change in the overall corporate organizational structure. In none of the situations did the CPO have free choice to select the supply organizational structure that he or she deemed appropriate for the circumstances. Rather, the supply organizational structure was forced to be congruent with the overall corporate structure. The challenge for supply executives, therefore, was to maximize the benefits of the organizational structure while minimizing the disadvantages.

Secondly, there are a number of implementation issues to consider when making a major organizational structure change in supply. Major changes affect the lives of many people and create an atmosphere of apprehension among the staff. Implementing change places significant pressures on the CPO, who not only has to worry about managing the day-to-day affairs of the supply department, but also successfully implementing the organizational change. The challenges associated with these issues frequently contribute to the need to seek assistance from consultants when implementing a major structural change.

Changes toward Centralization

When moving toward centralization, two concerns were sources of supply talent and information technology. During the transition, the source of supply talent at all levels of the supply function was a significant challenge. Experienced senior corporate-level supply personnel may not exist in-house. How and where to develop such organizational talent represented an important implementation issue. Some firms placed a greater priority on CPO credibility within the organization, as opposed to previous supply experience. Others identified new CPOs with previous supply experience to handle the change process. At the middle and junior levels, additional staff with specialized skills in areas such as contracting was required. Quite often, the existing supply talent in the decentralized organization was perceived to lack the required training or experience needed in the new centralized environment.

[3] Leenders and Johnson, *Major Structural Changes in Supply Organizations.*

Changes toward Decentralization

The CAPS research identified one implementation issue unique to the sites in the study moving toward decentralization: how to dismantle the centralized supply unit effectively. For example, Ontario Hydro created a shared services function that was responsible for negotiating corporatewide agreements and establishing and maintaining corporate purchasing policies, while the business units were responsible for materials management activities. The approach taken by Hoechst was to create a separate legal entity, Hoechst Procurement International, that would also offer purchasing services to other companies on a fee-for-service basis. The key objective in both situations was to preserve at least some of the organization's core supply capabilities and talent, while adapting to the new structural requirements of the company.

ORGANIZING THE SUPPLY GROUP

Once the corporate organizational structure is set, no matter what organizational design is chosen, delegation takes place within it. Whether the organization structure is based on functions, products, or business processes is immaterial; what really matters is that work must be assigned and executed in accordance with strategic plans and organizational goals. It follows logically that organizational planning and delegation are important segments of the integration of strategic goals and organizational designs.

The following sections describe the key aspects of supply organizational design, including the role of the chief purchasing officer, supply's status in the organization, and its reporting relationship and internal relationships. Even though the focus is on large supply organizations, many of the comments are also relevant for smaller supply organizations.

The Chief Purchasing Officer (CPO)

In a CAPS research study, the chief purchasing officer (CPO) is defined as the "most senior" or "top level" executive in a "firm's corporate (executive level) office *or* major division, such as a strategic business unit (SBU), who has formal authority and responsibility to manage his or her firm's (or SBU's) purchasing, buying or sourcing functions for the procurement of goods and services from external suppliers."[4] The chief purchasing officer's responsibilities may be divided and apportioned among subofficials and departments, but the functional responsibility and authority of the CPO should be definitely recognized. Moreover, functionalization implies that all the responsibilities reasonably involved in the supply function must be given to the CPO, covering the relevant supply network links as well as the full range of organizational needs. The essential principle is that there are certain universally recognized duties pertinent to this function and that these duties should be placed in a separate group equal in status with the other major functions of the organization.

The changes in supply management have affected everything from what the function is called to the titles of the people performing the tasks to the tasks that are performed.

[4] Thomas E. Hendrick and Jeffrey A. Ogden, *Chief Purchasing Officers' Compensation Benchmarks and Demographics: A 2001 Study of Fortune 500 Firms* (Tempe, AZ: Center for Advanced Purchasing Studies, 2002).

There is no common title for the individual who holds the top supply position in a large organization in North America. Depending on the role of supply in the organization, the reporting line, and where it is placed on the organization chart, the title may be chief purchasing officer, vice president, director, or manager. Attached to that may be purchasing, procurement, supply management, sourcing, strategic sourcing, or supply chain management. It is quite common to see CPO titles such as vice president, strategic sourcing and supply; vice president purchasing; vice president, supply chain management; or director, global procurement.

The titles in the cases used in this text provide a good range of titles in current use.

Profile of the CPO

The following profile of the average CPO emerged from the CAPS study.[5] The average CPO is a well-educated, 49-year-old male who has been at his organization for 12 years and CPO for a little over 3 years. He has over 14 years of experience in purchasing and a compensation package of salary plus bonus and health premium benefits of $282,000. He holds the title vice president and the title most likely includes the word *purchasing* or *procurement* in it, such as vice president, global procurement. Typically there are one to two levels between the CPO and the CEO. He probably reports to someone with a title of vice president or senior vice president with primary functional responsibility for finance, administration, or operations. The CPO may have overall management responsibility for nontraditional purchases such as corporate travel, food services, real estate, and printing. Additionally, the CPO might have responsibility for logistics (which includes inbound and outbound transportation, fleet management, warehousing, materials handling, order fulfillment, inventory management, supply/demand planning, and management of third-party logistics providers), quality, accounts payable, document/contract management, leadership of the supply process, materials, manufacturing, distribution, and facility management.

CPO Trends

Several trends have emerged over at least the last 10 years:

- Education levels are increasing. Almost all CPOs hold a bachelor's degree; about half a graduate degree, typically a master's in business.
- Diversity is lacking. CPOs continue to be predominately males in their late 40s.
- Reporting lines are changing. More CPOs report to senior vice presidents.
- CPOs are increasingly being hired from outside the organization rather than promoted from within.
- CPOs are increasingly being hired from functional areas other than purchasing.
- There is a shift from a bachelor's in business to engineering, coupled with an MBA.
- A small but growing number of CPOs have doctorates.
- The CPO role is still new in many organizations.
- When a new CPO replaces a current CPO, the current CPO often retires or leaves the company.

[5] Ibid.

Reporting Relationship

The executive to whom the CPO reports gives a good indication of the status of supply and the degree to which it is emphasized within the organization. If the chief purchasing officer has vice presidential status and reports to the CEO, this indicates that supply has been recognized as a top management function. The lower that supply reports in the organization, the less influence supply is likely to have on corporate strategy.

When supply is not given the same status as other functions, it must be placed under another senior functional executive. In many cases, supply reports to the chief financial officer because of the immediate impact of supply decisions on cash flows, the size of the annual spend, and the amount of money tied up in inventory. Organizational focus on strategic cost management also supports the decision to place supply under finance. In organizations where a high percentage of annual spend is for production requirements, supply often reports to the top manufacturing executive. In a shared services model, supply along with legal, accounting, human resources, and other functions might report to an administrative vice president. In a heavily engineering-oriented firm, the reporting relationship might be to the chief of engineering to get closer communication and coordination on product specification and quality control.

Factors that influence the level at which the supply function is placed in the organizational structure cover a broad spectrum. Among the major ones are

1. The amount of purchased material and outside services costs as a percentage of either total costs or total income of the organization. A high ratio emphasizes the importance of effective performance of the supply function.
2. The nature of the products or services acquired. The acquisition of complex components or extensive use of subcontracting represents a difficult supply problem.
3. The extent to which supply and suppliers can provide competitive advantage.

The important consideration in determining to whom supply should report relates to where it will be most effective in realizing its contribution to the organization's objectives. Supply should report at a level high enough in the organization so that the key supply aspects of strategic managerial decisions will receive proper consideration.

SUPPLY ACTIVITIES AND RESPONSIBILITIES

Supply management can be described as a series of activities that must be managed effectively for the organization to deliver best value to the final customer. According to the CAPS Research report, *Major Changes in Supply Chain Responsibilities,*[6] the changing roles and responsibilities of supply fall into four general categories: (1) what is acquired, (2) supply chain activities, (3) type of involvement in categories 1 and 2, and (4) involvement in corporate activities.

What Is Acquired

The items acquired by the supply group vary from organization to organization and items are added or deleted depending on circumstances in the buying organization. The acquisition

[6] Leenders and Johnson, *Major Changes in Supply Chain Responsibilities.*

segments include raw materials, standard and special direct purchases, MRO, capital, services, and resale. Nontraditional purchases are spend categories that have typically been managed outside of the purchasing and supply management process. In some organizations, purchasing activities are limited to production-related materials and services, leaving responsibility for nonproduction or indirect materials and services in the hands of users. The amount of annual spend that falls outside the management or control of supply ranges from a low of about 2 percent to a high of about 40 percent. This often includes large amounts for capital equipment, utilities, insurance, computers and software, travel, real estate, and construction services. Senior management in many organizations has recognized the significant opportunities from applying the skills of their supply group and the benefits of a structured sourcing process in the acquisition of nontraditional materials and services.

Supply Chain Activities

Supply has assumed greater responsibilities in a wide range of areas, including those not seen as traditional, as companies strive to leverage profit opportunities and create competitive advantage through their supply practices. Today's supply management organization has more responsibilities than the traditional "buying" activities once associated with the function. The activities handled by the supply function vary from firm to firm, even within the same industry. However, regardless of company size, there are a number of activities common to most supply organizations (see Table 2–3).

The addition or deletion of activities in any organization can be categorized as internally or externally focused. Internally focused activities include accounts payable, centralized coordination of purchasing, cost management, legal, materials management and logistics, production planning, quality, and supply budget and financial management. Externally focused activities may have either a supplier focus or a customer focus. Supplier-focused activities include inbound logistics, supplier development, raw material procurement for suppliers, supplier evaluation and communication, e-procurement, and outsourcing or subcontracting. Customer-focused activities include outbound logistics, involvement with new business development and new product development, and programs and customer bid support.

Type of Involvement

Supply can have no involvement or documentary, professional, or meaningful involvement in what is acquired and in supply chain activities. No involvement means supply is excluded completely. Documentary involvement requires the supply function to act as a recorder, a sender of purchase orders, or a receiver of bids, but important supply decisions are made outside supply. Professional involvement implies that supply professionals have the opportunity to exercise their expertise in important acquisition process stages. Meaningful involvement means that parties outside the supply group are willing and able to take supply considerations into account in managing their own areas of responsibility. They routinely and actively request input and assistance from supply personnel and, in turn, also are involved in supply decisions traditionally considered the prerogative of supply. One measure of meaningful involvement is the extent to which supply is expected to take part in major corporate activities.

TABLE 2–3
Supply Activities

Area of Responsibility	Activities
Purchasing/buying	• Creating contracts and supply agreements for materials, services, and capital items • Managing key purchasing processes related to supplier selection, supplier evaluation, negotiation, and contract management
Purchasing research	• Identifying better techniques and approaches to supply management, including benchmarking processes and systems • Identifying medium- and long-term changes in markets and developing appropriate commodity strategies to meet future needs • Identifying supply chain trends and opportunities for better materials and services
Inventory control	• Managing inventories and expediting material delivery • Establishing and monitoring vendor-managed inventory systems
Transportation	• Managing inbound and outbound transportation services, including carrier selection
Environmental and investment recovery/disposal	• Managing supply chain–related activities to assure compliance with legal and regulatory requirements and with company environmental policies • Managing disposal of surplus materials and equipment
Forecasting and planning	• Planning production and forecasting short-, medium-, and long-term requirements
Outsourcing and subcontracting	• Evaluating potential suppliers and negotiating contracts • Supporting the transition from internal production to external supply and vice versa
Nonproduction/nontraditional purchases	• Managing cost-effective delivery of nonproduction and nontraditional purchases, such as office supplies, security services, janitorial services, advertising, and insurance
Supply chain management	• Implementing and managing key supplier relationships and supplier partnerships, including supplier development and participation on cross-functional and cross-organizational teams • Developing strategies that use the supply network to provide value to end customers and contribute to organizational goals

Involvement in Corporate Activities

Major strategic corporate initiatives include mergers and acquisitions, new facility planning, new product development, outsourcing, revenue enhancement, technology planning, corporate e-commerce initiative, and corporate cost reduction initiative.

Influence of the Industry Sector on Supply Activities

The industry sector influences supply responsibilities. Firms that manufacture discrete goods such as cars, consumer electronics, apparel, and furniture face a significant number of dynamic, product-related pressures that affect the supply function and that are less likely to occur in commodity-oriented process industries. These pressures include changing consumer preferences, product innovation, and relatively short product life cycles. Purchased materials and services also represent a high percentage of the cost of sales for firms in discrete goods industries. For example, purchased materials and services can represent 80 percent of the average cost of an automobile. Consequently, firms in discrete goods industries are likely to have supply departments that play a key role in each step in the materials cycle, from product design to production.

The role of supply in process industry firms, such as oil and gas, chemicals, glass, and steel industries, is typically different compared to firms in discrete goods industries. Many process industry firms have two supply organizations: a specialized supply group, such as a commodity trading department, that frequently handles purchasing for important raw materials and a purchasing group responsible for the acquisition of materials, supplies, and services that support the operation of facilities. For example, it is common practice for crude oil acquisition in most large integrated oil companies to be handled by a commodity trading group, while other purchases are handled by the supply organization. As a result, although the cost of purchased materials and services might represent a substantial portion of the total cost of sales, the supply function for firms within processing industries is frequently excluded from the acquisition of the single most important raw material.

In the public, not-for-profit sector and service sectors, most purchases are for end use within the organization itself, with the exception of purchases for resale, such as in distribution and retail. In fast-growing organizations, capital purchases may represent a large percentage of total acquisition expenditures.

SUPPLY TEAMS

Corporate organization structures are leaner, flatter, more adaptive, and more flexible than in the past. Rigid functional structures have been replaced by a greater dependence on cross-functional teams that overlay the functional organization to push decisions lower in the organizational hierarchy. Teams bring together a number of people, often from different functional areas, to work on a common task. It is believed that teams provide superior results compared to individual efforts as a result of the range of skills, knowledge, and capabilities of team members. They also promote cross-functional cooperation and communication and may facilitate consensus building in the organization. Teams are used by a number of functions for a variety of purposes, such as improvements in quality, cost, or delivery; product development; process engineering; and technology management. They can be project-oriented or ongoing. Project teams are brought together for a limited time to achieve a specific goal or outcome, such as completion of a capital project or an e-commerce initiative. Ongoing teams continue indefinitely, such as a commodity-sourcing team that manages the process and the supplier relationship.

Leading and Managing Teams

Many teams fail to meet performance expectations. Changing to a team-based workplace requires a significant level of commitment and training of management and individual team members. Critical success factors include

- Supportive organizational culture, structure, and systems.
- A common compelling purpose, measurable goals, and feedback for individual and team.
- Organized for customer satisfaction rather than individual functional success.
- All functional areas involved in up-front planning, shared leadership roles, and role flexibility.
- The right people (right qualifications), in the right place (on a team that needed their skills), at the right time (when those skills were needed).
- A common, agreed-upon work approach and investment in a high level of communication.
- Dedication to performance and implementation with decisions delegated to the appropriate level.
- Integration of all relevant functional areas and various teams throughout the project life cycle.

Senior management often tries to combine the flexibility of decentralized supply management and the buying power and information sharing of centralized supply through the use of teams. Various types of purchasing and supply management teams may be used, including cross-functional teams, teams with suppliers, teams with customers, teams with both suppliers and customers, supplier councils (key suppliers), purchasing councils (purchasing personnel only), commodity management teams (purchasing personnel only), and consortia (pool buying with other firms).

Cross-Functional Supply Teams

Cross-functional teams consist of personnel from multiple functions focused on a supply-related task. It is generally believed that high-performing, cross-functional teams will get better results on the task, with greater benefit to the organization as a whole, at lower costs, in less time, with greater stakeholder buy-in. Effective cross-functional teams save time by allowing a simultaneous, rather than a sequential, approach. For example, if key stakeholder groups are involved in the development of a new process from concept through design, development, and rollout, the process may be better to start with, more widely accepted, and adopted quickly. The cycle time may be less than the nonteam approach but more of the work is concentrated at the beginning of the process.

Three important cross-functional supply teams are sourcing, new product development, and commodity management.

Sourcing Teams

A cross-functional sourcing team includes supply and representatives from other relevant functional areas. The team can focus on a wide range of projects including developing cost reduction strategies; developing local, business unit, or organizationwide sourcing strategies;

evaluating and selecting suppliers; performing value analysis; analyzing spend; and identifying consolidation opportunities.

New Product/Service Development Teams

Effective new product or service development processes can improve an organization's competitive position. Cross-functional teams can shorten development cycle times, improve quality, and reduce development costs by operating concurrently rather than sequentially. Rather than each functional area performing its task and passing the project off to the next functional area, the key functional groups—usually design, engineering, manufacturing, quality assurance, purchasing, and marketing—work on the new product development simultaneously. Because a large percentage of a product's cost is purchased materials, early supplier involvement is often needed. When surveyed, many supply managers report greater involvement in new product/service design and development.

Harley-Davidson, the motorcycle manufacturer, successfully uses cross-functional teams for sourcing and product development. Teams are formed for a platform or line of Harley-Davidson motorcycles and are responsible for the life cycle of their line. Each platform team consists of a program manager who is generally from the design community, as well as a lead from manufacturing, purchasing, and marketing. The platform team analyzes information from many sources and decides on the general design and style of the bike. Then the project is turned over to the company's engineering center of expertise, which is also a cross-functional team consisting of supply, engineers, suppliers, and others who work together to integrate all design components in a cost-effective, high-quality manner. Once the design is complete, the platform team is responsible for getting the end product into the hands of customers and accumulating and analyzing field reports, surveys of owner satisfaction levels, and marketing information.[7]

Commodity Management Teams

Commodity management teams are formed when expenditures are high and the commodity is complex and important to success. These are generally permanent teams that provide increased expertise, more cross-functional coordination and communication, better control over standardization programs, and increased communication with suppliers. They develop and implement commodity strategies aimed at achieving the lowest total cost of ownership. They engage in a number of activities, including supply base reduction, consolidation of requirements, supplier quality certification, management of deliveries and lead times, cost savings projects, and management of supplier relationships.

Cessna Aircraft Company created full-time, cross-functional commodity teams as part of a major change in its supply organization. Each team had representatives from seven different functional areas: purchasing, manufacturing, engineering, product design engineering, reliability engineering, product support, and finance. The mandate of the commodity teams was to drive supplier improvements and integration of suppliers into Cessna's design and manufacturing processes. Each commodity management team had annual strategic plans that were tied to the CEO's strategic objectives. The plan provided the long-term objectives, short- and long-term targets, and key processes and resource process maps.[8]

[7] "How Harley-Davidson Uses Cross-Functional Teams," *Purchasing,* November 4, 1999, p. 144.

[8] James P. Morgan, "Cessna Charts a Supply Chain Flight," *Purchasing,* September 7, 2000, pp. 42–61.

Teams with Supplier Participation

Supplier participation in cross-functional sourcing teams depends on the nature of the assignment. For example, it makes sense to include suppliers in teams assigned to develop supplier capabilities or improve supplier responsiveness, but not on teams assigned to evaluate and select new suppliers. Involving suppliers at the product design stage can produce substantial benefits and is common in discrete goods manufacturing industries, such as automotive and consumer electronics. The development of the Boeing 777 commercial aircraft made extensive use of supplier participation on cross-functional teams, enabling successful design and production in record time. Automotive manufacturers periodically give suppliers primary responsibility for designing major components, such as seating systems.

Intellectual property issues and confidentiality are perhaps the biggest obstacles to supplier participation, particularly when new product design is involved. Some firms ask suppliers to sign confidentiality agreements to minimize the potential effect of this obstacle on the team's effectiveness.

Teams with Customer Participation

In an effort to be truly customer-driven, some organizations include end customers on their teams. For example, when a commercial airframe maker designs a new passenger aircraft, it makes sense to have potential airline customers participate in the design team. They know best the characteristics a new aircraft must have from the airline perspective, given its anticipated passenger loads, route structures, maintenance plans, and passenger service strategies. If supply is also included in teams with end customers, there is a greater opportunity to deliver the greatest value in the shortest cycle time.

Co-location of Supply with Internal Customers

Locating buyers with internal customers, for example, engineering, can help to break down barriers between functions as individuals get to know, and learn to work with, each other. Close proximity fosters greater awareness that leads to better understanding of the goals, strategies, and challenges of each group. Also, internal customers are more likely to involve supply in decisions if the buyer is readily accessible when questions arise. Buyers can "sell" other departments on their worth by providing market intelligence including information on availability, suppliers, and specific commodities. The best selling point is a measurable outcome such as cost reduction, improved quality, or a better specification.

Co-location of Suppliers in the Buying Organization

As organizations look for ways to do more work with fewer people and achieve the productivity and competitiveness goals of the firm, they are increasingly looking to suppliers for expertise and assistance. Having key supplier personnel located in the buying organization who can function as buyer, planner, and salesperson can improve buyer–seller communications and processes, absorb work typically done by the firm's employees, and reduce administrative and sales costs.

Supplier Councils

A number of large firms, such as General Motors and Boeing, use supplier councils to manage supplier relationships. Supplier councils usually consist of 10 to 15 senior executives from the company's preferred supplier base, along with six to eight of the buying firm's top management. Supplier councils usually meet two to four times per year and deal with supply policy issues at the buying firm with the objectives of developing relationships and improving communication with the supply base. Supplier councils allow suppliers to be proactive participants in the supply management activities at the buying firm and can be useful forums to communicate strategies to key suppliers, identify problems with the supply base early on, and agree upon competitive targets in areas such as cost, quality, and delivery.

Supply Councils

Supply councils are generally comprised of senior supply staff and are established to facilitate coordination among the business units, divisions, or plants. Many firms use supply councils as a means of sharing information among decentralized units, or coordinating activities focused on a specific problem that might involve several supply groups. The goals of the council are to manage buyer–supplier relationships properly and to encourage continuous improvement.

For example, Wellman, a manufacturer and distributor of polyester fibers and PET resins, had a decentralized purchasing organization, where plant purchasing reported to the local manager at each site. The corporate purchasing council consisted of site purchasing leadership. It concentrated on standardizing purchasing processes, standardizing goods and services across sites, aggregating requirements and leveraging volume for lower prices, and simplifying and streamlining the materials process. The council also formulated annual business plans and objectives for purchasing.

Consortia

Purchasing consortia are a form of collaborative purchasing that is used by both public and private sector organizations as a means of delivering a wider range of services at a lower total cost. Purchasing consortia can take one of several forms, ranging from informal groups that meet regularly to discuss purchasing issues, to the creation of formal centralized consortia for the purpose of managing members' supply activities. Consortia are quite common in not-for-profit organizations, particularly educational institutions and health-care organizations. Interest in the concept in the for-profit sector was sparked by the ability to run an Internet-based consortium, called an electronic exchange or marketplace, and the lack of antitrust obstacles (e-marketplaces are discussed in Chapter 4 and antitrust issues in Chapter 12).

Savings through price reductions are a primary motivation for the creation and participation in purchasing consortia. Other benefits are opportunities for staff reductions, product and service standardization, improved supplier management capabilities, specialization of staff, and better customer service.

Despite the benefits, hesitation to participate in consortia may be due to concerns about[9,10]

[9] T. E. Hendrick, *Purchasing Consortiums: Horizontal Alliances among Firms Buying Common Goods and Services* (Tempe, AZ: Center for Advanced Purchasing Studies, 1997).

[10] P. Fraser Johnson, "The Pattern of Evolution in Public Sector Purchasing Consortia," *International Journal of Logistics: Research and Applications* 2, no. 1 (1999), pp. 57–73.

- *Antitrust issues.* Collaboration might be viewed as anticompetitive by the U.S. Department of Justice's Antitrust Division and/or the Federal Trade Commission.
- *Bureaucracy.* The consortium may become bureaucratic, difficult to manage, and costly to coordinate.
- *Complexity.* Fear that "open enrollment" will bring together buyers with widely diverse needs and philosophies toward buyer–seller relations, resulting in untenable complexity and dysfunction.
- *Competitors.* Fear that the competition might be allowed to join.
- *Confidentiality.* Disclosure of sensitive information. Therefore, most items purchased through consortia are nonstrategic, such as MRO components and routine services.
- *Supplier resistance.* Strong suppliers may resist participating in consortium arrangements.
- *Distribution channels.* Some believe existing distributors provide adequate pricing and services.
- *Equality.* A firm currently has preferred relationships with suppliers/free riding. The unequal size of member organizations can create difficulties with respect to the allocation of benefits.
- *Uncertainty.* Some were concerned costs would not decline and service levels would.
- *Standardization and compliance.* The degree of uniqueness of requirements and the costs of standardizing products and services.
- *Governance.* Loss of control and reporting relationships were concerns.

Successful consortia are able to address these hurdles by achieving the following six objectives:[11]

1. Reducing total costs for the members through lower prices, higher quality, and better services.
2. Eliminating and avoiding all real and perceived violations of antitrust regulations.
3. Installing sufficient safeguards to avoid real and perceived threats concerning disclosure of confidential and proprietary information.
4. Mutual and equitable sharing of risks, costs, and benefits to all stakeholders, including buying firms/members, suppliers, and customers.
5. Maintaining a high degree of trust and professionalism of the consortium stakeholders.
6. Maintaining a strong similarity among consortium members and compatibility of needs, capabilities, philosophies, and corporate cultures.

Conclusion

There is no one perfect organizational structure for supply. Its organizational structure will mirror the overall corporate structure. The challenge for supply executives is to maximize the benefits of their organizational structure, whether it is centralized, decentralized, or hybrid. Major research into organizational issues over the last decade has provided useful insights into innovative attempts to integrate the supply function and suppliers more effectively into organizational goals and strategies. No matter where the supply function is situated on the organization chart, each individual member of the supply organization has the opportunity to improve relations with internal customers and suppliers in an effort to make a greater contribution to organizational objectives.

[11] Hendrick, *Purchasing Consortiums.*

Questions for Review and Discussion

1. Relate the objectives of supply to (1) a company producing automobiles, (2) a large, fast-food restaurant chain, and (3) a financial institution.
2. What are the challenges faced by a supply manager working in a highly centralized structure?
3. How does specialization within supply differ in small and large organizations?
4. What are the reasons for giving the CPO a title and reporting line equal to marketing, engineering, or other key business functions?
5. What are indicators that supply is "meaningfully involved"?
6. What are the challenges in expanding the role of the CPO?
7. What implementation factors would you consider when asked to change the purchasing organization from a centralized to a hybrid structure? What factors would you consider if moving from decentralized to centralized?
8. How is team buying likely to affect the purchasing/supply function over the next decade?
9. Why and how would you go about setting up a consortium for the purchase of fuel oil, furniture, corrugated cartons, or office supplies?

References

Fearon, Harold E., and Michiel R. Leenders. *Purchasing's Organizational Roles and Responsibilities.* Tempe, AZ: Center for Advanced Purchasing Studies, 1995.

Giunipero, Larry C., and Dawn H. Percy. "World-Class Purchasing Skills: An Empirical Investigation." *Journal of Supply Chain Management,* Fall 2000, pp. 4–13.

Hendrick, Thomas E. *Purchasing Consortiums: Horizontal Alliances among Firms Buying Common Goods and Services.* Tempe, AZ: Center for Advanced Purchasing Studies, 1997.

Hendrick, Thomas E., and Jeffrey Ogden. *Chief Purchasing Officers' Compensation Benchmarks and Demographics: A 2001 Study of* Fortune *500 Firms*. Tempe, AZ: Center for Advanced Purchasing Studies, 2002.

Johnson, P. Fraser. "Supply Organizational Structures." Critical Issues Report, CAPS Research, August 2003.

Johnson, P. Fraser. "The Pattern of Evolution in Public Sector Purchasing Consortia." *International Journal of Logistics: Research and Applications* 2, no. 1 (1999), pp. 57–73.

Leenders, Michiel R., and P. Fraser Johnson. *Major Structural Changes in Supply Organizations.* Tempe, AZ: Center for Advanced Purchasing Studies, 2000.

Leenders, Michiel R., and P. Fraser Johnson. *Major Changes in Supply Chain Responsibilities*. Tempe AZ: Center for Advanced Purchasing Studies, 2002.

Murphy, David J., and Michael E. Heberling. "A Framework for Purchasing and Integrated Product Teams." *International Journal of Purchasing and Materials Management,* Summer 1996, pp. 11–19.

Case 2–1

Duchess University

In April, the purchasing department at Duchess University lost 3 of its 14 employees because of death and personal reasons. Jim Haywood, head of the purchasing department, saw these unexpected personnel changes as an opportunity to address an issue that had bothered him for a while: "Should I reorganize the structure of the department and, if so, how?"

COMPANY BACKGROUND: DUCHESS UNIVERSITY

Duchess University was a public institution, with about 3,000 full-time employees and about 25,000 students, that provided undergraduate and graduate education in all major academic disciplines. The total university budget was about $500 million and purchases were about $120 million. Currently, the university faced major challenges: increased demand for university education; at the same time many faculty members were nearing retirement and it was difficult to find replacements at acceptable costs. Moreover, the government had reduced its grants in recent years and had put a cap of 2 percent on tuition increases for the next five years, thus, constraining the university's major revenue generators.

THE PURCHASING DEPARTMENT

The Web site of the purchasing department stated its mission: "Our objective is to look after your needs. We want to provide you with the right goods or services, at the right time, at the right price, and on a continuing basis." To accomplish its goals, the department (1) purchased goods and services such as computer and business products, lab supplies, photocopiers, furniture, and travel for the university; (2) managed central supplies, which were bought in bulk, stored, and redistributed, as required; (3) was responsible for ensuring the economic and timely delivery of goods and services; (4) maintained an asset inventory; and (5) managed the disposal of goods.

Exhibit 1 provides the department organization chart. Junior buyers had a purchasing limit for a single purchase

EXHIBIT 1
Purchasing Department Organization Chart

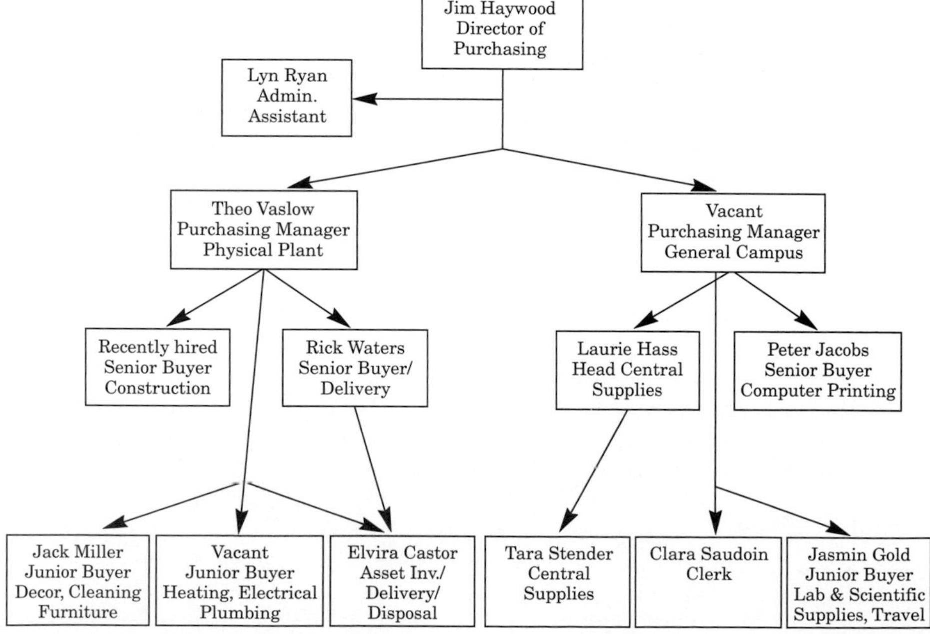

of $2,000; employees at the senior buyer level, $25,000. Purchasing managers had a purchasing limit of $50,000. Jim Haywood noted that the current department structure was a result of "patching up" in the last four years, in which the department had been extremely busy. In addition to its daily tasks, the department had to absorb the continuous introduction of software systems. The consistent work overload had prevented Jim Haywood from attending to his nondaily responsibilities, including a systematic revision of the department structure.

JIM HAYWOOD

Jim Haywood had assumed the position of director of purchasing six years earlier after working 17 years in the university's financial services area. As director of purchasing, he still reported to the director of financial services, with whom he had a good relationship. When Jim took over the purchasing department, it was in turmoil: The previous director had taken early retirement after senior management had voiced distrust in the department, and purchasing agents had strongly resisted changes to improve the department's efficiency. Moreover, the department staff was dispersed in two buildings.

When Jim came in, his goals included the reduction of the middle management layer (that is, the purchasing managers), the introduction of an online purchasing system, the integration of the department in one location, and the benchmarking of the department's performance. For the most part, Jim had achieved these goals. By January of the current year, through intra-university transfers, early retirement, and attrition, the number of purchasing agents had been reduced to two from six, and the total number of employees was 14, down from 20 in six years. PeopleSoft, a software package for business process applications, was in use. So far, however, PeopleSoft supported the current work processes, but reengineering to optimize PeopleSoft had yet to get under way. Moreover, all employees worked now in one location. Finally, Jim had introduced a Center for Advanced Purchasing Studies (CAPS) benchmarking system.

THE CURRENT SITUATION

At the end of April, Jim Haywood faced the following situation:

- In April, one purchasing manager had died; furthermore, a senior buyer had left after her husband was transferred, and a junior buyer had left after her husband retired. Jim had hired a replacement for the senior buyer position, but the replacement would not arrive until late May. He had not yet decided what to do with the remaining two vacant positions. Right now, his staff was down to 10 employees.
- CAPS data showed that the purchasing department had significantly improved over the past six years. For example, the total revenue per professional employee of $50 million was above the benchmark value of $30 million. Similarly, the total amount of purchases per buyer of $12 million had steadily improved over time and was now at the benchmark value. CAPS, however, also indicated that the department was still performing below average on several other parameters, such as cycle time and the number of suppliers per employee.
- After the consistent work overload during the previous four years, there was now an opportunity for reevaluating the department and catching up on nondaily responsibilities. Among other things, Jim reevaluated his goals for the department and its restructuring:

> "First, I want to reconsider the people issues in our department. I need to find a way to foster the careers of my employees. They have been with me for a long time, know what they do, and deserve recognition. Second, I still see room for improving the 'value added' in the department. We do too much work that does not increase our effectiveness. Third, we have to react to a current budget cut of 2 percent and future anticipated budget cuts between 3 percent and 5 percent."

  To share these goals and to get input on how to achieve them, Jim had already met with his superior. He also had had meetings with his three remaining senior employees—Theo Vaslow, Rick Waters, and Peter Jacobs—both individually and as a group. In addition, a staff meeting with all employees had taken place.

- In these meetings, several issues surfaced. Jim, as well as the purchasing agent Theo Vaslow, felt that they had to do too much supervising. Despite the reductions in personnel, the morale in the purchasing department was good. Most employees had been with the department for more than 10 years, and generally employee commitment to their department and their jobs was high. Jim generally viewed his employees as high performers who had done their best to keep the purchasing department running in extremely busy times because of the introduction of software systems. Some employees at the junior buyer level, however, had indicated their frustration about the lack

EXHIBIT 2 **Task List for the Purchasing Department**

Duchess University Purchasing Organizational/Responsibilities Review	
Task	**Expected Outcome**
• Eliminate the reprocessing of data.	• Free up people power; reduce costs.
• Analyze the purchasing data.	• Maximize purchasing effectiveness.
• Analyze the data from central supplies.	• Maximize purchasing effectiveness.
• Review the supplier master file.	• Save costs because of early payments.
• Eliminate forms (paperwork).	• Reduce costs.
• Update authorizations and limits system.	• Ensure functioning of the department.
• Train new university employees.	• Utilize resources outside the department on purchasing processes.
• Further develop the Web site by integrating software solutions.	• Reduce costs and speed up processes.
• Train purchasing employees on PeopleSoft.	• Improve effectiveness of personnel.
• Increase the number of systems contracts.	• Reduce costs.
• Review systems contracts that have ended.	• Reduce costs.
• Standardize purchasing processes across buyers.	• Achieve uniform best practices.
• Segregate procurement from nonprocurement activities.	• Improve daily operations.
• Rewrite job descriptions.	• Reflect past changes. Gain promotion compensation.

of promotion opportunities, as promotions to the senior buyer level led to salary increases of about 25 percent.

- On the basis of the meetings, Jim had generated a task list for achieving the goals, which is shown in Exhibit 2. Jim felt that now the goals and the task list were complete, but he was not sure how to implement them. He wondered to what extent restructuring the department would address issues on the task list.
- In September, the purchasing department would face an upgrade of PeopleSoft. Moreover, the department would have to gear up for Web-based processing of purchase requisitioning that would start within the next year. Jim stated:

> "Like in previous years, it is going to be tough. We will have to work very hard just 'to keep the train on the tracks' while implementing the new systems."

WHAT WAS NEXT?

Jim wanted to restructure the department before September. He asked himself: "What exactly should the outcome of the restructuring of the department be? And, if I changed the structure, how should I do it?"

Case 2–2

Roger Haskett

On June 26, 2004, Roger Haskett, director of purchasing for Morrow University in San Antonio, Texas, was evaluating a proposal negotiated by Professor Kahsay from the engineering faculty to upgrade computer equipment in his engineering lab. Roger was concerned that the proposal involved a capital lease arrangement, and even though there was no policy to prevent capital leases from being arranged, the university did not typically enter into such agreements.

EXHIBIT 1
Capital and Operating Leases

Capital Leases

If any of the following criteria are met, a lease must by classified as a capital lease:

1. Ownership of the property is transferred to the lessee at the end of the term, or
2. The lease contains an option to purchase the property for less than fair market value, or
3. The lease term is greater than 75 percent of the property's estimated economic life, or
4. The present value of the lease payments exceeds 90 percent of the fair market value of the property.

Operating Leases

Any lease that is not a capital lease is an operating lease.

MORROW UNIVERSITY

With more than 1,100 faculty members and almost 30,000 undergraduate and graduate students, Morrow University was recognized as a national leader in teaching as well as research. Through its 12 faculties and schools and four affiliated colleges, the university offered more than 60 different degree and diploma programs.

The purchasing department's mandate was to maximize the value of funds spent on supplies, equipment, and services; ensure ethical buying practices; maintain good supplier relations; and ensure compliance with the regulations governing taxes, accounting procedures, and other related university policies. The purchasing department was responsible for the acquisition of all goods and services for the university except for construction contracts, reading material offered by the library system, items offered for resale by the campus bookstore, and purchases for the food services department.

Most faculty and staff tended to handle their own purchasing needs for low-value purchases, which had been made easier with online purchasing applications. For purchases greater than $100,000, the purchasing department assigned a senior buyer to monitor and assist throughout the acquisition process. Senior buyers were available from three functional areas: business items, scientific items, and furniture/building items.

University procedures tried to maximize purchasing value and minimize vendor relations issues. Prior to acquiring goods or services with a value in excess of $7,500, two written quotes were required. Three quotes were required for acquisitions in excess of $10,000 and state policies required all acquisitions over $100,000 to be posted electronically to allow all potential vendors an opportunity to quote.

THE EQUIPMENT LEASE PROPOSAL

On June 22 the purchasing department received a proposal from Professor Kahsay to lease eight new Curtis processors for his engineering laboratory from Menard Leasing (Menard). The payment schedule called for an initial payment of $115,000 due on September 1, 2004; three annual payments of $90,000 due on March 1st of each of the subsequent three years; and a purchase option of $90,000 due on February 28, 2008. The total cost of the equipment would be $475,000, including interest. Given the nature and size of this request, Roger decided to deal with this request personally.

Even though there was no policy to prevent capital leases from being arranged, the university did not typically enter into capital leases. In general, the purchasing department considered capital leases an expensive and problematic purchase arrangement that should seldom be undertaken. Exhibit 1 describes the differences between capital and operating leases.

In a subsequent discussion with Professor Kahsay, Roger found out that Professor Kahsay had arranged a capital lease because he did not have sufficient funds within his annual operating budget to cover the cost of purchasing the equipment outright. Roger requested that Professor Kahsay change the lease to a purchase agreement with the equipment supplier. Roger wanted to pay cash for the net present value of the lease—approximately $425,000. However, Professor Kahsay was adamant that he should handle the acquisition out of his own budget and that any delays would jeopardize several important research projects. He said: "This is the only way we can stay within my budget and have the equipment arrive on time. Several of my doctoral candidates and I have important papers due for a worldwide conference and you are just blocking academic progress."

EXHIBIT 2
Conditional Sales Contract

MENARD LEASING

Attn: Roger Haskett

We are pleased to present the following proposal as a basis for further discussion concerning the financing by Menard Leasing of your planned equipment acquisitions. We appreciate the opportunity to make this proposal to you. Menard Leasing looks forward to working with you to complete this transaction.

LESSEE:	Morrow University
EQUIPMENT:	(2) Curtis SV1 Module with (4) 2.1 FJLOP Processors & Full Care Warranty until February 28, 2008 (as described in attached quotations).
TERM:	42 months, commencing September 1, 2004, or 15 days after delivery of processors.
ESTIMATED PAYMENT:	$115,000.00 due September 1, 2004, followed by 3 annual payments of $90,000.00 commencing March 1, 2005, payable in U.S. funds, with all applicable taxes.
ACTUAL PAYMENT:	The Estimated Monthly Payment is based on Menard's cost of funds on the date of this letter and, to arrive at the Actual Monthly Payment, it will be adjusted upward or downward to reflect changes in interest rates.
END OF LEASE CONDITIONS:	1) Purchase for $90,000.00 February, 28, 2008. 2) The absence of any material adverse changes in the Lessee's financial health or creditworthiness prior to the Funding Date. 3) The completion and due execution and delivery of Menard's standard form of Master Lease/Lease Arrangement, Delivery & Acceptance Certificate and other documents, as Menard may reasonably require, all such documents to be in form and substance satisfactory to Menard in all respects; such documents will supercede this letter once executed and delivered. 4) The acceptance of this proposal by the Lessee by June 28, 2004. 5) Lessee agrees to install and accept the Equipment set forth within ten (10) days of delivery or notify the Lessor of any problems with the Equipment within the ten days. Acceptance shall also be based on running the basic hardware and software diagnostics. In addition, Lessee agrees to accept partial shipment of the Equipment with the understanding that partial shipment shall include an operable system.

ACCEPTED this ________ day of June, 2004.

MENARD LEASING	MORROW UNIVERSITY
Pamela Switzer	(signature)
Pamela Switzer	(name/title)

DECISION

As of June 26, Roger had not yet signed the lease and both Professor Kahsay and Pamela Switzer, from Menard, were pressing for Roger to approve the contract (see Exhibit 2). However, Roger felt uncomfortable with the arrangement and wondered what action he should take.

Chapter Three

Supply Processes

Chapter Outline

Key Questions for the Supply Manager

Should we

- Make greater use of efficiency tools such as procurement cards to simplify and improve the purchasing process?
- Adopt an invoiceless payment system?
- Consider establishing a supplier-managed inventory program for MRO requirements?

How can we

- Handle lower-value purchases more efficiently?
- Streamline the process so that supply managers are more involved in the earlier stages of the process?
- Communicate more effectively with our internal business partners?

Management in many organizations is focused on identifying and streamlining key business processes to reduce costs, grow revenues, and manage assets. Business processes include the purchasing process, marketing process, accounts payable process, and research and development process. A process is a set of activities that have a beginning and an end, occur in a specific sequence, and have inputs and outputs. A process-oriented person considers the flow of information, materials, services, and capital throughout the entire process no matter how many different functions or departments touch the process. In a functionally oriented organization, people think about the part of a process for which their department is responsible. For example, in this chapter the supply management process is defined as starting with need recognition and ending with monitoring suppliers and relationships. The process has a series of distinctive steps including description of need, identification of potential sources, source selection and determination of terms, follow-up and expediting, receipt, payment, and monitoring. In a functionally oriented organization where supply personnel are not typically involved in the process until the identification of potential sources, they and the internal business partner may ignore the opportunity for supply and suppliers to add value in the need recognition and description stages. Waste is then driven into the process in the forms of unnecessary costs, long cycle times, and missed opportunities because the buying organization, operating out of *functional silos,* manages the process sequentially rather than simultaneously.

This chapter focuses on the critical aspects of a robust supply management process. The process must have structure and discipline. When developing or improving a purchasing/supply management process, the critical question is "Where, when, and how can supply personnel contribute to short- and long-term goals and strategies of the organization?" Once the basic process is understood, opportunities can be identified for technology applications to increase efficiency by streamlining the process without sacrificing effectiveness. Computerized purchasing systems, e-procurement, and electronic business-to-business (B2B) systems are addressed in Chapter 4. Remember, process first and technology last.

THE SUPPLY MANAGEMENT PROCESS

The supply management process requires a wide range of standard operating procedures to deal with the normal daily tasks. The large number of items, the large dollar volume involved, the need for an audit trail, the severe consequences of poor performance, and the potential contribution to effective organizational operations inherent in the function are five major reasons for developing a robust process. The acquisition process is closely tied to almost all other business processes included in an organization and also to the external environment, creating a need for complete information systems and cross-functional cooperation. The Internet and the availability of integrated software packages has had a substantial impact on the acquisition process and its management. Supply managers need to stay abreast of technological developments and be able to assess the fit of each new tool with the organization's goals and strategy. Considerable management skill is required to ensure continuing effectiveness.

Strategy and Goal Alignment

The first step in optimizing the supply process is building consensus within the organization around the opportunities to add value to the organization. This requires vertical and horizontal alignment of strategy and goals. If, for example, business unit strategy is out of sync with enterprise strategy, then decisions at the business unit level may benefit the business unit but fail to contribute to organizational strategy and goals. Horizontal alignment between and among functional areas also is required. For example, to attain profitability targets, the finance group may establish goals related to cash flow that lead to a payment policy that conflicts with the supply group's goal to contribute to profitability through long-term partnerships with key suppliers in which payment terms were a key negotiating point. Personnel at all levels in an organization must work to understand and align strategies and goals vertically and horizontally to maximize opportunities for the organization.

Individuals from many functions play valuable roles in a successful acquisition process. The users and specifiers of the good or service, often referred to as supply's internal customers, clearly play a role in recognizing and describing the need. They are usually the primary information sources for technical descriptions; volume requirements; and quality, delivery, and service targets as well as the budget owners. In some cases there is a hand-off of information once the internal customers have clearly defined the requirement. In other cases, purchasing/supply personnel bring market intelligence such as supply availability, price trends, new technology, and so on to the need recognition and description stages.

In Chapter 2, cross-functional sourcing teams, new product or service design teams, and commodity management teams were discussed. These are three situations where the internal customers and supply should interact as early as possible. Often, however, purchasing takes the lead role in analyzing and selecting the supplier(s) and determining price and other terms and conditions such as payment, delivery, quality, service, and so on. Often other functional areas step in as well. For example, expediting, shipping and receiving, legal, marketing, IS, engineering, and accounts payable all play a role in the process but are part of different functional areas with a different reporting line than purchasing. Each of these stakeholders has goals and objectives relative to the purchase, and when these conflict with one another, the total cost of owning, consuming, and disposing of a purchase may increase unnecessarily. Many senior managers work to develop a process orientation rather than a functional orientation. A cross-functional team (see Chapter 2) is one tool that can be used to foster a process orientation. Shared or common goals, objectives, and metrics also will encourage and motivate stakeholders from different functions to work together throughout the process.

Ensuring Process Compliance

In many organizations, increasing the rate of internal compliance with the supply process is a continuing challenge. The supply management executive team must get to the root causes of circumventing supply and develop strategies to eliminate or reduce these causes. The acquisition process must be developed to fit the organizational and supply structure discussed in Chapter 2. Process compliance is affected by organizational structure. If the organization is highly decentralized, with supply decision making located at the business unit, plant, mill, or division level, then a robust process would have to account for this structure. This environment would benefit from supply councils composed of site leaders. The council would work to standardize goods, services, and processes across sites; aggregate requirements and leverage volume for lower prices; simplify and streamline the materials management process; and formulate annual business plans and establish objectives for supply. Without a supply council and willing participation by site supply leaders, the organization might well end up with multiple suppliers of the same goods and services with disparate prices, terms, and conditions and varying levels of quality and service.

Even in a highly centralized organization there may be high levels of noncompliance in the form of maverick buying. The supply group can increase compliance through process improvements and consistently delivering results to internal business partners. In Chapter 4 technology tools are discussed that help to drive compliance. The culture of the organization also influences process compliance. In some situations, a mandate from top management to use the supply process will stop maverick buying. In other situations, mandates mean little in reality and it is left to supply personnel to convince and persuade users that it is in their best interest to comply.

Steps in the Supply Process

The supply process is basically a communications process. Determining what needs to be communicated, to whom, and in what format and timeframe is at the heart of an efficient and effective supply management process. It is essential for supply professionals to determine when, where, and how they can add value and when, where, and how they can extricate themselves from process steps that are best left to other people or to technology. The essential steps in the purchasing process are

1. Recognition of need.
2. Description of the need.
3. Identification and analysis of possible sources of supply.
4. Supplier selection and determination of terms.
5. Preparation and placement of the purchase order.
6. Follow-up and/or expediting of the order.

7. Receipt and inspection of goods.
8. Invoice clearing and payment.
9. Maintenance of records and relationships.

The fundamental steps in a robust purchasing and supply management process, and the rationale for each, are described below.

1. RECOGNITION OF NEED

Any purchase originates with the recognition of a definite need by someone or some system in the organization. The person responsible for a particular activity should know what the requirements of the unit are—what, how much, and when it is needed. This may result in a material requisition from inventory. Occasionally, such requirements may be met by the transfer of surplus stock from another department or division. Sooner or later, of course, the purchase of new supplies will become necessary. Some requisitions originate within the using department such as marketing and sales or engineering. Frequently, special forms will indicate the source of requisitions; where this is not the case, distinctive code numbers for each department may be used.

The supply department is responsible for helping to anticipate the needs of using departments. The supply manager should urge not only that the requirements be as nearly standard in character as possible and that a minimum of special or unusual orders be placed, but also that requirements be anticipated far enough in advance to prevent an excessive number of "rush" orders. Also, since the supply department is in touch with price trends and general market conditions, placing forward orders may be essential to protect against shortage of supply or increased prices. This means that supply should inform using departments of the normal lead time, and any major changes, for all standard purchased items. Early supply involvement and early supplier involvement (ESI), often as members of new-product development teams, brings in information that may result in cost avoidance/reduction, faster time to market, and greater competitiveness. As discussed in Chapter 2, many organizations are turning to cross-functional teams to bring different functional areas, and suppliers, into the process as early as possible. Since the greatest opportunity to affect value is in the need-recognition and description stages (product conception and design), the supply manager and supplier can contribute more in the need-recognition and description stages than later in the acquisition process. (See Chapter 5 for additional information on value creation.)

2. DESCRIPTION OF THE NEED

No purchaser can be expected to buy without knowing exactly what the internal customers want. For this reason, it is essential to have an accurate description of the need, the article, the commodity, or the service requested. Purchasing and the user, or the cross-functional sourcing team, share responsibility for accurately describing the item or service needed. If the user/buyer writes unclear or ambiguous descriptions, or overspecifies materials or quality levels, this will lead to unnecessary costs.

In many companies, the supply management process is split into mini-processes that are owned and managed by different functional areas of the organization. For example, internal users typically recognize and describe need, and after they have completed this process step to the best of their ability, the specification or description is shared with the buyer. By then, most of the cost and quality have been established. For example, if a car buyer recognizes her need as "I need to buy a new car" and describes the need as "a Honda gas-electric hybrid 5-speed two-seater," then the buyer has already established both the quality and most of the costs that she will incur over the life of the vehicle. There is little opportunity in the remaining steps of the process to reduce costs or affect quality to any significant degree. If, however, the buyer starts with a broader definition and description of her need and remains open to the intelligence and ideas of multiple stakeholders, she may end up making a decision that is better for her organization's goals and objectives. A sequential supply management process often leads to lengthy cycle time and unnecessary costs as the requirement is clarified through multiple iterations.

Types of Requisitions

There are several types of purchase requisitions including standard requisitions, traveling requisitions, and a bill of materials.

Standard Requisition

The following information should be included on a standard requisition:

1. Date.
2. Number (identification).
3. Originating department.
4. Account to be charged.
5. Complete description of material or service desired and quantity.
6. Date material or service needed.
7. Any special shipping or service-delivery instructions.
8. Signature of authorized requisitioner.

Some organizations include spaces on the requisition form for "suggested supplier" and "suggested price."

Traveling Requisition

Throughout time, people have adopted and adapted new technology to business processes. An early innovation was the traveling requisition used for recurring requirements and standard parts to reduce operating expenses. The traveling requisition is a simple form on cardstock that contains a complete description of the item. The requisitioner sends the card to purchasing when a resupply is needed, indicating quantity and date needed. Purchasing writes the PO; enters data on supplier, price, and PO number on the traveler; and sends it back to the requisitioner, who puts the card in the files until a subsequent resupply is needed. Traveling requisitions are still used in organizations that have not automated the purchasing process. More importantly, from a process perspective, the thinking and decision-making process of determining which items are appropriate for use on a traveling requisition and the flow of the information are useful when transitioning the process to an automated system.

Bill of Materials

Another variation is the bill of materials (BOM). It is used by firms who make a standard item over a relatively long period of time, as a quick way of notifying purchasing of production needs. A BOM for a toaster made by an appliance manufacturer would list the total number or quantity, including an appropriate scrap allowance, of parts or material to make one end unit, for example, a two-slice toaster. Production scheduling then merely notifies purchasing that it has scheduled 18,000 of that model into production next month. Purchasing then will "explode" the BOM (normally by a computerized system) by multiplying through by 18,000 to determine the total quantity of material needed to meet next month's production schedule. Comparison of these numbers with quantities in inventory will give purchasing the open-to-buy figures. In a firm that has developed a totally integrated materials computer system, in which long-term agreements containing supplier and pricing information have been entered into the database, the computer will generate order releases to cover the open-to-buy amounts. Use of the BOM system is a means of simplifying the requisitioning process where a large number of frequently needed line items are involved.

Flow of the Requisition

At a minimum, at least two copies of the requisition should be made: the original to be forwarded to the supply department and the duplicate retained by the issuer. In electronic purchasing systems, the need for audit trails and proper authorization remains, but they, obviously, are handled differently. It is a common practice to allow only one item to appear on any one purchase requisition, particularly on standard items. In the case of some special items, such as plumbing fittings not regularly carried in stock, several items may be covered by one requisition, provided they are for delivery at the same time. This simplifies recordkeeping, since specific items are secured from different suppliers, call for different delivery dates, and require separate purchase orders and treatment. In the case of firms operating with a computerized material requirements planning (MRP) system, the requisitions will be automatically computer generated.

It is important for the purchasing department to establish who has the power to requisition. Under no circumstances should the purchasing department accept requisitions from anyone other than those specifically authorized. Just as important is that all supplier personnel understand that a requisition is not an order.

All requisitions should be checked carefully before any action is taken. The requested quantity should be based on anticipated needs and should be compared to economical quantities. The delivery date requested should allow for sufficient time to secure quotations and samples, if necessary, and to execute the purchase order and obtain delivery. If insufficient time is allowed, or the date would involve additional expense, this should be brought to the attention of the requisitioner immediately. Consistent lack of adequate lead time is an indicator of a process problem that must be analyzed and resolved.

The procedure for handling requisitions on receipt in the purchase office is of sufficient importance to warrant citing an example from one organization. After being time-stamped, the proper specification card is attached to each individual requisition. If a contract already exists, the buyer marks all items covered by the contract, placing on the requisition the word *contract,* the name of the firm with which the order is to be placed, the price, terms, the FOB point (see Chapter 10, "Supplier Selection"), the total value, and the payment date, for the controller's information. The purchase order is then prepared, carefully checked with the specification card, the price, terms, and so on, before the order finally is mailed, faxed, or electronically transmitted to the selected supplier.

Early Supply and Supplier Involvement

For purchases that are of strategic or critical value to the buying organization, it is usually advisable to manage the process through a cross-functional sourcing team. For lower-value purchases, the buyer should question a specification if it appears that the organization might be served better through a modification. For example, the buyer might recommend a substitute if there are market shortages of the desired commodity or lower-priced or better alternatives are available. Since future market conditions play such a vital role, it makes sense to have a high degree of interaction between the purchasing and specifying groups in the early stages of need definition. At best, an inaccurate description may result in some loss of time; at worst it may have serious financial consequences and cause disruption of supply, hard feelings internally, lost opportunity for a product or service improvement, and loss of supplier respect and trust.

The terms used to describe desired articles or services should be uniform. The importance of proper nomenclature as a means of avoiding misunderstanding cannot be overemphasized. The most effective way to secure this uniformity is to maintain a database of common purchased items. Such files may be kept as a general catalog, which lists all the items used, and a stores catalog, which contains a list of all of the items carried in stock. Depending on the technological sophistication of the organization, such catalogs may be kept in an electronic file, on e-catalogs, in loose-leaf form, or in a card index. If such catalogs are adequately planned and properly maintained, they tend to promote the uniformity in description, reduce the number of odd sizes or grades of articles requisitioned, and facilitate accounting and stores procedures. However, unless such catalogs or their equivalents are properly planned, maintained, and actually used, they can be confusing and expensive beyond any benefits that could be derived from them. Tackling the preferences of internal users and convincing them that a standard item will suffice is an ongoing challenge for supply personnel.

3. IDENTIFICATION OF POTENTIAL SOURCES

Supplier selection constitutes an important part of the supply function, and involves the location of qualified sources of supply and assessing the probability that a purchase agreement would result in on-time delivery of satisfactory product and needed services before and after the sale. This step is discussed in detail in Chapters 6 and 7.

Issuing an RFx

When items are not covered by contract, the buyer has three options for soliciting business from potential suppliers: issuing a (1) request for quotation (RFQ), (2) request for proposal (RFP), or (3) request or invitation for bid (RFB). Since there are no commonly accepted definitions of these terms, it is important for buyers to communicate clearly to potential suppliers the process that will be followed to analyze and select a supplier. Many organizations use different solicitation tools depending on the complexity of the purchase, the dollar value, and the degree of risk they wish the supplier to bear.

Request for Quotation

Typically, an RFQ is issued in situations where the buyer and internal user can clearly and unambiguously describe the need, for example, by using a grade of material, stock-keeping unit (SKU), or commonly accepted terminology. In these cases, an RFQ would basically bring the comparison to one of price. With many commodities that are in constant use by an organization, particularly those for which there is an open and free market on which quotations can be obtained at practically any hour of the day, no problem is involved. The RFQ is sent out on standard inquiry blanks provided for this purpose. Where quotations are to be requested, a list of the names of potential suppliers will be written on the back of the requisitions. Standard inquiry forms are prepared, checked, signed, and mailed, faxed, or electronically transmitted to potential suppliers. When the quotations are received from the various suppliers, they will be entered on the quotation sheet and the buyer determines the supplier with whom the business is to be placed. The purchase order then is prepared and placed with the chosen supplier.

Request for Proposal

When the buyer has a more complex requirement and wants to draw on the supplier's expertise in developing and proposing a solution, an RFP would be more appropriate than an RFQ. Also, if the buyer is planning to use negotiation as the tool for determining price and terms then an RFP would be appropriate.

Requests for proposal typically include a more detailed package describing the needs of the buying organization and providing potential suppliers the opportunity to propose solutions to meet the requirements. For example, a buyer may issue an RFP for photocopying services for the entire organization including convenience copiers for each department and high-speed, high-volume copiers to be run by either in-house staff or supplier personnel. The RFP may provide potential suppliers the opportunity to propose multiple solutions to the buyer.

Request for Bid

A request for bid is similar to an RFP in terms of the bid specification package that is developed and sent to suppliers. If, however, the buyer is planning to use a competitive bid process without the opportunity to negotiate after bid receipt, then an RFB might be more appropriate. It is important to communicate to suppliers how the final selection will take place. Will this be a sealed competitive bid in which the contract will be awarded based on the lowest bid? Will the bids be the starting point from which negotiations will take place?

Linking Organizational and Category Strategy

Organizational strategy should be driven by final customer requirements. This, in turn, drives the development of category or commodity strategies. A number of issues should be considered when potential sources are identified by the sourcing team or individual. How important is the requirement in the short and long term? How risky is it to acquire in the marketplace? Should the business be given to a single source or multiple sources? Where should the supplier ideally be located: Locally? Domestically? Off-shore? What type of buyer–supplier relationship is desired? What are the basic requirements a supplier must meet to be considered as a source? These and similar questions position the decision in the context of the final customers' needs and wants and the organizational strategy.

4. SUPPLIER SELECTION AND DETERMINATION OF TERMS

Analysis of the quotes, bids, or proposals and the selection of the supplier lead to order placement. Since analysis of bids, quotations, and proposals and the selection of the supplier are matters of judgment, it is necessary to indicate here that they are logical steps in the supply process. Applicable tools range from a simple bid analysis form to complex negotiations. Supplier selection methods are discussed in Chapter 7 and determination of price and terms, through a variety of methods, is discussed in detail in Chapters 8 and 9.

5. PREPARATION AND PLACEMENT OF THE PURCHASE ORDER

Placing an order usually involves preparation of a purchase order form (see Figure 3–1) unless the supplier's sales agreement or a release against a blanket order is used instead. Failure to use the proper contract form may result in serious legal complications. Furthermore, the transaction may not be properly recorded. Therefore, even where an order is placed by telephone, a confirming written order should follow. At times, when emergency conditions arise, it may be expedient to send a truck to pick up items without first going through the usual procedure of requisition and purchase order. But in no instance—unless it is for minor purchases from petty cash—should materials be bought without documentation, written or computer-generated.

All companies have purchase order forms; in practice, however, all purchases are not governed by the conditions stipulated on the purchase order, but many are governed by the sales agreement submitted by the seller. Since every company naturally seeks to protect itself as completely as possible, responsibilities that the purchase order form assigns to the source of supply are, in the sales agreement, often transferred to the buyer. Naturally, a company is anxious to use its own sales agreement when selling its products and its own purchase order form when buying. Chapter 12 discusses the legal implications involved.

Format and Routing

Purchase order forms vary tremendously as to format and routing through the organization. The essential requirements on any satisfactory purchase order form are the serial number, date of issue, the name and address of the supplier receiving the order, the quantity and description of the items ordered, date of delivery required, shipping directions, price, terms of payment, and conditions governing the order.

These conditions are important and the question of what should and what should not be included is subject to a good deal of discussion. What actually appears on the purchase order form of any individual company is usually the result of experience. The items included in the conditions might:

FIGURE 3–1 Purchase Order

Source: Honeywell Flight Systems Division.

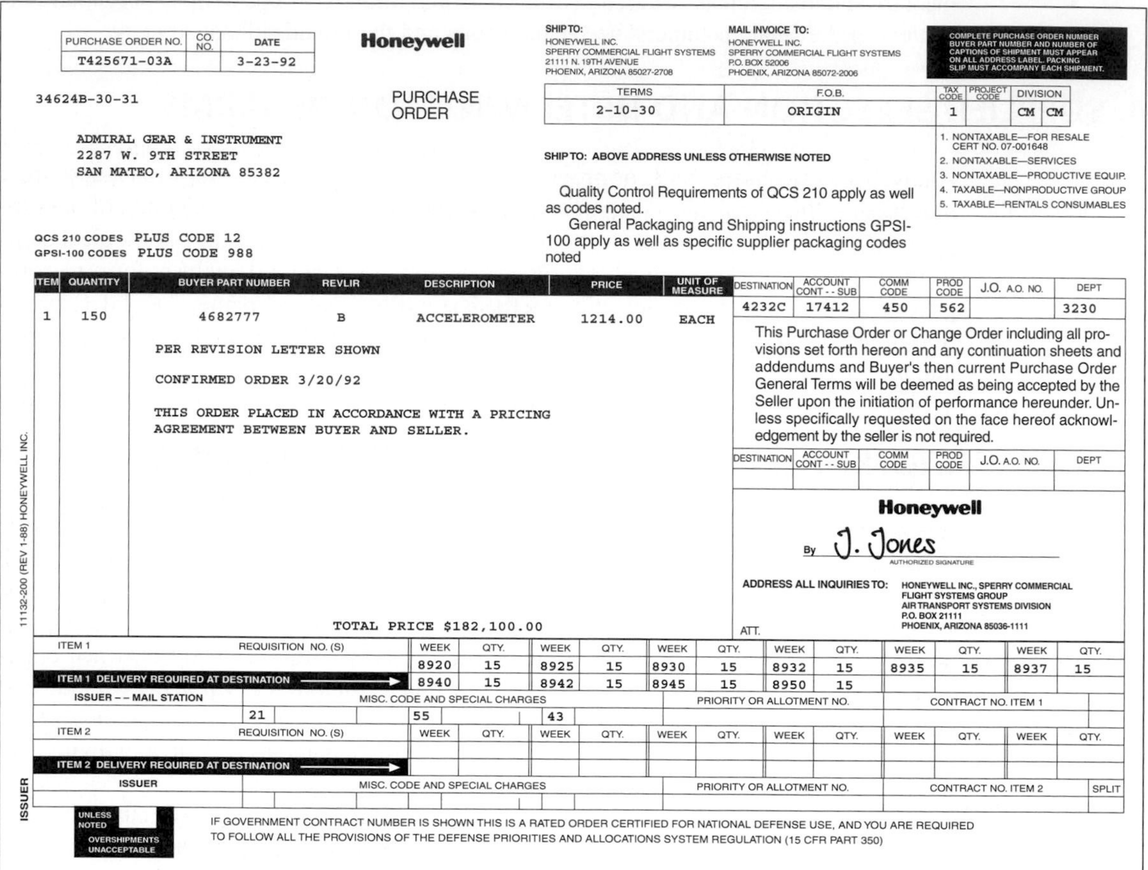

PURCHASE ORDER NO.	CO. NO.	DATE
T425671-03A		3-23-92

Honeywell

PURCHASE ORDER

SHIP TO:
HONEYWELL INC.
SPERRY COMMERCIAL FLIGHT SYSTEMS
21111 N. 19TH AVENUE
PHOENIX, ARIZONA 85027-2708

MAIL INVOICE TO:
HONEYWELL INC.
SPERRY COMMERCIAL FLIGHT SYSTEMS
P.O. BOX 52006
PHOENIX, ARIZONA 85072-2006

COMPLETE PURCHASE ORDER NUMBER BUYER PART NUMBER AND NUMBER OF CAPTIONS OF SHIPMENT MUST APPEAR ON ALL ADDRESS LABEL. PACKING SLIP MUST ACCOMPANY EACH SHIPMENT.

34624B-30-31

TERMS	F.O.B.	TAX CODE	PROJECT CODE	DIVISION	
2-10-30	ORIGIN	1		CM	CM

ADMIRAL GEAR & INSTRUMENT
2287 W. 9TH STREET
SAN MATEO, ARIZONA 85382

SHIP TO: ABOVE ADDRESS UNLESS OTHERWISE NOTED

1. NONTAXABLE—FOR RESALE CERT NO. 07-001648
2. NONTAXABLE—SERVICES
3. NONTAXABLE—PRODUCTIVE EQUIP.
4. TAXABLE—NONPRODUCTIVE GROUP
5. TAXABLE—RENTALS CONSUMABLES

Quality Control Requirements of QCS 210 apply as well as codes noted.
General Packaging and Shipping instructions GPSI-100 apply as well as specific supplier packaging codes noted

QCS 210 CODES PLUS CODE 12
GPSI-100 CODES PLUS CODE 988

ITEM	QUANTITY	BUYER PART NUMBER	REVLIR	DESCRIPTION	PRICE	UNIT OF MEASURE
1	150	4682777	B	ACCELEROMETER	1214.00	EACH

PER REVISION LETTER SHOWN

CONFIRMED ORDER 3/20/92

THIS ORDER PLACED IN ACCORDANCE WITH A PRICING AGREEMENT BETWEEN BUYER AND SELLER.

TOTAL PRICE $182,100.00

DESTINATION	ACCOUNT CONT - - SUB		COMM CODE	PROD CODE	J.O. A.O. NO.	DEPT
4232C	17412		450	562		3230

This Purchase Order or Change Order including all provisions set forth hereon and any continuation sheets and addendums and Buyer's then current Purchase Order General Terms will be deemed as being accepted by the Seller upon the initiation of performance hereunder. Unless specifically requested on the face hereof acknowledgement by the seller is not required.

DESTINATION	ACCOUNT CONT - - SUB		COMM CODE	PROD CODE	J.O. A.O. NO.	DEPT

Honeywell

By J. Jones
AUTHORIZED SIGNATURE

ADDRESS ALL INQUIRIES TO: HONEYWELL INC., SPERRY COMMERCIAL FLIGHT SYSTEMS GROUP
AIR TRANSPORT SYSTEMS DIVISION
P.O. BOX 21111
PHOENIX, ARIZONA 85036-1111

ATT.

ITEM 1 — REQUISITION NO. (S)

ITEM 1 DELIVERY REQUIRED AT DESTINATION →

WEEK	QTY.	WEEK	QTY.	WEEK	QTY.	WEEK	QTY.	WEEK	QTY.	WEEK	QTY.
8920	15	8925	15	8930	15	8932	15	8935	15	8937	15
8940	15	8942	15	8945	15	8950	15				

ISSUER - - MAIL STATION	MISC. CODE AND SPECIAL CHARGES			PRIORITY OR ALLOTMENT NO.	CONTRACT NO. ITEM 1
	21	55	43		

ITEM 2 — REQUISITION NO. (S)

ITEM 2 DELIVERY REQUIRED AT DESTINATION →

WEEK	QTY.	WEEK	QTY.	WEEK	QTY.	WEEK	QTY.	WEEK	QTY.	WEEK	QTY.

ISSUER	MISC. CODE AND SPECIAL CHARGES	PRIORITY OR ALLOTMENT NO.	CONTRACT NO. ITEM 2	SPLIT

UNLESS NOTED OVERSHIPMENTS UNACCEPTABLE

IF GOVERNMENT CONTRACT NUMBER IS SHOWN THIS IS A RATED ORDER CERTIFIED FOR NATIONAL DEFENSE USE, AND YOU ARE REQUIRED TO FOLLOW ALL THE PROVISIONS OF THE DEFENSE PRIORITIES AND ALLOCATIONS SYSTEM REGULATION (15 CFR PART 350)

11132-200 (REV 1-88) HONEYWELL INC.

ISSUER

Reduction 6%

1. Contain provisions to guard the buyer from damage suits caused by patent infringement.
2. Contain provisions concerning price, such as, "If the price is not stated on this order, material must not be billed at a price higher than last paid without notice to us and our acceptance thereof."
3. Contain a clause stating that no charges will be allowed for boxing, crating, or drayage.
4. Stipulate that the acceptance of the materials is contingent on inspection and quality.
5. Require in case of rejection that the seller receive a new order from the buyer before replacement is made.
6. Precisely describe quality requirements and the method of quality assurance/control.
7. Provide for cancellation of the order if deliveries are not received on the date specified in the order.
8. Contain conditions stating that the buyer refuses to accept drafts drawn against the buyer.

9. Have some mention of quantity, relating to overshipments or undershipments of the quantities called for. In certain industries, it is hard to control definitely the amount obtained from a production run, for example, printing, and in such instances, overruns and underruns are usually accepted within certain limits.
10. Provide for matters of special interest to the company, governing such matters as arbitration and the disposition of tools required in making parts.

Individual companies differ widely both in the number of copies of a purchase order issued and in the method of handling these copies. In a typical example, the distribution may be as follows: The original is sent to the supplier, sometimes accompanied by a duplicate copy to be returned by the supplier as an acceptance copy to complete the contract.

One copy is filed in the numerical PO file maintained by the purchasing department; another may be maintained in the supplier file. One copy is sent to the accounting department for use in the accounts payable process. A copy is sent to the stores department so it can plan for the receipt of the materials. A separate copy may be sent to the receiving department (if receiving and stores are organizationally separate) where it will be filed alphabetically by supplier and used to record quantities actually received when the shipment arrives. If the material is to go through incoming inspection (which normally would be raw material and production parts), a copy would be routed there also. It is obvious that a computerized system simplifies record keeping and access.

Giving or sending a purchase order does not constitute a contract until it has been accepted. The usual form of acceptance requested is that of an "acknowledgment" sent by the supplier to the purchasing department. Just what does constitute mutual consent and the acceptance of an offer is primarily a legal question. Generalizations concerning the acceptance of offers, as any lawyer will indicate, are likely to be only generalizations with many exceptions.

One further reason for insisting on securing an acceptance of the purchase order is that, quite aside from any question of law, unless the order is accepted, the buyer can only assume that delivery will be made by the requested date. When delivery dates are uncertain, definite information in advance is important if the buyer is to plan operations effectively.

Blanket and Open-End Orders

The cost of issuing and handling purchase orders may be reduced when conditions permit the use of blanket or open-end orders. A blanket order usually covers a variety of items. An open-end order allows for addition of items and/or extension of time. MRO items and production line requirements used in volume and purchased repetitively over a period of months may be bought in this manner.

All terms and conditions involving the purchase of estimated quantities over a period are negotiated and incorporated in the original order. Subsequently, releases of specific quantities are made against the order. In some instances, it is possible to tie the preparation of the releases into the production scheduling procedures and forward them to the purchasing department for transmission to the supplier, or the release may go from production scheduling direct to the supplier. It is not unusual for an open-end order to remain in effect for a year, or until changes in design, material specification, or conditions affecting price or delivery make new negotiations desirable or necessary. Figure 3–2 shows a form used to authorize release of materials on a blanket order.

FIGURE 3–2
Blanket Order Release

Source: Raytheon Company.

RAYTHEON

RAYTHEON COMPANY
SORENSEN OPERATION
SOUTH NORWALK, CONN.

BLANKET ORDER RELEASE
THIS NUMBER MUST APPEAR ON ALL DOCUMENTS AND PACKAGES

REQUISITION NO. | REQUISITIONED BY | UNIT | RELEASE DATE | PURCHASE ORDER NO. | RELEASE NO.

TO | SHIP VIA: UPS | ACCOUNT NO.

SHIP MATERIAL TO ABOVE ADDRESS UNLESS INDICATED OTHERWISE BELOW: SORENSEN | PROD. SHOP ORDER NO. | DELIVER MATERIAL TO (INTERNAL)

DELIVERY AT DESTINATION | VENDOR CODE: 620393 | MATERIAL CODE | TAXABLE: YES / NO: X | EXEMPTION NO.: 5151175

RECEIVED Date	RECEIVED Quantity	Item	Quantity Ordered	DESCRIPTION	Part Number	Qty	Net Unit Price

x INDICATES CONFIRMING ORDER
DATE YOUR
BLANKET ORDER TERMS AND CONDITIONS APPLY
TOTAL
RECEIVING DEPARTMENT USE ONLY

Supplier- or Vendor-Managed Inventory (SMI/VMI), Stockless Buying, or Systems Contracting

Supplier- or vendor-managed inventory, systems contracting, or stockless buying is a more sophisticated merging of the ordering and inventory functions than blanket contracts. Systems contracts rely on periodic billing procedures; allow nonpurchasing personnel to issue order releases; employ special catalogs; require suppliers to maintain minimum inventory levels, but normally do not specify the volume of contract items a buyer must buy; and improve inventory turnover rates.

This technique has been used most frequently in buying stationery and office supplies, repetitive items, maintenance and repair materials, and operating supplies (MRO). This latter class of purchases is characterized by many different types of items, all of comparatively low value and needed immediately when any kind of a plant or equipment failure occurs. The technique is built around a blanket-type contract that is developed in great detail regarding approximate quantities to be used in specified time periods, prices, provisions for adjusting prices, procedures to be followed in picking up requisitions daily and making delivery within a short time (normally 24 hours), simplified billing procedures, and a complete catalog of all items covered by the contract.

Generally the inventory of all items covered by a contract is stored by the supplier, thus eliminating the buyer's investment in inventory and space. Requisitions for items covered by the contract go directly to the supplier and are not processed by the purchasing department. The requisition is used by the supplier to pull stock, to pack, to invoice, and as a delivery slip. The streamlined procedure reduces paper-handling costs for the buyer and the seller and has been a help in solving the small order problem.

Some organizations use an electronic system in systems contracting that requires a data transmission terminal. The buyer or requisitioner simply indicates each item needed and the quantity required, which is transmitted electronically to the supplier's computer.

In some firms with large volume requirements from a specific supplier, that supplier stores items in the customer's plant as though it were the supplier's warehouse. The buyer's contact with the supplier is by computer, through a computer modem. The system would work as follows:

1. The buyer places the blanket order for a family of items, such as fasteners, at firm prices.
2. The supplier delivers predetermined quantities to the inventory area set aside in the buyer's plant. The items are still owned by the supplier.
3. The buyer inspects the items when they are delivered.
4. The computer directs storage to the appropriate bin or shelf.
5. The buyer places POs through the computer terminal, thus relieving the supplier's inventory records.
6. Pick sheets are computer prepared. The buyer physically removes the items from the supplier's inventory.
7. The supplier submits a single invoice monthly for all items picked.
8. The buyer's accounting department makes a single monthly payment for all items used.
9. The computer prepares a summary report, at predetermined intervals, showing the items and quantity used, for both the buyer's and supplier's analysis, planning, and restocking.

Systems contracting has become popular in nonmanufacturing organizations as well. It is no longer confined to MRO items and may well include a number of high-dollar-volume commodities. The shortening of the time span from requisition to delivery has resulted in substantial inventory reductions and greater organizational willingness to go along with the supply system. The amount of red tape has become minimal. Since the user normally provides a good estimate of requirements and compensates the supplier in case the forecast is not good, the supplier risks little in inventory investment. The degree of cooperation and information exchange required between buyer and seller in a systems contract often results in a much warmer relationship than is normally exhibited in a traditional arm's-length trading situation.

Third-Party MRO Suppliers

Some firms have developed contracts with third-party suppliers to provide all of their MRO requirements for the entire company or for a major division.

6. FOLLOW-UP AND EXPEDITING

After a PO has been issued to a supplier, the buyer may wish to follow up and/or expedite the order. At the time the order is issued, an appropriate follow-up date is indicated. In some firms, purchasing has full-time follow-up and expediting personnel.

Follow-up is the routine tracking of an order to ensure that the supplier will be able to meet delivery promises. If problems—for example, quality or delivery—are developing, the buyer needs to know this as soon as possible so that appropriate action can be taken. Follow-up, which requires frequent inquiries of the supplier on progress and possibly a visit to the supplier's facility, will be done only on critical, large-dollar and/or long lead-time buys. The follow-up often is done by phone, to get immediate information and answers, but some firms use a simple form, often computer generated, to request information on expected shipping date or percentage of the production process completed as of a certain date. Figure 3–3 shows a follow-up form.

Expediting is the application of pressure on a supplier to meet the original delivery promise, to deliver ahead of schedule, or to speed up delivery of a delayed order. It may involve the threat of order cancellation or withdrawal of future business if the supplier cannot meet the agreement. Expediting should be necessary on only a small percentage of the POs issued, for if the buyer has done a good job of analyzing supplier capabilities, only reliable suppliers—ones who will perform according to the purchase agreement—will be selected. And if the firm has done an adequate job of planning its material requirements, it should not need to ask a supplier to move up the delivery date except in unusual situations. Of course, in times of severe scarcity, the expediting activity assumes greater importance.

FIGURE 3–3
Follow-up Form

Source: Arizona Public Service Company.

aps.

PURCHASE ORDER FOLLOW-UP
(Please Rush Reply)
PURCHASING DEPARTMENT • P.O. BOX 21666 • PHOENIX, ARIZONA 85036

Date ____________
This is our ______ Request
Please Answer Immediately

REPLY TO ITEMS CHECKED BELOW BY
☐ This Form ☐ Wire ☐ Phone

Our Purchase Order No.	Request for Quotation No.	Your Invoice No.	Date	Amount	Your Reference

☐ 1. RUSH SHIPMENT. ADVISE EARLIEST DATE.
☐ 2. WHEN WILL SHIPMENT BE MADE? IF SHIPPED, ADVISE METHOD.
☐ 3. PLEASE TRACE SHIPMENT.
☐ 4. IF SHIPMENT HAS BEEN MADE, MAIL INVOICE, TODAY.
☐ 5. PLEASE MAIL RECEIPTED FREIGHT BILL.
☐ 6. WHY DID YOU NOT SHIP AS PROMISED? ADVISE WHEN YOU WILL SHIP.
☐ 7. WILL YOU SHIP ON DATE SHOWN ON PURCHASE ORDER?
☐ 8. RELEASE SHIPMENTS AS SHOWN UNDER REMARKS.
☐ 9. PLEASE MAIL US ACCEPTANCE COPY OR OUR PURCHASE ORDER.
☐ 10. PLEASE ACKNOWLEDGE OUR ORDER.
☐ 11. PLEASE MAKE YOUR SHIPPING DATE MORE SPECIFIC.
☐ 12. WHEN WILL BALANCE OF ORDER BE SHIPPED.
☐ 13. WHEN WILL PRICES BE SUBMITTED? PLEASE RUSH.
☐ 14. PLEASE MAIL SHIPPING NOTICE.
☐ 15. PLEASE INDICATE OUR PURCHASE ORDER NUMBER ON PAPERS REFERRED TO OR ATTACHED.
☐ 16. WE HAVE NO RECORD OF TRANSACTION COVERED BY INVOICE. ADVISE DATE OF SHIPMENT, NAME OF PERSON PLACING ORDER AND FURNISH SIGNED DELIVERY RECEIPT COPY.
☐ 17. INVOICE RETURNED HEREWITH.
☐ 18. INVOICE IS REQUIRED IN ________ COPIES.
☐ 19. PRICE OR DISCOUNT IS NOT IN ACCORDANCE WITH QUOTATION.
☐ 20. TERMS ON INVOICE ARE NOT IN ACCORDANCE WITH THE PURCHASE ORDER.
☐ 21. ENCLOSED INVOICE SENT TO US IN ERROR.
☐ 22. DIFFERENCE IN QUANTITY.
☐ 23. UNIT PRICE INCORRECT.
☐ 24. EXTENSION INCORRECT.
☐ 25. PURCHASE ORDER NO. LACKING OR INCORRECT.
☐ 26. SALES TAX DOES NOT APPLY – See reverse side of Purchase Order.
☐ 27. SHOULD BE BILLED F.O.B. DESTINATION.
☐ 28. HAVE YOU CONSIDERED THIS ORDER COMPLETE?
☐ 29. ____________

Reply: ____________

Vendor
By ____________

Purchasing
By ____________

510-00J

SEND WHITE AND PINK COPIES WITH CARBON INTACT. WHITE COPY IS RETURNED WITH REPLY.

Cost and Benefits

One of the costs of doing business with a supplier (and vice versa) is the cost associated with follow-up and expediting. Matching the degree and type of follow-up with the importance of the purchase to the organization is one form of risk assessment. Follow-up that does not reap a better return in the value added is merely another form of waste that should be eliminated. Likewise, the time spent by individuals to expedite orders should be captured and included in the total cost of ownership assessment. If an organization expends a lot of resources on expediting, it would be a prime target for root cause analysis and fishbone diagramming to identify the root causes and reduce or eliminate the need for expediting. Often, the analysis reveals that the need for expediting is driven by decisions made in the buying organization, not the supplier.

7. RECEIPT AND INSPECTION OF GOODS

The proper receipt of materials and other items is of vital importance. Many organizations have, as a result of experience, centralized all receiving under one department, the chief exceptions being large organizations with multiple sites. Receiving is so closely related to purchasing that, in many organizations, the receiving department is directly or indirectly responsible to the purchasing department. In firms where just-in-time inventory management systems have been implemented, materials from certified suppliers or supplier partners bypass receiving and inspection entirely and are delivered directly to the point of use. Further discussion of these arrangements is presented in Chapter 6, "Quantity and Inventory." Receiving also may be bypassed for small-value purchases.

The prime purposes of receiving are to

1. Confirm that the order placed has actually arrived.
2. Check that the shipment arrived in good condition.
3. Ensure the quantity ordered has been received.
4. Forward the shipment to its proper next destination be it storage, inspection, or use.
5. Ensure that proper documentation of the receipt is registered and forwarded to the appropriate parties.

In checking the goods received, it sometimes will appear that shortages exist either because material has been lost in transit or because it was short-shipped. Occasionally, too, there is evidence that the shipment has been tampered with or that the shipment has been damaged in transit. In all such cases, full reports are called for.

Normally one copy of the PO form, often with the quantity column masked out to force a count, is used for receiving. Receiving information then must be supplied to the purchasing department to close out the order, to inventory control to update the inventory files, and to accounts payable for the invoice clearance and payment. Some organizations use a separate receiving-slip form, rather than a copy of the PO, on which receiving records the date of receipt, supplier name, description of materials, and the receiving count. In organizations with an integrated computer materials system, receiving counts are entered directly into the computer data file.

Eliminating or Reducing Inspection

Clearly, the buying organization wants to do as little incoming inspection as possible. The goal is to build in quality at the design stage and ensure quality throughout the suppliers' processes so that incoming inspection can be eliminated or reduced. Chapter 5 on quality addresses the decisions related to quality and Chapter 8 discusses buyer–supplier relationships and programs such as certification programs that are designed primarily to ensure quality and reduce the risks associated with reducing or eliminating incoming inspection. In a just-in-time environment, production parts go from the receiving dock right into production. This is only possible when the supplier is capable of achieving the right level of quality consistently and the carrier is capable of hitting the delivery windows consistently. In other situations when quality is not assured, incoming inspection does occur and the buying organization must continually assess the need for inspection, determine the appropriate type of inspection, and carry it out in the most cost-efficient and effective way possible. Incoming inspection also may be associated with damage in transit and these situations would influence the carrier selection and the way in which quality is defined and assessed throughout the logistics process.

8. INVOICE CLEARING AND PAYMENT

The invoice constitutes a claim against the buyer and needs to be handled with care. Invoices commonly are requested in duplicate. Often invoices must show order number and itemized price for each article invoiced.

Procedures relating to invoice clearance are not uniform. In fact, there is a difference of opinion on whether the checking and approval of the invoice is a function of supply or accounting. Clearly, the invoice must be checked and audited. The arguments are that it relieves the supply department of the performance of a non-value-adding task, that it concentrates all the accounting work in a single office, and that it provides a check and balance between the commitment to buy and the payment to the supplier. The prime argument for having invoices checked by supply is that this is where the original agreement was made. If discrepancies exist, immediate action can be taken.

Where the invoice is handled by accounting, the following procedure is typical:

1. All invoices are mailed in duplicate by the supplier directly to the accounts payable department, where they are promptly time-stamped. All invoices then are checked and certified for payment, except where the purchase order and the invoice differ.
2. Invoices at variance with the purchase order on price, terms, or other features are referred to supply for approval.

Since the time required in supply to resolve minor variances might be more valuable to the organization than the dollar amount in dispute, many organizations use a decision rule that calls for payment of the invoice as submitted, providing the difference is within prescribed limits; for example, plus or minus 5 percent or $25, whichever is smaller. Of course, accounts payable should keep a record of the variances paid by supplier account to identify suppliers who are intentionally short-shipping.

If any of the necessary information is not on the invoice or if the information does not agree with the purchase order, the invoice is returned to the supplier for correction. Ordinarily, the buyer insists that, in computing discounts, the allowable period dates from the receipt of the corrected invoice, not from the date originally received.

In every instance of cancellation of a purchase order involving the payment of cancellation charges, accounting requires from supply a "change notice" referring to the order and defining the payment to be made before passing an invoice for such payment.

In cases where supply does the invoice checking, the following procedure applies: After being checked and adjusted for any necessary corrections, the original invoice is forwarded to accounting to be held until supply authorizes its payment. The duplicate invoice is retained by supply. As soon as supply obtains the receiving report, it checks that report against the invoice. If the receiving report and the invoice agree, supply keeps both documents until it receives assurance from inspection that the goods are acceptable. Supply then forwards its duplicate copy of the invoice and the receiving report to accounting, where the original copy of the invoice is already on file.

Aligning Supply and Accounts Payable

In many organizations, there is a lack of alignment between supply and accounts payable. On the supply side, suppliers are viewed as valuable contributors to the organization's success. As such, relationships with suppliers must be defined and cultivated. Living up to the terms and conditions of the contract is one indicator of the commitment to performance of both parties. When buyers negotiate payment terms and then their organization fails to live up to those terms, this should be seen as a serious breach by all functional representatives. However, often payment terms are not met. The root cause of late payment is typically one of two things: slow cycle time in the accounts payable process or conflict between finance policy and supply practice. In some organizations, accounts payable and supply have been put into one department to force goal alignment through structure and reporting relationship. In others, accounts payable and supply are put on a joint team to resolve the inconsistencies between the two groups and align the process.

Cash Discounts and Late Invoices

Sometimes suppliers are negligent about invoicing goods shipped, and it may be necessary to request the invoice to complete the transaction. On the other hand, payment of an invoice prior to the receipt of material is often requested. The question then is: When invoices provide for cash discounts, do you pay the invoice within the discount period, even though the material may not actually have been received, or do you withhold payment until the material arrives, even at the risk of losing cash discounts?

The arguments for withholding payment of the invoice until after the goods have arrived are as follows:

1. Frequently the invoice does not reach the buyer until late in the discount period and, on occasion, may even arrive after it. This situation arises through a failure on the part of the supplier to send the invoice promptly.
2. It is unsound buying practice to pay for anything until an opportunity has been given for inspection. The transaction has not, in fact, been completed until the material or part

has actually been accepted, and payment prior to this time is premature. In fact, legally, the title to the goods may not have passed to the buyer until acceptance of them.

3. In any event, the common practice of dating invoices as of the date of shipment should be amended to provide that the discount period runs from receipt of the invoice or the goods, whichever is later.

The arguments in favor of passing the invoice for payment without awaiting the arrival, inspection, and acceptance of the material are several:

1. The financial consideration may be substantial.
2. Failure to take the cash discounts as a matter of course reflects unfavorably on the credit standing of the buyer.
3. When purchasing from reputable suppliers, mutually satisfactory adjustments arising out of unsatisfactory material will easily be made, even though the invoice has been paid.

Streamlining the Receiving, Invoicing, and Payment Process

Some organizations, particularly those with integrated computer purchasing systems, question whether they need to receive an invoice at all, since the invoice provides no information that they do not already have and it is another piece of paperwork that costs money to handle. They notify their suppliers that payment, under the agreed-on cash discount schedule, will be made in a set number of days from receipt of satisfactory merchandise (and they may specify that payment will be made only after the complete shipment has been received). They simply then compare, in their computer system, the PO, the receiving report, and the inspection report; if they agree, then the computer prints a check at the receipt date plus the agreed-on payment term. Obviously, this requires that the receiving report be accurate; that the PO be fully priced, including taxes and cash discount terms; and that purchases be made FOB destination, since there is no way to enter in freight charges. The PO then is the controlling document. An additional enhancement is use of an electronic funds transfer system (EFT) where the buyer transmits payment information from its computer through a telephone modem to the bank's computer, and the funds are transferred to the supplier's bank account by account number and PO number.

9. MAINTENANCE OF RECORDS AND RELATIONSHIPS

After having gone through the steps described, all that remains for the completion of any order is to update the records. This operation involves little more than assembling and filing copies of the documents relating to the order and transferring to appropriate records the relevant information. The former is largely a routine matter. The latter involves judgment as to what records are to be kept and also for how long.

Most companies differentiate between the various forms and records as to their importance. For example, a purchase order constitutes evidence of a contract with an outside party and as such may well be retained much longer (normally seven years) than the requisition, which is an internal memorandum.

The minimum, basic records to be maintained, either manually or by computer, are

1. PO log, which identifies all POs by number and indicates the open or closed status of each.
2. PO file, containing a copy of all POs, filed numerically.
3. Commodity file, showing all purchases of each major commodity or item (date, supplier, quantity, price, PO number).
4. Supplier history file, showing all purchases placed with major large-total-value suppliers.
5. Outstanding contracts against which orders are placed as required.
6. A commodity classification of items purchased.
7. A database of suppliers.

Additional record files may include

1. Labor contracts, giving the status of union contracts (expiration dates) of all major suppliers.
2. Tool and die record showing tooling purchased, useful life (or production quantity), usage history, price, ownership, and location. This information may prevent the buyer from paying more than once for the same tooling.
3. Minority and small business purchases, showing dollar purchases from such suppliers.
4. Bid-award history file, showing suppliers asked to bid, amounts bid, number of no bids, and the successful bidder, by major items. This information may highlight supplier bid patterns and possible collusion.

Linking Data to Decisions

Supply data collection occurs throughout the process. Turning data into useable knowledge is a continuing challenge. In Chapter 4 a number of electronic tools are discussed that are designed to enable better decisions though information management. From a process perspective, it is important to think through exactly what decisions need to be made and then identify the relevant information, target the data sources, and determine how to capture, analyze, and disseminate information to decision makers. All too often, the problem is information overload, which leads to "analysis paralysis" rather than a lack of information holding up the process. What do we need to know and why? is the first question that should be asked. Metrics are discussed in detail in Chapter 13.

Managing Supplier Relationships

Internal and external relationships are affected throughout the supply process. They may be initiated, developed, damaged, or repaired. Attention should be given to the key supply chain stakeholders internally and externally throughout the process to build stronger and more productive relationships. It is also important to assess the status of key relationships periodically. Chapter 13 addresses metrics.

A SUPPLY PROCESS FLOWCHART

The way in which the supply process is operationalized depends in part on the nature of the purchase. The flowchart in Figure 3–4 demonstrates one way in which an organization

FIGURE 3–4
A Supply Process Flowchart

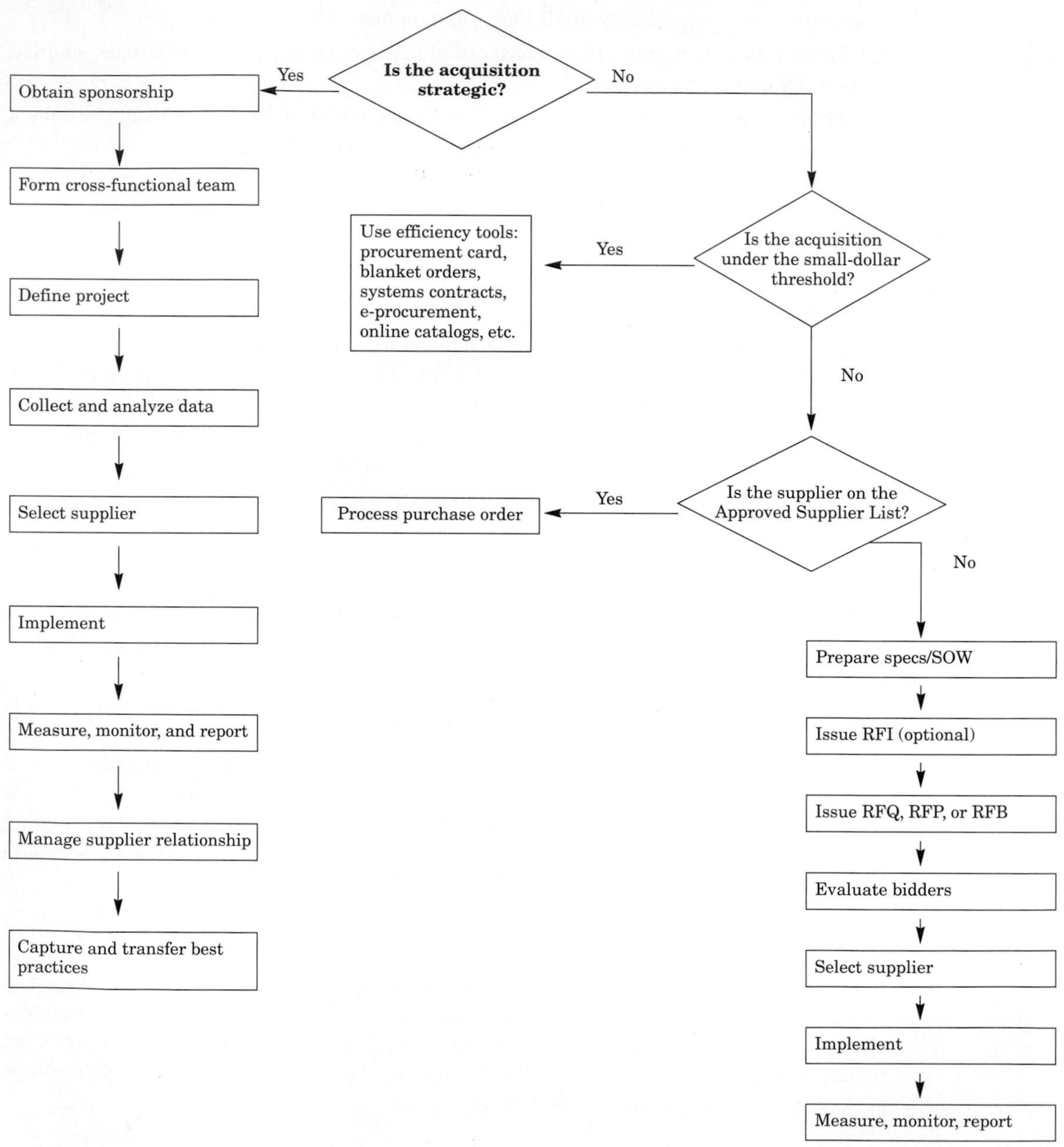

might customize the supply process based on different categories of purchases. In this example, the first cut is determining whether or not the purchase is strategic. While the exact definition may vary from organization to organization, a general description might be that a strategic purchase is one that is critical to the mission of the organization. This definition allows for high- and low-dollar-value purchases that are mission critical. For these purchases, it makes sense to spend more time, money, and resources in the sourcing process. For nonstrategic purchases (the right column of the flowchart), the first cut is made based on a small-dollar threshold. A second cut is made based on the availability of a prequalified supplier. Other ways to categorize purchases are discussed in Chapter 6.

RUSH AND SMALL-VALUE ORDERS

There are two continual realities in managing the supply needs of any organization. The first is the problem of rush or emergency orders. The second stems from the large number of small orders that inevitably represent the largest percentage of total purchase requirements, not in dollar terms but in variety.

Rush or Emergency Orders

Frequently, an excessively large number of requisitions will be received marked "rush." Rush orders cannot always be avoided; emergencies do arise that justify their use. Sudden changes in style or design and unexpected changes in market conditions may upset the most carefully planned material schedule. Breakdowns seemingly are inevitable, with an accompanying demand for parts or material that is not carried in stock.

There are, however, so-called rush orders that cannot be justified on any basis. They consist of those requisitions that arise because of (1) faulty inventory control, (2) poor production planning or budgeting, (3) an apparent lack of confidence in the ability of the supply department to get material to the user by the proper time, and (4) the sheer habit of marking the requests "rush." Whatever the cause, such orders are costly. This higher cost is due in part to the greater chance of error when the work is done under pressure. Rush orders also place an added burden on the seller, and this burden must directly or indirectly find its way into the price paid by the buyer.

What can be done to reduce the seriousness of the problem? For an excessive number of rush orders that are not actually emergency orders, the solution is a matter of education in the proper supply procedure. In one company, for example, when a rush requisition is sent, the department issuing the order has to explain to the general manager the reason for the emergency requirement and secure approval. Furthermore, even if the requisition is approved, the extra costs, so far as they can be determined, are charged to the department ordering the material. The result has been a marked reduction in the number of such orders. The use of preapproved suppliers, electronic catalogs, and e-procurement systems also may mitigate the problem by reducing the lead time for order processing and by allowing users to issue requests against an existing contract directly with the supplier.

Small-Value Orders and Efficiency Tools

Small-value orders are a continuing matter of concern in every organization. Most requisitions follow Pareto's Law, which says that about 70 percent of all requisitions amount to only about 10 percent of the total dollar volume. (Pareto's Law, also known as ABC analysis, is discussed in detail in Chapter 6, "Quantity and Inventory"). When organizations analyze their purchases, many find that roughly 70 to 80 percent of the transactions account for 10 to 15 percent of the dollars with most of the spend going to acquire maintenance, repair, and operating (MRO) supplies and general and administrative expenses, with low average transaction amounts. Many organizations spend as much to process the transaction for a $50 purchase as for a $5,000 one. One important consideration is the cost of the system set up to handle small orders versus the cost of the items themselves. Since the lack of a small item may create a nuisance totally out of proportion to its dollar value, assured supply is usually the first objective to be met.

Many approaches can be used to address the small order question. Typically they involve simplifying or automating the process or consolidating purchases to reduce the acquisition cycle time (time from need recognition to payment), reduce administrative cost, and free up the buyer's time for higher-value or more critical purchases. A few examples follow:

1. Vendor/supplier-managed inventory (VMI/SMI), stockless buying, or systems contracting can be used. This has occurred most widely in the purchase of MRO items. (See explanation earlier in this chapter.)
2. A procurement card (also called a purchasing card or a P-card) is a credit card that is provided to internal customers who use it to purchase directly from established suppliers.
3. Purchasing sets up blanket orders against which internal customers issue release orders; suppliers provide summary billing.
4. Electronic linkage is made with major suppliers either through an Internet-based electronic procurement system or an electronic data interchange (EDI) system. Ordering and reordering occur automatically once reorder points are established. (See Chapter 4.)
5. In reverse auctions, the buyer prequalifies suppliers and invites them to an online auction during which bidders submit bids and the buyer awards a contract for the predefined items for a set period of time.
6. Authority levels and bidding practices are adjusted, and telephone, fax, and auto-fax are used for ordering.
7. Integrated suppliers are used to provide a variety of supplies.
8. Low-value order placement is outsourced to third parties.
9. Persuasion may be employed to increase the number of standardized items requested.
10. The supply department holds small requisitions until a reasonable total, in dollars, has been accumulated.
11. A requisition calendar is established that sets aside specific days for the requisitioning of specific supplies, so that all requests for a given item are received on the same day. The calendar also may be so arranged that practically all the supplies secured from any specific type of supplier are requisitioned on the same day.

12. Invoiceless payments (self-billing) are arranged.
13. Users place orders directly.
14. A blank check purchase order is issued in which a signed, blank check is sent along with the PO. The supplier ships the full order, enters the amount due on the check, and cashes it. This reduces paperwork (receiving reports, inventory entries, and payments), saves postage, often enables a larger cash discount, and saves time in accounts payable.

Corporate Purchasing Cards

Corporate purchasing or procurement cards, or P-cards, are credit cards that are issued to internal customers (users) in the buying organization. The cards also can be merged with technology to be electronic commerce compatible and data sensitive to capture important information for buying organizations. Procurement cards are used primarily to reduce administrative costs and cycle time for low-dollar-value, indirect (nonproduction) materials, supplies, and services transactions. Holders of the card are given dollar limits and lists of preferred suppliers with whom purchasing has already negotiated prices and terms. P-cards automate many aspects of the system, thereby eliminating purchase orders and individual invoices and ensuring suppliers of fast payment, two or three days versus 30+ in a typical system. By moving the transaction activities to the user department, the purchasing cycle time is reduced and so is the cost of processing the transaction. Also, buyers (and accounts payable) are freed from the day-to-day transactions related to small-value purchases and can concentrate on higher-value purchases and supply management issues.

The primary perceived risk of P-cards is loss of control. Management wants assurance that only authorized persons will be issued the cards and that only appropriate purchases will be made from preferred suppliers. In response to these concerns, card issuers have instituted controls that (1) determine, at the point of sale, if the purchase meets preset dollar limits per card; (2) limit the number of transactions per day; (3) limit the value of a single transaction; and (4) determine if it is an approved supplier. While retail acceptance of the purchase cards is widespread worldwide, industrial suppliers have been slower to sign up for the programs. But the promise of fast payment and the potential for increased volume are leading to wider acceptance by industrial suppliers. Benchmark data indicate that organizations in most industries put a very low percentage of their spend on P-cards.

The most sophisticated card programs are able to (1) track and report sales tax information for audit purposes, (2) identify whether the supplier is a minority business owner, (3) capture specific product information, (4) identify which cost center should be charged for the purchase, and (5) include different types of purchases, including travel and entertainment expenses and fleet expenses.

POLICY AND PROCEDURE MANUAL

A policy and procedure manual is a carefully prepared, detailed statement of organization, duties of the various personnel, and procedures and data systems (including illustrative forms used, fully explained). A manual is an essential for the well-conceived training program for junior members. Furthermore, it adds an element of flexibility in facilitating the transfer of personnel from one job to another in case of vacation, illness, or temporary workload imbalances. The manual is also useful in explaining to nonsupply colleagues what and how things are done. The requirements of the Sarbanes-Oxley Act add greater importance to having internal controls, standardized processes, and consistent use.

Some managers feel that because their departments are not as large as those in bigger companies, there is no special need for a manual. They feel that everyone knows all that would be put in a manual anyway and hence there is no need for writing it all down. This argument overlooks the benefits gained in the actual task of preparing the manual.

The preparation of a manual is time-consuming and somewhat tedious, to be sure, but well worth the cost. Careful advance planning of the coverage, emphasis, and arrangement is essential, to include a clear definition of the purposes sought in issuing the manual and the uses to which it is to be put, for both of these have a bearing on its length, form, and content.

The preparer must decide whether the manual is to cover only policy or is to include also a description of the organization and the procedures, and if the latter, in how much detail. A collection of manuals now in use should be the starting point. Fortunately, excellent sample manuals that can serve as guides are available from a number of organizations.

When the general outline has been determined, the actual writing may be started. This work need not be done all at one time but section by section as the opportunity presents itself. It also is well to have the work thoroughly discussed and carefully checked, not only by those within the department itself but by those outside, such as engineering and production personnel, whose operations are directly affected. When a section is completed, that portion may provide the basis for a department discussion forum, not only for the sake of spotting errors and suggesting modifications before the material is actually reproduced but also to ensure that everyone understands its contents. This should be done prior to issue. When reproduced, a loose-leaf form may be found preferable, since it allows for easy revision. Another worthwhile step is to have the chief executive of the organization write a short foreword, endorsing the policy and practices of the department and defining its authority.

While many subjects might be covered in the manual, some of the more common are authority to requisition, competitive bidding, approved suppliers, supplier contacts and commitments, authority to question specifications, purchases for employees, gifts, blanket purchase orders, confidential data, rush orders, supplier relations, lead times, determination of quantity to buy, over and short allowance procedure, local purchases, capital equipment, personal service purchases, repair service purchases, authority to select suppliers, confirming orders, unpriced purchase orders, documentation for purchase decisions, invoice clearance and payment, invoice discrepancies, freight bills, change orders, samples, returned materials, disposal of scrap and surplus, determination of price paid, small-order procedures, salesperson interviews, and reporting of data.

Conclusion

The supply management process has come under increasing scrutiny because of the unrelenting focus on cost management and the realization that standardized processes and internal and external integration can lead to competitive advantage. Robust processes are the foundation of a successful supply organization. Without structured and disciplined supply processes, technology expenditures may leave the organization with too many tools and not enough integration or utilization.

Questions for Review and Discussion

1. Where in the supply process is there the greatest opportunity to add value and why?
2. What are the steps in a robust supply management process?
3. What contribution to purchasing efficiency might be effected through the use of (a) a corporate purchasing card, (b) the bill of material, and (c) supplier-managed inventory?
4. What approaches, other than the standard purchasing procedure, might be used to minimize the small-value-order problem?
5. When would you issue an RFP rather than an RFQ and why?
6. What records are needed for efficient operation of the purchasing function? How can data collection throughout the process help or hurt buyer–supplier relationships?
7. What are the costs and benefits of follow-up and expediting? Are there opportunities to reduce total cost of ownership at this stage of the process?
8. What topics should be covered in a policy manual?
9. Are rush orders ever justified? When? How should they be handled?
10. Where, and how, should invoices be cleared for payment within an organization?

References

Bovet, David, and Joseph Martha. *Value Nets: Breaking the Supply Chain to Unlock Hidden Profits.* New York: John Wiley & Sons, 2000.

Heijboer, Govert. *Quantitative Analysis of Strategic and Tactical Purchasing Decisions.* Enschede, The Netherlands: Twente University Press, 2003.

Hughes, Jon; Mark Ralf; and Bill Michels. *Transforming Your Supply Chain: Releasing Value in Business*. London: International Thomson Business Press, 1998.

Institute for Supply Management. Procurement Card Guide, Supplement to *Purchasing Today.* March 1998.

Institute for Supply Management. *Glossary of Key Purchasing and Supply Terms.* http://www.ism.ws, 2000.

Rozemeijer, Frank. *Creating Corporate Advantage in Purchasing*. Eindhoven, The Netherlands: Technische Universiteit Eindhoven, 2000.

Simchi-Levy, David; Philip Kaminsky; and Edith Simchi-Levy. *Designing & Managing the Supply Chain*. 2nd ed. New York: McGraw-Hill/Irwin, 2003.

Case 3–1

Mike Wesley

In April, Mike Wesley, the purchasing manager at Wesley Printing, was reviewing a coordination problem the company had experienced with a recent print job. Late delivery to an important customer had been avoided only as a result of special measures taken by company staff. However, these actions, while necessary under the circumstances, resulted in significant cost overruns. Mike knew that the company could not afford to encounter such problems in the future.

WESLEY PRINTING

Wesley Printing was a specialty printer producing pressure-sensitive and glue-applied paper labels for customers primarily in the food and beverage industry. Founded in 1905, the company was owned and managed by several descendants of the founder.

Wesley Printing competed on the basis of product quality and customer service. As a unionized shop, its cost structure was higher than that of many of its competitors. Several of Wesley's larger competitors preferred high-volume jobs, where customers typically made sourcing decisions on the basis of price. Smaller printing companies did not have the experience or resources to deal with difficult printing processes. Wesley emphasized a high level of service to its customers, working closely with them to achieve their objectives, willing to go out of its way to satisfy the customer, and being flexible in meeting very short lead times.

Meeting deadlines was very important to Wesley's customers. A shortage of labels at a customer's production line could result in downtime or expensive rework. The costs caused by such delays could be charged back to the printer, and the disruption to schedules made repeat business unlikely.

WESLEY'S ORGANIZATION

Wesley Printing was organized on the basis of functional groups. On the administration side, there were the sales, finance and accounting, purchasing, and estimating departments. On the operations side, there was the art department, where customer-provided artwork was retouched and adjusted; the camera department, which photographed the artwork on the large "process camera" in order to make the films; the plate department, where the films were used to produce printing plates for the presses; the press department, where the actual printing took place; the bindery department, where large sheets of labels were sheared or die-cut to correct size and shape; and finally the shipping and receiving department. A customer order moved sequentially through these departments, scheduled by the production manager. Scheduling was sometimes difficult because it was common for last-minute changes in customer requirements to make schedule alterations necessary.

THE FINE FOODS JOB

Monday, April 14

On Monday, April 14, the sales representative handling the Fine Foods account received a request for a quote on an unusual job. Instead of the usual flat label, Fine Foods wanted 60,000 small folded booklets, with a hole in one corner, through which passed a loop of string to enable it to be hung from the necks of condiment bottles. It was a rush job that had to be ready for a 7 a.m. production run the Tuesday of the following week, so that the client could have samples ready for a new product launch at a trade show. No schedule slippage could be tolerated.

The sales representative passed the order to the estimator, together with a sample booklet, in order to have a quotation prepared. The estimator knew that the job could be laid out such that an attachment on the press could fold the booklet as it was printed. Wesley did not have a drill suitable for making the holes, nor did they have equipment to insert the strings, so the estimator secured a quote from an outside bindery for those two parts of the job. The outside bindery agreed to complete its work by the following Monday morning if the job went ahead.

The finished quote was returned to the sales representative and a copy filed. The sales representative took the quote to the production manager to get a schedule commitment that the job would be done by Friday noon, in time to go to the outside bindery. The production manager agreed the commitment could be made.

Tuesday, April 15

The sales representative returned the quote to Fine Foods on Tuesday morning, and the client gave the job to Wesley, agreeing to send the artwork to arrive on Wednesday. The quote having been accepted, the file copy of the estimate and job specifications were retrieved and passed to the production manager, who scheduled the job and generated instructions for each production department. When the file was transferred, the sample was no longer in it. The production manager contacted the purchasing manager to have a purchase order prepared for the work to be done by the outside bindery. The purchasing manager sent the PO to the bindery, all the while assuming a simple flat tag was involved.

Wednesday, April 16

The artwork arrived and was duly processed by the art and camera departments. When the resulting films arrived at the plate maker, he laid the plates out in such a way that the booklets would not fold correctly if the press attachment was used. They would now have to be folded on a special folding machine, which Wesley did not have.

Thursday, April 17

The plates were sent to the press on Thursday afternoon for the print run, which was scheduled for the night shift. When the night shift press operator mounted the plates, he did not set up the folder attachment because the machine could not do the job properly. He assumed that alternate arrangements had been made for folding.

Friday, April 18

The full print run was completed in the morning and sent to Wesley's bindery, where the large sheets were cut to size, tied in blocks, and put in cartons for shipping to the outside bindery. The shipper, who prepared the shipment and assembled the paperwork instructions to go to the outside bindery, did not notice that the still unfolded booklets were not accompanied by any instructions for the bindery to fold them. The cartons of labels were sent to the outside bindery on Friday at noon.

Late Friday afternoon, the purchasing manager received a phone call from the manager of the bindery stating that the job arrived unfolded, that he had not contracted to fold them, and because he did not have the proper folding equipment, he intended to return the job. Mike and the sales representative were the only people in the office at that time and they both realized that if that happened, it would be impossible to meet the client's deadline.

Mike pleaded with the bindery manager to find some way to fill at least part of the order. The bindery manager agreed that if he could find enough labor to work around the clock all weekend, he could probably have a quarter of the order hand-folded and assembled by Monday evening. The sales representative called his contact at Fine Foods and imparted the news that, due to production difficulties, they would not be able to ship the full order on time, and would he be able to get by with a quarter of it? The customer replied that a quarter would not be enough, but he could get by with a third. Mike called the bindery manager and with more difficult persuasion got him to increase the quantity to a third.

Crews of people worked around the clock, hand-folding 20,000 little booklets. They were drilled and strung and were ready late Monday night. The Fine Foods account sales representative picked the booklets up from the bindery and personally delivered them to the production line at Fine Foods 150 miles away, a little before 7 o'clock the next morning.

After the Storm

Now that the emergency had passed, Mike felt it was important to find and correct whatever had gone wrong in their procedures that allowed such a slip-up to occur. He felt it was necessary to be able to assure both Fine Foods and the outside bindery that Wesley knew not only what had gone wrong, but also how to prevent it from happening again. This was the only way to assure both the customer and the supplier that they would not experience this kind of difficulty with Wesley in future dealings. It was also important for Wesley to prevent errors like this from happening again as all the extra costs involved in filling this order had caused a significant loss on the job.

Mike questioned how this had happened. The missing sample booklet was later found on the estimator's desk, but Mike felt that this was not the fault of a single person. All over the shop, mistakes had been made and not caught or corrected. Under pressure to be more efficient, Wesley was now turning out more work with fewer people than they had in the past. Mike wondered if production pressures no longer allowed the employees time to notice errors of omission. Wesley had recently completed all the documentation requirements to receive ISO 9000 certification, but that had not prevented this problem. Mike wondered what actions should be taken to prevent this kind of problem from happening again.

Case 3–2

UIL Inc.

In October, Jim Sinclair, materials manager for UIL Inc., was troubled by the amount of time consumed by processing rush orders. Jim wondered if inventory cages, eliminated several years earlier, would have to be reimplemented in some form, or whether he should try something different.

UIL

UIL manufactured custom equipment for a large variety of industries worldwide. UIL was a wholly owned subsidiary of Marin Inc., a large holding company. UIL functioned as an independent profit center responsible for its own purchasing, manufacturing, and sales functions. Capital was allocated to UIL from Marin on the basis that a levy would be charged to UIL's bottom line based on a percentage of capital utilized. Managers were then measured on their ability to maximize the final profit figure after the payments for use of capital had been paid to the parent. Otherwise, managers were free to make decisions regarding regular operations.

CURRENT MATERIALS REQUISITION SYSTEM

The UIL production operation required the requisition of a varied group of materials, ranging from items consumed on a regular basis, to items purchased sporadically, if not on a one-time basis. Under the current system, when workers on the plant floor required additional supplies, they would arrange for their requisition via Jim, the materials manager. Jim then had to issue a purchase order to a supplier to receive delivery of the required items.

The highest volume of orders existed in the Welding, Hardware, and Maintenance/Repair/Operating (MRO) areas. In these areas, individual items were inexpensive, often costing less than one dollar. Currently, items were held in stock with the quantity maintained within a minimum-maximum range. A computer system was used to track the number of items in stock and was supposed to indicate when inventory levels fell below the minimum level, thereby triggering an order by the materials manager.

GROWTH IN THE NUMBER OF PURCHASE ORDERS (POS)

Unfortunately, because inventory items in the three groups were so numerous yet inexpensive, employees were not motivated to keep inventory records current, and stockouts were frequent. These items, although trivial when available, would stop an area of operation when required. As a result, the materials manager was forced to issue a rush order to restock the supply. Lately, however, these rush orders had become a significant portion of the POs being issued and were consuming increasingly more of the materials manager's time. This was further aggravated by the portion of spend that this large number of POs represented. Jim's analysis showed that

Percentage of Total Spend	Spend Percentage of Total POs Issued
Less than 1%	Accounted for 25%
Less than 4%	60%
Less than 8%	73%
Less than 30%	94%

ELIMINATION OF INVENTORY CAGES

The traditional method of handling high-volume, low-cost items was with the use of inventory cages on the shop floor. An employee was assigned to a fenced-in inventory holding area or "cage" where production workers were able to request the items required. The cage manager would then be responsible for maintaining inventory levels of the items in the cage, giving the materials manager advanced notice of when orders would be required, and providing insight into ideal lot sizes. The cage manager could also maintain a degree of control as to the usage of the items.

Several years ago, Jim chose to eliminate the cages, citing the high cost of maintaining an employee to handle the inventory, particularly when the items being handled represented such a small cost to the company. Unfortunately, soon after the cages were eliminated, the instances where rush purchase orders to cover stockouts began to rise. Jim felt that the problem had grown to such proportions that he was not able to dedicate sufficient time to the remainder of the purchases, items that represented a much more significant proportion of total spend.

As a result, he concluded that the cages, in some form, might have to be reimplemented.

OUTSOURCING AS AN ALTERNATIVE

In October, Jim began exploring the alternative of allowing his suppliers to maintain inventory levels of the items in the three high-volume groups: MRO, Welding, and Hardware. This would be done by issuing a blanket purchase order for all of the items required in the class each month. All items in the class would be ordered from the same supplier under a single purchase order, resulting in a single invoice at the end of the month. This would reduce the number of purchase orders to 12 per year, per group, for a total of 36 transactions. In the period from January to October, this would have eliminated 637 transactions out of a total of 3,454 in this eight-month period.

Jim identified several disadvantages to the system. Currently, items within a class were purchased from many different suppliers, thereby providing an opportunity to shop around for the best quality and price. Under the proposed system, all the items would be purchased from the same supplier for a given class of products.

As well, it was the supplier that would come to the company premises and restock items. This presented the risk that the supplier would be motivated to overstock the shelves and poorly manage the inventory or even allow portions of the inventory to become obsolete. Poor management of inventory was even more likely because liability issues determined that the inventory would have to become the property of UIL at the time of delivery to the site, resulting in carrying costs to UIL. Jim felt that this risk could be minimized by setting minimum-maximum levels as before, and that he could still monitor the purchases being made, even if it was one month after-the-fact on the invoice.

The greatest benefit Jim recognized was the savings associated with not needing to hire someone to work in the cage. The suppliers would take on that responsibility and had already committed themselves to not raising their prices, despite the extra service provided. There was a risk, however, that over time, prices would rise due to the extra costs incurred by offering the materials-handling service. Jim could supply the parts he required, and if a relationship with one of the suppliers he selected deteriorated, he could replace them. But he was a bit worried that they would become dependent on one supplier's line of products, making a change to a new supplier more difficult.

THE DECISION

Jim had already interviewed several potential suppliers for the three product groups and was comfortable with his options. He was still not sure, however, if handing over this materials-handling function was a good idea. He knew that the standard cage method was a better alternative than the system currently used, but he had to decide if perhaps costs could be reduced further by this new option.

Case 3–3

Southeastern University

Heather Sloman, buyer in the purchasing department of Southeastern University, was preparing for a meeting with her boss, Glen Meredith, for later that day. Two days earlier, on April 6th, Glen had received a phone call from Walter Charbonneau, manager of the university registrar's office. Heather was surprised to learn from Glen that Walter had just bought a new piece of equipment for his department without following standard university purchasing policies. Glen asked Heather to look into the situation and get back to him with recommendations.

PURCHASING DEPARTMENT

Southeastern University was one of the largest universities in the state, with total enrolment of more than 25,000 graduate and undergraduate students and approximately 3,500 staff.

There were 12 faculties at the university, over 20 continuing education diploma and certificate programs, and three affiliated colleges. Purchasing was centralized, and the purchasing director, Blake Hyatt, reported to the university's vice president of administration.

The purchasing department was responsible for negotiating with suppliers, signing contracts with suppliers, and supervising the execution of contracts. Small-value purchases, those less than $100, could be handled out of petty cash. The purchasing department had also recently introduced a purchasing card, which could be used to acquire eligible goods and services with a value of less than $1,000.

The purchasing process began when a purchase request was submitted to the purchasing department. A clerk would stamp the requisition with the date and time received and checked it for proper signing authority. In some cases, it was necessary to forward the requisition to the research accounting section in the department of finance for account approval. Other information also was added to the requisition, such as tax and duty status, product classification, and supplier status.

Although the purchase requisition form provided an opportunity for the requisitioner to identify the preferred supplier, policy was to solicit at least two written quotations for purchases in excess of $7,500 and a minimum of three quotations for purchases in excess of $15,000. One of the buyers would prepare a request for quotation form (RFQ) and contacted approved suppliers. The RFQ form specified details, such as product or service description, quantities, FOB point, and terms of payment. Recent government legislation required that any RFQs in excess of $100,000 had to be posted on the Internet. After all bids were received and evaluated, the buyer would select the supplier and issue a purchase order.

The purchasing department maintained a list of approximately 1,200 approved suppliers, which was adjusted every three to five years. The selection criteria for becoming an approved vendor was based on the following weighted average evaluation system:

- Price, 50%
- Compliance with specifications, 25%
- Service, 20%
- Partnership, 5%

The purchasing department had three buying groups, and each group handled approximately 20 requests each day. (See Exhibit 1 for the organization chart.) In addition, approximately 250 contracts were rebid each year for ongoing purchases, such as snow removal

Exhibit 1 Organization Chart of the Purchasing Department

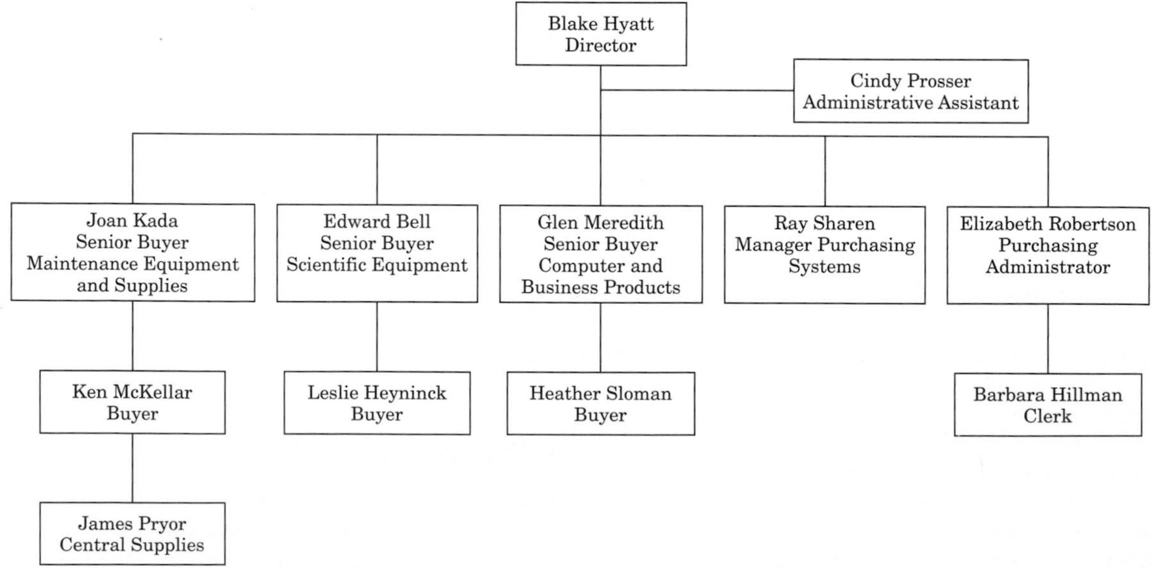

services and photocopier supplies. The total dollar volume of purchases amounted to $75 million of goods and services each year.

According to Heather Sloman, the main objective of the purchasing department was to achieve the greatest cost savings. She commented on the role of purchasing at the university: "Our training in purchasing allows us to negotiate the best deals for the university and help avoid wasting university money."

Although it was university policy that approval from the purchasing department was required before commitments could be made to suppliers, it was not unusual that university personnel contacted suppliers directly. Every year there were about 275 cases where contracts were signed with suppliers without prior approval of purchasing. Heather described what happened in these situations: "Most of the time, the only thing we can do is to call them and ask them to provide the details of the purchase. Usually the purchase has already been made, and there isn't much else that can be done."

THE FOLDING MACHINE ISSUE

The office of registrar handled about 160,000 pieces of mail a year. There were four major peaks of mailings each year: fees, admissions, records, and scholarships. As many as 50 to 60 people could be occupied manually stuffing envelops two days a month. A combination of full-time employees and temporary staff were used to perform this activity.

Walter Charbonneau had seen an advertisement in a flyer for an automatic folding machine, which could be used to eliminate some of the manual work in dealing with mass mailings. He later contacted a representative of the company and placed an order for the machine, at a cost of $14,000. Glen was notified shortly after the machine had arrived because Walter needed to make arrangements for payment. As far as Heather knew, the machine had arrived only in the last few days and had not been installed.

Heather found that the supplier of the folding machine was not on her approved supplier list. She then contacted three of her suppliers and received quotes of $10,000, $11,000, and $15,000 for similar equipment. The third quotation included one year of free service.

HEATHER'S OPTIONS

Heather recognized that some employees were going to ignore university policy from time to time and she had to be prepared to deal with such situations. However, if university staff failed to appreciate the benefits of sound purchasing practices, the university's centralized purchasing system would be undermined. When she spoke to Glen Meredith about the situation two days earlier, he said: "Let me know what we should do about this machine in the registrar's office. But also think about what else we can be doing to prevent these kinds of situations from happening again. These bad deals cost the university too much money each year. Besides, as a public institution, we must be extra careful to follow our procedures."

There were a number of alternatives Heather was considering regarding the equipment. One option was to simply keep the machine and pay the supplier. However, she felt the equipment could be returned, and if necessary she could negotiate a cancellation penalty with the supplier. Alternatively, Heather could go back to the supplier and use the quotations to negotiate a lower price.

Heather had about four hours before her meeting with Glen. As she sat down to prepare for the meeting, Heather thought about what she might say to Glen regarding avoiding future problems of this kind.

Chapter Four

Information Systems and Technology

Chapter Outline

Key Questions for the Supply Manager

Should we

- Use e-procurement tools for some or all of our purchases?
- Set up an intranet or extranet to help manage our purchases?
- Replace our EDI systems with XML?

How can we

- Decide which technology tools are most appropriate for the organization's categories of purchases?
- Make greater use of information technology and the Internet to simplify and improve the purchasing system and reduce costs?
- Use reverse auctions without damaging relationships with important suppliers?

In the past 25 years, there have been remarkable advancements in information technology used in the recording, transmission, analysis, and reporting of information within organizations and their supply chain networks. Even though there are still many unanswered questions when it comes to how e-commerce and the Internet will shape our economies, it is clear that all business processes and information systems used to manage tasks in all areas of business, including supply management, will be impacted.

The Internet, which was initially seen primarily as a tool for information sharing, is now seen as having tremendous potential for electronic commerce. Research by ISM/Forrester found that 89 percent of the respondents in their study used the Internet for the acquisition of indirect materials, while 72 percent used the Internet for direct materials. Despite the high adoption rate of Internet purchasing, the research also found that the average percentage of total purchases acquired via the Internet at these companies was only 12 percent for indirect materials and 13 percent for direct materials. Not surprisingly, the level of adoption of Internet-based purchasing was lower for the smaller companies in the study.[1]

Most people recognize the strategic importance of information and knowledge management, and that technology tools can improve efficiency and effectiveness when applied appropriately to a business process. Therefore, the decision maker must carefully assess the process to determine when and where the application of technology is most appropriate and what technology should be selected. If the process itself is flawed, then a process improvement program must be undertaken before the process is automated.

This chapter starts with the role of information systems in the organization and the potential ways that technology and Web-based applications might contribute to the efficiency and effectiveness of the acquisition process. The implications of technology and e-commerce for supply management are discussed. Lastly, a brief glossary of key terms and a detailed description of available technology is provided.

[1] Andrew Bartels, "ISM/Forrester Report on Technology in Supply Management: Q3 2003," Forrester Research Inc., 2003.

INFORMATION MANAGEMENT

There are four basic information flows involving supply. First, within the organization, information is sent to supply, including statements of need for materials and services to be obtained from outside the firm. Second, there are continuing requests for information available within supply for use by other functions in the organization. Such requests can involve information ranging from supplier pricing to purchasing forecasts used for cash flow budgeting. Third, information flows from external sources to supply. This information may come from suppliers (e.g., prices and deliveries) or from other sources (e.g., general market conditions and import duties). Fourth, information flows from supply to external sources, such as information to suppliers for materials and services requirements. In our interconnected world, supply must be able to manage effectively information flows involving both internal and external partners in the supply chain.

Information Systems[2]

Information systems are comprised of interconnected components that collect, process, and store raw data and distribute information to support decision making, control, and coordination within the organization. While information systems can be manual (e.g., paper-based), most information systems today rely on an information technology infrastructure, consisting of hardware and software, to operate its information systems.

Information system technology allows organizations to be connected with important partners in their supply chain networks. Capabilities to exchange reliable information with these partners quickly and cost effectively are essential for the improvement of supply chain performance.

Information systems can be classified into four types, each designed to serve the requirements and needs of the organization at different levels of management and across functions (see Figure 4–1). The strategic level comprises executive support systems (ESS); management-level systems consist of management information systems (MIS) and decision support systems (DSS); knowledge-level systems include knowledge work systems (KWS) and office automation systems (OAS); and transaction processing systems (TPS) are at the operational level.

Operational-level systems process data for the routine operations of the firm. Examples of operational-level systems for supply include generating POs, change orders, and requests for quotation; updating supplier lists; and maintaining commodity prices and supplier history files. Typically, transaction processing systems handle large volumes of repetitive data. These systems represent the foundation of the firm's information system hierarchy and downtime, for only a few hours, can create major problems.

Management information systems (MIS) are designed to provide reports and information to the management level of the organization to support activities related to planning, controlling, and decision making. MIS for the supply function include departmental budget information, supplier spend analysis, supplier performance reports, and raw material requirements forecasts.

[2] Adapted from K. C. Laudon, J. P. Laudon, and M. E. Brabston, *Management Information Systems: Managing the Digital Firm,* Upper Saddle River, NJ: Prentice Hall, 2002, pp. 40–47.

FIGURE 4–1 **Information Systems**

	Sales and Marketing	Operations	Finance	Accounting	Human Resources
			Strategic-Level Systems		
ESS	Sales planning	Operations planning	Financial forecasts	Corporate budget	H.R. planning
			Management-Level Systems		
MIS	Sales management	Inventory control	Capital expenditure analysis	Annual budget	Employee relocation analysis
DSS	Regional sales analysis	Production scheduling	SKU profitability analysis	Cost analysis	Union contract cost analysis
			Knowledge-Level Systems		
KWS	Engineering workstations	Graphics workstations		Managerial workstations	
OAS	Word processing	Document imaging		Electronic calendars	
			Operational-Level Systems		
TPS	Order tracking	Machine scheduling	Securities trading	Accounts receivable	Payroll
TPS	Order processing	Material control	Cash management	Accounts payable	Employee records

DSS, like MIS, are also at the management level and process data to assist in decision making. They do not merely present or analyze data: rather, DSS incorporate information into an analytical framework utilizing techniques such as mathematical relationships, simulations, or other algorithms. The outcome is definitive in nature and presents the results in either a deterministic or probabilistic fashion. DSS typically select alternative actions; management then considers the recommendation of the model with other variables (that may not be quantifiable) in arriving at a final decision. Examples are quotation analysis, price discount analysis, synthetic pricing, forecasting, and forward buying and futures trading models.

At the knowledge level, buyer workstations integrate a number of elements to create a total systems package that can result in increased effectiveness and productivity. The ideal technical components of a workstation are (1) an automated transaction system, linked to the company's databases, that performs routine purchasing activities; (2) access to decision-support software; (3) an expert systems element; and (4) personal productivity improvement software, word processing, spreadsheets, graphics, and database managers.

Firms with extensive international operations can benefit from developing *global databases,* which allow the firm to consolidate volumes and sourcing strategy. Developing these databases is difficult because of the significant investment, unreliable or nonexistent information networks in some countries, differing technical standards between countries, regulatory obstacles, and internal organizational obstacles. Considering the difficulties in coordinating efforts across multiple business units in North America, it is easy to imagine the further complications that arise when different countries, languages, cultures, and business cultures come into play. Some companies have adopted and implemented a single ERP system throughout global operations as a key step in the development of global processes.

INFORMATION SYSTEM TECHNOLOGY USE IN SUPPLY MANAGEMENT

Information system technology can provide seven important benefits to the organization:

1. Cost reduction and efficiency gains can be achieved by streamlining the purchasing processes and freeing up supply staff to do more value-adding work. Some organizations, such as Raytheon, have automated purchasing processes to reduce transaction costs by reducing the number of people touching the process and reducing the cycle time from need recognition to receipt of the good or service. Raytheon estimated its saving from the implementation of automation on low-value, noncritical items was $7 million in the first year.[3]
2. Quick and easy access to critical data in real time is helpful for sound decision making, makes it easier to identify supply problems earlier, and provides useful information for negotiations with suppliers.
3. Speedier communication with suppliers improves supply chain effectiveness and efficiency, especially when dealing with international suppliers. Faster turnaround times can lead to increased market share and lower inventories.
4. More time can be spent on strategic purchasing initiatives and focusing on important suppliers and supply projects because less time is required for administrative and tactical supply activities.
5. Improved information accuracy can be achieved by replacing manual systems with automation. The benefits can include lower inventories (e.g., safety stock), reduced stockouts, lower expediting costs, and improved customer satisfaction.
6. Integration of systems with other departments, suppliers, and customers can provide accurate information on a timely basis to assist with decision making in the areas of production planning and material requirements planning.
7. Enterprise systems provide control over how and where the money is spent. IBM uses its ERP system to feed information to its business database network where all spend data are housed and accessible by users. IBM's online spending tools help to ensure compliance with supply policies, including contract compliance and a significant reduction of maverick spending.[4]

It is no easy task, however, to decide which of the many available tools will best serve the organization's purposes, especially when technology is changing rapidly.

Software

To operate the computer, two types of software are needed. The first is the *systems software,* a group of programs provided by the computer manufacturer that runs the computer—starts it and makes the components work together. They do things such as copy information from one storage disk to another and cause the printer to work. The systems software currently is very adequate for the tasks at hand.

[3] A. E. Flynn, "Raytheon's Buyerless Tools," *Practix* 6, CAPS Research, March 2003.

[4] "IBM Tracks Benefits of Centralized Sourcing Data," *Purchasing*, March 21, 2002, pp. S2–S6.

Second is the *applications software,* which are the programs that manipulate data for a specific purpose, such as maintaining the open order file or taking supplier performance statistics and formatting them into a supplier performance evaluation analysis and report. There are a number of off-the-shelf purchasing software packages available. This software is constantly changing and improving, and the published guides to current programs appear frequently. These software programs may be designed for the exclusive use of supply, or they may be a module in an enterprise resource planning system designed to link together all of an organization's business processes.

Organizations typically have many different information systems designed to support the various needs of each function. Because these systems are designed to fill a particular purpose, they frequently do not "talk to each other," resulting in fragmentation of data in separate systems. Enterprise resource planning (ERP) software systems, such as SAP, Oracle, J. D. Edwards, and PeopleSoft, provide a corporate platform for information technology and include financial and operations applications. Enterprise systems collect data from key business processes and store them in a single comprehensive data repository where they are easily accessable. The enterprise application software market also includes enterprise relationship management, supply chain management, and electronic commerce programs. Most ERP systems offer "suites" of procurement applications, sometimes called *supplier relationship management systems*. Some companies, however, choose to implement specific modules rather than entire suites of software.

In addition to ERP systems, a number of application software procurement systems are available from a wide variety of systems developers, such as Ariba, i2, and FreeMarkets. These systems can be categorized into the following seven segments: spend analysis, supplier performance assessment, supplier identification sourcing, contract life-cycle management, procurement, order fulfillment tracking, and invoicing. Some vendors have solutions that support one or more of these processes.[5]

Rather than committing to expensive software solutions, some firms are opting to use software from application service providers (ASPs). Users can use ASP software by paying for a subscription or a per-transaction basis. Problems with ASPs include the high costs of ASP fees versus buying the software and difficulties integrating the online software with in-house software.

COMMONLY USED TECHNOLOGY TOOLS

There are a number of technological tools used in everyday supply operations, including fax machines, fax/modem, e-mail, and voice mail. While these tools are widely used in personal as well as business arenas, it is worth commenting on a few aspects of each.

Facsimile transmissions. Although e-mail has probably surpassed the fax in most workplaces, facsimile machines are a fast and convenient method of transmitting documents and other paper-based correspondence.

Fax/modem. The computer fax/modem card allows the user rapid transfer of data, graphics, and images using the computer and a conventional telephone line. The fax/modem can be used by purchasers for the conventional receipt and transmission of a

[5] A. Bartels, "Market Overview 2004: E-Procurement and E-Sourcing—What Will It Take to Break the Glass Floor in Demand?" Forrester Research, Inc., December 12, 2003.

fax, electronic mail (e-mail) with suppliers, and transmission of data files that can be downloaded and manipulated in spreadsheets or word processors without rekeying the data as required by conventional fax machines. Fax/modems are more cost-effective than fax machines because of the faster rates of data transmission.

Multifunction products (MFPs). MFPs combine fax as a feature on machines that print, scan, and tie into computer networks. One type of MFP is the Internet fax, which attaches a TIFF image to an e-mail message. The message can be viewed using graphics software, and because it is electronic, it can be viewed, stored, retrieved, and forwarded electronically. This eliminates the paper copy, unless the recipient chooses to print the file, and takes advantage of local telephone charges through an Internet service provider.

Electronic mail (e-mail). E-mail allows users to transmit messages back and forth within the organization and to external parties. E-mail can be used to communicate with suppliers, and, in some cases, is a means for suppliers to access and respond to requests for proposals (RFPs).

Voice mail. Voice mail is another communication tool that can, if used properly, save time, provide accurate information, improve communications between buyers and internal customers and suppliers, and cut down on "telephone tag." At its best, voice mail allows callers to communicate detailed information that the receiver can then respond to, in detail, or act on, without requiring a response. At its worst, voice mail turns both parties into receptionists who spend time copying down phone messages and then taking their turn at "telephone tag."

Bar coding. A bar code is a series of parallel rectangular bars and spaces arranged in a predetermined pattern to encode letters, numbers, and special characters. An optical character recognition device, or scanner, "reads" the information by passing a light beam across the bar code, sensing the width of the bars and transmitting the information into the computer, where it is decoded. Bar code information can include a wide array of data, such as product codes, date, location, and other identification data. Bar coding, or automatic identification systems, replaces data key entry with automatic data capture at the point of transaction and direct transmission to a computer or storage device. In supply, bar coding is particularly useful in receiving inbound materials and order generation. The benefits in receiving are quick and accurate data entry and faster checking and clearing of shipments. Automatic tracking of shipments throughout the system is simplified, and the receiving dock operates in a just-in-time (JIT) mode. The potential benefits of bar coding in order generation are labor savings, fewer errors and corrections, fewer disruptions due to material unavailability, and less need for safety stocks. Some large organizations, such as Wal-Mart and Target, have announced plans to use radio frequency identification (RFID) technology with large suppliers for certain applications instead of bar coding.

ELECTRONIC COMMUNICATION

Electronic Data Interchange (EDI)

Electronic data interchange, or EDI, allows computer-to-computer exchange between two organizations using agreed standards to structure the message data. Examples of documents exchanged via EDI include purchase orders, shipping notifications, shipping schedules, and invoices. EDI has been widely adopted in the manufacturing, transportation, and retailing sectors because it provides the advantages of fast turnaround time of large amounts of data, reduced administrative costs and data errors by eliminating rekeying of data, and secure transmission.

Despite the advantages and popularity of EDI, there have been two problems with this technology. Most EDI networks have traditionally relied on transmission over telecom lines using value-added network providers, or VANs. VANs route and manage EDI messages for customers, translating the messages so the trading partners can read them. The high costs of investing in the technology for EDI and the recurring costs related to VAN fees and telecom expenses made it difficult for most small and medium-sized businesses to justify the investment in EDI technology. Furthermore, although some attempts have been made at standardization, there are still a number of different EDI communication architectures in use.

Firms are looking to move some or all of their EDI transactions to the Internet because the cost of the technology is relatively low and it has become relatively easy to implement, allowing companies that do not have EDI capabilities to exchange information with those that have EDI and those that are not EDI-enabled. Instead of abandoning their existing EDI systems, companies can use Internet communication protocols to send electronic messages. These protocols can send files regardless of the format, and, because the files are sent over the Internet, the transmission time is faster and the company avoids telecom costs. Internet EDI is also more accessible to smaller companies because its costs are low and it does not require investments in sophisticated IT infrastructures. Firms can implement Internet EDI without involving a VAN, or the company can subscribe to a third-party Internet EDI service provider. Some well-established VANs, such as GEIS and Harbinger, have established Internet EDI products that allow subscribers to view files using their Web browser. The use of Internet EDI received a huge boost when, in August 2002, Wal-Mart mandated that all of its suppliers send and receive EDI data via the Web as of the end of 2003 using Applicability Statement 2 (AS2) technology.[6]

eXtensible Markup Language (XML)

When the Internet was first developed, HTML was used to arrange text and images on Web browsers. However, HTML is unable to distinguish between computer data presentation and the data itself. This means that HTML is good for sending electronic documents but inadequate for direct data exchanges between computers on the Web. Extensible markup language (XML), developed in 1998, uses identifying tags that allow information exchange without having to reformat the data for retrieval and viewing. Designed for Web-based data exchange, XML makes it possible for computers to automatically manipulate and interpret data without human intervention.

XML was believed to be the future for B2B computer communication among supply chain trading partners, replacing EDI. While some firms have adopted XML, it has not yet achieved widespread adoption. Concerns include implementation costs, security, and lack of standards, including the lack of standard tags and document type definitions (DTDs) for defining industry-specific data elements needed to execute specific transactions. Furthermore, many large organizations have invested heavily in EDI and are hesitant to change from an existing, proven system.

[6] A. Bednarz, "Internet EDI: Blending the Old and New," *Network World* 21, no. 8, February 23, 2004, pp. 29–30.

It would appear that the two standards, XML and EDI, will exist for the foreseeable future. Most firms will continue to use EDI systems where they work well and adopt XML where opportunities exist for cost or performance improvements.

Intranets and Extranets

Supply professionals are finding the Internet to be a tool of great importance. They can use the Internet to search, retrieve, and read computer files worldwide; exchange e-mail globally; search databases; access government sources; and search and purchase items from electronic catalogs, suppliers, and distributors.

An *intranet* is a single and widely assessable (for authorized users only) network set up to share information and communicate with company employees. It is a private, secure internal Web, based on Internet technologies. Intranets have the advantage of being easily scaleable and less costly and cumbersome to operate compared to the client/server networks of two decades ago.

Intranets can serve two functions: communicate information and facilitate collaboration among employees. Supply professionals can use intranets to communicate information and incorporate Web-based technology into the supply process. Intranets can be used to display supplier catalogs, such as for office supplies; provide lists of approved vendors; and post company supply policies. Supply processes can be enhanced by allowing employees to place orders via Web browsers, approving and confirming purchases electronically, and generating POs electronically. The main advantages of supply-based intranets are low transaction costs and reduced lead times.

An *extranet* is a private intranet that is extended to authorized users outside the company, such as suppliers. Extranets can be used to improve supply chain coordination and share information with key business partners. Through a Web-based interface, suppliers can link into a customer's systems and vice versa to perform any number of activities, such as check inventory levels, track the status of invoices, or submit quotes. Because the exchange of information is electronic, supply professionals are freed to spend time on value-added activities rather than entering data or checking on the status of shipments or payments to suppliers.

To help address problems with its business systems in accounts payable and procurement, Microsoft developed Web-based user-friendly supply systems, compatible with its SAP system. The first such system was MS Market (MSM), which was introduced in late 1996. It directed requisitioners to preapproved suppliers, provided assessments of their particular abilities, generated POs, and provided fiscal accountability through an online approval process. MSM also provided ordering assistance so that users with specific needs could quickly order, match invoices to orders, and arrange for electronic payment of suppliers. Between 1997 and 2003, enhancements were made to existing software tools and additional systems were added to the procurement suite. MS Spend allowed capture of spend data and analysis by supplier, customer, commodity, dollar amount, location, and about 40 other categories. MS Inquire allowed end-users and suppliers to look at the payment process via the Internet and provided end-users with accountability in approval of invoices. MS Vendor measured vendor performance and informed requisitioners of vendor competencies and ratings. MS Contract tracked Microsoft's contractual obligations with suppliers and calculated royalty and other obligation payments. In 1996, employees could wait four weeks for expense reimbursement. MS Expense streamlined the employee reimbursement process and removed accounts payable resources by providing online approval and coding of expense reports. As a result, employee expense reimbursements were settled in a matter of a few days.

The procurement software used by Microsoft provided valuable information for controlling the company's spend and implementing cost savings initiatives, streamlined and standardized procurement and accounts payable processes, increased transaction velocity and visibility, and clarified roles for users, approvers, and suppliers. In addition, the electronic procurement tools reduced transaction costs substantially: Staffing levels in the accounts payable and invoicing departments were reduced by more than 25 percent and 50 percent respectively. Meanwhile, approximately 20 supply people were redeployed from transactional activities to strategic procurement. The company estimated that the cost of processing a PO was reduced from approximately $60 per transaction in 1996 to less than $5 by 2002. Transaction cost savings represented a substantial financial impact: in fiscal year 2002, Microsoft issued approximately 500,000 POs and processed approximately 800,000 supplier invoices.[7]

E-Marketplaces

Business-to-business e-marketplaces are Web sites on which member companies buy and sell their goods and exchange information. The ISM/Forrester Report on Technology in Supply Management for the third quarter 2003 indicated that one-third of the survey respondents had bought some materials through an online marketplace.[8]

Public e-marketplaces are developed and owned by independent organizations and are "many-to-many" exchanges, and include sites such as Global Healthcare Exchange (GHE) and Theoilsite.

Industry-sponsored marketplaces are developed and owned by two or more industry players and can be aimed at a broad scope of supply chain activities, such as forecasting and replenishment, industry standards, or price discovery and clearing. These are also "many-to-many" exchanges and include Pantellos and Quadrem.

During the last decade, various forms of e-marketplaces rose and fell at a rapid rate and current projections are that major industries can only support one or two sites. In addition, e-marketplaces have changed their business models. Initially focused primarily on price discovery and clearing, these organizations now provide a range of software solutions and consulting services. Consequently, most e-marketplaces position themselves as "supply chain services" organizations.

Electronic or Online Catalogs

An online catalog is a digitized version of a supplier's catalog that allows buyers to view detailed buying and specifying information about the supplier's products and/or services through their computers' browsers. Product catalogs include two types of information: (1) product specification data and (2) transaction data. Product specification data are all the bits of information describing the products; transaction data are price, shipping and billing addresses, and quantity discounts. Product specification data are the same for all buyers, but

[7] M. R. Leenders, and P. F. Johnson, *Major Changes in CPO and CPO Reporting Line*, CAPS Research, forthcoming.

[8] Andrew Bartels, "ISM/Forrester Report on Technology in Supply Management: Q3 2003," Forrester Research, Inc., 2003.

transaction data must be customized to reflect the pricing and other terms and conditions negotiated with the supplier. For example, Business Depot, Dell Computer, and Cisco all provide customized versions of their catalogs for different buyers who have contracts with them.

When transitioning to an e-procurement application, ensuring online catalog accessibility is critical to the success of the program. This issue of catalog accessibility may become a factor in the supplier selection decision. The dilemma for the buyer is that the existing supplier, if there is one, may not have a digitized catalog. In this case the buyer has to decide if he or she wants to continue doing business with the supplier. If yes, the buyer has to take into account conversion time for the supplier to get the catalog online. If the buyer does not already have a relationship with a supplier, then the supplier selection decision can include a criterion that the supplier be e-commerce-enabled. However, the best supplier may not be e-enabled and the buyer may be making a mistake to put too much weight on this criterion.

Suppliers have a number of options available to digitize their catalogs. The same solutions provider that the buyer's organization uses can typically take the supplier's catalog, manual or electronic, and convert it to a suitable format. Alternatively, the supplier can purchase an out-of-the box software package and make the conversion or purchase the services of the software provider. If the buyer doesn't have an existing relationship with a supplier and does not wish to develop one, a data aggregator may be the answer. Data aggregators develop a library of product specifications from a variety of suppliers and then license organizations to use the product specifications and assist in developing the transaction data. Another approach is to use a catalog network in which a host company collects all the catalogs and customizes the transaction data for each buyer. The buyer can either pull the catalogs onto his or her server or access them from the host company. In some cases, the vendor will allow the buyer to "punch out" or access a supplier-hosted catalog.

As an alternative to using supplier catalogs, supply can create buyer-controlled catalogs that can combine information, such as pricing and specifications, from one or multiple vendors. Simple database software packages permit the creation of such catalogs and most enterprise resource planning (ERP) systems have features that permit the creation of customized catalogs. However, the responsibility is placed with the supply organization to update and maintain the catalogs. In-house catalogs permit the user to customize content in terms of supply options and pricing (or, alternatively, restrict purchasing options), the catalog can be integrated into the company's system to streamline the process and track spending patterns, the need for users to do comparison shopping is eliminated, and they support standardization and volume purchasing with approved suppliers.

RFID

Radio frequency identification (RFID) tags contain a chip and antenna that emit a signal, using energy from a radio frequency reader, which contains information about the container or its individual contents. There are a number of different types of RFID tags that vary widely in terms of memory, frequency, power source, and cost. The most common are passive, read-only tags, which currently cost in the range of $0.50 each, although the cost of this technology is expected to drop in coming years.

Already in use in a number of areas in our everyday life, such as employee identification badges and highway toll payment devices, RFID technology also has applications in supply management. Expecting to reduce their costs, several large retailers, such as Wal-Mart, Tesco, and Target, have announced plans to adopt RFID technology in their supply chain. Some of the potential benefits of this technology include the follwing manual counting and bar coding of incoming and outgoing material are eliminated; readers can automatically track inventory levels; identifying and picking inventory would be faster, easier, and more accurate; and spoilage could be reduced through improved stock rotation.

While many large companies will force their suppliers to invest in RFID technology, implementation of these systems promises to be challenging and costly and take years to complete. RFID will add another level of information and the firm's information systems must have the capability to capture, process, and analyze the data as they are collected. Implementation will necessitate additional investments in information technology and support from consultants and systems engineering specialists. Furthermore, implementing of RFID technology must be accompanied by appropriate process controls to achieve the benefits of inventory record accuracy.

ONLINE AUCTIONS

Auctions have been used for commercial transactions for centuries and there are many different types of auction methods. Generally, auctions can be classified on the basis of competition, between sellers or buyers; and forward or descending prices. For example, the Dutch flower auctions are an example of a declining price auction with competition between buyers, while a traditional English-style auction, involving the sale of equipment or furniture, is a rising price auction with multiple buyers. These various auction models have been married with Internet technology to provide purchasers with new techniques for determining price, quality, volume allocations, and delivery schedules with suppliers.

The October 2003 ISM/Forrester Report on Technology in Supply Management reported that 25 percent of survey respondents bought products or services through an online auction. The report also found that the ratio of the large organizations in the sample reported using online auctions compared to the small organizations was four to one.[9]

The actual Internet auction events can be conducted in a number of ways, including open offer auctions, private offer negotiations, posted prices, and reverse auctions.

In *open offer auctions,* suppliers can select the items they want to place offers on, see the most competitive offers from other suppliers for each item, and enter as many offers as they want up until a specified closing time. In *private offer auctions,* the buying organization offers a target price and quantity. Suppliers select the item(s) they wish to bid on and enter an offer by a specific time. The buyer evaluates each supplier's offer and enters a "status" for each item. The levels of status are *accepted:* the supplier is awarded the contract, contingent on final qualification; *closed:* the supplier may no longer submit offers for the item in question; *BAFO:* the supplier who receives electronically the best and final offer status may submit one more offer for the item; or *open:* the supplier may submit another offer. Bidding may be continued for as many rounds as necessary to accept or close all items. In *posted price auctions,* the buyer indicates the price that is acceptable and the first supplier that meets this price gets the award.

[9] Bartels, "ISM/Forrester Report on Technology in Supply Management: Q3 2003," Forrester Research Inc., 2003.

Reverse Auctions

A reverse auction is an online, real-time, declining-price auction between one buying organization and a group of prequalified suppliers. The bidding process is dynamic, where the suppliers compete for business by bidding against each other online using specialized software. Suppliers are given information concerning the status of their bids in real time, and the supplier with the lowest bid or (lowest total cost bid) is usually awarded the business.

When to Use Reverse Auctions

Reverse auctions are but one method for sourcing goods and services. When considering whether to use a reverse auction, prudent supply professionals evaluate the appropriateness of this method versus other sourcing techniques, such as RFPs/RFQs, sealed bids, face-to-face negotiations, or spot buys from the commodity markets. At a minimum, the following conditions should be in place in order to conduct a successful reverse auction:

1. Clearly defined specifications for the good or service, including technological, logistical, and commercial requirements.
2. Existence of a competitive market and a sufficient number of qualified suppliers willing to participate in the auction. Most companies believe that at least three suppliers are required, while using more than six suppliers may add unnecessary costs and complexity to the auction.
3. An understanding of the market conditions in order to set appropriate expectations for a reserve price.
4. Buyer and seller familiarity and competency using the auction technology.
5. Clear rules concerning how the auction will be conducted, such as conditions for extending the length of the auction and award criteria.
6. The buyer is prepared to switch suppliers if necessary.
7. The buyer believes that the current price is sufficiently high that the savings justify the use of a reverse auction.

Conducting Reverse Auction Events

Managing the reverse auction process involves three stages: preparation, the auction event, and implementation and follow-up. In the preparation stage, the purchaser must identify or certify appropriate suppliers, set the quality, quantity, delivery, and service requirements as well as the length of contract; train everyone involved (internal team members and supplier representatives) on the technology that will be used to run the auction; test the auction technology; and communicate how the auction will be conducted and the award criteria.

Reverse auction technology allows the buyer a variety of alternative approaches in terms of conducting auctions. For example, price visibility can be handled by showing rank order, percentage, or proportional differences. The technology also allows bid ranks to be adjusted for nonprice factors, such as differences in transportation costs or quality. Adequate planning and preparation frequently determine success or failure of an auction event.

Rules for conducting an auction event should be required upfront and strictly followed. The suppliers must understand how long the auction will run and the rules for extending the time period beyond the targeted closing time, often referred to as the "closing strategy." There are three types of closing strategies that can be used in an auction event: hard, soft, and unlimited. A hard closing strategy has a set time period without extensions, while soft close strategies permit short extensions if there is bidding activity in the last two to three minutes of the auction. Unlimited closing strategies allow unlimited extensions if there is activity within two or three minutes of the end of the auction. Understanding of supplier behavior is important when establishing a closing strategy.

Most reverse auction software allows suppliers and the buyer to communicate with each other during the auction. Such messages may or may not be visible to other suppliers participating in the event. Help desk support also should be available to provide technical assistance during the auction.

In the implementation and follow-up stage, the purchaser should announce the results to the supplier participants. Credibility by following the preestablished award criteria is important if the unsuccessful suppliers are to be encouraged to participate in future reverse auction events or become potential future suppliers. In addition, some suppliers may have questions regarding either the award process or future relationship with the buying firm.

In some cases, further negotiation or clarification may be required before the final contract is signed and it is important to complete such activities quickly, before the supplier starts to second-guess the commitment.

The leader of the reverse auction also should communicate with others in the organization concerning the outcome of the auction. For example, accounting will have to be notified if there is a change of vendors and/or pricing. In addition, new learnings from the event should be documented to improve the implementation of future reverse auctions.

Ethical Issues with Reverse Auctions

There are a number of ethical issues that buyers and sellers need to be concerned with when participating in reverse auctions. Potential ethical transgressions on behalf of buyers are:

1. Buyer knowingly accepts bids from suppliers with unreasonably low prices.
2. Buying firm submits phantom bids during the event to increase the competition artificially.
3. Buyer includes unqualified suppliers to increase price competition.

Some potential ethical issues involving suppliers are:

1. Suppliers act in collusion.
2. Suppliers bid unrealistically low prices and attempt to renegotiate afterwards.
3. Suppliers participate in the event but do not bid. This behavior is referred to as "bird watching" and is a strategy designed to collect market intelligence. Some reverse auction events have participation rules, where suppliers must enter bids before gaining access to the results.
4. Suppliers submit bids following the auction event in an attempt to secure the business.

Purchasers should always behave in an ethical manner and avoid the appearance of ethical conflicts in order to protect the reputation and integrity of their firm and individuals involved. Communicating clearly defined rules of the reverse auction upfront helps to avoid ethical misconceptions.

Potential Problems with Using Online Auctions[10]

Auctions represent one of many methods of price determination and there are a number of factors that supply professionals should consider when using any type of online auction:

Risks of interrupting good supply relationships. Committing a material or service to auction sends a signal to the supplier that the buyer has evaluated the supply relationship and is prepared to consider switching to a new source. It also implies that price, not service, is a determining factor. If the supply relationship is an important one and its performance must be assessed on factors other than only price/cost, then the tension created by using an auction may not produce the intended results. Furthermore, analysis should take into consideration nonprice factors, such as switching costs and supplier performance with respect to quality and delivery.

Risks of developing a poor reputation with the supply base. Extensive use of auctions, without consideration for the suitability of this method for the purchase involved, may send a signal to the supply base that the purchaser has a one-dimensional approach to supply management and is prepared to switch suppliers regularly on the basis of aggressive price/cost competition.

Costs of running the auction versus expected savings. The costs of running an auction can be high, regardless of whether or not a third party is hired to conduct the auction. Considerable time must be spent setting specifications, training suppliers, and setting up the technology. These costs must be weighed against the potential benefits. Firms may have to run several auctions each year to cover the fixed costs (e.g., software and training costs) associated with setting up to run reverse auctions. Consequently, supply professionals need to consider the breakeven point, in terms of reverse auction volume, for their reverse auction investment.

Cost savings potential of auctions versus traditional sourcing processes. There may be opportunities to achieve better outcomes in terms of price/cost, service, quality, or delivery through other means, such as negotiation, reengineering and value analysis, target pricing, or RFP/RFQ.

Significant up-front preparation and cost required compared to traditional RFP/RFQ. The costs associated with setting up and running the auction can be quite high compared to traditional RFP/RFQ methods of price determination.

Actual versus bid price discrepancies. Differences frequently exist between the close-of-auction price and the final contract price and cost. These differences can be caused by factors such as unforeseen costs related to the product or service being acquired, tooling, pilot testing, changes in design or specification, and switching suppliers as well as post-auction negotiation. An interesting paper by Hur and Mabert at the 2004 North American Research Symposium on Purchasing and Supply Management simulated reverse auction conditions over time. The conclusion was a minimum number of reverse auctions need to be held to justify the organizational learning and set-up costs.

[10] P. F. Johnson, "Supply Organizational Structures," CAPS Research, June 2003.

IMPLICATIONS FOR SUPPLY

From a supply management standpoint, the important thing to remember about e-procurement is that the buyer still plays a critical decision-making role in the process. The organization benefits from having supply personnel with the investigative and analytical skills to source, evaluate, and select suppliers; the influencing and persuading skills to negotiate the best deal for the organization; and a strategic and long-term planning approach to anticipate and prevent problems down the road. The transactional side, not the decision-making side, is streamlined and responsibility for actually placing orders is delegated to the user whenever possible.

Not all organizations have successfully implemented an e-procurement system for every step of the supply process. Furthermore, large organizations have been more aggressive than small and medium-sized enterprises in implementing e-procurement systems.

Clearly, these are exciting times for both those responsible for developing supply strategy and those tasked with implementation. In an environment of rapidly changing technology, it is difficult to predict exactly what the landscape will look like for supply managers in the future. It is, therefore, important to identify the key questions that decision makers in supply management must answer before embarking on an e-commerce path. These include:

1. *Should we be a leader or a follower?* The management of each organization must decide if it wishes to be an early adopter of new technology or if it prefers to see what emerges as the norm or standard. Early adopters of e-commerce tools often report that, despite the difficulties encountered, there are advantages to being further along than later adopters. Those who choose to wait tend to believe that the high risks and costs associated with adopting new technology in its infancy far outweigh whatever competitive advantages might be gained. Decision makers must assess a number of factors, including the organization's risk aversion and success level with technology implementation in the past, before moving forward.
2. *What should be acquired through e-commerce?* Should the organization purchase indirect materials, direct requirements, or both through e-commerce tools? Organizations that have enjoyed the benefits of buying indirect or MRO items through e-procurement are turning their attention to direct requirements. Supply managers must consider the characteristics of each category of purchase (see Chapter 6 for a discussion of purchase categories) to determine which goods or services might be successfully procured online. This analysis should include careful consideration of the existing and desired buyer–supplier relationship to ensure that the method of procurement does not adversely harm the relationship. Using technology to automate supply processes and integrate systems can lower transaction costs and free up time for supply professionals to work on value-added projects with important suppliers.
3. *What tools should we use to acquire those items?* A number of tools are available for streamlining the acquisition process. These range from lower-technology tools, such as procurement cards, to high-technology tools, such as online reverse auctions, online catalogs, and integrated e-RF*x* systems. A decision to adopt e-commerce for procurement does not necessarily mean that all the available tools will be adopted. The manager must determine the appropriateness of the tool to the type of material or service under consideration, the nature of the buyer–supplier relationship, and the comfort level of the internal stakeholders and the suppliers.

4. *Who should we use as a service provider(s)?* If the decision is made to use a third-party service provider, a careful assessment must be made of the available providers. On the technical side, several critical issues are compatibility with, or ease of migration from, existing software; scalability (can it grow with your needs); the supplier's technical reputation and experience with supply chain management; and expertise of the staff. Some of the key considerations beyond the technical issues are the long-term viability of the provider, user-friendliness of the software, fee structure, and service and support—offline and online.
5. *Should we enter into an alliance, and if so, what type, or work privately?* There are a number of alliance options available for e-commerce applications to supply management. Electronic purchasing can be done through a buyer-controlled system or through a neutral, third-party-controlled e-marketplace or trading hub. A number of factors must be considered, including the technical standards (interoperability and ease of data exchange), the degree of trust (confidence in the provider, confidentiality of information, system reliability, and uptime), and the cost and benefits of membership. On the seller side, the benefits may include improved service quality from more accurate and timely order processing, increased revenues from market expansion, and lower costs. For the buyer, participation in e-hubs may reduce transaction costs, increase competition through reduced search costs, and ultimately lead to lower costs.

Conclusion

As supply managers continue to transition to a more strategic role in many organizations, they also will continue to test and apply new technologies to the supply process. Although current surveys indicate that overall e-commerce adoption has been slower than anticipated due to the difficulties of internal and external integration and the lack of data standards, the future holds much promise for technology-enabled process improvements. The challenges are great, but those who see the opportunity for cost reductions, faster cycle times, and improved communication flows will continue to seek ways to use these new tools to their best advantage. Information systems and information technology enable a supply organization to contribute efficiently and effectively to organizational goals and strategies.

Glossary of Terms

Application service providers. Businesses that deliver and manage applications and computer services from remote computer centers to multiple users via the Internet or a private network.

Applications software. Programs that manipulate data for a specific purpose, such as maintaining the open order file or taking supplier performance statistics and formatting them into a supplier performance evaluation analysis and report.

Auction (see also **online reverse auction**). A seller with goods to sell invites multiple buyers to bid against each other at a set time and place to purchase the goods.

Bar code. A series of parallel rectangular bars and spaces arranged in a predetermined pattern to encode letters, numbers, and special characters.

Business-to-business (B2B). Electronic commerce between business entities.

Business-to-consumer (B2C). Electronic commerce between businesses and consumers.

Business-to-government (B2G). Electronic commerce between businesses and government agencies.

Data aggregators. Develop a library of product specifications from a variety of suppliers and then license organizations to use the product specifications and assist in developing the transaction data.

Decision-assisting (decision-support) systems. Process data to assist purchasing management in selecting from among alternatives.

Digital signatures. Short units of data bearing mathematical relationships to the data in the document's content that are transmitted using public key cryptography (PKI) programs. These programs create a pair of keys (one public key and one private key), and what the public key encrypts only the private key can decrypt. Alternatively, what the private key encrypts only the public key can decrypt. This assures confidentiality of information, and the digital signature allows the receiver to verify the sender of the data.

Document type definitions (DTDs). Definitions of industry-specific data elements needed to execute specific transactions.

E-commerce. A broad term meant to include any type of trading or business transaction that is handled electronically. This may be done through the use of the technology of the computer, including such tools as EDI, the Internet, intranets, and/or extranets, to streamline and enhance commercial transactions of both private and public sector entities.

Electronic data interchange (EDI). A closed system requiring a value-added network (VAN) to allow both buyer and seller to obtain and provide much more timely and accurate information.

Electronic or online catalog. A digitized version of a supplier's catalog that allows buyers to view detailed buying and specifying information about the supplier's products and/or services through their computers' browsers.

E-marketplaces. Web sites on which member companies buy and sell their goods and exchange information.

Enterprise spend management. Software that helps companies manage their spend by integrating spend data with analytics, sourcing, contract management, and tracking and reporting.

E-procurement applications. Web-based tools used to improve the efficiency and effectiveness of indirect or MRO purchases.

E-RFx. A generic term for electronic request for information (RFI), request for proposal (RFP), and request for quote (RFQ) systems.

ERP software systems. Provide a corporate platform for information technology and include financial and manufacturing applications. Examples include SAP, Oracle, J. D. Edwards, and PeopleSoft.

Expert systems. Provide decision-making assistance via an interactive question-and-answer session with a human.

eXtensible Markup Language (XML). A computer language that uses identifying tags that allow information exchange without having to reformat the data for retrieval and viewing.

Extranet. An organization's Web site that provides a limited amount of accessibility to persons outside the organization and often is used to link with actual and potential suppliers.

Firewall. Protective software used to prevent unauthorized access to confidential records.

Internet. The physical global network of computers, information servers, telephone lines, satellite links, signal routers, and the name and address codes that allow access to the World Wide Web. It is run mostly on a not-for-profit basis cooperatively by local and international organizations.

Intranet. A private Internet set up by a company to share data with workers and provide access to the larger Internet.

Mobile commerce or m-commerce. Electronic commerce conducted via wireless devices.

Online reverse auction or e-auction. A buyer wishes to purchase goods or services and invites multiple sellers to bid against one another in a declining price auction using the Internet.

Purchasing operating systems. Process data for the routine operations of the department, such as maintaining the status of purchasing actions; generating POs, change orders, and requests for quotation; filing and sorting supplier lists; and maintaining commodity, price, and supplier history files.

RFID. Radio frequency identification technology involving tags that contain a chip with information about the content of the container or its individual components.

Systems software. A group of programs provided by the computer manufacturer that runs the computer—starts it and makes the components work together.

World Wide Web (www). A term used to describe the network of billions of graphic hypertext documents or Web pages that are accessed from Web sites and hyperlinks connecting pages and Web sites.

Questions for Review and Discussion

1. What is EDI and what is XML? Explain the differences between the two systems. Why has XML not completely replaced EDI?
2. What should be considered before switching from an existing EDI system to a Web-based system?
3. What arguments would you use to convince a supplier to participate in a reverse auction?
4. In an organization not now using the Internet for purchasing, where would you start implementing a Web-based system?
5. How does the use of an e-procurement system change the nature of the skills and knowledge required of supply management personnel?
6. What kinds of software are needed for computer applications in purchasing? What is presently available?
7. What is the application of bar coding in the supply chain?
8. What are some of the major obstacles to faster adoption of e-commerce in supply management? What can be done to overcome these obstacles?
9. Why has there been difficulty in developing successful B2B exchanges or e-marketplaces? How do you think these issues will be resolved?
10. Why have some companies required their suppliers to use RFID technology? What are the potential benefits and costs of implementing this technology?
11. What possible improvements in purchasing and supply could the Internet offer in the future?

References

Bartels, Andrew. "ISM/Forrester Report on Technology in Supply Management: Q3 2003." Forrester Research Inc., 2003.

Beall, S., et al. *The Role of Reverse Auctions in Strategic Sourcing,* Tempe, AZ: CAPS Research, 2003.

DeHoratius, N. "Inventory Record Inaccuracy and RFID." *The 15th Annual North American Research Symposium on Purchasing and Supply Management Conference Proceedings*. Tempe, Arizona, March 2004, pp. 69–76.

Farhoomand, A., and P. Lovelock. *Global e-Commerce: Text and Cases*. Singapore: Pearson Education Asia, 2001.

Flynn, A. E. "Raytheon's Buyerless Tools." *Practix* 6. Tempe, AZ: CAPS Research, March 2003.

Hur, D., and V. A. Mabert. "Getting the Most Out of E-Auction Investment." *The 15th Annual North American Research Symposium on Purchasing and Supply Management Conference Proceedings*. Tempe, Arizona, March 2004, pp. 163–79.

Johnson, P. F. "Supply Organizational Structures." *Critical Issue Report*. Tempe, AZ: CAPS Research, June 2003.

Laudon, K. C.; J. P. Laudon; and M. E. Brabston. *Management Information Systems: Managing the Digital Firm*. Upper Saddle River, NJ: Prentice Hall, 2002.

Percy, D. H.; L. C. Giunipero; and L. M. Dandeo. "An Analysis of E-Procurement Strategy: What Role Does Corporate Strategy Play?" *13th Annual IPSERA Conference Proceedings*. Catania, Italy, April 2004, pp. C-216–27.

Case 4–1

Cable and Wireless plc (A)

Ninian Wilson, procurement process manager for Cable and Wireless plc in London, England, was evaluating his options for the company's first ever e-auction. It was July 10, and Ninian needed to settle on both the commodity and the e-auction service provider that he should use for the pilot project.

CABLE AND WIRELESS PLC

Cable and Wireless plc (C&W) was a leading global telecommunications company. Its core business unit, C&W Global, was a provider of Internet protocol (IP) and data services to business customers in the key markets of the United States, Europe, and Asia. C&W's global infrastructure provided a high-performance network that delivered integrated Internet, data, voice, and messaging communications to its customers. Its annual revenues were £9 billion and the company employed 55,000 people.

C&W had recently undertaken a thorough review of its assets and business strategy. As a result, management had sold a number of nonstrategic businesses and planned to reinvest the proceeds in network development and expansion in its IP and data services area, where it saw long-term growth opportunities.

THE E-PROCUREMENT INITIATIVE

Earlier in the year, an executive level group, the eGo team, had been formed to help guide C&W's transformation into an e-business. Don Reed, CEO Global Services, was the executive sponsor of the team, which focused on the e-enabling of C&W's customers, employees, partners, and suppliers and the links between these parties. The eGo team had a number of projects and initiatives under way, including e-procurement.

The goals of the e-procurement initiative were to (1) provide C&W employees with desktop e-transacting capabilities; (2) empower the procurement organization with e-enabling capabilities, such as e-auctioning; (3) free up supply resources through removal of non-value-adding activities, such as manual data rekeying; (4) reduce acquisition costs; and (5) reduce maverick buying. To develop an understanding of the full costs, benefits, and implications of implementing an e-procurement capability, a pilot project, called ¥o$, was initiated. Six C&W executives sat on the e-procurement steering committee, including Martin Ward, the Senior Vice President of Purchasing. Ninian Wilson was the program director for the e-auction component of the pilot.

COMMODITIES UNDER CONSIDERATION

Ninian's plan was to organize an online, real-time bid competition for a suitable commodity. He hoped that running an e-auction would provide insights into the reverse auction process and quantify cost-savings opportunities. Ninian commented, "The potential benefit is a cut in the price of a contract by as much as 20 to 30 percent, and this pilot will help us prove this."

As a starting point, Ninian looked at contracts that were coming to the end of their term and needed to be renewed. He identified archival services and marketing paper as potential candidates for the e-auction pilot.

ARCHIVAL SERVICES

C&W had six suppliers providing record storage services for its various operations in the U.K. representing a total annual cost of £133,000. Each of the suppliers was located in the greater London area and provided the same basic services: labeling, delivery, next-day retrieval, and storage. Several vendors had indicated that they would need price increases for the next contract.

Wendy Ellis, the commodity manager, had issued an RFQ two months prior, with the intention of consolidating requirements with a single vendor. Concerned that not all of the current vendors provided fireproof storage, Wendy added this feature to the RFQ, which she felt would add about £1,000 per year to the total cost. Each of the six current suppliers was asked to quote on C&W's archival storage requirements, and Clauws Records Services had submitted the lowest bid at a price of £423,000 for a 36-month contract.

MARKETING PAPER

C&W purchased approximately £4 million in paper worldwide used for marketing and sales literature. Its large spend in this area and the wide geographic coverage meant that C&W dealt with a number of paper merchants directly.

Ninian was aware that the contract for C&W's U.K. requirements for marketing paper was due to be revisited within the next month, and based on current prices, represented an annual spend of approximately £1.2 million. C&W did not currently have contracts in place for its requirements in Europe, the United States, or Asia and purchased its marketing paper in these regions from a large number of suppliers. However, the current U.K supplier, Engler Paper, had expressed an interest in working with C&W to expand its supply relationship to other regions.

Ninian felt that he could conduct an e-auction for C&W's global requirements or focus on its U.K. requirements only. He had identified seven potential suppliers, including two that had experience with e-auctions.

E-AUCTION SERVICE PROVIDERS

Ninian recognized that if he proceeded with an e-auction, he would have to make arrangements with an online bid service provider. His initial investigation had uncovered a large number of auction service providers that used a variety of different approaches. Eventually he narrowed his alternatives to two service providers.

IA-TECH was a U.S.-based e-procurement solutions provider with one of the three most popular types of software. It was one the world's largest providers of e-auction services and had conducted more than 250 reverse auctions for a number of firms in North America and Europe. IA-TECH proposed that it would charge a flat fee of £12,000 to conduct the auction for archival services, £25,000 for U.K. marketing paper, and £50,000 for C&W's total corporate requirements for worldwide marketing paper. IA-TECH's proposals were based on a maximum of six bidders.

e-Procure Systems was a relatively new e-auction service provider based in the U.K. e-Procure Systems had developed its own software and had conducted about 50 reverse auctions. It offered C&W two different pricing schemes. One option was a tiered commission structure of 3 percent for the first £500,000 of the contract, 2 percent for the second £500,000, 1 percent for the next £500,000 and .5 percent thereafter. Alternatively, e-Procure Systems also offered a risk-reward pricing structure, where it would take a fee of 15 percent of total savings from the e-auction over the existing cost.

Each of the service packages from IA-TECH and e-Procure Systems included training, support, and consulting, customization, and auction marketing. In order to proceed, Ninian knew that he needed to establish parameters for the e-auction service arrangement and select a service provider.

FINALIZING THE E-AUCTION

Ninian had several concerns. While he was satisfied that e-auctions could be useful for some commodities, he was uncertain which commodities were best suited for this procurement technique. Ninian was also uncertain as to how the suppliers would respond and knew that the suppliers would have to cooperate for the e-auction to be successful. Furthermore, Ninian needed to decide on the appropriate number of suppliers and determine which ones were best suited to participate.

Finally, this would be Ninian's first experience with an e-auction and, if he did decide to proceed, he knew it would be important to map out a game plan carefully. Not only did he need a commodity strategy, but he would also need to select an online bid service provider.

Ninian had a meeting with the e-Procurement Steering Group in two weeks, when he would be expected to present his recommendations.

Case 4–2

Establishing E-Business Standards at Deere & Company*

By the beginning of April 2000, Deere & Company, headquartered in Moline, Ill., had made the decision to shift Deere's $7 billion supply chain to an e-business model by 2003. Paul Morrisey, Manager of E-Business and Supply Management, was responsible for helping to establish common technology standards for the entire Deere supply chain. He needed to develop a preliminary plan for the establishment of those standards for a meeting with his boss in two weeks. Paul wondered what it would take to reach an agreement with suppliers and whether Deere was in a position to manage the supply chain electronically.

* This case, written by professor Steve Maranville, is reproduced with the permission of Deere & Company and NAPM.

DEERE & COMPANY

The 163-year-old Deere & Company was the only agricultural equipment company in the United States to have never changed hands. It was a highly decentralized company that operated more than 60 business units, sold products in more than 160 countries, and had 39,000 employees. In 1999, annual sales revenue had declined to $11.7 billion from a 1998 level of $13.8 billion. Even worse, profits had declined to $239 million from a 1998 level of $1.021 billion.

The company operated three different types of businesses. First, and largest, was Equipment Operations, consisting of agricultural, construction and forestry, and commercial and consumer lawn care. Second was Support Operations, comprised of power systems such as engines and transmissions, and service parts for Deere equipment. The third area was Financial Services—consisting of credit, which made financing and leasing agreements—and health care, which managed health care systems for 1,400 companies.

Each of Deere's 14 divisions currently purchased products independently, although there was a corporate coordinator of purchasing for some products who operated in an advisory capacity. Electronic Data Interchange (EDI) had been in place since the early '90s with 2,000 Deere suppliers representing 90 percent of domestic orders. However, there was a lack of global commonality in systems used. Every operating unit had developed its own method of using technology with suppliers.

Earlier, at Deere's annual meeting with major suppliers, Paul had heard complaints about the coordination problems in supply that existed within Deere. One supplier commented, "I get calls from 50 different people at Deere and they want 50 different things." A second major supplier said, "It's like there are 14 different companies all operating under the Deere name. If you want us to help you, help yourselves first."

Because Deere had no common, corporate supplier database, different divisions were purchasing the same products from the same supplier at different prices. Suppliers were successfully taking advantage of Deere's inability to coordinate purchase quantities.

PAUL MORRISEY

In more than 20 years, Paul Morrisey had moved successfully through a series of positions in manufacturing management at Deere. He came to corporate headquarters five years ago. Just before assuming his present position he completed a stint in marketing. For the past several months he'd been working on Deere's Internet and supply chain strategies. He believed that movement to e-business required a fundamental shift in thinking that had to be reflected in supply management processes. If done correctly, it could establish a sense of continuity throughout the supply chain. Paul had said, "We have to rethink our processes. We need to ask what would we do if we were a brand new company, rather than continuing to do what we've always done."

MOVEMENT TOWARD AN E-BUSINESS MODEL

Paul Morrisey's vision for an e-business integration of Deere's supply chain was:

> ". . . a pull system without much inventory. We have to figure out how to enable the supply chain to respond to a customer's needs quickly. As we fill the order we should collect additional information about the customer and mine the data to anticipate future customer needs. We need to fill the customer's order quicker than our competitors. And, we have to recognize that technology isn't the solution, it's the tool."

Paul categorized suppliers into three levels. The lowest level includes those suppliers with which Deere shares only information—communication, even if electronic, is at a fundamental level. The second level of suppliers are more sophisticated and are able to conduct e-commerce business transactions. The highest level includes those suppliers that are integrated partners and collaborate with Deere on product design. Only a very select group of suppliers were, or would be, brought to this level.

Different divisions at Deere had varying levels of technology in place. However, there were efforts in progress to establish common enterprise standards for EDI and to implement core transactions at all units. Notably, a common supplier database that was intended to be corporate-wide and used by all divisions was being developed. Previously, each individual unit had developed databases. This decentralization of data resulted in a lack of awareness about the overall nature of the business that Deere was doing with various suppliers. Paul believed that a transition from Deere's traditional purchasing model to strategic supply management via e-business would require the changes shown in Exhibit 1.

EXHIBIT 1
Establishing E-Business Standards at Deere and Company

Transitioning from Purchasing to Strategic Supply Management	
Traditional Purchasing Structure	**Strategic Supply Management**
Cost, quality, delivery	Total cost management
Coordinated purchasing	Strategic sourcing
Little assistance to suppliers	Supplier development
Deere product designs	Supplier integration in designs
Buy/sell relationships	Management relationships
Management of functions	Management of processes
Systems designed for internal use	Global integration of systems

Approximately 70 percent of Deere's product content was purchased, amounting to $7.1 billion in material. Management had set a goal for supply management to reduce the cost of purchased goods and services by $1.1 billion over the next three years.

There were 1,200 supply management employees worldwide. Seventy-eight percent of the work force was located in North America. In 1999, 82 percent of purchases originated in the United States; Europe accounted for 13 percent; South America for 2 percent; India, China, Africa, and Australia combined for another 2 percent; and Mexico accounted for the remaining 1 percent. While Deere's offshore purchases were small, efforts were under way to source more on the global market.

DEVELOPMENT OF A COMMON TECHNOLOGY

To help Deere establish technological standards for the entire company and its supply chain, the Deere Electronic Commerce Council was formed with the mission to ". . . drive global enterprise connectivity between Deere, its customers, and supply chain using secured, industry-standard information technology." Specific objectives were to move to 100 percent paperless, Web-based transactions, Web-based supplier collaboration on product development, and Web-based procurement.

In the past, not only had Deere failed to coordinate technological standards among its suppliers, it had failed to do so within its own company. The result was that some suppliers had to deal with different Deere divisions in different ways. Now, in order to integrate its supply chain, Deere had to establish common standards while resisting a Deere-specific solution. In other words, it had to develop or choose standards that could be used by suppliers on an industry-wide, or even multi-industry basis.

While some industry standards were available, they were far from complete. In addition, the software technology for fully integrating supply chains wasn't immediately available. Paul Morrisey believed there were pockets of good technology, but there was nothing to make it all come together. Deere had established initiatives to work with SAP, IBM, and Microsoft to develop applications for business-to-business Internet platforms, data warehousing, and Internet security.

As Paul thought about what he had to do, he realized he also would have to educate the leadership of the company on what was possible, bring business processes and technological systems into synch, and accomplish a cultural change among management that would allow Deere to operate in new ways.

Paul thought to himself that the difference between adopting the technology and changing the underlying culture is just like the difference between learning how to drive a different car and learning how to drive on the other side of the road. Learning how to drive a new car is a new skill, but learning how to drive on the other side of the road is a cultural change. Deere had to learn how to drive on the other side of the road. It wasn't about the technology; it was about being the best at what we do.

As he thought about these concerns, he reminded himself that his plan and recommendations were due to his boss in two weeks.

Case 4–3

Hemingway College

Catherine Barkley, manager of purchasing and accounts payable at Hemingway College in Fresno, California, stared at the latest e-mail from one of her staff. She had less than three months to take her department "live" on the new enterprise resource planning (ERP) system and problems continued to pour in. It was now April 6th and Catherine wondered what action she should take in light of the tight deadline she faced. Catherine was expected to make her recommendations to her boss, Dan Kavaliers, in a meeting the following day.

HEMINGWAY COLLEGE

Hemingway College was a community college with approximately 12,000 students. It offered training and educational programs in the areas of applied arts, business, health care, human services, hospitality, literacy, academic upgrading, life skills, computers, technology, apprenticeship, and English as a second language. All of its 78 post-secondary certificate and diploma programs remained popular and student intake was on the rise. The college prized itself on its trusted position within the community, citing that almost every fifth person in the city had passed through its classrooms.

Catherine reported to Dan Kavaliers, the vice president of finance and corporate services. She was responsible for a staff of 11 people, including four buyers, an accounts payable manager, four accounts payable clerks, a traffic and customs officer, and an administrative assistant. Most purchases were controlled centrally, although some departments had recently lobbied for a more decentralized structure.

RESOURCE PLANNING SYSTEM

Two years prior, senior management at Hemingway College decided to implement a new ERP system. Although the old systems provided the basic functionality required, they had become so antiquated and many vendors were discontinuing support for related software and hardware. It was also felt that this would be a good time to integrate various areas—finance, human resources, and student information—as well as upgrade to the latest technology in the market.

After a seven-month supplier evaluation process, a cross-functional senior management team, led by the vice president of finance and corporate services and the vice president of administration, selected an out of the box ERP package, EduSoft, which had been successfully installed in similar colleges across North America. The first group to get involved in the implementation of the new ERP system was finance, who implemented a new general ledger, including a coding structure for the new system. The next set of processes to be brought on the new system were the purchasing and accounts payable systems, as they tied in most closely with the general ledger. Successful implementation would ease the transition of the entire purchasing module, and in turn, that of other functional modules as well.

IMPLEMENTING THE PURCHASING MODULE

Catherine had held her first meeting with EduSoft staff the previous August to start planning the implementation. As team lead for implementing the purchasing module, she quickly realized that there were quite a few challenges ahead. The old in-house system had gradually evolved around the specific policies and needs of the purchasing department. EduSoft, however, had its own functional assumptions on policies and department needs built into the system. Catherine grappled with the issue of whether to try and change the EduSoft system to work with old established policies or to change policies in order to leverage EduSoft's streamlined built-in processes that seemed to have succeeded in other colleges. Catherine ultimately decided to implement the new streamlined systems, expecting that this decision would yield substantial long-term benefits.

From October to December of the previous year, the new purchasing and accounts payable system was tested for the availability of features and for access and security issues. In January, process mapping from the old system to the new one was finished off, and the new system looked set to be rolled out with all features implemented by the end of June.

TRAINING

During January and February, Catherine started weekly half-day meetings with staff to train them and give them hands-on exposure to the new system. This was important, as she needed to make the staff comfortable with the new system and achieve "buy-in." She planned to continue staff training throughout the summer since this was the best time for staff to get acquainted with the new system, as they were mostly free from the distractions of catering to everyday student requirements and issues. Currently, the staff training meetings typically lasted 15–20 minutes held every day or every second day, focused around specific issues that had come up while using the system, rather than the broad-based training sessions on policy and process change matters held earlier. So far, Catherine had been receiving a continual flow of problems encountered by staff trying to use the new system to deliver the functions they wanted.

IMPLEMENTATION SCHEDULE

The current schedule called for purchasing and accounts payable to complete implementation of its modules by the end of June in order that its systems would be functional for the start of the school year in August. The human resources department was scheduled to start implementation of its modules following purchasing, at the beginning of July, so that employee tax and income reporting information could start on January 1st the following year. The director of human resources and vice president of finance and corporate services were adamant that they wanted to avoid running two systems for employee records. Consequently, any delays in implementing the human resource modules would in turn set back overall system implementation by one year.

Delaying implementation of the purchasing and accounts payable modules also would create problems. Some old systems had been removed as part of the transition and reverting back to the old systems was not viewed as feasible.

ALTERNATIVES

In order to complete implementation of her department's modules on schedule, Catherine felt that she had at least two alternatives. First, Catherine believed that more staff time was needed to implement the modules than originally budgeted. This approach would require her to increase staff overtime dramatically and add temporary staff. Catherine would need to hold a one-week workshop with her staff to clear up systems problems and establish a new project plan. She estimated that staff overtime costs would be approximately $3,000 per week and four temporary staff, at a cost of approximately $2,000 per week, would be required. Even with the extra resources, Catherine remained concerned about the ability of her department to keep up with its normal activities, and ultimately staff burnout, if this alternative was adopted.

A second option would be to hire consultants from EduSoft to implement the modules. The consultants would require some support from Catherine's staff, but there would be no need for additional overtime or temporary staff beyond the current budget. In her conversations with representatives from EduSoft, they had indicated that she should budget $12,000 per week for this service. While this option was more convenient, Catherine was concerned about its higher costs and the implications of using a third party to implement the modules.

Catherine had a meeting scheduled with Dan Kavaliers the following morning at 9:00 a.m. and he was expecting an update from her and recommendations as part of a comprehensive plan that would ensure that implementation of the purchasing and accounts payable modules would occur by the end of June.

Chapter Five

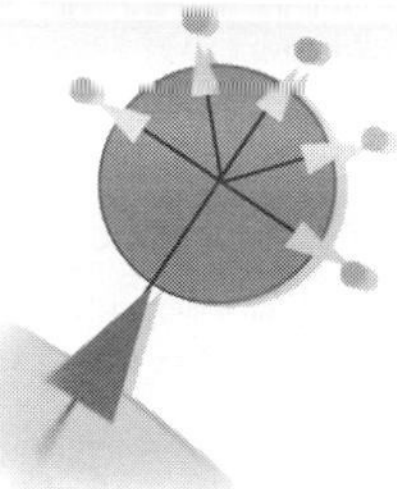

Quality, Specification, and Service

Chapter Outline

Key Questions for the Supply Manager

Should we

- Change our specification method?
- Initiate a six-sigma program?
- Certify suppliers?

How can we

- Improve customer satisfaction with quality?
- Reduce the costs of quality?
- Define "service" better?

Quality, quantity, delivery, price, and service are the five most common supply requirements. In this chapter, quality and service are addressed. Quantity, delivery, and price are discussed in the following chapters.

Quality has always been a major concern in supply management. The traditional definition of quality meant conformance to specifications. In the total quality management context, the definition was enlarged to represent a combination of corporate philosophy and quality tools directed toward satisfying customer needs. Even in its simplest definition, quality continues to represent significant challenges; in its broader context, it may well determine an organization's ability to survive and prosper in the years ahead.

DETERMINATION OF NEED

Every acquisition is intended to fill a need inside the purchaser's organization. Effective supply requires a full understanding of the function the acquisition is to fulfill, how the need is described, and how its quality is determined and measured.

Quality has taken on a special meaning in the past decades. While MRP and just-in-time or lean production have revolutionized the quantity, delivery, and inventory aspects of materials management, they also have required a new attitude toward quality. When no safety stock is available and required items arrive just before use, their quality must be fully acceptable. This extra pressure, along with all other good reasons for insisting on good quality, has sparked major efforts by purchasers to seek supplier quality assurance. In many cases, these efforts have involved supplier certification programs or partnerships, including the establishment of satisfactory quality control programs at the premises of those who supply the suppliers. Renewed interest in quality has reinforced the need for a team buying approach, the trend to supplier rationalization, cooperative buyer–supplier relations, longer-term contracts, and a reevaluation of the role of the price–quality trade-off in purchase decisions.

To understand the role of quality in procurement, it is necessary to determine how needs are defined, what constitutes a "best buy," and what action purchasers take to ensure that the right quality is supplied.

The first phase in any acquisition is to determine what is needed and why. Actually, this should be a three-step process. First, the organization's needs are established by focusing on the needs of its customers. Second, it is determined what the market can supply. Third,

FIGURE 5–1
The Transformation and Value-Added Chain

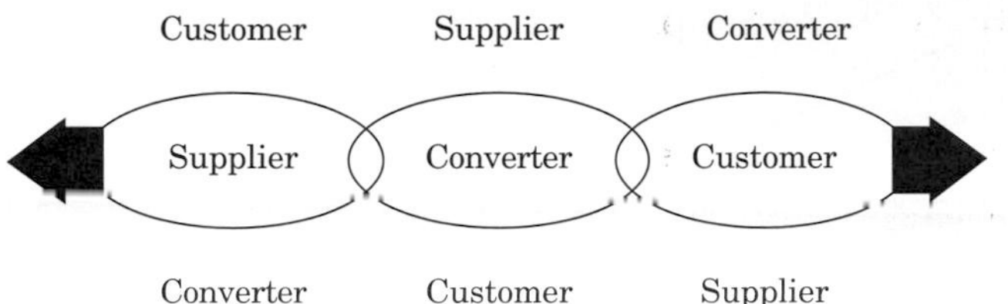

a conclusion is reached as to what constitutes good value under the circumstances. Frequently, steps one and two and, occasionally, all three steps are performed concurrently. The danger in proceeding through these steps too quickly is that vital information and analysis may be lost. Obviously, in complex purchases, the process may well go through these steps iteratively before a final decision is reached.

The quality concept argues that an organization's products or services are inseparable from the processes used to produce them. Just focusing on the product or service without examining the process that produces it is likely to miss the key to continuous improvement. If the process is not in statistical control and targeted for continuous improvement, the quality of the products or services produced is likely to suffer. This applies equally to the supply function as to the operations function of any organization.

Actually, every organization can be seen as part of a chain of organizations that has suppliers to one side and customers to the other. In further detail, every organization, by definition, performs three roles: customer, converter, and supplier (see Figure 5–1). As a converter, every organization needs to add value as its part of the chain.

The same idea can be applied on a micro level inside every organization. Each department or function itself is part of an internal chain performing the same three roles: customer, converter, and supplier to other internal functions and, in some cases, to external customers and suppliers. Here also, the value-added concept is important. Each department or function must add value and strive to minimize the cost of doing so by process control and continuous improvement in congruence with organizational goals and strategies.

Even in those organizations where traditional functions such as purchasing, production, and sales have given way to teams and functional boundaries have blurred or disappeared, the need for quality remains and the group must assume collective responsibility for it.

A continuous examination of the current and future needs of internal and external customers should result in the identification of current and future requirements to be procured. In theory, this sounds fairly simple; in practice, all kinds of difficulties exist.

Moreover, it has become generally recognized that about 70 percent of the opportunity for value improvement lies in the first two phases of the acquisition process: (1) need identification and (2) specification. Therefore, great attention needs to be paid to ensure that value opportunities are not overlooked (see Figure 5–2).

Early Supply and Supplier Involvement

Given the high opportunity to affect value during the need identification and specification stages, it is essential that supply considerations are brought to bear on decisions during these two stages. Early supply involvement and early supplier involvement (ESI) help assure that what is specified is also procurable and represents good value. Various organizational approaches, such as staffing the supply area with engineers, co-locating purchasing people in the engineering or design areas, and using cross-functional teams on new product development, have been used to address effective early supply involvement.

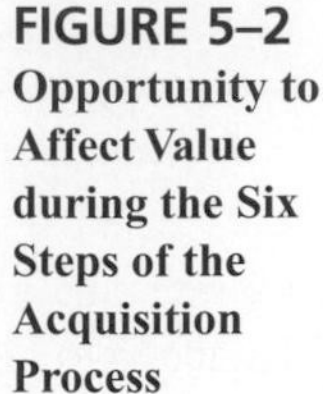

FIGURE 5–2 **Opportunity to Affect Value during the Six Steps of the Acquisition Process**

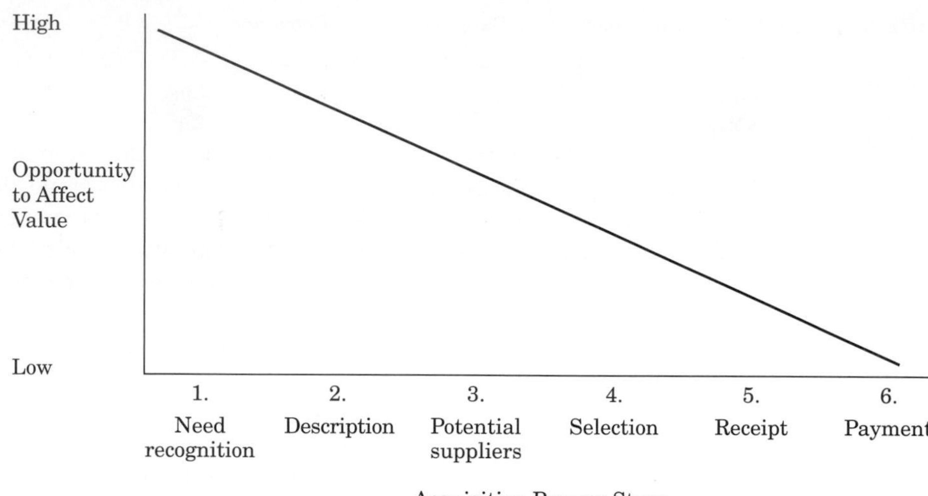

METHODS OF DESCRIPTION

The using, requesting, or specifying department must be capable of reasonably describing what is required to be sure of getting exactly what is wanted.

Although the prime responsibility for determining what is needed usually rests with the using or specifying department, the supply department has the direct responsibility of checking the description given. Purchasers should, of course, not be allowed to alter arbitrarily the description or the quality. They should, however, have the authority to insist that the description be accurate and detailed enough to be perfectly clear to every potential supplier. The buyer also must call to the attention of the requisitioner the availability of other options that might represent better value.

The description of an item may take any one of a variety of forms or, indeed, may be a combination of several different forms. For our discussion, therefore, *description* will mean any one of the various methods by which a buyer conveys to a seller a clear, accurate picture of the required item. The term *specification* will be used in the narrower and commonly accepted sense referring to one particular form of description.

The methods of description will be discussed in order:

1. By brand.
2. "Or Equal."
3. By specification.
   a. Physical or chemical characteristics.
   b. Material and method of manufacture.
   c. Performance or function.
4. By engineering drawing.
5. By miscellaneous methods.
   a. Market grades.
   b. Sample.
6. By a combination of two or more methods.

Description by Brand

There are two questions of major importance in connection with the use of branded items. One relates to the desirability of using this type of description and the other to the problem of selecting the particular brand.

Description by brand or trade name indicates a reliance on the integrity and the reputation of the supplier. It assumes that the supplier is anxious to preserve the goodwill attached to a trade name and is capable of doing so. Furthermore, when a given requirement is purchased by brand and is satisfactory in the use for which it was intended, the purchaser has every right to expect that any additional purchases bearing the same brand name will correspond exactly to the quality first obtained.

There are certain circumstances under which description by brand is desirable and necessary:

1. When, either because the manufacturing process is secret or because the item is covered by a patent, specifications cannot be laid down.
2. When specifications cannot be laid down with sufficient accuracy by the buyer because the supplier's manufacturing process calls for a high degree of that intangible labor quality sometimes called *expertise* or *skill,* which cannot be defined exactly.
3. When the quantity bought is so small as to make the setting of specifications or testing by the buyer unduly costly.
4. When end customers or users have real, even if unfounded, preferences in favor of certain branded items, a bias the purchaser may find almost impossible to overcome.

On the other hand, there are objections to purchasing branded items, most of them turning on cost. Although the price may often be quite in line with the prices charged by other suppliers for similarly branded items, the whole price level may be so high as to cause the buyer to seek unbranded substitutes. Thus, the purchaser may just as well prefer using trisodium phosphate over a branded cleaning compound costing 50 to 100 percent more.

A further argument, frequently encountered, against using brands is that undue dependence on brands tends to restrict the number of potential suppliers and deprives the buyer of the possible advantage of a lower price or even of improvements brought out by competitors.

"Or Equal"

It is not unusual, particularly in the public sector, to see requests for quotations or bids that will specify a brand or a manufacturer's model number followed by the words "or equal." In these circumstances, the buyer tries to shift the responsibility for establishing equality or superiority to the bidder without having to go to the expense of having to develop detailed specifications.

Description by Specification

Specification constitutes one of the best known of all methods employed. A lot of time and effort has been expended in making it possible to buy on a specification basis. Closely related to these endeavors is the effort toward standardization of product specifications and reduction in the number of types, sizes, and so on, of the products accepted as standard.

It is becoming common practice to specify the test procedure and results necessary to meet quality standards as part of the specification as well as instructions for handling, labeling, transportation, and disposal to meet environmental regulations.

Traditional advantages of buying with specifications include

1. Evidence exists that thought and careful study have been given to the need and the ways in which it may be satisfied.
2. A standard is established for measuring and checking materials as supplied, preventing delay and waste that would occur with improper materials.
3. An opportunity exists to purchase identical requirements from a number of different sources of supply.
4. The potential exists for equitable competition. This is why public agencies place such a premium on specification writing. In securing bids from various suppliers, a buyer must be sure that the suppliers are quoting for exactly the same material or service.
5. The seller will be responsible for performance when the buyer specifies performance.

Seven limitations in using specifications are

1. There are requirements for which it is practically impossible to draw adequate specifications.
2. The use of specifications adds to the immediate cost.
3. The specification may not be better than a standard product, readily available.
4. The cost is increased by testing to ensure that the specifications have been met.
5. Unduly elaborate specifications sometimes result in discouraging potential suppliers from placing bids in response to inquiries.
6. Unless the specifications are of the performance type, the responsibility for the adaptability of the item to the use intended rests wholly with the buyer.
7. The minimum specifications set up by the buyer are likely to be the maximum furnished by the supplier.

Specification by Physical or Chemical Characteristics

Specification by physical or chemical characteristics provides definitions of the properties of the materials the purchaser desires. They represent an effort to state in measurable terms those properties deemed necessary for satisfactory use at the least cost consistent with quality.

Specification by Material and Method of Manufacture

The second type of specification prescribes both the material and method of manufacture. Outside of some governmental purchases, such as those of the armed forces, this method is used when special requirements exist and when the buyer is willing to assume the responsibility for results. Many organizations are not in this position, and as a result, comparatively little use is made of this form of specification.

Specification by Performance or Function

The heart of performance specification is the understanding of the required functions. It is not easy to think of the basic function the item must perform. We tend to speak of a box instead of something to package in, a bolt instead of something that fastens. We think of a steak, instead of something to eat, and a bed, instead of something to sleep on.

Performance or function specification in combination with a request for proposal (RFP) is employed to a considerable extent, partly because it throws the responsibility for a satisfactory product back to the seller. Performance specification is results and use oriented, leaving the supplier with the decisions on how to make the most suitable product. This enables the supplier to take advantage of the latest technological developments and to substitute anything that exceeds the minimum performance required.

The satisfactory use of a performance specification, of course, is absolutely dependent on securing the right kind of supplier. It should be noted that it may be difficult to compare quotations and the supplier may include a risk allowance in the price.

Description by Engineering Drawing

Description by a blueprint or dimension sheet is common and may be used in connection with some form of descriptive text. It is particularly applicable to the purchase of construction, electronic and electrical assemblies, machined parts, forgings, castings, and stampings. It is an expensive method of description not only because of the cost of preparing the print or computer program itself but also because it is likely to be used to describe an item that is quite special as far as the supplier is concerned and, hence, expensive to manufacture. However, it is probably the most accurate of all forms of description and is particularly adapted to purchasing those items requiring a high degree of manufacturing perfection and close tolerances.

Miscellaneous Methods of Description

There are two additional methods of description: description by market grades and description by sample.

Description by Market Grades

Purchases on the basis of market grades are confined to certain primary materials. Wheat and cotton,[1] lumber, steel, and copper are commodities. For some purposes, purchase by grade is entirely satisfactory. Its value depends on the accuracy with which grading is done and the ability to ascertain the grade of the material by inspection.

Furthermore, the grading must be done by those in whose ability and honesty the purchaser has confidence. It may be noted that even for wheat and cotton, grading may be entirely satisfactory to one class of buyer and not satisfactory to another class.

Description by Sample

Still another method of description is by submission of a sample of the item desired. Almost all purchasers use this method from time to time but ordinarily—there are some exceptions—for a minor percentage of their purchases and then more or less because no other method is possible.

[1] For agricultural raw materials such as wheat and cotton, the grades are established by the U.S. Department of Agriculture. They include all food and feed products, the standards and grades for which have been established in accordance with the Federal Food and Drug Act, the Grain Standards Act, and other laws enacted by Congress. As will be noted later, establishing grades acceptable to the trade is essential to the successful operation of a commodity exchange.

Good examples are items requiring visual acceptance, such as wood grain, color, appearance, smell, and so on.

Combination of Descriptive Methods

An organization frequently uses a combination of two or more of the methods of description already discussed. The exact combination found most satisfactory for an individual organization will depend, of course, on the type needed by the organization.

Sources of Specification Data

Speaking broadly, there are three major sources from which specifications may be derived: (1) individual standards set up by the buyer; (2) standards established by certain private agencies, either other users, suppliers, or technical societies; and (3) governmental standards.

Individual Standards

Individual standards require extensive consultation among users, engineering, purchasing, quality control, suppliers, marketing, and, possibly, ultimate consumers. This means the task is likely to be arduous and expensive.

A common procedure is for the buying organization to formulate its own specifications on the basis of the foundation laid down by the governmental or technical societies. To make doubly sure that no serious errors have been made, some organizations mail out copies of all tentative specifications, even in cases where changes are mere revisions of old forms, to several outstanding suppliers in the industry to get the advantage of their comments and suggestions before final adoption.

Standard Specifications

If an organization wishes to buy on a specification basis, yet hesitates to undertake to originate its own, it may use one of the so-called standard specifications. These have been developed as a result of a great deal of experience and study by both governmental and nongovernmental agencies, and substantial effort has been expended in promoting them. They may be applied to raw or semimanufactured products, to component parts, or to the composition of material. The well-known SAE steels, for instance, are a series of alloy steels of specified composition and known properties, carefully defined, and identified by individual numbers.

When they can be used, standard specifications have major advantages. They are widely known and commonly recognized and readily available to every buyer. Furthermore, the standard should have somewhat lower costs of manufacture. They have grown out of the wide experience of producers and users and, therefore, should be adaptable to the requirements of many purchasers.

Standard specifications have been developed by a number of nongovernmental engineering and technical groups. Among them may be mentioned the American Standards Association, the American Society for Testing Materials, the American Society of Mechanical Engineers, the American Institute of Electrical Engineers, the Society of Automotive Engineers, the American Institute of Mining and Metallurgical Engineers, the Underwriters Laboratories, the National Safety Council, the Canadian Engineering Standards Association, the American Institute of Scrap Recycling Industries, the National Electrical Manufacturers' Association, and many others.

While governmental agencies have cooperated closely with these organizations, they have also developed their own standards. The National Bureau of Standards in the U.S. Department of Commerce compiles commercial standards. The General Services Administration coordinates standards and federal specifications for the nonmilitary type of items used by two or more services. The Defense Department issues military (MIL) specifications.

The American National Standards Institute (ANSI) is a private, nonprofit organization that administers and coordinates the U.S. voluntary standardization system. Its mission is to enhance U.S. global competitiveness and the American way of life by promoting, facilitating, and safeguarding the integrity of the voluntary standardization system.[2]

Developed by ANSI, NSSN, A National Resource for Global Standards, contains more than 250,000 references to standards from more than 600 developers worldwide. ANSI provides access to various U.S. and global standards on its Web site and can be a valuable resource for purchasers who need access to various standards.[3]

Government, Legal, and Environmental Requirements

Federal legislation concerning environmental factors, employee health and safety, security, and consumer product safety requires vigilance on the part of purchasing personnel to be sure that products purchased meet government requirements. The Occupational Safety and Health Administration (known as OSHA) of the U.S. Department of Labor has broad powers to investigate and control everything from noise levels to sanitary facilities in places of employment. The Consumer Product Safety Act gives broad regulatory power to a commission to safeguard consumers against unsafe products. Purchasing people have the responsibility to make sure that the products they buy meet the requirements of the legislation. Severe penalties, both criminal and civil, can be placed on violators of the regulations.

Loss Exposure

There are selective buying situations where the specifications may well expose the buying organization to risk. Robert S. Mullen, director of purchasing at Harvard University, cited the instance of a purchase of fireproof mattresses, costing only about $1,000 more in total, to avoid a multimillion dollar suit in case of student injury or death. Environmental risks represent another category.

Another form of loss exposure is related to the possibility of pilferage. The attractiveness of the requirements to consumers and the ease of resale may be reasons for theft. An alert purchaser can significantly cut down on losses by purchasing in smaller quantities, insisting on tamper-proof packaging, choosing the appropriate transportation mode, following the advice of security experts, and making sure that quantities are carefully controlled throughout the acquisition and disposal process.

STANDARDIZATION AND SIMPLIFICATION

The terms *standardization* and *simplification* are often used to mean the same thing. Strictly speaking, they refer to two different ideas. *Standardization* means agreement on definite sizes, design, quality, and the like. It is essentially a technical and engineering concept.

[2] American National Standards Institute, www.ansi.org, January 2001.

[3] See www.nssn.org or www.ansi.org.

Simplification refers to a reduction in the number of sizes, designs, and so forth. It is a selective and commercial problem, an attempt to determine the most important sizes, for instance, of a product and to concentrate production or use on these wherever possible. Simplification may be applied to articles already standardized as to design or size or as a step preliminary to standardization.

The challenge in an organization is where to draw the line between standardization and simplification, on the one hand, and suitability and uniqueness, on the other. Clearly, as economic and technological factors change, old standards may no longer represent the best buy. Frequently, by stressing standardization and simplification of the component parts, rather than the completed end product, production economies may be gained combined with individuality of end product. Simultaneously, procurement advantages are gained in terms of low initial cost, lower inventories, and diversity in selection of sources. The automotive industry, for example, has used this approach extensively to cut costs, improve quality, and still give the appearance of extensive consumer options.

Sasib, a manufacturer of equipment for the food and beverage industry, headquartered in Italy, found that product standardization was an important issue for its large global customers, such as Coca Cola and Heineken. The chief purchasing officer described the importance of standardization and the role of supply:

> Standardization is important to us, not just for leveraging purchases across the group, but also in terms of our ability to design and build a product for our customer that is consistent, regardless of where it is manufactured. We also want to be able to exchange and optimize manufacturing capacity. For example, we need to develop the flexibility to build machines in the U.S. that are designed in Europe and vice versa. More importantly, our customers are expecting standardization across our product lines. This can only be done if we use the same suppliers who can provide support everywhere in the world. Consequently, we use top-quality suppliers with global supply and service networks. Previously, the companies were dealing with local suppliers. Even in situations where divisions used common suppliers, prices and specifications differed substantially.[4]

QUALITY, SUITABILITY, AND BEST BUY

Practitioners often use the term *quality* to describe the notions of function, suitability, reliability and conformance with specifications, satisfaction with actual performance, and best buy. This is highly confusing.

Quality

Quality, in the simplest sense, refers to the ability of the supplier to provide goods and services in conformance with specifications. The area of inspection, discussed at the end of this chapter, covers this interpretation. Quality also may refer to whether the item performs in actual use to the expectations of the original requisitioner, regardless of conformance with specifications. Thus, it is often said an item is "no good" or of "bad quality" when it fails in use, even though the original requisition or specification may be at fault. The ideal, of course, is achieved when all inputs acquired pass this use test satisfactorily.

[4] Michiel R. Leenders and P. Fraser Johnson, *Major Structural Changes in Supply Organizations* (Tempe AZ: Center for Advanced Purchasing Studies, 2000).

Suitability

Suitability refers to the ability of a material, good, or service to meet the intended functional use. In a pure sense, suitability ignores the commercial considerations and refers to fitness for use. In reality, that is hardly practiced. Gold may be a better electrical conductor than silver or copper but is far too expensive to use in all but special applications. That is why chips are wired with gold and houses with copper. The notion of "best buy" puts quality, reliability, and suitability into a sound procurement perspective.

Reliability

Reliability is the mathematical probability that a product will function for a stipulated period of time. Complexity is the enemy of reliability because of the multiplicative effect of probabilities of failure of components. If failures occur randomly, testing is flexible because the same inference may be drawn from 20 parts tested for 50 hours as for 500 parts tested for 2 hours. Exceptions like the Weibull distribution (which accounts for the aging effect) and the bathtub curve (which recognizes the high probability of early failure, a period of steady state, and a higher probability of failure near the end of the useful life) also can be handled but require more complex mathematical treatment.

From a procurement standpoint, it is useful to recognize the varying reliabilities of components and products acquired. Penalties or premiums may be assessed for variation from design standard depending on the expected reliability impact.

Quality Dimensions

Considerable interest in the use of quality as a competitive tool has reawakened management appreciation of the contribution quality can make in an organization. On the supply side, how well suppliers perform may be crucial to the buying organization's own success in providing quality goods and services. A variety of surveys show that, in many organizations, at least 50 percent of the quality problems stem from goods and services supplied by suppliers. Moreover, management tools and techniques such as lean production, MRP, JIT, and stockless purchasing all require that what is delivered by a supplier conform to specifications. Furthermore, it is not realistic to insist that suppliers supply quality goods without ensuring that the buying organization's own quality performance is beyond reproach. This applies to the procurement organization, its people, policies, systems, and procedures as well. Quality improvement is a continuing challenge for both buyer and seller. Moreover, close cooperation between buying and selling organizations is necessary to achieve significant improvement over time.

Quality is a complex term, which, according to Professor David Garvin of the Harvard Business School, has at least eight dimensions:

1. *Performance*. The primary function of the product or service.
2. *Features*. The bells and whistles.
3. *Reliability*. The probability of failure within a specified time period.
4. *Durability*. The life expectancy.
5. *Conformance*. The meeting of specifications.
6. *Serviceability*. The maintainability and ease of fixing.
7. *Aesthetics*. The look, smell, feel, and sound.
8. *Perceived quality*. The image in the eyes of the customer.

Obviously, from a procurement point of view, the ninth dimension should be "procurability"—the short- and long-term availability on the market at reasonable prices and subject to continuing improvement.

"Best Buy"

The decision on what to buy involves more than balancing various technical considerations. The most desirable technical feature or suitability for a given use, once determined, is not necessarily the desirable buy. The distinction is between technical considerations that are matters of dimension, design, chemical or physical properties, and the like, and the more inclusive concept of the "best buy." The "best buy" assumes, of necessity, a certain minimum measure of suitability but considers ultimate customer needs, cost and procurability, transportation, and disposal as well.

If the cost is so high as to be prohibitive, one must get along with an item somewhat less suitable. Or if, at whatever cost or however procurable, the only available suppliers of the technically perfect item lack adequate productive capacity or financial strength, then, too, one must give way to something else. Obviously, too, frequent reappraisals are necessary. If the price of copper increases from $0.70 a pound to $1.50 or more, its relationship to aluminum or other substitutes may change.

The "best buy" is a combination of characteristics, not merely one. The specific combination finally decided on is almost always a compromise, since the particular aspect of quality to be stressed in any individual case depends largely on circumstances. In some instances, the primary consideration is reliability; questions of immediate cost or facility of installation or the ease of making repairs are all secondary. In other instances, the lifetime of the item is not so important; efficiency in operation becomes more significant.

The decision on what constitutes the best buy for any particular need is as much conditioned by marketing as by procurement and technical considerations. It should be clear that to reach a sound decision on the best buy requires all relevant parties—marketing, engineering, operations, and supply—to work closely together. The ability and willingness of all parties concerned to view the trade-offs in perspective will significantly influence the final decisions reached.

Determining the "Best Buy"

It is generally accepted that the final verdict on technical suitability for a particular use should rest with those involved in using, engineering, specifying, or resale. Supply's right to audit, question, and suggest must be recognized along with the need for early involvement of procurement during the design phase.

Supply fails to live up to its responsibility unless it insists that economic and procurement factors be considered and unless it passes on to those immediately responsible for specification suggestions of importance that may come as a result of its normal activities. The purchaser is in a key position to present the latest information from the marketplace that may permit modifications in design, more flexibility in specifications, or changes in manufacturing methods that will improve value for the ultimate customer. Cross-functional teams are preferable to an adversarial approach to "best buy" determinations.

The Cost of Quality

The old-fashioned management perspective was that the quality–cost curve was similar to the economic order quantity curve, or broadly U-shaped (see Figure 5–3). Under this

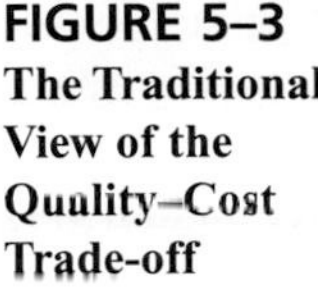

FIGURE 5–3
The Traditional View of the Quality–Cost Trade-off

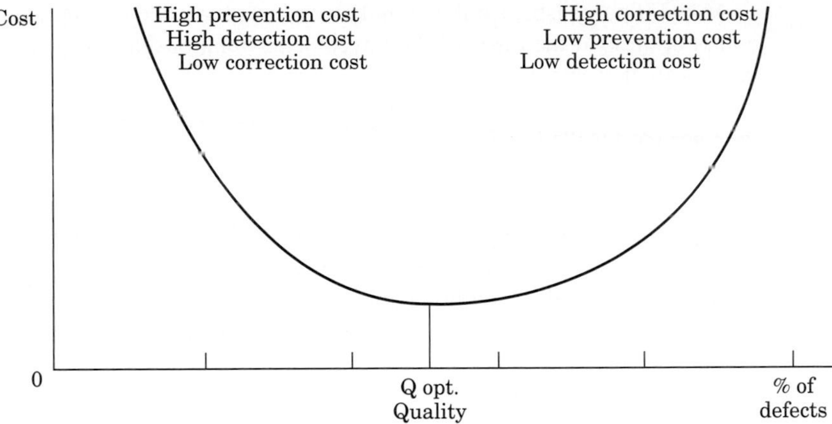

FIGURE 5–4
The Current View of the Quality–Cost Trade-off

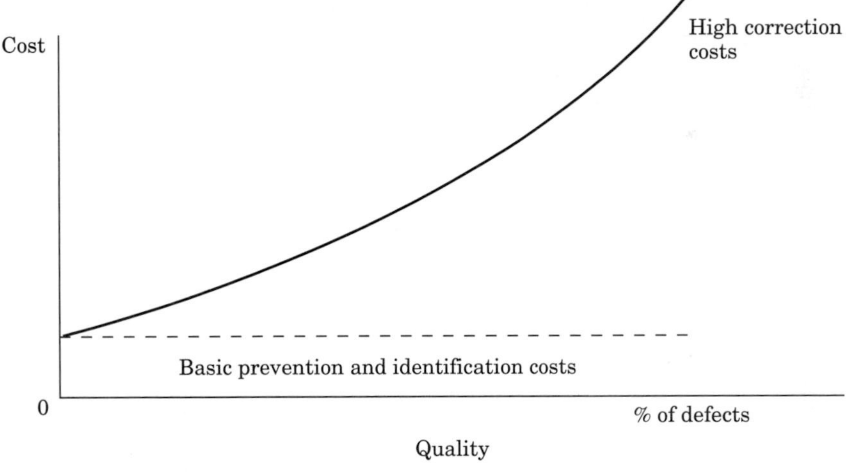

notion, it was considered acceptable to live with a significant defect level, because it was assumed that fewer defects would increase costs.

Thanks to the contribution of leaders like Deming, Juran, Shingo, and Crosby, a new perspective on quality and its achievability has emerged. This view of quality argues that every defect is expensive and prevention or avoidance of defects lowers costs (see Figure 5–4).

Interestingly enough, it used to be that purchasers were willing to pay more for higher-quality products or services, recognizing the benefits to the purchaser's organization, but also assuming that the supplier might have to incur higher costs to achieve better quality. If quality were "inspected in," this would indeed be a higher-cost solution. Deming argues that the stress in quality should be in making it right the first time, rather than inspecting quality in. Making it right the first time should be a lower-cost solution. Therefore, it is not unreasonable for a purchaser and seller to work together on achieving both improved quality and lower costs!

Many of purchasing's policies and procedures have been designed on the principle that competition is at the heart of the buyer–seller relationship. What keeps the seller sharp is the fear that another supplier might take away sales by offering better quality, better price, better delivery, or better service. The assumption was that a supplier switch was inexpensive for the purchaser and that multiple sourcing gave the purchaser both supply security and control over suppliers. The emergence of quality as a prime supply criterion challenges this traditional competitive view. It argues that it is very difficult to find a high-quality supplier and even more difficult to create a supplier who will continually improve quality. In fact, it may require extensive work of various experts in the purchasing organization, along with the appropriate counterparts in the selling organization, to achieve continuing improvement in quality. Under these circumstances, it is not realistic to use multiple sources for the same end item, to switch suppliers frequently, and to go out for quotes constantly.

Single sourcing has traditionally created considerable purchaser nervousness. The idea of sharing key organizational information with suppliers so that they can better plan, design, and service the purchaser's requirements is scary for procurement experts whose skills were honed on a competitiveness philosophy. The heart of a new approach to quality centers on the appropriate use of the hard tools, techniques, and mathematics of quality along with the soft tools of relationship building.

Perhaps the traditional view of quality stems from an economic environment of high demand and low worldwide competition in which defects were tolerated. Perhaps this was further abetted by an incomplete grasp of the real costs of quality and of poor quality. Unfortunately, in many organizations, these costs are well hidden and, therefore, difficult to consider in decision making. Four major cost categories applicable to quality are prevention, appraisal, internal failure, and external failure.

Prevention Costs

Prevention costs relate to all activities that eliminate the occurrence of future defects. These include such diverse costs as various quality assurance programs; precertifying and qualifying suppliers; employee training and awareness programs; machine, tool, material, and labor check-outs; preventive maintenance; and single sourcing with quality suppliers, as well as the associated personnel, travel, equipment, and space costs.

Appraisal Costs

Appraisal costs represent the costs of inspection, testing, measuring, and other activities designed to ensure conformance of the product or service. Appraisal costs might occur at both the seller's and buyer's organizations as each uses a variety of inspection systems to ensure quality conformance. If appraisal requires setting aside batches, or sending product to a separate inspection department, detection costs should include, aside from the inspection cost itself, extra handling and inventory tie-up costs in terms of space, people, equipment, materials, and associated reporting systems. (The advantages of using the supplier's QC reports and making it right the first time are evident.)

Internal Failure Costs

Internal failure costs are the costs incurred within the operating system as a result of poor quality. Included in internal failure costs are returns to suppliers, scrap and rework, lost labor, order delay costs including penalities, machine and time management, and all costs associated with expediting replacement materials or parts or the carrying of extra safety stock.

External Failure Costs

External failure costs are incurred when poor-quality goods or services are passed on to the customer and include costs of returns, warranty costs, and management time handling customer complaints. Unfortunately, when poor-quality parts are incorporated in assemblies, disassembly and reassembly costs may far outweigh the cost of the original part itself. When a defective product gets into the hands of customers or their customers, the possibility of consequential damages arises because a paper roll did not meet specifications, the printer missed an important deadline, a magazine did not reach advertisers and subscribers on time, and so on. There may be health or safety consequences from defective products. These costs are the most expensive because of the possible effects on individual customer goodwill and lost sales and profits. The loss of customers, the inability to secure new customers, and the penalties paid to keep existing customers are also part of external failure costs.

Morale Costs

One cost seldom recognized in an accounting sense is the morale cost of producing (or having to use) defective products or services. Aside from the obvious productivity impact, it may remove pride in one's work or the incentive to keep searching for continuing improvement. The motivation to work hard and well may be replaced by a "don't care" attitude.

An Overall Quality–Cost Perspective

It is so unpleasant to detail the costs of defective quality that the temptation is strong to ignore them. And that is exactly what many organizations have done for many years. They also have built these costs into internally accepted standards. As a consequence, the opportunity to improve quality is great in most organizations.

Some organizations have attempted to quantify the total cost of quality, and the outcome of such studies suggests that 30 to 40 percent of final product cost may be attributable to quality. Obviously, there is a huge incentive to tackle quality as a major organizational challenge.

Continuous Improvement

Continuous improvement, sometimes called by its Japanese name, *kaizen*, refers to the relentless pursuit of product and process improvement through a series of small, progressive steps and is an integral part of both JIT and TQM. Continuous improvement should follow a well-defined and structured approach and incorporate problem-solving tools such as Pareto analysis, histograms, scatter diagrams, check sheets, fishbone diagrams, control charts, run charts, and process flow diagrams.

The *plan–do–check–act cycle*, sometimes called the Deming Wheel, provides a good model for conducting continuous improvement activities. The data are collected and the performance target is set in the plan phase. Countermeasures are implemented in the do phase. Evaluation and measuring results of the countermeasures are performed in the check phase. The improvement is standardized and applied to other parts of the organization in the act phase.

Honda's BP Program is an example of applying a continuous improvement philosophy to supplier management. BP stands for best position, best productivity, best product, best price, and best partners. The BP is a 13-week process that focuses on waste elimination and is based on the principle that the people that perform the work are the greatest source of improvement ideas and creativity. Like all Honda improvement initiatives, BP follows Deming's plan–do–check–act cycle.[5]

ISO 9000 QUALITY STANDARDS AND THE MALCOLM BALDRIGE AWARD[6]

The International Organization for Standardization (ISO) in Geneva, Switzerland, tries to provide common standards across the world. The American National Standards Institute (ANSI) and the Canadian Standards Association (CSA) are North American members. The ISO 9000 quality standards were first adopted in 1987 and revised in 1994, and evolved quickly in Europe and later became popular in North America. By 2001, more than 300,000 organizations worldwide had been certified.

In December 2000, ISO announced significant revisions to its 9000 series, creating ISO 9000:2000. The traditional criticism of the ISO 9000 series since its initial release was that it did not check for actual customer satisfaction, nor did registration necessarily guarantee a quality product or service. The revisions aim to address these weaknesses and make ISO 9000 relevant for organizations in all sectors—services and manufacturing, profit and nonprofit organizations.

The most significant change in ISO 9000:2000 is the integration of ISO 9001, 9002, and 9003 into the new ISO 9001:2000. This is the only standard in the ISO 9000 family against which third-party certification can be carried. ISO 9004:2000, which is meant to be implemented following ISO 9001:2000, is a guideline standard that provides guidance for continuous improvement of quality management systems to achieve sustained customer satisfaction.

The revisions of ISO 9001:2000 and ISO 9004:2000 are based on eight quality management principles that reflect what the organizing committee considered best management practice: customer-focused organization, leadership, involvement of people, process approach, system approach to management, continual improvement, factual approach to decision making, and mutually beneficial supplier relationships.

The annual Malcolm Baldrige National Quality Award is intended to recognize U.S. organizations that excel in quality achievement and quality management, motivate U.S. companies to improve quality and productivity, provide standardized quality guidelines and criteria for evaluating quality improvement efforts, and provide guidance to U.S. organizations striving to make improvements by describing how winning organizations were able to achieve their successes. The diffusion of TQM practices is one of the most important aspects of the Baldrige Award, and the organization sends out more than 200,000 criteria packages each year.

[5] Dave Nelson, Rick Mayo, and Patricia Moody, *Powered by Honda* (New York: John Wiley & Sons, 1998).

[6] Information about the International National Standards Organization can be found on their Web site at www.iso.org.

The Baldrige Award evaluates both quality management programs and achievement of results, with heavy emphasis on total corporate financial performance. Some companies, such as Honeywell, Motorola, Southwest Bell, and Cummins Engine, have required their suppliers to use modified versions of the Baldrige criteria for quality measurement and evaluation.

In Canada, the government has initiated its own national quality awards program and, of course, in Japan, the Deming Prize carries a tremendous amount of international prestige; similar prizes are awarded in other countries.

TOTAL QUALITY MANAGEMENT (TQM)

Total quality management is a philosophy and system of management focused on customer satisfaction. In TQM the customer can be internal or external and is anyone in the supply chain who receives materials from a previous step in the chain. TQM begins with top management developing its vision for total quality, providing the commitment and support to strive for the realization of this vision, and reviewing and encouraging progress toward this achievement. According to the U.S. General Accounting Office, four important features of TQM are

1. Quality must be integrated throughout the organization's activities.
2. There must be employee commitment to continuous improvement.
3. The goal of customer satisfaction, and the systematic and continuous research process related to customer satisfaction, drives TQM systems.
4. Suppliers are partners in the TQM process.[7]

TQM stresses quality as the integrating force in the organization. For TQM to work, all stages in the production process must conform to specifications that are driven by the needs and wants of the end customer. All processes, those of the buyer and the suppliers, must be in control and possess minimal variation to reduce time and expense of inspection. This in turn reduces scrap and rework, increases productivity, and reduces total cost.[8] However, TQM is more than a philosophy and involves the use of several tools, such as quality function deployment (QFD) and statistical process control, in order to achieve performance improvements.

The following sections describe how quality management techniques are used and how they apply to the supply function.

QUALITY FUNCTION DEPLOYMENT (QFD)

Quality function deployment (QFD) is an important aspect of TQM and represents a method for developing new products that seeks to respond to pressures to introduce higher-quality new products at less cost and in less time. QFD, which has been used successfully by Toyota and many others, is based on teamwork and customer involvement and integrates marketing, design, engineering development, manufacturing, production, and purchasing in new-product development from the conception stage through final delivery. Through coordination and integration, rather

[7] F. Ian Stuart and P. Mueller Jr., "Total Quality Management and Supplier Partnerships: A Case Study," *International Journal of Purchasing and Materials Management* 30, no. 1 (Winter 1994), pp. 14–21.

[8] Stuart and Mueller, "Total Quality Management and Supplier Partnerships."

than the traditional sequential development approach, QFD allows the end customer's needs and wants to be communicated at the product development stage, and then drives the design and production stages. More time is spent up front in product development, but by accurately defining customer needs and wants, the total time spent on the design cycle is reduced because fewer design changes are made in later stages of the process. The four integrated stages of the QFD process are

1. *Product planning,* to determine design requirements.
2. *Parts deployment,* to determine parts characteristics.
3. *Process planning,* to determine manufacturing requirements.
4. *Production planning,* to determine production requirements.

Using the QFD methodology, buyer and supplier integration into the process can benefit the organization by (1) reducing or eliminating engineering changes during product development, (2) reducing product development cycle time, (3) reducing start-up cycle time, (4) minimizing product failures and repair costs over the product life, and (5) creating product uniformity and reliability during production.

From the perspective of supply management, well-functioning buyer–supplier relationships are a key contribution that purchasers and supply managers can make to the organizations' TQM and QFD efforts. Supply-base rationalization and closer relationships with key suppliers through partnering arrangements or strategic alliances go hand in hand with quality initiatives (see Chapter 19). The importance of matching purchasing performance measures to the strategic initiatives of the organization is also important if TQM and QFD are to be successful. For example, if purchasing's performance is measured on the basis of reduction in materials costs and operating efficiency rather than the quality of supplier relations, purchasers may be more inclined to buy on the basis of price alone, thereby undermining the quality initiatives of the firm. Integration of functions and processes throughout the firm, and with key suppliers, is a critical component of global competitiveness.

INSPECTION AND TESTING

Inspection and testing may be done at two different stages in the acquisition process. Before commitment is made to a supplier, it may be necessary to test samples to see if they are adequate for the purpose intended. Similarly, comparison testing may be done to determine which product is better from several different sources. After a purchase commitment has been made, inspection may be required to ensure that the items delivered conform to the original description.

Testing and Samples

Testing products may be necessary before a commitment is made to purchase. The original selection of a given item may be based on either a specific test or a preliminary trial.

When suppliers offer samples for testing, the general rule followed by purchasers is to accept only samples that have some reasonable chance of being used. Buyers are more likely to accept samples than to reject them, since they are always on the lookout for items that may prove superior to those in current use. For various reasons, however, care has to be exercised. The samples cost the seller something and the buyer will not wish to raise false hopes on the part of the salesperson. Sometimes, too, the buyer lacks adequate facilities for testing or testing may be costly to the buyer. To meet these objections, some organizations insist on paying for all samples accepted for testing, partly because they believe that a more representative sample is obtained when it is purchased through the ordinary trade channels and partly because the buyer is less likely to feel under any obligation to the seller. Some organizations pay for the sample only when the value is substantial; some follow the rule of allowing whoever initiates the test to pay for the item tested; some pay for it only when the outcome of the test is satisfactory. The general rule, however, is for sellers to pay for samples on the theory that, if sellers really want the business and have confidence in their products, they will be willing to bear the expense of providing free samples.

Use and Laboratory Tests

The type of test given also varies, depending on such factors as the attitude of the buyer toward the value of specific types of tests, the type of item in question, its comparative importance, and the buyer's facilities for testing. At times a use test alone is considered sufficient, as with paint and floor wax. One advantage of a use test is that the item can be tested for the particular purpose for which it is intended and under the particular conditions in which it will be used. The risk that failure may be costly or interrupt performance or production is, however, present. At other times a laboratory test alone is thought adequate and may be conducted by a commercial testing laboratory or in the organization's own quality control facility. For retailers, a test may be given in one or more stores to establish whether consumer demand is sufficient to carry the product.

The actual procedure of handling samples need not be outlined here. It is important to make and keep complete records concerning each individual sample accepted. These records should describe the type of test, the conditions under which it was given, the results, and any representations made about it by the seller. It is sound practice to discuss the results of such tests with supplier representatives so that they know their samples have received a fair evaluation.

Inspection

The ideal situation for inspection is, of course, one in which no inspection is necessary. This is possible because the quality assurance effort cooperatively mounted by the purchaser and the supplier has resulted in outstanding quality performance and reliable supporting supplier-generated records. Since not all organizations have reached this enviable goal, examining some of the more common ideas surrounding inspection and quality control is useful.

The purpose of inspection is to assure the buyer that the supplier has delivered an item that corresponds to the description furnished. When new suppliers are being tried, their products or services must be watched with particular care until they have proved themselves dependable. Unfortunately, too, production methods and skills, even of established suppliers, change from time to time; operators become careless; errors are made; and occasionally a seller may try to reduce production costs to the point where quality suffers. Thus, for a variety of reasons, it is poor policy for a buyer to neglect inspection methods or procedures. There is no point in spending time and money on the development of satisfactory specifications unless adequate provision is made to see that these specifications are lived up to by suppliers.

The type of inspection, its frequency, and its thoroughness vary with circumstances. In the last analysis, this resolves itself into a matter of comparative costs. How much must be spent to ensure compliance with specifications?

In setting specifications, it is desirable to include the procedure for inspection and testing as protection for both buyer and seller. The supplier cannot refuse to accept rejected goods on the ground that the type of inspection to which the goods would be subjected was not known or that the inspection was unduly rigid. Supplier and purchaser need to work out both the procedure for sampling and the nature of the test to be conducted. This way both supplier and purchaser should achieve identical test results, no matter which party conducts the test. Whereas in some situations purchasers may be more sophisticated in quality control and, in others, the suppliers, it is sensible for both sides to cooperate on this issue.

Commercial Testing Labs and Services

The type of inspection required may be so complicated or expensive that it cannot be performed satisfactorily in the buyer's or seller's own organization. In such cases it may be attractive to use the services of commercial testing laboratories, particularly in connection with new processes or materials or for aid in the setting of specifications. Also, the use of an unbiased testing organization may lend credibility to the results. For example, air, water, and soil samples are often sent to commercial labs to test for compliance with EPA standards.

Furthermore, standard testing reports of commonly used items are available from several commercial testing laboratories. They are the commercial equivalent of consumer's reports and can be a valuable aid.

Quality Assurance and Quality Control

The responsibility of a quality assurance group is not confined to the technical task of inspecting incoming material or monitoring in-house production. Obviously, it plays a key role in supplier certification. The quality group can initiate material studies. It can be called on to inspect samples provided by suppliers. Frequently it must investigate claims and errors, both as to incoming items and as to outgoing or finished products. It may examine material returned to stores to determine its suitability for reissue. Similarly, it may be called on to examine salvage material and to make a recommendation as to its disposition. Other duties include quality assurance and attendant efforts to help suppliers and their suppliers to design, implement, and monitor continuous quality improvement programs.

The structure and location of the quality assurance function constitute a relevant problem of administration. In most cases, the work of inspection is performed by a separate department whose work may be divided into three main parts: the inspection of incoming materials, the inspection of materials in the process of manufacture, and the inspection of the finished product. The assignment of this work to a separate department is supported partly on the ground that if the inspectors of materials in process and of the finished product report to the executive in charge of operations, there may be occasions when inspection standards are relaxed in order to cover up defects in production. In some organizations, the quality assurance function reports to the supply manager.

Inspection Methods

The current high interest in quality fueled by concern for customer satisfaction, cost, competitiveness, employee morale, and technological requirements reinforces the need for appropriate inspection methods.

A substantial specialized body of literature is available on the subject of quality control and inspection methods. In this text, only some of the basic quality control concepts will be indicated. Although the mathematics for statistical quality control have been well established for decades, their application has not been as widespread as might have been desirable. Over the past 30 years, various forms of *zero defects programs* have been initiated. The original efforts were largely attributable to defence and space programs, where the consequences of part failures were obviously very serious. Current thinking on quality reinforces the zero defects target as suppliers and purchasers both seek this goal for mutual benefit. If a purchaser could be certain that everything supplied by a supplier was defect-free, it would eliminate the need for overordering and for further inspection and enable immediate use of the materials or parts supplied. Such an ideal situation does not evolve without extensive management efforts. The procurement role in seeking supplier cooperation in the pursuit of the zero defect objective should not be minimized.

Similarly, materials personnel must be thoroughly familiar with the inspection methods commonly used inside their organization and by suppliers, so that they can reinforce their organization's quality efforts appropriately.

Inspection is expensive. If a part is of acceptable quality, inspection does not add to its value. Inspection represents a delay, a further addition of cost, and a possibility of error or damage in handling. Moreover, experience in organizations that have successfully pursued quality improvement programs shows significant productivity improvements have occurred simultaneously.

Because almost all output results for a manufacturing or transformation process of some sort, process control is the preferred approach to controlling product quality. Process control is a key aspect of TQM and is described in the following section.

PROCESS CONTROL

Dr. W. Edwards Deming, the well-known American quality control specialist, assisted Japanese manufacturers in instituting *statistical quality control* (SQC) beginning in the 1950s. Dr. Deming showed that most processes tend to behave in a statistical manner and that understanding how the process behaves without operator interference is necessary before controls can be instituted. Managing quality using SQC techniques involves sampling processes and using the data to establish statistically performance criteria and monitor processes.

Process capability refers to the ability of the process to meet specifications consistently. Since no process can produce the same exact results each time the activity is performed, it is important to establish what kind of variability is occurring and eliminate as much variability as possible. A process capability study identifies two types of variability: (1) the common causes or random variability and (2) special causes. *Statistical process control* (SPC) is a technique that involves testing a random sample of output from a process in order to detect if nonrandom changes in the process are occurring.

Common causes of variability may be machine, people, material, or method related. For instance, machine lubrication, tool wear, or operator technique would be common causes that result in inconsistent output. These common causes are often a natural part of the system. The only way to reduce common causes is to change the process. The output distribution about the mean quality level, taking into consideration common causes, results in the natural capability for a particular process.

Special causes or outside, nonrandom problems such as breakdown of machinery, material variation, or human error also must be identified and eliminated; otherwise, the output will fall outside the acceptable quality range. Statistical process control procedures are primarily concerned with detecting and, subsequently, eliminating special causes.

In determining whether or not a process is stable, the supplier must determine what the natural capability of the process is and whether or not the upper and lower capability limits meet the specifications of the buyer. When a process is "in control," the supplier can predict the future distributions about the mean. For a process to be capable and in control, all the special causes of variation in output have been eliminated and the variation from common causes has been reduced to a level that falls within the acceptable quality range specified by the buyer.

A process is capable when the process is in control, stable, and predictable and when the process averages a set number of standard deviations within the specifications.

In processes using repetitive operations, the quality control chart is invaluable. The output can be measured by tracking a mean and dispersion. The $\overline{X}$ (X-bar) chart is useful for charting the population means and the *R* chart the dispersion.

Upper (UCL) and lower (LCL) control limits can be set so that operator action is required only when the process or machine starts to fall outside of its normal desirable operating range. Figure 5–5 illustrates this "wandering" type of behavior at a steel mill. The rolling operation controls the thickness of the steel and each hour the operator collects thickness data

FIGURE 5–5
Control Chart

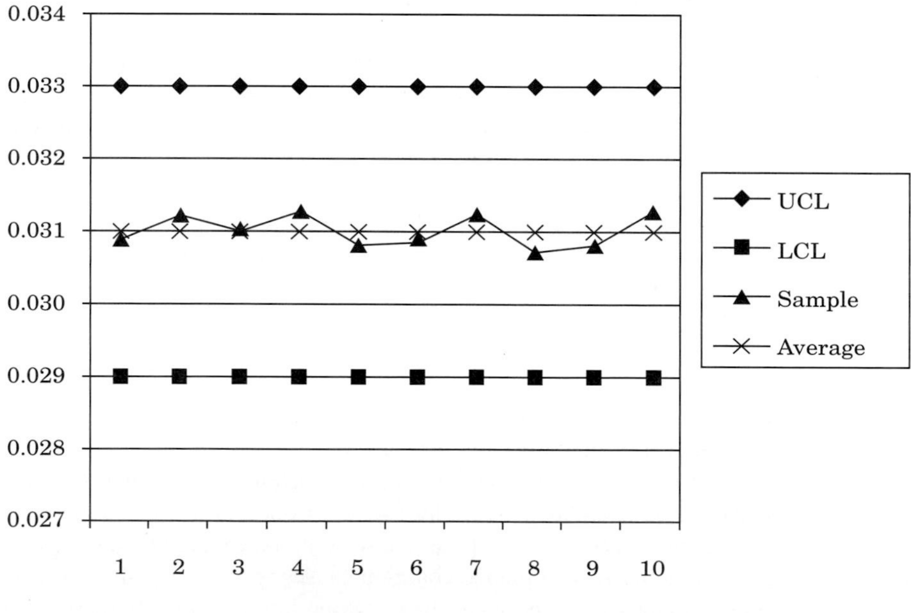

and enters on the $\overline{X}$ chart the means of samples taken from the process. An R chart is the plot of the range within each of the samples. If the mean or range falls outside its acceptable limits, the process is stopped and action is taken to determine the cause for the shift so that corrections can be made.

The control chart uses random sampling techniques and is well suited to most manufacturing and service operations producing large output and where it is not necessary to screen every item produced; for example, stamping steel parts or processing applications in an insurance office.

The first step in quality assurance is making sure that the supplier's process capability and the buyer's acceptable quality range mesh. If the natural range of the supplier's process is wider than the range of the buyer's quality requirements, then the buyer must negotiate with the supplier to have the supplier narrow the natural range through process improvements such as operator training or machine improvements. If it is not economically feasible or the supplier is unable or unwilling to make improvements for some reason, then the buyer may seek another supplier rather than incur the extra cost of inspection, rework, and scrap.

Cpk

The Cpk statistic is used to measure and describe machine or process capability relative to specification requirements by determining the percentage of parts that a process can produce within design specifications. Cpk is defined as the *lower* of either of the following:

$$\frac{\text{Upper tolerance limit} - \overline{X}}{\text{Process spread}} \quad \text{or} \quad \frac{\overline{X} - \text{Lower tolerance limit}}{\text{Process spread}}$$

$\overline{X}$ is the process mean and the process spread is equal to three standard deviations of the output values, or the spread on one side of the process average. The higher the Cpk, the more capable the process is of producing parts that are consistently within specification. A process with a Cpk of less than 1.0 is generally considered not capable, whereas above 1.0 it is capable. Purchasers can specify process capability expectations. Cummins Engine Company, for example, expects suppliers to meet a numeric Cpk of 1.67.

Six Sigma

Six sigma, or 6σ, originated by GE and Motorola, has become a quality initiative adopted by a number of organizations. Technically, 6σ or six standard deviations is very close to zero defects and corresponds to a Cpk value of 2.0.

Screening

There are basically two major types of quality checks on output. One is to inspect every item produced. The other is to sample.

It is traditionally held that 100 percent inspection, or screening, is the most desirable inspection method available. This is not true. Experience shows that 100 percent inspection seldom accomplishes a completely satisfactory job of separating the acceptable from the nonacceptable or measuring the variables properly. Actually, 200 or 300 percent inspection or even higher may have to be done to accomplish this objective. Depending on the severity of a mistake, an error of discarding a perfectly good part may be more acceptable than passing a faulty part. In some applications, the use of such extreme testing may increase the cost of a part enormously. For example, in certain high-technology applications, individual parts are required to be accompanied by their own individual test "pedigrees." Thus, a part that for a commercial application might cost $0.75 may well end up costing $50.00 or more and perform the identical function.

One of the many contributions of Shigeo Shingo in Japan was the development of foolproof, simple "poka yoke" devices that permit inexpensive, rapid 100 percent inspection to ensure zero defects. A simple example would be the three prong power cable connector that can only be inserted in the proper manner.

Sampling

The alternative to inspection of every item produced is to sample. How a sample is taken will vary with the product and process. The purpose is always to attempt to secure a sample that is representative of the total population being tested. Random sampling is one commonly used technique.

The method of taking a random sample will depend on the characteristics of the product to be inspected. If it is such that all products received in a shipment can be thoroughly mixed together, then the selection of a sample from any part of the total of the mixed products will represent a valid random sample. For example, if a shipment of 1,000 balls of supposedly identical characteristics is thoroughly mixed together and a random sample of 50 balls is picked from the lot and inspected and 5 are found to be defective, it is probable that 10 percent of the shipment is defective.

If the product has characteristics that make it difficult or impractical to mix together thoroughly, consecutive numbers can be assigned to each product, and then, through the use of tables of random sampling numbers (of which there are several) or a standard computer program, a sample drawn by number is chosen for detailed inspection.

The general rule that the statisticians believe should be observed when drawing a random sample is: Adopt a method of selection that will give every unit of the product to be inspected an equal chance of being drawn.

Sequential Sampling

Sequential sampling may be used to reduce the number of items to be inspected in accept–reject decisions without loss of accuracy. It is based on the cumulative effect of information that every additional item in the sample adds as it is inspected. After each individual item's inspection, three decisions are possible: accept, reject, or sample another item. A. Wald, one of the pioneers of sequential sampling development, estimated that, using his plan, the average sample size could be reduced to one-half, as compared to a single sampling plan.

In a simple version of sequential sampling, 10 percent of the lot is inspected, and the whole lot is accepted if the sample is acceptable. If the sample is not acceptable, an additional 10 percent may be inspected if the decision to reject cannot be made on the basis of the first sample.

Quality Software Programs

Many quality control software programs are available. They have resolved the tedium of extensive calculations and charts and provide a range of applications. Standard programs, for example, select sampling plans, calculate sample statistics and plot histograms, produce random selection of parts, plot operating characteristics (OC) curves, and determine confidence limits.

Adjustments and Returns

Prompt action for adjustments and returns made necessary by rejections are a responsibility of the purchasing department, aided by the using, inspection, or legal department.

Any nonconforming product, material, or equipment must be locked up to avoid the possibility of inadvertent processing, pilferage, or additional damage while its disposition is being deliberated. Some organizations use a material review board to decide how to deal with specific nonconforming materials.

The actual decision as to what can or should be done with material that does not meet specifications is both an engineering and a procurement question. It can, of course, be simply rejected and returned at the supplier's expense or held for instructions as to its disposition. In either case, the buyer must inform the supplier whether the shipment is to be replaced with acceptable material or whether other alternatives are being considered. Not infrequently, however, a material may be used for other than the originally intended purpose or substituted for some other grade. One alternative is to rework the material, deducting from the purchase price the cost of the additional processing involved. Also, particularly in the case of new types of equipment or new material to which the purchaser is not accustomed, the supplier may send a technical representative to the buyer's organization in the hope that complete satisfaction may be provided.

A problem growing out of inspection is that of the allocation, between buyer and seller, of costs incurred in connection with rejected material. The costs incurred on rejected materials may be divided into three major classes: (1) transportation costs, (2) testing cost, and (3) contingent expense.

The practice of allocating these costs varies considerably. The practice is affected to some degree by the kind of material rejected, trade customs, the essential economies of the situation, the buyer's cost accounting procedure, and the positions of strength of each organization. In practically all cases reported, transportation costs both to and from the rejection point are charged back to the supplier. Very few companies report inspection or testing costs as items to be charged back to the supplier. Such costs are ordinarily borne by the buyer and are considered a part of purchasing or inspection costs.

In many cases, contracts or trade customs provide that the supplier will not be responsible for contingent expense, yet this is perhaps the greatest risk and the most costly item of all from the buyer's standpoint. Incoming materials that are not of proper quality may seriously interrupt production; their rejection may cause a shortage of supply that may result in customer penalties, delay or actual stoppage of production, extra handling, and other expense. Labor and/or equipment time may be expended in good faith on material later found to be unusable. It is, in general, however, not the practice of buyers to allocate such contingent costs to the supplier. Some buyers, however, insist on agreements with their suppliers to recover labor, equipment, or other costs expended on the material before discovery of its defective character.

In a partnership mode, or with special quality programs in place at both the purchaser's and supplier's organizations, the frequency of defective materials or services decreases drastically. And the resolution of difficulties arriving from defective or late deliveries is usually handled in a highly professional and efficient manner, avoiding the nastiness of blame avoidance and litigation threats.

SUPPLIER CERTIFICATION

No matter how perfect the description of the need, the purchaser still needs to worry about whether the supplier will supply what is really required. Normally, this involves quality assurance programs, testing, inspection, and quality control.

Usually, before a new supplier is given an order, and often before a supplier is allowed to quote, the purchaser conducts a quality capability or quality assurance survey on the supplier's premises. The purpose is to ensure that the supplier is capable of meeting the specifications and quality standards required. Whereas this practice started in the military field, it is now common in all high-technology areas and in most larger organizations.

This survey, normally conducted by engineering, manufacturing, purchasing, and quality control personnel, will examine not only the supplier's equipment, facilities, and personnel but also the systems in place to monitor and improve quality. Also examined are the supplier's efforts to seek cooperation and compliance in quality standards from its suppliers and the supplier's commitment to ongoing quality improvement.

It is desirable to have continuing involvement with suppliers to evolve common quality standards, to agree on inspection methods, and to work out ways and means of improving quality while decreasing inspection and overall cost.

Clearly, the question as to whether to purchase only from certified suppliers extends well beyond quality considerations alone. In organizations pursuing partnerships with suppliers, quality certification is usually the first category of interorganizational alignment. It is evident in many industries that a minimum level of quality capability will be a standard requirement for any supplier and that corporate survival may depend on it.

The obvious target in improving quality is to have the right quality by making it right the first time, rather than inspecting the quality in. It is this pressure to create quality at its source that is behind all quality improvement programs. The same philosophy also should apply to the supply department itself and the purchaser's own organization. It is very difficult for a purchaser to insist that suppliers meet stringent quality requirements when it is obvious to the suppliers that the purchasing organization itself shows no sign of a similar commitment. The smartest thing for any purchasing department wishing to start a quality drive is to apply quality standards to its own performance on all of the phases in the acquisition cycle in which it is involved. Not only will this create familiarity with statistical quality control and quality standards in the purchasing department itself, but it also gives purchasing the right to ask for similar commitment by others.

SERVICE

Typically, purchasers think of supplier performance in terms of quality, quantity, delivery, price, and service when purchasing tangible requirements like raw material components, packaging, MRO items, capital equipment, or resale products. Thus, the accompanying service enhances the value of the purchase. Chapter 17 discusses the purchaser of services, and much of what is discussed in Chapter 17 is relevant to service as it accompanies tangible needs. Nevertheless, it is useful to combine in this chapter quality and service as separate from the purchase of a service without an accompanying product.

Although in practice many purchasers refer to a supplier as providing good service when the supplier delivers regularly on time, that is not the correct definition of service. Service may include design, recordkeeping, transportation, storage, disposal, installation, training, inspection, repair, and advice, as well as a willingness to make satisfactory adjustments for misunderstandings or clerical errors. Some purchasers include the supplier's willingness to change orders on short notice and be particularly responsive to unusual requests as part of their evaluation of the service provided. To cover some types of service, suppliers issue guarantees, covering periods of varying length.

If the service is vital to the success of the purchase, such as installation for equipment or training of operators, then it needs to be specified as part of the requirement. Service components like a helpful and pleasant attitude, though real, may be more difficult to quantify, yet distinguish one supplier from another.

Many suppliers specifically include the cost of service in the selling price. Others absorb it themselves, charging no more than competitors and relying on the superior service for the sale. One of the difficult tasks of a purchaser is to get only as much of this service factor as is really needed without paying for the excessive service the supplier may be obliged to render to some other purchaser. In many instances, of course, the service department of a manufacturing concern is maintained as a separate organization and profit center. Obviously, the availability of service is an important consideration for the buyer in securing the "best buy" at the outset.

Conclusion

Quality and service are two of the essential requirements for supply along with quantity, delivery, and price. The continuous pursuit of zero defects over many decades has evolved an impressive array of quality diagnostic and improvement tools. Making it right the first time rather than inspecting quality in is the prevailing wisdom.

Service goes beyond the essential tangible support a supplier is expected to provide such as installation of a new piece of equipment; most purchasers see service also as intangible reflecting responsiveness, flexibility, willingness to provide assistance in case of emergency, evidence of concern for continuous improvement, and friendliness. Thus, service is more difficult to specify, but very real in actual supplier–purchaser dealings. It is easy to promise and difficult to obtain. Both high quality and service form the basis for a longer-term successful relationship between a buyer and a seller and for supply chain cooperation and effectiveness.

Questions for Review and Discussion

1. Why should a purchaser be familiar with the mathematics of quality control and inspection?
2. What are the advantages of using performance specifications?
3. Why use supplier certification?
4. How could a quality philosophy be applied to a purchasing department?
5. What are the various costs associated with quality and why is it difficult to determine the magnitude of some of these costs?
6. Why was Deming so insistent on single sourcing?
7. What does it mean if a supplier is ISO 9000:2000 certified?
8. What are the trade-offs between 100 percent inspection and sampling?
9. What constitutes a best buy?
10. What are the advantages of specifying by brand? Disadvantages?

References

American National Standards Institute, www.ansi.org.

Askin, Ronald G., and Jeffrey B. Goldberg. *Design and Analysis of Lean Production Systems*. New York: Wiley, 2001.

Besterfield, Dale. *Quality Control*. 6th ed. Upper Saddle River, NJ: Prentice-Hall, 2001.

Bounds, Gregory. *Cases in Quality*. Burr Ridge, IL: Irwin, 1996.

Choi, Thomas Y., and Manus Rungtusanatham. "Comparison of Quality Management Practices: Across the Supply Chain and Industries." *Journal of Supply Chain Management,* Winter 1999, pp. 20–27.

International Standards Organization, www.iso.org.

Juran, Joseph M., and A. Blanton Godfrey. *Juran's Quality Handbook*. 5th ed. New York: McGraw Hill, 1999.

Leenders, Michiel R., and P. Fraser Johnson. *Major Structural Changes in Supply Organizations*. Tempe, AZ: Center for Advanced Purchasing Studies, 2000.

Nellore, Rajesh; Klas Soderquist; Gary Siddall; and Jaideep Motwani. "Specifications—Do We Really Understand What They Mean?" *Business Horizons,* November–December 1999, pp. 63–69.

Nelson, Dave; Rick Mayo; and Patricia Moody. *Powered by Honda*. New York: John Wiley & Sons, 1998.

Prahalad, C. K., and M. S. Krichman. "The New Meaning of Quality in the Information Age." *Harvard Business Review,* September–October 1999, pp. 109–118.

Ritzman, Larry P.; Lee J. Krajewski; and Robert D. Klassen. *Foundations of Operations Management.* Toronto: Pearson Prentice Hall, 2004.

Case 5–1

Bright Technology International

Bob Renwick, purchasing manager at Bright Technology International (BTI), was considering a quotation from Electronix for supply of MJ10012 transistors, in his Modesto, California, office. It was Tuesday, March 11th, and this was the third time this month he had been asked to consider a volume purchase for a component and he wondered what purchasing policies, if any, he should establish for such situations. Bob had to respond to the supplier's proposal before the end of the week, and he felt that the MJ10012 transistor purchase would provide a good basis in which to change the current approach used to acquire similar components.

COMPANY BACKGROUND

Headquartered in Hartford, Connecticut, BTI designed, manufactured, and marketed proprietary electro-optical instruments. Founded in the early 1980s, BTI went public in 1989. Company revenues had grown steadily and sales for the current fiscal year were expected to reach $10 million.

BTI's products were used around the world for medical research, health care, industrial process, quality control, environmental science, and other applications. The company focused exclusively on fluorescence instrumentation and distinguished itself in the marketplace by providing exceptional product support.

Fluorescence was a powerful technique for studying molecular interactions in analytical chemistry, biochemistry, cell biology, physiology, nephrology, cardiology, photochemistry, and environmental science. Applications included studying dynamics of the folding of proteins, measuring concentrations of ions inside living cells, studying membrane structure and function, investigating drug interactions with cell receptors, and fingerprinting oil samples. Its advantage over other light-based investigation methods was high sensitivity, high speed, and safety. BTI's products included spectrofluorometers and ratio fluorescence systems.

In recent years, the company had expanded internationally and it currently had sales and service centers in the United States, Canada, Germany, and the United Kingdom. Management expected that approximately 50 percent of its sales for the coming year would be outside the United States and Canada.

BTI had nine competitors. Eight of these were about the same size as BTI, while one other controlled nearly one-half of the market.

In total, BTI had approximately 80 employees, including 20 in Connecticut and 45 in Modesto. Manufacturing, engineering and R&D, and customer service functions resided at the Modesto facility.

PURCHASING AT BTI

Bob Renwick handled all purchasing for materials and services related to the production of BTI's products and reported to the plant manager. He had a background as a technician for a major telecom company before he joined BTI six years earlier.

Purchased components accounted for about 80 percent of cost of sales. Although Bob worked with more than 400 vendors, many of whom were located outside North America, approximately three-quarters of the total dollar value for his orders were for custom-designed components, while the balance of the orders were for basic items. He relied heavily on members of the engineering department, who were familiar with the suitability of suppliers to satisfy technical specifications for various components and for recommendations regarding new suppliers.

In recent years, there had been a trend of consolidation among the manufacturers of electrical components and optical parts, and the remaining players were mostly big companies with significant bargaining power. While there was still price competition for high-volume components, especially for large customers, suppliers tended to charge a premium when supplying small custom orders. For Bob, this trend meant increased prices for many of his components. To address this problem, he had worked with the engineering department to redesign certain products, eliminating some costly or hard-to-get components. However, engineering staff had not been able to solve this issue completely and occasionally customers specified certain types of subcomponents in their orders.

THE MJ10012 TRANSISTOR

The MJ10012 was a transistor used in the power supply for several of BTI's products. Each power supply needed two transistors and the annual demand for this kind of transistor had increased over the past few years. The expected demand for the coming year was estimated to be 2,000 units.

BTI had been using transistors manufactured by Steyn Technologies. However, a competitor, Abram Industries, acquired Steyn the previous year and the MJ10012 transistor was no longer part of the supplier's core product offering and its supply was currently handled through an independent distributor, Electronix.

Checking his records, Bob found that the MJ10012 transistor had been purchased in each of the last three years with the following price history:

Year	Price per Unit
Current quote	4.95
Previous year	3.50
Two years prior	2.00
Three years prior	1.69

Bob estimated that there was approximately a two months' supply in stock, and the supplier was quoting lead times of 30 days.

CONCLUSION

As Bob looked at the quotation from Electronix, he considered his alternatives. He was confident that there were other transistors on the market that provided similar performance capabilities, however, these products would have to be located, then tested and approved by engineering. If, on the other hand, he was going to buy the transistors from Electronix, how many should he order? The controller had indicated that it cost about $50 to process an order, and besides, Bob felt his time was best spent on other matters.

Bob had to make purchasing decisions about hundreds of different parts; and although the MJ10012 transistor decision was a minor one in terms of dollar amount, it represented a typical issue in the purchase of electrical and optical parts that was of growing concern to him. He wondered whether there was anything else he could do to deal with this and similar issues.

Case 5–2

Air Quality Systems Inc.

Patrick Wallace, plant manager at Air Quality Systems Inc. (AQS), in Richmond, Virginia, found himself confronted with a serious quality problem on the company's main product line. The foam insulation for a batch of heat recovery ventilation products manufactured at the plant had begun to peel off, making it likely that the equipment would malfunction. To make matters worse, Patrick also believed that it was likely that defective equipment had already been shipped to customers. It was Wednesday, August 6th, and Patrick knew that he had to react immediately to the problem.

THE COMPANY

Since the company's founding in 1984, AQS was committed to its mission to enhance the consumer's quality of life by creating, manufacturing, and marketing innovative energy-recovery products. It manufactured ventilation, air-cleaning, and heating equipment for residential and light commercial applications and had acquired a reputation in the industry for high quality and technological innovation.

Company management believed that its strengths lay in four key areas: design, assembly, steel fabrication, and the manufacture of aluminum heat recovery ventilators (HRV). AQS occupied a 65,000-square-foot, state-of-the-art manufacturing plant and was ISO 9001 registered. Facilities included a fully equipped laboratory and R&D area. Sales had increased consistently and were expected to reach $12 million in the current year, with sales of HRVs accounting for approximately two-thirds of the total.

Approximately 60 percent of the 3,400 parts used by AQS in its manufacturing operations were procured from suppliers, while the remaining 40 percent were produced in-house. Supply of the most critical components were single sourced, while sourcing decisions for less important commodity or commodity-like items were usually purchased on the basis of low cost, provided suppliers were able to meet expectations concerning quantity, delivery, and quality. Component parts were inspected by operators as part of their responsibilities in the assembly operations. As plant manager, Patrick was responsible for quality control and oversaw a staff of two technicians who handled product testing and addressed customer quality issues.

PRODUCTS AND CUSTOMERS

AQS sold more than 300 different products under the *AirPurity* brand name to large distributors. Distributors sold these products to wholesalers, who in turn sold to independent contractors. Contractors installed the products in homes and commercial buildings. Large wholesalers and contractors also could buy products directly from AQS.

Heat recovery ventilators moved stale air from inside the house to outdoors. At the same time, they drew in fresh air from outside and distributed it throughout the house or building, thereby replenishing the environment. As the two airstreams passed on either side of an aluminum heat exchanger, the heat from the outgoing air was transferred to the incoming air. The efficiency of the *AirPurity* HRV was such that virtually none of the warmth collected from the home was lost to the outside. In the summer, the HRV worked in reverse, removing heat from the incoming air and transferring it to the outgoing air. Residential units (with a capacity of 95–300 cubic feet per minute) were sold to homeowners, while commercial units (with a capacity of 500–2,500 cubic feet per minute) were sold to owners of large buildings, such as schools and offices. AQS products also could be used by homeowners in specific parts of the home, such as indoor pools and garages. A typical HRV residential unit cost between $550 and $750.

In addition to selling products under its own brand name, AQS also manufactured about 20 products for over a dozen large companies, which in turn sold these products under their own brand name. These companies included well-known names such as Honeywell, Lennox, and Sears.

THE QUALITY PROBLEM

The quality problem centered on the damper door for HRVs. The damper door was a steel door covered with foam insulation. The foam insulation consisted of a layer of PVC, a layer of foam, and a layer of adhesive. Suffolk Industries (Suffolk), a local manufacturer, supplied this product to AQS for all of its HRVs. In industry terminology, Suffolk was a "converter." It bought foam from a foam manufacturer, cut it into the required shape, and applied layers of PVC and adhesive to the product. It was placed on the damper door during the assembly operation at AQS, with the adhesive ensuring that it adhered to the door. Up until this point, the foam insulation supplied by Suffolk had proven to be of a reliable quality.

The converter business was not particularly capital-intensive, while foam manufacturing, on the other hand, was extremely capital-intensive. The product specified by AQS was ether foam, which required high concentrations of fire-retardant chemicals to make it heat-resistant to enable it to withstand the high temperatures used in the converter process. Other kinds of foam did not usually require high concentrations of fire-retardant chemicals.

The previous day, one of the operators in the assembly department noticed that the foam insulation was peeling off the damper doors in a batch of HRV equipment that had been manufactured recently and was awaiting shipment to customers. The foam was separating from the PVC layer, leaving a layer of adhesive on the door. The separation of the foam insulation was likely to cause the HRV unit to malfunction. After further investigation, Patrick expected that a similar problem might have occurred with some product that had already been shipped to customers, although he could not be sure at this point how long the quality problem had existed.

FUTURE COURSE OF ACTION

Patrick knew that he needed to act fast to resolve this problem and wondered about the appropriate course of action. Although the problem had been identified internally, he had not contacted either Suffolk or any of his customers. In the meantime, Patrick had stopped all HRV deliveries until the problem was resolved, although several customers currently waiting for deliveries would be disappointed about any delays. Hence, Patrick felt that resolving this matter quickly was paramount.

A further issue related to avoiding similar problems in the future. The company had expanded quickly over the past few years and Patrick wanted to protect the company's image of producing quality products. He wondered what, if anything, could be done to proactively avoid similar product-quality problems. Specifically, he wondered whether he should in-source supply of additional components or alternatively what changes he might consider for existing supply relationships.

Case 5–3

Synergy Metals Inc.

On Tuesday, October 21st, Jim Crawford, manufacturing manager at Synergy Metals in Mississauga, Ontario, Canada, received a phone call from Charles Herrick, quality manager at the DaimlerChrysler assembly plant in Brampton: "We've got another problem with the rings on your engine sprockets. This is the second time this problem has occurred in the last couple of months and I need you to look into this matter immediately and let me know within two days what you intend to do to prevent it from happening again."

SYNERGY METALS

Synergy Metals Inc. (Synergy) was a leading producer of powder metal components for the lawn, garden, and power equipment; automotive; home appliance; and aerospace industries. The company had grown significantly, mainly through acquisitions, in the past decade and employed more than 5,000 employees worldwide. Its product offerings included a wide range of powder metal parts, including bearings, gears, sprockets, and connecting rods. (See Exhibit 1.) Approximately 60 percent of its sales were automotive related.

The Mississauga plant was dedicated to manufacturing engine and transmission components for the automotive and commercial vehicle industries, and produced parts such as hubs, rotors, synchronizer rings, and sprockets. The plant used a traditional four-step manufacturing process for most of its powder metal products: powder blending, compaction, sintering, and sizing and coining. Some powder metal parts manufactured in the Mississauga plant were subsequently combined with other components to form large assemblies.

The Mississauga plant's customers include Ford, General Motors, DaimlerChrysler, Honda, and Toyota. Total employment at the plant numbered approximately 140 people with sales of approximately $18 million per year.

Jim Crawford had worked for Synergy for more than 15 years. He had started as the cost accounting supervisor, then moved to human resource management, and was promoted to his present position nearly eight years prior.

EXHIBIT 1 Synergy Products

THE ENGINE SPROCKET

The bankruptcy of a supplier in July had forced Jim to re-source part number B3755, engine sprocket ring. The B3755 was one component used in a "family" of several engine sprocket assemblies supplied to DaimlerChrysler and General Motors. This product line accounted for approximately two-thirds of the plant's total revenue and Synergy required approximately 20,000 B3755 rings each week.

The new supplier, Ecker Metal Products (Ecker), was selected based on its competitive pricing and because it also had ISO 9000 and QS 9000 certification. Ecker did not supply any other components to Synergy.

The re-sourcing process involved the purchase of technical drawings for $10,000 and some equipment for $20,000. The equipment consisted of a transfer system that was attached to the tooling. This system moved the rings between stages in the press during the manufacturing process. Although Synergy owned the tooling, the supplier had invested in the transfer system to reduce its labor costs.

QUALITY PROBLEMS

Immediately after the B3755 was re-sourced to Ecker, Jim received a call from DaimlerChrysler complaining of quality problems with the engine sprocket assembly. Jim followed company quality procedures, quarantining 100 percent of all stock affected by the complaint so it could be inspected before delivery to customers. Subsequent investigation found an intermittent problem with the B3755 part supplied by Ecker.

Jim and his quality manager, Yvonne Symons, met with their counterparts at Ecker the following week to review the problem and to ensure that appropriate corrective action was taken. The production manager at Ecker, Dave Catton, complained to Jim about the transfer system on the tooling, saying: "The transfer system that you gave us with the tooling doesn't work properly. The fingers don't always place the parts in the correct location in the tool, causing quality problems. Our operators try to catch the misformed parts, but they can't be expected to get them all. The only options are to remove the transfer system and go to a manual system or to invest in a new unit. Based on my experience, I figure it will cost about $25,000 for a new transfer system and likely take two months to have it built and installed. Removing the transfer system will add at least another $1.00 in labor."

Jim indicated that Synergy had never had a quality problem with the previous supplier and that he expected Ecker to work with the existing equipment, as stipulated in their contract. He explained that Synergy could not afford to invest in new equipment at this time and that he did not feel such an investment was required anyway. He reminded the management from Ecker at the meeting that they had reviewed the tooling and transfer system before quoting and subsequently accepting the job.

The meeting concluded with Dave Catton and the others from Ecker agreeing to work with the existing process. Ecker also agreed to increase the frequency of inspections until they became confident that the process was functioning properly.

DECIDING ON A COURSE OF ACTION

Early indications were that the latest quality problems were also related to the B3755 and Jim expected that Dave Catton would once again blame the transfer system for the problem. Jim was still reluctant to invest in a new system at this time because of the low margins on the engine sprockets.

Under the circumstances, Jim felt that he had to consider the option of finding a new supplier for the B3755. However, he was concerned that this alternative would take several weeks and be disruptive to production during the transition. Jim also had concerns regarding the cooperation that he might receive from Ecker if they knew the B3755 was being moved.

Before meeting with Ecker, Jim wanted to formulate his plan of action. He was aware that because this was the second occurrence in a relatively short period, Charles Herrick would expect a solid commitment that such problems would not occur again.

Chapter Six

Quantity and Inventory

Chapter Outline

Key Questions for the Supply Manager

Should we

- Change the way we forecast?
- Use vendor-managed inventories?
- Purchase our A items differently?

How can we

- Reduce our investment in supply chain inventories?
- Improve our inventory management?
- Obtain supplier cooperation for JIT?

Continuous improvement; speed to market; customer, employee, and supplier satisfaction; and global competitiveness require dedication to productivity and value-adding activities. These organizational goals drive management attitudes to quality, quantity, and delivery, with profound impact on the acquisition process. With respect to quantity and delivery considerations, the most telling evidence comes from inventory reduction and shortened lead times. Both can be accomplished by increasing frequency of deliveries, while decreasing the amount delivered at one time. Accompanying efforts in setup time reduction, just-in-time (JIT) systems, vendor-managed inventory systems, order cost reduction, EDI, and e-commerce are all part of the same drive.

The decisions of *how much* to acquire and *when* logically follow clarification of *what* is required. The natural response is to say, "buy as much as you need when you need it." Such a simple answer is not sufficient, however. Many factors significantly complicate these decisions. First, managers must make purchase decisions before, often a long time before, actual requirements are known. Therefore, they must rely on forecasts, not only of future demand but also of lead times, prices, and other costs. Such forecasts are rarely, if ever, perfect. Second, there are costs associated with placing orders, holding inventory, and running out of materials and goods. Third, materials may not be available in the desired quantities without paying a higher price or delivery charge. Fourth, suppliers may offer reduced prices for buying larger quantities. Fifth, shortages may cause serious disruptions.

In many organizations, the decision of how much to purchase and when is made more important by the close relationship between purchase quantity and scheduled use. It is necessary to distinguish between how much to buy in an individual purchase or release and what portion of total requirements to buy from an individual supplier. This chapter deals only with individual order quantities and inventory management; the allotment to suppliers is discussed in Chapters 10, 18, and 19.

INVENTORY MANAGEMENT

Quantity and delivery go hand in hand. Order less, deliver more frequently; order more, deliver less frequently. Every supplier performance evaluation scheme includes quantity and delivery as standard evaluation criteria. To ensure timely delivery, recognition needs to be given to the times required to complete each of the steps in the acquisition process discussed in Chapter 3. The ability to compress these times by doing them in parallel, by eliminating time-consuming and non-value-adding activities, by doing steps faster, and by eliminating delays can provide significant benefits. Much of the reengineering work in the supply area has focused on the acquisition process to make it more responsive and to reduce cycle time.

For the supply management function, the time-based strategies that are of importance in the quantity decision are ones that relate directly to the flow of materials, inventories (raw material, work-in-process, and finished goods), and related information and decisions. Competitive advantage accrues to organizations that can (1) successfully reduce the time it takes to perform activities in a process (reduce setup and cycle time) and (2) coordinate the flow of resources to eliminate waste in the system and ensure that materials and equipment arrive on time or just-in-time in economically sized batches.

Long lead times can occur in the design and development process, in the material acquisition to distribution of finished goods process, and in administrative support cycles (e.g., accounts payable, purchase order development/release cycle). Some of the causes of long lead times are waiting and procrastination, poorly engineered designs, the accumulation of batches prior to movement, inefficient and long physical flows with backtracking, and poor communication. Long lead times can impact decisions about *how much* to buy. Compressed cycle times and coordination of material and information flows can result in materials arriving just-*on*-time (e.g., when they were scheduled to arrive) or just-*in*-time (just prior to actual use or need). Material requirements planning–type (MRP) programs or kanban (pull systems) can be used to plan the timing and quantity of purchased materials and internally manufactured materials.

There are many causes for poor material flow coordination, including late, early, or no deliveries; low fill rate; material defects; scrap; uneven batch sizes; long lead times; production schedule changes; downtime; long setup/changeover times; infrequent updates of MRP systems; forecasts; and on-hand inventory accounting systems. Greater coordination of material and information flows both within the buying firm and its customers and between the buying firm and its suppliers (and their suppliers) can result in lower inventories and improvements in return on assets in the supply chain (see example in Chapter 1).

FUNCTIONS AND FORMS OF INVENTORIES

Understanding where (and why) inventory should be positioned in the supply chain can improve customer service, lower total costs, or increase flexibility. Proper inventory management requires a thorough understanding of both the functions and the forms of inventory.

The Functions of Inventory

Many purchases cover repetitive items often held in inventory. Thus, inventory policy has a great influence on purchase quantity decisions. The questions of how much to order, when, and how much to carry in stock are key decisions subject to continuous improvement examination along with the focus on quality and customer, employee, and supplier satisfaction. It is important in making delivery, inventory, or purchase order size decisions to understand why inventories exist and what the relevant trade-offs are. Inventories exist for many purposes, including:

- To provide and maintain good customer service.
- To smooth the flow of goods through the productive process.
- To provide protection against the uncertainties of supply and demand.
- To obtain a reasonable utilization of people and equipment.

The following classification of inventory functions reveals the multipurpose roles played by inventories.

Transit or pipeline inventories are used to stock the supply and distribution pipelines linking an organization to its suppliers and customers as well as internal transportation points. They exist because of the need to move material from one point to another. Obviously, transit inventories are dependent on location and mode of transportation. A decision to use a distant supplier with rail transport will probably create a far larger raw materials transit inventory than a decision to use a local supplier with truck delivery.

In *just-in-time* (JIT) production, a variety of means are used to reduce transit inventories, including the use of local suppliers, small batches in special containers, and trucks specifically designed for side loading in small quantities.

Cycle inventories arise because of management's decision to purchase, produce, or sell in lots rather than individual units or continuously. Cycle inventories accumulate at various points in operating systems. The size of the lot is a trade-off between the cost of holding inventory and the cost of making more frequent orders and/or setups. A mathematical description of this relationship, the economic order quantity, will be discussed later. In JIT, the need for cycle inventories is reduced by setup cost and time reduction.

Buffer or uncertainty inventories or safety stocks exist as a result of variability in demand or supply. Raw material, purchased parts, or MRO buffer stocks give some protection against the variability of supplier performance due to shutdowns, strikes, lead-time variations, late deliveries to and from the supplier, poor-quality units that cannot be accepted, and so on. Work-in-process buffer inventories protect against machine breakdown, employee illness, and so on. Finished goods buffers protect against unforeseen demand or production failures.

Management efforts to reduce supply variability may have substantial payoffs in reduced inventories. Options may include increasing supply alternatives, using local sources, reducing demand uncertainty, reducing lead time, or having excess capacity. Buffer inventory levels should be determined by balancing carrying cost against stockout cost.

Buying in expectation of major market shortages is a longer time-frame variation of buffer inventory. It may require large sums and top management strategic review. Chapter 8 discusses forward buying more fully.

Another class of buffer stock is that purchased in anticipation, but not certainty, of a price increase. In this case, the trade-off is between extra carrying costs and avoidance of higher purchase cost. This trade-off can be structured as shown in Figure 6–1. Obviously, intermediate levels of price increase and the timing of increases also will be identified. Other buffer stock trade-offs can be structured similarly.

Anticipation or certainty inventories are accumulated for a well-defined future need. They differ from buffer stocks in that they are committed in the face of certainty and therefore have less risk attached to them. Seasonal inventories are an excellent example.

FIGURE 6–1
Decision to Inventory in Anticipation of a Possible Price Increase

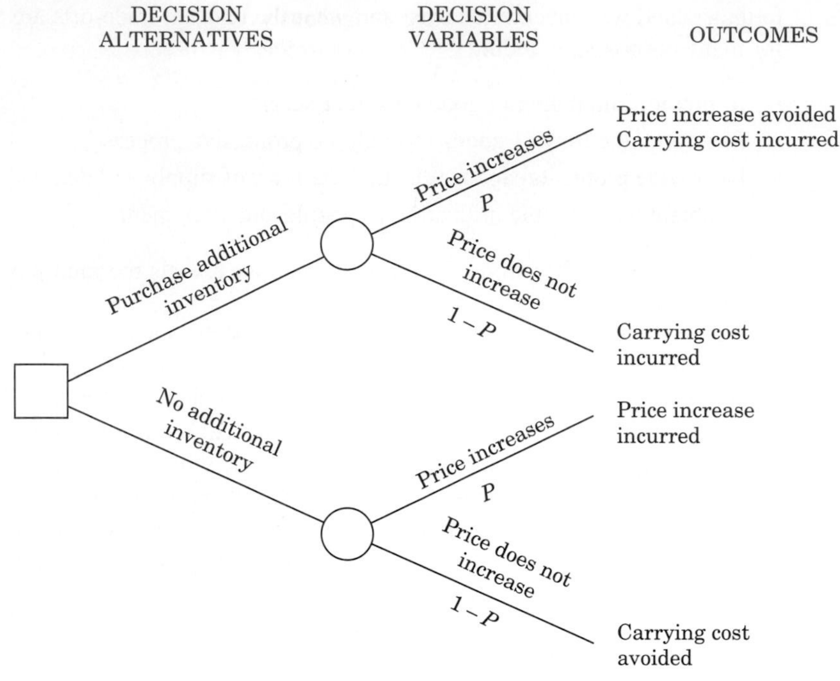

The stocking of commodities at harvest time for further processing during the year is a typical example. Reasons for anticipation stocks may include strikes, weather, shortages, or announced price increases.

The managerial decision is considerably easier than with buffer stocks because the certainty of events makes probability estimates unnecessary. Unfortunately, in times of shortages and rapid price increases, organizations may not be able to commit enough funds to meet the clear need for more anticipation stocks. Public organizations working under preestablished budgets may not be able to obtain authorization and funds. Many organizations that are short of working capital may be similarly frustrated.

Decoupling inventories make it possible to carry on activities on each side of a major process linkage point independently of each other. The amounts and locations of raw material, work-in-process, and finished goods decoupling inventories depend on the costs and increased operating flexibility benefits of having them.

All inventories perform a decoupling function, whether they be transit, cycle, buffer, or certainty inventories. When the prime purpose is to decouple, and space and time have been designed into the process to accommodate them, it is appropriate to recognize decoupling inventory as a unique category of its own. It gives flexibility and independence to both parties and is an excellent area for negotiations. Many contracts specify that a supplier maintain a certain finished goods inventory. A finished goods inventory performs a decoupling function between the supplier's manufacturing process and the customers' process.

By examining the functions of inventory, it is clear that they are the result of many interrelated decisions and policies within an organization. At any time, any of the inventory functional types will be physically indistinguishable from the others. Frequently, a particular item may serve many of the functions simultaneously. Why, then, classify inventories by function? The answer lies in the degree of controllability of each class. Some inventories are essentially fixed and uncontrollable, whereas others are controllable. A management directive to reduce total inventories by 20 percent, because of supply and marketing policies and prior commitments on cycle and seasonal inventories, could reduce decoupling and buffer inventories to nearly zero with potentially disastrous results.

The Forms of Inventory

Inventories may be classified by form as well as function; indeed, this classification is much more common. The five commonly recognized forms are (1) raw materials, purchased parts, and packaging; (2) work-in-process; (3) finished goods; (4) MRO items; and (5) resale items. Scrap or obsolete materials, although technically regarded as inventory, will not be considered here (see Chapter 11 dealing with investment recovery).

Raw materials, purchased parts, and packaging for manufacturers are stocks of the basic material inputs into the organization's manufacturing process. As labor and other materials are added to these inputs, they are transformed into work-in-process inventories. When production is completed, they become finished goods. In general, the forms are distinguished by the amount of labor and materials added by the organization. The classification is relative in that a supplier's finished goods may become a purchaser's raw materials.

For resource industries, service organizations, and public organizations, MRO inventories may be substantial. In resource industries, a significant portion of such inventory may be maintenance or repair parts to support the heavy capital investment base. In resale organizations, the main categories are goods for resale and inventories to maintain building and equipment. For many consumer goods industries, such as food and beverage, packaging represents a major purchase inventory category with substantial environmental implications.

Inventory Function and Form Framework

Combining the five forms and five functions of manufacturing inventory gives the 25 types of inventory that make up the inventory profile of an organization. They are presented in Figure 6–2 along with some of the managerial decision variables affecting each type. Not all inventory types will be present to the same extent in each organization; indeed, some may be completely absent. The 25 types make inventory control a more complex but a more easily focused task.

The behavior of inventories is a direct result of diverse policies and decisions within an organization. User, finance, production, marketing, and supply decisions can all have crucial influences on stock levels. Long-term fixed marketing or supply policies may render finished goods transit, raw materials transit, and cycle inventories quite inflexible, whereas short-term production scheduling may provide a great amount of flexibility of work-in-process inventories. Long-term supply contracts coupled with falling demand may lead to raw materials accumulation. Effective supply managers must recognize the behavior and controllability of each type of inventory in both the short and long terms. For effective supply management, they must also coordinate the policies and decisions of all functional areas.

Often managers use various informal rules of thumb in their decision making. A common one is turnover in number of times per year. The rule of thumb would dictate that as

FIGURE 6–2
Inventory Forms and Functions

Inventory Function	*Raw Materials, Purchased Parts, and Packaging* 1	*Work-in-Process* 2	*Finished Goods* 3	*MRO* 4	*Resale* 5
1 Transit (pipeline)	**Logistics Decisions**				
	Design of supply system, supplier location, transportation mode	Design of layout and materials handling system	Design of plant location and product distribution system	Supplier location, transportation mode, small shipments	Warehouse location, distribution, transportation mode
2 Cycle (EOQ, lots)	**Product/Process Design Decisions**				
	Order size, order cost	Lot size, setup	Distribution costs, lot sizes	OEM or not and order size	Order size and order cost
3 Buffer (uncertainty)	**Management Risk Level Decisions and Uncertainty**				
	Probability distributions of price, supply and stockout, and carrying costs	Probability distributions of machine and product capabilities	Probability distributions of demand and associated carrying and stockout cost	Probability distributions of breakdowns during use	Probability distributions of demand associated with carrying and stockout costs
4 Anticipation (price) (shortage)	**Price/Availability/Decisions and Uncertainty, Seasonality, Capacity**				
	Know future supply and demand price levels	Capacity, production costs of hire, fire, transfer, overtime, idle time, etc.	Demand patterns (seasonal)	Maintenance planning projects	Supply and demand patterns and price levels
5 Decoupling (interdependence)	**Production Control Decisions**				
	Dependence/ independence from supplier behavior	Dependence/ independence of successive production operations	Dependence/ independence from market behavior	Stock at vendor or at user	Stock at vendor or buyer stock

the use doubles, inventories should also double. However, a closer look must be taken at the components of that inventory.

Cycle inventories, produced in economic order lots (see the next section), increase proportionally to the square root of demand so, as demand doubles, cycle inventories should rise by a factor of only about 1.4. Ordering raw materials or storing them may have quite different cost structures from setting up machines, issuing production orders, or storing finished goods.

Transit inventories depend on supply and distribution networks. A change in the distribution system to accommodate extra volume could more than double or even reduce finished goods transit inventory. Anticipation stocks vary with the pattern of demand, not demand itself. Decoupling inventories may remain unchanged. Buffer inventories may increase or decrease in response to demand and supply instabilities. Many of these effects will balance each other out, but the point remains: Rules of thumb are crude ways of controlling inventory levels. Even if they seem to work, managers never know if they are the best available. Any set of rules must be interpreted intelligently and reevaluated and tested periodically.

Companies that have adopted lean supply practices achieve inventory reductions by eliminating the root cause for the purpose of holding the inventory. For example, cycle inventories are brought down by reducing setup times; decoupling inventories are reduced by better planning and better quality; and safety stocks are lowered because of lower supply and/or demand variability, reduced quality problems, or better on-time delivery performance. It is a continuing challenge to search for better ways to control inventories.

Managing Supply Chain Inventories

Decisions regarding what inventory to have in the supply chain and where to have it have important implications for customer service, working capital commitments, and ultimately profitability. Companies such as Dell, Wal-Mart, and Hewlett-Packard have demonstrated the opportunities to combine lean supply chains with high levels of customer service.

Supply chain inventory management involves managing information flows and establishing operational design of the physical flow of the goods and services. Managing information flows with supply chain partners is not an easy task. While information technology can be used to link customers quickly and efficiently, firms are frequently required to make major investments in new systems to ensure compatibility. (See Chapter 4 for a more detailed examination of information systems and information technology issues in supply chain management.)

However, coordinating information technology standards and software compatibility is just part of the challenge. Because most suppliers frequently deal with multiple customers, as opposed to focusing on a dominant downstream supply chain partner, issues relating to confidentiality must be addressed, affecting what information should be shared and when it should be communicated.

Operational design issues relate to production and fulfillment activities and can affect performance factors such as lead times, quality, and lot sizes. For example, flexible manufacturing processes that can respond quickly to customer orders may allow reductions in safety stock. Identifying appropriate modes of transportation is also important. Rail may provide the lowest cost, but trucking provides faster door-to-door service and opportunities to reduce transit inventories.

Finally, inventory fulfillment policies should take into account market conditions and the impact on supplier operations. Broad policies such as "we keep four weeks of inventory for all A items" ignores variability of demand or supply for product groups or families. It may be necessary to develop inventory level decision rules within group classifications to ensure that appropriate stocks are maintained.

Order policies based on percentage of total demand can lead to large fluctuations in demand at the supplier level, known as the "bullwhip effect." It can be addressed by sharing forecasts with suppliers so that they can plan production and have appropriate inventory available while keeping their costs low.

ABC CLASSIFICATION

A widely used classification of both purchases and inventories is based on monetary value. In the 19th century, the Italian Vilfredo Pareto observed that, regardless of the country studied, a small portion of the population controlled most of the wealth. This observation led to the Pareto curve, whose general principles hold in a wide range of situations. In materials management, for example, the Pareto curve usually holds for items purchased, number of suppliers, items held in inventory, and many other aspects. The Pareto curve is often called the 80-20 rule or, more usefully, ABC analysis, which results in three classes, A, B, and C, as follows when applied to inventory:

Class	Percentage of Total Items in Inventory	Percentage of Total Dollars Tied up in Inventory
A	10	70–80
B	10–20	10–15
C	70–80	10–20

These percentages may vary somewhat from organization to organization, and some organizations may use more classes. The principle of separation is very powerful in materials management because it allows concentration of management efforts in the areas of highest payoff. For example, a manufacturer with total annual purchases of $30.4 million had the following breakdown:

Number of Items	Percentage of Items	Annual Purchase Value	Percentage Annual Purchase Volume	Class
1,095	10.0%	$21,600,000	71.1%	A
2,168	19.9	5,900,000	19.4	B
7,660	70.1	2,900,000	9.5	C
10,923	100%	$30,400,000	100%	

FIGURE 6–3
ABC Classification of Inventory

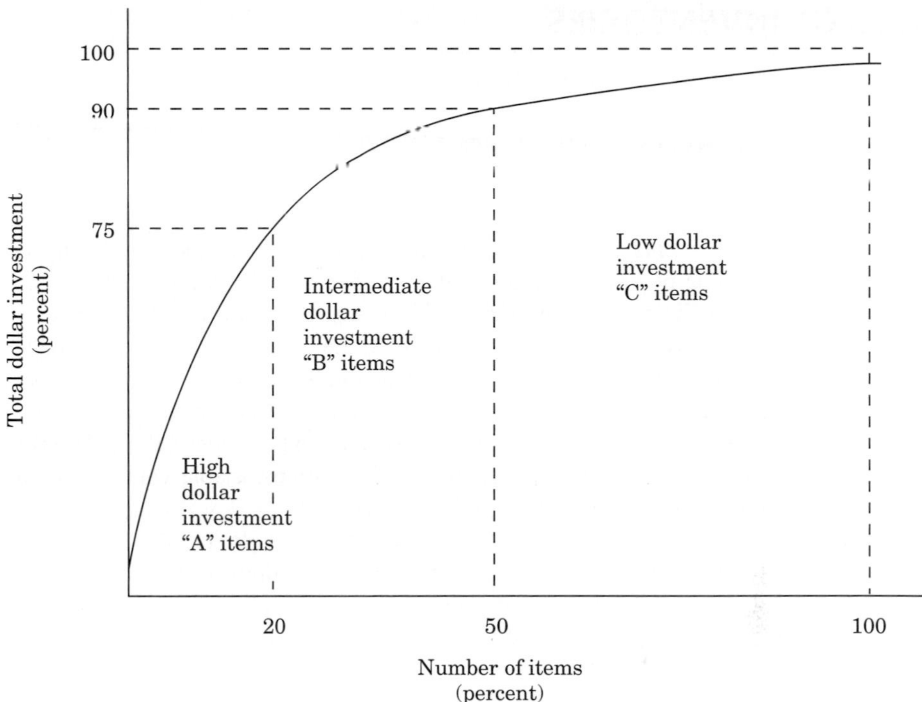

A similar analysis of the organization's inventories would be expected to show a similarly high portion of total value from a relatively small number of items.

Purchase value is a combination of unit price and number of units, so it is not sufficient to classify either high-priced or high-unit-volume items as A's on that basis alone. Annual value (e.g., Unit value × Annual value = Total annual value) must be calculated and a classification into three groups on this basis is a good starting point (see Figure 6–3).

How can a supply manager use such a classification? It pays to spend far more managerial time and effort on A and B items than on C items. Because supply assurance and availability are usually equally important for all items, it is common to manage C items by carrying inventories, by concentrating a wide variety of requirements with one or a few suppliers, by arranging stockless buying agreements or systems contracting, by using procurement cards, by exploiting e-catalogues, and by reviewing the items infrequently. These techniques reduce documentation and managerial effort (for most items) but maintain high service coverage.

A items are particularly critical in financial terms and are, therefore, barring other considerations, normally carried in small quantities and ordered and reviewed frequently. B items fall between the A and C categories and are well suited to a systematic approach with less frequent reviews than A items. It should be noted that some B or C items may require A care because of their special nature, supply risk, or other considerations.

COSTS OF INVENTORIES

Because of the high cost of carrying inventory, many systems have been developed to reduce stocks. Japanese manufacturers have spearheaded lean supply chain practices, including just-in-time systems. Nevertheless, it is useful to understand the nature and costs of inventories so that appropriate policies and procedures can be developed for specific organizational needs. North American organizations have begun to rely heavily on material requirements planning systems that have similar goals of reducing inventories wherever possible by having accurate, timely information on all aspects of the users' requirements, thorough coordination of all departments, and rigorous adherence to the system.

For every item carried in inventory, the costs of having it must be less than the costs of not having it. Inventory exists for this reason alone. Inventory costs are real but are not easy to quantify accurately. The relevance of cost elements in a given situation depends on the decisions to be made. Many costs remain fixed when the order size of only one item is doubled, but the same costs may well become variable when 5,000 items are under consideration. The main types of inventory costs are described below.

Carrying, holding, or possession costs include handling charges; the cost of storage facilities or warehouse rentals; the cost of equipment to handle inventory; storage, labor, and operating costs; insurance premiums; breakage; pilferage; obsolescence; taxes; and investment or opportunity costs. In short, any cost associated with having, as opposed to not having, inventory is included.

The cost to carry inventory can be very high. For example, recent estimates of the annual cost to carry production inventory ranged from 25 to 50 percent of the value of the inventory. Many firms do not do a very good job of estimating carrying costs. While there are several methods for calculating inventory carrying costs, the basic elements are (1) capital costs, (2) inventory service costs, (3) storage space costs, and (4) inventory risk costs.[1]

Once the firm has estimated its carrying costs as a percentage of inventory value, annual inventory carrying costs can be calculated as follows:

$$\text{(Carrying cost per year)} = \text{(Average inventory value)} \times \text{(Inventory carrying cost as a \% of inventory value)}$$

$$\text{Average inventory value} = \text{(Average inventory in units)} \times \text{(Material unit cost)}$$

$$\text{CC} = Q/2 \times C \times I$$

where

CC = Carrying cost per year
Q = Order or delivery quantity for the material, in units
C = Delivered unit cost of the material
I = Inventory carrying cost for the material, as a percentage of inventory value

[1] Doug M. Lambert, James R Stock, and Lisa M. Ellram, *Fundamentals of Logistics Management*, Burr Ridge, IL: McGraw-Hill/Irwin, 1998.

Ordering or purchase costs include the managerial, clerical, material, telephone, mailing, fax, e-mail, accounting, transportation, inspection, and receiving costs associated with a purchase or production order. What costs would be saved by not ordering or by combining two orders? Header costs are those incurred by identifying and placing an order with a supplier. Line item costs refer to the cost of adding a line to a purchase order. Most orders will involve one header and several line item costs. Electronic data interchange (EDI) and Internet-based ordering systems try to reduce ordering or purchase costs significantly as well as reduce lead time at the same time.

Setup costs refer to all the costs of setting up a production run. Setup costs may be substantial. They include such learning-related factors as early spoilage and low production output until standard rates are achieved as well as the more common considerations, such as setup, employees' wages and other costs, machine downtime, extra tool wear, parts (and equipment) damaged during setup, and so on. Both the purchaser's and vendors' setup costs are relevant. It should be pointed out that the reduction of setup costs and times permits smaller production runs and hence smaller purchaser order quantities and more frequent deliveries.

Stockout costs are the costs of not having the required parts or materials on hand when and where they are needed. They include lost contribution on lost sales (both present and future), changeover costs necessitated by the shortage, substitution of less suitable or more expensive parts or materials, rescheduling and expediting costs, labor and machine idle time, and so on. Often, customer and user goodwill may be affected, and occasionally penalties must be paid. The impact of stockouts on customers will vary. In a seller's market, an unsatisfied customer may not be lost as easily as in a buyer's market. In addition, each individual customer will react differently to a shortage.

In many organizations, stockout costs are very difficult to assess accurately. The general perception, however, is that stockout costs are substantial and much larger than carrying costs. Stockout costs, here discussed as they relate to inventory, are similar for late delivery or quantity shortfalls.

Variations in delivered costs are costs associated with purchasing in quantities or at times when prices or delivery costs are higher than at other quantities or times. Suppliers often offer items in larger quantities or at certain times of the year at price and transportation discounts. Purchases in small quantities or at other times may result in higher purchase and transportation costs, but buying in larger quantities may result in significantly higher holding costs. The quantity discount problem will be discussed in Chapter 9.

Many inventory costs may be hard to identify, collect, and measure. One can try to trace the individual costs attributable to individual items and use them in decision making. Usually such costs will be applicable to a broader class of items. A second approach is to forecast the impact of a major change in inventory systems on various cost centers. For example, what will be the impact on stores of a switch to systems contracting or vendor-managed inventories for some low-value items? Or what would be the impact of a just-in-time system on price, carrying, ordering, and stockout costs? Because most inventory models are based on balancing carrying, order, and stockout costs to obtain an optimal order and inventory size, the quality and availability of cost data are important considerations.

FORECASTING

Inventory management is complicated by the rapidly changing environment within which inventory and supply planning is carried out. Inventories always seem to be too big, too small, of the wrong type, or in the wrong place. With changing economic conditions, what is too little in one period may easily become too much in the next.

Forecasting is very much a part of the supply management picture and directly affects both quantity and delivery. Forecasts of usage, supply, market conditions, technology, price, and so on, are always necessary to make good decisions. The problem is how to plan to meet the needs of the future, which requires answers to questions such as Where should the responsibility for forecasting future usage lie? Should the supply management group be allowed to second-guess sales, production, or user forecasts? Should suppliers be held responsible for meeting forecasts or actual requirements? Should the supply manager be held responsible for meeting actual needs or forecasts?

In many organizations, the need for raw materials, services, parts, and subassemblies is usually derived from a sales forecast, which is the responsibility of marketing. In some service organizations and public agencies, the supply function often must both make forecasts and acquire items. In resale, the buyer may have to assess the expected sales volume (including volumes at reduced prices for seasonal goods), as well as make purchase commitments recognizing seasons. Whatever the situation, missed forecasts are quickly forgotten but substantial overages or shortages are long remembered. Supply managers are often blamed for overages or shortages no matter who made the original forecast or how bad the forecast was.

The real problem with forecasts is their unreliability. Forecasts will usually be wrong, but will they exceed or fall short of actual requirements and by how much? Continuous improvement methods can be applied to forecasting by tracking forecast accuracy and taking steps to eliminate root causes of forecast error.

To a supplier, a substantial variation from forecast may appear as a procurement ploy. If demand falls below forecast, the supplier may suspect that the original forecast was an attempt to obtain a favorable price or other concessions. Should demand exceed forecast, supplier costs may well increase because of overtime, rush buying, and changed production schedules. Purchasers need to share forecast uncertainty regularly with suppliers so that their quotations may take uncertainty into account. Such sharing is obviously impossible if buyers themselves are not aware of the uncertainty and its potential impact on the supplier. Forecasts also should be updated regularly.

Forecasting Techniques

There are many forecasting techniques that have been developed and an extensive literature that describes them. This section will review some briefly but will not describe any technique in detail.

Quantitative forecasting attempts to use past data to predict the future. One class of quantitative forecasting techniques, *causal models,* tries to identify leading indicators, from which linear or multiple regression models are developed. A carpet manufacturer might use building permits issued, mortgage rates, apartment vacancy rates, and so on, to predict carpet sales. Standard computer programs are used to develop and test such models. Chosen indicators are usually believed to cause changes in sales, although even good models do not prove a cause-and-effect relationship. Indicator figures must be available far enough ahead to give a forecast that allows sufficient time for managerial decisions.

A second quantitative forecasting class assumes that sales (or other items to be forecast) follow a repetitive pattern over time. The analyst's job in such *time series forecasting* is to identify the pattern and develop a forecast. The six basic aspects of the pattern are constant value (the fluctuation of data around a constant mean), trend (systematic increase or decrease in the mean over time), seasonal variations, cyclical variations, random variations, and turning points. Time series forecasting techniques include simple moving averages, weighted moving averages, and exponential smoothing.

One of the most common classes is the *qualitative* approach of gathering opinions from a number of people and using these opinions with a degree of judgment to give a forecast. Market forecasts developed from the estimates of sales staff, district sales managers, and so on, are an example. Such forecasts may also flow from the top down. The Delphi technique is a formal approach to such forecasting. Collective opinion forecasts lack the rigor of more quantitative techniques but are not necessarily any less accurate. Often, knowledgeable people with intimate market knowledge have a "feel" that is hard to define but that gives good forecasting results.

DETERMINING ORDER QUANTITIES AND INVENTORY LEVELS

In the following sections, some relatively simple theoretical models used to determine order quantities and inventory levels are discussed. The application of these models depends on whether the demand or usage of the inventory is dependent or independent. Dependent demand means the item is part of a larger component or product, and its use is dependent on the production schedule for the larger component. Hence, dependent demand items have a *derived demand.* Independent demand means the usage of the inventory item is not driven by the production schedule and is determined directly by customer orders, the arrival of which is independent of production scheduling decisions.

Fixed-Quantity Models

The classic trade-off in determining the lot sizes in which to make or buy cycle inventories is between the costs of carrying extra inventory and the costs of purchasing or making more frequently. The objective of the model is to minimize the total annual costs. In the very simplest form of this model, annual demand (R), lead time (L), price (C), variable order or setup cost (S), and holding cost percentage (K) are all constant now and in the future. When inventory drops to the reorder point (P), a fixed economic order quantity (Q) is ordered. Back orders and stockouts are not allowed.

Total cost is given as purchase cost, plus setup or order cost, plus holding cost, or

$$\text{TC} = RC + \frac{RS}{Q} + \frac{QKC}{2}$$

Using differential calculus, the minimum value of Q (also known as the EOQ) is found at

$$Q_{\text{opt}} = \sqrt{\frac{2RS}{KC}}$$

This is the value at which order cost and carrying cost are equal. Figures 6–4 and 6–5 show how costs vary with changes in order size and how inventory levels change over time using this model. As an example of the use of the model, consider the following:

R = Annual demand = 900 units
C = Delivered purchase cost = \$45/unit
K = Annual carrying cost percentage = 25 percent
S = Order cost = \$50/order

$$Q_{opt} = \sqrt{\frac{2RS}{KC}} = \sqrt{\frac{2 \times 900 \times \$50}{.25 \times \$45}} = 89 \text{ units}$$

FIGURE 6–4
Material Carrying and Order Costs

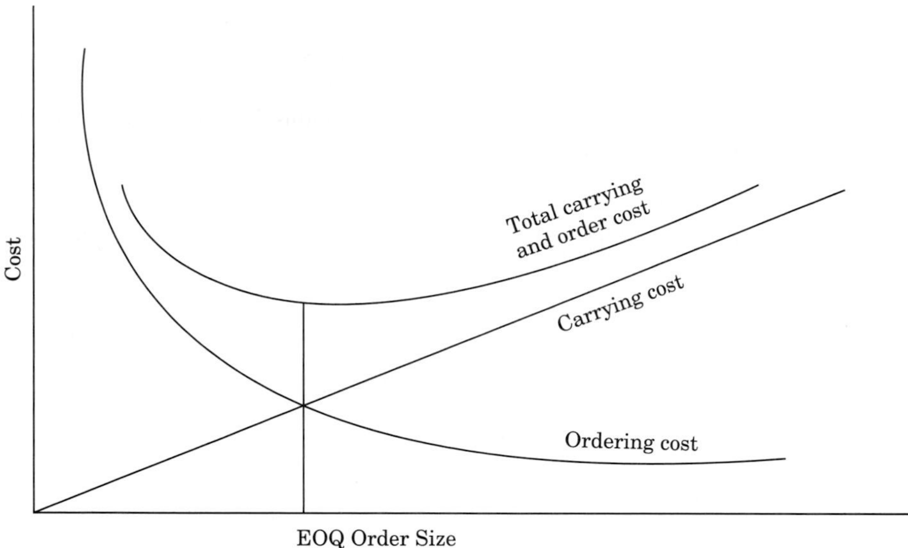

FIGURE 6–5
Simple Fixed Quantity Model

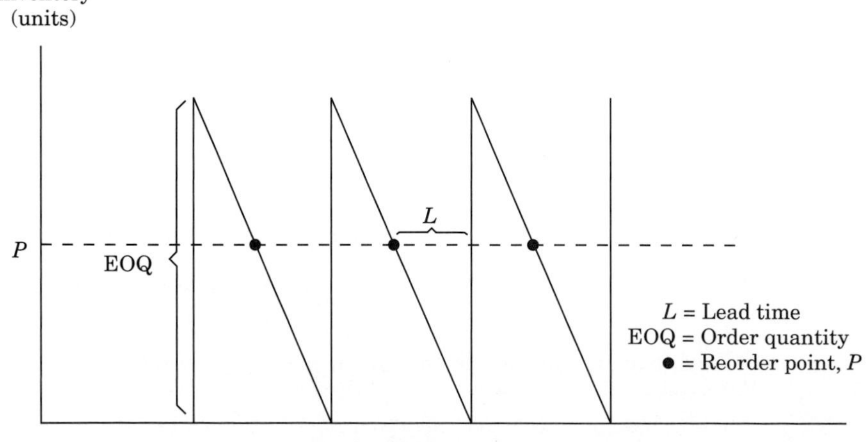

To determine the reorder point *P*, it is necessary to know the lead time *L*, which is 10 working days. Assuming 250 working days per year, the reorder point can be calculated as:

$$P = L \times \text{Daily demand} = L \times \frac{R}{250} = 10 \times \frac{900}{250} = 36 \text{ units}$$

This model suggests an order of 89 units whenever the inventory drops to 36 units. The last unit will be used just as the next order arrives. Average inventory will be 89/2 = 44.5 units. In practice, it might be advisable to keep some safety stock that must be added to the average inventory. Also, the bottom of the cost curve (see Figure 6–4) is relatively flat (and asymmetric) so that there might be advantages in ordering 96 (eight dozen) or 100 units instead. In this case, these quantities would cost approximately an additional \$2.50 and \$6.25, respectively, out of a total annual cost of about \$41,500. These costs are the additional ordering and carrying costs resulting from the additional units ordered.

The assumptions behind the EOQ model place some rather severe restrictions on its general applicability. Numerous other models have been developed that take into account relaxation of one or more of the assumptions. The reader may wish to refer to books on inventory management for a more extensive discussion.

Fixed-Period Models

In many situations, ordering every so often rather than whenever the stock reaches a certain level is desirable from an operations viewpoint. The scheduling of workload is easier when employees can be assigned to check certain classes of inventory every day, week, month, and so on.

In fixed-quantity models, orders are placed when the reorder point is reached, but in fixed-period models, orders are placed only at review time. The inventory level, therefore, must be adjusted to prevent stockouts during the review period and lead time.

Fixed-period models attempt to determine the optimal order period (*O*). The minimum cost period can be determined as follows. There are *R/O* cycles per year and, therefore, *T* (the fraction of the year) is *O/R*. This value of *O* can then be substituted in the EOQ formula to give:

$$T_{\text{opt}} R = \sqrt{\frac{2RS}{KC}} \quad \text{or} \quad T_{\text{opt}} = \sqrt{\frac{2S}{RKC}}$$

Using the values given for the previous example:

$$T_{\text{opt}} = \sqrt{\frac{2 \times 50}{900 \times 0.25 \times 45}} = 0.1 \quad \text{or} \quad 10 \text{ times per year}$$

For a year of 250 working days, this is 25 working days, or once every five weeks. The optimum order quantity, EOQ, is RT_{opt} or 90 units. This is the same result as before. Organizational procedures may make a review every four weeks or monthly more attractive. In this case, *T* would change to 0.08 and *O* to 72 at an additional cost of \$23.77 per year over the optimum value.

Probabilistic Models and Service Coverage

The aforementioned models assume that all parameters are known absolutely and do not change over time. It is far more common to have some variability in demand, lead times, supply, and so on. Probabilistic lot size models take these variations into account. The models are more complex than the deterministic ones above, but the probabilistic approach gives more information on likely outcomes.

Buffer or Safety Stocks and Service Levels

For buffer or safety stocks, the major decision variable is how much buffer inventory to carry to give the desired service coverage. The service coverage can be defined as the portion of user requests served. If there are 400 requests for a particular item in a year and 372 were immediately satisfied, the service coverage would be 372/400 = 93 percent.

Service coverage also can be defined as the portion of demand serviced immediately. If the 372 orders in the above example were for one unit each and the 28 other, unserviced ones, for five units each, the total yearly demand would be for 372 + 140 = 512 units. The service coverage would be 372/512, or 73 percent. It is obviously important to understand exactly what is meant by service coverage in an organization.

Holding a large inventory to prevent stockouts, and thus to maintain a high service coverage, is expensive. Similarly, a high number of stockouts are costly. Stockout costs are often difficult and expensive to determine but nevertheless real. Setting service coverage requires managers to make explicit evaluations of these costs so that the appropriate balance between carrying and stockout can be achieved.

Trade-offs between holding inventory and stocking out can be assessed quantitatively if accurate data are available, such as inventory holding costs, stockout costs, and demand or supply variability. However, because of the expense and difficulty of obtaining such costs and probability estimates for individual items, managers often set service coverage arbitrarily, typically about 95 percent, implying a ratio of stockout to holding costs of about 19 to 1. In practice, setting and managing service coverage is difficult because of the complexity of item classification, function, and interdependence. Service coverage need not be as high on some items as on others, but an item that may be relatively unimportant to one customer may be crucial to another. If the customer is an assembly line, low service coverage on one component makes higher service coverage on others unnecessary. Also, some customers will tolerate much lower service coverage than will others. Within an organization, internal departments are sometimes regarded as customers, and service coverage attained is one measure of supply management's effectiveness. It is useful to stress that service coverage and inventory investment are closely related. It becomes expensive to achieve high service coverage, and a high service coverage expectation without the necessary financial backup can lead only to frustration. Supply is, of course, also interested in service coverage as it pertains to supplier performance.

Service coverage can be used to determine the appropriate level of buffer inventory. The situation is shown in Figures 6–6 and 6–7. Four situations can arise as shown from left to right in Figure 6–6.

1. Only some of the buffer inventory was used.
2. No buffer inventory remained, but there was no stockout.
3. There was a stockout.
4. All the buffer inventory remained.

Figure 6–7 starts with an EOQ model except that it is not certain how many units will be used between placing and receipt of an order. Figure 6–7 targets desired service coverage

FIGURE 6–6
Fixed-Order-Quantity Model with Buffer Inventory and Variation in Demand

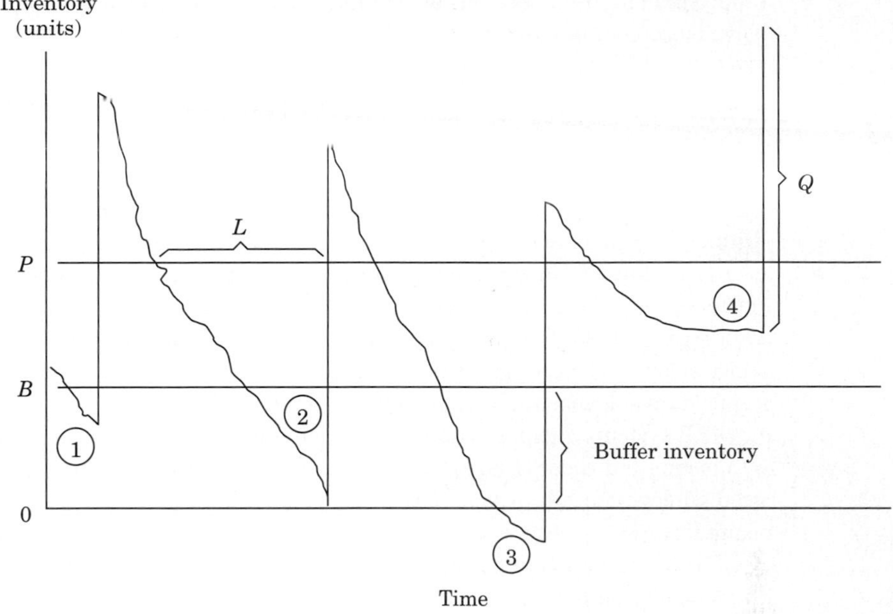

FIGURE 6–7
Determination of Buffer Inventory to Achieve Desired Coverage

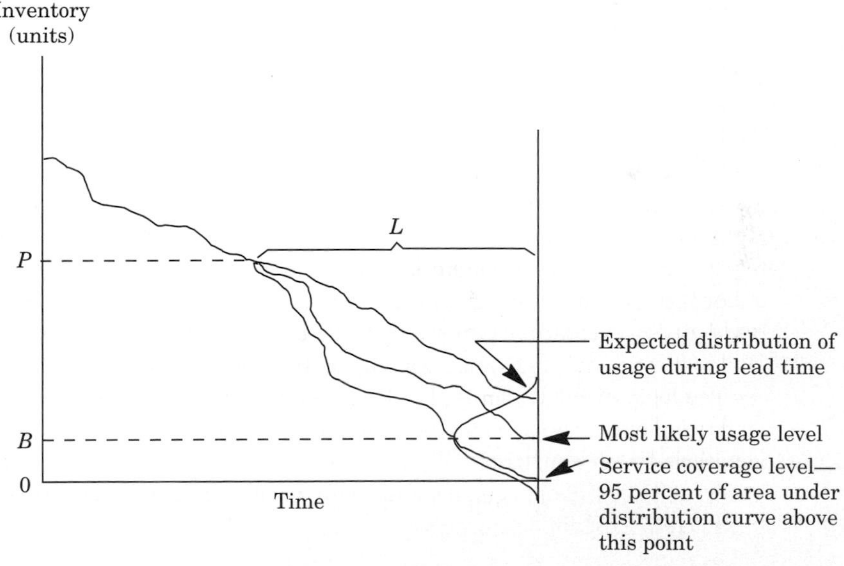

at 95 percent, given the standard deviation of average daily demand, an assumption of a normal demand distribution, and a most-likely usage level.

The complexity of probabilistic models increases greatly when lead times, usable quantities received, inventory shrinkage rates, and so on, also vary under conditions of uncertainty, when nonnormal distributions are observed, and when the variations change with time. Simulation models and other more advanced statistical techniques can be used to solve these complex situations.

MATERIAL REQUIREMENTS PLANNING (MRP)

One of the assumptions behind the lot-sizing models just described is that demand for the item being purchased or made is independent of all other demands. This situation is true for most manufacturers' finished goods. However, subassemblies, raw materials, and parts do not exhibit this independence. Demand for these items is dependent on the assembly schedule for finished goods. For example, each car assembled needs one windshield, one steering wheel, but four tires plus a spare. Similarly, many MRO items depend on maintenance schedules. Recognition of the existence of demand dependence lies behind the technique known as material requirements planning (MRP).

MRP systems attempt to support the activities of manufacturing, maintenance, or use by meeting the needs of the master schedule. In order to determine needs, MRP systems need an accurate bill of materials for each final product or project. These bills can take many forms, but it is conceptually advantageous to view them as structural trees.

Not all organizations have been successful in implementing MRP systems. Implementation may take years and involve major investments in training, data preparation, and organizational adjustments as well as in computer software and hardware. However, most organizations with successfully implemented systems feel that the reduced inventory, lead times, split orders and expediting, increased delivery promises met, and discipline resulting from MRP make the investment worthwhile. MRP systems allow rapid replanning and rescheduling in response to the changes of a dynamic environment.

MRP Inputs

There are three basic MRP inputs. The whole system is driven by the requirements forecast by time period (the master production schedule), which details how many end items are to be produced during a specified time period. The structured bill of materials (BOM) is the second input. The BOM uses information from the engineering and/or process records to detail the subcomponents necessary to manufacture a finished item. The third input is the inventory record, which contains information such as open orders, lead times, and lot-size policy so that the quantity and timing of orders can be calculated.

The logic of MRP allows simultaneous determination of how much and when to order. The calculations hinge on the assumptions that all information is accurate and known with certainty and that material will be ordered as required. MRP systems can help production meet schedules, avoid equipment downtime, adjust to order quantity changes, and identify the need to expedite late orders.

MRP Lot Sizing

Lot-sizing rules must be assigned to each item before the MRP plan can be computed. The selection of a lot-sizing rule is important because it affects inventory holding costs and operations costs, such as setup costs.

The four basic lot-sizing rules are lot-for-lot (L4L), economic order quantity (EOQ), least total cost (LTC), and least unit cost (LUC).

Lot-for-lot is the most common technique. It does not take into account setup costs, carrying costs, or capacity limitations. Lot sizing is based on producing net requirements for each period.

The EOQ lot-sizing technique balances inventory holding and setup (or order) costs. It uses the EOQ formula to set lot sizes, which requires estimates for annual demand, inventory holding costs, and setup (or order) costs.

The least-total-cost method compares the cost implications of various lot-sizing alternatives and selects the lot size that provides the least total cost. The LTC method is a dynamic lot-sizing technique.

The least-unit-cost method is also a dynamic lot-sizing method. It factors inventory holding and setup (or order) costs into the unit cost.

Lot sizing is a difficult issue when using MRP. Because most lost-sizing techniques require cost and annual demand information, accuracy of the data used will determine the effectiveness of the decisions made.

Modern MRP Systems

With advances in information systems technology, a number of improvements have been made to MRP systems that can help managers with planning and coordinating production and supply. One significant advance in MRP systems has been the addition of capacity requirements planning (CRP). CRP performs a similar function for manufacturing resources that MRP performs for materials. When the MRP system has developed a materials plan, CRP translates the plan into the required human and machine resources by workstation and time bucket. It then compares the required resources against a file of available resources. If insufficient capacity exists, the manager must adjust either the capacity or the master production schedule. This feedback loop to the master production schedule results in the term *closed-loop MRP* to describe this development.

The CRP module is often linked to a module that controls the manufacturing plan on the shop floor. The goal is to measure output by work center against the previously determined plan. This information allows identification of trouble spots and is necessary on an ongoing basis for capacity planning.

Manufacturing resource planning systems (MRP II) links the firm's planning processes with the financial system. MRP II systems combine the capability of "what if" production scenario testing with financial and cash flow projections to help achieve the sales and profitability objectives of the firm.

Many companies use enterprise resource planning systems (ERP), which include MRP modules, to integrate business systems and processes. ERP systems are software that allows all areas of the company—manufacturing, finance, sales, marketing, human resources, and supply—to combine and analyze information. ERP can provide a link from customer orders through the fulfillment processes. Therefore, fully implemented ERP systems allow supply to be aware of orders received by sales, manufacturing to be aware of raw material delivery status, sales to understand product or service lead times and availability, and financial transactions and commitments to be communicated directly into the financial accounting system. A thorough discussion of e-supply applications is provided in Chapter 4.

Consequently, a modern MRP system is thus a lot more than simply a device to calculate how much material to obtain and when to do so. It is an information and communication system that encompasses all facets of the organization. It provides managers with performance measures, planned order releases (purchase orders, shop orders, and rescheduling notices), and the ability to simulate a master production schedule in response to proposed changes in production loading (by, for example, a new order, delayed materials, a broken machine, or an ill worker). The integration required of such systems forces organizations to maintain highly accurate information, abandon rules of thumb, and use common data in all departments. The results are reduced inventory levels, higher service coverage, ready access to high-quality information, and, most importantly, the ability to replan quickly in response to unforeseen problems.

Supply Implications of MRP

The tight control required by MRP means that supply records regarding quantities, lead times, bills of material, and specifications must be totally accurate and tightly controlled. The on-time delivery required of MRP needs cooperation from suppliers. Purchasers therefore, must educate their suppliers to the importance of quantity, quality, and delivery promises to the purchaser. Such education should enable purchasers to reduce their safety stock.

Many MRP systems have purchasing modules that perform many of the routine clerical supply tasks, making supply's job more analytical and strategic. The long-term nature of the MRP planning horizon, typically a year, means longer-term planning for supply and the negotiation of more long-term contracts with annual volume-based discounts. These contracts have more frequent order release and delivery, often in nonstandard lot sizes. Quantity discounts on individual orders become less relevant in favor of on-time delivery of high-quality product.

Purchasers must understand the production processes both of their own organizations and of their suppliers. The tighter nature of MRP-using organizations increases the responsibility on supply to be creative and flexible in providing assistance to minimize the inevitable problems that will occur in supply lines. The MRP system provides purchasers with an information window to production scheduling so they are better able to use judgment in dealing with suppliers. Because of the reduced resource slack that results from MRP, purchasers must incorporate de-expediting into their activities as well as the more usual expediting role. The integrating and forward-looking nature of MRP means an increase in specialization in the supply department. For example, the buyer-planner is a person who uses MRP to assure smooth functioning of the interface between the purchaser's and supplier's processes. Also, specialization will be based on finished product line outputs rather than on raw material inputs.

In contrast to MRP, just-in-time production methods can achieve many of the goals of MRP in conjunction with MRP or on a stand-alone basis.

LEAN SUPPLY AND JIT

Lean supply is an approach where relationships with suppliers are managed based on a long-term perspective so as to eliminate waste and add value. It is based on Japanese manufacturing concepts pioneered by Toyota. Lean systems have been adopted in many organizations, under a variety of names, such as the Delphi Manufacturing System at the automotive parts maker Delphi Corporation. However, the Toyota production system is generally recognized as the best model of lean operations.

The most popular system that incorporates the lean philosophy is *just-in-time (JIT)*. Under a JIT system, components, raw materials, and services arrive at work centers exactly as they are needed. This feature greatly reduces queues of work-in-process inventory. The goals of JIT production are similar to those of MRP—providing the right part at the right place at the right time—but the ways of achieving these goals are radically different and the results impressive. Whereas MRP is computer based, JIT is industrial engineering based. JIT focuses on waste elimination in the supply chain, and there are many JIT features that are good practice in any operation, public or private, manufacturing or nonmanufacturing.

In JIT, product design begins with two key questions: Will it sell? and Can it be made easily? These questions imply cooperation between marketing and operations. Once these questions have been answered positively, attention turns to design of the process itself. The emphasis is on laying out the machines so that production will follow a smooth flow. Automation (often simple) of both production and materials handling is incorporated wherever possible. Frequently, U-shaped lines are used, which facilitate teamwork, worker flexibility, rework, passage through the plant, and material and tool handling. In process design, designers strive to standardize cycle times and to run a constant product mix, based on the monthly production plan, through the system. This practice makes the production process repetitive for at least a month.

The ability to smooth production implies very low setup and order costs to allow the very small lot sizes, ideally one. JIT treats setup and order costs as variable rather than as the fixed costs implied by the EOQ equation. By continuously seeking ways to reduce setup times, the Japanese were the first to have managed impressive gains. Setups, which traditionally required three to four hours, have been reduced to less than a minute in some JIT facilities. These dramatic improvements have been achieved by managerial attention to detail on the shop floor; the development and modification of special jigs, fixtures, tools, and machines; and thorough methods training. Setup simplification is aided by their willingness to modify purchased machines, their acquisition of machines from only a few sources, and their frequent manufacture of machines in-house—often special purpose, light, simple, and inexpensive enough to become a dedicated part of the process. Order costs, conceptually similar to setup costs, have similarly been reduced.

One of the necessary corollaries of having components and materials arrive just as they are needed is that the arriving items must be perfect. In JIT, a number of interrelated principles are used to ensure high-quality output from each step in the production process.

First, responsibility for quality rests with the maker of a part, not with the quality control department. In addition, workers and managers habitually seek improvement of the status quo, striving for perfection. Quality improvements are often obtained from special projects with defined goals, measures of achievement, and endings. Also, workers are responsible for correcting their own errors, doing rework, and so on.

Second, the use of production workers instead of quality control inspectors builds quality in rather than inspecting it in. This feature and the small lot sizes allow every process to be controlled closely and permit inspection of every piece of output. Workers have authority to stop the production line when quality problems arise. This aspect signifies that quality is a more important goal of the production system than is output.

Third, JIT insists on compliance to quality standards. Purchasers reject marginally unacceptable items and visit supplier plants to check quality on the shop floor for themselves. Because such visits are frequent, JIT manufacturers document their quality in easily understood terms and post the results in prominent places. This process forces the manufacturer to define quality precisely.

JIT control of quality is helped by the small lot sizes that prevent the buildup of large lots of bad items. JIT tends to have excess production capacity so that the plants are not stressed to produce the required quantities. In the same vein, machines are maintained and checked regularly and run no faster than the recommended rates. Plant housekeeping is generally good. The quality control department acts as a quality facilitator for production personnel and suppliers, giving advice in problem solving. This department also does some testing, but the tests tend to be on final products not easily assignable to a single production worker, or special tests requiring special equipment, facilities, knowledge, or long times not available to personnel on the shop floor. Automatic checking devices are used wherever possible. Where necessary, sample lots are chosen to consist of the first and last units produced rather than a larger, random sample. Analytical tools include the standard statistical techniques, often known by workers, and cause-and-effect diagrams to help solve problems.

JIT requires great dedication by both workers and managers to hard work and helping the organization. JIT workers must be flexible. They are trained to do several different jobs and are moved around frequently. The workers are responsible for quality and output. Workers continuously seek ways to improve all facets of operations and are rewarded for finding problems that can then be solved.

In summary, JIT is a mixture of a high-quality working environment, excellent industrial engineering practice, and a healthy focused factory attitude that operations are strategically important. The order and discipline are achieved through management effort to develop streamlined plant configurations that remove variability. The JIT system has often been described as one that "pulls" material through the factory rather than pushing it through. The use of a kanban system as a control device illustrates this point well.

Kanban Systems

Kanban is a simple but effective control system that helps make JIT production work. Kanban is not synonymous with JIT, although the term is often incorrectly so used and the two are closely related. *Kanban* is Japanese for *"card";* the use of cards is central to many Japanese control systems, including the one at Toyota, whose kanban system has received much attention.

Kanban systems require the small lot size features of JIT and discrete production units. The systems are most useful for high-volume parts used on a regular basis. They are much less useful for expensive or large items that cost a lot to store or carry, for infrequently or irregularly used items, or for process industries that don't produce in discrete units.

Two types of kanban systems exist: single card and double card. In double-card systems, two types of cards (kanban) exist: conveyance (C-kanban) and production (P-kanban). Single-card systems use only the C-kanban. The two-card system's operation uses the following rules.

1. No parts may be made unless there is a P-kanban authorizing production. Workers may do maintenance, cleaning, or work on improvement projects until a P-kanban arrives rather than making parts not yet asked for. Similarly, C-kanban controls the transport of parts between departments.

2. Only standard containers may be used, and they are always filled with the prescribed small quantity.
3. There is precisely one C-kanban and one P-kanban per container.

The system is driven by the user department pulling material through the system by the use of kanban. The main managerial tools in this system are the container size and the number of containers (and therefore kanban) in the system. The control is very precise, flexible, and responsive. It prevents an unwanted buildup of inventory. For example, the actual assembly of parts into a complete finished product provides the "pull" for more parts to be produced.

JIT and Inventory Management

Inventories often exist to cover up problems in supply or inside the organization. For example, a buffer inventory can protect a user from poor quality or unreliable delivery from a marginal supplier. In JIT, the deliberate lowering of inventory levels to uncover such malpractices forces an organization to identify and solve the underlying problems or causes for high and undesirable inventories. This deliberate inventory reduction is often seen by some managers as a form of organizational suicide, a willingness to put continuity of supply, service, or operation at risk. However, enough organizations have experimented with this concept (and survived) to show the merits of this practice. Diagrammatically, this lowering of inventory levels is frequently shown as a seascape of inventory with sharp rocks of different heights underneath, representing the problems or malpractices that need to be exposed sequentially.

JIT Implications for Supply Management

JIT has become sufficiently entrenched as a concept that its applicability is not in question, only the extent to which it should be applied. Many companies are working closely with their suppliers to implement JIT.

There are a number of implications of JIT for supply management. One of the obvious includes the necessity to deal with suppliers of high and consistent quality and with reliable delivery. This implies that concentrating purchases with fewer nearby suppliers may be necessary. The frequent delivery of small orders may require a rethinking of the inbound transportation mode. For example, it is normal to have a trucker follow a standard route daily to pick up, from 6 to 20 different suppliers, small lots in a specially designed side-loading vehicle. Having delivery arranged directly to the place of use eliminates double handling. Special moving racks designed for proper protection, ease of counting, insertion, and removal also help improve material handling. A lot of supplier training and cooperation is required to assist in the design and operation of an effective JIT system.

In the minimum sense, JIT can refer to arranging for delivery just before a requirement is needed. In this context, JIT has wide applicability beyond manufacturing—in public, service, and other nonmanufacturing organizations. Reliability of delivery reduces the need for buffer or safety stock, with the benefits that arise out of such inventory reduction.

In JIT there is a close cooperation between supplier and purchaser to solve problems, and suppliers and customers have stable, long-term relationships. In keeping with the JIT philosophy, suppliers, usually few in number, are often located close to their customers to facilitate communication, on-time delivery of small lots of parts, low pipeline and safety stocks, and low supply costs. The situation in many JIT companies is much like extensive backward vertical integration. The organizations have close coordination and systems integration that smooth operations. The job of a purchaser in the JIT environment is that of a facilitator, negotiator, communicator, and innovator.

Conclusion

Supply chain effectiveness is totally dependent on the assurance that quality, quantity, and delivery are consistently perfect. Both quantity and delivery involve lot-sizing and inventory decisions that, in turn, affect costs, productivity, flexibility, and customer satisfaction. To complicate matters even further, uncertainty rears its ugly head and forecasts are unreliable. Despite major advances such as MRP and JIT, the challenges of quantity and delivery continue to occupy supply managers all over the world.

Questions for Review and Discussion

1. Of what interest is ABC analysis?
2. What is a master production schedule and what role does it perform?
3. Why is it expensive to carry inventories?
4. In a typical fast-food operation, identify various forms and functions of inventory. How could total investment in inventories be lowered? What might be the potential consequences?
5. What are transit inventories?
6. What is a kanban and why is it used?
7. What problems do inaccurate usage forecasts create for buyers? For suppliers?
8. What is the difference between JIT and MRP?
9. Why would anyone prefer to use a fixed-period reordering model over a fixed-quantity one?
10. Describe sources of variability in the supply chain. How does variability increase supply chain costs?

References

Davis, M. M.; N. J. Aquilano; and R. B. Chase. *Fundamentals of Operations Management.* 4th ed. New York: McGraw-Hill/Irwin, 2003.

Lambert, D. M.; J. R. Stock; and L. M. Ellram. *Fundamentals of Logistics Management.* Burr Ridge, IL: McGraw-Hill/Irwin, 1998.

Lyman, S. B. "Supplier Classification Systems." *Inside Supply Management* 14, no. 7 2003, pp. 10–11.

Nelson, D.; P. E. Moody; and J. Stegner. *The Purchasing Machine: How the Top Ten Companies Use Best Practices to Manage Their Supply Chains.* New York: The Free Press, 2001.

Ritzman, L. P.; L. J. Krajewski; and R. D. Klassen. *Foundations of Operations Management.* Toronto: Pearson Education Canada, 2004.

Stunza, T. "Prepping the Supply Base for Leaner Supply Systems." *Purchasing* 128, no. 9 2000, pp. 62–68.

Womack, J. P., and D. T. Jones. "From Lean Production to the Lean Enterprise." *Harvard Business Review* 27, no. 2 (1994), pp. 93–103.

Case 6–1

Connecticut Circuit Manufacturers

It was the morning of February 1, when Jack Veber, Senior Buyer at Connecticut Circuit Manufacturers (CCM), received a phone call from a large customer complaining that an order had not been delivered on time. Since this was not the first such occurrence, Jack knew that he would be expected to present recommendations that addressed this problem at the general management meeting the following day.

CONNECTICUT CIRCUIT MANUFACTURERS

Connecticut Circuit Manufacturers was established in June 1980 and specialized in circuit board design and assembly. CCM manufactured two product lines: Contract Products and Design Products.

CCM had manufactured Contract Products since the company first began operation in 1980. Contract Product customers provided the design of the circuit board and CCM manufactured the circuit board in specified quantities. CCM expected to sell 4,000–5,000 units of Contract Products. Sales of Contract Products had grown consistently at 10 percent per year, and this growth rate was expected to continue in the next three years.

Design Products were introduced seven months ago. For Design Products, CCM was responsible for the design of the circuit board as well as for production. As with Contract Products, Design Products were manufactured in quantities specified by the customer. Annual sales of Design Products for the current year were expected to be 500–1,000 units. The company anticipated a rapid 40 percent per annum growth rate of this product line in the next three years.

Management of CCM had been the same since the company was founded in 1980. All members of the management team were middle-aged entrepreneurs who spent the majority of their time exploring new opportunities for the company. Management was very open with employees and encouraged them to voice concerns and recommendations that related to company improvement and growth.

The manufacturing of circuit boards was a competitive industry, and margins on a single circuit board were small. CCM had three local competitors who manufactured high-quality circuit boards at competitive prices.

PRODUCTION

CCM assembled circuit boards in batches, and production lot sizes were based on confirmed customer orders. Assembly operations varied among products and were based on design specifications and material requirements.

A range of raw materials were used in circuit board assembly, including integrated circuits, resistors, printed circuit boards, connectors, cables, and fasteners. Consequently, the production department at CCM worked very closely with the buying group with respect to inventory management. It was the buyer's responsibility to ensure that all supplies required for production were available in inventory.

Recently, production reached full capacity with a single shift. The company was growing and expectations were for rapid growth due to the introduction of Design Products. CCM added a second shift in February that increased capacity to 7,000 units.

Twelve suppliers were currently providing CCM with the commodities required for circuit board production. The majority of these suppliers had enjoyed a long-term relationship with CCM. However, management felt that under current market conditions, additional suppliers could be developed to provide similar levels of quality, price, and service.

THE CCM SUPPLY GROUP

Jack Veber was hired as Senior Buyer by CCM on November 30. In his new role, Jack Veber was responsible for ensuring that all resistors and cables were available when needed for production. Jack Veber spent the majority of his time managing relationships with suppliers and keeping track of customer orders and deadlines. In order to keep inventory costs down, Jack Veber had to make sure that excess inventory of these items was kept to an absolute minimum.

Prior to coming to CCM, Jack Veber spent five years as an intermediate buyer at a large local manufacturer. His responsibilities at his previous employer included purchasing all commodities for two specific customers. Jack Veber gained experience in purchasing all types of commodities and claimed this was the main reason he was offered the position as Senior Buyer at CCM.

Along with Jack Veber, another Senior Buyer and one Junior Buyer handled purchasing at CCM. The other Senior Buyer was Al Cooper, who had been with CCM for 15 years. His responsibilities included purchasing all types of integrated circuits and connectors and printed circuit boards. As integrated circuits and printed circuit boards were expensive to keep in inventory, Al Cooper spent the majority of his time keeping track of integrated circuit board requirements for production and managing existing relationships with integrated circuit board suppliers.

Tim LeBlanc was the Junior Buyer. He started with CCM two years ago, immediately after graduating with a purchasing degree from a local college. Due to limited experience, Tim LeBlanc had minimal purchasing responsibility. His main role was to assist the Senior Buyers by providing them with required production information. Tim was also responsible for purchasing all types of screws, nuts, and washers. Ideally, as Tim gained experience, he would be given more purchasing responsibility.

In February, CCM had five customers. Three of these customers were regular Contract Product customers and two were Design Product customers. Contract Product customers had an ongoing business relationship with CCM. These customers tended to be sensitive to product quality, price, and on-time delivery.

Design Product customers were mainly conscious of product quality and customer service. The main features of customer service as defined by these customers were on-time delivery and effective customer relations. The company also hoped to attract new customers for its Design Products and expected that Design Product business would lead to additional Contract Product business.

THE GENERAL MANAGEMENT MEETING

As part of becoming better acquainted with CCM's requirements, Jack Veber had gathered some information and created summary tables provided in Exhibits 1 and 2. He did not know yet whether these might be useful in rethinking CCM's supply strategy and execution.

The phone call he received earlier that morning was from Customer E complaining about a late delivery. Several weeks earlier, a similar phone call was received from Customer A.

Jack Veber had a meeting with upper management the next day at the general management meeting. Upper management was already aware of the complaint made by Customer A and would most likely be made aware of Customer E's complaint before tomorrow's meeting. Jack Veber was eager to determine what factors might

EXHIBIT 1 **Connecticut Circuit Manufacturers: Annual Component Purchases**

Item Name	Annual Orders (parts)	Buyer	Total Annual Purchases
Integrated circuits	50,000	Cooper	$250,000
Resistors	500,000	Veber	$50,000
Printed circuit boards	7,000	Cooper	$105,000
Connectors	14,000	Cooper	$35,000
Cables	8,000	Veber	$24,000
Screws, nuts, washers	448,000	LeBlanc	$15,680

EXHIBIT 2 **Connecticut Circuit Manufacturers Annual Purchases for Each Customer**

Item Name	Customers					
	A*	B	C	D	E*	Total
Integrated circuits	15	10	20	3	25	73
Resistors	15	40	18	12	10	95
Printed circuit boards	4	3	5	1	7	20
Connectors	2	4	3	1	5	15
Cables	2	2	2	0	4	10
Screws, nuts, washers	8	12	10	10	10	50
Total # items	46	71	58	27	61	263
Total material value	$135,000	$50,000	$80,000	$14,680	$200,000	$479,680

* Design product customers.

have led to the delivery problems but had no specific information yet. During the general management meeting, Jack Veber planned to present his analysis and provide recommendations that would reduce the possibility of similar problems occurring in the future.

Case 6–2

Abbey Paquette

As it approached 5 P.M. on Friday, August 15, Abbey Paquette, Purchasing Agent for the Chicago-based Pentz International Inc., contemplated the events of the last five days. Abbey and her team had spent a week collecting information that might help them respond to a request that had come directly from the company president to make a drastic reduction in the $2.5 million annual inventory carrying cost. Abbey was now wondering how to proceed.

COMPANY BACKGROUND

In the mid-1920s, a group of five talented young engineers developed and refined a process to extrude aluminum tube into a continuous helical fin over a variety of liner tubes. The resulting bimetal fin tubing worked as an extremely effective component in large-scale heat exchangers. The extended heat transfer surface of these tubes enabled the group's heat exchanger products to find applications in the pulp and paper, power generation, electrical transmission and distribution, and other process-related industries.

In 1928, based on the success of the group's heat exchanger products, Pentz International Inc. (PII) was established in Chicago, Illinois. As the combination of the fin-tube and time-proven heat exchanger designs gained wider recognition, PII's business grew in both the United States and international markets. By the 1980s PII's heat transfer products were being used in a wide variety of industrial applications all over the world, including hydroelectric installations in Australia, electric transmission and distribution systems in Europe, giant water-pumping systems in the United States, and several waste-to-energy facilities in the Middle East.

PII had operated as a distinct entity under various ownerships during the company's growth and evolution. In September 1990, PII was acquired by Belgian-based Redmain Industries and became a member of the Redmain Heat Transfer Group. Redmain Industries was one of the largest privately held corporations in Europe, with over 15,000 employees worldwide. Under Redmain ownership, PII became a world-leading designer and manufacturer of a wide range of specialized heat transfer equipment. Employment at the plant grew to 240 people, and current-year sales were forecasted to be $50 million.

PURCHASING AT PII

Abbey Paquette was responsible for purchasing and materials management activities at the plant. She negotiated contracts with suppliers, scheduled deliveries, and managed raw material inventories. A major challenge presented by these responsibilities was carrying sufficient inventories to ensure that material was always available for manufacturing operations. Abbey recognized, however, that holding material in inventory unnecessarily could be expensive for the company.

EDICT FROM THE NEW PRESIDENT

Abbey had arrived at the office early Monday morning and was surprised to find many people already hard at work. She checked her e-mail, as she did first thing every morning, and discovered a personal e-mail from Isaac Chisholm, PII's new president, that simply read:

> "Presently this site's annual inventory carrying costs are close to two and a half million—this number should be reduced to zero by year-end. Please get back to me with some suggestions on how we may approach this goal. I offer my full support in this initiative."

Isaac Chisholm had taken over as president of PII on August 3 with a mandate to improve PII's poor financial performance. Within just a few days, several drastic changes were already apparent.

After reading the e-mail, Abbey's heart sank as she began to think about what an enormous request had just been made. She realized that the fact that inventory levels had been allowed to reach such levels reflected very poorly on her and, consequently, Abbey was anxious to solve the problem. Her immediate reaction was to contact the company's other purchasing agent, Karen Black. Karen and Abbey agreed that they needed to clear their schedules and dedicate the following week entirely to identifying what could be done. They enlisted the support of the production manager, Kathleen Deholihan, and the accounting manager, Marty Sullivan.

THE INVESTIGATION

Carrying Costs

The group met with the company controller, David Ellis, on Tuesday morning. During the meeting, David explained to the team that the term "carrying cost" referred to money that was tied up in inventory but that could otherwise be applied to other "value-added activities." It also included, according to David, other costs such as handling, storage, and obsolescence. He indicated that PII used a rate of 20 percent for calculating inventory holding costs. David went on to point out that the value of the materials and the length of time in inventory contributed to inventory carrying costs.

David also reminded Abbey and the others that PII incurred costs each time an order was placed. He estimated that the variable costs of placing an order with a supplier were about $50.

Inventory Tracking and Control

When the team began to investigate the present inventory tracking and control procedures, Abbey and Karen were shocked to discover that the database from which they drew their inventory information and based decisions for new component orders was filled with outdated and inaccurate information. It was discovered that the inventory clerk had been fired a few months earlier and had not been replaced. Instead, the forklift drivers who "pulled" components from the warehouse for use in manufacturing were expected to enter the information into the database regarding what they had removed from stock.

One of the forklift drivers, Rick, indicated that when things were busy in production, he just jotted information on a pad of paper about what had been pulled, and then entered the information when things slowed down a bit. He admitted that, at times, engineers and other line operators pulled parts themselves without recording the information.

Recognizing that the existing inventory data were suspect, the team decided to dedicate two full days, Wednesday and Thursday, to completing an inventory count. When the count was completed, the team discovered a number of inventory record errors, including several charges to inventory carrying costs for items that were no longer in stock.

Supplier Agreements

After a grueling couple of days involved in the inventory count, the team turned their attention to analyzing supplier agreements. Abbey and Karen found that many of the supplier agreements were based on large batch orders. For example, PII ordered component BD-517 from a local supplier at a cost of $26.75 each, with a minimum order quantity of 2,000 pieces. However, weekly usage of the BD-517 was approximately 500 pieces.

DEVELOPING A PLAN

By Friday, Abbey felt that the team had accomplished a lot since Monday. She now had to turn her attention to deciding what steps needed to be taken next. Long hours had been spent updating the database, but Abbey knew that rehiring a clerk would not be possible in the present environment and, consequently, she wondered what she should do in order to improve the situation. She also recognized that in order to reduce inventory carrying costs, PII's investment in raw materials would have to be reduced. Before she could go home to her family and relax for the weekend, Abbey knew she had to come up with a definitive plan of action that she could present to Isaac Chisholm Monday morning.

Case 6–3

Sedgman Steel

Alice McKenzie, the production material control supervisor at Sedgman Steel, in Syracuse, New York, sat at her desk preparing for a meeting with her boss, Isaak Theissen. Isaak, the director of materials management at Sedgman, was concerned about the large amount of raw material inventory and had asked Alice earlier in the week to investigate the situation. It was now Wednesday, August 17th, and Alice had promised to provide a preliminary report to Isaak on Friday afternoon.

COMPANY BACKGROUND

Sedgman Steel Inc. was a large diversified North America–based manufacturing company, with annual sales of approximately $1.7 billion. The Syracuse operation employed 125 people and supplied cut-to-length steel tubing and steel sheets to automotive and automotive parts companies.

Customers provided Sedgman with the specifications for the material, which included the chemical composition (e.g., carbon content) and material thickness. Cut-to-length tubing specifications included inner and outer diameter conditions. Raw material was supplied from one of two sources. Integrated steel companies supplied large steel coils, which were placed in leveling and straightening equipment and cut to length. The sheets were stacked on wooden pallets, banded, and shipped to cusvbtomers, usually on a just-in-time (JIT) basis.

Steel tubing was supplied from a Sedgman tube manufacturing facility in Michigan. Tubing arrived in standard lengths of 24 feet and was cut to length on computer-controlled cutting equipment. Tubing was loaded on customer-supplied containers and also shipped on a JIT basis.

Steel purchasing was an important activity at Sedgman Steel Inc., and for the most part was handled at the plant level in the company. Steel and tubing purchases at the Syracuse plant represented approximately $65 to $70 million each year, and the purchasing manager there worked closely with sales to make sure that material costs were properly reflected in selling prices. Customer contracts were negotiated in spring each year.

MATERIAL CONTROL

The material control department was responsible for incoming and outgoing transportation, inventory control, production planning and scheduling, and customer order fulfillment. Overall, the Syracuse plant had a dozen customers, to which it supplied approximately 350 different products. Sedgman routinely dealt with about 15 steel suppliers, while its sister plant in Michigan was the sole supplier of tubing.

Policy was to have raw material available at least two weeks in advance of production. Raw material deliveries also were scheduled to accommodate full truckload shipments of about 80,000 pounds.

Three years prior, Sedgman had contracted its warehousing and transportation services to a third-party logistics organization, Fehr Logistics Company. Fehr was responsible for providing inbound and outbound transportation services and managing the 50,000-square-foot warehouse adjacent to the manufacturing facility.

The contract with Fehr specified staffing levels and hours of operation and provided the supplier with a profit based on a percentage of its total costs. After some initial problems, management was generally satisfied with its relationship with Fehr.

RAW MATERIAL INVENTORY

Isaak Theissen had become concerned regarding the large amount of raw material inventory. Inventory records for July indicated that there was approximately $20 million of inventory on-hand, and on Tuesday he had asked Alice to investigate, commenting that: "Our customers certainly don't carry this amount of inventory. Why should we? I want you to look into the situation and see what we can do to fix it."

Earlier in the day, Alice decided to pay a visit to the warehouse and was surprised with what she saw. The warehouse was completely full with coils of steel and bundles of raw tubes. Several trailers were parked outside waiting to be unloaded. In addition, there appeared to be a shortage of staff at the warehouse. The normal complement was eight, but Alice only identified five people.

PREPARATION FOR THE MEETING

As Alice prepared for the Friday meeting, she made a list of issues that she would have to address with Isaak. Based on what she knew so far, Alice agreed that opportunities existed to reduce the amount of inventory, but Isaak would want specific targets and the timing identified. Furthermore, he would also need assurances that the inventory levels could be reduced without affecting operations or customer service.

Recognizing the importance of the project, Alice had blocked off the next two days. She wondered what steps she should take next.

Chapter Seven

Transportation and Delivery

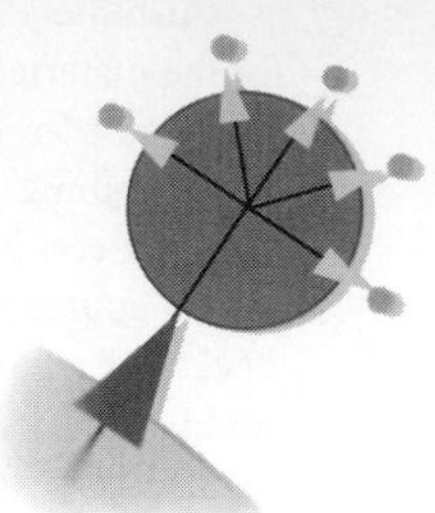

Chapter Outline

Key Questions for the Supply Manager

Should we

- Designate method of shipment and carrier, or let the supplier do it?
- Use FOB origin or FOB destination terms, or some other designation?
- Outsource some or all of the logistics function to a third party?

How can we

- Develop an effective logistics strategy?
- Identify value-added logistics services that will reduce our overall costs?
- Ensure that we attain the optimum mix of reliability, costs, and service from transportation and logistics service providers?

Purchased goods must be transported from the point where they are grown, mined, or manufactured to the place where they are needed, with inventories held at a minimum amount, to ensure production and customer service. The emphasis on reducing costs and cycle time throughout supply chains highlights the importance of inventory velocity and increases the need for competitive transportation and other logistics services as an alternative to maintaining costly inventories. Advances in information technology, coupled with the speed of Internet communications, have greatly enabled the flow of real-time information and the reduction of inventory throughout supply chains. In Chapter 4 we discussed technology issues and inventory management was covered in Chapter 6. In this chapter, delivery and transportation issues are covered.

Logistics activities are a vital part of our economies. Total business logistics costs in the United States in 2002 were estimated at $910 billion, or about 8.7 percent of GDP. These costs were divided into inventory carrying costs, transportation costs, and administrative costs. While this is an impressive amount, business logistics costs in the United States have actually been declining over the past two decades as a percentage of GDP, dropping from a high of 16.2 percent in 1981.[1] A number of factors have contributed to declining logistics costs, including deregulation of the transportation sector, technology advances and e-commerce, and greater emphasis in organizations to improve supply chain processes and practices.

Supply plays a vital role in delivery of goods and services in the supply chain. Supply may have direct functional responsibility for some logistics responsibilities, such as arranging in-bound transportation with suppliers or responsibility for supervising warehousing and stores. Meanwhile, others in the organization, such as marketing, may turn to supply to assist in establishing relationships with third-party logistics (3PL) service providers to operate distribution facilities and warehouses. Consequently, supply's role in delivery can involve functional oversight and logistics services acquisition.

The purchase of logistics services demands a high degree of skill and knowledge if the costs of movement are to be minimized while at the same time meeting service needs.

[1] R. V. Delaney and R. Wilson, *14th Annual State of Logistics Report*, June 2003.

Due to the complexity of the logistics industry and the significantly larger number of alternatives available as a result of deregulation, getting the best value for an organization's transportation and logistics dollar involves much more than simply "getting the best rate."

ORGANIZATION FOR LOGISTICS DECISIONS

The management of inventory in motion and at rest is referred to as logistics. Logistics is defined by the Council of Logistics Management as "that part of the supply chain that plans, implements, and controls the efficient, effective flow and storage of goods, services, and related information from the point of origin to the point of consumption in order to meet customers' requirements."[2] Logistics costs can be divided into three categories—inventory carrying costs, administrative costs, and transportation—with transportation accounting for the bulk of the costs.

Due to the large number of dollars involved in the movement of goods into and out of an organization and the potential effect on profits, most large firms have a separate logistics services department with specialists in areas such as selection of carriers and routing, expediting, packaging, and handling claims in the case of loss or damage to goods during shipment. In the very large firm, the logistics function may be specialized even further, based on the purpose of shipment. For example, an automobile producer may have three separate departments: one concerned with incoming materials shipments, one making the decisions on in-plant and interplant materials movement, and the third concerned with the shipment of finished goods through the distribution channels to customers. In an organization operating under the materials management concept, the transportation or logistics manager may have responsibility for all types of materials movement. This person must recognize that storage, handling, and shipping of raw materials and finished goods does not add value to the product. Instead, it is a key cost element in the operation of the firm and should be managed to minimize costs, within the parameters of needed service.

In the medium-sized and smaller organization, the number of logistics decisions may not be large enough to warrant a full-time logistics specialist. Here the transport decisions are handled by the buyer or supply manager. This means that the buyer must have enough knowledge to make decisions on preferred free on board (FOB) terms, selection of carriers and routing, determination of freight rates, preparation of necessary documentation, expediting and tracing of freight shipments, filing and settling of claims for loss or damage in transit, and payment procedures for transport services received. This person must make these decisions in light of their impact on other areas such as inventory levels, carrying costs, and the use of capital.

FOB TERMS AND INCOTERMS

The term *FOB* stands for *free on board,* meaning that goods are delivered to a specified point with all transport charges paid. There are several variations in FOB terms, as Table 7–1 shows. Shipping terms and the responsibilities of buyer and seller in international contracts are covered by Incoterms (see Chapter 14), which were first originated in 1936 by the

[2] Council of Logistics Management (CLM), "*Definition of Logistics*," http://www.clm1.org.

TABLE 7–1 **FOB Terms and Responsibilities**

FOB Term	Payment of Freight Charges	Bears Freight Charges	Owns Goods in Transit	Files Claims (if any)	Explanation
FOB origin, or FOB freight collect	Buyer	Buyer	Buyer	Buyer	Title and control of goods passes to buyer when carrier signs for goods at point of origin
FOB origin, freight prepaid	Seller	Seller	Buyer	Buyer	
FOB origin, freight prepaid and charged back	Seller	Buyer	Buyer	Buyer	Seller pays freight charges and adds to invoice
FOB destination, freight collect	Buyer	Buyer	Seller	Seller	Title remains with seller until goods are delivered
FOB destination, freight prepaid	Seller	Seller	Seller	Seller	
FOB destination, freight prepaid and charged back	Seller	Buyer	Seller	Seller	Seller pays freight charges and adds to invoice
FOB destination, freight collect and allowed	Buyer	Seller	Seller	Seller	Buyer pays freight charges and deducts from seller's invoice

International Chamber of Commerce and continue to be updated, most recently in 2000. The selection of the FOB point is important to the purchaser, for it determines four things:

1. Who pays the carrier.
2. When legal title to goods being shipped passes to the buyer.
3. Who is responsible for preparing and pursuing claims with the carrier in the event goods are lost or damaged during shipment.
4. Who routes the freight.

The claim that FOB destination is always preferable because the seller pays the transportation charges is incorrect. While the seller may pay the transportation charges, in the final analysis the charges are borne by the buyer, because transportation costs will be included in the delivered price charged by the supplier. In effect, if the buyer lets the supplier make the transportation decisions, then the buyer is allowing the supplier to spend the buyer's money.

In purchases from international suppliers, FOB is an Incoterm meaning *free on board (named port of shipment),* and the seller passes title to the goods to the buyer when the goods are passed over the rail of the ship. The ocean carrier typically does not provide any insurance on goods in transit; therefore, it is important when goods are bought FOB origin for the buyer to ensure that adequate insurance coverage is provided. The two marine freight terms commonly used are *CFR* and *CIF*. CFR, *cost and freight,* is similar to FOB origin, with freight charges paid by the seller. However, under CFR the buyer assumes all risk and should provide for insurance. CIF, *cost, insurance, and freight,* means that the seller will pay the freight charges and provide appropriate insurance coverage. This is similar to FOB destination, freight prepaid. In some instances, the buyer may wish to obtain equalization of freight charges with the nearest shipping point of the seller, or some competitive shipping point. In that case, the following clause can be used: "Freight charges to be equalized with those applicable from seller's shipping point producing lowest transportation cost to buyer's destination." For a more detailed discussion of Incoterms, see Chapter 14.

TRANSPORTATION

Depending on the type of goods being moved, transportation may account for as much as 40 percent of the total cost of the item, particularly if it is of relatively low value and bulky, such as agricultural commodities or construction materials. But in the case of very-high-value, low-weight, and bulk electronics goods, transport costs may be less than 1 percent of total purchase costs. It is not unusual in many firms to find that a significant percent of their purchase expenditures go for transportation costs. While target savings vary from firm to firm, many have found that only a modest effort to manage transportation services more efficiently will result in substantial savings.

If minimization of costs were the only objective in buying transportation services, the task would be easy. However, the transportation buyer must look not only at cost but also at service provided. For example, items are purchased to meet a production schedule, and the available modes of transport require different amounts of transport time. If items are shipped by a method requiring a long shipment time, inventory may be exhausted and a plant or process shut down before the items arrive. Also, reliability may differ substantially among various transportation companies; service levels, lost shipments, and damage may vary greatly between two different carriers. The buyer should use the same skill and attention in selecting carriers as used in selecting other suppliers. The effects of transportation deregulation have made the carrier selection and pricing decision far more important today.

In addition, JIT purchasing systems (Chapter 6), global sourcing (Chapter 14), and outsourcing (Chapter 18) make logistics decisions more crucial. With JIT, deliveries must be on time, with no damage to the items in transit, because minimal inventories are maintained. Inventory cost savings should offset additional transportation costs from a supplier providing fast, reliable deliveries. With global sourcing, extended lead times and distances place additional pressure on the transport decision maker. The option to outsource some or all of the logistics function also adds complexity to the analysis of options and the management of inventory at rest and in motion.

With deregulation of the transportation industry and the development of intermodal service, the focus for the transport buyer has shifted from mode of transport to breadth of service, information systems, timeliness (reliability and speed), and rates. Breadth refers to the ability of a carrier to handle multiple parts of the logistics process, including transportation, warehousing, inventory management, and shipper–carrier relationships.

Because of the importance of speed—in terms of both providing reliable, consistent, on-time service and moving goods through the system quickly—shippers are seeking core carriers with whom they can develop closer relationships to reduce cycle time. The development of information systems and the application of e-commerce tools to both inbound and outbound transportation also contribute to timeliness and breadth of service. Shippers are demanding improved communications and information systems to facilitate tracking and expediting orders. Because delays in the supply chain may lead to higher inventory levels and increase total cost, the whole logistics process is viewed as an area where cost avoidance and cost reductions will reap bottom-line rewards.

Outsourcing, or using third party logistics service (3PL) providers, has become increasingly popular as organizations downsize, focus on core competencies, and seek partnerships or alliances with key suppliers. The 3PL industry grew rapidly following deregulation of the transportation sector, with an estimated market size of $65 billion in the United States in 2002, up from $31 billion in 1995.[3] 3PLs provide a wide range of logistics services for their clients, with the most popular being warehousing, outbound and inbound transportation, freight bill auditing and payment, freight consolidation and distribution, cross-docking, product marking, and packaging and returns.[4]

Supply's Involvement in Transportation

The involvement of the supply function in transportation decisions is significant and growing as a result of the added alternatives opened up by deregulation. Supply involvement is in two areas. The first is direct functional responsibility within the organization for any one or several logistical activities, such as transportation, warehousing, receiving, or inventory control. A 2004 study by CAPS Research found that in 284 large organizations, inbound traffic reported to purchasing in 56 percent of the firms, compared to 51 percent in 1995 and 40 percent in 1987. In the case of the outbound traffic function, it reported to supply in 43 percent of the firms in 2003, which also was up from the 39 percent that reported to supply in 1995 and 31 percent in 1987.

A second area of supply involvement is working with managers from other functions, such as operations or marketing, in devising solutions with suppliers of logistics services to improve customer service, lower costs, increase flexibility, or improve quality.

Transportation Regulation and Deregulation

Government regulation in the transportation sector in both the United States and Canada has been focused in two areas: economic and safety/environmental. For nearly 100 years, the U.S. and Canadian transportation sectors operated under a strict regulatory environment that controlled rates, routes, carrier services, and geographic coverage. These economic regulations were controlled at the federal, state, and provincial levels, and while government policies evolved over time, the objectives were to ensure that transport services were available in all geographic areas without discrimination, establish rules for new forms of transportation, provide market stability and supply, and control prices and services in the face of monopoly power. Since the late 1970s, governments in Canada and the United States and elsewhere in the world have embraced a policy and legislative agenda of deregulation. Today, the U.S. and Canadian transportation sectors are essentially deregulated, with shippers able to negotiate rates, terms, services, and routes with service providers.

[3] R. V. Delaney and R. Wilson, *14th Annual State of Logistics Report*.

[4] C. J. Langley, G. R. Allen, and G. R. Tyndall, "Third-Party Logistics Study: Results and Finding of the 2001 Sixth Annual Study," Cap Gemini Ernst & Young, 2001.

While economic regulations have been eliminated for the most part, carriers must adhere to an ever-increasing number and range of safety and environmental regulations, such as transportation of dangerous goods, vehicle emissions, and working conditions. Government regulation also has established new standards for security at airports and ports since the tragic events of 9/11. For example, the International Ship and Port Facility Code sets new standards for ship verification, certification, and control to ensure that appropriate security measures are implemented.

As changes occur in the political, social, economic, and technological landscape, governments will continue to reassess transportation policies and regulations. Supply managers must keep abreast of actual and potential regulatory changes because of the potential significant impact on the organization's supply chain.

TRANSPORTATION CARRIERS

While deregulation has reshaped the transportation sector, some terminology is still used to describe carriers that is based on the legal designations under regulation: common carriers, contract carriers, exempt carriers, and private carriers. While these legal designations technically no longer exist, they still provide guidance in terms of the role and function of each group.

Common carriers offer transportation service to all shippers at published rates, in a nondiscriminatory basis, between designated points. Under deregulation, however, common carriers have considerable flexibility in establishing rates and routes.

A contract carrier is a for-hire carrier that provides service to a limited number of shippers and operates under specific contractual arrangements that specify rates and services. Generally, rates for contract carriers are lower compared to common carriers because volumes are typically higher with individual shippers and scheduling is usually more predictable.

Exempt carriers are also for-hire carriers, but they are exempt from regulation of rates and services. This status was originally established to allow farmers to transport agriculture products on public roads, but this status has been broadened over the years to include a number of different products by a variety of modes. Under deregulation, most carriers can be considered exempt from rate restrictions.

A private carrier provides transportation for its company's own products and the company owns (or leases) all related equipment and facilities. In a regulated environment, private carriers had the advantages of not being restricted by regulations and the flexibility that this status offered. Today, common and contract carriers enjoy the same flexibility and many companies have chosen to outsource transportation services as a result.

The five basic modes of transportation are motor, rail, air, water, and pipeline. Supply professionals need to understand the characteristics of each mode in order to assess tradeoffs when making transportation decisions. A brief description of each follows.

Motor Carriers

Motor carriers, or trucks, are the most flexible mode of transportation and account for approximately 80 percent of transportation expenditures by U.S. firms. This mode offers the advantage of point-to-point service, over any distance, for products of varying weight and size. Compared to other modes, service is fast and reliable, with low damage and loss rates. Consequently, motor carriers are the preferred mode for organizations operating under a just-in-time system.

Motor carriers can be divided into three categories: (1) less-than-truck-load (LTL), (2) truckload (TL), and (3) small parcel, ground. LTL shipments are typically of short haul compared to TL shipments, while the cost per hundredweight (cwt) is generally higher compared to TL shipments over the same distance.

Rail Carriers and Intermodal

Rail carriers once dominated the transportation sector, but their share of the transportation market has declined steadily since World War II. Rail carriers are relatively inflexible and slow and have higher loss and damage rates, compared to motor carriers. However, rail has the advantage of lower variable operating costs, which makes it attractive for hauling large tonnage over long distances.

Intermodal freight services are divided between containers on flatcars (COFC) and truck trailers on flatcars (TOFC), sometimes referred to as piggyback systems. This segment allows carriers to take advantage of the relative strengths of two modes. For example, shipments can benefit from the long-haul economies of rail, while accommodating door-to-door service attributes of truck. Additional benefits include shorter terminal delays and lower damage rates due to less handling. Since intermodal service was completely deregulated, attractive arrangements often are possible, and growth in this mode has been substantial.

Air Carriers

The primary advantage of airfreight is the speed. Airfreight is costly and also must be combined with trucks to provide door-to-door service. Consequently, products best suited for this mode are of high value and/or extremely perishable. Although airfreight volume has increased over the past two decades, most shippers still regard this mode as premium emergency service.

Water Carriers

Although most international trade uses water carriers, referred to as international deep sea transport, this mode is also used domestically in inland water and coastal systems and lakes. Although inexpensive compared to other modes, water carriers are slow and inflexible. Similar to rail, waterway transportation is best suited for hauling large tonnage over long distances, and is frequently used for bulk commodities such as coal, grain, and sand. Furthermore, compared to other modes, water carriers are disadvantaged because of the need for suitable waterways, ports, and handling equipment. Water carriers also must team up with motor carriers to provide door-to-door service.

Many waterway shipments involve the use of containers. Containers also can be transported via truck or rail from the point of origin and to the final destination.

Pipelines

Since pipelines can only transport products in either a liquid or gaseous state, the use of this mode of transport is quite limited. However, once the initial investment in the pipeline is recovered, the variable costs of operation are relatively low.

Selection of Mode and Carrier

Normally, the buyer will wish to specify how purchased items are to be shipped; this is the buyer's legal right if the purchase has been made under any of the FOB origin terms. If the purchaser has received superior past service from a particular carrier, it then becomes the preferable means of shipment.

As one would expect, shippers are most concerned that the carrier meet its delivery promises (deliver on schedule), provide the movement service without damaging the goods at a competitive cost. On the other hand, if the shipper has relatively little expertise in the traffic area and the supplier has a skilled logistics department, it might be wise to rely on the supplier's judgment in carrier selection and routing. Also, in a time of shortage of transport equipment (e.g., railroad cars, trucks, or ocean freight), the supplier may have better information about the local situation and what arrangements will get the best results. And, if the item to be shipped has special dimensional characteristics, requiring special rail cars, the supplier may be in a better position to know what's available and the clearances needed for proper shipment.

Each form of common carrier transportation—rail, truck, air, and inland water—has its own distinct advantages for shippers in respect to speed, available capacity, flexibility, and cost. By the same token, each mode has inherent disadvantages. For example, comparing air with truck transport, air has the advantage in terms of speed; truck transport can accommodate greater volume and has lower rates and greater flexibility in terms of delivery points. The astute buyer must recognize such advantages/limitations and arrive at the best overall balance, considering the needs of the organization.

After determining the mode of transport, a decision must be made on a specific carrier and the specific routing of the shipment. The factors to be considered when selecting mode of shipment, carrier, and routing include the following:

Required delivery time. The required date for material receipt may make the selection of mode of shipment quite simple. If two-day delivery from a distant point is needed, the only viable alternative probably is air shipment. If more time is available, other modes can be considered. Most carriers can supply estimates of normal delivery times, and the purchaser also can rely on past experience with particular modes and carriers. Time-definite services are in demand as organizations focus on time-based competition and JIT inventory management systems.

Reliability and service quality. While two carriers may offer freight service between the same points, their reliability and dependability may differ greatly. One carrier may (1) be more attentive to customer needs; (2) be more dependable in living up to its commitments; (3) incur less damage, overall, to merchandise shipped; and (4) in general be the best freight supplier. The buyer's past experience is a good indicator of service quality.

Available services. As the demand for third-party logistics services grows, shippers want services like warehousing and inventory management in addition to transportation services. In addition, carriers and 3PLs may offer access to data that can be used to improve inventory management practices or to provide better customer service.

Type of item being shipped. If the item to be shipped is large and bulky, a particular mode of transportation may be required. Special container requirements may indicate only certain carriers who have the unique equipment to handle the job. Bulk liquids, for example, may indicate railroad tank car, barge, or pipeline. Also, the safety requirements for hazardous materials may make certain carriers and routings impractical or illegal.

Shipment size. The postal service, and companies such as Federal Express and United Parcel Service, or airfreight forwarders can move items of small size and bulk. Larger shipments probably can be moved more economically by rail or truck.

Possibility of damage. Certain items, such as fine china or electronics equipment, by their nature have a high risk of damage in shipment. In this case, the buyer may select a mode and carrier by which the shipment can come straight through to its destination, with no transfers at distribution points to another carrier. It is part of the buyer's responsibility to ensure that the packaging of goods is appropriate for both the contents and mode of transport.

Cost of the transport service. The buyer should select the mode, carrier, and routing that will provide for the safe movement of goods, within the required time, at the lowest total transport cost. Also, the buyer may make certain trade-offs in purchasing transportation, just as trade-offs are made in selecting suppliers for other purchases.

Carrier financial situation. If any volume of freight is moved, some damages will be incurred, resulting in claims against the carrier. Should the carrier get into financial difficulty, or even become insolvent, collection on claims becomes a problem. Therefore, the buyer should avoid those carriers who are on the margin financially. While in an era of deregulation there are many new entrants in the transportation industry, there also are many exits, and the number of bankruptcies—combined with changes in the laws and regulations governing transportation—may cause shippers to get hit with undercharge bills years after the service was provided.

Handling of claims. Inevitably, some damage claims will arise in the shipment of quantities of merchandise. Prompt and efficient investigation and settlement of claims is another key factor in carrier selection.

Private fleets. One alternative to using a common carrier might be to use private or leased equipment. A private carrier does not offer service to the general public. Many companies have elected to contract for exclusive use of equipment; and some have established their own trucking fleet through use of either company-owned or leased tractors and vans.

The use of a private fleet is a type of make-or-buy decision. Maintaining a private fleet gives the firm greater flexibility in scheduling freight services. It can be economically advantageous, but unless the equipment can be fully utilized through planned back-hauls of either semifinished or finished goods, it may turn out to be more costly than use of the common carrier system.

RATES AND PRICING

The economic realities of transportation costs can be summarized succinctly. Transportation costs increase as distance, quantity, and speed increase. These realities are reflected in the carrier's rates and pricing arrangements.

The two categories of carrier rates are line haul rates and accessorial rates. Line haul rates are charged for moving products to a nonlocal destination and can be grouped into four categories: (1) class rates, (2) exception rates, (3) commodity rates, and (4) miscellaneous rates. Today, most rates between shippers and carriers are negotiated, and the distinctions between rate classifications have become blurred.

As with other purchases, carriers offer lower rates if the quantity of an individual shipment is large enough. Both rail and motor carriers offer discounts for full carload (CL) or truckload (TL) shipments. These will be substantially less per hundred weight (cwt) than less-than-carload (LCL) or less-than-truckload (LTL) quantities. If the shipper can consolidate smaller shipments to the same destination, a lower rate may be available (called a *pool car*). In some instances, shippers may band together through a shippers' association to get pool car transport rates.

The unit train is another innovation by which the shipper gets a quantity discount. By special arrangement with a railroad, a utility company, for example, is provided one or more complete trains, consisting of 100-plus coal cars, that run shuttle between the coal mine and the utility's place of use. This speeds up the movement, and the materials are moved at an advantageous commodity rate. Four basic types of rate discounts have developed; the buyer in some instances can take advantage of one or more of them and possibly enjoy substantial savings.

1. Aggregate tender rates provide a discount if the shipper will group multiple small shipments for pickup or delivery at one point.
2. Flat percentage discounts provide a discount to the shipper if a specified total minimum weight of less-than-truckload shipments is moved per month, encouraging the shipper to group volume with one carrier.
3. Increased volume–increased discount percentage is applied if a firm increases its volume of LTL shipments by a certain amount over the previous period's volume.
4. Specific origin and destination points provide a specified discount if volume from a specified point to a specified delivery point reaches a given level.

Demurrage charges (sometimes also called detention charges for motor carriers) often are incurred by shippers or receivers of merchandise. This simply is a daily penalty charge for a rail car or a motor van that is tied up beyond the normal time for loading or unloading. If demurrage were not charged, some firms would use the carrier's equipment as a free storage facility. In most instances, the daily demurrage rate becomes progressively higher the longer the car or trailer is tied up, until it gets almost prohibitive. A shipper can enter into an averaging agreement with a carrier, whereby cars or vans unloaded one day early may be used to offset cars that are unloaded a day late. In an averaging agreement, settlement is made monthly. If the shipper owes the carrier, payment must be made; if the carrier owes the shipper, no payment is made, but instead the net car balance starts at zero in the new month. The supply department should be aware of the normal number of rail cars or vans that can be unloaded each day and attempt to schedule shipments in so that they do not "back up" and result in payment of demurrage penalties.

OTHER TRANSPORTATION SERVICE PROVIDERS

In addition to the carriers already described, there are a number of other transportation service options available to shippers.

Expedited transportation refers to any shipment that requires pickup service and includes a specific delivery guarantee. In the United States, this is typically less than five days. Shipments may move via domestic air, ground parcel, less-than-truckload, or air-export services.

Under deregulation, competition for small-shipment services has become intense. Buyers now can use some of the standard supply techniques, such as systems contracts, aggressive negotiation, multiple sourcing, quotation analysis, target pricing, and vendor evaluation, to get better purchasing arrangements with carriers. Competition is intense among express carriers as they move to cross over into the heavy-lift air cargo market. The emerging integrated carriers, those with their own aircraft like Federal Express and UPS, are capturing a larger share of the market. Volume discounts, tracking systems, and ground networks are the distinguishing factors.

Another growth area is same-day service, which is being developed by express carriers such as Airborne Express, UPS, and Federal Express. The same-day niche is growing rapidly and expanding into the international market. The users of same-day service range from the entertainment, advertising, and legal industries to manufacturers. The same-day service is used when the cost of not having a critical part or document is greater than the amount spent on same-day service.

Freight forwarders buy dedicated space on scheduled carriers, providing benefits of lower rates than the shipper might otherwise receive and providing one point of contact for shipments that may span two or more modes and carriers. Freight forwarders can specialize as domestic or international, or by mode, such as airfreight or surface transportation. Freight forwarders can provide a number of value-added services. For example, domestic surface freight forwarders consolidate small shipments into rail cars and piggyback trailers and arrange for motor carrier pickup and delivery.

Brokers charge shippers a fee for arranging transportation services with a carrier. The broker will act as the shipper's agent in negotiating rates and service arrangements. In instances where the shipper has limited familiarity with the transportation market and carrier options, brokers can provide the necessary expertise to oversee negotiations with carriers.

Customshouse brokers are used for importing products. They ensure that documentation is accurate and complete, and can provide a variety of other services, such as providing estimates of landed costs, payments to foreign suppliers, and insurance.

DOCUMENTATION IN FREIGHT SHIPMENTS

There are several kinds of documents used when shipping products.

The *bill of lading* is the key document in the movement of goods. It contains information about the products being shipped including weight and quantity, the origin of the shipment, contract terms between the carrier and shipper, and the final destination. Each shipment must have a bill of lading, which is the contract, spelling out the legal liabilities of all parties, and no changes to the original bill of lading can be made unless approved by the carrier's agent in writing on the bill of lading. Signed by both the shipper's and carrier's agents, the bill of lading is proof that shipment was made and is evidence of ownership. It is a contract and fixes carrier liability; normally it will be kept by the party who has title to goods in transit, for it must be provided to support any damage claims. As with most other documentation, electronic versions and online systems management are common in many organizations.

There are several variations on the bill of lading. The uniform straight bill of lading is the complete bill of lading and contains the complete contract terms and conditions. The straight bill of lading–short form contains those provisions uniform to both motor and rail. Short bills are not furnished by carriers but instead are preprinted by shippers. The unit bill of lading is prepared in four copies; the extra copy is the railroad's way-bill. This way-bill moves with the shipment and may be of assistance in expediting freight movement. The uniform order bill of lading is printed on yellow paper (the other bills of lading must be on white paper) and is called a sight draft bill of lading. It is a negotiable instrument and must be surrendered to the carrier at destination before goods can be obtained. Its primary use is to prevent delivery until payment is made for the goods. To obtain payment, the shipper must provide a sight draft, along with the original copy of the bill of lading, to its bank; when the draft clears, the bank gives the bill of lading to the shipper, who then can obtain delivery of the merchandise.

The freight bill is the carrier's invoice for services provided. In addition to providing the total charges for the shipment, the freight bill typically lists the origin and destination, consignee, items, and total weight. Carriers are not obligated to extend credit to shippers and freight bills can be prepaid or collect (e.g., freight charges paid upon arrival of the shipment).

A shipper must provide its carrier with a detailed description, in writing, of any loss or damage that occurs in a shipment. A *freight claim* is a document submitted to recoup financial costs from shipment loss or damage. There is not a standard freight claim form, but most of the information provided in the claim is available on the bill of lading.

The carrier's liability for loss and damage varies depending on the service provided and the contractual terms between the shipper and the carrier. Most freight claims must be submitted within nine months of delivery (or reasonable delivery in the event of loss), but the carrier contract terms could stipulate a different filing period.

If the merchandise is being shipped under any of the FOB origin terms, the buyer will have to pursue the claim. If the shipment is FOB destination, the supplier must process the claim, but because the merchandise is in the buyer's hands, the buyer will have to supply much of the information to support the claim.

Unconcealed loss or damage is referred to in situations when it is evident on delivery that loss or damage has occurred. Such damage or loss must be noted on the carrier's delivery receipt and signed by the carrier's delivering agent. If this is not done, the carrier may maintain that it received a "clear receipt" and not admit any liability. It is a good idea for the receiving department to have a camera available, take one or more photos of the damaged items, and have them signed by the carrier's representative.

In contrast, *concealed loss or damage* refers to situations when merchandise is found short or damaged after the container is opened. The unpacking should be discontinued, photos should be taken, and the carrier's local agent should be requested to inspect the items and prepare an inspection report.

Concealed loss or damage claims often are difficult to collect because it is hard to determine whether the loss or damage took place while the shipment was in the carrier's possession or whether it occurred before the shipment was delivered to the carrier.

Freight Audits

A careful audit of paid freight bills will often uncover instances of overpayment to the carrier. Savings from freight bill audits may range from 5 to 20 percent of the charges depending on the commodity shipped.

In the larger firm, in-house freight bill audit capability often is available. In the smaller firm, the use of an outside freight audit consultant, referred to as a *traffic consultant* or *rate shark,* can be used. These organizations will examine all paid freight bills in an attempt to spot overpayment due to wrong classification, wrong rate, duplicate payment, or calculation errors. When overpayments are found, the rate shark will process a claim with the carrier. The agreement with the shipper typically is that the rate shark retains a percentage of the dollars recovered. Due to the complexity of the freight purchase area, even a company with a sophisticated, well-trained traffic staff probably pays some overcharges and, with the advice of an outside auditor, could generate substantial recoveries. And with the rate shark, if nothing is recovered no payment is made.

A prepayment audit should be performed to make corrections before making payment, and a post-payment audit will protect the shipper within the confines of the three-year moratorium. Carriers (and bankruptcy trustees) also perform carrier audits to determine if any undercharges occurred. Carriers also have a limited time to adjust the bills and collect payment for undercharges.

EXPEDITING AND TRACING SHIPMENTS

As with the normal purchase of goods and services, expediting means applying pressure to the carrier in an attempt to encourage faster-than-normal delivery service. The carrier often can and will provide faster service to assist the shipper in meeting an emergency requirement, provided such requests are made sparingly. Expediting should be done through the carrier's general agent and, if at all possible, the carrier should be notified of the need for speed as far in advance of the shipment as possible.

Tracing is similar to follow-up, for it attempts to determine the status (location) of items that have been shipped but have not yet been received, and thus are somewhere within the transportation system. Tracing also is done through the carrier's agent, although the shipper may work right along with the carrier's agent in attempting to locate the shipment. If tracing locates a shipment and indicates it will not be delivered by the required date, then expediting is needed.

With new technology tools, such as global positioning systems, Internet-based communications, and bar coding, tracing can be done faster and more accurately. Some carriers are able to provide online freight information systems that include the ability to track shipment status in real time.

DEVELOPING A TRANSPORTATION AND LOGISTICS STRATEGY

The changes in the regulatory environment of transportation, advances in information management systems, and the growing concern with managing both upstream (suppliers) and downstream (end customers) in supply networks have brought rapid and continuous change to logistics management. The same principles of effective purchasing and supply management can and should be applied to logistics services. Development of a logistics strategy should include

Value analysis of alternatives. A service requirement value analysis may turn up totally adequate, lower-cost transport arrangements.

Price analysis. Rates vary substantially and decisions should be made only after consideration of all possibilities. Competitive quotes should be obtained. Negotiation of big-ticket transportation is possible.

Consolidation of freight, where possible. Volume discounts may reduce transport costs substantially. Systems contracts and blanket orders may be advantageous. If JIT purchasing is in use or being implemented, consolidation of several JIT suppliers may be cost-effective.

Analysis and evaluation of suppliers. Carrier selection and evaluation systems can provide data needed for better decision making. Four areas to evaluate are (1) financial, (2) management, (3) technical/strategic, and (4) relational, or overall corporate relationship between carrier and shipper.

Reassessment of the possibilities of using different transport modes. This would include using private trucking and intermodal transportation, such as piggybacking. The savings often are substantial.

Development of a closer relationship with selected carriers. Data that enable better planning of transport requirements should be shared to take advantage of the specialized knowledge of both buyer and carrier. A reduced carrier base and partnerships or logistics alliances might be considered.

Cost analysis/reductions. Long-term contracts; partnerships; third-party involvement; freight consolidation; demurrage; packaging; and service, quality, and delivery requirements offer opportunities for cost reductions.

Outsourcing, third-party logistics, contracting out. As organizations downsize, focus on core competencies, and face time-based competition, the decision to contract with a company or several companies to provide complete logistics services should be considered.

Safety considerations. Safety issues may be related to downward pressure on driver's income since deregulation, and to shipper demands that may result in shippers and carriers agreeing to unrealistic, legally unattainable delivery schedules. These pressures may lead to drivers falsifying log books to conceal violations of hours worked and miles driven, and to accidents involving commercial vehicles. Avoidance of safety problems should be a key element in the strategy.

Environmental factors. Growing concerns over clean air and water, the transport of hazardous materials, and fuel/energy consumption also must be taken into account.

Conclusion

Transportation costs represent a significant expense at most organizations and, in a deregulated environment, there are a wide range of service options available. Not only do logistics and transportation services represent a significant cost, they also affect customer service levels through availability of products, investments in infrastructure such as warehouse networks and trucks, and responsibilities within the supply chain for activities such as expediting and filing claims for loss or damaged goods.

Supply has a dual role in managing transportation and logistics activities. In many companies, supply has functional responsibility for logistical activities such as inbound transportation, warehousing, and packaging. Supply also is expected to work with others in the organization, such as marketing and operations, in managing outsourced agreements with third-party logistics suppliers. Astute supply managers, therefore, should be familiar with the basic concepts of transportation and logistics in order to appreciate the implications of their decisions, such as arranging transportation of raw materials from suppliers or negotiating logistics outsourcing contracts with a 3PL.

Questions for Review and Discussion

1. How has transportation deregulation affected the purchase of logistics services?
2. What factors should be considered in selecting a mode of transportation? A carrier?
3. How do firms organize to handle the logistics function?
4. Why might an organization decide to outsource all or some of its logistics activities to a third party?
5. What types of transportation damage might occur and how should each be handled?
6. What kinds of shipping needs are best met by a courier and why?
7. What are the use and significance of the bill of lading?
8. What does FOB mean? What variations are there in FOB terms?
9. Why should a buyer audit payments for freight purchases?
10. What strategies should be developed to effectively manage the logistics function?
11. How would logistics decisions be affected by a JIT purchasing arrangement?
12. Under what circumstances might a buyer prefer each of the following carriers: TL, LTL, air, water, rail, intermodal?

References

Ballou, Ronald H. *Business Logistics Management.* 5th ed. Upper Saddle River, NJ: Prentice Hall, 2004.

Bowersox, D. J.; D. J. Closs; and M. B. Cooper. *Supply Chain Logistics Management*. New York: McGraw-Hill/Irwin, 2002.

Coyle, J. J.; E. J. Bardi; and C. J. Langley Jr. *The Management of Business Logistics: A Supply Chain Perspective*. 7th ed. Toronto, Canada: Thomson, 2003.

Incoterms 2000. New York: International Chamber of Commerce (ICC) Publishing Inc., 2000.

Johnson, James C.; Donald F. Woods; Daniel L. Wardlow; and Paul R. Murphy Jr. *Contemporary Logistics.* 7th ed. Upper Saddle River, NJ: Prentice Hall, 1999.

Ramburg, Jan. *ICC Guide to Incoterms 2000.* New York: International Chamber of Commerce (ICC) Publishing Inc., 2000.

Stock, James R., and Douglas M. Lambert. *Strategic Logistics Management.* 4th ed. New York: McGraw-Hill/Irwin, 2001.

Case 7–1

Great Western Bank

The Great Western Bank of San Diego placed an order for 12 special-purpose accounting machines with the Data-Max Corporation of Cincinnati, Ohio. Great Western and Data-Max agreed to a firm-fixed price of $9,500 per unit, FOB the shipping point (Cincinnati). In the purchase order, the bank's purchasing agent designated a particular carrier (Yellow Freight) and Data-Max returned a signed acknowledgement copy without change in any of the terms and conditions.

On completion of the 12 units three months later, Data-Max shipped them via a different common carrier than Yellow Freight. At the time of shipment, an invoice was mailed to Great Western. To take advantage of the 2 percent cash discount, Great Western paid the invoice immediately, as was its custom. The machines had not yet arrived.

Unfortunately, as the truck was passing through Illinois, the driver lost control; the vehicle was involved in an accident, and the truck and contents were destroyed. The 12 machines were a total loss.

The buyer, on contacting Data-Max relative to the loss, was told: "Look, we sold these machines to you F.O.B. Cincinnati, and title passed at the time they were loaded on the carrier. That's the law." At this point, the buyer pointed out that Data-Max had not shipped via the carrier specified on the purchase order. To this Data-Max replied: "Sure, that's true. But we saved you money by shipping via a less expensive transportation method. [This was, in fact, true.] Furthermore, you acknowledged and accepted our action by paying our invoice, for the invoice clearly stated the date and method of shipment. It is your responsibility to work out any adjustment for the loss directly with the truck line."

Case 7–2

Geo Products

In early April, Sharon Lee, supervisor of purchasing and transportation at Geo Products (Geo) in Georgia, had to decide on the future transportation needs of the company. Increased sales would place significant demands on the company's resources, including transportation. As a result, Sharon had been asked by the plant manager to develop a suitable transportation strategy by April 15.

INDUSTRY

Geo manufactured kitchen and bathroom cabinets and mirrors. Geo competed in the upper end of the market, manufacturing high-quality products. Based on current sales forecasts, management expected Geo to double its output over the next 12 months.

Most of the big players in the industry had a linear relationship between transportation expenses and revenue. It was estimated that an average relationship would be 20:1 and varied depending on the distance the product was shipped.

COMPANY BACKGROUND

Geo was a subsidiary of Star Corporation (Star). Star, a financial holding company, had two manufacturing operations in Canada and four in the United States. The Georgia plant was intended to meet market demand in the southeastern states.

Georgia plant operations ordered supplies and services based on confirmed customer orders and promised delivery dates. The plant produced approximately 30,000 units last year.

Approximately nine years prior, the Georgia plant had an exclusive third-party contract with a transportation company that provided on-site support. However, at that time, the company was faced with intense competitive pressures and looked for other, more cost-effective alternatives. As a result, Geo negotiated with Eastern Leasing Company (Eastern) to lease two trucks and to provide transportation services through a separate trucking services company (TSC). Under the arrangement with Eastern, Geo contacted TSC when shipments required delivery. Although only two trucks were officially leased by Geo, TSC was flexible in providing more trucks and drivers when necessary.

TRANSPORTATION ACTIVITIES

Regular weekly deliveries were made to customers in the southern states. The routes for each truck were specified, with one customer typically being visited once per week. Occasionally, two visits per week were necessary when extra orders were placed and all units could not be filled in the first shipment.

Payment to TSC was made on a per mile basis, whereas Geo's customers were charged $11 per unit for delivery, regardless of the size and number of units delivered or ordered. Payment to the leasing company was $1/mile whether the trailer was full or half-empty. Last year, Geo spent approximately $200,000 on TSC fees and paid approximately $160,000 to Eastern as part of the lease arrangement.

When the quantity to be delivered was not large enough for a whole trailer or delivery dates did not fit with the pre-planned route, Geo would hire the services of other common carrier truck lines. In these situations, Geo was charged on the basis of weight or square footage. These shipments took longer for delivery because common carriers typically made a number of stops for other companies also sharing the trailer before reaching Geo's final destination. Last year, Geo spent about $80,000 on LTL loads.

THE TRANSPORTATION DECISION

Because of the forecast increase for the coming 12 months, Sharon was concerned that the company might not be able to meet the future market requirements with the existing two trucks. She felt that a number of possible alternatives existed. First, she could continue with the current approach and use common carriers to handle the additional volume. A second alternative was to lease an additional truck from Eastern. Finally, she could restructure the existing arrangement and negotiate a contract with a carrier to provide on-site service.

Sharon knew she had to develop a plan to support the projected growth at the Georgia plant for the April 15 meeting with the plant manager.

Case 7–3

Penner Medical Products

Neil Bennett, warehouse manager at Penner Medical Products (Penner), in Rockford, Illinois, was concerned about rising costs and delays associated with shipments arriving from an important Canadian supplier. Ken McCallum, the general manager, had asked Neil to look into the situation and get back to him with recommendations. It was Monday, April 14th, and Neil knew that Ken expected to see his plan by the end of the week.

PENNER

Penner was a medical supplies distributor and retailer, supplying small and medium-sized medical practices for more than 50 years. Company sales were $30 million and Penner employed approximately 120 people. Management expected a 10 percent increase in sales over the following five years. Penner sold a wide range of products, such as blood pressure gauges, tongue depressors, scalpels, and specialized furniture. Customers could purchase products either through Penner's five retail locations, all of them within a 200-mile radius of Rockford, or order directly from its central warehouse. The company took orders from customers either over the phone or through its Web site.

Although Penner was a family-owned business, retirement of key family members resulted in the hiring of several professional managers to run the company. Ken McCallum had been with the company for less than one year and was anxious to exploit opportunities to improve profitability.

Penner's main warehouse was a 30,000-square-foot building, normally filled with merchandise in excess of $2 million. The warehouse was staffed by a manager, two receivers, two drivers for local deliveries to customers, two shippers, and two stock pickers, one of whom was also occasionally asked to drive the company's two-ton truck, the biggest delivery vehicle available. Warehouse workers were paid an average of $15.00 per hour.

Neil Bennett started with Penner as a stock picker and was able to progress though the organization as a result of his effort and dedication. He was promoted to warehouse manager eight months earlier.

STINSON DISTRIBUTION COMPANY

Rising costs and missed delivery dates from an important supplier in Ontario, Canada, Stinson Distribution Company (Stinson), had been a concern for some time. A medium-sized company, Stinson had a long-term relationship with Penner, supplying a wide variety of specialized equipment for medical offices. Stinson produce high-quality products and was Penner's only supplier of this equipment.

Missed delivery dates and incomplete orders from Stinson were resulting in customer complaints and lost sales. Furthermore, transportation costs were well over budget and senior management viewed inventory levels as excessive. The controller indicated to Neil that inventory holding costs were 15 percent.

Two days per week, Penner's two-ton truck was sent to Stinson, traveling across the border at Detroit. Under ideal conditions, the one-way trip took 9 to 10 hours, and the truck, although empty in the first leg of the trip, was typically fully loaded with approximately $15,000 in goods on its way back to Rockford. The controller indicated that the cost of operating the two-ton truck was $55 per hour, including fuel, insurance, and administrative overhead. Neil observed that fuel costs had increased dramatically lately. He had tried to share the trips to Ontario with other local businesses to cut down transportation costs, but such efforts had been sporadic.

Concerns regarding security since 9/11 had resulted in delays at the Detroit border crossing, extending shipping times and costs for Penner. The duration and timing of delays at the border were highly variable and could last anywhere from 30 minutes to several hours. Furthermore, incomplete paperwork could add to these problems, since customs officials had become very thorough when reviewing documentation. Neil estimated that approximately 25 percent of the goods from Stinson were delayed as a result of paperwork problems.

The two-ton truck was also in demand to supply materials to Penner's customers, making scheduling deliveries increasingly difficult. Neil had recently resorted to using United Parcel Services (UPS) to handle rush orders from Stinson, with an appreciable cost premium. He observed that: "At least UPS never messes up the paperwork and gets the product here on time." Penner was also currently paying $1,000 per month to rent space at a warehouse in Windsor used to prepare shipments to cross the border.

EVALUATING OPPORTUNITIES

Neil recognized that his meeting with Ken McCallum was still five days away but wanted to get started working on the problem right away. Ken had indicated, "This problem is costing us a lot of money every day we let it continue. I want a plan in place at the end of the week that will convince me that the problem is going to get fixed quickly."

Chapter Eight

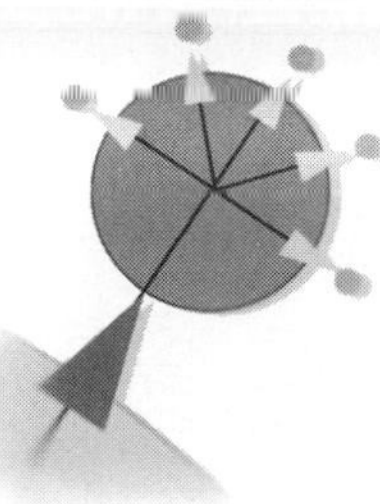

Price

Chapter Outline

Key Questions for the Supply Manager

Should we

- Use competitive bidding as our principal means of price determination?
- Use supplier price lists in determining prices?
- Use forward buying?

How can we

- Spot and combat price fixing?
- Use the futures market to hedge the purchase of raw materials?
- Know when to allow price changes during a contract?

Determination of the price to be paid is a major supply decision. The ability to get a "good price" is sometimes held to be the prime test of a good buyer. If by "good price" is meant greatest value, broadly defined, this is true.

While price is only one aspect of the overall supply job, it is extremely important. The purchaser must be alert to different pricing methods, know when each is appropriate, and use skill in arriving at the price to be paid. There is no reason to apologize for emphasizing price or for giving it a place of importance among the factors to be considered. The purchaser rightly is expected to get the best value possible for the organization whose funds are spent.

While competitive bidding can be used for some purchases, purchasing in the commodities market requires a much different approach and buyer skill set. This chapter examines how suppliers set prices and techniques that can be used to establish and adjust prices. Chapter 9 complements the material covered in this chapter by addressing supplier cost analysis, discounts, and negotiation.

RELATION OF COST TO PRICE

Every supply manager believes the supplier should be paid a fair price. But what does "fair price" mean? A fair price is the lowest price that ensures a continuous supply of the proper quality where and when needed.

A "continuous supply" is possible in the long run only from a supplier who is making a reasonable profit. The supplier's total costs, including a reasonable profit, must be covered by total sales in the long run. Any one item in the line, however, may never contribute "its full share" over any given period, but even for such an item the price paid normally should at least cover the direct costs incurred.

A fair price to one seller for any one item may be higher than a fair price to another or for an equally satisfactory substitute item. Both may be "fair prices" as far as the buyer is concerned, and the buyer may pay both prices at the same time.

Merely because a price is set by a monopolist or is established through collusion among sellers does not, in and of itself, make that price unfair or excessive. Likewise, the prevailing price need not necessarily be a fair price, as, for example, when such price is a "black" or "gray" market price or when it is depressed or raised through monopolistic or coercive action.

The supply manager is called on continuously to exercise judgment as to what the "fair price" should be under a variety of circumstances. To determine this fair price, he or she must have experience (data) and common sense. In part, of course, accuracy in weighing the various factors that culminate in a "fair and just price" is a matter of capitalizing on past experience and thorough knowledge of the processes used to produce the item, and the costs associated with them, as well as logistics costs such as storage, transportation, and other relevant costs.

Meaning of Cost

Assuming this concept of a fair price is sound, what are the relationships between cost and price? Clearly, to stay in business over the long run, a supplier must cover total costs, including overhead, and receive a profit. Unless costs, including profit, are covered, eventually the supplier will be forced out of business. This reduces the number of sources available to the buyer and may cause scarcity, higher prices, less-satisfactory service, and lower quality.

But what is to be included in the term *cost?* At times it is defined to mean only direct labor and material costs, and in a period of depressed business conditions, a seller may be willing merely to recover this amount rather than not make a sale at all. Or cost may mean direct labor and material costs with a contribution toward overhead. If the cost for a particular item includes overhead, is the latter charged at the actual rate (provided it can be determined), or is it charged at an average rate? The average rate may be far from the actual rate.

Most knowledgeable businesspeople realize that determining the cost of a particular article or service is not a precise process. In manufacturing industries there are two basic classifications of costs: *direct* and *indirect.*

Direct costs usually are defined as those that can be specifically and accurately assigned to a given unit of production; that is, direct materials, such as 10 pounds of steel, or direct labor, such as 30 minutes of a person's time on a machine or assembly line. However, under accepted accounting practices, the actual price of the specific material used may not be the cost that is included in figuring direct material costs. Because the price paid for material may fluctuate up or down over a period of time, it is common practice to use a so-called standard cost. Some companies use as a standard cost for materials the last price paid in the immediately prior fiscal period. Other companies use an average price for a specific period.

Indirect costs are those incurred in the operation of a production plant or process, but that normally cannot be related directly to any given unit of production. Some examples of indirect costs are rent, property taxes, machine depreciation, expenses of general supervisors, data processing, power, heat, and light. Indirect costs often are referred to as *overhead.* They may be fixed or variable.

Classification of costs into variable, semivariable, and fixed categories is a common accounting practice and a necessity for any meaningful analysis of price/cost relationships. Most direct costs are ***variable costs*** because they vary directly and proportionally with the units produced. For example, a product that requires 10 pounds of steel for one unit will require 100 pounds for 10 units.

Semivariable costs may vary with the number of units produced but are partly variable and partly fixed. For example, more heat, light, and power will be used when a plant is operating at 90 percent of capacity than when operating at a 50 percent rate, but the difference is not directly proportional to the number of units produced. In fact, there would be some costs (fixed) for heat, light, and power if production were stopped completely for a period of time.

Fixed costs generally remain the same regardless of the number of units produced. For example, real estate taxes will be the same for a given period of time regardless of whether one unit or 100,000 units are produced. Several accounting methods can be used to allocate fixed costs. A common method is to apply a percentage of direct costs in order to allocate the cost of factory overhead. Full allocation of fixed expenses will depend on an accurate forecast of production and the percentage used. Obviously, as full production capacity is reached, the percentage rate will decline.

Factory overhead often is based on some set percentage of direct labor cost because, historically, labor represented the largest cost element. Although this rarely is true any longer, standard cost accounting often has not changed. Selling, general, and administrative expense is based on a set percentage of total manufacturing cost. The following example illustrates the typical product cost buildup in a manufacturing setting.

Direct materials	$ 5,500
+ Direct labor	2,000
+ Factory overhead*	2,500
= Manufacturing cost	**$10,000**
+ General, administrative, and selling cost	1,500
= Total cost	**$11,500**
+ Profit	920
= Selling price	**$12,420**

*Factory overhead consists of all *indirect* factory costs, both *fixed* and *variable.*

We now can define costs as so many dollars and cents per unit based on an average cost for raw material over a period of time, direct labor costs, and an estimated volume of production over a period of time on which the distribution of overhead is based.

If this definition of cost is acceptable, then a logical question is, whose cost? Some manufacturers are more efficient than others. Usually all sell the same item at about the same price. But should this price be high enough to cover only the most efficient supplier's costs, or should it cover the costs of all suppliers? Furthermore, cost does not necessarily determine market price. When a seller insists that the price must be a given amount because of costs, this position is not really justified. In the final analysis, goods are worth and will sell for what the market will pay.

Moreover, no seller is entitled to a price that yields a profit merely because the supplier is in business or assumes risk. If such were the case, every business automatically would be entitled to a profit regardless of costs, quality, or service. Unless a seller can supply a market with goods that are needed and desired by users and can supply them with reasonable efficiency, that seller is not entitled to get a price that even covers costs.

How Suppliers Establish Price

Depending on the commodity and industry, the market may vary from almost pure competition to oligopoly and monopoly. Pricing will vary accordingly. For competitive reasons, most firms are not anxious to disclose just how prices are set, but the two traditional methods are the cost approach and the market approach.

The Cost Approach

The cost approach to pricing says the price should be a certain amount over direct costs, allowing for sufficient contribution to cover indirect costs and overhead and leaving a certain margin for profit. For the purchaser, the cost approach offers a number of opportunities to seek lower-cost suppliers, to suggest lower-cost manufacturing alternatives, and to question the size of the margin over direct costs. Negotiation, used with cost-analysis techniques, is a particularly useful tool.

The Market Approach

The market approach implies that prices are set in the marketplace and may not be directly related to cost. If demand is high relative to supply, prices are expected to rise; when demand is low relative to supply, prices should decline. This, too, is an oversimplification. Some economists hold that large multinational, multiproduct firms have such a grip on the marketplace that pure competition does not exist and that prices will not drop even though supply exceeds demand. In the market approach, the purchaser must either live with prevailing market prices or find ways around them. If nothing can be done to attack the price structure directly, it still may be possible to select those suppliers who are willing to offer nonprice incentives, such as holding inventory, technical and design service, superior quality, excellent delivery, transportation concessions, and early warning of impending price and product changes. Negotiation, therefore, may center on items other than price.

Many economists hold that substitution of like but not identical materials or products is one of the most powerful forces preventing a completely monopolistic or oligopolistic grip on a market. For example, aluminum and copper may be interchanged in a number of applications. The aluminum and copper markets, therefore, are not independent of one another. The purchaser's ability to recognize these trade-offs and to effect design and use changes to take advantage of substitution is one determinant of flexibility. Make or buy (or outsource) is another option. If access to the raw materials, technological process, and labor skills is not severely restricted, one alternative may be for an organization to make its own requirements to avoid excess market prices.

Sometimes purchasers use long-term contracts to induce the supplier to ignore market conditions. This approach may be successful in certain instances, but it is normal for suppliers to find ways and means around such commitments once it becomes obvious that the prevailing market price is substantially above that paid by their long-term customers.

GOVERNMENT INFLUENCE ON PRICING

The government's role in establishing price has changed dramatically. The role of government has been twofold. The government can have an active role in determining prices by establishing production and import quotas and regulating the ways that buyers and sellers are allowed to behave in agreeing on prices. Because other governments are active in price control and have, in a number of situations, created dual pricing for domestic use and exports, it is difficult to see how the U.S. and Canadian governments will be able to ignore their position. Prices may be determined by review or control boards or by strong moral suasion. They are likely to be augmented by governmental controls such as quotas, tariffs, and export permits.

Governments influence prices of utilities that offer common services, such as electricity and water, and set prices on licenses and goods and services provided by government-run organizations, such as postal services. Energy deregulation is still in its infancy but will be an interesting and challenging area for purchasers to watch. The U.S. Postal Service also is undergoing changes as it forges alliances with private-industry competitors. What these changes will mean in terms of pricing and negotiation opportunities remains to be seen.

Legislation Affecting Price Determination

United States

The federal government has taken an active interest in how a buyer and seller agree on a price. The government's position largely has been a protective role to prevent the stronger party from imposing too onerous conditions on the weaker one or preventing collusion so that competition will be maintained.

The two most important federal laws affecting competition and pricing practices are the Sherman Antitrust and Robinson-Patman acts. The Sherman Antitrust Act of 1890 states that any combination, conspiracy, or collusion with the intent of restricting trade in interstate commerce is illegal. This means that it is illegal for suppliers to get together to set prices (price fixing) or determine the terms and conditions under which they will sell. It also means that buyers cannot get together to set the prices they will pay. The Robinson-Patman Act (Federal Anti-price Discrimination Act of 1936) says that a supplier must sell the same item, in the same quantity, to all customers at the same price. It is known as the "one-price law." Some exceptions are permitted, such as a lower price (1) for a larger purchase quantity, providing the seller can cost justify the lower price through cost accounting data; (2) for moving distress or obsolete merchandise; or (3) for meeting the lower price of local competition in a particular geographic area. The act also goes on to state that it shall be illegal for a buyer *knowingly* to induce or accept a discriminatory price. However, the courts have been realistic in their interpretation of the law, holding that it is the job of the buyer to get the best possible price for his or her company, and that as long as he or she does not intentionally mislead the seller into giving a more favorable price than is available to other buyers of the same item, the law is not being violated.

If the buyer feels a seller is violating either the Sherman Act or the Robinson-Patman Act, a charge detailing the violation can be made to the Federal Trade Commission (FTC), which was set up to investigate alleged improprieties. From the buyer's standpoint, bringing a seller's actions to the government's attention has few advantages. Since most of the time the government's reaction is relatively slow, the need for the item may be gone and conditions may be substantially changed by the time the complaint is decided. Most sellers would view the lodging of a complaint as a particularly unfriendly act, making it difficult for the organization to maintain a reasonable future relationship with that particular supplier. For this reason, complaints are not common, and most are lodged by public buying agencies rather than corporations.

Canada

Canadian federal pricing legislation differs from U.S. legislation, but it has essentially the same intent. It prohibits certain pricing practices in an attempt to maintain competition in the marketplace and applies to both buyers and sellers. Violation of the statute is a criminal offense. Suppliers or buyers may not "conspire, combine, agree, or arrange with another person" to raise prices unreasonably or to otherwise restrain competition. It does not prevent the exchange of data within a trade or professional association, providing it does not lessen price competition. Bid rigging is a per se violation, which means that the prosecution need only establish the existence of an agreement to gain a conviction; there is no requirement to prove that the agreement unduly affected competition. It is also illegal for a supplier to grant a price concession to one buyer that is not available to all other buyers (similar to the U.S. Robinson-Patman Act).

Quantity discounts are permitted, as are one-time price cuts to clear out inventory. As in the United States, the Canadian buyer who knowingly is on the receiving end of price discrimination also has violated the law. With regard to price maintenance and the purchase of goods for resale, it requires that a supplier should not, by threat or promise, attempt to influence how the firms that buy from it then price their products for resale.

TYPES OF PURCHASES

Analysis of suppliers' costs is by no means the only basis for price determination. What other means can be used? Much depends on the type of product being bought. There are seven general classes:

1. *Raw materials.* This group includes the so-called *sensitive commodities,* such as copper, wheat, and crude petroleum, but also steel, cement, and so forth.
2. *Special items.* This group includes items and materials that are special to the organization's product line and, therefore, are custom ordered.
3. *Standard production items.* This group includes such items as bolts and nuts, many forms of commercial steel, valves, and tubing, whose prices are fairly stable and are quoted on a basis of "list price with some discount."
4. *Items of small value.* This group includes items of such small comparative value that the expenditure of any particular effort to check price prior to purchase is not justified. Maintenance, repair, and operating supplies (MRO) fall in this class.

The other three classes, which are not discussed in detail here because they either are covered elsewhere in or are outside the scope of this text, are:

5. *Capital goods.* These purchased items are accounted for as a capital asset and expensed out through depreciation, rather than being expensed immediately at the time of purchase or use. The purchase of these equipment and construction items is discussed in Chapter 16, "Capital Goods."
6. *Services.* This category of purchases is very broad and includes many types of services, such as advertising, auditing, consulting, architectural design, legal, insurance, personnel travel, copying, security, and waste removal. Purchase of services is covered in Chapter 17, "Services."
7. *Resale.* This category can be subdivided into two groups:
   a. Items that formerly were manufactured in-house but have been outsourced to a supplier and now are brought in complete. An example would be the major appliance maker that markets a microwave oven but no longer manufactures the product. Instead it buys the microwave oven complete, under its own brand name. The decision process for these items is the same as presented in this book.
   b. Items sold in the retail sector, such as the clothing sold in the general-line department stores; the food sold through supermarkets; the tools sold in hardware stores; and the tires, batteries, and accessories sold in gasoline/filling stations.

   Obviously the dollar amount involved in the purchase of these resale items is tremendous. The people who buy these items typically are called merchandise managers, for they first must decide what will sell. Based on this assessment, they then make their buying decisions. Since this text concentrates on industrial and institutional buying, there is no detailed coverage of merchandise buying, although many of the same supply principles and practices apply.

Raw Materials/Sensitive Commodities

Raw materials and commodities are normally quoted at market prices, which fluctuate daily. For these items, the price at any particular moment probably is less important than the trend of the price movement. The price can be determined readily in most instances because many of these commodities are bought and sold on well-organized markets. Prices are reported regularly in many of the trade and business journals, such as *Iron Age, Chemical Marketing Reporter,* and *The Wall Street Journal.* These publications and other sources also are readily available online, giving the interested buyer instantaneous access. For example, the price of gold is quoted daily and reported extensively in the media.

These quoted market prices also can be useful in developing prices-paid evaluation systems and price indexes for use in price escalator clauses.

To the extent that such quoted prices are a fair reflection of market conditions, the current cash price is known and is substantially uniform for a given grade. Yet, it is common knowledge among buyers that such published market quotations usually are on the high side, and the astute buyer probably can get a lower price. A company's requirements for commodities of this sort usually are sufficiently adjustable so that an immediate order is seldom a necessity, and purchase can be postponed if the trend of prices is downward.

The price trend is a matter of importance in the purchase of any type of commodity, but it is particularly important with this group. Insofar as "careful and studious timing" is essential to getting the right price, both the type of information required as a basis for such timing and the sources from which the information can be obtained differ from those necessary in dealing with other groups of items. Commodity study research, discussed in Chapter 13, is particularly useful in buying these items.

Special Items

Special items include the large variety of purchased parts or special materials peculiar to the organization's end product or service. Make or buy is always a significant consideration on these items because of their proprietary nature. Prices normally are obtained by quotation because no published price lists are available. Subcontracts are common, and the availability of compatible or special equipment, skilled labor, and capacity may be significant factors in determining price. Because large differences may exist between suppliers in terms of these factors and their desire for business, prices may vary substantially between suppliers. Each product in this group is unique and may need special attention. A diligent search for suppliers willing and able to handle such special requirements, including an advantageous price, may pay off handsomely.

Standard Production Items

The third group of items includes those standard production items whose prices are comparatively stable and are likely to be quoted on a basis of list-less-certain-discounts. This group includes a wide range of items commonly obtainable from a substantial list of sources. The inventory problems related to this class of requirements are largely routine. Changes in price do occur, but they are far less frequent than with raw materials and are likely to be moderate. Prices usually are obtained from online or hard-copy catalogs or similar publications of suppliers, supplemented by periodic discount sheets.

It should not be concluded from this that such purchases are unimportant or that the prices quoted should not be examined with care. Quite the contrary is true. The items are important in themselves; the annual dollar volume of purchases is often impressive; and real attention needs to be paid to the unit price. When a requisition is received by supply, the first step commonly would be to refer to past purchase records as the first source of information. If the material in question has been regularly purchased or orders have been placed for it recently, an up-to-date price record and catalog file will give all the information pertaining to the transaction, such as the various firms able to supply the commodity, the firms from which purchases have been made, and the prices paid. This information will be sufficiently recent and reliable to enable the buyer to place the order without extended investigation. However, if the buyer does not feel justified in proceeding on the basis of this information, a list of available suppliers from supplier files, catalogs, the Internet, and other sources can be assembled and quotation requests can be sent to potential suppliers. Online auctions (seller-initiated) or reverse auctions (buyer-initiated) are also being used by some organizations seeking a more efficient means of purchasing standard items (see Chapter 4).

Good sources for current prices and discounts are sales representatives. Few manufacturers rely wholly on catalogs (online or hard copy) for sales but follow up such material with visits by their salespersons.

A sales representative may quote the buyer a price while in the buyer's office, and the buyer may accept by issuing a purchase order (PO). There likely will be no problem, although legally the salesperson probably doesn't have agency authority, and the offer made by the salesperson does not legally commit the selling company *until* it has been accepted by an officer of the selling company. If the buyer wishes to accept such an offer, and to know that the offer is legally binding, he or she should ask the salesperson to furnish a letter, signed by an officer of the selling company, stating that the salesperson possesses the authority of a sales *agent.*

Small-Value Items

The fourth group of commodities for the purpose of price determination includes items of such small value, comparatively speaking, that they do not justify any particular effort to analyze the price in detail. These often are referred to as maintenance, repair, and operating (MRO) supplies. Every supply department must buy numerous items of this sort; yet these items do not in themselves justify a catalog file, even when such catalogs are available, nor do they represent enough money to warrant sending out for individual quotations. Actually, the pricing problem on such items is handled in a variety of ways; the following constitutes an excellent summary of these procedures.

As discussed in Chapter 4, a number of organizations have experienced success in procuring MRO items through e-procurement systems. While the actual transaction is handled electronically, most of the advantages come from applying good supply practices, such as consolidating and standardizing requirements and reducing the number of suppliers.

It is also common practice to send out unpriced orders for such items. Another common practice is to indicate on the order the last price paid, this price being taken from the record of purchases or past purchases if the last purchase was not too far back. Other buyers make a practice of grouping these small items under some blanket order or systems-contract arrangement or on a cost-plus basis with suppliers who undertake to have the materials in inventory when needed, and who are willing to submit to periodic checking as to the fairness of the prices they charge. Procurement cards also are used to allow internal customers to purchase small-value items from designated suppliers. (See Chapter 3 for a discussion of blanket orders, systems contracting, and procurement cards, and Chapter 4 for a discussion on e-procurement.)

In most cases, sources of supply for these items are local, and current prices often are obtained by telephone, by fax, or online and then placed on the face of the purchase order so they become a part of the agreement. The most common practice of all, however, is perhaps to depend on the integrity of the suppliers and to omit any detailed checking of the proper price on items of small value. Many supply managers believe that their best assurance is the confidence they have in carefully selected sources of supply, and they feel secure in relying on their suppliers to give them the best available price without requiring them to name the price in advance, and without checking it when the invoice is received.

One method for controlling prices for these small-dollar items consists of the practice of spot-checking. This means the selection of an occasional item that then is carefully investigated to develop the exact basis on which the supplier is pricing. Discovery of unfair or improper prices by such spot checks is considered a reason for discontinuing the source of supply, who is discovered to be taking advantage of the nature of the transaction in pricing. Perhaps a more effective way to buy items of small value, such as those included in the MRO group, is to use the systems-contracting and third-party supplier techniques described in Chapter 3.

Somewhat similar to the small-value purchase problem is the emergency requirement. Here, as for example with equipment breakdown, time may be of much greater value than money, and the buyer may wish to get the supplier started immediately, even though price has not been determined. The buyer may decide merely to say "start" or "ship" and issue an unpriced purchase order. If the price charged on the invoice is out of line, it can be challenged before payment.

THE USE OF QUOTATIONS AND COMPETITIVE BIDDING

Quotations normally are secured when the size of the proposed commitment exceeds some minimum dollar amount, for example, $1,000. Governmental purchases commonly must be on a bid basis; here the law requires that the award shall be made to the lowest *responsible* bidder. (See Chapter 15, "Public Supply Management," for a detailed discussion of competitive bidding.) In industrial practice, quotations may be solicited with a view to selecting those firms with whom negotiations as to the final price will be carried on.

The extent to which competitive bidding is relied on to secure an acceptable price varies widely. On the one hand, it is a common practice for buyers of routine supplies, purchased from the same sources time after time, to issue unpriced orders. The same thing occasionally happens in a very strong seller's market for some critical item when prices are rising so rapidly that the supplier refuses to quote a fixed price. Whenever possible, however, price should be indicated on the purchase order. In fact, from a legal point of view, a purchase order *must* contain either a price or a method of its determination for the contract to be binding. When it is decided to ask for competitive bids, certain essential steps are needed. These are a careful initial selection of dependable, potential sources; an accurate wording of the request to bid; submission of bid requests to a sufficient number of suppliers to ensure a truly competitive price; proper treatment of such quotations, once received; and a careful analysis of them prior to making the award.

The first step is to select possible suppliers from whom quotations are to be solicited; this amounts, in fact, to a preliminary screening of the sources of supply. It is assumed that the bidders must (1) be qualified to make the item in question in accordance with the buyer's specifications and to deliver it by the desired date, (2) be sufficiently reliable in other respects to warrant serious consideration as suppliers, (3) be numerous enough to ensure a truly competitive price, but (4) not be more numerous than necessary. The first two of these qualifications have been considered in our discussion of sources. The *number* of suppliers to whom inquiries are sent is largely a matter of the buyer's judgment. Ordinarily, at least two suppliers are invited to bid. More often, three or four are invited to submit bids. A multiplicity of bidders does not ensure a truly competitive price, although under ordinary circumstances it is an important factor, provided that the bidders are comparable in every major respect and provided that each is sufficiently reliable so that the buyer would be willing to purchase from that supplier.

The buyer normally will exclude from the bid list those firms with whom it is unlikely that an order would be placed, even though their prices were low. Sometimes bids are solicited solely for the purpose of checking the prices of regular suppliers or for inventory-pricing purposes. It should be remembered, however, that a company is put to some expense—at times, a very considerable one—when it submits a bid. It should not be asked to bear this cost without good reason. Moreover, the receipt of a request to bid is an encouragement to the supplier and implies that an order is possible. Therefore, purchasers should not solicit quotations unless placement of a purchase order is a possibility.

Having decided on the companies that are to be invited to bid, the purchaser in an off-line process sends a general inquiry, in which all the necessary information is set forth. A complete description of the item or items, the date on which these items are wanted, and the date by which the bid is to be returned are included. In many instances, a telephone inquiry is substituted for a formal request to bid.

Subsequent to the mailing of an inquiry but prior to the announcement of the purchase award, bidders naturally are anxious to know how their quotations compare with those of their competitors. Because sealed bids, used in governmental purchasing, are not commonly used in private industry, the purchaser is in a position to know how the bids, as they are received, compare with one another. However, if the bids are examined on receipt, it is important that this information be treated in strictest confidence. Indeed, some buyers deliberately keep themselves in ignorance of the quotations until such time as they are ready to analyze the bids; thus they are in a position to tell any inquiring bidder truthfully that they do not know how the bid prices compare. Even after the award is made, it probably is the better policy not to reveal to unsuccessful bidders the amount by which they failed to meet the successful bid.

In many entities in the public sector, the entire bid process has been automated. Bid packages and specifications are made available online, bidders submit their bids and proposals online, and the bid opening and award are communicated electronically. The cycle time reductions and other cost savings obviously can be great if the automated process is efficient.

This process is quite similar when it is an online bidding situation. In the case of an online auction, the potential sources are also prequalified and invited to take part in the online bidding. The auction, or event, is set for a specific date and time period much like the deadline and bid opening deadlines in an off-line process. The success of the auction depends in large part on the quality of the bid specifications and the ability of the person and process to prequalify suppliers. Bidders can see, online, the actual bid amounts but not who the bidders are. (See Chapter 4.)

Firm Bidding

The reason for the confidential treatment of bid price information is its connection with a problem practically all buyers have to face, namely, that of "firm bidding." Most firms have a policy of notifying suppliers that original bids must be final and that revisions will not be permitted under any circumstances. Exceptions are made only in the case of obvious error.

Particularly in times of falling prices, suppliers, extremely anxious to get business, try by various devices to ensure that their bids will be the lowest. Not infrequently they have been encouraged in this procedure by those purchasers who have acceded to requests that revisions be allowed. Unfortunately, it is also true that there are buyers who deliberately play one bidder against another and who even seek to secure lower prices by relating imaginary bids to prospective suppliers. The responsibility for deviations from a policy of firm bidding must be laid at the door of the purchaser as well as the supplier.

A policy of firm bidding is sound and should be deviated from only under the most unusual circumstances. To those who contend that it is impossible to adopt such a policy, the answer is that it actually is the practice followed in many organizations. The advantage of firm bidding as a general policy, however, needs no particular explanation. If rigidly adhered to, it is the fairest possible means of treating all suppliers alike. It tends to stress the quality and service elements in the transaction instead of the price factor. Assuming that bids are solicited only from honest and dependable suppliers and that the buyer is not obligated to place the order with the lowest bidder, it removes from suppliers the temptation to try to use inferior materials or workmanship once their bid has been accepted. It saves the purchaser time by removing the necessity for constant bargaining with suppliers over price.

An exception to the firm bidding approach is one where the buyer wants both parties (seller and buyer) to have the flexibility to clarify and define specifications and prices further after the initial bids are received. The buyer will notify all the sellers, at the time the initial bid request is made, that after the initial bids are received, the buyer may enter into discussions concerning any aspects of the requirement with one or more of the bidders, and then request best-and-final-offers (BAFOs). Some public buying agencies now also are permitted to use this approach.

Occasionally the buyer may, after reviewing the bids submitted, notify the bidders that all bids are being rejected and that another bid request is being issued, or that the item will be bought through a means other than competitive bidding. This may be done if it is obvious that the bidders did not fully understand the specifications, if collusion on the part of the bidders is suspected, or if it is felt that all prices quoted are unrealistically high.

Determination of Most Advantageous Bid

Typically, a bid analysis sheet is used to array the bids of all suppliers and the particulars of each bid (see the Hampton Manor case in Chapter 17 and the Loren case in Chapter 19), or the bids are viewed electronically in real time during an online auction. But after the bids have been submitted and compared, which should be selected? The lowest bid customarily is accepted. The objective of securing bids from various sources is to obtain the lowest price, and the purpose of supplying detailed specifications and statements of requirements is to ensure that the buyer receives the same items or services irrespective of whom the supplier may be. Governmental contracts must be awarded to the lowest bidder unless very special reasons can be shown for not doing so.

However, there are several cases in which the lowest bidder may not receive the order. Information received by the buyer subsequent to the request for bids may indicate that the firm submitting the lowest bid is not reliable. Even the lowest bid may be higher than the buyer believes justifiable. Or there may be reason to believe there was collusion among the bidders.

There are other reasons why the lowest bid is not always accepted: plant management, engineering, or using departments may express a preference for a certain manufacturer's product. Possibly a slight difference in price may not be considered enough to compensate for the confidence ensured by a particular supplier's product. A small difference in price may not seem to justify changing from a source of supply that has been satisfactory over a long period; yet the bid process may have been considered essential in ensuring that the company was receiving the proper price treatment.

Selecting the supplier, once the quotations are received, is not a simple matter of listing the bidders and picking out the one whose price is apparently low, because the obvious price comparisons may be misleading. Of two apparently identical bids, one actually may be higher than the other. One supplier's installation costs may be lower than another's. If prices quoted are FOB origin, the transportation charges may be markedly different. One supplier's price may be much lower because it is trying to break into a new market or is trying to force its only real competitor out of business. One supplier's product may require tooling that must be amortized. One supplier may quote a fixed price; another may insist on an escalator clause that could push the price above a competitor's firm bid. These and other factors are likely to render a snap judgment on comparative price a mistake.

Collusive Bidding

A buyer also may reject all bids if it is suspected that the suppliers are acting in collusion with one another. In such cases, the proper policy to pursue is often difficult to determine, but there are various possibilities. Legal action is possible but seldom feasible because of the expense, delay, and uncertainty of the outcome. Often, unfortunately, the only apparent solution is simply to accept the situation with the feeling that there is nothing the buyer can do about it anyway. Another possibility is to seek new sources of supply either inside or outside the area in which the buyer customarily has purchased materials or services. Resorting to substitute materials, temporarily or even permanently, may be an effective means of meeting the situation. Another possibility is to reject all the bids and then to attempt, by a process of negotiation or bargaining with one or another of the suppliers, to reduce the price. If circumstances make the last alternative the most feasible, a question of ethics is involved. Some supply managers feel that when collusion among suppliers exists, it is ethical for them to attempt to force down suppliers' prices by means that ordinarily would not be adopted.

The Problem of Identical Prices

It is not unusual for the buyer to receive identical bids from various sources. Because such bids may indicate intensive competition on the one hand and discrimination or collusion on the other, the purchaser must take care in handling such situations. Some of the situations that tend to make identical or parallel prices suspect are when:

1. Identical pricing marks a novel break in the historical pattern of price behavior.
2. There is evidence of communication between sellers or buyers regarding prices.
3. There is an "artificial" standardization of the product.
4. Identical prices are submitted in bids to buyers on complex, detailed, or novel specifications.
5. Deviations from uniform prices become the matter of industrywide concern—the subject of meetings and even organized sanctions.

The purchaser can take four different types of action to discourage identical pricing. The first is to encourage small sellers who form the nonconformist group in an industry and are anxious to grow. The second is to allow bidders to bid on parts of large contracts if they feel the total contract may be too large. The third is to encourage firm bidding without revision. And the fourth is to choose criteria in making the award so as to discourage future identical bids. If identical bids have been received, the buyer can reject all bids and then either call for new bids or negotiate directly with one or more specific suppliers.

However, if it is decided that the contract should be awarded at this time, various alternatives are available. It may be given to:

1. The smallest supplier.
2. The one with the largest domestic content.
3. The most distant firm, forcing it to absorb the largest freight portion.
4. The firm with the smallest market share.
5. The firm most likely to grant nonprice concessions.
6. The firm whose past performance has been best.

Competitive bidding attempts to obtain a fair price for items bought; the forces of competition are used to bring the price down to a level at which the efficient supplier will be able to cover only production and distribution costs, plus make a minimum profit. If a supplier wants the order, that supplier will "sharpen the pencil" and give the buyer an attractive quote. This places a good deal of pressure on the supplier.

However, for the bid process to work efficiently, several conditions are necessary: (1) There must be at least two, and preferably several, qualified suppliers; (2) the suppliers must want the business (competitive bidding works best in a buyer's market); (3) the specifications must be clear, so that each bidder knows precisely what is being bid on, and so the buyer can easily compare the quotes received from various bidders; and (4) there must be honest bidding and the absence of any collusion between the bidders. When any of these conditions is absent—that is, a sole-source situation, a seller's market, specifications that are not complete or subject to varying interpretations, or suspected supplier collusion—then negotiation is the preferred method of price determination. (See Chapter 9.)

PROVISION FOR PRICE CHANGES

Many long-term contracts contain provisions for price changes. The contract normally provides for no price changes for a fixed period of time after which a price change may become possible with a minimum notice period (see Loren case in Chapter 19). The actual provisions for price changes include a variety of options.

Guarantee against Price Decline

For goods bought on a recurring basis and for raw materials, the contract may be written at the price in effect at the time the contract is negotiated. The contract then provides for a reduction during a subsequent period if there is a downward price movement in the marketplace. The contract normally specifies that price movement will be determined by the list price reported in a specific business or trade publication or on a Web site. The buyer is more likely to be influenced by such guarantees when they are offered in an effort to overcome reluctance to buy, induced by a fear that prices are likely to drop still further.

Price Protection Clause

When a buyer enters into a long-term contract for raw materials or other key purchased items with one or more suppliers, the buyer may want to keep open the option of taking advantage of a lower price offered by a different supplier. This might be done by either buying from the noncontract supplier or forcing the contract supplier(s) to meet the lower price now available from the noncontract suppliers. Therefore, a price protection clause may be incorporated into the contract specifying that: "If the buyer is offered material of equal quality in similar quantities under like terms from a responsible supplier, at a lower delivered cost to the buyer than specified in this contract, the seller on being furnished written evidence of this offer shall either meet the lower delivered price or allow the buyer to purchase from the other supplier at the lower delivered price and deduct the quantity purchased from the quantity specified in this contract."

Escalator Clauses

The actual wording of many escalator clauses provides for either an increase or decrease in price if costs change. Clauses providing for escalation came into common use during many of the hyperinflation years in the 1970s when suppliers believed that their future costs were so uncertain as to make a firm quotation either impossible or, if covering all probable risks, so high as to make it unattractive, and perhaps unfair, to the buyer.

In designing any particular escalator contract, several general and many specific problems—such as the proportion of the total price subject to adjustment; the particular measures of prices and wage rates to be used in making the adjustment; the methods to be followed in applying these averages to the base price; the limitations, if any, on the amount of adjustment; and the methods for making payment—will be encountered. In times of price stability, escalation usually is reserved for long-term contracts, on the principle that certain costs may rise and that the seller has no appreciable control over this rise. In times of inflation, shortages, and sellers' markets, escalation becomes common on even short-term contracts as sellers attempt to ensure themselves of the opportunity to raise prices and preserve contribution margins. Changes in material and direct labor costs generally are tied to one of the published price and cost indexes, such as those of the Bureau of Labor Statistics or one of the trade publications, such as *Iron Age* or the *Chemical Marketing Reporter*. Finding a meaningful index to which escalation may be tied is a real problem in many instances. Because most escalation is automatic once the index, the portion of the contract subject to escalation, the frequency of revision, and the length of contract have been agreed to, the need for care in deciding on these factors is obvious.

The following is an illustrative escalator clause:

Labor

Adjustment with respect to labor costs shall be made on the basis of monthly average hourly earnings for the (Durable Goods Industry, subclass Machinery), as furnished by the Bureau of Labor Statistics (hereafter called the Labor Index). Adjustments shall be calculated with respect to each calendar quarter up to the completion date specified in contract. The percentage increase or decrease in the quarterly index (obtained by averaging the Labor Index for each month of the calendar quarter) shall be obtained by comparison with the Labor Index for the base month. The base month shall be____ 200____. The labor adjustment for each calendar quarter as thus determined shall be obtained by applying such percentage of increase or decrease to the total amount expended by the contractor for direct labor during such quarter.

Materials

> Adjustment with respect to materials shall be made on the basis of the materials index for Group VI (Metals and Metal Products), as furnished by the Bureau of Labor Statistics (hereafter called the Materials Index). Adjustments shall be determined with respect to each calendar quarter up to the completion date specified in the contract. The percentage of increase or decrease in the quarterly index (obtained by averaging the Materials Index for each month of the calendar quarter) shall be obtained by comparison with the Materials Index for the base month. The base month shall be____ 200____. The material adjustment for each calendar quarter shall be obtained by applying to the contract material cost the percentage of increase or decrease shown by the Materials Index for that quarter.

A buyer who uses escalator clauses must remember that one legal essential to any enforceable purchase contract is that it contain either a definite price or the means of arriving at one. No contract for future delivery can be enforced if the price of the item is conditioned entirely on the will of one of the parties. The clauses cited earlier would appear to be adequate. So too are those clauses authorizing the seller to change price as costs of production change, provided that these costs can be reasonably determined from the supplier's accounting records.

Other Price Options

In Chapter 15, a variety of contract options with respect to price are discussed, including firm-fixed-price (FFP), cost-plus-fixed-fee (CPFF), cost-no-fee (CNF), and cost-plus-incentive-fee (CPIF).

Most-Favored-Customer Clause

Another commonly used price protection clause (sometimes referred to as a "most-favored-nation clause") specifies that the supplier, over the duration of the contract, will not offer a lower price to other buyers, or if a lower price is offered to others, it will apply to this contract as well.

CONTRACT CANCELLATION

In practice, cancellations usually occur during a period of falling prices. At such times, if the price has declined since the placing of the order, some buyers may try to take advantage of all sorts of loopholes in the purchase order or sales agreement to reject merchandise. To avoid completion of the transaction, they take advantage of technicalities that under other circumstances would be of no concern to them whatsoever. One can have sympathy for the buyer with a contract at a price higher than the market price. There is little justification, however, for the purchaser who follows a cancellation policy under this situation. A contract should be considered a binding obligation. The practice referred to is an instance of "sharp practice," which hopefully is becoming less and less prevalent as the years go by. There may be occasions when a buyer justifiably seeks to cancel the contract, but to do so merely because the market price has fallen is not one of them.

In some instances, the buyer knows when the purchase order is placed that the customer for whose job the materials are being bought may unexpectedly cancel the order, thus forcing cancellation of purchase orders for materials planned for the job. This is a common risk when purchasing materials for use on a government contract, for appropriation changes often force the government to cancel its order, which results in the cancellation of a great many purchase orders by firms who were to have been suppliers to the government under the now-canceled government contract. Or severe changes in the business cycle may trigger purchase-order cancellations. If cancellation is a possibility, the basis and terms of cancellation should be agreed on in advance and made part of the terms and conditions of the purchase order. Problems such as how to value, and what is an appropriate payment for, partially completed work on a now-canceled purchase order are best settled before the situation arises.

FORWARD BUYING AND COMMODITIES

Forward buying is the commitment of purchases in anticipation of future requirements beyond current lead times. Thus, an organization may buy ahead because of anticipated shortages, strikes, or price increases. As the time between procurement commitment and actual use of the requirement grows, uncertainties also increase. One common uncertainty is whether the actual need will be realized. A second concern is with price. How can the purchaser ascertain that the price currently committed is reasonable compared to the actual price that would have been paid had the forward buy not been made?

Commodities represent a special class of purchases frequently associated with forward buying. Almost all organizations purchase commodities in a variety of processed forms. For example, an electrical equipment manufacturer may buy a substantial amount of wire, the cost of which is significantly affected by the price of copper. Many organizations buy commodities for further processing or for resale. For them, the way they buy and the prices they pay for commodities may be the single most important factor in success. Prices for selected commodities are reported daily in *The Wall Street Journal* and many other sources, in hard copy or on the Internet.

Forward Buying versus Speculation

All forward buying involves some risk. In forward buying, purchases are confined to actually known requirements or to carefully estimated requirements for a limited period of time in advance. The essential controlling factor is need. Even when the organization uses order points and order quantities, the amount to be bought may be increased or decreased in accordance both with probable use and with the price trend, rather than automatically reordering a given amount. Temporarily, no order may be placed at all.

This may be true even where purchases have to be made many months in advance, as in the case of seasonal products, such as wheat, or those that must be obtained abroad, such as cocoa or coffee. Obviously, the price risk increases as the lead time grows longer, but the basic reasons for these forward commitments are assurance of supply to meet requirements and price.

Speculation seeks to take advantage of price movements. At times of rising prices, commitments for quantities beyond anticipated needs would be called speculation. At times of falling prices, speculation would consist of withholding purchases or reducing quantities purchased below the safety limits, and risking stockouts as well as rush orders at high prices, if the anticipated price decline did not materialize.

At best, any speculation, in the accepted meaning of the term, is a risky business, but speculation with other people's money has been cataloged as a crime. It is supply's responsibility to provide for the known needs to the best advantage possible at the time, and to keep the investment in unused materials at the lowest point consistent with safety of operation. Purchasers can buy forward, but should not speculate or gamble.

Organizing for Forward Buying

The organization for determination and execution of policy with regard to long-term commitments on commodities whose prices fluctuate varies widely depending on the organization's size, financial strength, and the percentage of total cost represented by those volatile commodities. Risk management is a key issue in commodity acquisition. In some instances, the CEO exercises complete control, based almost wholly on personal judgment. In other cases, although the CEO assumes direct responsibility, a committee provides assistance.

Some organizations designate a person other than the supply manager, whose sole responsibility is over price-sensitive materials and who reports directly to top management. In a large number of firms, the supply manager controls the inventory of such commodities. In a few companies, almost complete reliance for policy execution is placed in the hands of an outside agency that specializes in speculative commodities.

The soundest practice for most organizations would appear to be to place responsibility for policy in the hands of a committee consisting of the top executive or general manager, an economist, a risk manager, and the supply manager. Actual execution of the broad policy as laid down should rest with the supply department.

Control of Forward Buying

Safeguards should be set up to ensure that commodity commitments will be kept within proper bounds. The following checks set up by one leather company are given merely as an illustration: (1) Forward buying must be confined to those hides that are used in the production either of several different leathers or of the leathers for which there is a stable demand. (2) Daily conferences are held among the president, treasurer, sales manager, and hide buyer. (3) Orders for future delivery of leather are varied in some measure in accordance with the company's need for protection on hide holdings. Because the leather buyer is willing to place orders for future delivery of leather when prices are satisfactory, this company follows the practice of using unfilled orders as a partial hedge of its hide holdings. In general, the policy is to have approximately 50 percent of the total hides the company owns covered by sales contracts for future production of leather. (4) A further check is provided by an operating budget that controls the physical volume of hides rather than the financial expenditures, and that is brought up for reconsideration whenever it is felt necessary. (5) There is a final check that consists of the use of adequate and reliable information, statistical and otherwise, as a basis for judging price and market trends.

This particular company does not follow the practice of hedging on an organized commodity exchange as a means of avoiding undue risk, though many companies do. Nor does this company use any of the special accounting procedures, such as last-in, first-out or reproduction-cost-of-sales, in connection with its forward purchases.

These various control devices, regarded as a unit rather than as unrelated checks, should prove effective. They are obviously not foolproof, nor do they ensure absolutely against the dangers inherent in buying well in advance. However, flexibility in the administration of any policy is essential, and, for this one company at least, the procedure outlined combines reasonable protection with such flexibility.

In organizations requiring large quantities of commodities whose prices fluctuate widely, the risks involved in buying ahead, under some circumstances, may be substantially minimized through the use of the commodity exchanges.

The Commodity Exchanges

The prime function of an organized commodity exchange is to furnish an established marketplace where the forces of supply and demand may operate freely as buyers and sellers carry on their trading. An exchange that has facilities for both cash and futures trading also can be used for hedging operations. The rules governing the operation of an exchange are concerned primarily with procedures for the orderly handling of the transactions negotiated on the exchange, providing, among other things, terms and time of payment, time of delivery, grades of products traded, and methods of settling disputes.

In general, the purposes of a commodity exchange will be served best if the following conditions are present:

1. The products traded are capable of reasonably accurate grading.
2. There are a large enough number of sellers and buyers and a large enough volume of business so that no one buyer or seller can significantly influence the market.

In order for a commodity exchange to be useful for hedging operations, the following conditions also should be present:

1. Trading in "futures"—the buying or selling of the commodity for delivery at a specified future date.
2. A fairly close correlation between "basis" and other grades.
3. A reasonable but not necessarily consistent correlation between "spot" and "future" prices.

All of these conditions usually are present on the major grain and cotton exchanges, and in varying degrees on the minor exchanges, such as those on which hides, silk, metals, rubber, coffee, and sugar are traded. Financial futures also permit a firm to hedge against interest rate fluctuations, which are one of the strongest factors affecting exchange rate fluctuations.

One of the most easily accessed sources of information about futures and options prices is the commodities section carried Monday through Friday in *The Wall Street Journal.* It reports prices from the major exchanges, from the United States and Canada (e.g., Chicago Board of Trade and Winnipeg Commodity Exchange) and international (e.g., London International Financial Futures Exchange and Sydney Futures Exchange). Each of the major commodity trading exchanges has a Web site that provides real-time information for quotes, charts and historical data, and news.

The commodities traded on the exchanges vary; if the volume is not large enough, a given commodity will drop off the exchange either temporarily or permanently. However, the following agricultural items, metals, petroleum products, and currencies normally are among those listed on any given day: corn, oats, soybeans, soybean oil, wheat, canola, cattle, hogs, pork bellies, cocoa, coffee, sugar, cotton, orange juice, copper, gold, platinum, silver, crude oil, heating oil, gasoline, natural gas, Japanese yen, Euro, Canadian dollar, British pound, Swiss franc, Australian dollar, and Mexican peso.

In most cases, the prices quoted on the exchanges and the record of transactions completed furnish some clue, at least, to the current market price and to the extent of the trading in those commodities. They offer an opportunity, some to a greater extent than others, of protecting the buyer against basic price risks through hedging.

Limitations of the Exchanges

There are limitations to these exchanges as a source of physical supply for the buyer. In spite of a reasonable attempt to define the market grades, the grading often is not sufficiently accurate for manufacturing purposes. The cotton requirements of a textile manufacturer are likely to be so exacting that even the comparatively narrow limits of any specific exchange grade are too broad. Moreover, the rules of the exchange are such that the actual deliveries of cotton do not have to be of a specific grade but may be of any grade above or below basic cotton, provided, of course, that the essential financial adjustment is made. This also holds true for wheat. Millers who sell patented, blended flours must have specific types and grades of wheat, which normally are purchased by use of a sample.

There are other reasons why these exchanges are not satisfactory for the buyer endeavoring to meet actual physical commodity requirements. On some of the exchanges, no spot market exists. On others there is a lack of confidence in the validity of the prices quoted. Crude rubber, for example, is purchased primarily by tire manufacturers, a small group of very large buyers. On the hide exchange, on the other hand, a majority of hides sold are byproducts of the packing industry, offered by a limited number of sellers. An increase or a decrease in the price of hides, however, does not have the same effect on supply that such changes might have on some other commodities.

It is not asserted that these sellers use their position to manipulate the market artificially any more than it is asserted that the buyers of rubber manipulate the market to their advantage. In these two cases, however, the prices quoted might not properly reflect supply and demand conditions.

Hedging

The advantage of the commodity exchanges to a manufacturer is that they provide an opportunity to offset transactions, and thus to protect, to some extent, against price and exchange risks. This commonly is done by *hedging.*

A hedging contract involves a simultaneous purchase and sale in two different markets, which are assumed to operate so that a loss in one will be offset by an equal gain in the other. Normally this is done by a purchase and sale of the same amount of the same commodity simultaneously in the spot and futures markets.

Hedging can occur only when trading in futures is possible. A simple example of hedging to illustrate the above statement follows:

In the Cash Market	In the Futures Market
On September 1:	
Processor buys 5,000 bushels of wheat shipped from country elevator at \$4.00 per bushel (delivered Chicago)	Processor sells 5,000 bushels of December wheat futures at \$4.10 per bushel
On October 20:	
Processor sells Flour based on wheat equivalent of 5,000 bushels priced at \$3.85 per bushel (delivered at Chicago)	Processor buys 5,000 bushels of December wheat futures at \$3.95 per bushel
Loss of 15¢ per bushel	Gain of 15¢ per bushel

In the foregoing example, it is assumed that the cash or spot price and the futures price maintained a direct correlation, but this is not always the case. Thus, there may be some gain or loss from a hedging operation when the spread between the spot price and the futures price does not remain constant. *Hedging can be looked on as a form of insurance, and, like insurance, it is seldom possible to obtain 100 percent protection against all loss, except at prohibitive costs.* As the time between the spot and future declines, the premium or discount on the future declines toward zero (which it reaches when spot = future). On seasonal commodities, this decline in price differential usually begins six to eight months in advance. Under certain circumstances, this phenomenon can make "risk-free" speculation possible. For example, when the speculator has access to a large amount of money, at least three times the value of the contract, and when a six- to eight-month future premium exceeds the sum of contract carrying cost and inventory and commission cost, the "speculator" can buy spot and short the future with a precalculated profit. Volume on the exchange should be heavy for this kind of operation.

While there are other variations of the techniques used in hedging, the one simple example is sufficient for the present discussion of forward and speculative buying.

Successful hedging on an exchange requires skill, experience, and capital resources. This suggests certain limitations imposed on small organizations. It also explains why organizations using large amounts of a certain commodity often own memberships on the exchange that deals in that commodity. A representative of the firm may then be constantly on the watch for advantageous opportunities for placing, withdrawing, or switching hedges between months and can translate this judgment into action immediately. To be successful, the actual procedure of hedging calls for the close observation of accumulating stocks of the commodity, the consequent widening or narrowing of the spreads between prices quoted on futures contracts, and the resulting opportunities for advance opening and closing of trades. These factors are constantly shifting on the exchanges. The skill of the hedger is reflected in the ability to recognize and grasp these momentary opportunities.

Hedging may not always be helpful or advantageous to the purchaser. One obstacle to a wider use of the exchanges is the lack of understanding by potential users as to when and how to use them. Another limitation is the vacuum effect when one of the relatively few large commodity brokers goes bankrupt, pulling some clients along.

Moreover, most brokers have not shown extensive interest in the industrial market. Most brokers probably will admit that they can barely afford to service a straight hedger because they may have to send out six monthly position statements and four or more margin calls for a single round turn commission, while their faithful "traders" will often maintain a substantial cash account and net them several round turn commissions per month with a minimum of bookkeeping.

Furthermore, many managers still view futures trading with suspicion and tend to blame past mistakes on the system rather than managerial errors of judgment. The large variations in commodity prices in recent years may well have sensitized a number of managers to the opportunities in futures trading, where before there seemed little need to be involved.

Sources of Information Regarding Price Trends

On what is the buyer's judgment as to price trends based? Roughly speaking, there are five general sources of information, all subject to marked limitations with respect to their value and dependability. Most of the organizations listed below have online services that permit access to data on a real-time basis.

One source of information consists of the services of specialized forecasting agencies, such as Moody's Investors Service. A second source is the commodity exchanges, which typically provide historical information about prices and volumes. Most exchanges also provide access to reports by government agencies and some analysts.

The third source includes a wide variety of governmental and other published data, such as the *Federal Reserve Bulletin,* the *Survey of Current Business, BusinessWeek, Barron's,* and *The Wall Street Journal.* Trade magazines also are helpful in particular industries and are typified by such publications as *Iron Age* and *Chemical Market Reporter.* Probably the most-watched indicator of industrial purchase prices is the producer price index (PPI) compiled and released monthly by the Bureau of Labor Statistics. It previously was called the wholesale price index (WPI). The PPI is a family of indexes that measure the average change over time in selling prices received by U.S. domestic producers of goods and services. It measures price changes from the perspective of the seller and is available in three types of classification: industry-based, commodity-based, and stage-of-processing-based. A companion measure, also produced monthly by the Bureau of Labor Statistics, is the consumer price index (CPI). The CPI is based on the prices from the perspective of the end purchaser.

The fourth source comprises the highly unscientific—but nevertheless valuable, if properly weighted—information derived from sales representatives, other buyers, and others with whom the buyer comes in daily contact.

The fifth source of information is the purchasing manager indexes for the United States and Canada. Each month, ISM releases the Manufacturing *Report on Business* (ROB) and the nonmanufacturing ROB. In Canada, the Ivey Purchasing Managers Index is also released monthly. Both of these reports provide a useful service by presenting a composite reading by supply managers across the United States or Canada in a number of areas, such as prices, inventory levels, lead times, new orders, production, and employment.

Conclusion

Price determination can be a tricky issue. The method of price determination should be influenced by what is being bought and the characteristics of the supply market at that particular point in time. Knowing how to set prices, establishing appropriate strategies for price adjustments, and managing supply price risk are important skills for supply managers. Buyers that rely on competitive bidding and one-year contracts for every purchase will miss opportunities for achieving lower total costs.

Two topics closely related to price determination are cost analysis and discounts and negotiation, which are covered in the next chapter.

Questions for Review and Discussion

1. What is the significance of the Sherman Antitrust and the Robinson-Patman acts to the industrial buyer?
2. What advantages does the competitive bid process have as a method of price determination?
3. How is supplier cost related to supplier price?
4. What are the various ways by which prices are determined?
5. What methods can the buyer use to establish price for (*a*) sensitive commodities, (*b*) special items, (*c*) standard production items, and (*d*) items of small value?
6. Distinguish between direct and indirect costs. How can the buyer analyze these costs?
7. What can the buyer do if he or she suspects collusion on the part of suppliers?
8. Why might a buyer wish to hedge a commodity purchase? How would the buyer do that?
9. Does hedging remove all risk?
10. What is the difference between forward buying and speculation?

References

Dubois, A., and A. C. Pedersen. "Why Relationships Do No Fit into Purchasing Portfolio Models—A Comparison between the Portfolio and Industrial Network Approaches." *European Journal of Purchasing & Supply Management* 8, no. 1 2002, pp. 35–42.

Gelderman, C. J., and A. J. van Weele. "Strategic Direction through Purchasing Portfolio Management: A Case Study." *Journal of Supply Chain Management* 28, no. 2 2002, pp. 30–38.

Handfield, R. B., and S. L. Straight. "What Sourcing Channel Is Right for You?" *Supply Chain Management Review* 7, no. 4 2003, pp. 62–70.

Mabert, V. A., and T. Schoenherr. "An Online RFQ System: A Case Study." *Practix* 4. Tempe, AZ: CAPS Research, March 2001, pp. 1–6.

Schlosser, M. A., and G. A. Zsidisin. "Hedging Fuel Surcharge Price Fluctuations." *Practix* 7. Tempe, AZ: CAPS Research, May 2004, pp. 1–5.

Zsidisin, G. A., and L. M. Ellram. "An Agency Theory Investigation of Supply Risk Management." *Journal of Supply Chain Management* 39, no. 3 2003, pp. 15–29.

Case 8–1

MasTech Inc.

Robert Fisk, purchasing manager for MasTech Inc. of Detroit, Michigan, was preparing for a meeting the following day with the plant general manager, Andrew Ross. MasTech, a Tier 1 supplier for the auto industry, was under tremendous cost pressures from its customers, and Robert had to recommend whether the company should change its steel supplier for an important product.

COMPANY BACKGROUND

MasTech Inc. was a division of Omron Corporation, a large North American automotive parts manufacturer with annual sales of $10 billion. Omron's customers included General Motors, Ford, and DaimlerChrysler as well as several Japanese and European automakers. It employed 50,000 people, working in 170 plants throughout North America, Europe, and Asia. Omron used a decentralized philosophy, and each plant was evaluated as a profit center.

MasTech supplied a variety of stamped-metal components to automotive assembly plants in Michigan, and its annual sales were $280 million. Each plant had its own purchasing department responsible for all direct and indirect materials purchases.

Robert Fisk had been the purchasing manager for MasTech for the last 10 years. Working under Robert's direct supervision was a senior materials buyer, a materials buyer, and an expeditor. Robert paid personal attention to steel contracts because steel accounted for approximately 60 percent of total costs.

THE FORD CROSS-MEMBER CONTRACT

Suppliers in the automotive industry provided engineering and technical support to their customers during product development. Once in production, suppliers were expected to provide defect-free products with JIT delivery. Furthermore, the automakers specified annual cost reductions that typically ranged from 3 to 5 percent.

Four years previously, MasTech had won the bid to produce a cross-member part for the frame of a new Ford truck model that went into production two years later. The contract specified annual cost reductions of 3 percent over the life of the contract.

The cross-member required a total of 130,000 tons of steel annually, which was purchased from a major mill, Uxbridge Steel (Uxbridge). MasTech, which used Uxbridge as a supplier for several components, negotiated a price of $30 per hundredweight, FOB MasTech.[1] As was standard practice in the industry, Uxbridge used Vaughan Steel Processing (Vaughan) to do all its secondary processing: pickling, slitting, and edge trimming. The steel was shipped to MasTech directly after processing at Vaughan.

MasTech's steel suppliers were required to make deliveries according to a fixed schedule, sometimes as frequently as every 4 to 8 hours. If deliveries were not made according to the schedule, MasTech could face machine down-time and risk delaying shipments to customers. Robert estimated that it cost MasTech $1,500/hour per line to be idle, while costs of idling a car assembly plant were about $300,000 per hour.

SUPPLY PROBLEMS

Robert Fisk was concerned about Vaughan's delivery performance. Since production started on the cross-member, Vaughan had been able to supply only 75 percent of MasTech's requirements and Robert had been forced to turn to alternate sourcing, incurring a 10 percent price premium. Robert commented, "Vaughan won't carry the inventory I think they should, and as a result they miss a lot of our deliveries."

Demand for steel had been strong the past two years, but indications were that the market was beginning to weaken. Consequently, Robert asked Colgon Steel to quote on MasTech's cross-member requirements. Colgon had not been profitable in recent years and was anxious to secure additional volume. Robert received a quote of $24.75 per hundredweight for unprocessed steel, FOB Ashgrove Steel Processing (Ashgrove).

Ashgrove indicated that it would charge MasTech $4.75 per hundredweight for processing and delivery. Although MasTech had never used Ashgrove for its steel processing requirements, the company did have a good reputation. Ashgrove was a relatively small processor, but

[1] hundredweight = price per 100 pounds

the president indicated that they would add another line just for MasTech's business.

ALTERNATIVES AVAILABLE TO ROBERT

Robert indicated to Uxbridge that he was market testing the steel for the Ford cross-member and asked his supplier to revisit their pricing. As a result, Uxbridge agreed to drop the price of the finished product to $29.75 per hundredweight and offered to sell unprocessed steel at $24.75 per hundredweight FOB Ashgrove.

Andrew Ross was expecting a large part of the contractual 3 percent price reduction to come from a reduction in steel costs. In advance of his meeting with Andrew, Robert needed to decide what action he should take and to identify the savings he expected would accrue to MasTech.

Case 8–2

Chevron Corporation: *The PC Selection Team*

Jean Wolcott, alliance manager, Chevron Information Technology Company, was preparing for the second meeting of the Desktop Life Cycle Management Team, scheduled for Friday, April 25, at the San Ramon, California, office complex. It had been decided during the first team meeting, held the previous day, that the Chevron Supplier Quality Improvement Process (CSQIP) framework should be followed to select a supplier for desktop computers. The meeting on Friday would focus on assessing factors that might influence the total costs of operating desktop computers at Chevron Corporation. It was now April 23, and Jean wanted to make her own assessment of total cost factors in advance of the session two days hence.

CHEVRON CORPORATION

Chevron Corporation was a publicly held, worldwide petroleum and chemical company headquartered in San Francisco, California. One of the world's largest integrated petroleum companies, Chevron operated in more than 90 countries and employed approximately 34,000 people.

Ken Derr, chairman and CEO of Chevron, strongly believed that decentralization and empowerment should be the philosophical base for a major reorganization at Chevron. Thus, four major operating companies (OpCos) were identified: a U.S. upstream company called Chevron Production Company (CPDN); a U.S. downstream company called Chevron Products Company (CPDS); all of Chevron's non–North American upstream activities, organized under Chevron Overseas Petroleum Inc. (COPI); and Chevron Chemicals Company (CCC), which remained essentially unchanged. Each OpCo was expected to operate within Chevron's framework of corporate values, policies, and financial guidelines, but had considerable autonomy for the development and execution of business plans that had to be approved at the Chevron corporate level.

Chevron Information Technology Company (CITC), headquartered in Chevron Park, San Ramon, California, provided information technology support to Chevron locations worldwide. As part of a previous corporate reorganization, some IT responsibilities, such as control over network architecture, hardware, and software, had been distributed to the OpCos. Consequently, each OpCo had its own information technology group, which meant that CITC's involvement with individual business units varied substantially. Furthermore, a common standard for information technology did not exist within the company currently. Dave Clementz, president of CITC, described the situation:

> Chevron found itself with a conglomeration of hundreds of different personal computers and software programs. The variety of configurations, life cycles, and service contracts posed serious usage and maintenance issues for the company. Our network was not providing us the service capabilities that we needed and was becoming increasingly expensive to maintain. For example, because we did not have a standard software program, even simple activities, such as opening documents, could be a problem.
>
> Last year, a consensus began to develop that we needed to assess our distributed IT philosophy. As a result, we formed a broad-based group from the various business units to examine Chevron's IT strategy. It became known as the "Vision Study." One of its important recommendations was the creation of a universal, high-performance computer network worldwide. Our Global Information Link Project, which we called the "GIL" Project, was our means of accomplishing this objective.

THE GIL PROJECT

The GIL Project started in March. Its main objective was to establish a flexible and reliable IT infrastructure by standardizing all aspects of the network and computing environment at Chevron Corporation worldwide. GIL would connect more than 30,000 desks across more than 700 worksites in more than 90 countries. Ed Miller was named GIL project manager, responsible for coordinating the project teams set up to make recommendations concerning each of the major areas of Chevron's IT infrastructure, such as operating systems, servers, software, telecommunications, and desktop systems. Ed would also be responsible for overseeing GIL implementation.

Tom Bell was the team leader responsible for recommending the desktop computer system that Chevron would adopt as part of the GIL Project. The members of the Desktop Life Cycle Management Team were Marjorie Ferrer and Pete Sandoval, from Chevron Production Company; Mike Jochimson and Joe Panto, from CITC; Faith Bovard, from finance; Shelli Peacock, from Chevron Petroleum Technology; and Jean Wolcott, from purchasing.

The Desktop Life Cycle Management Team was a critical component of the GIL Project, as described by Tom Bell:

> Our team's involvement was considered critical to the GIL Project on two dimensions. First, the desktop standard impacted several of the other GIL activities. The other GIL teams needed to know which hardware standard had been approved before they could complete their assignments. You might say that we were on the critical path.
>
> The second aspect was financial. It was expected that the IT investments associated with the GIL Project would represent an initial investment of approximately $150 million. We anticipated that the desktop hardware portion would make up about $90 million. Spending this kind of money meant that we would need approval from the Board of Directors.

Tom Bell made the following observations regarding the involvement of Ed Miller:

> Ed was the ideal selection for the position of GIL project manager. He had a high energy level and was focused on the project objectives, but Ed also had an ability to use his relaxed style to keep things in perspective for those around him. Ed also insisted on empowering the team leaders. He was involved in key decisions but relied heavily on the judgment of the project teams.

THE CHEVRON PRODUCTION COMPANY IT STANDARD

Chevron Production Company (CPDN) was responsible for Chevron's North American upstream operations, consisting of exploration and production facilities. CPDN conducted a study two years ago that resulted in the establishment of a desktop standard with a personal computer (PC) and laptop from Global Technology Company (GTC). Last year, CPDN replaced all of its desktop machines and leased approximately 20 million worth of GTC equipment. Tom Bell commented on the CPDN experience:

> Management at CPDN recognized the benefits of standardization early. They went through a detailed study and settled on a laptop and a PC from Global Technology Company. Tricon Inc. was selected as the reseller, responsible for delivering the equipment, installation, asset disposal, and warranty service. The selection of GTC did not come as a surprise. They are one of the world's largest computer technology companies with total revenues of about $60 billion, and Tricon is one of their largest distributors and a global technology services company. We wanted to leverage the experience of CPDN regarding desktop systems and made sure they were involved on our team.

OUTCOME OF THE FIRST TEAM MEETING

The Chevron Desktop Life Cycle Management Team held its first meeting on April 22. During that meeting Tom Bell reviewed the team objectives and schedule.

The team's first objective was to evaluate appropriate desktop supply alternatives and make a recommendation concerning appropriate cost-effective desktop standards for both PCs and laptops. This recommendation would include the selection of a supplier or suppliers for desktop systems. Chevron currently had approximately 25,000 PCs and 5,000 laptops in use in its worldwide operations. Four manufacturers supplied approximately 90 percent of the computers currently in use at Chevron: GTC, Saba Computer Company, Vytec Inc., and Cassin Technologies. Saba was a global manufacturer and developer of computer equipment and systems, networking products, printers, scanners, and support and maintenance services. Its head office was located in San Diego, California, [illegible] the company had annual revenues of $40 billion. [illegible] with its head office in San Antonio, Texas, was a low-cost manufacturer of computer hardware and had annual revenues of approximately $25 billion. Cassin, with annual revenues of $10 billion, sold all of its computers directly to end consumers, bypassing the industry's traditional distribution network. Cassin's head office was in Houston, Texas.

The second team objective dealt with timing of the project. It was important that the team complete its assignment before June 20. Any delays beyond this date would affect other GIL project teams.

Jean Wolcott was asked to lead the next meeting scheduled for April 25, when the entire team would use CSQIP to evaluate its supply options.

CSQIP

The basic premise behind CSQIP was that Chevron would gain competitive advantage by forming mutually beneficial alliances with world-class suppliers, characterized by shared business objectives, strategies to accomplish those objectives, a system of metrics for measuring progress, and ongoing teamwork and communication between customer and supplier. CSQIP supplier alliances were reserved for goods and services that offered the greatest potential for cost savings, typically high-expenditure, high-complexity materials and services. It could be applied to either an existing supply relationship or to a new purchase decision. CSQIP had been successfully applied to a number of products and services, such as line pipe, control valves, trucking, lubricants, copiers, and underwater services. The Alliance Improvement Teams had produced average savings of 8 to 10 percent, and as much as 25 percent of the contract value in the services arena. Currently, Chevron was expected to spend $2.6 billion under its alliance program.

Total cost of ownership was a primary driver of the CSQIP process, based on the belief that poor quality increased costs. Consequently, while price was recognized as important, it was regarded as only one element of the supply relationship. Under the CSQIP process, total cost of ownership was described as all direct and indirect costs incurred over the life of a material or service, such as engineering, inventory, installation and testing, operations and maintenance, and retirement or disposal.

Chevron had a number of alliance managers trained in the CSQIP procedure. These individuals provided direct assistance, CSQIP training, and expertise within departments or OpCos.

THE CSQIP STEPS

CSQIP involved a number of steps, which could be divided into two phases: supplier selection and process improvement. Each step in the process involved specific activities. See Exhibit 1 for an outline of the CSQIP steps and Exhibit 2 for main issues addressed during the supplier selection phase.

EXHIBIT 1 **CSQIP Steps**

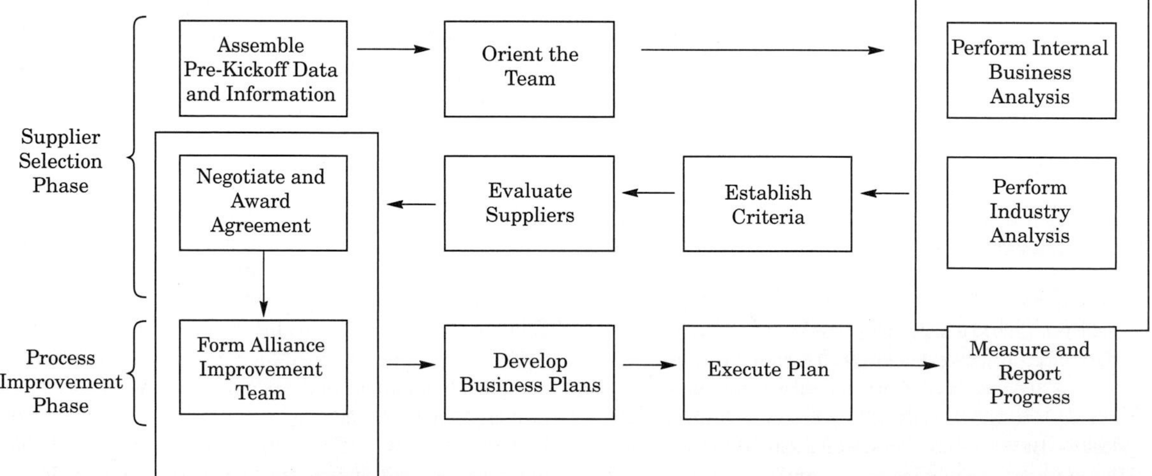

EXHIBIT 2 **CSQIP Process Activities**

Assemble Pre-Kickoff Data and Information and Orient the Team	
Assemble data	• Collect information relating to the anticipated purchase, such as existing volumes, suppliers, outstanding contracts
Orient the team	• Define project scope and team authority • Establish what the project has been designed to accomplish and why it is important • Establish project objectives, including costs and financial benefits • Determine project timing and schedule
Perform Internal Business Analysis	
Develop initial supplier selection criteria	• Brainstorming exercise to develop initial list of criteria for supplier selection
Evaluate total cost of ownership drivers	• Collect data from internal and external sources that provide information regarding total cost of ownership • Brainstorming exercise to explore total cost factors • Refine supplier selection criteria
Perform Industry Analysis	
Evaluate industry structure	• Evaluate structure of the supply chain in the industry, including manufacturers, wholesalers, and distributors • Determine which companies are leaders within their industry segments • Develop an initial supplier list
Establish Criteria	
Establish supplier evaluation criteria	• Finalize criteria to be used in the evaluation of potential suppliers
Evaluate Suppliers	
Create questionnaire and assign points	• Develop detailed questionnaire to be completed by potential suppliers • Assign weights to each question
Develop supplier list	• Finalize supplier list based on industry assessment and supplier evaluation criteria
Evaluate responses	• "Score" supplier responses and rank suppliers
Create shortlist of suppliers	• Create shortlist of suppliers for on-site visits
Prepare for on-site visits	• Identify new questions or requirements for clarification of information • Prepare agenda for meeting(s)

PREPARING FOR THE NEXT TEAM MEETING

Although the team did not have much time to complete its assignment, Jean knew that its recommendations would be scrutinized thoroughly. The review process would involve three stages. First, the team's recommendations would be presented to CITC management for review and approval. An executive group, the Outsourcing Guidance Review Team, responsible for technology policy within Chevron, would also have to review the proposal. This committee included Dave Clementz; Don Paul, vice president technology and environmental affairs; Marty Klitten, CFO; and Ron Kiskis, corporate vice president. Finally, given the size of the expenditure, the team's recommendations had to be formally adopted by the Chevron Board of Directors.

Jean had asked to lead the meeting on April 25, during which time the team would concentrate on the internal business analysis step in the CSQIP framework and create a list of factors that might affect the total cost of ownership of operating desktop computers at Chevron. During this session, each member of the team would be expected to help create a list of factors contributing to the total cost of ownership as part of a brainstorming exercise. Jean and the team would then use this information to help develop criteria for evaluating potential suppliers.

In order to be fully prepared for the meeting herself and because she had never tried to apply the total cost of ownership concept to the acquisition of computers, Jean decided to think through on her own what cost factors might apply to desktop PCs and laptops.

Case 8–3

Commodity Purchasing Game

In this game, you will have the chance to try your skill as a commodity purchaser. You will be using information similar in type to that available to Ms. Martin, the purchasing manager of a well-known chocolate bar corporation.

Because raw material accounts for 50 percent of the cost of producing a chocolate bar, the purchasers in the chocolate bar business have a great deal of responsibility on their shoulders.

Among other functions, Ms. Martin, at the beginning of each month, has to decide how many pounds of cocoa should be purchased during the coming weeks of that month. When doing this, she takes into account the expected need of the production department, the time of the year, the inventory on hand, the cost of short supply, the cost of carrying inventory, and, finally, the commodity market trends, more specifically, cocoa.

You will be able in this game to make similar decisions, although the game will be a simplified version of the actual situation. The most important features of this simplification are, first, it will not be possible for you to buy cocoa after the first day of the month (you are allowed to purchase cocoa only once a month—on the first day); and, second, it will not be possible for you to buy cocoa on the futures market.

COCOA NEED

Company sales, and industry sales in general, are very much influenced by seasonal factors. Because the chocolate has a tendency to melt in the warm months of the year, sales usually slow down during the summer months and rebuild very quickly in the fall when the manufacturers start their promotion again. For the last six years, July has been the slowest month for sales and September the biggest.

Because chocolate bars have a limited shelf life, and because it is company policy to supply freshly made chocolate bars to the retailers, it is company practice not to stockpile finished goods. Actually, chocolate bars sold in one month have to be produced in the same month.

In the last five years, the company's cocoa need has grown almost constantly. Cocoa requirements have increased 200 percent in this five-year period. Last year's cocoa purchases were 4.76 million pounds. An average of the cocoa requirements for the last three years, broken down per month, is shown in Exhibit 1. The curve shown is only the average of the experience of many years. In any given year, the monthly percentage of total need might vary ∓ 3 percentage points from what is given by the curve. For example, January's figure of 10 percent is really the midpoint of a possible low of 7 percent and a possible high of 13 percent.

From past experience, Ms. Martin knows that the production department uses approximately 60 percent of the total yearly cocoa purchases in the last six months of the year. And, moreover, 55 percent of this last six months' need is used in September and October.

Production scheduling is done on a weekly basis. Ms. Martin has no precise idea of what the actual total monthly production need for cocoa will be on the first day of that month, other than from her judgment of need level of prior periods and from consideration of the general shape of the need curve shown in Exhibit 1.

RAW MATERIAL

Cocoa, the basic raw material in chocolate, has an especially volatile price, and there is no way to hedge

EXHIBIT 1
Cocoa Need per Month by the Production Department

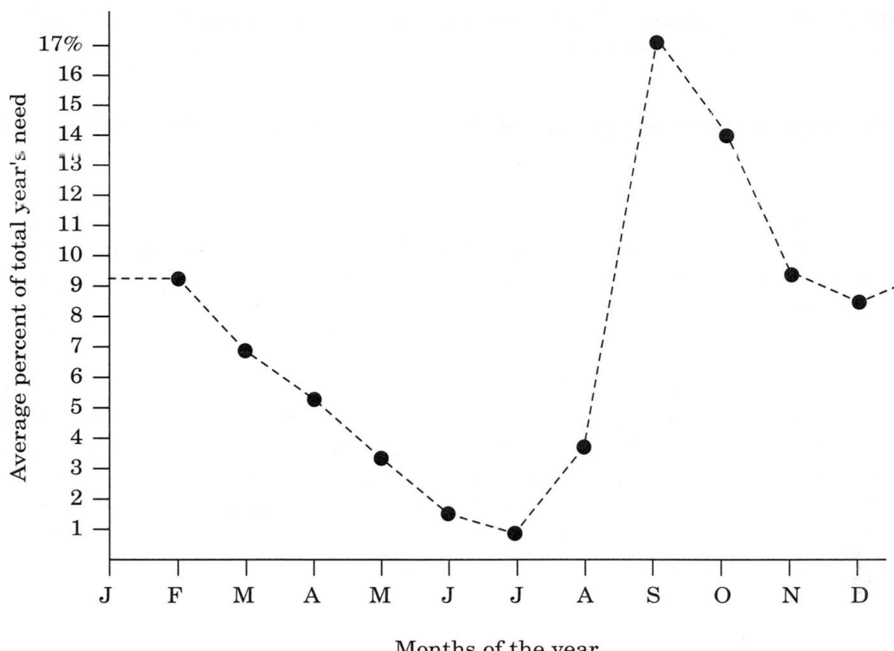

completely against the wide price swings. Chocolate comes from cocoa beans, a crop subject to wide production fluctuations with a stable and generally rising demand. Furthermore, it takes 7 years for new cocoa trees to come into production (15 years to reach full production), and drought and disease can sharply reduce supply in a matter of months or even weeks.

Using the company's expected sales and expenses for the year, Ms. Martin estimates that when she pays 48 cents a pound for cocoa, the contribution per pound purchased is 13 cents, and any increase in the price paid for cocoa has a direct reverse effect on the amount of contribution and vice versa. (If she pays 49 cents per pound, then the contribution would be one cent less, or 12 cents, etc.)

In order to be as efficient as possible in her predictions of future cocoa prices, Ms. Martin keeps informed by means of trade journals; she follows the futures market closely and studies the past performance of cocoa prices.

As of October 1, Ms. Martin has assembled the information given in Exhibits 2, 3 and 4. Company policy does not allow her to carry an inventory of more than 1.2 million pounds of raw cocoa in her monthly ending inventory. The company is short of funds, and the president is not anxious to exceed borrowing limits set by the bank.

COSTS INVOLVED

In deciding on purchasing alternatives, Ms. Martin bears in mind several costs which she knows to be fairly accurate. These costs are inventory costs and stockout costs.

Inventory Costs

Storage cost for one pound of raw material is 0.4 cent per month. This amount takes into account interest on tied-up capital, insurance, deterioration, and direct handling expense. Ms. Martin knows that over the period of a season, inventory carrying charges can reasonably be calculated on the basis of inventory on hand at the end of each month.

Stockout Costs

Ms. Martin also considers stockout costs. A stockout cost occurs whenever the production demand for raw cocoa in a particular month is greater than the available raw cocoa in inventory. For example, if 50,000 pounds of raw cocoa are on hand at the beginning of the month, 50,000 pounds are purchased, and the need during the month totals 110,000 pounds, then a stockout of 10,000 pounds occurs. The company then has to place rush orders for raw cocoa and, consequently, is forced to pay a cent per pound premium.

EXHIBIT 2 Size of Upcoming Crops Hold Key to Cocoa Prices (October 1)

Prices of cocoa beans have risen 8 percent since September 22. The increase follows a roller-coaster ride which took the market from a long-term low in July of last year to a 39-month peak in mid-July of this year, then down again by some 21 percent.

Harvesting of the main crop in Ghana, the world's largest cocoa producer, reportedly has been delayed by adverse weather. In addition, recent rains may have reduced yields in several African-producing areas. Black pod disease reportedly has hit the Brazilian crop, and Russia has told Ghana it wants early deliveries of the 100,000 long tons of cocoa pledged for this season and of cocoa on which Accra defaulted last season. Ghana, in turn, has requested an extension of one month or more for deliveries on sales contracts with the United States and Europe that were originally scheduled for the current quarter.

Future Boost

Renewed buying interest by large manufacturers, coupled with trade and speculative purchases, helped boost cocoa futures. However, the extent to which supplies tighten in the next month or two will depend greatly on the size of invisible stocks and of future government purchases from African growers, who have been given an incentive through purchase price increases by the Cocoa Marketing Boards.

The current New York spot prices of Accra (Ghanaian) cocoa beans, at 24 cents per pound, compares with quotes of 44.50 cents on September 22, 33.50 cents a year ago, and a peak 56.50 cents on July 14 of the current year. During the 10-week price slump, the open interest in New York cocoa futures shrank from a record 38,054 contracts (30,000 pounds each) on August 10 to fewer than 28,700 contracts; it now aggregates 29,500 contracts.

On the New York Cocoa Exchange, the December future currently is selling at around 45.04 cents, up from 40.44 cents on December 22. The March option is quoted at around 46.22 cents, against 41.84 cents on September 22. The May future is selling at 47.08 cents. The distant December option is at 49.44 cents.

British Bean Experts

According to London's Gill and Duffus, Ltd., unfavorable weather held this year's world cocoa bean crop to 1,214,000 long tons, 20 percent below a year earlier. In the face of this dip, relatively attractive prices and rising incomes are expected to push the current year's world cocoa bean grindings (not to be confused with actual consumption) to a record 1,414,000 long tons. This is 83,000 long tons (6.2 percent) above that of last year.

Allowing 1 percent for loss in weight, output seems to be lagging anticipated grindings by a record 212,000 long tons. This being the case, the October 1 world carryover of cocoa beans, which is estimated at around 366,000 long tons, is barely a three-month supply. Nine years ago, a similar drop to a three-month supply saw prices average 68 cents, far above the current market.

On the eve of the coming season, the trade lacks accurate information on the size of the major new African crops. During recent months, African governments have sold ahead a large portion of the prospective new main crop at prices well above those of a year ago. Ghana's advance sales are placed above 275,000 long tons, some 100,000 more than last year, at prices ranging between 46 cents and 52 cents a pound.

Prior to the recent reports of adverse weather, the trade generally estimated the coming season's world cocoa output at around 1,300,000 long tons, some 60,000 to 86,000 tons above last season. This includes this year's prospective main and mid crops in Ghana of between 435,000 and 475,000 long tons versus 410,000 tons last year, and a record 572,000 long tons two years ago. Guess estimates for Nigeria range between 200,000 and 210,000 tons, against 182,000 last season, and a record 294,000 tons two years ago, but may fail to account fully for losses due to the country's tribal unrest. Output from the Ivory Coast is tentatively forecast at between 120,000 and 150,000 tons, up from 112,000 tons last season, and close to its record of 145,000 tons.

Bad weather and pod rot, a fungus that causes seed to rot, have caused the experts to drop their estimates on the Brazilian crop to 130,000 or 135,000 long tons, down from 158,000 tons of last season. Recent reports indicate that the crops in other Latin American countries also will lag last season's levels, which may drop next season's yields for our Southern neighbors some 60,000 to 75,000 tons below the 283,000 tons of last year. Adding everything together, the coming season's cocoa bean harvest is likely to range between 1,250,000 and 1,350,000 long tons, which would be a good deal smaller than the current year's anticipated world cocoa bean grindings.

How closely output matches next year's consumption is the key to the cocoa market. Bulls on cocoa believe that prices have not been high enough to discourage the steady rise in usage. They attribute the July to September slump mainly to forecasts of increased crops, tight money, and the large open interest which invited volatile prices.

EXHIBIT 3 **Cocoa Spot Price and Cocoa Futures Market (October 1)**

	Futures Market
December	45.04
March	46.22
May	47.08
July	47.84
September	48.62
December (next year)	49.44

Spot Price: 48.0 cents per pound.

EXHIBIT 4 **Past Performance of Cocoa on the Commodity Market**

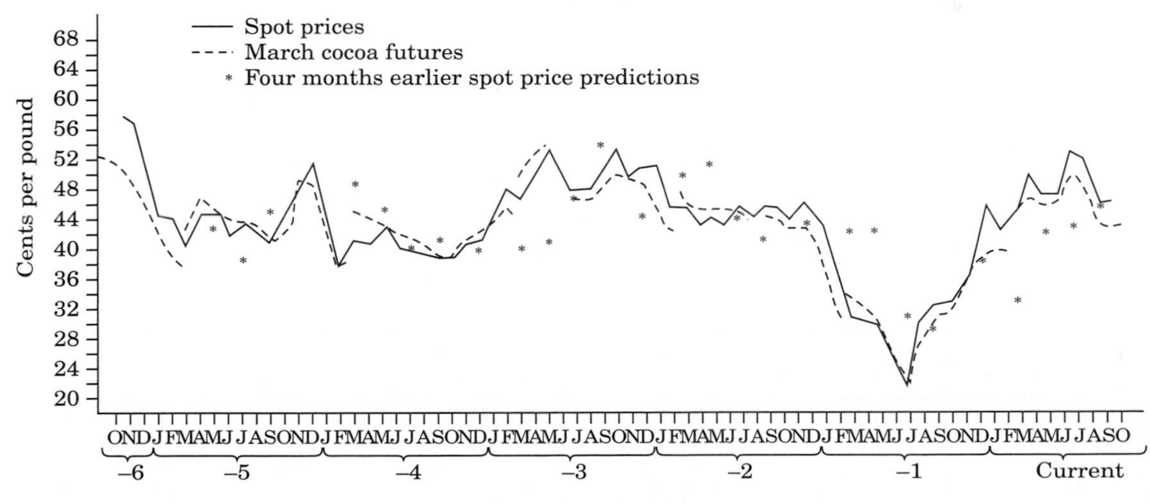

Ms. Martin's Commission

The president of the company was convinced that incentives for executives were important. Therefore, part of Ms. Martin's salary was based on her performance as a cocoa purchaser. She receives a 5 percent commission on the monthly net contribution to profits.

Net monthly contribution = Monthly contribution − Monthly stockout costs (or monthly inventory carrying costs)

CLOSING INVENTORY TARGET

At the end of the game, each group is expected to have a closing inventory of 200,000 pounds of raw cocoa. Every group who fails to reach this 200,000 pound target will be penalized in the following way.

1. For every pound in excess of the aforementioned target:

   As in every other month, the company will have to pay an inventory carrying cost, and, moreover, there will be an extra charge of 6.0 cents per pound over the 200,000 pound target.

2. For every pound short in relation to the aforementioned target:

   The company will have to pay 6 cents per pound and will have to buy sufficient cocoa at the September 1 spot price to bring the inventory level to 200,000 pounds.

HOW TO PLAY THE GAME

In the actual conduct of this game, teams will be used to make the purchasing decisions normally made by Ms. Martin. On the first day of each month, each team will decide on the quantity of cocoa to be purchased. This decision will be made by the team by whatever means it chooses. Thus, a prediction from a plot of past month's performance might be used by some teams, a pure guess by others. In making the decision, teams will want to consider both the possibilities of future needs and the inventories now on hand as well as their forecast of cocoa spot price behavior.

After each team has made its purchasing decision for the coming month, the instructor will announce the next month's price and actual consumption during the past month. Given this information, teams can calculate, using Exhibit 5, all of the necessary costs and, finally, the "net commission of the purchaser." They can then decide how much cocoa, if any, to purchase for the next month.

The object of the game is to increase as much as possible the purchaser's cumulative commission over 12 months. This means that teams will have to decide whether it

EXHIBIT 5 **Result Form**

	Stock on hand at start of month in lbs. = ending inventory of previous month	Purchases in lbs.	Total available for production in lbs. (3 = 1 + 2)	Production requirements in lbs.	Ending inventory in lbs. (5 = 3 − 4) Cannot be less than 0 or greater than 1,200,000 lbs. Penalty for any excess of $2,000 in commission plus excess contribution.	Stockout in lbs. (6 = 4 − 3 if greater than 0)	Stockout costs (7 = 6 × $.06)	Inventory carrying costs (8 = 5 × $.004)	Contribution per lb. purchased	Total monthly contribution (10 = 2 × 9)	Total monthly costs (11 = 7 + 8)	Net monthly contribution (12 = 10 − 11) (can be negative)	Monthly commission on contribution (13 = 5% × 12) (can be negative)	Cumulative commission (14 = 13 + 14) previous month	
	1	2	3	4	5	6	7	8	9	10	11	12	13	14	
August	50M	350M	400M	450M	0	50M	$3,000	0	7.0¢	$24,500	$3,000	$21,500	$1,075	($1,075)	
September	0	1,100M	1,100M	900M	200M	0	0	$800	12.8¢	$140,800	$800	$140,000	$7,000	($8,075)	← $0
October	200M														
November															
December															
January															
February															
March															
April															
May															
June															
July															
August															
September															

would be cheaper in the long run to incur some inventory or stockout costs, depending on their predictions of the cocoa price behavior on the commodity market. At the end of each month, every team's results will be shown on the screen in front of the class and, at the end of the twelfth month, the class will discuss each team's method of predicting sales and cocoa prices. Teams will probably find it advantageous to split the work of making sales estimates, calculating costs and profit, and estimating the next period cocoa spot price.

Summary of Important Points to Remember When Playing the Game

1. Purchases can be made only on the first day of the month.
2. You cannot buy cocoa on the futures market.
3. It is a company practice to purchase cocoa on the first day of each month.
4. It is not possible to carry an inventory of more than 1.2 million pounds of raw cocoa. Penalty for excess of $2,000 in commission and excess stock will be returned to the vendor with a 6 cent penalty per pound on top of the $2,000 penalty.
5. At a purchase price of 48 cents per pound, the cocoa will bring a contribution of 13 cents. This contribution is directly related to the purchase price. (A 1-cent increase in the cost results in a 1-cent decrease in the contribution, and vice versa.)
6. There is an inventory carrying cost and a stockout cost that are directly deducted from the contribution amount to give the net contribution.
7. There is a closing inventory target of 200,000 pounds.

Result Form Used

To make the keeping of results easier for each team, a form has been distributed (see Exhibit 5). The exact steps in using this form are shown on the form itself.

Example

Each team member should carefully trace the proceedings as outlined in the following example to understand all of the steps involved in playing and recording the game.

Ms. Martin has already used the "Result Form" to record the operating results of the two months prior to October. On August 1, Ms. Martin had to decide how many pounds of cocoa should be purchased. Knowing the spot price on August 1 was 54 cents a pound, she thought, after consulting the trade journals and studying the futures market, that the prices would go down; therefore, she decided to purchase cocoa to supply the need of the current month only. She then consulted the production need curve and came to the conclusion that the need of that month would be approximately 300,000 pounds. Knowing that she had 50,000 pounds of cocoa in inventory, and wanting to keep a safe margin, she purchased 350,000 pounds of cocoa at the price of 54 cents per pound. She then entered the following figures on the "Result Form."

Column (1) = 50,000 pounds (from column (5) previous month)
Column (2) = 350,000 pounds
Column (3) = 400,000 pounds
Column (4) = 450,000 pounds
Column (5) = 0 pounds
Column (6) = 50,000 pounds
Column (7) = $3,000
Column (8) = $0
Column (9) = $0.07
Column (10) = $24,500
Column (11) = $ 3,000
Column (12) = $21,500
Column (13) = $ 1,075
Column (14) = $ 1,075

At the end of the month of August, Ms. Martin received from the production department the exact figure of the month's requirements, 450,000 pounds. Because there were only 400,000 pounds of cocoa in inventory, the company had to make a last-minute order to another supplier of cocoa at a premium of $0.06/lb. With this information, Ms. Martin could now calculate her net commission according to the company's norms. She entered the following figures on the "Result Form."

Column (1) = 0 pounds (from column (5) previous month)
Column (2) = 1,100,000 pounds
Column (3) = 1,100,000 pounds
Column (4) = 900,000 pounds
Column (5) = 2000,000 pounds
Column (6) = 0 pounds
Column (7) = $0
Column (8) = $800
Column (9) = $0.128
Column (10) = $140,800
Column (11) = $800
Column (12) = $140,000
Column (13) = $7,000
Column (14) = $8,075

EXHIBIT 6 Report Form

Decision Report		Result Report
Month 1	Group #	Last month's results net commission $ ....
Purchases	pounds of cocoa	Cumulative commission to date $ ....

Start of the Game

The game proper starts on October 1. At the beginning of the game there are 200,000 pounds of cocoa on hand. It is now up to each team at this time to decide on the coming year's purchases and, thus, start playing the game. We will assume that the cumulative commission of $8,075 to the end of September has been paid to Ms. Martin and that each team will start again from zero. Please use Exhibit 6 as the sample for your group's reporting form, which should be handed in to the instructor each period.

Case 8–4

Price Forecasting Exercise*

You and ____ other members of the class have been asked to forecast the price of a commodity on ____. So that your organization may take the most advantageous procurement action possible, your organization needs $5 million worth of this commodity for delivery between ____ and ____. The amount—$5 million worth—is based on the spot price of this commodity on ____. Your report must address the following four questions:

Question 1. What is the current ____ spot price of this commodity, based on what quotation? What is the specification of the commodity, and what is the minimum amount of purchase required for the quoted price to hold? How much in weight or volume does $5 million represent?

Question 2. What is the current futures for ____?

Question 3. What spot price do you forecast for this commodity on ____? Why?

Question 4. In view of your forecast, what recommendations would you make to the executive committee of your organization with regard to the purchase of this commodity? Would you advise buying now and taking delivery now, or later? Would you hedge? Would you delay purchase? Anything else? What savings do you forecast from your recommendation?

QUALIFICATIONS

1. The commodity selected may not be a pegged price in the market in which you are purchasing. It must be a freely fluctuating price, and it must be traded on a recognized commodity exchange. Prices must be reported daily in an accessible news source.
2. Approval for a selected commodity must come from the instructor. No two teams may select the same commodity. Commodity selection is on a first-come, first-served basis.
3. Foreign exchange rates may be an important consideration in your decision.
4. This report has four parts:
   a. A written report (in at least two copies) to be handed in on ____ before 4:30 p.m.
   b. A five-minute class report to be presented orally during class on ____.
   c. A written evaluation report (in at least two copies) to be handed in before 4:30 p.m., ____, including the ____ actual spot price. The evaluation should compare a savings (loss) estimate in view of the recommended action for the weight calculated in the report.

* Your insturctor will supply the missing information, dates, etc.

d. A one-minute report on ____ highlighting the evaluation.

5. Group names and commodity selections to be submitted no later than 4:30 p.m., ____.

SPECIAL REMARKS

1. The amount of $5 million is in U.S. dollars. Exchange rates with foreign currencies have to be considered as part of this problem.
2. There is a commission charge for every commodity. Please determine what this is for your commodity and include it in your calculations.
3. In the case of purchase and storage ahead, the carrying cost is 2 percent per month.
4. If the market has a daily variation and quotes high and low closing for the day, please be consistent and use the same type of quotation throughout.
5. Use the same source (publication) for your future price and your spot price.

Chapter Nine

Cost Management, Discounts, and Negotiation

Chapter Outline

Key Questions for the Supply Manager

Should we

- Use target pricing?
- Negotiate with our suppliers or accept their existing terms and conditions?
- Take advantage of a volume or cash discount offered by a supplier?

How can we

- Understand what it costs our suppliers to manufacture their products?
- Make a cost analysis on all of our large-dollar purchase items?
- Achieve our objectives in a negotiation with an important supplier?

The profit leverage effect of supply (discussed in Chapter 1) lays the foundation for the role of supply in helping the firm meet strategic goals of continuous improvement, customer service, quality, and increased competitiveness. Leveraging the potential of supply requires fully exploiting all opportunities to reduce, contain, or avoid costs, resulting in the lowest total cost of ownership and, hopefully, leading the organization to becoming the low-cost producer of high-quality goods and services. Supply management can contribute to attainment of low-cost-producer status by its management of internal and external costs. Methods of streamlining the acquisition process and reducing internal costs associated with acquisition were discussed in Chapters 2 and 3. This chapter focuses on managing external costs.

As the status of the supply function in well-managed companies has increased in importance, a more professional attitude has developed in the people responsible for the operation of the function. As the professional competence of the personnel has increased, greater use has been made of the more sophisticated tools available to the business decision-making executive. Negotiation and cost management techniques are prime examples of this developing professionalism.

In the long run, companies need suppliers that provide the lowest total costs, not necessarily the lowest prices. Consequently, a focus on costs, as opposed to prices, allows purchasers to make informed decisions and identify opportunities to reduce waste in the supply chain. However, understanding "what the numbers tell us" is only part of the battle. Effective buyers also need to understand how and when to use information effectively in a negotiation setting with important vendors. This chapter describes cost management techniques, examines discounts, and explains basic negotiation concepts. Cost management and negotiation represent a power combination for supply professionals.

COST MANAGEMENT

Some supply managers believe they are not justified in going very far into suppliers' costs. They take this position for several reasons: (1) In many cases, suppliers do not know their costs, and it would be useless to inquire about them; (2) the interpretation of cost calls for an exercise of judgment, and differences of opinion would arise even if all the figures were available; (3) some suppliers will not divulge cost information; (4) the seller's costs do not determine market prices; and (5) the buyer is not interested in the supplier's costs anyway; the primary concern is getting the best price consistent with quality, quantity, delivery, and service. If a seller offers a price that does not cover costs, either in ignorance or with full recognition of what it is doing, the matter is the seller's problem and not the buyer's.

However, unless a buyer has some idea of a supplier's costs, at least in a general way, it is difficult to judge the reasonableness of the supplier's prices. Furthermore, the position that the buyer is neither concerned with nor responsible for suppliers who offer merchandise below cost must recognize two things: first, good suppliers need to cover their costs to survive and prosper; and, second, prices may subsequently rise materially above cost as suppliers fight for financial survival.

The party in the strongest position in a negotiation session is the one with the best data. Recognizing the importance of cost, it is common practice for the purchaser to make the best estimate possible of the supplier's costs as one means of judging the reasonableness of the price proposed.

Many larger firms have cost analysts within the supply area to assist in analyzing supplier costs in preparation for negotiation. Some companies use cost-based pricing, a cost modeling system used by purchasers to determine total cost. These cost estimates must be based on such data as are available. The prices of raw material entering into the product are commonly accessible and the amounts required are also fairly well known. For component parts, catalog prices often offer a clue. Transportation costs are easily determined. The buyer's own engineers should provide data on processing costs. General overhead rates can be approximated.

Overhead costs generally consist of indirect costs incurred in the manufacturing, research, or engineering facilities of the company. Equipment depreciation typically is the largest single element in manufacturing overhead. It is important to know how these overhead costs are distributed to a given product. If overhead is allocated as a fixed percentage of direct labor costs and there is an increase in labor costs, overhead costs can be unduly inflated unless the allocation percentage is changed.

The growing tendency for industry to become more capital intensive has increased the relative percentage of overhead versus direct labor and materials. Because some items in the overhead, such as local real estate taxes, are attributable to the location of the supplier and others are properly seen as depreciation or investment at varying technological and economic risk levels, the analysis and allocation of these costs to individual products are particularly difficult.

Both tooling costs and engineering costs often are included as a part of general manufacturing overhead, but it is wisest to pull them out for analysis as separate items since each may account for a relatively large amount of cost. The buyer wants to know what it should cost a reasonably efficient supplier to build the tooling and own the completed tooling, what its life expectancy (number of units) is, and whether the tooling can be used with equipment other than that owned by the supplier. Only with such information can the buyer guard against being charged twice for the same tooling.

General and administrative expense includes items such as selling, promotion, advertising, executive salaries, and legal expense. Frequently there is no justification for the supplier to charge an advertising allocation in the price of a product manufactured to the buyer's specifications.

Material costs can be estimated from a bill of material, a drawing, or a sample of the product. The buyer can arrive at material costs by multiplying material quantities or weight per unit by raw material prices. Sometimes a material usage curve will be helpful. The purpose of the curve is to chart what improvement should occur from buying economies and lower scrap rates as experience is gained in the manufacturing process. Use of price indexes and maintenance of price trend records are standard practice.

Direct labor estimates are not made as easily as material estimates. Even though labor costs are normally labeled direct for machine operators and assembly-line workers, in reality they tend to be more fixed than most managers care to admit. Most organizations prefer not to lay off personnel, and there are strong pressures to keep the so-called direct labor force reasonably stable and employed. This means that inventories and overtime often are used to smooth fluctuations in demand and also that labor cost becomes at least semivariable and subject to allocation.

Product mix, run sizes, and labor turnover may affect labor costs substantially. The greater the mix, the shorter the lot size produced, and the higher the turnover, the greater the direct labor costs will be. These three factors alone may create substantial cost differences between suppliers of an identical end product. Geographical considerations also play a large part because differences in labor rates do exist between plant locations. Such differences may change dramatically over time, as the rapid increases in direct labor rates in Japan and Germany have demonstrated. The astute cost analyst will estimate the supplier's real labor costs, taking the above considerations into account.

Total Cost of Ownership

The purchaser should estimate the total cost of ownership (TCO) before selecting a supplier. Broadly defined, total cost of ownership for non-capital goods acquisition includes all relevant costs, such as administration, follow-up, expediting, inbound transportation, inspection and testing, rework, storage, scrap, warranty, service, downtime, customer returns, and lost sales. The acquisition price plus all other associated costs becomes the total cost of ownership. A total cost approach requires the cooperation of engineering, quality, manufacturing, and supply to coordinate requirements such as specifications and tolerances that affect the supply decision. Early supplier involvement also is essential to ensure cost-effectiveness.

TCO models attempt to determine all the cost elements, thereby revealing opportunities for cost reduction or cost avoidance for each cost element, rather than merely analyzing or comparing prices. The difficulty lies in identifying and tracking these cost elements and using the information appropriately to compare different suppliers. (See also life cycle costing in Chapter 16.)

The concept of TCO acknowledges that acquisition price is merely one part of the costs associated with owning a good or procuring a service. While the most obvious reason for using TCO is to identify the actual cost of the supply decision, TCO also can be used for a number of other possible reasons: (1) to highlight cost reduction opportunities; (2) to aid supplier evaluation and selection; (3) to provide data for negotiations; (4) to focus suppliers on cost reduction opportunities; (5) to highlight the advantage of expensive, high-quality items; (6) to clarify and define supplier performance expectations; (7) to create a long-term supply perspective; and (8) to forecast future performance.

There are a number of methods for estimating the total cost of ownership. Each firm must develop or adopt a method of cost modeling that best fits the needs of the organization. In close buyer–supplier relationships, the seller may willingly share cost data with the buyer. In other situations, the buyer or sourcing team may have to develop its own cost model to prepare for negotiations. There are many approaches to cost modeling, from informal ones to highly sophisticated, complex computer models. Firms typically use either *standard cost models,* which are applied to a variety of supply situations, or *unique cost models,* which are developed for a specific item or situation.[1]

One way of analyzing cost elements is demonstrated by a model that refers to three cost components: (1) pretransaction costs (e.g., identifying need, qualifying sources, and adding supplier to internal systems), (2) transaction costs (e.g., purchase, inspection, and administrative costs), and (3) post-transaction (e.g., defective parts, repairs, and maintenance).[2] The acquisition price is broken down into the individual cost elements from which the price is derived. Each of these cost elements then can be analyzed by the buyer for areas of reduction or avoidance. Cost elements are both tangible and intangible, meaning that many are difficult to estimate.

The notion that an attempt should be made to identify and analyze all costs of ownership drives many of the supply strategies discussed in this book. For example, longer-term, closer buyer–supplier relationships; partnering arrangements and alliances; and early supplier and purchaser involvement all can facilitate total cost modeling, improve negotiations and decision making, and result in increased competitiveness for the firm.

Target Pricing

Target pricing is experiencing growing use in North America. Target pricing focuses the attention of everyone in the organization on designing costs out of products rather than on eliminating costs after production has begun. This concept is a logical extension of the quality movement that forwarded the perspective that it makes sense to build something right the first time. Basically, in target pricing, the organization establishes the price at which it plans to sell its finished product, then subtracts out its normal operating profit, leaving the target cost that the organization seeks. The target cost is then further subdivided into appropriate cost sectors such as manufacturing, overhead, and materials and services. Supply becomes responsible for working with suppliers to achieve the materials and services target. For example, if the end product is a manufactured item that will be sold for $200, and purchased goods represent 60 percent of each dollar in sales revenue, then supply would be responsible for $120 of the $200 selling price. If it is determined that a 10 percent reduction in price is desirable because of the expected impact on sales revenue, then supply would be responsible for securing a 10 percent reduction in its portion of the costs ($120) of the item, or $12. This means purchased materials, on a unit basis, should not exceed $108. This becomes the target materials cost in the pricing structure.

Target pricing results in companywide cost reductions, in (1) design to cost, on the part of design engineering; (2) manufacture to cost, on the part of production; and (3) purchase

[1] Lisa Ellram, "A Taxonomy of Total Cost of Ownership Models," *Journal of Business Logistics,* vol. 15, no. 1, 1994, pp. 171–91.

[2] Lisa Ellram, "Total Cost of Ownership: Elements and Implementation," *International Journal of Purchasing and Materials Management,* Fall 1993.

to cost, on the part of supply. From the standpoint of supply, target pricing can be beneficial by providing a means of documenting specific price reductions needed from suppliers, demonstrating supply's contribution to the pricing goals of the firm, and documenting supply's contribution on a product-by-product basis. To be effective, target pricing works best when the customer has clout in the supply chain; when there is loyalty between buyer and seller, as in a partnering arrangement or alliance; and when the supplier also stands to benefit from the cost reductions.

The cost reductions on the part of the supplier conceivably can come from several areas: the supplier can seek reductions in overhead expenses and/or general and selling and administrative expenses; the supplier can improve efficiencies in labor as measured by the learning curve; or the supplier can seek labor and material cost reductions. This last option requires the supplier to pass down these techniques to *its* suppliers in the supply chain. Overall, target pricing provides supply with (1) a measurable target for supply performance, (2) a yardstick for measuring cost reductions, and (3) a means of measuring the supplier's efficiency. As with all cost analysis tools, the expected benefits from the target costing process must exceed the costs associated with conducting the analysis.

Target pricing cannot occur in a vacuum. To be successful, the effort requires cross-functional team efforts, early supplier and early supply involvement, concurrent engineering, and value engineering. In a CAPS study, *The Role of Supply Management in Target Costing,* the companies participating in the study reported that they used target costing to increase competitiveness, increase cooperation with suppliers and get earlier supplier involvement, and improve cost management.[3]

The Learning Curve or Manufacturing Progress Function

The learning curve provides an analytical framework for quantifying the commonly recognized principle that one becomes more proficient with experience. Its origins lie in the aircraft industry in World War II when it was empirically determined that labor time per plane declined dramatically as volume increased. Subsequent studies showed that the same phenomenon occurred in a variety of industries and situations. Although conceptually most closely identified with direct labor, most experts believe the learning curve or manufacturing progress function is actually brought about by a combination of a large number of factors that include:

1. The learning rate of labor.
2. The motivation of labor and management to increase output.
3. The development of improved methods, procedures, and support systems.
4. The substitution of better materials, tools, and equipment or more effective use of materials, tools, and equipment.
5. The flexibility of the job and the people associated with it.
6. The ratio of labor versus machine time in the task.
7. The amount of preplanning done in advance of the task.
8. The turnover of labor in the unit.
9. The pressure of competition to do tasks better, faster, cheaper.

[3] Lisa M. Ellram, *The Role of Supply Management in Target Costing,* Tempe, AZ: CAPS Research, 1999.

We know the manufacturing progress function happens; its presence has been empirically determined a sufficient number of times that its existence is no longer in doubt.

The learning curve has tremendous implications for cost determination and negotiation. For example, take a 90 percent learning curve. The progress is logarithmic. Every time the volume doubles, the time per unit drops to 90 percent of the time per unit at half the volume. Suppose we wish to purchase 800 units of a highly labor-intensive, expensive product that will be produced by a group of workers over a two-year period. The 100th unit has been produced at a labor time of 1,000 hours. With a 90 percent learning curve, the labor time for the 200th unit would drop to 900 hours and the 400th unit to 90 percent of 900 hours, or 810 hours per unit.

It is important to recognize that the choice of learning curve, be it 95, 90, 85, or 80 percent or any other figure, is not an exact science. Normally, fairly simple tasks, like putting parts into a box, tend to have a learning curve close to 95 percent. Medium-complexity tasks often have learning curve rates between 80 and 90 percent, while highly complex tasks tend to be in the 70 to 80 percent range.

The learning curve implies that improvement never stops, no matter how large the volume becomes. The potential of the learning curve in supply management has not yet been fully explored. It is a powerful concept. Progressive discounts, shortened lead times, and better value can be planned and obtained through its use. The learning curve is used along with target pricing to set progressively lower price targets for future deliveries.

Activity-Based Costing

Traditional cost accounting introduces distortions into product costing because of the way it allocates overhead on the basis of direct labor. In the past, when labor costs often were the largest cost category, this allocation made sense. However, as the cost of materials has eclipsed labor costs as the single largest cost factor, accountants have looked for other ways to allocate overhead.[4] Basically, activity-based costing (ABC) tries to turn indirect costs into direct costs by tracking the cost drivers behind indirect costs. One of the biggest hurdles in ABC is the cost of tracking indirect costs and translating them into direct costs, compared with the benefits of being able to assign these costs to specific products more accurately. In ABC, manufacturing overhead is divided into costs that change in response to unit-level activities (in proportion to the number of units produced), batch-level activities (in proportion to the number of batches produced), and product-level activities (that benefit all units of a product). The remainder are true fixed costs and are allocated the same way as in traditional cost accounting.

It is easy for those trying to apply the ABC concept to collect too much detail and be unable to make much sense out of it. Even so, it is a powerful tool and one that has many implications for supply management.

Buyers can use activity-based costing as a tool to reduce supplier costs by eliminating nonvalue-adding activities, reducing activity occurrences, and reducing the cost driver rate. To accomplish these goals, buyers must collect data from suppliers on activities (specific tasks), cost drivers (a metric to measure activity), cost driver rates (rate at

[4] This section is drawn largely from John C. Lere and Jayant V. Saraph, "Activity-Based Costing for Purchasing Managers' Cost and Pricing Determinations," *International Journal of Purchasing and Materials Management,* Fall 1995, pp. 25–31.

which cost is incurred), and units of cost driver (the amount of activity). Buyers then can determine which activities add value and should occur, and which do not add value and should be eliminated. Even if an activity is deemed value-adding, it may be possible to reduce the number of times the activity occurs, thereby reducing cost. For example, receiving inspection may be rated as nonvalue-adding and targeted for elimination, or it may be deemed value-adding but the number of receipts requiring inspection may be reduced, thereby reducing costs. Lastly, the cost of the activity itself may be targeted as an area for improvements in efficiency through value analysis and system redesign.

DISCOUNTS

Discounts represent a legitimate and effective means of reducing prices. The most commonly used types of discounts are cash discounts, multiple discounts, quantity discounts, and cumulative or volume discounts. They may be offered by suppliers or negotiated by purchasers.

Cash Discounts

Cash discounts are granted by virtually every seller of industrial goods, although the actual discount terms are a matter of individual trade custom and vary considerably from one industry to another. The purpose of a cash discount is to secure the prompt payment of an account.

Most sellers expect buyers to take the cash discount. The net price is commonly fixed at a point that will yield a fair profit to the supplier and is the price the supplier expects most customers to pay. Those who do not pay within the time limit are penalized and are expected to pay the gross price. However, variations in cash discount amounts frequently are made without due regard for the real purpose for which such discounts should be granted and are used, instead, merely as another means of varying prices. If a buyer secures a cash discount not commonly granted in the past, he or she may be sure that the net result is merely a reduction in the price, regardless of the name used. On the other hand, a reduction in the size of the cash discount is, in effect, an increase in the price.

Cash discounts, therefore, sometimes raise rather difficult questions of price policy, but if they are granted on the same terms to all buyers and if postdating and other similar practices are not granted to some buyers and denied to others, then the supply department's major interest in cash discounts is confined largely to being sure they are called to the attention of the proper financial managers. The purchaser ordinarily cannot be held responsible for a failure to take cash discounts because this depends on the financial resources of the organization and is, therefore, a matter of financial rather than supply policy. The purchaser should, however, be very careful to secure such cash discounts as customarily are granted. It is a part of the buyer's responsibility to see that inspection is made promptly, that goods are accepted without unnecessary loss of time, and that all documents are handled expeditiously so all discounts quoted may be taken. A discount of 2 percent if payment is made within 10 days, with the gross amount due in 30 days, is the equivalent of earning an annual interest rate of approximately 36 percent. If the buying company does not pay within the 10-day discount period but instead pays 20 days later, the effective cost for the use of that money for the 20 days is 2 percent (the lost discount).

Because there are approximately 18 20-day periods in a year, 2% × 18 = 36%, the effective annual interest rate.

To establish the exact date by which payment must be mailed to deduct the cash discount from the payment amount, and to avoid the confusion that often results from handling incorrectly prepared supplier invoices, some firms include a clause in their purchase order specifying that "determination of the cash discount payment period will be calculated from either the date of delivery of acceptable goods, or the receipt of a properly prepared invoice, whichever date is later."

Some customers will take the cash discount even when they are paying after the discount date. Part of the buyer's responsibility is to ensure that his or her organization lives up to the terms and conditions of the contract. This will mean working with other functional areas to ensure that payment is made in a timely manner.

Trade Discounts

Trade discounts are granted by a manufacturer to a buyer because the purchasing firm is a particular type of distributor or user. In general, they aim to protect the distributor by making it more profitable for a purchaser to buy from the distributor than directly from the manufacturer. When manufacturers have found that various types of distributors can sell their merchandise in a given territory more cheaply than they can, they usually rely on the distributors' services. To ensure that goods will move through the channels selected, the distributor is granted a trade discount approximating the cost of doing business.

However, trade discounts are not always used properly. Protection is sometimes granted distributors not entitled to it, because the services that they render manufacturers, and presumably customers, are not commensurate with the discount they get. Generally speaking, buyers dealing in small quantities who secure a great variety of items from a single source or who depend on frequent and very prompt deliveries are more likely to obtain their supplies from wholesalers and other distributors receiving trade discounts. With the larger accounts, manufacturers are more likely to sell directly, even though they may reserve the smaller accounts in the same territory for the wholesalers. Some manufacturers refuse to sell to accounts purchasing below a stipulated minimum annual volume.

Discounts often are available to a buyer who also purchases aftermarket requirements (replacement parts for units already sold). The supplier may put the buyer who wishes to buy items that will be sold to the aftermarket into one of several price classifications: (1) an OEM (original equipment manufacturer) class, (2) a class with its distributors, or (3) a separate OEM aftermarket class. Aftermarket suppliers often do special packaging, part numbering, or stocking, which may justify a special price schedule. The buyer needs to know what price classifications the supplier uses and the qualifications for placing the buyer in a particular classification.

Multiple Discounts

In some industries and trades, prices are quoted on a multiple discount basis. For example, 10, 10, and 10 means that, for an item listed at \$100, the actual price to be paid by the purchaser is (\$100 − 10%) − 10%(\$100 − 10%) − 10%[(\$100 − 10%) − 10%(\$100 − 10%)] = \$100 − \$10 − \$9 − \$8.10 = \$72.90. The 10, 10, and 10 is, therefore, equivalent to a discount of 27.1%. Tables are available listing the most common multiple discount combinations and their equivalent discount.

Quantity Discounts

Quantity discounts may be granted for buying in particular quantities and vary roughly in proportion to the amount purchased. From the seller's standpoint, the justification for granting such discounts is usually that quantity purchasing results in savings to the seller, enabling a lower price to the buyer who has made such savings possible. These savings may be of two classes: (1) savings in marketing or distribution expense and (2) savings in production expense.

The savings in marketing or distribution expense arise because it may be no more costly to sell a large order than a small one; the billing expense is the same; and the increased cost of packing, crating, and shipping is not proportional. When these circumstances exist, a direct quantity discount not exceeding the difference in cost of handling the small and the large order is justified. Transport savings (e.g., truckload versus nontruckload) are classical examples of quantity discounts.

There may be substantial savings in production costs as a result of securing a large order instead of a small one. For instance, setup costs may be the same for a large order as a small one; material costs may be lower per unit.

From the buyer's viewpoint, the question of quantity discounts is intimately connected with that of inventory policy. While it is true that the larger the size of a given order, the lower the unit price likely will be, the carrying charges on the buyer's larger inventory are more costly. Hence, the savings on the size of the order must be compared against the increased inventory costs.

The Price-Discount Problem

A normal situation in supply occurs when a price discount is offered if purchases are made in larger quantities. Acceptance of a larger quantity provides a form of anticipation inventory. The problem may be solved in several ways. Marginally, the question is: "Should we increase the size of our inventory so that we obtain the benefits of the lower price?" Put this way, it can be analyzed as a return on investment decision. The simple EOQ model is not of much assistance here because it cannot account for the purchase price differential directly. It is possible to use the EOQ model to eliminate some alternatives, however, and to check the final solution. Total cost calculations are required to find the optimal point.

The following problem is illustrative of the calculation:

R = 900 units (annual demand)
S = $50 (order cost)
K = 0.25 or 25 percent (annual carrying cost)

Sample Calculations for the Price-Discount Problem

	100	200	400	800
Total annual price paid	$40,500	$38,700	$37,350	$36,000
Carrying cost	562	1,075	2,075	4,000
Order cost	450	225	112	56
Total cost	41,512	40,000	39,537	40,056
Average inventory	$2,250	$4,300	8,300	16,000
EOQ (units)	89	92*	93*	94*

* Not feasible

C = \$45 for 0–199 units per order
\$43 for 200–399 units per order
\$41.50 for 400–799 units per order
\$40 for 800 and more units per order

A simple marginal analysis shows that in moving from 100 per order to 200, the additional average investment is \$4,300 − \$2,250 = \$2,050. The saving in price is \$40,500 − \$38,700 = \$1,800, and the order cost saving is \$450 − \$225 = \$225. For an additional investment of \$2,050, the savings are \$2,025, which is almost a 100 percent return and is well in excess of the 25 percent carrying cost. In going from 400 to 800, the additional investment is \$7,700 for a total price and order savings of \$1,406.25. This falls below the 25 percent carrying cost and would not be a desirable result. The total cost figures show that the optimal purchase quantity is at the 400 level. The largest single saving occurs at the first price break at the 200 level.

The EOQs with an asterisk are not feasible because the price range and the volume do not match. For example, the price for the second EOQ of 92 is \$45. Yet, for the 200 to 400 range, the actual price is \$43. The EOQ may be used, however, in the following way. In going from right to left on the table (from the lowest unit price to the highest price), proceed until the first valid EOQ is obtained. This is 89 for the 0 to 199 price range. Then the order quantity at each price discount about this EOQ is checked to see whether total costs at the higher order quantity are lower or higher than at the EOQ. Doing this for the example shown gives us a total cost at the valid EOQ level of 89 of:

Total annual price paid	\$ 40,500
Carrying cost	500
Order cost	500
Total cost	\$ 41,500

Because this total cost at the feasible EOQ of 89 units is above the total cost at the 200 order quantity level and the 400 and 800 order levels as well, the proper order quantity is 400, which gives the lowest total cost of all options.

The discussion so far has assumed that the quantity discount offered is based on orders of the full amount, forcing the purchaser to carry substantial inventories. It is preferable, of course, from the purchaser's standpoint to take delivery in smaller quantities but to still get the lower discount price. This might be negotiated through annual contracts, cumulative discounts, or blanket orders. This type of analysis also can identify what extra price differential the purchaser might be willing to pay to avoid carrying substantial stocks.

Quantity Discounts and Source Selection

The quantity discount question is of interest to many buyers for a second reason: All quantity discounts, and especially those of the cumulative type, tend to restrict the number of suppliers, thereby affecting the choice of source.

Because there is real justification for quantity discounts when properly used, the buyer should obtain such discounts whenever possible. Ordinarily they come through the pressure of competition among sellers. Furthermore, an argument may be advanced that such discounts are a matter of right. The buyer is purchasing goods or merchandise, not crating, or packing materials, or transportation. The seller presumably should expect to earn a profit not from those wholly auxiliary services but rather from manufacturing and selling the merchandise processed. These auxiliary services are necessary; they must be performed; they must be paid for; and it is natural to expect the buyer to pay for them. But the buyer should not be expected to pay more than the actual cost of these auxiliary services.

When an attempt is made to justify quantity discounts on the basis that they contribute to reduced production costs by providing a volume of business large enough to reduce the overhead expenses, somewhat more cautious reasoning is necessary. It is true that in some lines of business the larger the output, the lower the overhead cost per unit of product. It also may be true that without the volume from the large customers, the average cost of production would be higher. However, the small buyers may place a greater total proportion of the seller's business than do the large ones. So far as production costs are concerned, therefore, the small buyers may contribute even more toward that volume so essential to the per-unit production cost than does the larger buyer.

Another contention is that large customers ordering early in the season, or even prior to the time actual production of a season's supply begins, should be granted higher discounts because their orders keep the facility in production. Such a buyer probably may be entitled to a lower price than one who waits until later in the season to order. However, such a discount, because it is justified by the early placement of an order and therefore should be granted to every buyer placing an early order regardless of its size, is not properly a quantity discount but is a time discount.

Cumulative or Volume Discounts

Another type of quantity discount is cumulative and varies in proportion to the quantity purchased; however, instead of being computed on the size of the order placed at any one time, it is based on the quantity purchased over a period of time. Such discounts are commonly granted as an incentive for continued patronage. It is hoped they will induce a purchaser to concentrate purchases largely with a single source rather than distributing them over many sources, thus benefiting the company offering the discount. Generally speaking, the purchaser should not scatter orders over a number of sources, for distributing one's orders over many sources is uneconomical and costly. No supplier, under such circumstances, is likely to give the same careful attention to the buyer's requirements as it would if it felt it were getting the larger portion of the purchaser's business.

The use of cumulative discounts must meet the same cost justification rules under the Robinson-Patman Act as other quantity discounts. However, as long as the buyer is not knowingly accepting or inducing discriminatory quantity discounts, then the responsibility for justification rests solely with the seller.

Cumulative discounts, if provided in the form of a payment by the supplier after the specified contract date, can provide tangible evidence of purchasing savings, especially if the discounts were not included in budgets or standard costing systems.

It may be easier for a supplier to provide a discount to a purchaser than a lower price. This allows the supplier to keep established list prices unchanged and distinguish between various classes of purchasers.

NEGOTIATION

Negotiation is the most sophisticated and most expensive means of price determination. Negotiation requires that the buyer and supplier, through discussion, arrive at a common understanding on the essentials of a purchase/sale contract, such as delivery, specifications, warranty, prices, and terms. Because of the interrelation of these factors and many others, it is a difficult art and requires the exercise of judgment and tact. Negotiation is an attempt to find an agreement that allows both parties to realize their objectives. It must be used when the buyer is in a single- or sole-source situation; both parties know that a purchase contract will be issued and their task is to define a set of terms and conditions acceptable to both. Because of the expense and time involved, true negotiation normally will not be used unless the dollar amount is quite large.

Negotiating a fair price should not be confused with *price haggling.* Supply managers generally frown on haggling and properly so, for in the long run the cost to the buyer far outweighs any temporary advantage. For a purchaser to tell a sales representative that he or she has received a quotation that was not, in fact, received or that is not comparable; to fake telephone calls in the sales representative's presence; to leave real or fictitious bids of competitors in open sight for a sales representative to see; to mislead as to the quantity needed—these and similar practices are illustrations of those unethical actions so properly condemned by the codes of ethics of the Institute for Supply Management (ISM) and the Purchasing Management Association of Canada (PMAC) and other supply associations around the world.

Negotiation need not result in a lower price. Occasionally, there may be revision upward of the price paid, compared with the supplier's initial proposal. If, in the negotiation, it becomes clear that the supplier has either misinterpreted the specifications or underestimated the resources needed to perform the work, the buyer will bring this to the supplier's attention so the proposal may be adjusted accordingly. A good contract is one that both parties can live with, and under which the supplier should not lose money, providing its operation is efficient. When a purchaser cooperates in granting increases not required by the original supplier proposal, the buyer then is in a position to request decreases in prices if unforeseen events occur that result in the supplier's being able to produce the material or product at a substantial savings.

Negotiation Strategy and Practice

Reasonable negotiation is expected by buyer and seller alike. It is within reasonable bounds of negotiation to insist that a supplier:

1. Operate in an efficient manner.
2. Keep prices in line with costs.
3. Not take advantage of a privileged position.

4. Make proper and reasonable adjustment of claims.
5. Be prepared to consider the special needs of the buyer's organization.

While negotiation normally is thought of as a means of establishing the price to be paid, and this may be the main focus, many other areas or conditions can be negotiated. In fact, *any* aspect of the purchase/sale agreement is subject to negotiation. A few of these areas are:

1. Quality	2. Support	3. Supply	4. Transportation	5. Price
• Specification compliance • Performance compliance • Test criteria • Rejection procedures • Liability • Design changes • Packaging	• Technical assistance • Product research, development, and/or design • Warranty • Spare parts • Training • Tooling • Packaging • Data sharing, including technical data • MIS	• Lead times • Delivery schedule • Consignment stocks • Expansion options • Supplier inventories • Cancellation options	• FOB terms • Carrier • Commodity classification • Freight allowance/ equalization • Multiple delivery points	• Purchase order price • Discounts • Escalation provisions • Exchange rate terms • Import duties • Payment of taxes • Countertrade credits

The discussion of some of the elements and considerations that affect the price of an item makes it obvious that negotiation can be a valuable technique to use in reaching an agreement with a supplier on the many variables affecting a specific price. This is not to say that all buying/selling transactions require the use of negotiations. Nor is the intention to indicate that negotiation is used only in determining price. Reaching a clear understanding of time schedules for deliveries, factors affecting quality, and methods of packaging may require negotiations of equal or greater importance than those applying to price.

A list of some of the various kinds of purchasing situations in which the use of negotiations should prove valuable follows:

1. Any written contract covering price, specifications, terms of delivery, and quality standards.
2. The purchase of items made to the buyer's specifications. Special importance should be attached to "first buys," because thorough exploration of the needs of the buyer and the supplier often will result in a better product at a lower price.
3. When changes are made in drawings or specifications after a purchase order has been issued.
4. When quotations have been solicited from responsible bidders and no acceptable bids have been received.
5. When problems of tooling or packaging occur.
6. When changing economic or market conditions require changes in quantities or prices.

7. When problems of termination of a contract involve disposal of facilities, materials, or tooling.
8. When there are problems of accepting any of the various elements entering into cost-type contracts.
9. When problems arise under the various types of contracts used in defense and governmental contracting.
10. When cost analysis shows a significant gap between market price and costs.

Framework for Planning and Preparing for Negotiation

Success in negotiation largely is a function of the quality and amount of planning that has been done. Figure 9–1 presents a model of the negotiation process. The basic steps in developing a strategy for negotiation are:

1. Develop the specific objectives (outcomes) desired from the negotiation. This is done by gathering relevant information and than generating, analyzing, evaluating, and selecting alternatives.
2. Gather pertinent data. Here is where cost analysis comes into play.
3. Determine the facts of the situation. A fact is defined as an item of information about which agreement is expected. For example, if the supplier's cost breakdown states that the direct labor rate is $20.10 per hour, and you agree, that is a fact.
4. Determine the issues. An issue is something over which disagreement is expected. The purpose of negotiation is to resolve issues so that a mutually satisfactory contract can be signed. For example, if the supplier claims the manufacturing burden rate is 300 percent of direct labor costs, but your analysis indicates a 240 percent burden rate is realistic, this becomes an issue to be settled through negotiation.
5. Analyze the positions of strength of both (or all) parties. For example, what is the supplier's capacity, backlog, and profitability? How confident is the supplier of getting the contract? Is there any time urgency? The process of analyzing strengths helps the negotiator establish negotiation points, helps avoid setting unrealistic expectations, and may reveal

FIGURE 9–1
Model of the Negotiation Process

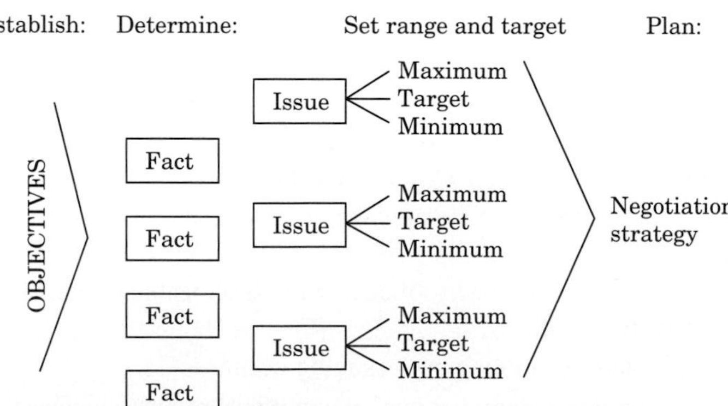

ideas for strategies. The negotiator (or team) should be able to generate a list of 12 to 24 points for either side through a brainstorming process.

6. Set the buyer's position on each issue and estimate the seller's position on each issue based on your research. What data will be used to support the buyer's position? What data might support the seller's position? Two questions should be asked after analyzing positions of strength: (*a*) "Whose position is stronger?" and (*b*) "Which points give each side the most strength?" The answer to the first question should help determine how realistic the objectives are and if they need to be changed or clarified. The answer to the second question tells the negotiator what his or her key points will be in the negotiation and what to expect from the other side. If done well, this information allows the negotiator to prepare counterarguments. By estimating the range of acceptable results for both buyer and seller, the negotiator can determine, first, if there is a zone of overlap, meaning negotiation is feasible and likely to result in an agreement; or, second, if there is a gap between the objectives of the parties (see Figure 9–2). If there is a gap, the negotiator must determine if it can be closed, and if not, whether negotiation even makes sense in this particular situation.
7. Plan the negotiation strategy. Which issues should be discussed first? Where is the buyer willing to compromise? Who will make up the negotiation team (it frequently is composed of someone from both engineering and quality control, headed by the buyer)? Establishing a range and a target for each objective sets reasonable objectives that the negotiator feels can be achieved. The tactics used in the actual negotiation may mean starting out at a more extreme position than the negotiator truly believes is achievable. The decision about tactics should be based on the negotiator's understanding of the situation and the parties involved in the negotiation. If

FIGURE 9–2
The Zone of Negotiation

1. The seller and purchaser overlap.

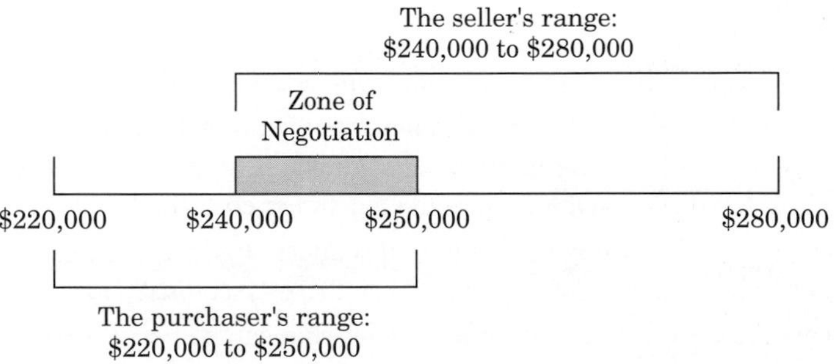

2. The seller and purchaser do not overlap.

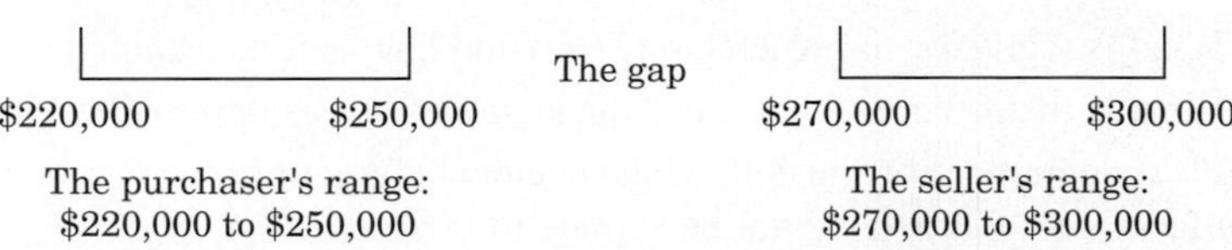

the goal of negotiation is performance, then the *way* negotiation is conducted is important because it affects the intention to perform. If the tactics used leave the other party feeling negative toward the negotiator or the results, there may be little commitment to the agreement or to solving any problems that might arise during the life of the contract.

8. Brief all persons on the team who are going to participate in the negotiations.
9. Conduct a dress rehearsal for the people who are going to participate in the negotiations.
10. Conduct the actual negotiations with an impersonal calmness.

All negotiation has an economic as well as a psychological dimension. It is important to satisfy both of these dimensions to achieve a win-win result. The trends toward teaming, single sourcing, partnering, and empowerment reinforce the need for supply personnel to be superior negotiators, both with suppliers and with others in their own organization. Actually, negotiations inside one's own organization to obtain cooperation and support for supply initiatives may be more challenging than those with suppliers.

Conclusion

Supply professionals concerned with contributing effectively to organizational goals and strategies need to be concerned with managing costs instead of prices. Beating up suppliers for unreasonable price concessions can be as damaging as "leaving too much on the table" in a negotiation with an important vendor. Understanding where and how supply chain costs can be reduced or eliminated can represent an opportunity to gain competitive advantage.

Discounts offer an interesting opportunity for buyers and sellers to achieve their objectives.

Negotiation and supplier cost analysis complement each other. Cost analysis identifies the opportunity and secures the result. The skilled supply professional not only understands the value of reliable supplier cost data but is also resourceful in collecting such information and capable of using it effectively in a negotiation.

Questions for Review and Discussion

1. What is cost-based pricing? How and why is it be used?
2. What are the major cost categories that you would include when estimating a supplier's cost for a manufacturing item? How would you estimate such costs if the supplier was either unwilling or unable to provide a detailed cost breakdown?
3. What are cash discounts, quantity discounts, trade discounts, and cumulative discounts? Should the buyer attempt to use these discounts? How?
4. When, and how, is negotiation used, and what can be negotiated?
5. What is a learning curve and how can it be used?
6. Why do firms use target pricing? How are target prices established?
7. What is activity-based costing (ABC) and how can the buyer use ABC to reduce costs?
8. What is total cost of ownership (TCO) and how is it determined?
9. What is the difference between "managing costs" as opposed to "managing prices"?
10. Please comment on the following statement: Target pricing can only be used for manufactured items and cannot be applied to services.

References

Cooper, Robin, and Regine Slagmulder. *Target Costing and Value Engineering.* Portland, OR: Productivity Press, and Montvale, NJ: The IMA Foundation for Applied Research Inc., 1997.

Ellram, Lisa M. *The Role of Supply Management in Target Costing*. Tempe, AZ: CAPS Research, 1999.

Ellram, Lisa. *Strategic Cost Management in the Supply Chain: A Purchasing and Supply Management Perspective*. Tempe, AZ: CAPS Research, 2002.

Ellram, Lisa. "A Taxonomy of Total Cost of Ownership Models." *Journal of Business Logistics* 15, no. 1, 1994, pp. 171–91.

Ellram, Lisa. "Total Cost of Ownership: Elements and Implementation." *International Journal of Purchasing and Materials Management,* Fall 1993.

Ferrin, B. G., and R. E. Plank. "Total Cost of Ownership Models: An Exploratory Study." *Journal of Supply Chain Management*, 38 no. 3, 2002, pp. 18–29.

Fisher, Roger, and Danny Ertel. *Getting Ready to Negotiate: The Getting to Yes Workbook.* New York: Penguin Books, 1995.

Fisher, Roger; William Ury; and Bruce Patton. *Getting to Yes: Negotiating Agreement Without Giving In.* New York: Penguin Books, 1991.

Lewicki, R. J.; D. M. Saunders; and J. W. Milton. *Negotiation*. 3rd ed. Burr Ridge, IL: McGraw-Hill/Irwin, 1999.

Ury, William. *Getting Past No: Negotiating Your Way from Confrontation to Cooperation.* New York: Bantam Books, 1993.

Case 9–1

Deere Cost Management

On Wednesday, February 18th, Jim Elsey, cost management specialist at Deere & Company in Moline, Illinois, received a call from Glen Lowery, sales manager in the Agricultural Products Division:

> Jim, I need you to look into our costs on the gatherer chain. Our margins have really shrunk and we need to do something about this problem. Get back to me and let me know what you think.

THE GATHERER CHAIN

Deere & Company (Deere) manufactured and distributed a full line of agriculture equipment as well as a broad range of construction and forestry equipment and commercial and consumer equipment. The company had annual sales of $14 billion with operations in more than 160 countries.

A popular product sold by the Agricultural Products Division was a conveyor system. Materials placed on the front end of the conveyor sat on the gatherer chain, which carried the material to the opposite end. The gatherer chain was joined together in links, fastened by pins, and included small hooks that helped to carry the material. It sat on rollers that required regular lubrication to keep the conveyor system in good working condition.

The Agricultural Products Division had produced the conveyor system for several years, with only slight modifications in its design. As standard practice for each product, Deere sold replacement parts, including gatherer chains, through its dealer network. It was the

EXHIBIT 1
Profitability Analysis for Gatherer Chain

	Two Years Ago	Last year	Current Year Budget
Aftermarket price	$ 40.00	$ 36.25	$ 30.00
Purchase cost	$ 21.25	$ 22.61	$ 24.12
Cost–price ratio	53%	62%	80%
Unit sales	475,000	410,000	350,000

intention of management to ensure that its aftermarket products were price competitive. As a result, the sales department regularly benchmarked pricing for its products.

Jim learned that the gatherer chain was purchased from Saunders Manufacturing (Saunders), a supplier located in Decatur, Illinois. Saunders was a family-owned business run by Wayne Saunders, the son of the company's founder. Saunders had a long-term relationship with Deere and Wayne had a reputation as a tough, successful businessman who had grown the company to the point where it now employed approximately 300 people.

Reviewing the sales margin for the gatherer chain, Jim could see why Glen was concerned. Over the past three years, the sales revenue and margin had been declining steadily (see Exhibit 1). The budgeted selling price for the current year was based on the need to match the price set by a major competitor.

FINANCIAL ANALYSIS

Jim arranged a meeting the following day with Susan Tessier, from purchasing, and Jose da Costa, from engineering. During the meeting, Jim laid a gatherer chain on the conference room table and asked Jose to estimate the raw material content. After a little bit of work, Jose estimated that the product consisted of approximately 11.6 pounds of steel and 46 pins that joined the links. He also expected that Saunders would have approximately a 20 percent scrap rate, for steel only, as part of their normal production cost. Jose also commented that Saunders could use general-purpose equipment for the manufacturing and assembly process.

Susan then pulled out her material cost file and made the following observations:

> We just finished negotiations with our steel suppliers and expect to pay approximately $28.00 per hundredweight for this type of material. I am also buying the same pins for a couple of our Divisions, and I figure Saunders is paying about 3.5¢. Don't forget that for this part we pay the freight, which usually costs about 3 percent of the purchase price, and they pay the packaging.
>
> We have looked around for other suppliers for this part and haven't been able to find anyone that capable of beating the current price. Saunders has been a good supplier. Their quality and on-time delivery performance have been excellent. I wouldn't want to lose them as a supplier.

Following the meeting, Jim examined the Annual Survey of Manufacturers, published by the U.S. Department of Commerce. Within the report was a breakdown of manufacturing costs, as a percentage of sales, for U.S. companies in Saunders' industry code. According to data from the previous year, the breakdown was material, 42 percent; direct labor; 13 percent; indirect labor, 6 percent; and overhead, 20 percent.

SUPPLIER NEGOTIATION

Glen felt that the budgeted cost–price ratio for the gatherer chain was unacceptable and was anxious to see what could be done to address the problem. He remarked to Jim that

> The competition is pretty strict about maintaining a 50–50 cost–price ratio on their product lines. Why is it they can sell this product for $30.00 and we can't match their cost structure?

Jim felt that he had gathered enough information to do some preliminary analysis. However, he was aware that he needed to think about how he could use the information in his negotiation with the vendor. Susan had indicated that Wayne Saunders had been a tough negotiator, with a "take it or leave it" attitude regarding pricing, and had been unwilling to share any specific cost information to justify his requests for price increases.

Case 9–2

McMichael Inc.

Art Flynn, packaging buyer for McMichael Inc. (MI), was working on an import substitution project involving a local minority supplier. He was concerned, however, that his efforts would be fruitless since his original proposal had been flatly rejected by the plant manager as too expensive.

McMichael Inc., a medium-sized company, had over the years specialized in prescription skin-care products, a market niche in which it had developed an excellent reputation. About three years ago, after extensive testing, MI had introduced a new facial cream in a special package that allowed for precise measurement of the quantity dispersed. The container, manufactured by a French firm for a different application, was fairly expensive at an FOB MI's factory cost of $0.36. What concerned Art Flynn even more, however, were the quality and delivery problems encountered. Communications with the manufacturer were difficult and Art had the impression the manufacturer did not seem to care much about MI's business, which, as Art knew, was only a small proportion of their total volume produced.

With the cooperation of MI's marketing, engineering, production, and quality control personnel, Art had found a local minority supplier who appeared capable of meeting MI's requirements. This custom molding firm, OSA Inc., was owned by Bert Wood, a bright engineer, who had purchased the firm several years earlier when the previous owner wished to retire. OSA Inc. had its own tool and die manufacturing operation as well as its own molding shop. It depended heavily on automotive contracts, a situation Bert Wood wished to correct by acquiring more nonautomotive business. In conjunction with MI's engineers, Bert Wood had worked out a mold design for the cream dispenser and included several suggestions for minor improvements. The cost of the mold was $56,000, an investment Bert Wood was in no position to make and that MI would have to absorb up front. Bert Wood quoted a unit price of $0.27 based on purchase quantities of 30,000 units at a time and an annual volume estimated at 300,000 units. Bert Wood had submitted a cost breakdown of this quote as follows:

Resin	16¢
Labor	3¢
Overhead*	8¢
	27¢

*Overhead breakdown:

Power	1¢
Depreciation	1¢
Interest	3¢
Space, insurance, light and heat, taxes, supervision	3¢

When Art submitted this quote along with the request for a $56,000 mold investment up front, the plant manager and treasurer both turned it down, arguing the 24-month payback on the mold was far too long and that the company had better investment opportunities with a 12-month payback.

Art was disappointed, because he had hoped this project would assist in helping him meet his savings target for the year. When he talked the idea over with his manager, Louise Moffat, she suggested he give it another try. She said: "I am sure that if you can get the mold payback down to 15 months, you will get a warmer reception. There are not that many deals around this company that pay for themselves in one year." She also suggested Art talk to marketing to see if some other products could use the same packaging and to the production scheduling group to check if different production quantities could be ordered.

When Art talked to the marketing people, he found out that the package was ideal for another product to be introduced shortly and with an annual demand estimated at 100,000 units. Marketing had been uneasy about using the French package because of the difficulties encountered with it and assured Art that if he could get a reliable domestic source, this option would be highly attractive.

The scheduling group, for a number of years, had used a modified MRP system. When Art discussed the new package idea with them, they told him that if the new product and the older one were to be packaged in the same package, a total package requirement of about 40,000 units would make sense and that the master production schedule could easily be adjusted to run the two products in conjunction.

Art also discussed the situation with the resin supplier, who indicated that his quote to Bert Wood had been based on the lot size of 30,000 packages, but that a 40,000 unit lot would fall into a new price bracket 5 percent lower than the originally quoted price.

Art wondered just what effect all of this new information would have on his original proposal. He knew that Bert Wood had been adamant about his $0.27 quote. Bert Wood had said: "I know I am classified as a minority supplier. But I don't want to hide behind that fact. I want no special favors from any of my customers. Nor am I in a position to make special gifts to anyone else. I have had to borrow at what I consider to be ridiculously high interest rates to buy this company. Now I have to make it pay off. My $0.27 price is as low as I can go, as far as I can see."

Chapter Ten

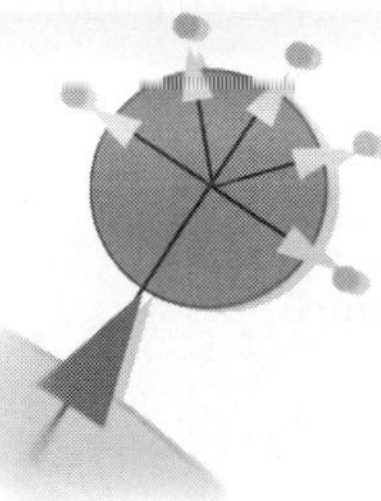

Supplier Selection

Chapter Outline

Key Questions for the Supply Manager

Should we

- Use cross-functional sourcing teams to select suppliers?
- Use one or more suppliers?
- Switch from informal to formal supplier evaluation?

How can we

- Reach agreement with internal business partners on evaluation criteria and weighting?
- Balance financial and nonfinancial factors when selecting suppliers?
- Be sure that we choose the best supplier available?

Effective sourcing decisions form the basis of sound supply for any organization. These decisions should be driven by a sourcing strategy that is directly linked to organizational strategy, goals, and objectives. Many organizations have adopted the term *strategic sourcing* to capture the linkage between sourcing strategy and organizational strategy. A strategic sourcing process considers suppliers and the supply base integral to an organization's competitive advantage. It is important to define clearly the term *strategic* and establish what makes a purchase or a supplier strategically important to the organization. Typically, a strategic purchase is one that is mission-critical. The good or service has the potential to either help or hinder the attainment of the organization's mission. Categorizing purchases into strategic and nonstrategic buckets is a first step in the strategic sourcing process. This type of categorization drives the decisions throughout the sourcing and selection process including the allocation of resources to any specific buy. Without this categorization, the supply manager or sourcing team may overinvest resources, time, and attention in tactical or operational purchases and underinvest in strategic ones.

The development of supply strategy is addressed in Chapter 20 and commodity strategy is covered in Chapter 13, "Research and Metrics." In this and Chapters 18 and 19, the major factors influencing supplier choice and development are discussed. This chapter focuses on finding and evaluating suppliers and examining issues of supplier number, location, and size. Chapter 18 examines make or buy, insourcing, and outsourcing, while Chapter 19 focuses on supplier relations and supply chain management.

THE SUPPLIER SELECTION DECISION

The decision to place a certain volume of business with a supplier should always be based on a reasonable set of criteria. The art of good purchasing and supply management is to make the reasoning behind this decision as sound as possible. Normally, the analysis of the supplier's ability to meet satisfactory quality, quantity, delivery, price/cost, and service objectives governs this decision. Some of the more important supplier attributes related to these prime criteria may include past history, facilities and technical strength, financial status, organization and management, reputation, systems, procedural compliance, communications, labor relations, and location. Obviously, the nature and amount of the purchase will influence the weighting attached to each objective and hence the evidence needed to support the decision. For example, for a small order of new circuit boards to be used by engineers in a new-product design, quality and rapid delivery are of greater significance than price. The supplier should probably be local for ease of communication with the design engineers and have good technical credentials. However, for a large printed circuit board order for a production run, price would be one key factor, and delivery should be on time, but not necessarily unusually fast. Thus, even on requirements with identical technical specifications, the weighting of the selection criteria may vary. It is this sensitivity to organizational needs that separates the good supply manager from the average. The one result every buyer wishes to avoid is unacceptable supplier performance. This may create costs far out of proportion to the size of the original purchase, upset internal relationships, and strain supplier goodwill and final customer satisfaction.

Decision Trees

The supplier selection decision can be seen as decision making under uncertainty and can be represented by a decision tree. Figure 10–1 shows a very simple, one-stage situation with only two suppliers seriously considered and two possible outcomes. It illustrates, however, the uncertain environment present in almost every supplier choice and the risk inherent in the decision. To use decision trees effectively, the buyer must identify the options and the criteria for evaluation and assess the probabilities of success and failure. This simple tree could apply to a special one-time purchase without expectation of follow-on business for some time to come.

The more normal situation for repetitive purchases is shown in Figure 10–2. Whether the chosen source performs well or not for the current purchase under consideration, the future decision about which supplier to deal with next time around may well affect the present decision. For example, if the business is placed with supplier C and C fails, this may mean that only A could be considered a reasonable source at the next stage. If having

FIGURE 10–1
A Simple One-Stage Supplier Selection Decision

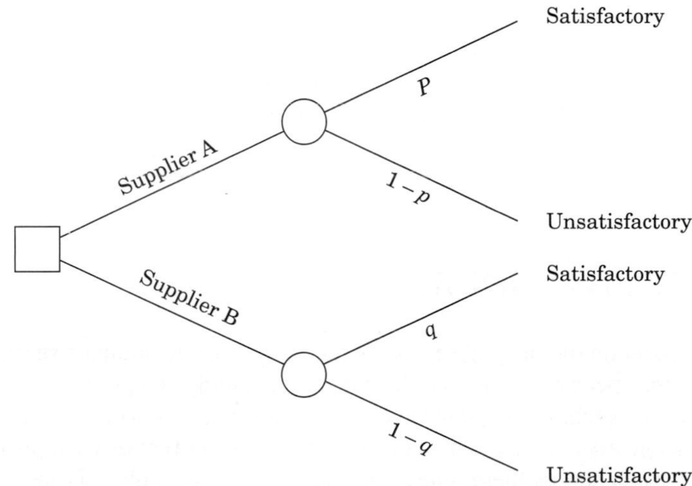

FIGURE 10–2
Simplified Three-Stage Decision Tree for Supplier Selection

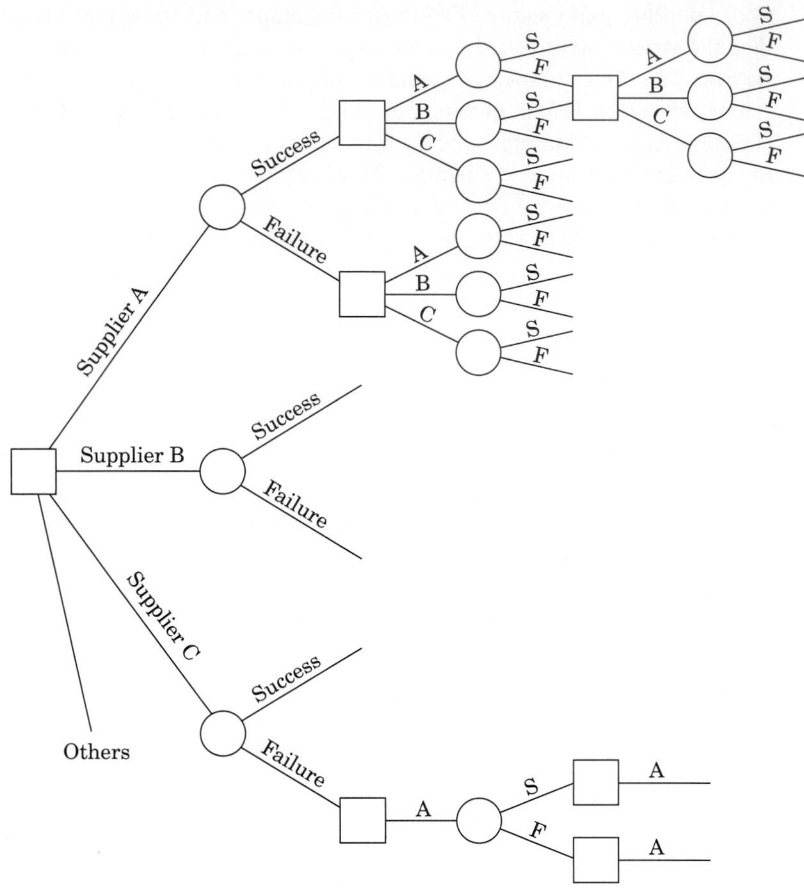

A as a single source, without alternatives, is not acceptable, choosing C as the supplier at the first stage does not make any sense.

It is necessary to consider the selection decision as part of a chain of events, rather than as an isolated instance. This addition of a time frame—past, present, and future—makes the sourcing decision even more complex. However, as long as the objective of finding and keeping good sources is clearly kept in mind, the decision can be evaluated in a reasonable business context.

IDENTIFYING POTENTIAL SOURCES

The identification of potential sources is a key driver of the ultimate success or failure from a performance perspective. Research on decision making and problem solving indicates that the chances of reaching an optimal decision depend in large part on the decision maker's ability to generate alternatives. When faced with a problem, typically people quickly identify a few alternatives, assess them, select the "best" one, and implement the selection. In many cases, the "truly best" solution was never considered because it was the 5th or 10th or 15th alternative that was never identified. Therefore, sourcing teams should determine how to build a comprehensive knowledge base of potential suppliers.

Information Sources

Knowledge of sources is a primary qualification for any effective buyer. Online searches, e-catalogs, and company Web sites are the most common tools used today. Other sources include trade journals, advertisements, supplier and commodity directories, sales interviews, colleagues, professional contacts, and the supply department's own records.

Online Sources

The Internet and the World Wide Web provide a rapidly growing and ever-changing body of information for supply professionals. The challenge for most buyers is not finding information, but identifying, sorting, analyzing, and using relevant information. The following brief list contains Web addresses for some sites of interest to supply.

Chemical Abstracts. http://www.chemistry.org/acs/ This is the home page of the American Chemical Society. There is also a members-only section that requires a membership/access fee.

Institute for Supply Management (ISM). http://www.ism.ws Many of the resources are available to members only. The site includes the monthly manufacturing and non-manufacturing Reports on Business, considered leading indicators of economic activity in the United States, and the JPMorgan Global PMI Reports on Manufacturing and Services.

Purchasing Management Association of Canada (PMAC). http://www.pmac.ca The site includes the Ivey Purchasing Managers' Index, a leading indicator of economic activity in Canada.

Ivey Purchasing Managers Index. http://iveypmi.uwo.ca The Richard Ivey School of Business at the University of Western Ontario manages the Canadian Purchasing Managers Index. The index includes goods, services, and government.

Government of Canada. http://www.canada.gc.ca/ The home page for the Canadian government with links to any Canadian government department.

Primark Financial Information Division. http://www.primark.com Provides financial information on U.S. and international companies through flexible delivery platforms.

U.S. Securities and Exchange Commission. http://www.sec.gov All companies in the United States who file their quarterly 10Q and annual 10K reports are on this database.

D&B. http://www.dnb.com D&B provides basic company reports online for a fee, and company's location and products gratis.

Thomas Register. http://www.thomasregister.com The most comprehensive online resource for finding companies and products manufactured in North America. Services include online order placement, viewing and downloading of millions of computer-aided design (CAD) drawings, and viewing thousands of online company catalogs and Web sites. It includes listings for over 173,000 companies in the United States and Canada and over 8,000 online supplier catalogs and Web links.

Worldpages.com. http://www.worldpages.com This is an Internet and Yellow Pages directory company with listings in the United States and Canada, and links to more than 350 international directories. It also links to a directory of toll-free (800/888) numbers in the United States.

World Wide Yellow Pages. http://www.yellow.com/ This is a worldwide listing of companies.

Ziff Davis Media Publications. http://www.zdnet.com This is a resource for information on e-commerce.

Catalogs

A well-managed purchasing and supply department must have catalogs of the commonly known sources of supply, covering the most important materials in which a company is interested. The value of catalogs depends largely on presentation form, accessibility, and frequency and extent of use. Electronic catalogs (discussed in Chapter 4) are increasingly used. The advantage of e-catalogs is that both buyers and internal customers have ready access to them and they can be customized to include the prices and other terms and conditions negotiated by the buyer with the seller. Management of e-catalog content is as serious an issue as management of hard-copy catalogs. Advances in online catalog management continue to increase the ease of access and improve the form of presentation.

The accessibility of catalog content is driven by the manner in which it is indexed and filed, a not-so-simple task even with online catalogs. Catalogs are issued in all sorts of sizes and formats, which makes them difficult to handle. Proper indexing of catalogs is essential. Some companies still use microfilm files and loose-leaf binders with sheets especially printed for catalog filing; others use a form of card index. Indexing should be according to suppliers' names as well as products listed. It should be specific, definite, and easily understandable. Distributors' catalogs contain many items from a variety of manufacturing sources and offer a directory of available commodities within the distributors' fields. Equipment and machinery catalogs provide information about specifications and the location of a source of supply for replacement parts as well as new equipment. Catalogs frequently provide price information and many supplies and materials are sold from standard list prices or by quoting discounts only. Catalogs are also used as reference books by internal customers.

Trade Journals

Trade journals also are a valuable source of information as to potential suppliers. The list of such publications is, of course, very long, and the individual items in it vary tremendously in value. Yet, in every field, there are worthwhile trade magazines, and buyers read extensively those dealing with their own industry and with those industries to which they sell and from which they buy. These journals are utilized in two ways. The first use is to gain general information from the articles that might suggest new products and substitute materials as well as information about suppliers and their personnel. The second use is a consistent perusal of the advertisements to stay current on offerings.

Trade Directories

Trade directories are another useful source of information. They vary widely in their accuracy and usefulness, and care must be exercised in their use. Trade registers, or trade directories, are volumes that list leading manufacturers, their addresses, number of branches, affiliations, products, and, in some instances, their financial standing or their position in the trade. They also contain listings of the trade names of articles on the market with names of the manufacturers, and classified lists of materials, supplies, equipment, and other items offered for sale, under each of which is given the name and location of available manufacturing sources of supply. These registers are organized by commodity, manufacturer, or trade name. Standard directories include the Thomas Register (http://www.thomasregister.com), MacRae's Blue Book (http://www.macraesbluebook.com), and Kompass publications (http://www.kompass.com).

Trade directories of minority- and women-owned business enterprises can assist purchasers with a goal or requirement to increase the percentage of contracts awarded to these firms. For example, the Central Contractor Registration (www.ccr.gov) simplifies the federal contracting process by creating an integrated database of small, disadvantaged, 8(a), and women-owned businesses that want to do business with the government. Searches can be based on SIC codes, keywords, location, quality certifications, business type, and ownership race and gender. Diversity Information Resources (www.diversityinforesources.org) fosters minority economic development through the publication of directories of minority- and women-owned businesses with access to a database of over 9,800 certified M/WBE suppliers, veteran, service-disabled veteran, and HUBZone suppliers. A number of organizations also certify businesses as minority- and women-owned, including the Women's Business Enterprise National Council (WBENC) (http://www.wbenc.org); the National Women Business Owners Corporation (NWBOC) (http://www.nwboc.org); the National Minority Supplier Development Council (NMSDC) (http://www.nmsdc.org); and, in the public sector, the Office of Small and Disadvantaged Business Utilization (OSDBU) (http://osdbuweb.dot.gov).

Sales Representatives

Sales representatives may constitute one of the most valuable sources of information available, with references to sources of supply, types of products, and trade information generally. One challenge for supply personnel is balancing the need to meet with sales representatives with other responsibilities and time constraints. It is essential to develop good supplier relations, which begin with a friendly, courteous, sympathetic, and frank attitude toward the supplier's salesperson. After contact, relevant information should be captured in a format that can be easily accessed and used effectively. Some organizations develop routing mechanisms on their Web sites to alleviate the time pressure on buyers and sellers by providing information about how to do business with the organization and routing callers to the appropriate person.

Supplier and Commodity Databases

Information from any source, if of value, should be captured. For example, an index of catalogs makes it easy to access a needed catalog. Two common databases are of suppliers and commodities. The supplier database includes information on each active supplier including locations and contact information, open orders and past orders, supplier performance scorecards, and other pertinent information that might be of value to future decisions. Supplier databases may be managed online, in a simple computer file, or in a card file.

A commodity database classifies material on the basis of the product and includes information related to the sources from which the product has been purchased in the past, perhaps the price paid, the point of shipment, and a link or cross-reference to the supplier database. Miscellaneous information is also given, such as whether specifications are called for, whether a contract already exists covering the item, whether competitive bids are commonly asked for, and other data that may be of importance. Accompanying files dealing with sources are, of course, those relating to price and other records. Some of these have already been discussed in earlier chapters, and others will be discussed later. The information management aspects of enterprise resource planning (ERP) systems and e-procurement systems are discussed in Chapter 4.

Visits to Suppliers

Some supply managers feel that visits to suppliers are particularly useful when there are no difficulties to discuss. The supply manager can talk with higher-level executives rather than confining discussion to someone who happens to be directly responsible for handling a specific complaint. This helps to cement good relations at all levels of management and may reveal much about a supplier's future plans that might not otherwise come to the buyer's attention. Such a visitation policy does raise certain problems not found in the more routine types of visits, such as who should make the visits, how best to get worthwhile information, and the best use of the data once obtained. Experience has indicated that the best results come from (1) developing, in advance, a general outline of the kinds of information sought; (2) gathering, in advance, all reasonably available information, both general and specific, about the company; and (3) preparing a detailed report of the findings after the visit. When the visits are carefully planned, the direct expense incurred is small compared with the returns.

Samples

In addition to the usual inquiries and a plant visit, samples of the supplier's product can be tested. This requires thinking about the "sample problem." Frequently, a sales representative for a new product urges the buyer to accept a sample for test purposes. This raises questions as to what samples to accept, how to ensure a fair test of those accepted, who should bear the expense of testing, and whether or not the supplier should be given the results of the test. (See "Testing and Samples" in Chapter 5.)

Colleagues

Frequently, internal business partners are valuable sources of information about potential sources of supply. Purchase requisitions may invite the requisitioner to identify potential sources.

References

Often buyers will include a request for references in the RFQ, RFP, or RFB. To get the most useful information possible, it is the job of the interviewer to set the parameters for the interview. First, make sure that the reference is a company of similar size and objectives. Second, talk to people with firsthand knowledge of the supplier's performance. Third, ask open-ended questions that allow the reference to describe the performance of the supplier and the relationship. For example, a new customer might be asked about the implementation process: "Did it go smoothly? Tell me about a time things weren't going according to plan. How did the supplier deal with the problem or change?" A veteran customer might be asked about the supplier's actions to stay competitive or to continuously improve: "Tell me about a time when the supplier initiated an improvement that also benefited you (the customer)?" Past customers might be asked about the transition process to another supplier: "When you switched suppliers, how did the original supplier handle the transition of information? materials? etc.?"[1] Potential sources need to be evaluated.

THE EVALUATION OF POTENTIAL SOURCES

Obviously, the evaluation of an existing supplier is substantially easier than the evaluation of a new source. Since checking out a new supplier often requires an extensive amount of time and resources, it should be done only for those suppliers who stand a serious chance of receiving a significant order. Where such a potential supplier competes with an existing supplier, the expected performance of the new source should, hopefully, be better than that of the existing one. The use of trial orders has been mentioned as a popular means of testing a supplier's capability, but it still fails to answer the question as to whether the trial order should have been placed with a particular source at all. Even though a supplier may complete a trial order successfully, it may not be an acceptable source in the long run.

The evaluation of potential sources, therefore, attempts to answer two key questions:

1. Is this supplier capable of supplying the purchaser's requirements satisfactorily in both the short and long term?
2. Is this supplier motivated to supply these requirements in the way the purchaser expects in the short and long term?

The first question can be largely answered on a technical basis. The second probes the human side. Why should supplier personnel give special attention to this purchaser's requirements?

In evaluating potential sources, the most common major factors are technical or engineering capability, manufacturing or distribution strength, financial strength, and management capability.

Technical, Engineering, Manufacturing, and Distribution Strengths

Technical and engineering capability, along with manufacturing strength, impinge on a number of supply concerns. The most obvious factor is the quality capability of the supplier. It is possible, however, that a company capable of meeting current quality standards may still lack the engineering and technical strengths to stay current with technological advances. Similarly, manufacturing may lack capacity, or the space to expand, or the flexibility to meet a variety of requirements. Presumably, the reason for selecting one supplier over another is because of greater strengths in areas of importance to the purchaser. The evaluation of the

[1] Chuck Stefanosky, "Don't Be Afraid to Dig Deep," *Purchasing Today*, November 1999, pp. 10–11.

supplier, therefore, should focus not only on current capability, but also on the supplier's future strengths. Only in very large organizations might the supply group have sufficient technical strength to conduct such supplier evaluations on its own. Normally, other functions such as engineering, manufacturing, internal users, or quality control provide expert assistance to assess a potential supplier on technical and manufacturing strengths.

Should the supplier be a distributor, the stress might be more on distribution capability. The nature of the agreements with the distributors supplying manufacturers, their inventory policies, systems capability and compatibility, and ability to respond to special requirements would all be assessed, along with technical strengths of the personnel required to assist the purchasing organization to make the right choices among a series of different acceptable options. A number of distributors have developed strong supplier/vendor managed inventory programs, permitting organizations the option of outsourcing the total MRO supply function and reducing the total supply base significantly.

Management and Financial Evaluation

As the tendency toward greater reliance on single sources for a longer period of time continues, along with greater interest in materials requirements, just-in-time production, and strategic sourcing, a potential supplier's management strengths take on added significance. From the supply point of view, the key question is: Is the management of this supplier a corporate strength or a weakness? This will require a detailed examination of the organization's mission, its corporate values and goals, its structure, qualifications of managers, management controls, the performance evaluation and reward system, training and development, information systems, and policies and procedures. It is also useful to have an explanation as to why the supplier's management believes it is managing well and an indication of its most notable successes and failures. A functional assessment of strengths and weaknesses in areas like marketing, supply, accounting, and so on, will substantiate the overall picture. For example, in a contract where the supplier spends a substantial percentage of total volume on raw materials and parts with outside suppliers or subcontractors, the supply group of the buying organization would be best suited to evaluate the supplier's procurement system, organization, procedures, and personnel. This is especially important when assessing supply chains that consist of multiple tiers of suppliers.

Supplier documentation and personal visits by the sourcing team are typically required. For large contracts in large organizations, the sourcing team's formal report detailing the management strengths and weaknesses of potential suppliers may be the deciding factor in the selection process.

The financial strengths and weaknesses of a supplier obviously affect its capability to respond to the needs of customers. The buyer must determine the extent of the financial assessment appropriate for each purchase. As discussed earlier in this chapter, the critical question is: Is the product or service strategic? If so, then the supplier is strategically important and a full financial analysis is necessary. While short-term alternatives may lessen the risks, the strategic nature of the purchase indicates the need for complete understanding of the long-term risks and opportunities from the supplier's financial situation. Many supply managers focus on early warning systems to alert them to changes in the financial situation of key suppliers that may affect the buying organization. This allows them to step in and work with the supplier or strengthen their contingency plans should the supplier's situation worsen.

There are often substantial opportunities for negotiation if the purchaser is fully familiar with the financial status of a supplier. For example, the offer of advance payment or cash discounts may have little appeal to a cash-rich source but be highly attractive to a firm short of working capital. A supplier with substantial inventories may be able to offer supply assurance and a degree of price protection at times of shortages that cannot be matched by others without the materials or the funds to acquire them.

Individual financial measures that may be examined include, but are not limited to, credit rating, capital structure, profitability, ability to meet interest and dividend obligations, working capital, inventory turnover, current ratio, and return on investment. Presumably, financial stability and strength are indicators of good management and competitive ability. Financial statements, therefore, are a useful source of information about a supplier's past performance. Whether the supplier will continue to perform in the same manner in the future is an assessment the purchaser must make, taking all available information, including the financial side, into account. Some of the financial ratios that a buyer may want to take a look at include profit and loss, inventory turnover, accounts receivable turns, and current ratio (see Chapter 13, "Research and Metrics," for a detailed discussion of these metrics and their uses). This information is available from Dun & Bradstreet (http://www.dnb.com) and Hoover's (http://www.hoovers.com). For privately held companies, the buyer may have difficulty accessing sufficient financial information depending on the buyer's strength in the relationship.

There is general agreement among supply executives that a supplier's management capability and financial strength are vital factors in source evaluation and selection. Even after a satisfactory evaluation of management, financial, and technical strengths of a supplier has been completed, the question remains as to what weight should be accorded to each of the various dimensions. Also, should the supply manager take the initiative in insisting that the supplier correct certain deficiencies, particularly on the management or financial side?

Many examples exist that illustrate the need for supplier strength. These are normally related to the long-term survival of the company. Small suppliers are frequently dependent on the health, age, and abilities of the owner-manager. Every time this individual steps into an automobile, the fate of the company rides along. The attitudes of this individual toward certain customers may be very important in supply assurance.

Most long-term and significant supplier–buyer relationships are highly dependent on the relationships and communication channels built by the respective managers in each organization. Unless each side is willing and able to listen and respond to information supplied by the other side, problems are not likely to be resolved to mutual satisfaction.

SUPPLIER EVALUATION METHODS

Once the buyer or sourcing team has narrowed the list of potential sources, a decision has to be made about the final selection process. Often, the buyer or sourcing team is comparing a current supplier with a performance record to potential suppliers with only secondhand performance information. A current supplier is one that has passed through earlier supplier screening efforts and subsequently received, at a minimum, one order. Most buyers tend to separate current suppliers into at least two categories: those that are so new to the supply base there is insufficient performance data to assess and established suppliers who have proven to be reliable, good sources over time. Both groups are evaluated continuously, formally and informally. Nevertheless, it is common practice to pay special attention to new sources who have not yet established a proven track record of satisfactory performance over time under a variety of market conditions.

The evaluation and selection process can be highly informal or highly structured and formalized depending on the nature of the purchase. In this section, several methods are discussed, including informal, categorical, and weighted-point evaluations.

Informal and Semiformal Evaluation and Rating

Informal evaluation includes assessments of the supplier by internal users and others anywhere in the buying organization where such contact takes place. "How are things going with supplier X?" is a typical question that can and should be asked by supply personnel when in contact with others in their own organization. Similarly, information gleaned from conversations at professional meetings, at conferences, and from the media can be useful in checking out and comparing such personal impressions. A knowledgeable buyer will have accumulated a wealth of such information on suppliers and will always be on the alert for signs that new information may affect the overall assessment of a supplier. In fact, in most small organizations, almost all evaluation of current sources is carried out informally. When users and buyers are in daily personal contact and feedback on both satisfactory and unsatisfactory supplier performance is quick, such informality makes a lot of sense.

In larger organizations, however, communication lines are stretched, supply personnel and internal users may be in different locations, and large contracts may be negotiated by a centralized purchasing group or a prime contractor located at a primary facility, while daily supplier contact is handled at various locations. If suppliers are also large, requirements in different locations of the country or the world may be met with varying degrees of success by different plants belonging to the same supplier. As the buyer–supplier network grows in complexity, the need to have a more-formal system for evaluating current sources also increases.

Executive Roundtable Discussions

One simple semiformal supplier evaluation tool is the regular, annual discussion between top executives in the buying organization and those of the supplier. Normally, these top-level discussions are confined to major suppliers of major or strategic requirements. The presence of top executives of both sides lends weight to the occasion and permits discussion of past performance; future expectations; economic, social, and technological trends; long-term plans; and so on, in a high-level context. The chief purchasing officer (CPO) normally takes the lead in organizing and facilitating such sessions and invites the appropriate executives to take part. These roundtable discussions can help cement relationships between the buyer and supplier at a high level, and when repeated over time can provide invaluable information for both sides. They would normally, but not exclusively, take place at the buying organization.

Obviously, the number of such high-level sessions must be limited. Equivalent lower-level sessions for suppliers further down on the priority list also have considerable merit and permit a regular update in a broader context than the normal supplier–purchaser contacts geared to specific current orders.

Formal Supplier Evaluation and Rating

Accompanying the trends of supply base rationalization, strategic sourcing, and closer relations with key suppliers is the growing sophistication in supplier performance rating. Often, continuous improvement is tracked along with more traditional factors such as quality, quantity, delivery, and price. In other cases, suggestions for product or service redesign, value chain improvements, willingness to work on supply-chain teams, assistance in investment recovery or disposal, or the development of anything that would provide better value for the ultimate customer may be tracked and recorded. In evaluating current sources, the question is: How well did the supplier do? To use this information in future supplier selection decisions, the key question is: What is the supplier's performance likely to be in the future?

Most formal supplier rating approaches attempt to track actual performance over time. Advances in purchasing process software allow for easier tracking on a real-time basis and greater performance visibility. As orders are delivered, quality, quantity, delivery, price, and service objectives and other terms and conditions are tracked. Thus, corrective action can be taken as needed on the existing contract. Also, when it is time to place another order, the past record can be used to assess whether the same supplier should again be seriously considered or not. A simple scheme for smaller organizations might include a notation only as to whether these factors were acceptable or not for specific orders received. More detailed evaluations include a summary of supplier performance over time.

It is normal to track a supplier's quality performance closely and in sufficient detail to pinpoint corrective action. In many organizations, only certified suppliers are considered for potential future business and extensive evaluations on quality and other dimensions of supplier attributes and performance are carried out accordingly (see Chapter 5).

Delivery performance of a current supplier is fairly easily tracked if good records exist of delivery promises and actual receipts and few modifications have been made on an informal basis. In a JIT mode, nonperformance on delivery is just as critical as unsatisfactory quality and actual delivery is closely monitored. In the example below, different levels of delivery performance are described and assigned a category rating (excellent, good, fair, poor).

Excellent:	*a.* Meets delivery dates without expediting.
	b. Requested delivery dates are usually accepted.
Good:	*c.* Usually meets shipping dates without substantial follow-up.
	d. Often is able to accept requested delivery dates.
Fair:	*e.* Shipments sometimes late; substantial amount of follow-up required.
Poor:	*f.* Shipments usually late; delivery promises seldom met; constant expediting required.

Quantifying the assessment is often preferred because it signifies an attempt to remove subjectivity from the process. Some performance areas, such as delivery, are more easily quantified than others, such as service. For example, the on-time delivery window might be defined by a particular company as anywhere between two days early and zero days late as committed to master scheduling. Deliveries are tracked and performance is rated according to a preestablished rating system. For example, delivery may be worth 15 out of 100 points, which means that delivery performance carries 15 percent of the weight of the decision. Points for on-time delivery might be allocated as follows:

15 points	> 98% on-time
10 points	95–97.9% on-time
5 points	90–94.9% on-time
0 points	< 90% on-time

Actual price performance of a supplier is easily tracked, as discrepancies between agreed-to prices and those actually invoiced by suppliers should normally be brought to supply's attention anyway. Price ratings of suppliers are, therefore, often of a comparison type, actual price versus target, or actual price versus lowest price received from other suppliers supplying the same requirement. Assessment of total cost of ownership from one supplier to another is more difficult to track, and often far more important than year-over-year price savings. Estimating total cost for a potential supplier rather than a current one is even more difficult and adds a level of complexity to the decision process.

It is in the service area that perhaps the most judgment is called for. Opinions need to be collected on the quality of technical assistance, supplier attitude, and response time to requests for assistance, support staff qualifications, and so on. It is normal, therefore, to have a relatively simple rating scheme for service, such as outstanding, acceptable, and poor, along with explanations regarding specific incidents to explain these ratings. Efforts should be made to create objective assessments of service performance including clearly defined service levels and metrics. A key driver in satisfactory service performance is clear and unambiguous descriptions of the required service level included in statement of work.

It is even more difficult to establish metrics to assess supplier performance or projected performance in areas of strategic importance, such as innovation. Measures of innovation at an organizational level might include the percentage of sales attributable to new products or services, the number of new patents or new products successfully introduced, or gross margins from new products compared to gross margins from existing products. Measuring supply and suppliers' direct and indirect contribution to these metrics is an ongoing challenge.

Weighted Point Evaluation Systems

Many organizations rate suppliers by assigning points and scales to each factor and each rating. Where several sources supply the same goods or services, such schemes permit cross-comparisons. Outstanding performance of a supplier can then be rewarded with additional business, while poor performance may result in the development and implementation of a performance improvement plan, or lead to less business with the supplier, or possibly dropping a supplier altogether. The IPC case in Chapter 13 provides a good example of a weighted point evaluation system and how it applies to a specific supplier.

Several issues are of concern with weighted point evaluation systems. The typical process for developing a weighted point evaluation system is to to the organization from this particular sourcing decision. This strategy drives the process. At this stage of the assessment, a number of issues must be addressed at a high-level, strategic perspective. A more thorough analysis of some of these criteria may take place at the next level of evaluation. These issues include

1. Should we use a single source, dual sources, or more than two?
2. Should we buy from a manufacturer or a distributor?
3. Where should the supplier be located?
4. Relative to our organization, should the supplier be small, medium, or large?
5. Are there social, political, ethical, legal, or environmental issues we should consider?
6. Should we purchase for a supplier?
7. Should we purchase for company personnel?
8. What risks might the organization expose itself to?

Single versus Multiple Sourcing

Should the buyer rely upon a single supplier or utilize several? The answer to this question must be the very unsatisfactory one, "It all depends."

Briefly, the arguments for placing all orders for a given item with one supplier are as follows:

1. Prior commitments, a successful past relationship, or an ongoing long-term contract with a preferred supplier might prevent even the possibility of splitting the order.
2. The supplier may be the exclusive owner of certain essential patents or processes and, therefore, be the only possible source. Under such circumstances, the purchaser has no choice, provided that no satisfactory substitute is available.
3. A given supplier may be so outstanding in the quality of product or in the service or value provided as to preclude serious consideration of buying elsewhere.
4. The order may be so small as to make it not worthwhile to divide it.
5. Concentrating purchases may make possible certain discounts or lower freight rates that could not be had otherwise.
6. The supplier will be more cooperative, more interested, and more willing to please if it has all the buyer's business.
7. When the purchase of an item involves a die, tool, mold charge, or costly setup, the expense of duplicating this equipment or setup is likely to be substantial.
8. Deliveries may be more easily scheduled.
9. Just-in-time production, stockless buying or systems contracting, or EDI may be used.
10. Effective supplier relations require considerable resources and time. Therefore, the fewer suppliers the better.
11. Single sourcing is a prerequisite to partnering.

On the other hand, there are arguments for multiple sourcing—provided, of course, that the sacrifice is not too great:

1. It has been traditional practice to use more than one source, especially on the important requirements, even though in the United States single sourcing has been the trend for years.

1. Identify the factors or criteria for evaluation.
2. Determine the importance of each factor.
3. Establish a system for rating each supplier on each factor.

The relevant factors or decision criteria should be determined in the context of the chase and the sourcing strategy for that item. Clearly, most organizations track major pliers more closely than those sources deemed to have less impact on organizational formance. Some organizations use annual dollar volume as a guide toward such cate rization, for example, identifying A, B, and C sources, much the same as inventories can classified using the Pareto distribution (see Chapters 3 and 6). Some organizations adc special category of "critical" goods or services regardless of dollar volume, where unsati factory performance by a supplier might result in serious problems for the organization. Th purpose of such categorization is to fit each category with an appropriate supplier ratin scheme. For example, for a high-value, high-volume purchase over a long-term contract, th buyer may include factors such as the supplier's management, human resources, and information systems fit. For a C-item (low dollar value, high volume), the critical factors may be delivery, availability, convenience, and price. There are a number of ways to assign weight to the factors. One is to assign percentages to each factor for a total of 100 percent.

Obviously, the selection of the factors, weights, and form of measurement will require considerable thought to ensure congruence between the organization's priorities for this product class and the rating scheme's ability to identify superior suppliers correctly. For different product classes, different factors, weights, and measures should be used to reflect varying impact on the organization.

In a fully computerized system, all supplier performance data would be entered as orders were received, and the buyer (and the supplier in some cases) should have online access so as to be able to discuss the supplier's performance at any time. Suppliers need to be informed as to how they stand on the rating scale. Improved performance on the part of the supplier often results from the knowledge that its rating is lower than some competitor's or falls short of a set target.

LINKING SOURCING WITH STRATEGY

From these various sources of information, the buyer is able to make up a list of available suppliers from whom the necessary items can be acquired. The first level of analysis is finding out which suppliers might be able to meet the buying organization's requirements. The second level of analysis is determining which of these the supply manager or sourcing team is willing to seriously consider as a source. For items that are high risk and high value, the investigation may be drawn out and extensive, requiring the collaboration of supply, internal users, and technical experts such as engineering, quality control, systems, and maintenance on a formal or informal team. The cost of analysis greatly outweighs the advantages for items that are inexpensive and consumed in small quantities.

Narrowing the list has implications beyond the decision and can and will impact the buying organization throughout the life of the contract. In an effective strategic sourcing process, the hard work is all on the front end. A category- or commodity-sourcing strategy should be in place and address all the factors that influence the ability to maximize value

2. Knowing that competitors are getting some of the business may tend to keep the supplier more alert to the need for giving good prices and service.
3. Assurance of supply is increased. Should fire, strikes, breakdowns, or accidents occur to any one supplier, deliveries can still be obtained from the others for at least part of the needs.
4. The purchasing organization has developed a unique capability for dealing with multiple sources.
5. It avoids supplier dependence on the purchaser.
6. The purchasing organization obtains a greater degree and volume of flexibility, because the unused capacity of all the suppliers may be available.
7. Even in situations involving close and cooperative supplier relationships, it is possible to make backup arrangements so that supplier X specializes in product Q and backs up supplier Y, who specializes in product R and backs up supplier X.
8. Strategic reasons, such as military preparedness and supply security, may require multiple sourcing.
9. Government regulations may insist that multiple suppliers, or small or minority sources, be used. If there is high risk associated with a small or single-minority source, multiple sourcing may be necessary.
10. Sufficient capacity may not be available to accommodate the purchaser's current or future needs.
11. Potential new or future suppliers may have to be tested with trial orders, while other sources receive the bulk of the current business.
12. Volatility in the supply market makes single sourcing unacceptably risky.

Genuine concern exists among supply executives as to how much business should be placed with one supplier, particularly if the supplier is small and the buyer's business represents a significant portion of the seller's revenue. It is feared that sudden discontinuance of purchases may put the supplier's survival in jeopardy, and, yet, the purchaser does not wish to reduce flexibility by being tied to dependent sources. One simple rule of thumb traditionally used was that no more than a certain percentage, say 20 or 30 percent, of the total supplier's business should be with one customer.

If a decision is made to divide an order among several suppliers, there is then the question of the basis on which the division is to be made. The actual practice varies widely. One method is to divide the business equally. Another is to base the allocation on geographical coverage. Another is to place the larger share with a favored supplier and give the rest to one or more alternates. In the chemical industry, as in a number of others, it is common practice to place business with various suppliers on a percentage of total requirements basis. Total requirements may be estimated, not necessarily guaranteed, and there may not even be a minimum volume requirement. Each supplier knows what its own percentage of the business amounts to, but may not be aware who the competition is or how much business each competitor received if the number of sources exceeds two. There is no common practice or "best" method or procedure, although renewed interest in single sourcing is consistent with a number of current trends, especially the quality movement, partnerships, and strategic sourcing.

Manufacturer versus Distributor

Should a buyer purchase from the manufacturer directly or from some trade channel such as a wholesaler, distributor, or even a retailer? Occasionally, various types of trade associations pressure buyers to patronize the wholesaler, distributor, or mill supply house. The real issue is often closely related to buying from local sources. The question is not primarily one of proximity to the user's plant but rather one of buying channels.

The justification for using trade channels is found in the value-added services that they render. If wholesalers are carrying the products of various manufacturers and spreading marketing costs over a variety of items, they may be able to deliver the product at the buyer's plant at a lower cost, particularly when the unit of sale is small and customers are widely scattered or when the demand is irregular. Furthermore, they may carry a stock of goods greater than a manufacturer could afford to carry in its own branch warehouse and therefore be in a better position to make prompt deliveries and to fill emergency orders. Also, they may be able to buy in car- or truckload lots, with a saving in transportation charges, and a consequent lower cost to the buyer.

Local sentiment may be strongly in favor of a certain distributor. Public agencies are particularly susceptible to such influence. Sometimes firms that sell through distributors tend, as a matter of policy, to buy whenever possible through distributors.

On the other hand, some large organizations often seek ways of going around the supply house, particularly where the buyer's requirements of supply items are large, where the shipments are made directly from the original manufacturer, and where no selling effort or service is rendered by the wholesaler. Some manufacturers operate their own supply houses to get the large discount. Others have attempted to persuade the original manufacturers to establish quantity discounts—a practice not unlike that in the steel trade.

Still others have sought to develop sources among small manufacturers that do not have a widespread distribution organization. Some attempts have been made to secure a special service from a chosen distributor, such as an agreement whereby the latter would add to its staff "two people exclusively for the purpose of locating and expediting nuisance items in other lines." A similar arrangement might place a travel agent directly on the purchaser's premises to improve service. Systems contracting and stockless purchasing systems depend heavily on concentrating a large number of relatively small purchases with a highly capable distributor.

Ultimately, every participant in the value chain needs to add value. This guiding principle should apply also to the selection of nonmanufacturers in the distribution network.

Geographical Location of Sources

Shall purchases be confined as largely as possible to local sources, or shall geographical location be largely disregarded? Most buyers *prefer* to buy from local sources. This policy rests on two bases. First, a local source can frequently offer more dependable service than one located at a distance. For example, deliveries may be more prompt both because the distance is shorter and because the dangers of interruption in transportation service are reduced. Knowledge of the buyer's specific requirements, as well as of the seller's special qualifications, may be based on an intimacy of knowledge not possessed by others. There may be greater flexibility in meeting the purchaser's requirements; and local suppliers may be just as well equipped as to facilities, know-how, and financial strength as any of those located at more distant points. Thus, there may well be sound economic reasons for preferring a local source to a more distant one. In just-in-time production systems, proximity of the supplier's plant to that of the purchaser is vital. For example, automotive manufacturers encourage suppliers to relocate plants closer to automobile assembly operations.

A second basis for selecting local sources rests on equally sound, although somewhat less tangible, grounds. The organization owes much to the local community. The facility is located there, the bulk of the employees live there, and often a substantial part of its financial support, as well as a notable part of its sales, may be local. The local community provides the company's personnel with their housing, schools, churches, and social life. Executives are constantly asked by local business owners or managers at local professional and social gatherings why they are not receiving any business. To recognize these facts is good public relations. Therefore, if a local source of supply can be found that can render a buyer as good a value as can be located elsewhere, it should be supported. Moreover, buyers should attempt to develop local sources when potential exists.

This policy has two complicating elements. One is supply's primary responsibility to buy well. Emotion should rarely supplant good business judgment because in the long run it will hurt the local community. A second complication arises through the difficulty of defining "local." Technological changes have affected not only the size and distribution of the centers of population but also the commercial and business structure, resulting, among other things, in a widening of market areas and hence the sources from which requirements can be obtained. Therefore, what once might properly have been called local has, for many areas and many items, become state, provincial, or national. There is no easy rule by which a buyer can decide the economic boundaries of the local community. As e-commerce activities grow, the boundaries of time and space will shrink even more. As it becomes easier to access information about potential suppliers and to move information between and among organizations, it also may become easier to do business with international suppliers (see also Chapter 14, "Global Supply").

Supplier Size

Should a purchaser have the option of buying from a large, medium, or small supplier, which size of supplier should be favored? How does the size of the purchasing organization affect the decision? A matrix of relative sizes can be developed (see Figure 10–3). The size and nature of the requirement also may affect the decision, as it is general wisdom that the larger the requirement, the larger the supplier should be. Generally, smaller suppliers tend to be local for those smaller requirements where flexibility, speed of response, and availability tend to be more important than price. Larger suppliers tend to be more appropriate for high-volume requirements where technology, quality, and total cost of ownership may be critical. And medium suppliers fall in between. The trouble with generalizations is that exceptions abound. Small suppliers tend to fill niches that the larger ones cannot or may have chosen not to cover. According to *Hispanic Business* magazine, the leaders of its fastest-growing 100 companies focus on a strategy of focusing on, and filling, one niche in the marketplace.

Small suppliers have traditionally shown a loyalty and service deemed impossible from larger suppliers, but the customer service focus of many larger organizations is trying to attack this perception. Small suppliers tend to depend on the management of a key

FIGURE 10–3 Relative Purchaser and Supplier Size

Purchaser Size	Supplier Size
Small	Small
	Medium
	Large
Medium	Small
	Medium
	Large
Large	Small
	Medium
	Large

owner-manager and this person's health and attitude will affect the risk of doing business. Larger organizations tend to have greater stability and greater resources, reducing the day-to-day risk of supplier performance.

Interest in diversity of customers, employees, and suppliers has renewed interest in the large purchaser–small supplier interface and the role of education, assistance, and continuing watchfulness on the part of supply to help the supplier succeed. Advances in technology present both opportunities and challenges to small business owners. The Internet is available to anyone with a computer and a modem, yet many small business owners fear that the costs of e-commerce will be prohibitive.

Social, Political, and Environmental Concerns

Noneconomic factors may have a significant bearing on sourcing decisions. These include social, political, and environmental concerns (see Chapter 12, "Supply Law and Ethics," for a more detailed discussion). In a 2000 CAPS Research study, Carter and Jennings defined the purchasing manager's involvement in the socially responsible management of the supply chain as "a wide array of behaviors that broadly fall into the category of environmental management, safety, diversity, human rights and quality of life, ethics, and community and philanthropic activities."[2]

Social

Most organizations recognize that their existence may affect the social concerns of society. Some social problems can be addressed through supply policy and actions. For example, it is possible to purchase certain services or goods from social agencies employing recovering addicts, former prisoners, or those with physical and mental disabilities. It is possible to purchase from suppliers located in low-income areas or certain geographical areas of high unemployment. Government legislation requiring suppliers on government contracts to place a percentage of business with designated minority- or woman-owned businesses has forced many purchasers to undertake searches for such suppliers. Many supply managers have initiated assistance and educational programs to make their minority-sourcing programs work.

[2] Craig R. Carter and Marianne M. Jennings, *Purchasing's Contribution to the Socially Responsible Management of the Sypply Chain* (Tempe, AZ: Center for Advanced Purchasing Studies, 2000), p. 7.

For example, the secretary of the Department of Energy (DOE) established a mentor-protégé program in which prime contractors help energy-related small minority businesses increase their capabilities in return for subcontracting credit and other incentives. In one sense, these early reverse marketing efforts provided useful insights into the process of developing partnerships with larger suppliers as well. Companies in the private sector often engage in these actions voluntarily out of a sense of corporate social responsibility and to gain strategic advantage. For example, Detroit's big three automotive manufacturers have positioned supplier diversity as a strategic advantage because they see the connection between from whom they buy and to whom they sell. By helping to develop the economy of the ethnic community through its supplier development programs, it also is increasing the purchasing power of the community's members. Supplier development is addressed in Chapter 19.

There are problems and opportunities when exercising purchasing power in the social area. Balancing the often-conflicting goals of the organization (lowest total cost with social responsibility) and assessing and mitigating the risks presented by supplier diversity programs add a level of complexity to what already may be a complex sourcing decision. Most supply managers agree that the "deal" must make good business sense. There are a number of resources and publications available to link buyers and minority and women business owners including

- The U.S. Small Business Administration (SBA), http://www.sba.gov.
- The National Minority Supplier Development Council and its regional purchasing councils, http://www.nmsdcus.org.
- *Minority Business Entrepreneur (MBE)* magazine, http://www.mbemag.com.
- *Hispanic Business* magazine, http://www.hispanicBusiness.com.

Political

The basic question in the political area is: Should the acquisition area be seen as a means of furthering political objectives? Public agencies have long been under pressure of this sort. "Buy local" is a common requirement for city and state purchasing officials. "Buy American" is a normal corollary requirement. The attempt by the Canadian government to spread purchases across the country, approximately in line with population distribution, is another example. For military purposes, the U.S. government has a long-standing tradition of support and development of a national supply base to afford security protection in the case of conflict, and recently to reward other countries for their support of U.S. initiatives.

The question always arises as to how much of a premium should be paid to conform with political directives. Should a city purchasing agent buy buses from the local manufacturer at a 12 percent premium over those obtainable from another state or country? The debate over offshore outsourcing has raised the political stakes and many public entities are passing legislation to prevent offshore outsourcing that results in a loss of jobs domestically. Politics aside, whether this behavior is good for the economy in the long run is an ongoing debate.

For private industry, political questions are also present. Should the corporation support the political and economic aims of the governing body? Governments have little hesitation on large business deals to specify that a minimum percentage should have domestic content. In the aerospace and telecommunications industry, for example, foreign orders are often contingent on the ability to arrange for suitable subcontracting in the customer's home country. It is interesting that governments have no fear to tread where private industry is forbidden to walk. Multinationals often find themselves caught in countries with different political views. U.S. companies for many years have not been allowed to trade with Cuba, yet their subsidiaries in other countries face strong national pressure to export to Cuba the same products that the U.S. parent is not allowed to sell from U.S. soil. The same holds for purchasing from countries with whom trade is not encouraged by the government. American subsidiaries frequently find themselves caught between the desire of the local government to encourage local purchases and the U.S. government, which encourages exports from the parent or the parent's suppliers. The growing role of government in all business affairs is likely to increase difficulties of this kind in the future. Their resolution is far from easy and will require a great deal of tact and understanding.

Environmental

Sustainability is the ability to achieve economic prosperity while protecting the natural systems of the planet and providing a higher quality of life for its people. To accomplish this, decision makers must consider the role of four types of capital: financial capital (cash, investment, and monetary instruments), manufactured capital (infrastructure, machines, tools, and factories), human capital (labor and intelligence, culture, and organization), and natural capital (resources, living systems, and ecosystem services). Supply managers play a key role in an organization's sustainability initiatives in product or service design, sourcing and contracting, and asset or investment recovery. Consequently, supply's role in helping to achieve this goal needs to be examined carefully.

The first issue is: How can our organization design products and services that directly or indirectly contribute to sustainability? The second issue is: How can our organization purchase materials, products, or equipment that directly or indirectly contribute to sustainability? How can the supply group raise sustainability questions when others in the organization fail to do so? The third issue is: How can we purchase from sources, domestic or international, that we know are committed to sustainability and sound practices? These are not easy questions answered glibly out of context. It is possible to evade the issue by putting government in the control seat, saying, "as long as government allows it, it must be all right." A practical consideration is that government may shut down a polluting supplier with little notice, endangering supply assurance.

Environmental supply chain strategies range from merely trying to avoid violations to including environmental considerations from the design stage forward. The preferred hierarchy is (1) source reduction—design or use less, (2) reuse—multiple use of same item such as a package or container, (3) recycle—reprocess into raw material, (4) incinerate—at least extract energy, but create CO_2 pollution at a minimum, and (5) landfill—require space and transportation to store with potential impact on land and water. The introduction of gas-electric hybrid vehicles and the development of fuel cell technology are examples of source-reduction initiatives. "Designing for recycling" requires manufacturers of appliances and automobiles to design products for ease of disassembly to allow for recovery of useful materials. In the automobile industry, this represents a particularly difficult challenge. Much of the weight-reduction emphasis to improve government-required fuel ratings has come about by the substitution of lightweight, but difficult to retrieve and recycle, plastics for heavier but easily recycled metal parts.

Obviously, suppliers can aid substantially in addressing these priorities to minimize the environmental impact of the purchaser's and their customer's requirements (see also Chapter 11, "Investment Recovery"). In many organizations, supply's role as an information link between environmentally affected individuals, internal functions, and suppliers in the handling of waste and hazardous materials has been established already. U.S. federal regulations, for example, for chemicals as to (1) transportation, (2) use, and (3) disposal of hazardous materials, have created a need for comprehensive hazardous materials management and information systems (HMMIS). Workplace right-to-know legislation and emergency preparedness requirements further reinforce the need for HMMIS.

There are many organizations and programs available to support the efforts of supply managers. For example, since 1982, Rocky Mountain Institute (RMI) has worked with corporations, governments, communities, and citizens to help solve problems, gain competitive advantage, increase profits, and create wealth through the more productive use of resources. RMI's Research & Consulting team helped a semiconductor manufacturer improve its buildings and equipment in ways that also radically reduced energy costs and carbon emissions; showed urban planners how to spur economic development through better building design and water infrastructure; and helped conceive a successful floor-covering service utilizing resource-efficient, closed-loop industrial processes with an innovative business model.

The U.S Environmental Protection Agency (http://www.epa.gov) offers programs and tools that contribute to sustainability in the areas of planning and practices, scientific tools and technology, and measuring progress. Its 2000 publication, *The Lean and Green Supply Chain: A Practical Guide for Material Managers and Supply Chain Managers to Reduce Costs and Improve Environmental Performance,* illustrates the efficiency-enhancing opportunities that arise when companies incorporate environmental costs and benefits into mainstream materials and supply chain management decision making. It provides introductory guidance on how to identify these costs and benefits and how to adjust existing information systems and analysis techniques to better account for this significant category of costs. The EPA's *Sector Strategies Program* seeks industrywide environmental gains through innovative actions taken with a number of manufacturing and service sectors. The Office of Policy, Economics and Innovation (OPEI) works with participating trade associations, EPA programs and regions, states, and other groups to find sensible solutions to sector-specific problems. The EPA's Environmental Accounting Project provides tools for calculating the environmental costs of nonprevention approaches and the economic benefits of pollution prevention. The project makes available a number of case studies, benchmarking projects, and calculation and spreadsheet tools for conducting environmental cost analysis for business decision making (http://www.epa.gov/oppt/acctg/).

The U.S. National Recycling Coalition (http://www.nrc-recycle.org) represents all the diverse interests committed to the common goal of maximizing recycling to achieve the benefits of resource conservation, solid waste reduction, environmental protection, energy conservation, and social and economic development. For example, it sponsors the Electronics Recycling Initiative to promote the recovery, reuse, and recycling of obsolete electronic equipment and to encourage the design, manufacture, and purchase of environmentally responsible electronic equipment.

Internationally, the ISO 14000 certification, developed along the lines of ISO 9000, is a process for certifying the environmental management system of an organization. In a 1999 CAPS Research report, *ISO 14000: Assessing Its Impact on Corporate Effectiveness and Efficiency,* respondents from ISO 14000–certified plants reported that other than lead times, certification has a large, positive impact on the perceived efficiency and effectiveness of the organization's environmental management system.[3]

Strategic supply management is all about maximizing opportunities and minimizing risks. In the area of environmental impact and sustainability, there are many opportunities for supply managers who are at the forefront of environmental awareness. By being ahead of, rather than behind, legislative requirements, opportunities to tap government financial support and public recognition for innovative experiments may exist. The simple fact is that almost every supplier selection decision is likely to be impacted by environmental considerations.

Joint Purchasing with Supplier

If the buying organization has more leverage in the marketplace and more efficient purchasing processes, it may be advantageous to buy certain requirements for suppliers. Although the purchaser will incur some additional expense, there would be a net gain to both parties in the transaction and some agreement about shared cost savings. The close relationship that would exist between the suppliers and purchasers, furthermore, would enable the supply manager to know more about the production costs of suppliers and to ascertain whether or not it was paying a fair price for the products. The purchaser, moreover, would be sure of the quality of the materials used and would increase buying power. If quality problems occur later, however, the supplier may determine that quality difficulties stem from the poor quality of material supplied. With a reduction in the number of buyers in the market for the raw materials, there would be less false activity and thus greater price stability. This last reason is rather important. Frequently, when a large company requests bids from individual suppliers, they in turn enter the material markets to make inquiries about prices and quantities available. If six suppliers are bidding on an offer, their preliminary inquiries for material required to fill the prospective order will be multiplied six times.

Purchasing for Company Personnel

Another problem faced by most supply departments is deciding to what extent it is justified in using its facilities to obtain merchandise for employees of the organization or for its executives at better terms than they could individually obtain. Some companies not only sell their own merchandise to their employees at a substantial discount and also allow them to buy at cost any of the merchandise bought by the company for its own use, but go even further and make it possible for employees to obtain merchandise that the company itself neither makes nor uses.

[3] Steven A. Melnyk, Roger Calantone, Rob Handfield, Robert Sroufe, and Frank Montabon, *ISO 14000: Assessing Its Impact on Corporate Effectiveness and Efficiency* (Tempe, AZ: Center for Advanced Purchasing Studies, 1999).

There are some reasons why a company should pursue a policy of employee purchasing. Under certain circumstances, of course, it is imperative that a company make some provision for supplying its employees with at least the necessities of life, a condition particularly true in remote mining and lumbering locations. A policy of employee purchasing, it is also argued, provides the means for increasing real wages at little or no cost to the company. It may increase the loyalty of the employees to the organization and thus form part of the fringe benefits. Employees often feel they are entitled to any considerations or advantages the company can obtain for them. Furthermore, whatever the procurement manager may think about the general practice, it is often somewhat difficult to refuse a request from a top executive to "see what can be done about a discount."

Many companies, on the other hand, have steadfastly refused to adopt such a policy. There is some question of just how much prices are really reduced compared with the prices of the chain store, the supermarket, the discount store, and other low-cost distribution outlets. Some ill will toward the company may be aroused, since the ordinary retailer is likely to feel that the company is entering into direct competition or at least is bringing pressure to grant discounts to the organization's employees.

Unfortunately, few people realize how difficult it is for a purchasing department to handle numerous small requests of a personal nature. It is a time-consuming and unrewarding task, since a complete market search is almost impossible, and any quality, price, or service troubles arising from the purchase are always brought back to those involved.

Risk Assessment

Every organization's management makes decisions about the risks it is willing to take in light of the expected returns. It takes actions to avoid, mitigate, transfer, insure against, limit, or explicitly assume risk. For the buyer or supply manager, it is essential to consider each decision in the context of the organization's risk profile.

Research into buyers' risk assessment behavior shows that the perceived risk of placing business with an untried and unknown supplier is high. Likewise, the perceived risk associated with routine, repetitive purchases is much less than the risk of new or less standard acquisitions. In general, the risk is seen to be higher with unknown materials, parts, equipment, or suppliers and with increased dollar amounts. Commodity managers can take a number of actions to avoid, mitigate, transfer, limit, or insure against risk. For example, a buyer may attempt to transfer risk by asking for advice, such as engineering judgment, or by seeking additional information, including placing a trial order, or hedging in the commodities market. The buyer may require bid bonds, performance bonds, or payment bonds to insure against risk, or avoid risk by not doing business with suppliers in certain countries, or mitigate risk by dual or multiple sourcing rather than single sourcing. The buyer may limit risk by negotiating payment terms that allow progress payments when certain milestones are met but withhold a percentage of the payment until completion and acceptance of the service provided. When a buyer takes an action such as selecting a supplier, or switching suppliers, or agreeing to certain terms and conditions, he or she should take these actions with the explicit understanding of both the risk at which the decision puts the organization, the return expected, and the balance between the two.

Strategy Development

Risk assessment is a key step in strategy development. Supply risks can be assessed in several ways. Pareto analysis (see Chapter 6), which compares dollar volume to variables such as percent of suppliers, percent of inventory, and number of orders, focuses strategy development on high dollar purchases. Portfolio analysis typically includes supply market risks in the assessment and focuses attention on the value-generating capability of a purchase in light of the risks of acquiring the purchase in the marketplace. While there are numerous two-by-two matrices in existence, Figure 10–4 is a classic example of this approach. From this analysis, the actual goods and services purchased by an organization can be placed in the appropriate quadrant, broad strategies can be developed by quadrant, specific commodity strategies can be developed for each commodity in a quadrant, and decisions then can be made as to the most appropriate sourcing strategy and tools for each category.

Noncritical and leverage purchases share the same market risk, between low and medium, which means there are multiple suppliers and market forces to keep prices competitive. Since the items are fairly standard, quality is comparable and substitutes are available. Therefore, convenience, ease of acquisition, low acquisition costs, and delivery systems may be the most important decision criteria. As the required volume of standard items increases, leverage opportunities increase and price per unit becomes a critical variable. Volume gives the buying organization more power in the marketplace and the supply manager focuses on developing strategies to leverage volume and scale. The supply manager may develop a strategy to move items from the noncritical to the leverage category by bundling items differently, standardizing purchases, or consolidating the supply base. These moves push the

FIGURE 10–4 **Supply Risks and Dollars Extended**

Source: Peter Kraljic, "Purchasing Must Become Supply Management," *Harvard Business Review,* September–October 1983.

MARKET RISK	Low VALUE → High	
High	**Bottleneck** • Unique specification • Supplier's technology is important • Production-based scarcity due to low demand and/or few sources of supply • Substitution is difficult • Usage fluctuates and is not routinely predictable • Potential storage risk	**Strategic** • Continuous availability is essential to the operation • Custom design or unique specifications • Supplier technology is important • Few suppliers with adequate technical capability or capacity • Changing source of supply is difficult • Substitution is difficult
Low	**Noncritical** • Standard specification or "commodity" type items • Substitute products readily available • Competitive supply market with many suppliers	**Leverage** • Price per unit is key because of volume • Substitution is possible • Competitive supply market with several sources
	Low	High

item to the right on the value or *x*-axis and result in price savings from increasing volume. These initiatives usually focus attention on internal processes and business relationships as supply develops the means to analyze and consolidate spend that is often dispersed throughout the organization.

The items in the leverage category merit special attention because they represent the "low-hanging fruit" that companies pick when they begin to focus attention on purchasing and supply management. Many of the e-business tools discussed in Chapter 4 are especially appropriate in managing leverage purchases. By reducing the supply base to as few as the risk profile indicates is appropriate, the supply manager can generate price savings that free up cash for other uses such as reallocating to support or generate revenue growth.

Bottleneck purchases, which are medium to high risk to acquire, represent a difficult category to manage because of the uniqueness built into the specification. Interestingly, often it is the decisions made by members of the buying organization that elevate the risk. The more unique or customized the good or service, the more difficult it is to acquire. One of supply's objectives discussed in Chapter 2 was to standardize wherever possible. The challenge of fulfilling this objective is felt most strongly when managing bottleneck purchases; for example, if an organization wants to develop supply management training for its global supply group of 2,500 people located in 25 countries across multiple time zones, cultures, and languages. If the company sends out an RFP to solicit proposals and requires highly customized courses, there will be few providers with the capabilities to do the job and the proposals and quotes will reflect this complexity. If the internal training design team can develop a statement of work that clearly delineates the standard course content from the customized content, they in effect will reduce the risk (and cost) of acquisition. The challenge for the manager of bottleneck goods and services is as much an internal challenge as an external one. The supply manager must work with internal business partners to determine the appropriate level and type of customization required to satisfy the needs and wants of the final customer. Any uniqueness that is not valued by the final customer is waste and should be eliminated. This is clearly a high-risk decision because the cost of building in unnecessary uniqueness can be quite high, and the cost of eliminating a unique characteristic that the final customer truly values may be even more costly. The tools to extract value from this category include cross-functional and cross-organizational teams, value analysis, total cost modeling, and customer relationship management. For example, automotive manufacturers have successfully standardized many parts across both make and model of car without harming the perceptions of buyers or the company's pricing strategy. Bottleneck purchases represent cost reduction or savings opportunities that require concerted cross-functional and often cross-organizational effort to realize.

Strategic purchases represent both the greatest risk and the greatest reward opportunity for an organization and its supply network. Strategic purchases share the same characteristics of bottleneck purchases in that they often are highly customized or possess some characteristic that limits the number of viable suppliers. The difference is that strategic purchases have the greatest potential to help or hurt attainment of the organization's mission. For example, if the mission of the organization is summed up in a phrase such as "Select and Use," then any purchase that drives a potential customer to select and use a product might be considered strategic. This might include the ingredients in a detergent, or the artwork on the packaging, but not the office supplies used in general operations. The acquisition of strategic purchases and management of strategic spend historically have been handled by many people outside of the purchasing and supply organization. For example, jet fuel for an airline or energy supplies for certain manufacturing concerns may represent both high-dollar and high-value purchases and those with primary ownership of these purchase categories were business specialists with technical rather than supply management skills. The trend is toward joint ownership of strategies, goals, objectives, metrics, and accountability for these purchases. Supply brings expertise such as supply base knowledge, negotiating skill, contract development and management skill, and the ability to build and manage a long-term relationship to complement the technical knowledge of the internal business partner. The tools and techniques applied to strategic purchases include total cost modeling, value analysis and engineering, cross-functional teams, and strategic alliances. Many of the efficiency tools and process improvements described in Chapters 3 and 4 free up time for supply personnel to focus resources and human talent on the acquisition and management of strategic purchases.

Conclusion

Before a buyer or sourcing team can make a final supplier selection, a decision on all the important questions of strategy just discussed must be reached: whether to patronize a single or several sources of supply; whether to buy directly from the manufacturer or through a distributor; whether to buy wholly from local sources; what weight to give social, political, and environmental concerns; and how to assess risks.

A sourcing strategy can then be decided upon. Chapters 18 and 19 deal with additional considerations such as make or buy and supplier relations. The next chapter addresses the transportation and logistics issues in organizations.

Questions for Review and Discussion

1. How might a supply manager assess the risks of a specific purchase category or supplier?
2. What considerations must be made before establishing a joint purchasing agreement with a supplier?
3. Why is the trend toward single sourcing? What are the disadvantages to this trend?
4. What is a weighted point evaluation system? Why is it used?
5. Why might it be preferable to buy from a distributor or wholesaler rather than directly from the manufacturer?
6. What are the advantages of purchasing from small local sources?
7. When might it be appropriate to conduct an informal, rather than a formal, supplier evaluation?
8. What are the similarities and differences between evaluating new and existing sources of supply?
9. Why is purchasing focusing more attention on a supplier's management as part of the evaluation process? How might this evaluation be conducted?
10. How might social, political, or environmental issues impact a supplier selection decision?

References

Carter, Craig R., and Marianne M. Jennings. *Purchasing's Contribution to the Socially Responsible Management of the Supply Chain.* Tempe, AZ: CAPS Research, 2000.

Carter, Joseph R., and Ram Narasimhan. *Environmental Supply Chain Management.* Tempe, AZ: CAPS Research, 1998.

Flynn, Anna E. *"Knowledge-Based Supply Management."* In *The Purchasing Handbook,* ed. J. L. Cavinato and R. G. Kauffman, Chapter 8. 7th ed. New York: McGraw-Hill: 2005.

Hawken, Paul; Amory Lovins; and L. Hunter Lovins. *Natural Capitalism: Creating the Next Industrial Revolution.* Boston: Little, Brown and Company, 1999.

Krause, Daniel R., and Robert B. Handfield. *Developing a World Class Supply Base.* Tempe, AZ: CAPS Research, 1999.

McIvor, Ronan, and Marie McHugh. *"Partnership Sourcing: An Organization Change Management Perspective." Journal of Supply Chain Management,* 2001.

Case 10–1

Quotech Inc.

"Should we go with Castle Metals' lower quote, or favor Marmon Keystone's proven reliability?" pondered Emily Trent, purchasing agent for Quotech Inc., a Cleveland-based manufacturer of materials handling equipment. It was May 1 as she prepared for her meeting the next day with Larry Pilon, sales representative from Marmon Keystone. At stake was an order for up to $700,000 of tubing that needed a decision within a week.

UNITED DOMINION INDUSTRIES AND QUOTECH INC.

Quotech Inc. was one of three companies comprising the Materials Handling Division (MHD) of Halgus Holdings (HH). HH total sales for last year were $2.15 billion, producing $98.4 million in net income. The Materials Handling Division represented approximately 18 percent of HH's sales.

Last year, the MHD reported a profit of $42 million on sales of $388 million, compared to the preceding year's figures of $38.9 million and $349 million respectively. Most of the growth in sales and earnings was attributable, however, to recent acquisitions. According to the company annual report, last year had been a disappointing year for HH, despite double-digit sales growth from its existing operations as well as from newly acquired companies. HH had suffered price erosion in its markets. The situation made cost-reduction measures vital for HH. Nicholas Whitehead, the president of HH, had gone on record as saying, "There are definitely opportunities for supply chain savings."

Last year, HH adopted the PEP program designed to achieve additional improvement in the company's operations. Cost reduction and containment were identified as key components of the PEP initiative, responsible for the maintenance of HH's competitive position.

PURCHASING AT QUOTECH

In addition to Emily, the Purchasing Department at Quotech comprised Frank Wilson, director of purchasing, and Rhonda Bates, buyer. Together, they were responsible for deciding on Quotech's $17 million in manufacturing component purchases. HH's company structure and its PEP initiative called for close coordination between operating units within a division. As such, the purchasing personnel at Quotech were in close touch with their counterparts in Canada and Virginia. Doing so had proven a good strategy, as purchase consolidation measures and the consequent increase in volume-based buying power had squeezed savings of $500,000 in the first quarter of 2000 alone. Given company objectives, and the success in achieving reduction in costs, the reliance on a consolidated purchase ordering process was expected to continue.

THE SOURCING SELECTION ISSUE

The issue currently demanding Emily's attention was the sourcing of the division's requirement for 2 7/8″ tubing. She was the lead buyer for the division. The tubing in question was a standard material for a variety of products. While not a mission-critical component, tubing that did not meet vendor specifications could cause equipment malfunction. Furthermore, like most manufacturing components, the supplier's inability to meet production demands on a timely basis could result in costly assembly line shutdowns. As such, the role of the supplier was not trivial. While each of the three companies comprising the division had historically sourced its purchases independently, top management's cost reduction imperative had changed this practice. As such, the current order was worth up to $700,000 and represented a consolidated purchase meant to satisfy all companies' tubing requirements for the coming year.

QUOTECH'S CURRENT SUPPLIER: MARMON KEYSTONE

Marmon Keystone was part of the U.S.-based Marmon Group of companies. Its local arm was based in Akron and had been a supplier of components to Quotech for the past decade. Emily had been very satisfied with Marmon Keystone, thanks to Doug Elliott, its sales representative. Doug made it a point to visit with Emily at appropriate intervals, inquiring about Quotech's sourcing needs, if any. Over the course of their relationship, Doug had become a trusted partner supplier to Emily, making good on Marmon Keystone's promises of reliable product quality and on-time delivery, two attributes that were very important to Quotech.

As it was not possible to develop detailed product specifications for every component, and a lot depended on the supplier's ability to provide components based on an "eyeball" evaluation at the vendor's plant premises, Doug Elliott had built an enviable record for himself and his firm. Quotech's Supplier Performance Tracking System indicated that over the last three years, there was evidence of just one MGA (product return) to Marmon Keystone, which was rectified immediately. Furthermore, Marmon Keystone had, in effect, taken on Quotech's inventory handling by performing the warehousing function on behalf of Quotech. This service spared Emily a big headache and saved Quotech a significant amount annually. One incident, particularly, stood out in Emily's mind as she evaluated Marmon Keystone. On one of his visits, Doug had noted the low inventory on an unrelated component and suggested filling the order. This proactive commitment to Quotech's interest on his part was yet to be imitated by any other suppliers.

Two years ago, when Doug Elliott was promoted to the position of general manager at Marmon Keystone, he specifically instructed his replacement, Larry Pilon, to "take special care of this account." Larry had been true to his word and had continued the tradition of value creation and vendor satisfaction that his predecessor had displayed. This prompted Emily to attribute Marmon Keystone's success as a supplier to institutional rather than person-specific reasons. With annual sales of almost $300,000 to Quotech, it was not surprising that Marmon Keystone was among its top 20 suppliers, while Quotech was probably among Marmon Keystone's top 10 customers.

CASTLE METALS

Castle Metals had come to the attention of Emily through John Stevenson, the purchasing manager at the Canadian company. Emily knew very little about Castle Metals. Records indicated that the firm did not appear among the top 50 suppliers to the Toronto plant. Further investigation into the Canadian company's purchases last year indicated $300,000 from Marmon Keystone.

Neither Quotech nor the Canadian company had any history of dealing with Castle Metals. However, both firms had different sourcing needs in that the Canadian company was more of a "specialty shop" requiring multiple variations of basic components in small quantities. In contrast, Quotech had standard sourcing requirements and tended to purchase higher quantities of more standardized components. It was felt that Castle Metals could serve both companies' diverse needs from its Mississauga, Ontario, plant. Moreover, Castle Metals' bid for the tubing had undercut Marmon Keystone's by $18,000. To Emily's surprise, John Stevenson and her Virginia counterparts believed Castle Metals should be the supplier for the 2 7/8″ tubing. While surprised by the decision, she nevertheless realized that it could be based on the need to source products from multiple suppliers to "keep them honest."

CONCLUSION

Emily considered the sourcing decision as well as the "consolation" she could award the "losing" firm. Her records indicated that the Canadian location sourced $240,000 in components and the Virginia plant also had further tubing requirements. Given that both Castle Metals and Marmon Keystone had branches in all three locations, the possibility existed that she could use either as a supplier for those requirements. "What do I tell Larry?" thought Emily, as she planned for the meeting.

Case 10–2

Bid Evaluation

On August 4, Matt Roberto, Custom Equipment's (CE) newly hired buyer, was preparing for a meeting with the purchasing manager the following day. He had received four bids for CE's cable and wire business and was wondering if the bid evaluation criteria he had developed earlier were still appropriate and what action to recommend next.

BIDDING PROCESS

Given his limited experience at CE, Matt decided that going out for bid would be the best idea because he was not personally familiar with any of the electrical suppliers that sold wire and cable to CE.

The package that Matt had distributed contained a list of all wire and cable products used annually and a usage forecast for the coming year. Suppliers were asked to provide pricing, terms, delivery method, and their current stock situation of products of concern to CE. Pricing and ability to accommodate CE's requirements were important considerations, as were return policies. Suppliers were asked to include any innovative ideas on how to improve service to CE.

Ten potential electrical suppliers had been asked to bid for CE's entire yearly wire and cable requirements. Suppliers invited to participate in the Wire Management Program (WMP) were chosen based on CE's confidence in their ability to quote all of CE's requirements for wire and cable. All suppliers were local, so distance to CE's plant was not considered to be a factor.

Completed bids were submitted to CE from the four most capable suppliers because the other six suppliers could not adequately satisfy all of CE's needs. Although Matt believed the other six companies to be quite capable, most claimed that they could not satisfy all of CE's requirements. Licensing agreements, the size of the company, and willingness to stock certain products could be reasons for this. However, Matt believed four bids still made for a competitive bid environment.

Some suppliers had asked about the possibility of supplying alternative products with nearly identical features, especially as a substitute to CE's request for "Newflex" cable. Due to licensing agreements, only Premier Cable Corporation (PCC), Bannister Electric, and Eastern Electric could supply Newflex. Some suppliers, such as State Electric, could supply "Kelvin" cable as an alternative to Newflex. Many large-customer companies purchased Kelvin cable in place of Newflex, claiming Kelvin to be more effective in high-intensity applications.

EXHIBIT 1 **Supplier Overview**

	Vendor			
Vendor Aspects	**PCC**	**Eastern**	**State**	**Bannister**
Target market (small, regional)	Specialized	Med.–large	Small–medium	Med.–large
Supply	Custom	Volume	Custom/volume	Volume
Positioning (quality, leader)	Service	Availability	Service	Availability
Cost base	1 location	3 locations	1 location	Many locations
Sales	$14 mil/year	$117 mil/year	$51 mil/year	$225 mil/year
MRP	No	Yes	No	Yes
Reputation	Good	Good	Very good	Good
Payment terms	Net 15 days	Net 45 days	Net 30 days	Net 30 days
Management	Fair/weak	Good	Good	Good
ISO certification	Began process	Certified	Registered	Certified

EXHIBIT 2 Criteria for Bid Evaluation

Criteria	Weight	PCC	Eastern	State	Bannister
Past performance*	20	17	14	16	0
Price	35	30	27	24	33
Terms	15	10	13	12	12
Delivery (from order to arrival)	15	10	12	15	0
Future EDI & EFT	10	0	10	10	10
Inventory buy-back**	5	2	5	5	4
Total	100	69	81	82	59

* As judged by the receiving manager.
** Inventory buy-back was a figure based on the number of dollars willing to credit for current CE wire and cable stock.

The CE bid also included a list of currently held obsolete stock in CE's warehouse. Due to changes in customer specifications, CE's warehouse contained some wire and cable stock that was no longer used for its projects. The stock still had resale value, and Matt's manager wanted the bidding electrical companies to submit a buy-back value as part of their quotes. She estimated the value of the inventory to be $5,000.

From his discussions with CE's receiving manager with regard to the performance records kept for ISO 9001 purposes, Matt had completed an analysis and comparison of the suppliers prior to receiving the submitted bids (see Exhibit 1). He had also developed the criteria with which to evaluate the submitted bids. Matt had also assigned weights to each criterion (see Exhibit 2). Given the nature of CE's business, Matt wanted the evaluation to be a realistic reflection of what was most critical to CE's operations. He took the total value of each bid, separated it into wire and cable, respectively, and created a bid summary with which to analyze the pricing of each bid (see Exhibit 3).

ELECTRICAL COMPONENT SUPPLIERS

Below are descriptions of the four electrical suppliers that submitted completed bids to Custom Equipment.

Premier Cable Corporation (PCC)

PCC was a small electrical supplier that specialized in cable and cable accessories. It had been servicing the automotive and robotics industries for nine years. PCC's reputation was based on its service. It had a five-year relationship with CE and was currently supplying CE with all of its Newflex cable requirements.

PCC wanted to continue to supply CE with Newflex cable in the future. However, it was worried about bidding against larger suppliers on commodity wire products because it did not possess the economies of scale of the larger suppliers. The president was quoted as saying, "It's hard to do both high-end cable and commodity wire products together." Because of its size, PCC had no intention of installing any new computer systems in the coming year, and it also did not have much use for CE's obsolete stock wires and cables.

Delivery from PCC's facility was made through a courier. CE received delivery of its orders 3–4 days from order placement. PCC could provide 24-hour service if necessary, but at an extra cost. Many Newflex cables were held in stock at PCC. Nonstocked cables could be couriered overnight from the Newflex manufacturing plant in New Jersey. Because many of CE's requirements were urgent, it was reassuring to have PCC as a supplier. The owner and sales representative wore beepers on the weekends in case of customer emergencies.

EXHIBIT 3 Bid Summary

Bidder	Wire Products*	Cable Products*	Buy-Back of CE's Stock	Total
Premier Cable Corp.	$322,762	$519,435	$(2,000)	$840,197
Eastern Electric	$295,841	$558,233	$(5,000)	$849,074
State Electric	$305,593	$577,152	$(5,000)	$877,745
Bannister	$285,090	$538,791	$(4,000)	$819,881

*All prices fixed for one year, unless there is a fluctuation of greater than $0.10/lb. in the price of copper.

PCC's sales representative provided great service and returned all calls promptly, according to comments from some CE buyers. Another buyer had also informed Matt that PCC's delivery times were fair for nonrush items. The organization was very responsive and interested in pleasing its customers. One of PCC's customers that Matt had spoken with described the company as "service oriented . . . cost issues come later. They're willing to work with pricing. . . . quality is never an issue."

Eastern Electric

Eastern Electric (Eastern) was a well-established electrical distributor located about 30 miles away. It was a large organization that desired all of CE's electrical business. Eastern's top priority was product availability, which it met with its size and dealer network. Eastern's pricing was competitive, and its management team was professional and friendly. It was sometimes difficult to get a hold of the inside sales representative. Response time to requests had occasionally been slow in the past. On average, delivery took 2–3 days from order. CE could receive up to three deliveries from Eastern each day because it operated its own fleet of delivery trucks; however, they usually contained the components ordered a few days prior. Eastern's size and detailed order fulfillment processes could impede its ability to process rush orders.

Matt visited Eastern Electric's central wire warehouse and was impressed by the amount of products it held in stock, including Newflex cable. It had the latest computer systems. Eastern Electric had not been a major player in CE's wire and cable business in the past, although it supplied many other electrical components on a daily basis.

Bannister

Bannister was a very large wire and cable supplier that began operations in the early 1950s. It had not done any recent business with Custom Equipment, for which Matt could not find any specific reason. Therefore, CE's receiving manager had no current records of performance. Order fulfillment was performed through the use of courier delivery services. Some of Bannister's key customers were very large, prominent customers. These companies used large quantities of wire and cable.

The sales representative was friendly but gave a lot of "general" answers to Matt's questions. He seemed interested in obtaining CE's business but unfamiliar with basic inventory concepts, which surprised Matt. Matt got the initial impression that CE would not be the Bannister representative's most valued customer.

By chance, Matt met and spoke with a former employee of Bannister a few days later, who described the organization as being "too big . . . not fast . . . everything needs to be documented and this can cause problems with rush deliveries. However, it prides itself on product availability and competitive pricing."

State Electric

State Electric was a small electrical supply company that had been dealing with CE for eight years. Its founder and its sales representative had both originally been employed by Eastern Electric but had resigned 11 years ago to start State Electric. State was currently supplying CE with most of its wire requirements.

State's primary focus was service. Delivery times were excellent, usually same-day or next day for stock items, according to CE's receiving manager. Otherwise, delivery would usually take 2–3 days. State was recently planning to implement new computer systems to serve its customers better. Its outside sales representative was always available to answer questions or give advice, and he personally visited Custom Equipment every few days. Matt observed that his presence was well appreciated by CE's engineers and employees, and everyone seemed to like him.

Of the four bidding suppliers, State could not supply Newflex cable. Instead, it wanted to supply CE with Kelvin cable, which was more expensive but supposedly equally effective. Some concern arose regarding this replacement cable because it had not been fully tested on a CE job as of yet. State held two "lunch and learn" seminars at CE to educate the engineers and purchasing agents about the Kelvin company and its products. These helped to familiarize all concerned with Kelvin products and gave the engineers at CE an opportunity to inspect the products and ask technical questions.

Another potential difficulty with Kelvin cable was that there were numerous jobs with Newflex as the customer-specified cable. If CE wanted to use Kelvin products, it would need written permission from the customer. CE would first have to try the Kelvin cable on a nonspecified job. To help convince CE to try the new cables, the representatives from State and Kelvin together agreed to supply an entire job with Kelvin products free of charge. This offer was significant considering that the cable for an average CE project cost between \$8,000 and \$12,000.

SELECTION CRITERIA

Even before the bids had been sent out, Matt had identified a set of evaluation criteria and weights. Now that he had received the bids, Matt wondered if the need criteria and weights needed revision, and which supplier he should recommend to the purchasing manager at the next day's meeting.

Case 10–3

Somers Office Products Inc.

George Bellows, purchasing manager of Somers Office Products (Somers), in Calgary, Alberta, was considering whether he needed to switch suppliers. Fairmont Canada, one of Somers's primary suppliers, had just announced that they were being acquired by MSC Inc., a direct competitor of Somers.

SOMERS OFFICE PRODUCTS INC.

Somers Office Products had been established as a dealer in stationery in 1920 and had functioned as a family business until 1975, when it was acquired by the current management group. Somers operated two retail outlets, but the bulk of its sales were to commercial customers. The company continued to be privately owned and operated at a profit. It operated a warehouse and total employment was about 80 people, most of whom were in sales.

The company had three product segments: office supplies, office furniture, and office design services. Office supplies constituted the largest segment and included items such as stationery, paper, and forms. One of the fastest-growing lines was computer supplies, such as printer cartridges.

SUPPLIERS

The office supplies industry was very price competitive and the trend for resellers, such as Somers, was for a higher level of use of wholesalers, rather than direct purchases from manufacturers. Large wholesalers, who could generally offer pricing levels similar to those received directly from the manufacturers, competed on the basis of value-added services, such as next-day delivery.

As a reseller, Somers purchased office supplies through a variety of channels but relied on two distributors, Fairmont Canada and Roancroft Stationers. Fairmont Canada specialized in computer supplies and had annual sales of $150 million (CAD). Roancroft, a large U.S.-based company with sales of $3.5 billion (USF), provided Somers with a wide range of office supplies. Both suppliers had invested heavily in technology that provided opportunities for customers to view catalogs and to place orders online.

DISTRIBUTION

Somers provided its customers with catalogs that were regularly supplemented with fliers. Somers' office supply orders were, for the most part, met from inventory. The company had a fill rate of almost 98 percent and thus provided a very high service level to its customers.

To achieve a high level of customer service without maintaining excessive inventory levels, Somers had developed close working arrangements with Roancroft and Fairmont Canada. For example, while Somers maintained approximately 4,500 items in inventory, Roancroft maintained inventories in over 25,000 items. Somers supplied catalogs to its customers that included products supplied by Roancroft, and customer orders were sent from Somers to Roancroft on a daily basis by electronic data interchange (EDI). Any orders sent by 4:30 p.m. would be delivered to Somers (or directly to a customer, if required) by 10 a.m. Customer orders were then combined at the Somers warehouse and shipped the following day.

Fairmont Canada provided Somers with access to more than 100 manufacturers and stocked over $20 million of products in inventory. Orders received by 5 p.m. were shipped that day.

FAIRMONT CANADA ACQUISITION

On April 3, MSC Inc., a direct competitor of Somers, announced that it was acquiring Fairmont Canada, a subsidiary of the U.S.-based Fairmont Inc. At the same time, it was also announced that Roancroft was acquiring the U.S. wholesale operations of Fairmont Inc.

Recently, Fairmont Inc. had expanded its activities to direct, end-user sales through a subsidiary that sold computer supplies through e-catalogs over the Internet. Many resellers considered this expansion of Fairmont Inc. as direct competition with their own activities and believed that Fairmont Inc. had gained an unfair advantage in the marketplace.

THE DECISION

The extent to which Fairmont Canada would pursue direct sales activities was still unclear to George, who was concerned that terminating its relationship with the supplier would require restructuring of processes and client relationships. One option available to Somers was to use Wahby International, a U.S.-based supplier of computer supplies that George had been using on a limited basis. Wahby provided catalogs with Internet ordering and order-tracking capabilities and had entered into a partnership with FedEx to provide a very high level of shipping response capability. The company stated in its corporate mission a total commitment to support its resellers and that it avoided any direct sales to end users. Wahby had sales of $1 billion (USF), but unfortunately, it did not have a strong presence in Canada, and George was concerned about leaving the company exposed to a single supplier of computer supplies.

George knew that Wayne Fitzsimmons, president of Somers, would expect a strategy to be developed quickly in reaction to the news concerning Fairmont Canada. Meanwhile, Somers was considering its own expansion into e-commerce as a defensive move against the new competition in the field and as a means to lower its costs. However, the establishment of a Web site catalog was still in the planning stage and an upgrade of their computer system would be needed.

Chapter Eleven

Investment Recovery

Chapter Outline

Key Questions for the Supply Manager

Should we

- Use an online auction as a means of disposing of scrap, surplus, and excess materials and equipment.
- Centralize responsibility for investment recovery?
- Attempt to use scrap, surplus, and excess materials in-house?

How can we

- Improve the investment recovery process?
- Reduce the quantities of materials and equipment to be disposed of?
- Make business decisions that are financially superior and environmentally sound?

Managers are concerned with the effective, efficient, and profitable recovery and disposal of scrap, surplus, obsolete, and waste materials and assets generated within the firm. In recent years, disposal problems have become more complex and important as companies face increasingly stringent environmental legislation and rising disposal costs. The focus on the entire supply chain means that managers must look for return loops to recapture their initial materials investment through remanufacturing, repair, reconfiguration, and recycling. Added to this is the need to develop and use new methods for avoiding the generation of solid waste products in the first place and better means of disposing of wastes that are discharged into the air and waterways, causing pollution. Cleaning up pollution is expensive and so avoiding the purchase, use, emission, or disposition of hazardous materials is the basis of a sound environmental management approach. This approach also puts supply in a critical position within the organization.

While this chapter analyzes and discusses the supply department's role in environmental management systems, the alert supply executive also must keep abreast of new technology concerned with avoiding and eliminating causes of pollution. Materials no longer can be selected and used without considering their eco-efficiency (e.g., improving material utilization per unit of production, their recyclability, and their potential for generating hazardous waste). The need for environmentally protective waste management and the need to reduce the amount of waste generated have led to development of the concept of an integrated waste management system. This plan calls for source reduction (eliminating unnecessary discards before they enter the waste stream), recycling (returning a product to commerce), resource recovery (burning trash and recovering energy), and landfills (providing the final disposal option for materials that cannot be reclaimed).

Not only does the proper sale of scrap, surplus, and waste result in additional income for the seller, it also prevents pollution and serves to conserve raw material resources and energy. For example, every ton of iron and steel scrap recycled saves one-and-one-half tons of iron ore, one ton of coke, and one-half ton of limestone, plus the energy required to convert the raw materials into virgin product. This scrap is collected for beneficial reuse, conserving impressive amounts of energy and natural resources in the recycling process.

Thus, investment recovery requires attention to environmental issues and regulations (e.g., hazardous waste disposal) and the ability to identify opportunities to recover revenues or reduce costs (e.g., through recycling or new means of disposal). In many organizations, investment recovery is the responsibility of the supply function.

NORTH AMERICAN ENVIRONMENTAL INITIATIVES

Why are environmental issues of concern to supply managers? For one thing, the people of the United States consume approximately 25 percent of the world's resources despite representing only 5 percent of the world's population. Both business and government leaders should consider the impact of these numbers.

The U.S. and Canadian governments have enacted a number of important regulations and many of these affect the supply function. Important among these regulations in the United States are four pieces of federal legislation: (1) the Resource Conservation and Recovery Act; (2) the Toxic Substances Control Act; (3) the Comprehensive Environmental Response, Compensation and Liability Act; and (4) the Clean Air Act. In Canada, the major pieces of environmental legislation are the Environmental Protection Act and the Water Resources Act. Among the implications of government environmental legislation for supply is that:

1. Purchasers contracting for waste disposal may want to (*a*) ensure that a disposal supplier is competent and reputable and has an EPA permit, (*b*) require the supplier to warrant that employees are trained in handling the specific waste, and (*c*) insist on the right to inspect the facility and the EPA permit.
2. Purchasers should require suppliers to warrant that any chemical or chemical mixture they provide is listed by the EPA.
3. Purchasers must track the amount and type of chemicals that enter and leave the plant and consult the Material Safety Data Sheets (MSDS).
4. Purchasers can choose environmentally friendly products; establish criteria for supplier selection that limit purchases from suppliers that sell damaging products; and be alert to alternatives, substitutes, or new technology that may help their companies meet the goals of government legislation.

The U.S. government provides details of its major environmental laws on the Environmental Protection Agency (EPA) Web site (http://www.epa.gov).

Environmentally Preferable Purchasing

Recognizing that the U.S. government is one of the largest consumers of goods and services in the world, the EPA developed the Environmentally Preferable Purchasing (EPP) program. EPP requires all federal procurement officials to assess and give preference to those products and services that are environmentally preferable. To support the program, a database was created containing environmental attribute information for a wide range of products. Although this program was developed for federal agency procurement, commercial purchasers also will find the information useful.

Voluntary Compliance Programs

The EPA is attempting to develop a more comprehensive program designed to hold down the costs of environmental continuous improvement. The goals are to develop an industry-by-industry approach, coordinate rule making, simplify record keeping and reporting requirements, permit streamlining, and review enforcement/compliance objectives.

Toward those goals, the EPA has developed a wide range of voluntary compliance programs. Detailed information on these programs is also available on the EPA Web site. Of particular interest to supply managers is the Environmental Accounting Project, which provides accounting tools and techniques for incorporating environmental, health, and safety costs and benefits into business decision making. Its Web site address is http://www.emawebsite.org.

ISO 14000 ENVIRONMENTAL STANDARDS

ISO 14000, similar to ISO 9000 in management principles, focuses on environmental issues. One is not a prerequisite for the other. ISO 14000 standards were introduced in 1996, and more than 60,000 companies worldwide had been certified as of December 2003, including approximately 3,500 U.S. locations and 1,300 Canadian locations.[1]

ISO 14000 standards describe the basic elements of an effective environmental management system (EMS) and do not replace federal, state, and provincial environmental laws and regulations. The standards include creation of a corporate environmental policy, setting of objectives and targets, implementaion of a plan to achieve the objectives and targets, performance measurement and corrective action, and continuous improvement. ISO 14000 standards are process, not performance, focused. They describe how a company can implement an EMS and achieve its objectives and targets.

The ISO 14000 series consists of standards related to EMS (ISO 14001 and ISO 14004) and standards related to environmental management tools, such as environmental auditing, environmental performance evaluation, environmental labeling, and life-cycle assessment. These standards are divided into the two general categories, shown in Figure 11–1. The EMS standards provide the framework for the management systems, and the life-cycle assessment standards focus on evaluation and analysis of products and processes.[2]

FIGURE 11–1 **ISO 14000 Framework**

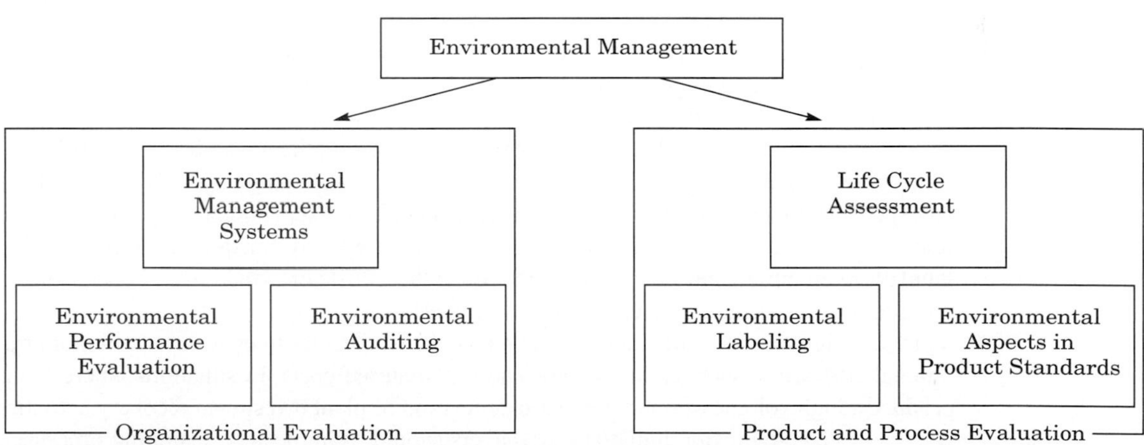

Source: Steve Melnyk et al., ISO 14000: *Assessing Its Impact on Corporate Effectiveness and Efficiency*, Tempe, AZ: Center for Advanced Purchasing Studies, 1999.

[1] ISO World, http://www.ecology.or.jp/isoworld/english/analy14k.htm, May 2004.

[2] Steven Melnyk et al., *ISO 14000: Assessing Its Impact on Corporate Effectiveness and Efficiency*, Tempe, AZ: Center for Advanced Purchasing Studies, 1999.

There are several reasons why supply managers should be concerned with the ISO 14000 standards. In the long run, firms with EMS should provide lower costs and offer fewer problems to their customers. From a total cost perspective, firms that control waste and conserve energy as part of an EMS are not only being environmentally responsible, they also should be more efficient. They also have less risk of exposing their customers to legal liabilities associated with violation of state and federal environmental legislation. (Chapter 12 covers the legal aspects of supply.) Furthermore, purchasers should avoid dealing with firms that may provoke a strong negative reaction because of poor environmental performance.

BENEFITS OF EFFECTIVE DISPOSAL

It is surprising that more attention has not been given by organizations to the whole problem of investment recovery and disposal. There are several reasons. One of the most important is that *scrap* suggests something that has no value and the junk man can take away—in other words, something a company is willing to sell if it can get anything for it, but, if not, it is willing even to pay somebody to haul away. Another reason is that many companies are not large enough to maintain investment recovery departments because the amounts of scrap and surplus they generate do not appear great enough to warrant particular attention.

The emphasis on managing a network of supply chain partners leads to a number of cost reduction opportunities in areas that may have been previously neglected by management. Environmental safety and health is one such area. Some of the ways in which supply can simultaneously achieve cost reductions and make improvements in environmental performance are: (1) reducing the obsolescence and waste of maintenance, repair, and operating (MRO) supplies through better materials and inventory management; (2) substantially reducing the costs from scrap and materials losses; (3) lowering the training, handling, and other expenses for hazardous materials; (4) increasing revenues by converting wastes to byproducts; (5) reducing the use of hazardous materials through more timely and accurate materials tracking and reporting systems; (6) decreasing the use and waste of chemicals, solvents, and paints through chemical service partnerships; and (7) recovering valuable materials and assets with efficient materials recovery programs.

Scrap is often a potential source of profit, and, therefore, the most obvious contribution of properly managed disposal activities is cost recovery. Directing residuals to landfills is an expensive disposal option, with tolling costs at landfills exceeding $200 per ton in some regions. Furthermore, associated costs, such as handling and transportation, make using landfills even more expensive. Firms can reduce their costs or avoid cost increases by examining ways to reduce or reuse their scrap materials.

Disposition costs are often ignored by managers who prefer to concentrate on more traditional cost areas, such as direct labor and raw material costs. In situations where firms produce a high volume of scrap, regular examination of plant investment recovery activities can lead to cost-reduction initiatives. Managers should examine scrap handling processes, segregation activities, logistics costs, and fees charged by dealers, brokers, and processors.

Governments, shareholders, and consumers are pressuring firms to develop and implement policies that protect the natural environment, which has been referred to as the "greening" of business. Most industrialized countries are setting aggressive recycling targets for their industries. Such pressures have been particularly strong in Europe, where Germany has passed ambitious legislation that imposes responsibility for recycling consumer waste on manufacturers.[3] Supply managers can make a contribution by identifying materials suitable for recycling or reuse, examining alternative and innovative disposal options, and securing raw materials that maximize production yields.

Notable examples of firms that have begun to successfully integrate environmental management practices within their supply chain include Xerox, DaimlerChrysler, and IBM. Xerox's Asset Recycle Management Program successfully diverts 90 percent of all materials and components for its end-of-life photocopiers through reuse, remanufacturing, and recycling. The company estimates that this program generated annual savings of $300 to $400 million. Meanwhile, DaimlerChrysler estimates that it saved $4.7 million per year at one manufacturing facility in Michigan through the implementation of a new scrap management system set up by OmniSource. Scrap metal from DaimlerChrysler is returned to steel suppliers and recycled.[4]

Supplier selection should play a major role in corporate environmental management strategies. IBM has developed a process whereby environmental matters are incorporated into the supplier selection process. IBM considers: (1) the environmental impact of purchases with respect to how they will affect its processes and products, (2) the impact that its suppliers have on the environment, and (3) opportunities for recyclable components.[5]

CATEGORIES OF MATERIAL FOR DISPOSAL

No matter how well a company is managed, some excess, waste, scrap, surplus, and obsolete material will develop. Every organization tries, of course, to keep such material to a minimum. But try as it may, this never will be wholly successful. The existence of this class of material is the result of a wide variety of causes, among which are overoptimism in the sales forecast, changes in design and specifications, errors in estimating usage, inevitable losses in processing, careless use of material by factory personnel, and overbuying resulting from attempts to avoid the threat of rising prices or to secure quantity discounts on large purchases.

We are not presently concerned with the methods by which excess, waste, scrap, or obsolete material may be kept at a minimum; these already have been discussed in connection with proper inventory, standardization, quality determination, value analysis, and forward buying. The immediate problem has to do with the disposition of these materials when they do appear. We first need to distinguish among the six categories of material for disposal.

[3] Amy Halpert, "Germany's Solid Waste Disposal System: Shifting the Responsibility," *Georgetown International Environmental Law Review,* Fall 2001, pp. 135–59.

[4] Robert D. Klassen and P. Fraser Johnson. "The Green Supply Chain," in *Understanding Supply Chains: Concepts, Critique and Futures,* ed. Roy Westbrook and Steve New, Oxford, UK: Oxford University Press, 2004.

[5] Lisa Ellram and Wendy Tate, "IBM's Supply-Base Efforts toward Sustainability," *Practix,* CAPS Research, August 2003.

Excess or Surplus Materials

Excess (or surplus) material is that stock that is in excess of a reasonable requirement of the organization. It arises because of errors in the amount bought or because anticipated production did not materialize. Such material may be handled in various ways. In some cases it can be stored until required, particularly if the material is of a nonperishable character, if storage costs are not excessive, and if there is a reasonable expectation that the material will be required in the future. Occasionally it may be substituted for more active material. Or, if the company operates a number of plants, it may be possible to transfer the excess to another plant. There are times, however, when these conditions do not exist and when prompt sale is desirable. The chances for change in the style or design may be so great as to diminish considerably the probability that this particular material may be required. Or it may be perishable. Factory requirements may be such as to postpone the demand for large amounts of this material so far into the future that the most economical action is to dispose of it and repurchase at a later date.

Obsolete Material or Equipment

Obsolete material differs from excess stock in that, whereas the latter presumably could be consumed at some future date, the former is unlikely ever to be used inside the organization that purchased it. For example, company calendars in the stockroom become outdated. Material becomes obsolete as a result of a change in the production process or when some better material is substituted for that originally used. Once material has been declared obsolete, it is wise to dispose of it for the best price that can be obtained.

Although material or equipment may be obsolete to one user, this need not mean that it is obsolete to others. For example, a company could replace old machines with others that are more modern and more productive. However, the discarded machines may still have value for some other manufacturer in the same type of business or in some other industry, representing a profit-making opportunity for the company wanting to dispose of the obsolete equipment. Similarly, an airline may decide to discontinue using a certain type of airplane. This action makes not only the plane but also the repair and maintenance parts inventory obsolete. But both may have substantial value to other airlines or users of planes.

Rejected End Products

Because of the uncertainties of the production process, or because of complex end-product quality specifications, a certain percentage of completed products may be rejected by outgoing quality control as unsatisfactory. In some instances these finished products can be repaired or reworked to bring them up to standard, but in other instances it is not economic to do so. The semiconductor industry is a good example; because of the technological complexities of the process, the "yield" on a particular production line may be such that only 70 percent of the finished devices measure up to end-product specifications.

The rejected products may then be sold to users who do not require the normal quality in purchased items. These might be classified as factory seconds. One problem is that if the end product is identified with a name or trademark, unscrupulous buyers may then turn around and remarket the item as one that measures up to the stated quality requirements for the original item. To avoid this, the sales contract may include a statement that "the buyer agrees and warrants that the product will not be resold in its present form or for its original usage application." If the seller does not feel this contract clause provides adequate protection, then the firm may find it necessary to destroy the rejected items (as is done in the pharmaceutical industry), remove the distinguishing mark or identification, or melt the product down to recover any valuable metal content.

Scrap Material

Scrap material differs from excess or obsolete stock because it cannot properly be classified as new or unused. Scrap is a term that may be applied to material or equipment that is no longer serviceable and has been discarded. Another form of scrap is represented by the many byproducts of the production process, such as fly from cotton spinning; warp ends from weaving; ferrous and nonferrous metal scrap from boring, planing, and stamping machines; flash metal from the foundry process; or paper cuttings from the binding process, as when this book was bound. Start-up adjustment scrap is frequently significant, and in industries like papermaking, paper converting, printing, and polyethylene pellet manufacturing, it is one major reason for a significant price increase for small custom orders. The faster and the more automated the equipment, the higher the start-up scrap will be as a percentage of the total material used in small orders. Commonly, items of this class, which are a normal part of the production process, are considered a form of scrap; such material frequently may be salvaged. In the metal industries, the importance of scrap in this form has a definite bearing on costs and prices. For instance, a selection from among forgings, stampings, or castings may depend on the waste weight. The waste weight to be removed in finishing plus labor costs of removing it may make a higher-priced article the better value. In turning brass parts, the cost of the material (brass rod) may be greater than the price of the finished parts because the recovered brass scrap is such an important element in the cost. Indeed, scrap is so valuable as an element in cost that it is not unusual for the purchase contract on nonferrous metals to include a price at which the scrap will be repurchased by the supplier.

Scrap metals normally are separated into ferrous and nonferrous categories. Ferrous includes those products conceived from iron and generally are attracted by the scrap man's geiger counter (an ordinary magnet). The ferrous group consists of scrap steel, cast iron, white iron, and so on. The nonferrous group includes four broad families: (1) red metals, which are copper based; (2) white metals, which are aluminum, tin, lead, or zinc based; (3) nickel alloys; and (4) precious metals—for example, gold, silver, and palladium—known as exotics. Industry standards have been established for the grading of ferrous and nonferrous scrap materials, such as copper, steel, glass, and paper.

There are some 1,500 scrap dealers and brokers in the United States who buy, broker, and/or process scrap commodities, including metals, paper, plastics, glass, rubber, and textiles. The dealer or broker acts as an intermediary between the seller (normally the supply department) and the final buyer (such as a steel mill). These organizations can be an important service provider to manufacturing companies that generate a large amount of scrap and by-products as part of the normal manufacturing process by installing in-plant equipment for residual handing, hauling the material, and selling the scrap.

Waste

Waste is material or supplies that have been changed during the production process and, through carelessness, faulty production methods, poor handling, or other causes, have been spoiled, broken, or otherwise rendered unfit for further use or reclamation. There is a form of waste not due to obsolescence and yet not a result of carelessness or poor handling. Waste, for example, may occur by the fact that the material is not up to specifications because of faulty machinery or breakdowns, or because of unforeseen chemical action. In some instances, waste can be defined simply as the residue of materials that results from the normal manufacturing process and that has no economic (resale) value (unlike scrap, which does have value). An example is the smoke produced by burning fuel, or cutting oil that has become so badly contaminated as a result of the normal manufacturing process that it cannot be reclaimed. However, what is waste today and has no current economic value may change tomorrow. For example, years ago the natural gas produced in crude oil production was waste and was flared off in the oil fields because it had no sales value; today it has substantial economic value.

Hazardous Waste

Hazardous waste is discarded material that exhibits certain specific hazardous characteristics, such as toxic, ignitable, corrosive, or dangerously reactive substances. Because of supply's role in the acquisition of materials and the disposal of waste, purchasers should consider the total cost of hazardous waste for the company. These costs include direct cleanup costs, disposal costs (rapidly rising due to a landfill shortage), administrative and legal costs, and new plant and equipment costs (to reduce waste and deal with contaminated plants).

The Institute of Scrap Recycling Industries proposes the following action plan, which undoubtedly would involve supply:[6]

Phase I: Develop an inventory of products containing toxic heavy metals.

Phase II: Consider how best to handle the hazardous materials that have the potential to contaminate currently nonhazardous waste.

Phase III: Define how best to encourage the future substitution of nonhazardous materials for the hazardous materials used now and previously used.

Phase IV: Consider how best to deal with those materials that pose long-term hazardous waste threats and for which no substitutes appear economically feasible.

The U.S. Department of Transportation regulates all hazardous materials transport under the Hazardous Materials Transportation Act (HMTA). In Canada, the Federal Department of Transport is responsible for administration of the Transportation of Dangerous Goods Regulations. Purchasers play a key role in transferring information required by the Hazard Communication Standard (HCS) or "right-to-know" law developed by the Occupational, Safety and Health Administration (OSHA). Material Safety Data Sheets (MSDS) provide the information necessary to recognize potential health hazards to employees and the community at large. The purchaser should request an MSDS from the manufacturer or supplier, perform a hazard evaluation considering the need for the chemical against the potential hazard to employees and the community, and, if necessary, develop sourcing and usage alternatives. The MSDS should be kept on file.

[6] The Institute of Scrap Recycling Industries, "Dealing with Potential Hazardous Waste and Potentially Non-Recyclable Materials," http://www.isri.org.

Laws and regulations for hazardous materials also cover packaging and movement of hazardous materials. The HMTA requires facilities to follow certain packaging, labeling, loading, routing, and emergency planning requirements.

Differences of opinion may exist as to the exact definitions of scrap, excess, and waste. From the standpoint of the supply manager who has to dispose of the material, these differences are secondary. The objective is to realize as large a return as possible from the safe disposal of these items.

RESPONSIBILITY FOR MATERIAL DISPOSAL

The question of who bears the responsibility for the management of material disposal in an organization has more than one answer. In large companies where substantial amounts of scrap, obsolete, surplus, and waste materials and equipment are generated, a separate department may be justified. The manager of such a department may report to the general manager or the production manager. In some companies there is, within the manufacturing department, a separate investment recovery, salvage, or "utilization" division to pass on questions about possible reclamation. Indeed, the place of the "investment recovery" division is well-established among many larger firms. This division is primarily a manufacturing rather than a sales division and is concerned with such duties as the development of salvage processes; the actual reclamation of waste, scrap, or excess material; and the reduction of the volume of such material. Most companies depend on the supply department to handle disposal sales.

A study of purchasing organizational relationships, conducted in 2003 by the CAPS Research, covered the practices of 284 major organizations in the United States and Canada. That study found that supply was responsible for scrap/surplus disposal/inventory recovery in 56 percent of the firms.

Legitimate reasons for assigning disposal of materials to the purchasing/materials management function include (1) they possess knowledge of price trends; (2) contact with salespeople is a good source of information as to possible users of the material; (3) familiarity with the company's own needs may suggest possible uses for, and transfer of, the material within the organization; and (4) unless a specific department is established within the firm to handle this function, supply is probably the only logical choice.

In large and highly diversified organizations, there is a great need for the coordination of salvage disposal if the best possible results are to be obtained. Where a corporate supply department is included in the home-office organization structure, even if only in a consulting relationship with the various divisions of the company, available information and records and established channels of communication should help to ensure that salvage materials generated in any part of the company are considered for use in all parts of the company before being offered for sale.

Because the social and financial stakes are high and because of the complexity of laws and regulations, turnkey environmental contracting is a possible option for small- to medium-sized waste generators with needs that are too diverse or too small to be handled directly by treatment, storage, or disposal facilities.

The general conclusion is that, except in the cases of companies with separate salvage or investment recovery departments, management has found the supply department, because of its knowledge of original suppliers, materials, markets, prices, and possible uses, in a better position than other departments of the company to salvage what can be used and to dispose of what cannot.

KEYS TO PROFITABLE DISPOSAL

Obviously, the optimum solution would be not to generate materials that need disposal. While this is not totally possible, every effort should be made, through good planning and taking advantage of modern technology, to minimize the quantity of material generated.

The disposition of all kinds of obsolete, scrap, and surplus materials always should be handled to reduce the net loss to the lowest possible figure or, if possible, achieve the highest potential gain. The first thought, therefore, should be to balance against each other the net returns obtained from each of several methods of disposition. Thus, excess material frequently can be transferred from one plant to another of the same company. Such a procedure involves little outlay except for packing, handling, and shipping. At other times, by reprocessing or reconditioning, material can be salvaged for use within the plant. Such cases clearly involve a somewhat larger outlay, and there may be some question as to whether, once the material has been so treated, its value, either for the purpose originally intended or for some substitute use, is great enough to warrant the expense.

Because the decision whether to undertake the reclamation of any particular lot of material is essentially one of production costs and of the resultant quality, it should be—and commonly is—made by the production or engineering departments instead of by supply or the scrap department. The most the supply manager can do is to suggest that this treatment be considered before the material is disposed of in other ways.

DISPOSAL CHANNELS

There are several possible means of material disposal. In general, the options are, in order of maximum return to the selling company:

1. Use elsewhere within the firm on an "as is" basis. An attempt should be made to use the material "as is," or with modification, for a purpose other than that for which it was purchased; for example, substitution for similar grades and nearby sizes, and shearing or stripping sheet metals to obtain narrower widths. In the case of a multidivision operation, periodically each division should circulate to all other divisions a list of scrap/surplus/obsolete material and equipment; arrangements then may be made for interplant transfer of some of the items. In some organizations with an enterprise resource planning (ERP) system (see Chapter 4), a national and even global database can be developed for individuals from the same organization to post and purchase spares, obsolete materials, and excess supplies from one another more efficiently and cost-effectively.

2. Reclaim for use within the plant. As a result of the materials shortages of the early 1970s, the environmental movement of the 1980s, and new recycling processes of the 1990s, many firms have become interested in the possibilities of recycling materials such as paper, copper, zinc, tin, aluminum cans, and precious metals. For example, can the material be reclaimed or modified for use by welding? Welding has become a very important factor in disposing of materials to advantage. Defective and spoiled castings and fabricated metal parts can be reclaimed at little expense; short ends of bar stock and pipe can be welded into working lengths; and worn or broken jigs, fixtures, and machine parts can be built up or patched. Furthermore, castings and fabricated metal parts can be reduced in size by either the arc or acetylene cutting process. Or perhaps a steel washer(s) could be stamped out of a piece of scrap (referred to as off-fall) that is a normal output of the production process. Precious metal scrap often is shipped to a precious metal refiner, who processes it back into its original form and returns it for use as a raw material, charging the supply department a tolling charge for its services.

The opportunities for recycling, and thereby reducing the waste stream, extend beyond municipal recycling systems and include programs that "close the loop" by collecting the material, turning it into cost-competitive, high-quality, recycled content products and selling them back to the purchaser.

3. Sell to another firm for use on an "as is" basis. Can any other manufacturer use the material either "as is" or with economical modification? It should be noted that sales can often be made directly to other users who may be able to use a disposal item in lieu of a raw material they currently are buying. Or one firm's surplus or obsolete equipment may solve another firm's equipment requirements nicely. A good example of this is the market that has existed for years for DC-9 aircraft, which are obsolete for one air carrier and are bought for use by supplemental or commuter airlines. In some cases, and particularly prevalent in public agencies, surplus or obsolete equipment and vehicles are sold at public auction. Some companies permit employees to buy, as part of their employee relations program, used equipment or surplus materials at preset prices. If this is done, adequate controls should be established to ensure that the return to the firm is at a reasonable level and that all interested employees are treated fairly.

4. Return to supplier. Can it be returned to the manufacturer or supplier from whom it was purchased, either for cash or for credit on other later purchases? A great deal of steel scrap is sold by large-quantity purchasers directly back to the mills, who use it as a raw material in the steel production process. Normally, the firm using this disposal avenue must be a large consumer. In the case of surplus (new) inventory items, the original supplier may be willing to allow full credit on returned items.

5. Sell through a broker. Brokers can handle the sale of scrap, surplus, and obsolete equipment and materials. Their role is to bring buyer and seller together, for which they take a commission. Much metal scrap is disposed of through this channel. Brokers also exist to handle the purchase and sale of obsolete, surplus, used, and rebuilt equipment and typically specialize by either industry—for example, bakery—or type of equipment—for example, computers. This medium often is used by the selling organization and may present interesting alternatives for the buyer in the equipment acquisition process. Most used equipment brokers have Web sites that provide information about equipment availability and pricing.

6. Sell to a local scrap or surplus dealer. All communities of any size will have one or more scrap dealers. The return from sale through this channel likely will be low, for four reasons: (1) There may be only one dealer, a noncompetitive, sole buying source; (2) the dealer assumes the risk of investment, holding, and attempting to find a buyer; (3) the profit margin for assuming this risk may be quite high; and (4) extra movement and handling, which is costly, is involved.

7. Donate, discard, or destroy the material or item. In some instances, a firm may decide to donate used equipment to an educational or charitable organization, taking a tax deduction. A number of nonprofit clearinghouses distribute goods to schools and charities. Because the tax aspects of such contributions are complex, the advice of tax counsel should be obtained as part of the decision process.

If no buyer or user can be found for the item, the firm may have to dispose of the item. This can be quite costly because of the landfill shortages and the liability posed by potential environmental hazards. Caution should be taken to protect the environment and to ensure that disposal methods for dangerous materials do not create a safety hazard to the public. The Investment Recovery Association, an international nonprofit trade association of firms with established investment recovery programs, provides assistance in disposing of recyclable products, capital assets, and surplus materials.

Most items can be disposed of profitably by use of imagination, creative thinking, and problem solving. Recent research on the importance of environmental considerations in strategic supply and supply chain management indicates that avoidance of violations is still the primary focus. Yet many organizations are coming up with creative and cost-effective ways to handle investment recovery challenges.

DISPOSAL PROCEDURES

When selling scrap and surplus materials, adequate procedures must be established that will protect the company from loss due to slipshod methods, dishonest employees, and irregular practices on the part of the purchaser. These procedures must cover a broad range of activities, including segregation and storage, weighing and measuring, delivery, negotiation, supplier selection, and payment.

Contamination of scrap with foreign materials will often significantly reduce its recovery value. If two types of scrap, for example, steel and copper scrap, are mixed, the return per pound on sale likely will be less than the lowest-priced scrap, because any buyer must go to the expense of separating the scrap before processing. Consequently, scrap should be segregated, prepared, and analyzed systematically during the various stages of the production process in order to protect its value.

Scrap can be segregated by type, alloy, grade, size, and weight, and should be done at the point where the scrap is generated. This requires proper planning and organization of segregation activities, which includes providing instructions to employees at collection points. Training programs also can be used to help company employees identify and separate scrap materials. Plants, not the dealers or the processors, should control the collection and classification of scrap materials, and company personnel should be familiar with the grades of scrap produced. Periodic studies should be conducted to evaluate the most effective methods of disposing of scrap in light of changing volumes and different mixes of scrap grades.

Adequate controls should be in place for accurate reporting and payment. All sales should be approved by a department head, and cash sales should be handled through the cashier and never by the individual whose duty it is to negotiate the sale. All delivery of byproducts sold should be accomplished through the issuing of an order form, and a sufficient number of copies should be made to provide a complete record for all departments involved in the transaction. The shipping department should determine the weight and count, and this information should be sent directly to the accounts receivable department.

The department responsible for the performance of this function should maintain a list of reputable dealers in the particular line of material or equipment to be disposed of and should periodically review this list. At frequent intervals, the proper plant official should be instructed to clean up the stock and report on the weights and quantities of the different items or classes of items ready for disposal.

A common procedure is to send out invitations to four or five dealers to call and inspect the lots and quote their prices FOB factory yard. Such transactions usually are subject to the accepted bidder's check of weights and quantities and are paid for in cash before removal. Not infrequently, acceptable and dependable purchasers with whom satisfactory connections have already been established are relied on as desirable purchasers, and no bids are called for from others. Technology tools are increasingly applied to investment recovery programs. Companies are using the Internet and intranets to advertise the sale of surplus and obsolete equipment and materials.

If a firm generates large amounts of scrap materials consistently, the bidders may be asked to bid on the purchase of this scrap over a time period of six months to a year. It is generally advisable to rebid or renegotiate such contracts at least annually to encourage competition. However, when establishing contract duration, plants need to consider the associated transaction costs. Not only are there administrative costs of soliciting bids, other costs need to be taken into account, such as possible production interruptions as equipment provided by the old processor is replaced by the new processor. Plants often negotiate long-term agreements with their processors in order to encourage investment in equipment viewed as beneficial by plant management.

Often the disposal agreement will have an escalator clause in it, tying the price to changes in the overall market, as reported in a specifically designated independent market index, such as AMM.com. The market prices of many types and grades of scrap materials can vary widely over a relatively short time period, which is the reason for the use of escalator clauses. For example, over the five-month period between April and September 2003, the price of scrap steel in Chicago, No. 2, bundles, increased from $85 per ton to $100 per ton (18 percent) while the price of post-consumer corrugated paper decreased from $75 per ton to $62.50 per ton (17 percent).[7]

The contract for sale of scrap items should include price and how determined, quantities involved (all or a percentage), time of delivery, FOB point, cancellation privileges, how weights are determined, and payment terms. For reporting purposes, revenues associated with the scrap disposal activities should be credited to separate accounts, as opposed to netting them against a purchase or expense account. The practice of netting scrap revenues against raw material costs may be justified for statement presentation purposes, but such revenue should be itemized on management statements and budgets.

SELECTING THE RIGHT DISPOSAL PARTNER

Selection of the appropriate firm to handle waste and scrap removal can be a challenging, yet critical, task. First, most scrap materials can be sold. However, supply managers are

[7] American Metal Market, "*Recycling Manager*," AMM.com, April and September 2003.

used to buying, not selling, materials. Second, hazardous materials must be properly disposed of; failure to do so can result in substantial fines and cleanup costs. This requires an understanding of regulatory issues surrounding residual disposition. Third, disposal methods have implications for the general manufacturing operation. Decisions, such as segregation, impact a plant's processing operations and influence its cost structure. Consequently, traditional supply precepts do not always apply when selecting a firm to handle disposal activities.

In most situations, plants must rely on support from scrap dealers to help manage elements of their disposal activities. As a result of the costs associated with regulatory noncompliance, generators of scrap and waste must be aware of what happens to the material after it leaves the company premises. Consequently, only approved processors, dealers, or brokers should be used, with qualification based on a range of possible criteria: secondary processing and waste treatment capabilities and capacity; size and capacity of truck fleet; ability to provide dependable service; problem-solving capabilities; ability to provide destruction of scrap products in order to avoid entry into the market; and financial stability. Assessing the financial stability of the dealer, broker, or processor often requires obtaining a list of credit references or obtaining a credit report from an organization such as Dun & Bradstreet.

The volume of scrap or waste material has a significant influence on how companies choose to manage their disposal activities. Plants with high volumes often support disposal activities with dedicated staff and employ a greater level of resources in the disposition process. Depending on volume, logistics systems also differ. For example, plants that generate a high volume of a particular grade of scrap may find it cost-effective to utilize rail transportation or specialized highway trailers.

Every effort should be made to obtain maximum competition from sources available to buy scrap or surplus material. Unfortunately, the number of potential users and buyers of scrap in a particular area may be small, resulting in noncompetitive disposal situations. Supply should actively attempt to find new buyers and encourage then to compete in terms of price paid and services provided.

Investment recovery involves supplier management issues, which have implications for the overall performance of the firm. Measuring total costs of disposition is useful as a means of identifying a range of opportunities to work with disposal partners with the objective of improving activities. For example, in a cooperative relationship, joint problem-solving efforts can be utilized by the plant and scrap investment buyer as a response to changing issues. Make-or-buy decision criteria can be applied to determine the appropriate mix of activities for the plant; these activities should be reevaluated regularly to adapt to changing situations.

Conclusion

Virtually every firm faces the challenge of disposing of materials or equipment at some point, and in most organizations, this responsibility is given to supply. The potential benefits of effective investment recovery and disposal programs to organizations are numerous and include recovery of raw materials, cost reduction and avoidance, improved company image, compliance with government regulations, and resource conservation. Managing investment recovery and disposal requires familiarity with environmental issues and regulations and the capability to establish appropriate reverse supply chain flows that capture opportunities for revenue recovery and provide cost-effectiveness.

Questions for Review and Discussion

1. Why is investment recovery often a responsibility of the supply department?
2. How can the firm obtain maximum return from disposal of unneeded items?
3. What specific procedures should supply use to dispose of unneeded items?
4. What are the channels used in disposing of items? What are the advantages of each?
5. What is the difference between surplus material, obsolete material, rejects, scrap, waste, and hazardous waste? How do investment recovery and disposal practices differ between these six categories?
6. Where can you achieve cost reductions in disposal and investment recovery activities? What are the major cost drivers?
7. How do environmental concerns affect the disposal of scrap, surplus, and obsolete materials?
8. How can the Internet be used to facilitate investment recovery programs?
9. How can environmental matters be incorporated into supplier selection?

References

Carter, Craig R., and Marianne M. Jennings, *Purchasing's Contribution to the Socially Responsible Management of the Supply Chain,* Tempe, AZ: CAPS Research, 2000.

Carter, Joseph R., and Ram Narasimhan, *Environmental Supply Chain Management,* Tempe, AZ: Center for Advanced Purchasing Studies, 1998.

Ellram, Lisa, and Wendy Tate, "IBM's Supply-Base Efforts Toward Sustainability," *Practix,* CAPS Research, August 2003.

The Environmental Protection Agency (EPA), *The Lean and Green Supply Chain: A Practical Guide for Materials Managers and Supply Chain Managers to Reduce Costs and Improve Environmental Performance,* EPA 742-R-99-003, February 2000, http://www.epa.gov.

The Environmental Protection Agency (EPA), *Enhancing Supply Chain Performance with Environmental Cost Information: Examples from Commonwealth Edison, Andersen Corporation, and Ashland Chemical,* EPA 742-R-99-002, April 2000, http://www.epa.gov.

Institute of Scrap Recycling Industries, *Scrap Recycling: Where Tomorrow Begins,* http://www.isri.com.

Melnyk, Steven; Roger Calantone; Rob Handfield; R. L. Tummala; Gyula Vastag; Timothy Hinds; Robert Sroufe; Frank Montabon; and Sime Curkovic, *ISO 14000: Assessing Its Impact on Corporate Effectiveness and Efficiency,* Tempe, AZ: Center for Advanced Purchasing Studies, 1999.

Performance Benchmarks for Investment Recovery, Tempe, AZ: Center for Advanced Purchasing Studies, 2001.

Case 11–1

Miltec Inc.

Susan Atkins, vice president of supply at Miltec Inc., was concerned about the forthcoming move to the new corporate head office. This would create a disposal challenge as all office furnishings in former locations became surplus.

Miltec, a large, fast-growing electronics company, would complete its new head office building in downtown Los Angeles in another three months. The building had already drawn favorable reviews from the local community for its advanced architectural design, incorporating energy-saving concepts as well as the open office format. Because of Miltec's rapid growth, its offices had been spread over eight different locations, mostly in rented quarters. It was hoped that the new 27-story tower would heighten the corporation's visibility and image while bringing all office employees under the same roof. The architect and the new building task force have decided to furnish all offices with new furniture and fixtures to complement the design of the building. As a consequence, all furnishings in the "old" locations would become surplus. Plans called for staged "moving in" of all departments over a four-month period. Leases in old locations were expiring accordingly.

Susan Atkins did not know how much furniture was involved. Some dated back to 1973 when the company was founded. Susan suspected that a large portion was not tagged properly, even though Miltec had an asset identification and tagging program. She also suspected most pieces would have been fully depreciated on the company's books.

According to corporate guidelines, purchasing was responsible for disposal of all capital assets subject to certain authorizations from budget unit heads and corporate officers depending on the asset's value. The vice president of administration had requested Susan pay special attention to the corporate manual clause: "Surplus items may be sold to Miltec employees at market or trade-in value. Notices of available items must be posted on all bulletin boards." Susan suspected this request might have something to do with the beautiful Early American cherry office set in the vice president's office. Susan was also aware many Miltec employees had a sentimental attachment to their furnishings and that they might welcome a chance to purchase such items for their personal use.

Other relevant corporate instructions regarding disposal included

- Surplus capital assets may be donated to charitable organizations. All such requests must be approved by the vice president of administration.
- It is the responsibility of the corporate supply department to obtain the highest possible return for all surplus items.

One of Susan's assistants suggested that all surplus furnishings be stored in a local warehouse until all moves were complete. At that point it would be clear what items and how many were available. Unused furniture dealers could then be invited to bid on the whole lot. Warehouse space could probably be rented for about $10,000 a month.

Susan had never before faced a disposal of this magnitude and wondered how she should proceed.

Case 11–2

Ornex

On June 3 Greg Saunders, materials manager at Ornex, a parts manufacturer in Detroit, Michigan, heard the company had not been awarded a large new contract it had expected from its main automotive customer. Greg had ordered a substantial shipment of customized metal powder in anticipation of this contract, and now he wondered how to dispose of the raw material on hand.

ORNEX

Ornex, an automotive parts manufacturer, had been supplying North American automobile companies for four decades. Some of the products manufactured included transmission gears, hubs, and crank shafts. The plant employed approximately 150 people, and Ornex manufactured 12 different automotive parts.

Ornex's mission was "to produce world-class competitive products that exceed our customers' expectations in quality, cost, and delivery through people, teamwork, and technology."

RAW MATERIALS PURCHASING

Ornex obtained metal powders from two major sources: 60 percent of its requirements came from FE Metal Powders Inc. based in Quebec, and the remainder from Simpsons Powders Inc. based in the United States. Both of these suppliers performed rigorous tests on their metal powders, and Greg considered these two companies to have the highest quality raw materials in the industry.

Because of the high demand for metal powders, delivery schedules varied depending on the type of product requested by Ornex. Delivery normally took 10 weeks for standard products and up to 16 weeks for special formulations of metal powders. Thus, long lead times required extensive inventory planning. Moreover, occasionally raw material had to be ordered prior to confirmation of a customer contract.

The metal powder suppliers recognized the difficulties with material planning and offered most parts manufacturers a consignment period of 60–120 days. The consignment clause meant that Ornex only paid for powder it used. Thus, if a metal powder had been purchased for a major job prior to the acceptance of a bid, and if that job was awarded to a competitor, the powder could be returned as long as it was unused and had been purchased in the last two to four months. However, consignment did not apply to any type of customized order.

THE NEW CONTRACT

In July of the previous year, Ornex had submitted a bid to manufacture "races," a new type of transmission part for its primary automotive customer. If the bid were accepted, production would have to begin the following March. Due to the long raw material lead time, Greg placed an initial order for the customized raw iron powder in early November. FE Metal Powders was selected to provide 400,000 pounds of powder at a cost of $0.60 per pound. After the 16-week waiting period, the 400,000 pounds would be delivered in monthly shipments of 100,000 pounds each.

By March however, Greg still had not received contract confirmation. The iron powder began to accumulate in inventory, but Greg was not concerned because the plant had adequate space. However, on June 3 the automobile company awarded the bid to a competing automotive supplier. Greg immediately requested the cancellation of all remaining deliveries. FE Metal Powders agreed to cease all shipments, but at this late date Ornex had already acquired 300,000 pounds of customized raw iron. This inventory had been purchased on credit. The supplier would be demanding payment by the end of the month.

THE CURRENT SITUATION

Greg wondered what his best option was with respect to the 300,000 pounds of metal powder already in Ornex's inventory. He could see at least two options. First, Ornex could return the inventory. FE Metal Powders understood the nature of this/or the company's dilemma and verbally agreed to take back the inventory. FE Metal Powders would act as a selling agent and try to resell the inventory to another parts manufacturer. Ornex would be required to pay a commission of $0.20 per pound. This would protect FE Metal Powder from future loss if it could not resell the customized powder. Even though this would mean a loss for Ornex, this alternative was worth considering.

If the customized powder could not be used within one-and-a-half years, or if the seal on the package were broken, the powder could develop rust. If rust balls developed, this would burden the company with further costs for screening out the rust if the powder was to be used.

Greg also was considering keeping the inventory on hand. Greg anticipated that 100,000 pounds of the customized powder could be used in the near future. However, the remaining stock probably would not be completely cleared out for another 18 months. Greg knew that inventory carrying costs at Ornex were usually calculated at 2 percent per month of the value of the inventory. There was adequate space to hold the powder in the current facilities, but the real concern was rusting of the unused powder. Greg knew that the longer the packages remained sitting in inventory, the greater the probability that the packages could be broken. He also recognized that if this alternative was chosen, a payment schedule for the powder would have to be negotiated with FE Metal Powders.

Chapter Twelve

Supply Law and Ethics

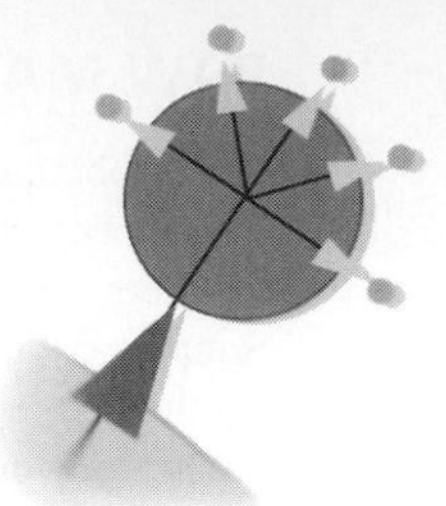

Chapter Outline

Key Questions for the Supply Manager

Should we

- Put all purchase agreements in writing?
- Develop and support a set of principles of social responsibility?
- Use alternative dispute resolution in large-dollar purchase agreements?

How can we

- Minimize the organization's legal and ethical exposure?
- Minimize our own personal liability for purchase actions?
- Avoid legal disputes with suppliers?

All supply communications, agreements, and understandings internally and externally have ethical and legal implications. A professional supply manager does not require the training of a lawyer or an ethicist but should understand the basic principles of commercial law and ethics. Such understanding should enable recognition of problems and situations that require professional counsel and also provide the knowledge to avoid pitfalls in day-to-day operations. As a strategic player in the organization, the supply manager must always be looking to maximize opportunities and minimize risks for the organization. Keeping an eye on the legal and ethical horizons is one way supply professionals can contribute to the organization.

Seldom will either buyer or seller resort to the courts to enforce a purchase contract or assess financial damages. In those infrequent situations where formal legal action is the last resort, the legal costs can be high and the outcome uncertain. *The competent purchaser wishes to avoid such situations and will take legal action only as a last resort.* A knowledge of the law of contracts will help the supply manager avoid such legal involvement and position the organization to successfully pursue, or defend itself against, such lawsuits.

Ensuring that the supply process is conducted ethically and in a socially responsible manner is another way in which supply professionals must contribute to the organization's success. Recent events have once again put ethical behavior in the spotlight. Ethical purchasing and supply behavior will help the supply manager avoid ethical breaches and position the organization to capitalize on its reputation.

LEGAL AUTHORITY

What is the supply officer's legal status? Briefly, he or she has the authority to attend to the business of supply in accordance with the instructions given by his or her employer. These instructions usually are broad in character. There should be, and in all progressive organizations there is, a clear understanding as to what the supply officer is expected to do. This normally is covered by a job description (see Figures 2–2 and 2–3 for sample job descriptions). A clear understanding of duties is good business policy strengthened by the law's assumption that an agreement exists between the agent and the employer as to the scope of the authority. The supply officer has a right to expect from the employer a clear understanding as to duties and responsibilities; the supply officer, in turn, is expected to perform these duties in a loyal, honest, and careful manner, fulfilling the obligations to the employer, from a legal point of view. In agreeing to render service to an employer, there is no implied agreement that no errors will be made, for some errors are incidental to all vocations.

By special stipulation, the supply manager may even assume responsibility to the principal for the risks from honest error, but such arrangements are rare. Nevertheless, when a person accepts an appointment to serve as an agent for the principal, the implication exists that the person possesses the necessary skill to carry out the work. In some cases, a very high degree of skill is demanded and accepting an appointment under such circumstances implies the necessary skill. There are, of course, many possible modifications of this general statement. The supply officer becomes liable to the employer when damage occurs through active fault or through negligence. Difficulties arise in attempting to define what negligence is, although in general it may be said to constitute an "omission of due care under given circumstances."

The supply officer also has an obligation to keep his or her employer informed about specific actions taken to perform the purchasing function, and report resultant outcomes from these actions. In addition, records must be kept and an accounting made for any funds or property handled. If the purchaser does not fulfill these obligations, his or her employer may sue for damages.

Since the supply officer is acting as an agent for the company he or she represents, it follows that the officer is in a position to bind the company within limits. Actually, of course, the power of an agent to bind the principal may greatly exceed the right to do so. This right is confined by the limits assigned, that is, in accordance with the actual authorization; power to bind the principal, however, is defined by the *apparent* scope of authority, which in the case of most supply officers is rather broad.

Unauthorized purchasers, for example, an engineer who agrees to buy something from a salesperson, acquires apparent authority as soon as the company ratifies the purchase by receiving and making payment. The engineer now has indefinite apparent authority to buy similar products from the same supplier for similar dollar amounts. Each time the company ratifies an unauthorized purchase a valid contract is created and apparent authority is created. This is commonly referred to as *maverick buying.* In many organizations, the number of people with apparent authority and the volume of dollars spent by such maverick buyers is great enough to undermine the integrity of the supply process and jeopardize supply's relationship with suppliers. Procurement card programs, which give limited authority to nonpurchasers, set spending limits, and designate what can and cannot be purchased, are an effective and legal means of giving limited authority to persons outside the purchasing department, thus allowing supply professionals to focus on more critical goods and services.

Furthermore, to avoid personal liability, it must be made clear to the person with whom the buyer deals that the purchaser is acting as an agent. In fact, the law requires even more if purchasers are not to be held personally liable; not only must they indicate that they are acting as agents but also the person with whom they are dealing must agree to hold the principal responsible, even though the latter is at the moment unknown.

The actual authority delegated to an agent is not limited to those acts that, by words, the agent is expressly and directly authorized to perform. Every actual authorization, whether general or special, includes by implication all such authority as is necessary, usual, and proper to carry through to completion the main authority conferred. The extent of the agent's implied authority must be determined from the nature of the business to be transacted. These powers will be broad in the case of one acting as a general agent or manager. It is the duty of the third party dealing with the agent to ascertain the scope of the agent's authority. Statements of the agent as to the extent of powers cannot be relied on by the third party. Any limitation on the agent's power that is known to the third party is binding on the third party.

PERSONAL LIABILITY

The supply officer may be held personally liable under certain conditions when signing contracts. These conditions include (1) when he or she makes a false statement concerning authority with intent to deceive or when the misrepresentation has the natural and probable consequence of misleading; (2) when agents perform a damaging act without authority, even though they believe they have such authority; (3) when he or she performs an act that is itself illegal, even on authority from the employer; (4) when he or she willfully performs an act that results in damage to anyone; and (5) when he or she performs a damaging act outside the scope of his or her authority, even though the act is performed with the intention of rendering the employer a valuable service. In each of these cases, the supplier ordinarily has no recourse to the company employing the agent, since no valid contract existed between the seller and the purchasing firm. Since such a contract does not exist, the only recourse the supplier has is to the agent personally.

The principal may still be held legally liable in instances where the purchaser acted within apparent scope of authority but outside actual scope if the seller did not know that there were limitations on the actual authority. Under these circumstances, the purchaser probably is in the wrong and is, of course, answerable to the principal. The purchaser also may be answerable to the seller on the ground of deceit, or the charge that he or she is the real contracting party, or for breach of the warranty that he or she was authorized to make the precise contract he or she attempted to make for the principal.

Moreover, suits have been brought by sellers against supply managers when it was discovered that the latter's principal was for some reason unable to pay the account. For example, such conditions have arisen when (1) the employer became insolvent or bankrupt; (2) the employer endeavored to avoid the legal obligations to accept and pay for merchandise purchased; or (3) the employer became involved in litigation with the seller, whose lawyers decided that the contract price could be readily collected personally from the supply manager.

Although a supply officer should never attempt to perform the duties of a competent lawyer, he or she should keep informed about court decisions and changes in laws that affect his or her actions. Purchasing trade publications normally report court decisions and major changes in laws that have an impact on the performance of the supply function.

Supply officers are personally liable for the commission of any illegal act, even though they are unconscious of the illegality of the act and though it is done under the direction of the employer. A purchaser is not likely to commit an illegal act consciously, but under stress of severe competition, in an effort to secure as favorable terms as possible for his or her company, he or she may run afoul of the law unintentionally. It is well to remember that the antitrust acts apply to buyers as much as to sellers. The U.S. Supreme Court has held that these acts are applicable to all attempts to restrain trade, even though the restraint is exercised on those not engaged in the same line of business and is based on purchasing activities rather than selling activities—provided that the net result of the act is to restrain competition.

AUTHORITY OF SUPPLIERS' REPRESENTATIVES

Another important consideration is the authority of the sales representative of a company with which the supply officer is transacting business. Subject to the many exceptions arising out of varying circumstances, the courts have consistently held that although an employer is bound by all the acts of an agent acting within the scope of the employment, a salesperson's ordinary authority is simply to solicit orders and to send them to his or her employer for ratification and acceptance. Therefore, the supply officer should know definitely whether or not a salesperson has the authority to conclude a contract without referring it to the company that he or she represents.

Even if a supplier does not authorize its salesperson to enter into binding contracts, and although the company may do nothing to lead others to believe that its representative has such power, yet if the salesperson does enter into a contract with a buyer, that contract is likely to be held valid unless the seller notifies the buyer within a reasonable time that the salesperson has exceeded his or her authority. In other words, a contract results because the conduct of the seller is interpreted as acceptance. If the purchaser wishes assurance that the salesperson does have authority to sign the contract for the supplier, it is a simple matter to request a letter, signed by an officer of the supplier firm, specifying that the salesperson has the authority of a sales agent.

False statements on the part of the seller or its representative regarding the character of the merchandise being purchased cause the contract to become voidable at the option of the other party. It is true that this "undoubted right" to rely on sellers' statements is at best a highly qualified right, the value of which depends on the circumstances surrounding the transaction. However, aside from any legal question that is involved under ordinary circumstances, the seller is likely to be sufficiently jealous of its reputation and goodwill to make substantial concessions.

THE UNIFORM COMMERCIAL CODE

A uniform body of law governing the sale of goods within a country and between countries minimizes the risks associated with the acquisition process. Uniform laws provide a set of rules for making and interpreting contracts, and for understanding the obligations and remedies of parties to the contract. It makes it easier and more economical to buy and sell raw materials, commodities, and manufactured goods. Uniform laws also allow buyers and sellers to mold their contracts to their specifications. Without uniform laws, there is greater room for uncertainty and disputes. The sales law of one state, province, or country often differs from that of another. Where there is doubt about the rules that apply, the parties cannot be sure of their rights and obligations. Such uncertainty breeds inefficiency and ill will.

In the United States, the American Law Institute and the National Conference of Commissioners on Uniform State Laws jointly sponsor the revisions and preparation of the Uniform Commercial Code (UCC). The UCC is a comprehensive modernization of various statutes relating to commercial transactions. In Canada, the Uniform Law Conference spearheads the Commercial Law Strategy, which is designed to modernize and harmonize commercial law in Canada, with a view to creating a comprehensive framework of commercial statute law that will make it easier to do business in Canada. The U.N. Convention on Contracts for the International Sale of Goods (CISG) purports doing the same thing at an international level. If the buyer feels that legal problems may arise in dealing with a supplier outside the country, the purchase contract then should specify under which country's laws the dispute would be adjudicated. If both countries have adopted the CISG, it will apply unless both parties agree to something else. Canada, for example, does not have a standardized set of commercial laws for the entire country. Quebec has its own set of laws dealing with property and civil rights based on the Napoleonic Code.

In the United States, many federal, state, and local statutes govern purchasing practice, but Article 2 of the UCC covers most of the transactions involving purchase and sale of goods. The UCC resulted from the joint efforts of the American Law Institute and the National Conference of Commissioners on Uniform State Laws. Since the first publication of the Uniform Commercial Code in 1952, it has undergone numerous revisions and refinements with the latest edition in 2003. The UCC applies only to legal situations arising in the United States. All states have adopted some form of UCC Article 2. Even though Louisiana law is based on the Napoleonic Code, not English common law, the state has adopted most of the provisions of the UCC. Purchasers may want to include separate terms relating to the goods portion of the contract, so that the UCC applies to that portion of the contract.

Article 2 of the UCC applies to transactions in goods (Article 2-102) by merchants, where a merchant is "a person who deals in goods of the kind or otherwise by his occupation holds himself out as having knowledge or skill peculiar to the practices or goods involved in the transaction or to whom such knowledge or skill may be attributed by his employment of an agent or broker or other intermediary who by his occupation holds himself out as having such knowledge or skill."[1] A buyer is defined as a person who buys or contracts to buy goods, and a seller is a person who sells or contracts to sell goods (Article 2-103).

The Purchase Order Contract

A valid contract is based on four factors:

1. Competent parties—either principals or qualified agents.
2. Legal subject matter or purpose.
3. An offer and an acceptance.
4. Consideration (bargained-for exchange).

[1] Uniform Commercial Code, Article 2-104 (2003).

The purchase order generally contains the buyer's offer and becomes a legal contract when accepted by the supplier. Many purchase order forms have a copy that includes provision for acknowledgment or acceptance. There has never been universal agreement on how detailed the terms and conditions that are printed on the purchase order should be. Some companies' forms use the reverse side to spell out the complete terms and conditions that apply to any transaction. This is commonly referred to as boilerplate or *a framework agreement*. Some companies may include a separate sheet detailing terms and conditions applying to that specific order. Other companies provide only for the very basic items necessary for a valid offer and depend on the provisions of the UCC for proper legal coverage. The supply officer should rely on company legal counsel to determine the policy to be followed.

An offer can be equally valid if made by a seller either in writing or verbally. Such an offer becomes a legal contract when accepted by the buyer. Regardless of whether an offer is made by the buyer or the seller, it can be modified or revoked before it is accepted. However, an offer in writing that includes an assurance that the price will remain firm for a specified period may not be revoked prior to the expiration of the period. Under the UCC, if a seller makes a firm offer to sell, it generally must be held open for a "reasonable" time period. This reasonable time period generally has been held to be three months, unless a shorter period is stated by the seller at the time the offer was made.

The courts generally have held that advertisements and price lists do not constitute legal offers unless specifically directed to the buyer or unless an order placed on the basis of the advertisement or price list is specifically accepted by the supplier.

Acceptance of Orders

Since the purchase order form or the sales contract is intended to include all the essential conditions surrounding the transaction, it is customary to include in the agreement a statement such as, "Acceptance of this order implies the acceptance of conditions contained thereon." The purpose of such a provision is to make all the conditions legally binding on the seller and to avoid cases in which the seller advances the defense that he or she was not aware of certain conditions. Similar statements are found in practically all purchase agreements to warn that there are conditions attached on the front or back of the contract.

Having placed an order with a supplier, the supply officer wishes to ensure that the order has been accepted. It is customary to insist on a supplier acknowledgment, usually in written form. It is not uncommon to incorporate, as a part of the contract, a clause requiring that the acceptance be made in a particular manner, in which case a form is enclosed with the order and the purchase order contains a clause that stipulates: "This order must be acknowledged on the enclosed form." In e-procurement systems, both the purchase order and the acknowledgment are transmitted electronically.

It is important to know when an offer either of sale or of purchase has been accepted. As a matter of law, the person making an offer may demand, as one of the conditions, that acceptance be indicated in a specific manner. Ordinarily, however, when an offer is made, the offeror either expressly or by implication requires the offeree to send the answer by mail, facsimile, or other electronic transmittal. When the answer is duly posted, faxed, or electronically transmitted, the acceptance is communicated and the contract is completed from the moment the letter is mailed, the telegram is sent, or the fax or the electronic document complete with a digital signature is transmitted. Any reasonable manner of acceptance is satisfactory, unless the offeror makes it clear that acceptance must be made in a particular manner. Acceptance may be "in any manner and by any medium reasonable in the circumstances."[2]

The increased use of facsimiles (fax), electronic data interchange (EDI), digital signatures, and Web-based purchasing systems to send bids, purchase orders, and contracts requires buyers and sellers to agree on procedures and terms and conditions to prevent disputes that might end up in court.

Sometimes the supplier may use an acknowledgment form of its own, which may conflict with some of the conditions stated in the purchase order. Often in such situations, a careful comparison is not made of all conditions stated in the offer with all conditions stated in the acceptance. If litigation subsequently occurs between buyer and seller, application of Article 2-207 of the UCC may resolve the question:

(1) A definite and seasonable expression of acceptance or a written confirmation which is sent within a reasonable time operates as an acceptance even though it states terms additional to or different from those offered or agreed upon, unless acceptance is expressly made conditional on assent to the additional or different terms.

(2) The additional terms are to be construed as proposals for addition to the contract. Between merchants such terms become part of the contract unless:

(a) the offer expressly limits acceptance to the terms of the offer;

(b) they materially alter it; or

(c) notification of objection to them has already been given or is given within a reasonable time after notice of them is received.

(3) Conduct by both parties which recognizes the existence of a contract is sufficient to establish a contract for sale although the writings of the parties do not otherwise establish a contract. In such case the terms of the particular contract consist of those terms on which the writings of the parties agree, together with any supplementary terms incorporated under any other provisions of this Act.[3]

A clause that would materially alter the contract and result in surprise or hardship if incorporated without express awareness by the other party is, for example, one that negates standard warranties that usually apply, or one that requires quantity guarantees where the usage of the trade allows greater quantity leeway. If the additional or different terms do not materially alter the deal, then they will be incorporated into the contract unless the other party objects to them within a reasonable time. Thus, if the buyer does not wish to get into a dispute as to whether the seller's acceptance materially alters any of the provisions of the original offer, on the face of the purchase order (PO) should be typed a statement that "Absolutely no deviations from the terms and conditions as contained in this offer will be permitted."

Purchases Made Orally—Statute of Frauds

Most professional buyers have occasion to place orders over the telephone or orally in person. However, Article 2-201 of the UCC specifies that

[2] Ibid., Article 2-206.

[3] Ibid., Article 2-207.

1. Normally there must be some written notation if the price of the order for the sale of goods is $500 or more.
2. If the seller supplies a memorandum that is not in accordance with the buyer's understanding of the oral order, he or she must give a notice of objection to the supplier within 10 days of receipt of the memorandum to preserve his or her legal rights.[4]

When an alleged oral agreement is partially performed—for example, 1 of 10 lots is delivered and then the purchaser cancels—the partial performance can validate the contract, but only for the amount already accepted. An exception to this falls under the doctrine of *promissory estoppel,* which says if one party "relied to its detriment" on the promises made by the other party, the entire contract may be validated. Some type of writing is needed to demonstrate that a contract exists, but performance, partial or complete, removes the requirement for writing either for the partial or complete fulfillment of the contract. Both the buyer and seller may rely on the doctrine of promissory estoppel, which is an exception to the statute of frauds.

To safeguard against misunderstandings when in a conversation with a supplier, say, "This is not an order" if seeking information only; instruct suppliers not to begin work without authorization; and document all changes made after the purchase order has been issued.

Inspection

One important right of the buyer is that of inspecting the goods before acceptance. This rule gives the buyer an opportunity to determine whether or not the goods comply with the contract description. It is well established that buyers who inspect goods *before* entering into a contract of sale are put on guard and are expected to use their own judgment with respect to quality, quantity, and other characteristics of the merchandise. The UCC states that "when the buyer before entering into the contract has examined the goods or the sample or model as fully as he desired or has refused to examine the goods there is no implied warranty with regard to defects which an examination ought in the circumstances to have revealed to him."[5]

Where a purchaser accepts merchandise after inspection, either as to quality or quantity, the buyer ordinarily is prevented from raising an issue with respect to these points. Also, a seller cannot be held responsible for the failure of equipment to perform the work that the buyer expected of it, if the latter merely provides material specifications without indicating to the seller the purpose to which the equipment or goods are to be put. In some purchase contracts, payment may be required before the buyer has had an opportunity to inspect the goods; for example, payment may be made before the seller actually ships the goods. Payment in this case does not constitute an acceptance of the goods or impair the buyer's right to inspect or any of the buyer's remedies on breach of contract.[6] In a JIT or ship-to-stock arrangement where goods are not inspected, the buyer needs to specify in the written contract a time frame for notification of defects since the UCC does not cover these situations completely.

[4] Ibid., Article 2-201.

[5] Ibid., Article 2-316(3).

[6] Ibid., Article 2-512.

The courts generally have held that if a purchaser is not sufficiently experienced to be able to judge adequately the goods inspected, or if he or she relies on a fraudulent statement made by a seller and purchases in consequence of that fraudulent statement, the buyer then may rescind the contract or hold the seller liable for damages.

Acceptance and Rejection of Goods

The acceptance of goods is an assent by the buyer to become the owner of the goods tendered by the seller. Any words or acts that indicate the buyer's intention to become the owner of the goods are sufficient. If the buyer keeps the goods and exercises rights of ownership over them, acceptance has taken place, even though the buyer may have expressly stated that the goods are rejected. If the goods tendered do not comply with the sales contract, the buyer is under no duty to accept them; but if the buyer does accept the goods, he or she does not thereby waive the right to damages for the seller's breach of contract. If the buyer accepts goods that do not comply with the sales contract, the seller must be notified of the breach within a reasonable time. What is a "reasonable time" is determined by normal commercial standards.[7] Recent legal rulings indicate that if the buyer tells the supplier about a problem and even if the supplier tries to fix the problem but the buyer fails to specifically give notice "of breach," the supplier may have room for legal negotiating.[8]

In the event the seller delivers goods or the tender of delivery fails in any way to conform to the contract, the buyer has the option to (1) reject the whole shipment, (2) accept the whole shipment, or (3) accept part of the shipment and reject the balance. Rejection, of course, must be within a reasonable time after delivery and the seller must be notified promptly. The buyer must hold the goods, using reasonable care, until the seller has had sufficient time to remove them.[9] The question of whether to reject goods delivered under a particular order may arise from various causes and may be dealt with in a variety of ways. For instance, the goods may be late, may have been delivered in the wrong amount, or may fail to meet the specifications. The important thing to keep in mind is that the purchaser wants the goods. A lawsuit, therefore, is not desirable, even though the buyer may be granted any one of the commonly recognized judicial remedies for breach of contract, such as money damages or insistence on performance. Legal action is uncertain and often costly, may take a great deal of time, and may cause the loss of a good supplier.

The supply officer, therefore, usually seeks other means of adjustment. Several courses are open. The first question is the seriousness of the breach. If not too serious, a simple warning to the supplier may be adequate. If the goods received are usable for some purpose, even though not quite up to specifications, a price adjustment can be worked out to the mutual satisfaction of the buyer and the seller. Sometimes the goods, though not usable in the form received, may be reprocessed or otherwise made usable by the supplier, or by the purchaser at the supplier's expense. If the goods are component parts, they may be replaced by the supplier. If equipment is involved, or even processed material that is incapable of being efficiently used in its present form, the supplier may correct the defects at the

[7] Ibid., Article 2-607.

[8] William A. Hancock, "The UCC Notice Requirement," *NAPM Insights,* October 1990, p. 8.

[9] UCC, Articles 2-601 and 2-602.

user's plant. Or, as a last resort, the goods may be rejected and shipped back to the supplier, usually at the supplier's expense.

In some cases, purchasers use a full-payment check to settle a dispute. In this case the purchaser sends a check for what he or she believes covers the goods, less the cost of the defect, and writes the words "Payment in Full" to indicate that this is a settlement. The supplier, under the UCC, can cash the check and write "under protest" or "without prejudice" to protect its rights to try to collect the balance due. The courts recently have ruled that there is an offer and acceptance, hence a valid contract, if the check and notice were sent to a specific person who knowingly cashes the check. If, however, the check was sent to accounts receivable or some other routine processing area of the supplier's company, there would not be a real acceptance, and the supplier would still have rights to try to collect or settle the balance with the buyer.

Warranties

The rules governing warranty arrangements between buyer and seller have advanced from *caveat emptor* (let the buyer beware) to the legal provisions of the UCC, which recognize four types of warranties:

1. Express warranty.
2. Implied warranty of merchantability.
3. Implied warranty of fitness for a particular purpose.
4. Warranty of title.[10]

Essentially,

Express warranties include promises, specifications, samples, and descriptions pertaining to the goods that are the subject of the negotiation.

Implied warranty of merchantability has to do with the merchantable quality of goods, and the applicable UCC statutes have developed out of mercantile practices. Accepted trade standards of quality, fitness for the intended uses, and conformance to promises or specified fact made on the container or label are all used as measures of marketable quality.

Implied warranty of fitness for a particular purpose usually results from a buyer's request for material or equipment to meet a particular need or accomplish a specific purpose. The UCC provides that "where the seller at the time of contracting has reason to know any particular purpose for which the goods are required and that the buyer is relying on the seller's skill or judgment to select or furnish suitable goods, there is . . . an implied warranty that the goods shall be fit for such purpose."[11] If the buyer provides detailed specifications for the item requested, the seller is relieved of any warranty of fitness for particular purpose.

Warranty of title ensures that there are no liens against the title to the goods and the goods are free from patent or copyright infringement.

[10] Ibid., Articles 2-312, 2-313, 2-314, and 2-315.

[11] Ibid., Article 2-315.

Under the UCC, suppliers may still write disclaimers or exclusions to warranties.[12] To exclude express warranties, suppliers may include a clause stating that "no express warranties have been made by the supplier except those specifically stated in this contract." To exclude implied warranties, suppliers must put the disclaimer in writing in a conspicuous place. Typical language is, "No implied warranties of merchantability or fitness for a particular purpose accompany this sale." A general disclaimer may be made by labeling the sale "as is" or "with all faults." Also, if the buyer examines the goods before the sale, the buyer is bound by all defects found and those the buyer should have found.[13]

Title to Purchased Goods

The professional purchaser should have a clear understanding of when the title of goods passes from the seller to the buyer. Normally, there will be an agreement on the FOB (free on board) point, and the buyer receives title at that point. Articles 2-319 and 2-320 of the UCC cover the legal obligations under the various shipping terms (FOB, FAS, CIF, and C&F). On capital goods it is particularly important for tax and depreciation reasons to establish title before the tax year ends.

If the buyer specifies a particular carrier for transportation of goods, the seller is responsible for following the buyer's instructions, which are part of the contractual agreement, subject to any substitution necessary because of the failure of the specified carrier to provide adequate transportation services. Of course, the seller must promptly notify the buyer of any substitutions made. If the buyer elects not to specify a particular carrier, the seller then may choose any reasonable carrier, routing, and other arrangements. Whether or not the shipment is at the buyer's expense, as determined by the FOB term used, the seller must see to any arrangements, reasonable in the circumstances, such as refrigeration, watering of livestock, protection against cold, and selection of specialized cars.

In some instances, the buyer is given possession of the goods prior to the passing of a legal title. This is known as a *conditional sales contract* and the full title passes to the buyer only when final payment is made. This procedure permits a buyer to obtain needed material or equipment now and pay at some future time.

Protection against Price Fluctuations

Cancellations can be the direct result of action by the buyer. They arise in two ways, the first of which is not recommended. It comes about because the buyer, if compelled to live up to the agreement, would lose money. Conditions may have changed or sales may have fallen off. Therefore, the buyer no longer wants the goods. The market price may have dropped and the buyer could now buy the goods for less money. Faced with these conditions, the buyer seeks some form of relief. He or she becomes extremely watchful of deliveries and rejects goods that arrive even a day late. Inspection is tightened, and failure to meet any detail in the specifications is seized on as an excuse for rejection. Such methods should never be followed by a good supply officer.

The second form of cancellation may arise in a perfectly legal and ethical manner, through evoking a clause—occasionally inserted in purchase contracts—that seeks to guarantee against price decline. In purchasing goods subject to price fluctuations, it is in

[12] Ibid., Article 2-316

[13] Gaylord A. Jentz, J.D., "Exclusion of Warranties," *NAPM Insights,* July 1991, p. 8.

the interest of the buyer to be protected against unreasonable price changes. Occasionally a long-term contract is drawn up that leaves the determination of the exact price open until deliveries are called for. To meet these conditions, a clause such as the following may be incorporated in purchase contracts:

> Seller warrants that the prices stated herein are as low as any net prices now given by you to any customer for like materials, and seller agrees that if at any time during the life of this order seller quotes or sells at lower prices similar materials under similar conditions, such lower prices shall be substituted for the prices stated herein.

These stipulations against price decline are not confined to purchase agreements; under some circumstances the buyer may receive price reductions on the seller's initiative. An example of this type of clause is the following:

> Should the purchaser at the time of any delivery, on account of this contract, be offered a lower price on goods of equal quality and in like quantity by a reputable manufacturer, it will furnish the seller satisfactory proof of same, in which event the seller will either supply such shipment at the lower price or permit the buyer to purchase such quantity elsewhere, and the quantity so purchased elsewhere will be deducted from the total quantity of this contract. Should the seller reduce its prices during the terms of this contract, the buyer shall receive the benefit of such lower prices.

Such clauses are legally enforceable and frequently work to the buyer's advantage. However, the administrative problems in seeing to it that these clauses are lived up to may be substantial.

Cancellation of Orders and Breach of Contract

Once a contract is made, it is expected that both buyers and sellers will adhere to the agreement. Occasionally one or the other seeks to cancel the contract. Ordinarily this is a more serious problem for the seller than it is for the buyer. Occasionally a seller may wish to avoid complying with the terms of an agreement such as refusing to manufacture the goods or delaying the delivery beyond the period stipulated in the agreement. The rights of the purchaser under these circumstances depend on the conditions surrounding the transaction. The seller is likely to be able, without liability, to delay delivering purchased goods when the buyer orders a change in the original agreement that may delay the seller in making delivery.

If the seller fails to make delivery by the agreed time, the purchaser, without obligation, may refuse to accept delivery at a later date. However, the attempt to secure what the buyer might consider reasonable damages resulting from a breached sales contract is likely to be difficult, since the courts experience a good deal of trouble in laying down rules for the guidance of the jury in estimating the amount of damages justly allowed a buyer who sustains financial losses resulting from a seller's failure to fulfill a contract of sale. If there is a general rule, it is that the damages allowable to a purchaser if a seller fails to deliver goods according to contract are measured by the difference between the original contract price and the market value of the merchandise at the time when the buyer learned of the breach of contract and at the place where the goods should have been delivered, together with any incidental and consequential damages provided in Article 2-715.[14]

The seller is sometimes confronted by an attempted cancellation on the part of the buyer. It is not unusual, therefore, to find in the sales contract the following clause: "This

[14] UCC, Article 2-713.

contract is not subject to cancellation." As a matter of fact, the inclusion of such a clause has little practical effect, unless it is intended to indicate to the purchaser that if he or she attempts to cancel, a suit for breach of contract may be expected.

However, in a very strong seller's market, where the breach of contract by the seller is related to failure to deliver on a promised date or even to abide by the agreed price, the practical alternatives open to the buyer are almost nil. The latter still wants the goods and may be unable to acquire them from any other supplier on time or at any better price. Much the same restriction, in fact, exists even where the contract provides for the option of cancellation by the buyer. The purchaser wants goods, not damages or the right to cancel. Since the chances of getting them as promptly from any other supplier are slight, the buyer is likely to do the best he or she can with the original supplier provided, of course, that bad faith as to either price or delivery is not involved.

COMMON LAW AND THE PURCHASE OF SERVICES

Common law governs the purchase of services. This includes contracts solely for services and when services are bundled with goods and the service portion equals more than 50 percent of the value of the contract. Common law originated in England and became the foundation of U.S. law in the original 13 colonies. It is not based on written rules of law but rather the law of the courts as expressed in judicial decisions. Common law develops over time as courts make decisions on a case-by-case basis, developing what is known as "case law." In deciding cases, judges look to prior judicial decisions for established precedents and make adaptations only to account for changing conditions and societal needs. Judicial precedents derive their force from the doctrine of *stare decisis* [Latin for stand by the decided matter], that is the previous decisions of the highest court in the jurisdiction are binding on all other courts in the jurisdiction.

The common law system has both flexibility and stability. Flexibility comes as changing conditions make decisions inapplicable except as analogy and the courts turn to other English-speaking (common law) judicial experiences. Stability derives from general acceptance of certain authoritative materials. When the courts fail to address changing conditions, statutes are enacted that supercede common law. Typically, however, in statutory interpretation, the courts have recourse to the doctrines of common law.

Supply managers who contract for services must understand that while common law provides them with general guidelines for contracting for services, it does not offer much in terms of performance obligations. Because the parties to a service contract cannot refer to a set of rules to govern performance, they must ensure that each and every performance requirement and expectation is clearly defined in the contract. Many service contracts start with a performance-based specification and the process of writing the specification should help to achieve this goal.

E-COMMERCE AND THE LAW

The growth of e-commerce has led to both hope and despair in many quarters. Some fear that it will lead to a greater divide between the haves and have-nots, both between and within nations. Others, such as the governments of Japan and the United States, believe that it will lead to wider economic growth. In 1998, the United States and Japan issued a Joint Statement on Electronic Commerce that recognized that electronic commerce will be "an engine of economic growth in the Twenty-first Century. . . and e-commerce will enhance the standard of living of citizens in the United States and Japan as well as the rest of the globe." The joint statement went on to say, "The Governments of the United States and Japan recognize the importance of working together to promote global electronic commerce." Four general principles were endorsed:

1. The private sector should lead in the development of electronic commerce and in establishing business practices.
2. Both governments should avoid imposing unnecessary regulations or restrictions on electronic commerce. . . .
3. Governments should encourage effective self-regulation through codes of conduct, model contracts, guidelines, and enforcement mechanisms developed by the private sector.
4. Cooperation and harmonization among all countries, from all regions of the world and all levels of development, will assist in the construction of a seamless environment for electronic commerce.[15]

The growth of e-commerce also raised the question of whether or not existing laws sufficiently address the legal ramifications of this new way of doing business. The governments of many countries as well as the U.N. Commission on International Trade Law (UNCITRAL) and the European Union have focused on the legal aspects of e-commerce. In some countries, it is believed that a legal structure must be developed first before the government allows and encourages the spread of e-commerce. In other countries, such as the United States, e-commerce was quickly adopted by many businesses and the law came later. The UCC does not contain any specific sections related to e-commerce because the review committee decided the wording of the law allowed for new forms of communication. There are, however, other laws at the federal and state level that address e-commerce.

Electronic Signatures

One of the critical issues in e-commerce transactions was the legality of electronic or digital signatures for contractual purposes. The term *digital signature* is used generically here to mean electronic authentication of documents. The telecommunications ministers of the 15 member nations of the European Union (EU) passed the Electronic Signature Act, which grants digital signatures the same legal status as written ones. It must be approved by each EU government before going into effect. Japan enacted the Japanese Law Concerning Electronic Signatures and Certification Services on May 24, 2000. In Canada each of the provinces (except Nunavut) has passed e-commerce legislation that includes electronic signature provisions.

In the United States, a number of states have passed legislation on electronic signatures, but the passage of the Electronic Signatures in Global and National Commerce Act, Public Law No. 106–229 (E-Sign Act) in June 2000 was an attempt to develop uniform rules across the country. The E-Sign bill was introduced to regulate interstate commerce by electronic means by permitting and encouraging the continued expansion of electronic commerce

[15] *Joint Statement on Electronic Commerce by U.S. and Japan,* found on Web site of McBride Baker & Coles, http://www.mbc.com/ecommerce.

through the operation of free market forces, and for other purposes. This statute grants online legal or financial agreements signed with a digital signature or chain of electronic code equivalent legal status with handwritten signatures and paper documents. It also included electronic recordkeeping provisions.

The important features of the U.S. law are (1) technology-neutral standards that prevent governments from legislating a specific type of technology and (2) party autonomy or the right of businesses to "freedom of contract" in determining the terms and conditions specified in a transaction. Technology-neutral means that parties entering in electronic contracts can choose the system they want to use to validate an online agreement.

Uniform Electronic Transactions Act

The Uniform Electronic Transactions Act (UETA) was approved and recommended for enactment by the National Conference of Commissioners on Uniform State Laws in July 1999. UETA validates the use of electronic records and electronic signatures. At least half the states have adopted it. The federal E-Sign Act allows a state to preempt the Act if it has enacted UETA. UETA and the E-Sign Act bear many similarities and in some situations the language of UETA was borrowed by the authors of the E-Sign bill. However, there are differences. UETA is more comprehensive than E-Sign and addresses some topics differently. UETA contains provisions for the following issues that are not dealt with in the E-Sign Act:

- *Attribution.* An electronic record or signature is attributed to a person if it was an act of that person.
- *Effect of other state law.* UETA recognizes that an electronic signature is just as effective, valid, and enforceable as paper. However, questions of authority, forgery, and contract formation are determined by other state law.
- *Effect of party agreement.* The parties to the contract are free to enter into agreements concerning their use of electronic media.
- *Send and receive.* UETA ties the determination of when an electronic record is sent or received to the communications systems used by the parties to the contract.
- *Effect of change or error.* E-Sign does not contain provisions for dealing with mistakes in electronic communications, while UETA does contain such provisions for breaches in security procedures and mistakes made by an individual dealing with an electronic agent. Unless otherwise specified, the rules of mistake apply.
- *Admissability.* UETA specifies that electronic records cannot be excluded as evidence solely because they are in electronic format.[16]

Antitrust and E-Marketplaces

As discussed in Chapter 4, a business-to-business e-marketplace is an Internet exchange where goods are traded. Both the Federal Trade Commission (FTC) and the U.S. Department of Justice have raised questions about the potential for price fixing and collusion. Two different types of e-marketplaces exist. The first type, the ones run by a neutral third party in

[16] Patricia Brumfield Fry, "A Preliminary Analysis of Federal and State Electronic Commerce Laws," UETA Online, http://www.uetaonline.com/docs.

which buyers pool their requirements for specific items, such as office supplies, are not under scrutiny. The second type, industry sites owned and operated by competitors who together represent more than 50 percent of an industry market share, raise antitrust concerns. Three activities cause the concern: (1) the potential for sharing information among competitors that may allow for price increase or the development of a monopoly, (2) the danger of one buyer or a consortium of buyers acting as one to coerce a supplier to accept a price lower than what would occur in a competitive market, and (3) suppliers that may not be in a position to freely decide not to participate.[17]

Supporters of industry e-marketplaces argue that firewalls can be used to protect against competitor's sharing information. Such e-marketplaces also are compared to Internet shopping malls where direct competitors co-locate and share expenses for things like security. Well-crafted B2B operating rules may be enough to eliminate concerns, and traditional antitrust analysis is feasible.

INTELLECTUAL PROPERTY LAWS

In the Knowledge Age, more and more wealth is derived from intellectual capital. Thus, the legal issues associated with who actually owns intellectual capital are of greater concern. According to the World Intellectual Property Organization (WIPO), intellectual property (IP) refers to creations of the mind: inventions, literary and artistic works, and symbols, names, images, and designs used in commerce. Intellectual property is divided into two categories. Industrial property includes inventions (patents), trademarks, industrial designs, and geographic indications of source. Copyright includes literary and artistic works such as novels, poems, and plays; films; musical works; artistic works such as drawings, paintings, photographs, and sculptures; and architectural designs. Rights related to copyright include those of performing artists in their performances, producers of phonograms in their recordings, and those of broadcasters in their radio and television programs.

According to WIPO, the emerging issues in intellectual property range from the Internet to health care to nearly all aspects of science and technology and literature and the arts. Their research has dealt with intellectual property issues related to access to drugs and health care, small and medium-sized enterprises, electronic commerce programs and activities, Internet domain disputes, genetic resources, and traditional knowledge and folklore. WIPO is an international organization dedicated to promoting the use and protection of intellectual property. Headquartered in Geneva, Switzerland, WIPO is one of the 16 specialized agencies of the United Nations. It has 180 nations as member states and administers 23 international treaties dealing with different aspects of intellectual property protection. Information on WIPO can be found at http://www.wipo.int.

Copyright Law

The U.S. Copyright Act is federal legislation enacted by Congress to protect the writings of authors. As technology has changed, the term "writings" has expanded and the Copyright Act now reaches architectural design, software, the graphic arts, motion pictures, and sound recordings. A copyright gives the owner the exclusive right to reproduce,

[17] American Bar Association Committee on Cyberspace Law, *"Antitrust: B2B e-Marketplaces," Legislative Reporters,* found at http://www.abanet.org/buslaw/cyber/legislation/anti.html.

distribute, perform, display, or license his or her work. The owner also receives the exclusive right to produce or license derivatives of his or her work with limited exceptions for types of "fair use," such as book reviews. To be covered by copyright, a work must be original and in a concrete "medium of expression." Under current law, works are covered whether or not a copyright notice is attached and whether or not the work is registered. The Copyright Office of the Library of Congress administers the act.

Patents

Patents are granted by the U.S. Patent Office (or a similar agency in other countries) to provide the inventor/developer the sole rights of making, using, and selling the item in question—and denying others the right to also do so, unless the inventor decides to sell the patent rights. An invention must be novel, useful, and not of an obvious nature. Such "utility" patents are issued for four general types of inventions/discoveries: machines, human-made products, compositions of matter, and processing methods. Changing technology has led to an ever-expanding understanding of what constitutes a human-made product leading to additions to the Patent Act for design and plant patents. Patents are normally issued for a nonrenewable period of 20 years, measured from the date of application. Unless otherwise agreed between buyer and seller, if a supplier regularly deals in a particular line of goods, that supplier implicitly warrants that the goods delivered do not infringe against the patent rights of any third party. However, when the buyer orders goods to be assembled, prepared, or manufactured to his or her own specifications, and if this results in an infringement of a patent or trademark, then the buyer may be liable to legal action. There is, under such circumstances, a tacit representation on the part of the buyer that the seller will be safe in manufacturing according to the specifications, and the buyer then is obliged to indemnify the seller for any loss suffered.[18] If a charge of patent infringement is made against the buyer, he or she must notify the supplier promptly so that the charge can be defended, or settlement made, in a timely manner. Also, if a seller attempts to include a patent disclaimer clause in the sales contract, the buyer should be extremely cautious in accepting such a clause, since there may be costly litigation if patent infringement has occurred.

An even more delicate matter may arise when a buyer requests a supplier to manufacture an item, to the buyer's specifications, that includes a new idea, process, or product that has not yet been awarded patent protection. This often happens in the high-technology industries. The buyer does not want to lose the right to the new development and possible subsequent financial rewards. The buyer's purchase contract should address this matter with an appropriate protection clause, formulated with advice of legal counsel.

Two recent developments in patent law are of interest to supply managers.[19] First, the danger of infringing broadly worded patents, such as those related to e-commerce technology, has decreased dramatically as a result of a recent ruling by a federal appeals court. Second, under a new rule enacted by the U.S. Patent and Trademark Office (USPTO), proprietary information contained in patent applications will now be made public 18 months after the application is filed. Also under this new rule, if an organization believes a patent application to be too broad, the organization may submit written materials to the USPTO

[18] UCC, Article 2-312(3).

[19] Timothy Baumann, "New Developments in Patent Law," *Purchasing Today,* April 2001, p. 26.

in an attempt to persuade the USPTO that the patent application should not be allowed to issue as a patent.

Trademarks

A trademark is a logo, brand name, or design that is new or distinctive enough to market or represent a company or its goods and services. It provides protection to the owner of the mark by ensuring the exclusive right to use it to identify goods or services, or to authorize another to use it in return for payment. The period of protection varies, but a trademark can be renewed indefinitely beyond the time limit on payment of additional fees. Trademark protection is enforced by the courts, which in most systems have the authority to block trademark infringement.

In a larger sense, trademarks promote initiative and enterprise worldwide by rewarding the owners of trademarks with recognition and financial profit. Trademark protection also hinders the efforts of unfair competitors, such as counterfeiters, to use similar distinctive signs to market inferior or different products or services. The system enables people with skill and enterprise to produce and market goods and services in the fairest possible conditions, thereby facilitating international trade.

Industrial Design

An industrial design is the ornamental or aesthetic aspect of an article including its three-dimensional features, such as the shape or surface of an article, or two-dimensional features, such as patterns, lines, or color. Industrial designs are applied to a wide variety of products of industry and handicraft such as clinical and medical instruments, luxury items, housewares, electrical appliances, vehicles, and architectural structures. To be protected under most national laws, an industrial design must appeal to the eye. It does not protect any technical features of the article to which it is applied.

Geographical Indication

A geographical indication is a sign used on goods from a specific geographical origin that possess qualities or a reputation due to its origin. It may be used for a variety of agricultural products, such as "Tuscany" for olive oil produced in a specific area of Italy or "Roquefort" for cheese produced in France.

PRODUCT LIABILITY

Product liability refers to the liability of any or all parties along the manufacturing supply chain for damage caused by that product. This includes the manufacturer of component parts, an assembling manufacturer, the wholesaler, and the retail store owner. Liability suits have been filed over inherent defects in products that caused harm to a consumer of the product.

Product safety and product liability considerations have become much more important due to increased government regulations and judicial interpretations of the existing laws. Although generally thought of as relating to tangible goods, the definition has expanded to include intangibles (gas), naturals (pets), real estate (house), and writings (navigational charts). This has magnified the involvement and responsibility of purchasing managers, as firms attempt to reduce the financial threat arising from product liability problems.

Claims can be based on negligence, strict liability, or breach of warranty of fitness. Product liability is generally considered a strict liability offense, which means that the defendant is liable when it is shown that the product was defective. No amount of care on the part of the manufacturer exonerates it from its legal liability if it is demonstrated that the product was defective. There are three types of relevant product defects: design defects, manufacturing defects, and defects in marketing. Design defects occur when a product may perform its function but is inherently dangerous due to a design flaw. Manufacturing defects occur during the construction or production of the item. Defects in marketing result from improper instructions and failures to warn consumers of latent dangers in the product.

Since the United States does not have a federal products liability law, state statutes apply. The U.S. Department of Commerce has promulgated a Model Uniform Products Liability Act (MUPLA) for voluntary use by the states. The law of products liability is found mainly in common law (case law) and in Article 2, Sections 314–315 of the Uniform Commercial Code, which deal with implied and express warranties of merchantability.

Part of the strategic role of supply managers is to minimize organizational risk. Taking a more active role in designing for procurability and sustainability is one way for supply managers to be more strategic. Considering potential risks and associated costs throughout the life of a product can help the organization avoid product liability suits. In the sourcing, evaluating, selecting, contracting, and receiving stages, there are opportunities to recognize and deal with potential product liability. The earlier in the process this is done, the better from a cost and reputation standpoint. This requires close internal working relationships with design, engineering, quality control, manufacturing, and marketing, to ensure that the organization is not being unreasonably exposed to product liability lawsuits. The increased application of strict liability tests and the lack of federal product liability laws mean that an organization may assume greater liability based on the actions of the purchaser. Hence, supply managers must ensure defect-free materials and components capable of performing a full range of applications and uses, in compliance with relevant standards, tests, and criteria for product safety.

ALTERNATIVE DISPUTE RESOLUTION

Alternative dispute resolution (ADR) refers to any means of settling disputes outside of the courtroom, including arbitration, mediation, early neutral evaluation, and conciliation. As burgeoning court queues, rising costs of litigation, and time delays continue to plague litigants, more states have begun experimenting with ADR programs. Some of these programs are voluntary; others are mandatory.

Title 9 of the U.S. Code establishes federal law supporting arbitration. It is based on Congress' plenary power over interstate commerce. Where it applies, its terms prevail over state law. There are, however, numerous state laws on ADR. Thirty-five states have adopted the Uniform Arbitration Act as state law. Thus, the arbitration agreement and decision of the arbiter may be enforceable under state and federal law. In 1970, the United States joined the U.N. Convention on the Recognition and Enforcement of Foreign Arbitral Awards.

The Office of Dispute Resolution coordinates the use of ADR for the Department of Justice. The office is responsible for ADR policy matters, ADR training, assistance to lawyers in selecting the right cases for dispute resolution, and finding of appropriate neutrals to serve as mediators, arbitrators, and neutral evaluators. The office also coordinates the Interagency ADR Working Group, an organization that promotes the use of ADR throughout federal executive branch agencies.

The two most common forms of ADR are arbitration and mediation.

Commercial Arbitration

Regardless of the type of contract, disputes will arise. These disagreements are annoying, but in terms of cost and time, it usually is not advantageous to go to court over them. In the majority of cases, they are settled by buyers and sellers through negotiation. If no negotiated agreement is reached, to avoid resorting to a court of law, arbitration clauses are included in commercial contracts. These provide that an impartial arbitrator, or panel of arbitrators, will listen to the evidence and then render a judgment, which both parties have agreed in advance to accept without appeal. This is less costly and time-consuming than court action. Arbitration is a simplified version of a trial involving no discovery and simplified rules of evidence. Either both sides agree on one arbitrator, or each side selects one arbitrator and the two arbitrators elect the third to comprise a panel. Arbitration hearings usually last only a few hours and the opinions are not public record. Arbitration has long been used in labor, construction, and securities regulation but is now gaining popularity in other business disputes.

There are prepared arbitration clauses that are valid, irrevocable, and enforceable under the arbitration laws of certain states. For matters under the jurisdiction of the federal courts, there is the Federal Arbitration Law. Even in states that do not have such laws, it is possible to demand arbitration if provision is made for the necessary procedure in the contract, and if there is a statute making "*future* disputes" the subject of binding arbitration agreements.

The use of arbitration clauses in contracts is a reasonable measure of protection against costly litigation. To ensure this protection, the following questions should be asked about arbitration clauses that are to be incorporated in commercial agreements:

1. Is the clause in the proper form under the appropriate arbitration laws? Unless properly drawn, it may not be legally valid, irrevocable, and enforceable.
2. Does the clause fully express the will of the parties or is it ambiguous? If it is uncertain in its terms, the time and expense involved in determining the scope of the clause and the powers of the arbitrators under it may destroy its value or increase costs.
3. Does the clause ensure the appointment of impartial arbitrators? If a person serving as arbitrator is an agent, advocate, relative, or representative of a party, or has a personal interest in the matter being arbitrated, the award rendered may be vacated by the court on the ground of evident corruption or partiality on the part of an arbitrator.
4. Does the clause provide adequately, by reference to the rules of an association or otherwise, for a method of naming arbitrators, thus safeguarding against deadlocks or defaults in the proceedings? If not, the actual hearing of the dispute may be unduly delayed, and the practical value of the arbitration may be defeated.

Mediation

Mediation is an even less formal alternative to litigation than arbitration. Mediators are individuals trained in negotiations who bring opposing parties together and attempt to work out a settlement or agreement that both parties accept or reject. Mediation is used for a wide gamut of case types.

Internal Escalation

A third form of alternate dispute resolution might best be called internal escalation. It may be agreed by both buyer and seller that if a dispute arises, the first round of resolution will fall to the purchaser and sales representative. If they cannot resolve the matter, their supervisors will get together and so on, with the final round between the top executives of both organizations. Only when they fail to agree will other forms of dispute resolution be pursued.

THE SARBANES-OXLEY ACT

The Sarbanes-Oxley Act (2002) is the public company accounting reform and investor protection act. Several sections of the Act might impact supply management. Section 401a requires off-balance-sheet transactions and obligations to be listed. For supply management this might include long-term purchase agreements such as multiyear supplier-managed inventory programs, cancellation and restocking charges, and lease agreements. Section 404 requires the creation and maintenance of viable internal controls that the SEC has ruled include policies, procedures, training programs, and other processes beyond financial controls. For supply management this might include insecure and unreliable communications such as e-mails used to communicate with trading partners, poor purchase commitment visibility, and inventory write-offs. Section 409 requires timely reporting of material events that impact financial reporting. Supply events that might meet the threshold of materiality include late supplier deliveries, ERP system crashes that disrupt shipments, and poor inventory accuracy.

ETHICS

Ethics comes from a Greek work *ethika,* which means "character" or "custom" and relates to the principles or standards of human conduct, sometimes called *morals* (Latin *mores,* "customs"). Ethics, as a branch of philosophy, is considered a normative science, because it is concerned with norms of human conduct. Each individual makes decisions out of an ethical framework. Each organization creates an ethical framework as part of its organizational culture that drives and constrains behavior. Numerous factors influence ethics, including family, education, religion, peers, gender, age, socioeconomic status, culture, and experience. When a group of diverse people are brought together in one organization, it is important to consciously create an ethical culture. This culture is documented by the standards of conduct in a code of ethics. It is brought to life by the attitude, behavior, and practices of company leaders as well as each individual in the organization, especially when ethical challenges occur. It is reinforced by the procedures put in place to monitor ethical behavior and by the language used in the course of doing business.

Purchasing represents the exchange of money for goods and services. Often, a very large amount of money is involved in this exchange. It is, therefore, vital that the transactions associated with the procurement process be carried out at the highest ethical level. Unfortunately, temptation is always present where large amounts of money are involved. Sometimes suppliers will go to considerable lengths to secure business and resort to unethical practices, such as bribes or large gifts. Sometimes unscrupulous purchasers take advantage of their privileged position to extract personal rewards that are unethical as well as illegal. Clearly, both suppliers and purchasers are responsible for ensuring that unethical conduct is not tolerated. Both PMAC and ISM have codes of ethics and principles and standards of purchasing practice that guide the professional behavior of their members. (See Figure 12–1 and 12–2.)

FIGURE 12–1 **Excerpts from the PMAC Code of Ethics**

VALUES AND NORMS OF ETHICAL BEHAVIOUR

A. Values

Members will operate and conduct their decisions and actions based on the following values:

1. *Honesty/Integrity.* Maintaining an unimpeachable standard of integrity in all their business relationships both inside and outside the organizations in which they are employed;
2. *Professionalism.* Fostering the highest standards of professional competence amongst those for whom they are responsible;
3. *Responsible Management.* Optimizing the use of resources for which they are responsible so as to provide the maximum benefit to their employers;
4. *Serving the Public Interest.* Not using their authority of office for personal benefit, rejecting and denouncing any business practice that is improper;
5. *Conformity to the Laws.* In Terms of:
   A. The laws of the country in which they practice;
   B. The Institute's or Corporation's Rules and Regulations
   C. Contractual obligations.

B. Norms of Ethical Behaviour

1. To consider first, the interest of one's organization in all transactions and to carry out and believe in its established policies.
2. To be receptive to competent counsel from one's colleagues and be guided by such counsel without impairing the responsibility of one's office.
3. To buy without prejudice, seeking to obtain the maximum value for each dollar of expenditure.
4. To strive for increased knowledge of the materials and processes of manufacture, and to establish practical procedures for the performance of one's responsibilities.
5. To participate in professional development programs so that one's purchasing knowledge and performance are enhanced.
6. To subscribe to and work for honesty in buying and selling and to denounce all forms of improper business practice.
7. To accord a prompt and courteous reception to all who call on a legitimate business mission.
8. To abide by and to encourage others to practice the Professional Code of Ethics of the Purchasing Management Association of Canada and its affiliated Institutes and Corporation.
9. To counsel and assist fellow purchasers in the performance of their duties.
10. To cooperate with all organizations and individuals engaged in activities that enhance the development and standing of purchasing and materials management.

RULES OF CONDUCT

In applying these rules of conduct, members should follow guidance set out below:

A. *Declaration of Interest.* Any personal interest which may impinge or might reasonably be deemed by others to impinge on a member's impartiality in any matter relevant to his or her duties should be immediately declared to his or her employer.

B. *Confidentiality and Accuracy of Information.* The confidentiality of information received in the course of duty must be respected and should not be used for personal gain; information given in the course of duty should be true and fair and not designed to mislead.

C. *Competition.* While considering the advantages to the member's employer of maintaining a continuing relationship with a supplier, any arrangement which might prevent the effective operation of fair competition should be avoided.

D. *Business Gifts and Hospitality.* To preserve the image and integrity of the member, the employer and the profession, business gifts other than items of small intrinsic value should not be accepted. Reasonable hospitality is an accepted courtesy of a business relationship. The frequency and nature of gifts or hospitality accepted should not be allowed whereby the recipient might be or might be deemed by others to have been influenced in making a business decision as a consequence of accepting such hospitality or gifts.

E. *Discrimination and Harassment.* No member shall knowingly participate in acts of discrimination or harassment towards any person that he or she has business relations with.

F. *Environmental Issues.* Members shall recognize their responsibility to environmental issues consistent with their corporate goals or missions.

G. *Interpretation.* When in doubt on the interpretation of these rules of conduct, members should refer to the Ethics Committee of their Institute or Corporation.

FIGURE 12–2 **ISM Principles and Standards of Ethical Supply Management Conduct**

LOYALTY TO YOUR ORGANIZATION
JUSTICE TO THOSE WITH WHOM YOU DEAL
FAITH IN YOUR PROFESSION

From these principles are derived the ISM standards of supply management conduct. (Global)

1. Avoid the intent and appearance of unethical or compromising practice in relationships, actions, and communications.
2. Demonstrate loyalty to the employer by diligently following the lawful instructions of the employer, using reasonable care and granted authority.
3. Avoid any personal business or professional activity that would create a conflict between personal interests and the interests of the employer.
4. Avoid soliciting or accepting money, loans, credit, or preferential discounts, and the acceptance of gifts, entertainment, favors, or services from present or potential suppliers that might influence, or appear to influence, supply management decisions.
5. Handle confidential or proprietary information with due care and proper consideration of ethical and legal ramifications and governmental regulations.
6. Promote positive supplier relationships through courtesy and impartiality.
7. Avoid improper reciprocal agreements.
8. Know and obey the letter and spirit of laws applicable to supply management.
9. Encourage support for small, disadvantaged, and minority-owned businesses.
10. Acquire and maintain professional competence.
11. Conduct supply management activities in accordance with national and international laws, customs, and practices, your organization's policies, and these ethical principles and standards of conduct.
12. Enhance the stature of the supply management profession.

Approved January 2002

Most large organizations in their policies and procedures will deal specifically with standards of behavior of purchasing personnel and their relations with suppliers. Many organizations are moving to a congruent position that equates the treatment of customers, employees, and suppliers as identical. Simply stated: "every customer, employee, and supplier of this organization is entitled to the same level of honesty, courtesy, and fairness." Buyers are urged to behave in a manner that reflects the organization's wishes.

Several areas are especially important to establish and maintain the reputation of the supply group and the organization. These are perceptions, conflict of interest, gifts and gratuities, relationships with suppliers, and reciprocity.

Perceptions and Conflict of Interest

Perception is often as important as reality. If a buyer's action is perceived by others to be inappropriate, then both the buyer's and the organization's reputations may be harmed. Because of this danger, everyone in supply must think about how an action will appear to others. Through conscious behavior, supply personnel can avoid ethical entanglements. Whether or not to accept entertainment, gifts, and gratuities is a prime area related to perceptions. Many purchasers argue that their decision will not be swayed by a free lunch. Others argue that even if the buyer knows the entertainment did not influence the decision, others (especially rejected bidders and personnel in other functions) may not be so sure. There is also the concern that any perceived imbalance in a relationship will subconsciously motivate the parties to move to parity. For example, after accepting several dinner invitations, most people feel a sense of obligation to return the favor. How does one know for sure that one can remain objective after receiving gifts and entertainment from a salesperson.

Another area that touches on the issue of perception is that of conflict of interest. There are situations where two parties cannot agree on the existence of a conflict. Often, the person involved truly believes that he or she can remain objective despite having conflicting interests. It may never be proven otherwise, but the perception of others may be that the business interest was sacrificed for personal interest. For example, a supply professional may be in a decision-making position that involves a friend or family member's business. No matter how thorough a job the person does, there will be those who will always believe the business was won on personal and not professional relationships.

Gifts and Gratuities

Attempts to influence decisions unfairly are directed not only toward supply personnel. Managers, supervisors, and others in production, marketing, information systems, engineering, or elsewhere who are directly responsible for, or largely influence, decisions regarding types of requirements to be procured are also approached. Even though the buyer is not directly influenced, the buyer's task is affected. So serious do some organizations consider this whole problem that they forbid any employee to receive any gift, no matter how trivial, from any supplier, actual or potential. In organizations where nonsupply personnel are allowed to receive or extend entertainment and gifts and supply personnel are not, the resulting environment can undermine the integrity of the supply process as sales representatives focus their attention on those outside the supply group who they believe can influence the decision. An astute sales representative can quickly determine who the real decision maker is and how serious the buying organization is about following its own processes. The impact on total cost of ownership is often overlooked by those who argue that there is no harm done in accepting gifts and entertainment.

Looked at from the sales perspective, a salesperson's job is to influence and persuade decision makers. This can be done most effectively by knowing the product or service and the potential customer's needs and wants, and presenting proposals that represent good value. People learn about others and their situation by spending time with them. They also build a relationship and a foundation of trust. The easiest way is to spend time together in a social setting. The challenge is to find ways to foster the development of trust and mutual understanding of the goals and objectives of each other's organization while maintaining a professional relationship. In buyer–supplier partnerships or strategic alliances, this issue becomes even more pronounced. Now the supplier may be a single source in a long-term deal that brings together people from the two organizations on a regular, sometimes daily, basis. These situations require special attention to ensure that the business focus is maintained.

How, then, shall the supply manager deal with the problem of excessive entertainment and gifts in any one of its varied and subtle forms? This practice is designed to influence the decision maker by creating a sense of obligation through gifts, entertainment, and even open bribery. It is, of course, often difficult to distinguish between legitimate expenditures by suppliers in the interest of goodwill and illegitimate expenditures made in an attempt to place the buyer under some obligation to the supplier. In these borderline cases, only ordinary common sense and a clearly written code of conduct can provide the answer.

The Institute for Supply Management (ISM) and the Purchasing Management Association of Canada (PMAC) in their codes of ethics strongly condemn gratuities beyond token gifts of nominal value. It is true, however, that every year a small number of cases are uncovered of individuals who do not abide by this code, thereby placing the whole profession under suspicion. Part of the blame must clearly lie with those who use illegal enticements to secure business. For example, a salesperson calls on a purchaser and invites him or her out to lunch so they may discuss a transaction without losing time or as a matter of courtesy. Such action is presumed to be in the interests of goodwill, although the cost of the lunch must be added to the selling price. An attractive but inexpensive gift may be given by the supplier's company to adorn the desk of the buyer. The supplier's name appears on the gift, and therefore it is construed as advertising. The sales representative may send a bottle of wine or sporting event tickets after a deal has been completed.

It is but a step from this type of effort to entertaining a prospective buyer at a dinner, followed perhaps by a theater party. The custom of giving simple gifts may develop into providing much larger ones. It is difficult to draw the line between these different situations. In some organizations, the supply manager or buyer frequently refuses to allow sales personnel to pay for luncheons or at least insists on paying for as many luncheons as do prospective sellers.

Aside from its economic aspects, the practice of commercial bribery is involved in many legal cases. Fundamentally, the rulings on commercial bribery rest on the doctrine of agency. Any breach of faith on the part of the agent, who has always been recognized by law as keeping a fiduciary position, is not permitted; therefore, the agent's acceptance of a bribe to do anything in conflict with the interests of its principal is not permitted by law.

The evils of commercial bribery are more far-reaching than would at first appear. Although originating with only one concern, bribery is rapidly likely to become a practice of the entire industry. A producer, no matter how superior the quality of goods or how low its price, is likely to find it difficult to sell in competition with concerns practicing bribery. The prices paid by the buyer who accepts bribes are almost certain to be higher than they would be under other circumstances. Defects in workmanship or quality are likely to be smoothed over by the buyer who accepts bribes hidden from his or her employer. Materials may be deliberately damaged or destroyed to make products of some manufacturers who do not offer bribes appear unsatisfactory. There is no point in going further into an analysis of this practice. It takes many forms, but regardless of the guise in which it appears, there is nothing to be said for it.

Even though bribery is outlawed in North America, it may flourish in other parts of the world, legally or not. The spectacular revelations about the bribery involved in the UN sponsored oil for food program in lraq were a sad reminder of the pervasiveness of such practices.

Promotion of Positive Relationships with Suppliers

Most organizations have policies and procedures concerning the relations between the supply office and suppliers' representatives. Purchasing and supply management associations in many countries around the world have adopted their own codes of ethics governing the relationship between supplier and purchaser. All of them are based on the requirement that both supplier and purchaser need to deal ethically with one another to ensure a sound basis for business dealings. Thus, courtesy, honesty, and fairness are stressed and buyers are urged to behave in such a fashion as to reflect the organization's wishes. Normally, this includes seeing suppliers without delay, being truthful in all statements, covering all elements of procurement in order that the final understanding may be complete, not asking suppliers to quote unless they have a reasonable chance at the business, keeping specifications fair and clear and competition open and fair, respecting the confidence of suppliers with regard to all confidential information, not taking improper advantage of sellers' errors, cooperating with suppliers in solving their difficulties, and negotiating prompt and fair adjustment in cases of dispute. It is also expected that a buyer be courteous in stating rejection of bids with explanations that are reasonable but not betray confidential information, answer inquiries promptly, and handle samples, tests, and reports with prompt, complete, and truthful information. Lastly, all codes of ethics stress a need to avoid all obligations to sellers except strict business obligations.

Occasionally, sales representatives attempt to bypass purchasing because they believe it may be to their advantage to do so. If the supplier secures an order without the knowledge and agreement of purchasing, internal dissension may be created, as well as resentment against the sales representative. The short-term gain may turn into a long-term loss. Although supply personnel are expected to be well acquainted with the organization's operations, equipment, materials, and varied requirements, and to be qualified to pass on the practicality of suggestions and proposals that may be made by sales representatives and technical people, the supply manager does not, as a rule, have the background that constitutes the basis for the technical person's special knowledge. In these situations, cross-functional sourcing teams are used and different team members may manage the supplier relationship for their primary area of concern. The team approach lessens the fears of individual members that others will make decisions that are not in their best interests.

In a partnering relationship or a buyer–supplier alliance, it is normal to have a substantial amount of regular direct contact between supplier personnel and nonsupply people in the buyer's organization. Direct contacts are not normally part of the supplier selection decision but are essential to the effective execution of the contract and maintenance of a superior working relationship.

Reciprocity

Under what circumstances, if at all, shall trade relations or reciprocity be practiced? A general definition of *reciprocity* is: "Reciprocity is the practice of giving preference in buying to those suppliers who are customers of the buying company as opposed to suppliers who do not buy from the company." From a supply management perspective, reciprocity is unacceptable when it involves purchasing items under conditions that will result in higher prices or inferior service. It is debatable as to how far it should be practiced, *assuming that conditions of price, service, and quality are substantially the same.*

The case against any general use of reciprocity rests on the belief that the practice is at variance with the sound principles of either buying or selling. The sale of a product or service must be based on the qualities of the product sold and of the service attending the transaction. There is only one permanent basis for a continuing customer–supplier relationship: the conviction on the part of the buyer that the product or service of a particular seller is the one best adapted to the need and is the best all-around value available. As long as the sales department concentrates its attention on this appeal, it will find and retain permanent customers.

Few purchasers would object to reciprocal buying on the basis that quality, service, and price must be equal. In practice, abuse is practically certain to creep in. For instance, buyers are urged to buy from X not because X is a customer but because X is Y's customer and Y is our customer, and Y wants to sell to X.

The normal expectation of a seller using reciprocity as an argument is that the purchaser is willing to grant price, quality, or delivery concessions. In North America, reciprocity is on shaky legal grounds, and the U.S. Supreme Court has upheld the Clayton Act under Section 7 that reciprocity is restrictive to trade and creates unfair competition.[20]

On an international scale, a form of reciprocity is practiced widely by governments who insist on "offsets." For example, a foreign company may receive a government contract on the condition that it meets stringent local content requirements. Thus, the supplier is forced to develop new sources, often at substantial cost, to secure the business. Furthermore, such foreign contracts often involve barter, since the purchaser insists on paying with raw materials or locally manufactured goods. (See Chapter 14, "Global Supply.")

SOCIAL RESPONSIBILITY

Corporate social responsibility is defined by Business for Social Responsibility (BSR) as "achieving commercial success in ways that honor ethical values and respect people, communities, and the natural environment." BSR is a global nonprofit organization that promotes

[20] The case is *FTC v. Consolidated Foods,* 380 U.S. 592 (1965).

cross-sector collaboration and contributes to global efforts to advance the field of corporate social responsibility. For many organizations, the first step toward social responsibility is to develop and adopt principles of social responsibility. Following that, BSR reports that a comprehensive set of policies, practices, and programs is integrated into business operations, supply chains, and decision-making processes throughout the company and wherever the company does business. It includes responsibility for current and past actions as well as future impacts. The focus may vary by business, by size, by sector, and even by geographic region. Typically it includes issues related to business ethics, community investment, environment, governance, human rights, marketplace, and workplace.

Becoming a socially responsible enterprise is difficult when operating in one country, and daunting when operating globally. The variety of stakeholders, customs, business norms, practices, legal systems, and ethical frameworks make it difficult to balance the interests of all stakeholders. For example, is it socially responsible to move jobs offshore to low-wage countries? What if wages are subsistence level and mandated by the laws of the country? Is the employer responsible for wage rates in another country? Those in countries where job opportunities and incomes have been severely restricted might have a different view of offshore jobs than those in the country losing jobs. Should the focus be on what is "socially responsible" in the country where the company is headquartered or in all the countries in which it sells its products or services, or in the cities in which most of its operations are located? Putting the principles of social responsibility to work is an ongoing challenge and one that touches supply managers in a very real way.

For example, in its "*Sustainability Report 2003,*" Netherlands-based Royal Philips Electronics NV, Europe's largest consumer electronics maker, introduced provisions requiring its 50,000 suppliers to adhere to minimum expectations for sustainability performance. This includes labor standards that include health and safety protections, unionizing rights, and nondiscrimination; ban the use of child labor in accordance with the International Labor Organization Conventions; and achieve the International Standards Organization (ISO) 14001 environmental management certification standard. Philips chief procurement officer Barbara Kux says, "The outsourcing of manufacturing activities means extending ethical, social and environmental standards related to those activities toward our suppliers." Kux adds, "The overall approach is one of finding solutions through open and honest discussions with the supplier, but if no satisfactory solution can be found, suppliers can expect that this will affect the business relationship." Philips will introduce a self-assessment tool to help suppliers measure their sustainability performance, and beginning in 2005, the company plans to conduct supplier checks to verify the self-assessments.[21]

The strongest support for social responsibility is a demonstrated correlation between progressive social, environmental, and governance practices and policies that financially outperform others in a sector. A growing number of analysts report on sector performance on this basis. Triple-bottomline reporting is one policy that social responsibility advocates support. This policy requires companies to report on financial concerns, as well as how the company takes environmental and social concerns into business practices. One widely recognized model for reporting is the Global Reporting Initiative (GRI). One indication of the importance of corporate social responsibility is the annual Dow Jones Sustainability Indexes (DJSI) launched in 1999. In 2003, 50 new companies were added and 40 were

[21] William Baue, "Philips Extends Sustainability Expectations to Suppliers, Including Child Labor Ban," *SocialFunds.com* , http://www.socialfunds.com, March 29, 2004.

deleted based on the assessment that they had not kept pace with sustainability best practices. The 2003 annual review also found that the DJSI World Index outperformed the mainstream market financially since the last review in September 2002. Such outperformance bolsters the business case for considering sustainability in investment decisions. A shift in market perceptions also supports the case as private and institutional investors adapt economic, environmental, and social criteria to reflect the impact of sustainability issues on long-term shareholder value

The Institute for Supply Management (ISM) developed a set of social responsibility principles and practices specifically directed at supply professionals. They are designed to benefit the workplace, the individual, the organization, and the community in the following areas: community, diversity, environment, ethics, financial responsibility, human rights, and safety. The document includes a supply management audit for social responsibility.

Conclusion

Supply professionals play both a strategic and an operational role in the organization. The strategic role is to maximize opportunities and minimize risks for the organization. The operational role is to execute the strategies in the most efficient and effective way possible. Monitoring the legal and ethical environment is one area where supply contributes strategically and operationally. The supply manager is well-positioned to spot potential legal and ethical opportunities and risks.

Questions for Review and Discussion

1. What is corporate social responsibility and how does this issue affect supply managers?
2. Under what conditions is it realistic for a buyer to cancel a contract? For a seller to cancel a contract?
3. Does a supplier have to accept a PO exactly as offered by the buyer to create a legally binding contract?
4. What is alternative dispute resolution? When and how should it be used?
5. Does a salesperson have basically the same legal authority as a buyer? If not, how is it different?
6. What are the legal rights of the buyer if goods delivered by a supplier do not measure up to the specifications?
7. Under what conditions might purchasers be held personally liable for contracts they enter into?
8. Is an oral contract legally enforceable? Under what conditions?
9. What authority does a purchasing agent have to make decisions that are binding on the principal? What responsibility do purchasing agents have for the consequences of their decisions?
10. What actions can the purchasing agent take to protect intellectual property rights and avoid legal action?
11. What can supply managers do to minimize the company's risk of a product liability lawsuit?
12. What legal issues would you want to consider before setting up an e-procurement system in a company?
13. Where does the borderline fall between gratuities and bribery?

References

American Arbitration Association. *Dispute-Wise*[SM] *Business Management: Improving Economic and Non-Economic Outcomes in Managing Business Conflicts.* 2003. http://www.adr.org.

American Arbitration Association. *Drafting Dispute Resolution Clauses 1: A Practical Guide* 2004. http://www.adr.org.

Business for Social Responsibility. http://www.bsr.org.

Global Reporting Initiative. http://www.globalreporting.org.

King, Donald B., and James J. Ritterskamp Jr. *Purchasing Manager's Desk Book of Purchasing Law, 1999 Supplement.* 3rd ed. Englewood Cliffs, NJ: Prentice Hall, 1999.

Office of Dispute Resolution, U.S. Department of Justice. http://www.usdoj.gov/odr.

Smedinghoff, Thomas J. (ed.); Andrew R. Basile Jr.; and Geoffrey Gilbert. *Online Law: The SPA's Legal Guide to Doing Business on the Internet.* Chicago: Addison-Wesley, 1996.

Uniform Commercial Code: Official Text and Comments. Philadelphia, PA: American Law Institute and National Conference of Commissioners on Uniform State Laws, West Publishing Company, 2003.

World Intellectual Property Organization (WIPO). http://www.wipo.int/.

Wydick, Richard C. *Plain English for Lawyers.* 4th ed. Durham, NC: Carolina Academic Press, 2001.

Case 12–1

Brassco

On March 2, Harry Jones, materials manager of Brassco, received a letter from a supplier who was refusing Harry's request to terminate Brassco's linen laundering contract. Jones firmly believed that the contract contained an exit clause that could be executed with proper notice, but his supplier had a different interpretation.

BRASSCO PURCHASES

With 280 employees and $100 million in sales annually, Brassco manufactured copper fittings for a variety of industrial users. As materials manager, Harry Jones was responsible for purchases of about $70 million, of which about 60 percent were for raw materials.

LAUNDERING

Recently the state government had launched a new environmental initiative to reduce landfill waste by 50 percent over a five-year period. The government indicated that one method of achieving this goal would be through an aggressive application of "The 3Rs" of reducing, reusing, and recycling, and that regular company audits would be performed in accordance with the regulation. In keeping with this mandate, Brassco attempted to reduce its daily waste production by, among other initiatives, replacing many of its disposable paper products with reusable linen equivalents.

Harry Jones observed that the excessive use of paper towels in the plant was creating significant waste each day. By replacing these towels with their linen counterparts, he was able to make progress toward the environmental goal. However, as a result of the change, he required a laundering service to maintain the program.

Currently, Brassco had a rental and laundering contract with Riddirt for floor mats, uniforms, protective garments, and gloves, which amounted to about $40,000 annually. Harry decided to ask Riddirt to quote on the new contract, but he also asked several other commercial launderers to quote on both the new linen towel contract and the existing Brassco laundering requirements. Harry believed that administration and coordination effort could be reduced if all of Brassco's laundering needs were single sourced.

EXHIBIT 1
Selected Quotes for Brassco Laundering

	New Linen Towel Service	Existing Uniform Rental and Cleaning
Able Cleaners	$40,500	$38,000
Cleano	no bid	32,200
Wilkens	no bid	30,100
Riddirt	no bid	40,000*

*Not a re-bid; current contract price.

THE BIDS

To Harry's surprise, only one company, Able Cleaners, was able to quote on the towel contract, while several companies, including Able, quoted on the remaining cleaning needs of Brassco. (See Exhibit 1.)

Unfortunately, Able Cleaners was not the lowest overall bidder because a combination of two suppliers resulted in a lower overall dollar cost to Brassco. What was even more surprising for Harry was that Riddirt's current contract price of $40,000 for floor mats and clothing was about 30 percent higher than the lowest alternate option.

TERMINATION OF RIDDIRT CONTRACT

Consequently, Harry decided to terminate the Riddirt agreement. On review of the Riddirt contract he had on file, Harry noted that Clause 5 regarding the term of the rental service agreement stated:

> The Agreement shall be in force for a period of five years from the date hereof, and thereafter for an equal period, unless terminated by written notice by either party prior to sixty days before the contract expiration date.

On March 1, he, therefore, sent a fax to Riddirt, stating:

> Please accept this fax as written notification to terminate our existing agreement effective May 20. . .

A DIFFERENCE OF OPINION

Early the following morning, Harry received a response from Riddirt indicating they were unwilling to accept Brassco's request for termination. In their opinion, it was in clear violation of the signed contract. They explained that Brassco was locked in for a minimum five-year term, which would not expire for another two years. Further, Riddirt believed that the contract clearly outlined that unless Brassco provided notice 60 days prior to the contract end date, the service agreement would automatically be renewed for a subsequent five-year term.

Harry was frustrated and uncertain how to proceed. He knew that contract law was complex. However, in his evaluation of the contract, which had been negotiated prior to his arrival at Brassco, he understood that he could terminate his obligation to Riddirt any time prior to the last 60 days of the five-year term. He was also frustrated by the automatic rollover clause, as he wondered what would have resulted if the bidding process had never happened and his attention hadn't been drawn to the contract's details.

Case 12–2

Lancaster Life Insurance Co.

Glenn Williamson, purchasing manager at Lancaster Life Insurance Co., had failed to award one of Lancaster's long-time group insurance clients a printing contract. Six months later, the printer was threatening to change insurers, and Lancaster's sales representative covering the printer was on the phone demanding action.

LANCASTER LIFE INSURANCE CO

Lancaster had premiums of $1.5 billion and earnings of $65 million during the past year. Lancaster's products were distributed by 2,261 of the company's own sales representatives through the head office and 155 regional offices. The company's annual report stated that such key profitability ratios as mortality experience, interest rate spreads, and loss ratios were at satisfactory levels. Nevertheless, the economic climate had caused a considerable slowing of business growth. The following table shows premiums and earnings contributions by product line.

Product Line	Premiums ($ millions)	Earnings Contribution ($ millions)
Individual insurance	618	24.1
Retirement products	456	11.8
Employee benefits*	326	11.6
Reinsurance and other	109	17.0
Total	1,509	64.5

*Group insurance (typically includes some combination of health, vision, dental coverage, etc. as well as life insurance).

GROUP INSURANCE PRODUCTS

Group insurance was essentially a commodity product, purchased by a firm to include in its employee benefit package. Clients purchased group insurance on the basis of price for a given level of service quality. Its smaller margins and lack of customer loyalty meant that group insurance was considered by the sales force to be a tougher business than individual insurance. Approximate commissions on a group policy were in the 3 percent range, compared to 7 percent on an individual policy. While individuals changed life insurers relatively infrequently, businesses, especially larger ones, were a much less stable customer base.

PURCHASING DEPARTMENT

Lancaster's highly centralized purchasing department fell under the umbrella of Corporate and Administrative Services. The purchasing department bought all non-computer-related supplies, from business forms to photocopiers to company cars, for the entire Lancaster organization and its sister firms. Total purchases amounted to about $100 million per year. Glenn Williamson managed a staff of 18 general buyers and specialized forms managers.

Supplies used on a regular basis, or "stock" purchases, were stored in a central warehouse. Regional offices ordered supplies on a rotating schedule, and shipments were made to 10 to 12 offices per day. Williamson valued the inventory in the warehouse at approximately $2 million. The purchasing department was responsible for the acquisition of $20 million of supplies annually. The forms managers oversaw the printing and inventory levels of approximately 3,500 different business forms and advertising brochures.

The purchasing department viewed itself as providing a service to head office and the regional offices, its major clients. The main goal of the department was to obtain the best value for its purchasing dollar. Williamson defined this as getting the necessary quality for the lowest possible price and worked continuously to reduce costs without sacrificing quality. For the past 10 years, suppliers had been chosen on the basis of a bidding process to encourage competitive pricing and service. Under this process, suppliers were encouraged to quote their best price for a predetermined level of quality and service, and the lowest price won the contract.

In Lancaster's experience, centralized purchasing was much more cost-effective than having regional offices buying their own supplies. As Williamson explained, "Who is going to get the better price—an office administrator buying one photocopier or an experienced purchaser buying 20 photocopiers?"

Because Lancaster provided life insurance to so many different people, Williamson was very conscious of the public relations responsibilities of the purchasing department. "The suppliers are all existing clients or potential clients. We need to be seen as giving people a fair chance."

MASTER PRINTER INC

Master Printer had supplied advertising brochures to Lancaster for many years. Williamson described the historical relationship:

> They used to just walk into the Marketing Department and walk out with the contract. No competition. Nothing. So they could charge what they liked. Now, I'm not saying they were gouging us. Their quality and service were always very good. They just were not pricing competitively. Then, 10 years ago, the purchasing department got more teeth, and we started getting quotes from the suppliers. Within two years, Master Printer's sales to Lancaster dropped to about 20 percent of their previous levels. The company wasn't doing well, so then a couple of years ago it came under new ownership.

> We got a call from the group rep covering them last spring, asking why Master Printer had not been awarded a particular contract. I guess their management was upset at not getting it and was turning up the heat on the sales rep. Maybe threatening not to renew their $100,000 plus policy. So I told the rep that their bid was $6,000 higher than the five other bids. Everyone else was bidding around $22,000. Anyway, it seemed to satisfy him. That was the last I heard of it.

RECIPROCAL BUYING

Reciprocal buying issues, or the pressure to purchase from a particular supplier in order to ensure that the supplier also remained a group or personal client, were not new in the business. The pressure on the purchasing department from sales reps and their managers was, however, becoming stronger and more frequent as the recession deepened and competition, particularly for group business, intensified. "Times are tough," commented Williamson. "They want the policy, and some of those reps will promise anything to get it. So where does that leave us?"

Williamson found that Lancaster's policy with respect to reciprocal buying offered little concrete guidance: "It says 'All other things being equal, we will favor our clients,' but what are 'all other things'? And if we are only going to buy from our clients, then do we tell that to all potential bidders? And if we do that, then why would a non-client bid? So up go the prices."

On Tuesday morning, November 17, the sales representative covering Master Printer phoned again for Glenn Williamson. Master Printer's management was going to take its insurance business somewhere else. This was *Lancaster's* client and *his* client, and who did the idiots in purchasing think they were? He worked his butt off and here was Williamson driving away his clients! What was Williamson going to do about it? How did Williamson plan to get his client back? He was going to take this as high as he needed to go. He wanted action *now*.

Chapter Thirteen

Research and Metrics

Chapter Outline

Key Questions for the Supply Manager

Should we

- Recognize supply research as a formal activity?
- Benchmark our supply processes?
- Develop a consistent, formal system for evaluating supply performance?

How can we

- Measure supply's contribution more effectively?
- Get internal validation for the budgetary impact of supply's performance?
- Prepare more accurate budgets?

In a rapidly changing environment, innovation and improvements in productivity can best be managed if we look at what might be possible, develop comprehensive plans, evaluate accomplishments and shortfalls, and report outcomes. So far in this text, the discussion has primarily focused on identifying the contribution that supply can make to the organization and determining how to make that contribution. Two additional activities must be performed: (1) research to develop and operationalize the plans and metrics and (2) communication of supply's contribution internally and externally.

The changing demands and increasing expectations of supply have led to a need for supply managers with broader and deeper knowledge and skill sets. Research skills are needed throughout the supply process, first to collect, analyze, and synthesize information that might assist in need recognition and description; next to identify potential suppliers in light of organizational goals and objectives; then to perform the supplier selection process, manage the supplier relationship throughout its life, and measure the results of these activities.

Metrics also need to be established to capture results as they occur throughout the process. Many of the traditional metrics of purchasing performance focused more on efficiency measures such as price per unit or cost to process a purchase order than on effectiveness measures such as congruence with corporate goals or customer satisfaction. In Chapter 1, supply's contribution was described as strategic, operational, direct, and indirect. Metrics should capture the contribution along each of these dimensions. The challenge is to develop metrics that put supply's contributions in a language that speaks to the audience—internally to senior management and internal business partners and externally to stakeholders such as stockholders, the community, suppliers, and other supply chain members.

This chapter covers supply research, budgets, and performance metrics. It considers the need for supply managers to measure, evaluate, and report on their performance and the requirements senior management places on the supply process for credible results.

ORGANIZING FOR SUPPLY RESEARCH

Supply research is the systematic collection, classification, and analysis of data as the basis for better supply decisions. Figure 13–1 shows some of the data (information) that might be required for effective buying decisions.

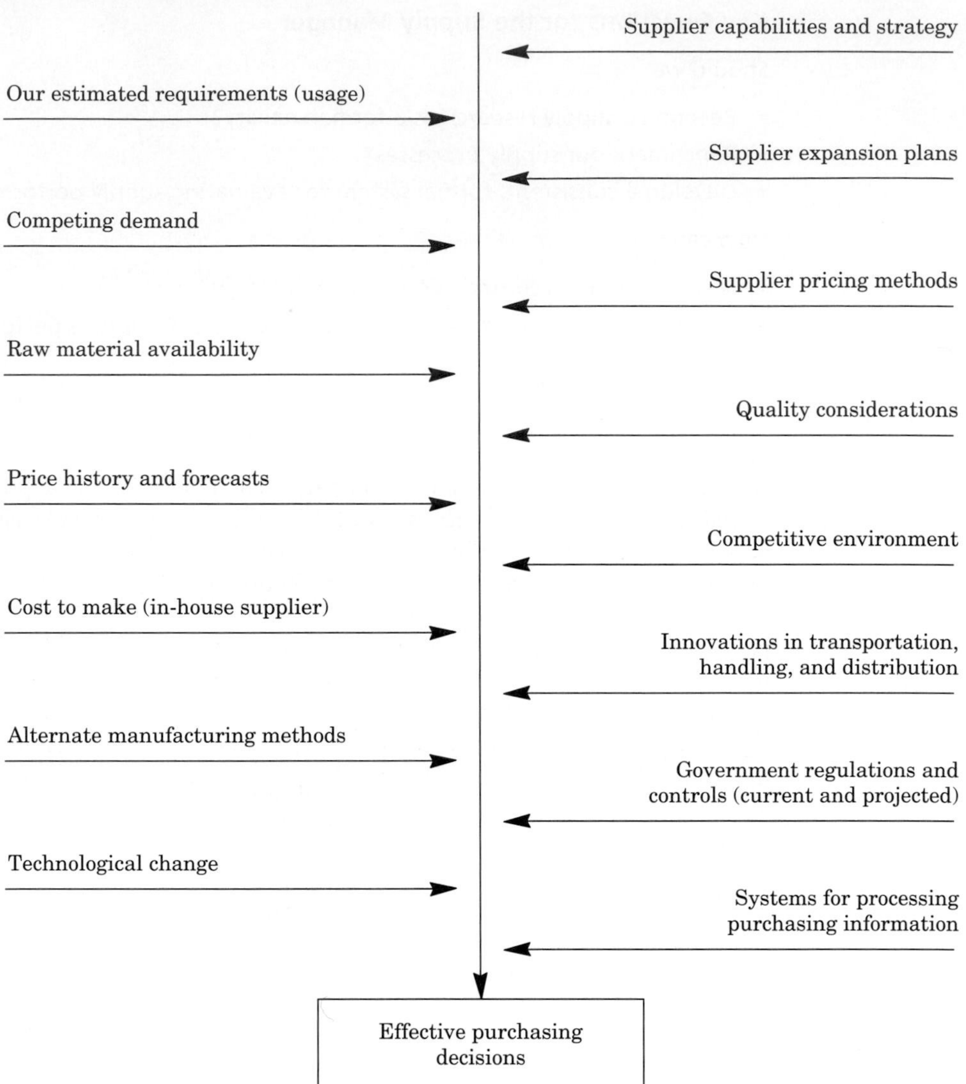

FIGURE 13–1
Ingredients of Effective Buying

The studies conducted in supply research include projects under the major research headings of

1. Purchased materials, products, or services (value analysis).
2. Commodities.
3. Suppliers.
4. Supply processes.

Considerable attention has been given to a similar activity in the counterpart function of marketing research. Marketing research generally is well accepted in all medium- to large-sized firms as a necessary ingredient in decision making, and it has produced significant results for those firms that practice marketing research systematically. Supply research, if approached in an organized manner, also has the potential for generating major improvements in supply decision making.

A firm could conduct supply research in one of three ways: (1) full-time research positions, (2) inclusion of research as a part-time responsibility of supply personnel, or (3) cross-functional teams to bring an expanded knowledge base to the research process.

Full-Time or Part-Time Research Positions

As with its counterpart function, marketing research, there are persuasive arguments for the assignment of full-time personnel to perform supply research. These positions typically are titled purchase analyst, cost management specialist, value analyst, or commodity specialist. (See Figure 13–2 for an example of a job description for a supply cost management specialist at Deere and Company).

A thorough job of collecting and analyzing data requires blocks of time, and in many supply departments the buyers do not have this time. They are fully occupied finding workable solutions to immediate problems. Furthermore, many areas of supply research, such as economic studies and analysis of business processes, require in-depth knowledge of research techniques. These research techniques call for a level of skill not possessed by the typical buyer, primarily because research skill typically is not one of the criteria used in selecting persons for buying positions.

The supply researcher must take a broad view of the overall effects of supply decisions on operating results. The buyer, on the other hand, may be so engrossed in his or her own responsibility area that the big picture goes unrecognized.

In this model of full-time research staff, supply decisions are made by the buyer or business owner based on the data, analysis, and recommendations of the researcher. Conflict may develop between the researcher and the decision maker; thus the recommendations of the researcher may not receive fair consideration and the value of the efforts will be negated. The part-time researcher model is based on the argument that the buyer is the most familiar with the goods and services acquired and should be responsible for supply research.

Cross-Functional Teams

The division of the supply function into operational and strategic elements, coupled with downsizing and flattening of the organization, has led to an increased use of cross-functional sourcing teams that do the research and planning but do not actually do the buying. This model is somewhat of a compromise between the full-time supply analyst and the part-time buyer-researcher. Such teams have titles such as sourcing team, commodity management team, or value analysis team. (See Chapter 2 for more detail.)

The difficulty with the team approach is that it is hard to pinpoint responsibility for results when it is diffused over a number of individuals. However, the team approach can work satisfactorily, provided that (1) team members are carefully selected to ensure that each really has something to contribute, (2) the team has strong leadership (from a functional point of view, it probably should be someone from the supply area), (3) a specific set of objectives and expectations of results is formulated and communicated to each member and the team as a whole, (4) each team member's normal job responsibilities are rearranged to give that person the time and the resources necessary to ensure results, and

FIGURE 13–2
Deere and Company Job Description for Supply Cost Management Specialist

JOHN DEERE

Job Title: Supply Cost Management Specialist
Department: Supply Management
Supervises: None, may facilitate/lead team activities
Job Function: Enabling the design and procurement processes to obtain the best value from the supply base.

Primary Duties:

1. Develop cost models and tables for direct materials to be used for
   —Evaluating cost competitiveness of product designs.
   —Creating product target costs on a part-by-part basis.
   —Creating supplier target costs to enable fact-based negotiations.
   —Highlighting potential cost reduction areas.
2. Utilize cost management techniques to give accurate and timely cost evaluations of designs on a part-by-part basis.
3. Support Strategic Sourcing in meeting or exceeding product cost goals for direct material.
4. Support Strategic Sourcing in all aspects of cost reduction activities including
   —Utilizing cost management techniques to determine potential areas for cost reduction.
   —Tracking, forecasting, and budgeting for cost reduction of Order Fulfillment Process (OFP) cost activities.
   —Facilitating the JD CROP (John Deere Cost Reduction Opportunities Process) at the unit level.
   —Participating or facilitating the Compare and Share process with Strategic Sourcing and the Value Improvement process.
5. Participate or lead enterprise-level cost management activities such as cost modeling or training

(5) performance evaluation and reward systems foster team participation and overall team performance. If any of these five conditions is not present, less than optimum outcomes are almost certain.

SUPPLY RESEARCH OPPORTUNITIES

The types of data that bear on a major supply decision are numerous and many different items may be purchased; therefore, the number of possible supply research projects is almost infinite. However, even a company with full-time supply analysts has limited resources and must use some method of deciding which supply-research projects should have top priority.

The following is a list of criteria that are used by firms to decide where they will direct their research effort. This is not intended to be in priority order (although the most widely used method is the "top dollar" criterion).

1. *Value of product or service.* Top dollar (current or projected).
2. *Product profitability.* Red dollar (unprofitable end product).
3. *Price/cost characteristics.* Infrequent price changes, frequent or seasonal price fluctuations, end-product cost not competitive, raw materials costs rising at a greater rate than selling price of product.
4. *Availability.* Limited number of suppliers, new suppliers adding to available supply, possibility of international sourcing, possibility of in-house manufacture or outsourcing.
5. *Quality.* Have had quality or specification problem.
6. *Data flows.* Information for decisions often inaccurate, late, or unavailable; cost of data is excessive.

Research projects typically fall into one of four categories: (1) purchased materials, products, or services; (2) commodities; (3) suppliers; and (4) supply processes.

Purchased Materials, Products, or Services

Research is typically conducted on purchased materials, products, or services to ensure that the best value-creating decision is made. These research projects include

1. *Specification.* Analysis of current specifications compared to the final customers' required performance level to eliminate unneeded attributes or unnecessarily high levels of performance, and to enable competitive sourcing.
2. *Standardization.* Review of how specific products are used and consideration of using one item to fill the needs for which multiple items currently are purchased.
3. *Substitution.* Analysis of the technical and economic ramifications of using a different item than the one presently purchased.
4. *Packaging.* Investigation of processes and materials to determine the optimal method of meeting requirements.
5. *Supplier switching.* Analysis of opportunities to improve value with a different supplier.
6. *Investment recovery.* Analysis of disposal methods (including recycling), channels, and techniques to isolate those that will provide greatest net return to the firm.
7. *Lease or buy.* Collection of data on the advantages and disadvantages of each alternative so that the most attractive decision can be identified.
8. *Make or buy and continue making or outsource.* Comparison of economic and managerial outcomes from each alternative to make an informed choice.

Two techniques are useful when researching purchased materials, products, or services: value analysis and target costing.

Value Analysis

Value analysis is the first supply research method to receive major worldwide attention, publicity, and acceptance. Originally developed by Lawrence D. Miles at General Electric, value analysis (VA) was widely accepted in U.S. industry and in Japan, where it is cited as a cornerstone of Japan's cost-effective manufacturing system. Japan gives the Miles Award to those firms making the most effective use of value analysis. Although initially used as a purchasing tool, value analysis is now applied to both goods and services.

Value analysis compares the *function* performed by a purchased item with the *cost* in an attempt to find a better-value alternative. The first step is to select a part, material, or service to analyze; next, to form a cross-functional value analysis team (often including a supplier); and finally, to define the function of the item or service in a verb and noun combination. For example, if the can that holds a soft drink is selected for value analysis, its function might be defined as "holds liquid." This approach encourages creative thinking and keeps the team from locking onto the existing solution, an aluminum can, as the only solution. Value analysis is a systematic approach that can be an ongoing part of the supply management process.

The standard value analysis approach is to pose and provide detailed answers to a series of questions about the item currently purchased. Figure 13–3 details this approach and lists standard value analysis questions.

Many discrete goods' manufacturers, such as consumer electonics and automotive companies, use value analysis. For example, Ford has been using value analysis for many years. Three-day workshops are conducted in its Value Analysis Center with cross-functional teams made up of Ford design and release engineers, an assembly process expert, the installation engineer at the plant, the supplier's engineer, a Ford purchaser, a Ford cost estimator, and a finance estimator from the supplier. Larry Denton, the director of the Ford Value Analysis Center described the process as follows: "You have the part on the table and you have a competitor's part, tear down boards, and a team of about 10 people with a professional facilitator to go through and brainstorm ideas on how to lower cost. We use the value equation $V = F/C$ (value = function over cost)." The objective is to enhance the function of the part while keeping cost constant, or reduce the cost and maintain the same function.[1]

In many instances, a higher-priced item than necessary is purchased because of time pressure or rapidly changing technology and manufacturing methods. The distinction is often made that *value analysis* is done on purchased items used in the ongoing production process and *value engineering* focuses on value improvement opportunities in the design stage. The value analysis process is the same at both stages. Obviously, value engineering to arrive at the best value specification and design that will adequately perform the function is the most efficient way to do the job, but unfortunately this analysis, due to time pressures, often is not done.

Moreover, after a product has been on the market for a while, greater certainty about demand, new technological options, or suppliers may become available, and prices of key materials or components may have changed. Therefore, a careful value analysis after the original design may reveal surprising opportunities for value improvement, even if the original design had been carefully value engineered. Value analysis techniques are equally applicable to services, supply processes, and e-commerce activities.

[1]"Ford Stresses Value Analysis to Lower Cost," *Purchasing,* March 7, 1996, pp. 54–55.

FIGURE 13–3 **The Value Analysis Approach: Comparison of Function with Cost**

I. Rationale: VA is a systematic and creative approach to improve value without impairing quality.
II. Select a relatively high-cost or high-volume purchased item to value analyze. This item can be a component, material, or service that is believed to cost more than it should.
III. Thoroughly describe how the item is used and what is expected of it—its *function*. Define the function in a verb-noun, two-word combination, such as "holds liquid."
IV. Ask the following questions of the item:
   1. Does its use contribute value?
   2. Is its cost proportionate to its usefulness?
   3. Can basic and secondary functions be separated?
   4. Have functional requirements changed over time?
   5. Does it need all its features?
   6. Is there anything better for the intended use?
   7. Are the original specs realistic under today's conditions?
   8. Can the item be eliminated?
   9. If the item is not standard, can a standard item be used?
   10. If it is a standard item, does it completely fit the application or is it a misfit?
   11. Does the item have greater capacity than required?
   12. Is there a similar item in inventory that could be used?
   13. Can the weight be reduced?
   14. Have new materials or designs been developed that would alter performance of the product?
   15. Are closer tolerances specified than are necessary?
   16. Is unnecessary machining performed on the item?
   17. Are unnecessary fine finishes specified?
   18. Is commercial quality specified?
   19. Can the item be made cheaper internally?
   20. If being made internally, can the item be purchased for less?
   21. Is the item properly classified for shipping purposes?
   22. Can cost of packaging be reduced?
   23. Are suppliers of the item being asked for suggestions to reduce cost?
   24. Do material, reasonable labor, overhead, and profit total its cost?
   25. Will another dependable supplier provide it for less?
   26. Is anyone buying it for less?
V. Following the Initial Analysis:
   1. Where practical, get samples of the proposed item(s).
   2. Select the best possibilities and propose changes.
VI. Follow-up: Were the expected benefits realized?
VII. Outcome: *A thorough study is almost certain to uncover many potential savings!*

Target Costing

Target costing is an approach that starts with the selling price of a final product or service minus the desired operating profit to arrive at a pool of money available for all costs. Responsibility for cost pools is allocated to functions throughout the organization. The supply group further allocates materials and services costs to establish cost targets and assign responsibility to buyers, commodity managers, and sourcing teams. These people develop plans and strategies to achieve the cost targets with suppliers. Effective target costing requires establishing detailed cost breakdowns and performing value analysis to determine how the function of the product or service can be achieved at the targeted cost. Cross-functional teams of engineers, supply, cost analysts, and supplier personnel are often used to attain target costs.

Honda of America credits target costing as one of the major contributing factors to its profit turnaround in the mid-1990s. Purchased components from suppliers represent 70 to 80 percent of Honda's cost of sales. The Honda sales group sets the selling prices for new models, and based on the estimated profit margin, target costs are set for each of the parts in the automobile. The target costing process begins at the design phase, using cost models developed by R&D and procurement staff, and the target costs are used to evaluate supplier costs to determine their accuracy. Individual target costs are set before design drawings are authorized. In effect, the target costs represent the budget for the new vehicle.[2]

Commodities

The term *commodity* can be used in several ways. In the strictest sense, a commodity is a raw material that is traded on a commodities market, such as flour, steel, or copper. In many organizations, the term is used more broadly to describe a purchase category such as computers, travel, or printed circuit boards. Therefore, commodity studies may be performed on major raw materials as well as manufactured items, such as motors or semiconductors. Typically, commodity research focuses on items that represent a significant percent of annual spend, but it may be conducted on smaller spend commodities if they are in critically short supply or strategic. This research is designed to predict the short- and long-term future supply environment. It should provide the basis for making sound decisions and present supply and senior management with relatively complete information about future availability and price. This area probably is the most sophisticated in terms of difficulty and skills needed to do a good job.

A comprehensive commodity study should include analyses of these major areas: (1) current and future status of the company as a buyer; (2) production process alternatives; (3) uses of the item; (4) demand; (5) supply; (6) price; and (7) strategy to reduce cost and/or ensure supply. The information resulting from a commodity study should

1. Provide a basis for making sound procurement decisions.
2. Present supply management and top management with information concerning future supply and price of purchased items.

Figure 13–4 provides a set of guidelines that might be used to make a commodity study.

Some companies do sophisticated commodity research, resulting in a well-documented strategic purchase plan. While a planning horizon of from five to 10 years is the norm, some firms make a 15-year rolling forecast, updated each year. If a firm makes a 15-year strategic marketing plan, it makes sense to couple this with a strategic supply forecast and plan, for in the long term the acquisition of an adequate supply of critical materials may be the crucial determinant in the organization's success in meeting its market goals. Firms need to make realistic estimates of price trends so that they can plan their strategy of adjusting material inputs to counter this trend. Also, the availability of many commodities is questionable due to dependence on offshore sources whose stability may be doubtful due to international politics and depletion of reserves.

[2] Lisa Ellram, *The Role of Supply Management in Target Costing* (Tempe, AZ: Center for Advanced Purchasing Studies, 1999).

FIGURE 13–4 Commodity Study Guidelines

The completed commodity study should provide data and/or answers for each of the following categories to the extent required by the particular commodity. Additional items may also be very pertinent.

I. *Current and future status.* Includes a description of the commodity, its current usage and forecast of future requirements, suppliers, price, terms, annual expenditures, mode of transport, and current contracts.

II. *Production process.* Includes how the item is made, the materials used, the supply/price status of these materials, the labor required, the current and future labor situation, alternative production processes, and the possibility of making the item, including costs, time factor, and production problems.

III. *Uses of the item.* Includes primary use(s), secondary use(s), possible substitutes, and the economics of substitution.

IV. *Demand.* Includes the firm's current and future requirements, inventory status, sources of forecast information and lead times, and competing demand—current and projected—by industry, by end-product use, and by individual firm.

V. *Supply.* Includes current producers—location, reliability, quality, labor situation, capacity, distribution channels, and strengths and weaknesses of each supplier; total (aggregate) supply situation, current and projected; and external factors—import issues, government regulations, technological change forecast, and political and ecological trends/problems.

VI. *Price.* Includes economic structure of producing industry, price history and future forecast, factors determining price, cost to produce and deliver, tariff and import regulations, effects of quality and business cycle changes on price, estimated profit margins of each supplier, price objectives of suppliers, potential rock-bottom price, and price variance among user industries.

VII. *Strategy to reduce cost and/or assure supply.* Includes considering forecasted supply, usage, price, profitability, strengths and weaknesses of suppliers, the company's position in the market, and its plan to lower cost and to assure supply. It also includes consideration of the option to make the item in-house, use a short-term or long-term contract, acquire or develop a producer, find a substitute, import, hedge, perform value-engineering/analysis, and negotiate volume commitments with suppliers.

VIII. *Appendix.* Includes general information such as specifications, quality requirements and methods, freight rates and transportation costs, storage and handling, raw materials reserve; and statistics, for example, price, production, and purchase trends.

Suppliers

While the first two research areas—purchased materials, products, or services and commodities—were directed primarily at the item being purchased, the third area is directed at the source of the item. The previous two areas were the *what;* this one concerns *from whom.* Obviously, the buyer or sourcing team is better able to select or create best-in-class supply sources and to prepare for and successfully conduct supplier negotiations with more knowledge about present and potential suppliers and their method of operation and market position. Likewise, it is only through structured and formalized supplier performance measurement systems that supply managers can assess the results of their selection decision and use that information in future decisions. With greater discipline, consistency, and focus across the organization, the supply group can better capture and communicate the contribution of suppliers and supply to the organization's strategy.

Chapter 10, "Supplier Selection," addresses the issue of supplier evaluation in detail. The main point of that chapter was that each purchase must be assessed according to its value to the organization's final customers and the risk associated with the acquisition. Comparisons between and among suppliers for any given good or service may focus on any number of factors including supplier competitiveness in terms of price, contract terms and conditions, delivery/supply assurance, quality, replenishment programs, service, and technology. Clearly, effective supplier research for either selection or performance metrics requires alignment of research objectives with organizational strategy to ultimately deliver value to the final customer.

There are 9 specific topic areas in the category of supplier research. Many of these areas were explored in greater detail in Chapter 10.

Analysis of Financial Capacity

A key tool in risk assessment is the investigation of the financial health of current and potential suppliers. This assessment should predict the risk level the buying organization faces based on the probability of the supplier encountering financial problems, identify the potential effects on the buying firm, and enable the buyer to develop risk minimization strategies. Often, the finance department conducts this analysis, but in some cases it is the responsibility of supply analysts or a cross-functional team. Either way, if the dollar value and risk are high, then the analysis must be thorough and complete. For example, purchasers of computer software and hardware from substantial manufacturers have been surprised suddenly to find that their supplier "has gone bankrupt."

Analysis of Production Facilities

In the quest for lowest total cost, it is important to collect data on the supplier's physical facilities, emphasizing capacities and limitations. Review and analysis of production processes may lead to process improvements and cost savings. (See Chapter 17, "Services," for a discussion of the analysis of service providers.)

Finding New Supply Sources

It is often worthwhile to search for new suppliers. Research and long-range planning may lead to reverse marketing where the buying firm persuades a supplier to develop the ability to meet the buyer's needs now and in the future. Chapter 10, "Supplier Selection," and Chapter 19, "Supplier Relations," address sourcing and reverse marketing.

Supplier Cost Analysis

Supplier cost analysis (along with value analysis) has become a common research focus, because it produces large and immediate savings. Estimates of supplier costs can be developed for both products and services and should include direct material, direct labor, engineering, tooling, plant/facilities overhead, general and administrative expense, logistics/distribution costs, and profit. Understanding a supplier's cost structure is a powerful tool in negotiations, effective management of supply chain costs, determination of a fair and reasonable price, establishment of target prices, and evaluation of the efficiency of processes. See Chapter 9, "Cost Management and Negotiation," for more details.

Relationship Classification

By forming a partnering arrangement or strategic alliance with a single source, both buyer and seller can focus on joint problem solving, process improvements, and increased profitability. Developing closer relationships with single sources can reduce risks by binding together the futures of the two organizations in a way that encourages cooperation, trust, and commitment to mutual success. Analyzing the supplier's management capabilities and anticipating all contingencies is essential before negotiating a complete contractual agreement.

Quality Assurance of Purchased Materials

It is useful to develop a system with suppliers to reach agreement on quality standards, arrive at quality yields, determine training needs of supplier production and quality personnel, establish a system for mutual tracking of quality performance, and determine needed corrective action. Quality-related metrics might include parts per million (PPM), A-ranked parts rejections, and slippage in quality or delivery targets.

Supplier Perception Survey

A systematic survey of suppliers' perceptions about the buying firm and its supply process and practices can identify how the buyer/seller relationship could be improved. This information can be used to review and modify supply organization and policy.

Supplier Sales Strategy

A better understanding of a supplier's objectives and the means it is using to achieve these goals allows the buyer to anticipate the supplier's actions. The supplier can then design a supply strategy to provide for continued supply at lowest total cost.

Countertrade

Many countries have countertrade clauses in government contracts requiring local content, usually specified as a percentage or as a fixed-dollar-value amount. This essentially is a barter agreement, and some supply analysts are responsible for gathering and analyzing the data that form the basis for such agreements. (See Chapter 14 for a detailed discussion.)

Supply Processes

Adequate knowledge about purchased items and their suppliers are important in attaining maximum value from the purchasing dollar. This knowledge does not, however, ensure that the supply transactions will be handled in the most efficient manner. Efficient supply processes reduce the supply operating expense. Research may be conducted to improve administration of the process, ensure speed and cost-effectiveness by eliminating unnecessary steps, and automate where possible through Internet and intranet applications. Specific topic areas include the requisition to pay flowpath and may focus on any or all of the steps in the process. (See Chapters 3 and 4 for a detailed discussion about supply processes and technology applications.)

According to quality guru W. Edwards Deming, it is poor processes, not people, that are typically the cause of problems. However, good people are instrumental in transforming a poor process into an excellent one. Therefore, the supply department's hiring, retraining, retaining, and succession planning are important aspects of supply processes.

Assessing Research Results

Supply research can contribute substantially to the ability of the supply department to cope successfully with future materials uncertainties, growing services spend, and the demands for greater supply effectiveness.

SUPPLY PLANNING PROCESS

The actual supply planning process starts with information derived from the annual sales forecast, production forecast, and general economic forecast. The sales forecast will provide a total measure of the requirements of materials, products, and services to be acquired by purchasing; production forecasts will provide information on the location at which the materials, products, and services will be required; and the economic forecast will provide information useful in estimating general trends for prices, wages, and other costs.

In most organizations, less than 20 percent of the number of line items purchased account for over 80 percent of the dollars spent. Once high-value purchases have been identified, the broad forecast can be broken down into specific plans. The next step is to make price and supply availability forecasts for each of the major categories or commodities.

The estimates of material and service consumption are broken down into monthly and quarterly time periods. These quantities are checked against inventory control data that take into account lead times and safety stocks and compared to price trend and availability forecasts to develop a buying plan. Market conditions must be considered. If the forecasts predict ample supply availability and a possible weakening in prices, a probable buying policy will be to reduce inventories to the lowest level that is economically feasible. If, however, the forecasts predict a short supply and increasing price trend, the buying strategy needs to ensure availability through stock on hand, contractual agreements, or forward buying. In forecasting trends that will affect the availability and price of component parts, the conditions expected for the forecasted period in the industries in which the parts' suppliers operate also must be considered.

After the monthly and quarterly unit quantities and estimated price per unit are tabulated and modifications made as a result of developing a buying plan, individual buyers make an analysis of the items for which they are responsible. Further modifications in prices may be made because of the objectives or target cost that they have established to guide their activities for the period.

Any uncertainty, such as in lead times, or requirements forecasts make planning difficult.

SUPPLY BUDGETS

The supply budgeting process should start with a review of supply goals and objectives, followed by a forecast of action and resource needs to meet the goals, and then the development of a budget. Four separate supply budgets are commonly developed:

Materials (operations) purchase budget. The materials or operations budgeting process begins with an estimate of expected operations, based on sales forecasts and plans. Investments in materials can be substantial, and shortages can lead to expensive stockouts.

The primary advantage of the materials budget-planning process is that it identifies cash flow commitments and isolates problems well in advance of their occurrence. Sensitivity analysis can provide management an opportunity to explore and/or develop alternatives. Typically the materials purchase budget has a planning horizon of one year or less, except in the case of high-dollar, complex, long-production-cycle products, such as aircraft or power plants where a multiyear budget is needed.

MRO budget. The MRO budget covers a purchase plan, typically for a 12-month period, for maintenance, repair, and operating supplies. The large number of individual line items makes it infeasible to budget for each item; past ratios such as MRO cost adjusted by anticipated changes in inventory and general price levels are used.

Capital budget. The capital expenditure plan often has a multiyear horizon, based on the firm's strategic plan for product lines, market share, and new ventures. Decisions can be made on projected capital purchases based on production needs, obsolescence of present equipment, equipment replacement needs, and expansion plans. Considerations in capital budgeting include length of supplier lead times, cost of money, anticipated price escalation, and the need for progress payments to equipment suppliers.

Administrative or operating budget. The annual administrative budget, based on anticipated operating workloads, includes all of the expenses incurred in the operation of the supply function. This includes salaries and wages; space costs, including heat and electricity; equipment costs; information technology charges; travel and entertainment expense; office supplies; educational expenditures for supply personnel; postage, telephone, and fax charges; and subscriptions to trade publications. Last fiscal year's budget is compared to actual expenditures to reconcile any substantial differences. Typically, this comparison is done monthly to control operating expenses and detect problem areas promptly. After reviewing the past history, the next fiscal period budget is prepared to make provisions for salary increases, personnel additions or deletions, and estimates of all other expenses as anticipated by the requirements of the supply plan. The final budget is then coordinated with the organization budget.

PERFORMANCE MEASUREMENT SYSTEMS

The supply function, as a major decision area in the allocation of most organizations' resource stream, should be a "major player" in developing overall strategy, executing this strategy, and capturing the results for future decisions. In this text we address three fundamental questions: (1) How can the supply function contribute effectively to organizational objectives and strategy? (2) How can the organizational objectives and strategy properly reflect the contribution and opportunities offered in the supply arena? (3) How can the contribution of supply be captured and communicated? The third question is the focus of this section.

The Value of Supply Metrics

For supply to exert the influence needed to produce results, it needs the respect and support of the CEO. While an increasing number of senior executives recognize that a properly organized supply function, staffed by competent employees, is capable of significant contributions, others remain unconvinced that, if given the opportunity, supply can deliver significant results. To receive recognition as a major contributor to organizational success, supply's contribution must be effectively captured and communicated. It is a major challenge to improve supply performance metrics and evaluation methods and to get validation of supply's results.

The benefits of a careful appraisal of supply performance are many: (1) It focuses attention on the priority areas, making it more likely that objectives will be realized; (2) it provides data for taking corrective action, if needed, to improve performance; (3) by isolating problem areas, it should help to develop better internal relationships; (4) it spotlights training needs of personnel; (5) the possible need for additional resources, for example, personnel or information technology, is documented; (6) it provides information to senior management about supply's contribution; and (7) those people performing at a better-than-normal level can be identified and rewarded, which should improve motivation in the organization.

The Challenges

The old adage, "if you don't measure it, you can't manage it," still applies today. Most managers recognize both the need for performance appraisal and the difficulty in developing meaningful supply metrics and methods of evaluation. Research in organization theory and human behavior has demonstrated that, to attain effective results, there must be a clear definition of the purpose and objectives or goals expected of the function and its employees. A major problem in many organizations has been the lack of clearly defined objectives for the supply department and its personnel. Unless it can be determined what is to be evaluated, the question of how to evaluate has little meaning. Therefore, the first challenge is establishing clear objectives.

Setting Objectives

The chief purchasing officer has the responsibility for determining general objectives for the function and the coordination of such objectives with the strategic objectives of the company. An underlying assumption is that the designated metrics support the organizational mission. Identifying industry-accepted performance metrics and linking them to the organizational mission is a critical first step in developing an effective supply performance measurement system. In addition, there must be a quality process for managing improvement, a link to recognition and rewards systems for supply personnel, internal business partners, and suppliers.

Once established, the overall targets are provided to subordinates as general guidelines for decision makers to use to establish the objectives that will govern their activities for some period of time. When properly administered, the individual's objectives act as a motivating force to give direction to work and subsequently a basis for appraising performance. An individual's motivation and satisfaction from accomplishing objectives is driven in part by the degree of responsibility the individual exercises in establishing and implementing objectives.

Two areas of performance measurement are necessary in a world-class supply organization: supplier performance measurement and supply management performance measurement. These are closely related because supply's main focus is capturing the contribution of suppliers to the organization. The following sections address these areas.

Measuring Supplier Performance

Collection and analysis of performance data is the basis for determining how good a job the supplier is doing. This information also allows for more intelligent decisions about sources for rebuys and more useful feedback to current suppliers about areas of improvement. In partnering arrangements or alliances, the performance of the supplier is assessed regularly to reveal cycle time reductions, opportunities for process improvements, cost reduction, and quality and service improvements. Regular performance assessment is a catalyst for continuous improvement.

There are many metrics that may be included in a supplier performance measurement system. Some organizations limit metrics to a few critical metrics, while others develop systems that track hundreds. There should be a clear link between data and decisions to avoid expending excessive resources capturing information that is never used by decision makers. Some of the more common metrics are discussed in the following section.

Key Supplier Performance Indicators

Direct measures quantify supplier performance at the time work is completed. Examples are on-time delivery, number of rejects, increase in sales after a marketing campaign, and cycle time to develop a specific product/service/technology in a development stage. Automation of real-time metrics such as on-time delivery measures and careful selection of more time-consuming data collection activities help to reduce the time spent measuring results.

The supplier scorecard may include a summary statement of the supplier's cost, quality and timeliness performance and a compilation of satisfaction surveys, real-time metrics, variance of invoice amounts to estimates or contract negotiated rates, and other contract-related terms.

Price is one of the most common metrics in supply and supplier performance assessment. There are a number of different ways to measure price performance. These include old price versus new price, lowest acceptable initial bid versus final price, actual versus budget, and supplier quote versus final quote. Another useful means of evaluating the reasonableness of prices actually paid is to compare actual price to an index of market prices. This can provide a good reading on whether the trend of prices paid is better or worse than that being experienced by the overall market.

Supply Management Performance Metrics

Capturing supply management's contribution to the organization is a necessary and challenging task. Traditionally, firms have concentrated on analyzing their own internal trends, by comparing their current supply performance with their own past performance, to determine improvement. Increasingly, senior supply executives are focusing on developing metrics that capture both the hard-dollar contribution and the "soft" or indirect supply contributions discussed in Chapter 1. Interesting efforts are being made to capture supply's contribution along three dimensions: revenue enhancement, asset management, and cost management. Supply managers also are working with finance and internal business partners to validate supply's contribution.

Each organization has its own unique needs, and measures must be tailored to fit the situation. However, there are 12 guidelines managers should follow to establish a measurement system:

1. Metrics need to be designed for use at a point in time.
2. Each organization has specific measurement needs at a given point in time.
3. Measures should address financial results, supplier performance, IT systems, and internal practices and policies.
4. Measures must change frequently.
5. Trend analysis often is useful.
6. Measures should not be overdone or underutilized.
7. Measures are only tools.
8. Benchmarking is a source of new ideas and measures.
9. Senior management must see value in the measures used.
10. Measures can show the effectiveness of supply and identify areas needing improvement.
11. The credibility of measures must be ensured.
12. Continuous improvement in supply depends on measurement.

Supply management performance can be measured according to any number of metrics. Three key issues must be addressed: (1) setting targets, (2) establishing effective metrics, and (3) getting internal validation.

Setting Targets

In the planning process, initiatives and targets can be identified for the following fiscal year. For example, cost savings initiatives can be identified and prioritized jointly with internal business partners. In some organizations, these savings are built into budgets and become part of operating plans. During the year, supply personnel track savings, which are validated by finance and internal business partners. The finance manager ensures acceptance of the volumes used and timing of the savings and judges between cost savings and cost avoidance.

One of the key evaluation tools used in most organizations is the budgetary process. If the materials purchase, MRO, capital, and purchasing administrative budgets are carefully prepared, based on realistic assumptions about the future, they do provide a reasonable standard against which actual expenditures can be compared. If significant variances between budget (standard) and actual have occurred, in the absence of documented evidence that the assumptions on which the budget was based have changed, then a judgment can be made that performance was either superior or less than satisfactory, depending on whether the variance was positive or negative.

Standard costs also are used in many organizations to evaluate the supply department's pricing performance. Standard costs should be set based on anticipations of future overall market price movements; to do this with any degree of realism, supply must have a major input in setting such price/cost standards. If the standards are set solely by cost accounting, based almost completely on historical cost performance, then they lose much of their utility as a standard for judging performance. But if realistic standards are set, taking into account overall economic and market trends, then a practical and useful standard for measuring price effectiveness is provided.

ESTABLISHING METRICS

Metrics can be grouped into two broad categories, efficiency and effectiveness. Supply executives must determine the key performance indicators for supply in alignment with the key performance indicators for the organization as a whole.

Efficiency Metrics

The traditional approach to measuring supply performance focused on efficiency, which emphasizes price and departmental operating efficiency. Performance measures include purchased material price reductions, operating costs, and order processing time. As discussed in Chapter 1, purchasing makes a direct contribution to the bottom line of the firm because of the profit-leverage effect of purchasing. Efficiency or operating metrics attempt to capture how efficient the supply process is. The required information varies by the type of industry but typically includes total dollar volume of purchases, total dollars spent for department operating expenses, and total number of purchase orders issued.

These figures may be used to calculate average figures and percentages to show

1. Average dollar cost of the purchase orders written as

$$\frac{\text{Dollar cost of operating the department}}{\text{Number of POs written}}$$

2. Operating costs as a percentage of total dollar volume of purchases.
3. Operating costs as a percentage of total dollar volume of sales.

Comparing the above figures and ratios with similar figures for previous time periods provides some perspective on the efficiency of the supply function. However, these reports are of little use in providing a basis for evaluation of how effectively the supply function is providing the materials and equipment needed at the lowest total cost, considering quality, service, and the needs of the user. Note that the lowest price is not necessarily the lowest total cost.

Effectiveness Metrics

Effectiveness metrics attempt to measure how well something is done. These measures include evaluating direct and indirect contributions to final customer satisfaction, profit, revenue enhancement, or asset management. En-route or interim measures might include the quality of supplier relations or levels of internal business partner satisfaction. The benefits may come from reductions in operating costs or materials costs, enhancements in the performance of others (quality improvements in materials that lead to fewer defects and more satisfied end customers), shorter lead times, faster time-to-market, and/or increased sales due to increased value in the eyes of the end customer.

Operating Reports

Supply operating reports are prepared on a regular basis—monthly, quarterly, semiannually, or annually—and can be classified under the following headings and include

1. Market and economic conditions and price performance.

   a. Price trends and changes for the major materials and commodities purchased. Comparisons with (1) standard costs where such accounting methods are used, (2) quoted market prices, and/or (3) target costs, as determined by cost analysis.[3]
   b. Changes in demand–supply conditions for the major items purchased, and the effects of labor strikes or threatened strikes.
   c. Lead time expectations for major items.
2. Inventory investment changes.
   a. Dollar investment in inventories, classified by major commodity and materials groups.
   b. Days' or months' supply, and on order, for major commodity and materials groups.
   c. Ratio of inventory dollar investment to sales dollar volume.
   d. Rates of inventory turnover for major items.
3. Purchasing/supply operations and effectiveness.
   a. Cost reductions resulting from supply research and value analysis studies.
   b. Quality rejection rates for major items.
   c. Percentage of on-time deliveries.
   d. Number of out-of-stock situations that caused interruption of scheduled production.
   e. Number of change orders issued, classified by cause.
   f. Number of requisitions received and processed.
   g. Number of purchase orders issued.
   h. Employee workload and productivity.
   i. Transportation costs.
4. Operations affecting administration and financial activities.
   a. Comparison of actual departmental operating costs to budget.
   b. Cash discounts earned and cash discounts lost.
   c. Commitments to purchase, classified by types of formal contracts and by purchase orders, aged by expected delivery dates.
   d. Changes in cash discounts allowed by suppliers.

Measures of supplier relations require looking at the relationship from both sides. Measures of supplier performance include the traditional aspects of quality, delivery, and cost, but also more qualitative dimensions such as communication and cooperation. The quality of the service provided to the supplier by the buying organization also is measured.

Using end-customer satisfaction as a measure of the effectiveness of supply makes a lot of sense because the actions of supply affect customer satisfaction. In reality, the true impact of supply may be difficult to determine.

Many of the more valuable contributions made by supply and suppliers are difficult to measure. These include attempting to capture supply's contribution to increasing speed to market, asset/resource utilization, increase in cost avoidance, process improvements, improved level of service, revenue generation, and new product/service value engineering.

If supply is to make a strategic contribution to the competitiveness of the organization, it must focus on quality, cost, customer service, and cycle time. To this end, supply must emphasize the creation of a competitive supply base and capture suppliers' contributions to competitive advantage.

[3] One useful means of evaluating the reasonableness of prices actually paid is to compare actual price to an index of market prices. This can provide a good reading on whether the trend of purchasing's prices paid performance is better or worse than that being experienced by the overall market.

Cost Metrics

Cost management is widely recognized as a key performance area for supply. Most people recognize that price paid is only one component of the total cost of ownership. Efforts to develop metrics that effectively capture the total cost impact of a decision or action often fall short. There are four cost categories that might be measured: (1) cost savings, (2) cost reductions, (3) cost avoidance, and (4) process cost savings. Reportable savings might come from discounts, payment terms, renegotiations of prices, deferrals of payments, extended payment terms, standardization, supplier participation, process improvements, alternate material suggestions, change of shipment routings, design/specification changes, and innovative logistics.

Validating Results

Internal validation of results has become a goal of many senior supply executives. Often, supply is responsible for developing and implementing savings initiatives and capturing the year over year savings. Finance adds credibility by validating the impact of the savings on profit or loss considering factors such as inflation, volume, market movement, and so forth. Internal business partners confirm credibility by signing off on the reported savings, while signifying joint ownership and accountability for goals and outcomes. Any discrepancies between targets and outcomes can be discussed and resolved jointly.

Appraising Team Performance

Effective team performance, like effective individual performance, is more likely to occur if specific goals and objectives are established for the team as a whole and if evaluation and reward systems, such as salary increases, promotions, and bonuses, foster participation and performance. Managers in many organizations struggle to develop appraisal and reward systems that foster team participation and output without ignoring individual performance.

Evaluating team performance can be tricky. Three options are possible:

1. Each team member's manager evaluates the individual. However, the manager may be relatively uninvolved in the team and evaluating from a distance. Also, different managers may evaluate similar performance differently. The lack of consistency may result in lessened commitment and lowered morale of the team members.
2. Team members evaluate each other. This ensures that those closest to the team activities perform the evaluations. However, the team members may not be truly objective in evaluating the overall team performance.
3. A joint evaluation or 360-degree process is used. Team members evaluate each other (including the team leader); the team leader evaluates each member; and an external manager evaluates overall team performance.

Supply Performance Benchmarking

Benchmarking is a process of evaluating a company's work methods, processes, service levels, or products against meaningful standards to answer the question, "How are we doing, compared to other firms?" Averages and ranges for specific metrics provide data for analysis to allow a company to make better decisions about those changes needed to develop industry best practices and, in turn, superior performance. Industry standards for *overall* firm performance (such as profit, sales, and return on assets) long have been available through published financial reports. But performance numbers for the purchasing/supply function have not been available because of competitive concerns. However, in today's globally competitive business environment, it is essential to monitor an organization's performance relative to its competitors.

Performance benchmarking measures *what* results organizations have achieved in their purchasing/supply activities, and process benchmarking attempts to determine *how* an organization achieves results. To conduct a process benchmarking study, practices used by top-performing organizations are identified and a team visits the top performer in an attempt to identify its best practices. Because no two organizations are identical, direct comparisons are difficult to make. A performance benchmarking study is required to identify the superior performers. In 1989 CAPS Research began collecting data from organizations to develop purchasing performance benchmarks or standards for measuring quality or value.

As of early 2004, CAPS Research had benchmarking reports available for aerospace and defense, banking, cable telecommunications, carbon steel, chemical, computer and telecommunications equipment, diversified food, DOE contractors, electronics, engineering and construction, higher education, investment recovery, life insurance, machinery, mining, municipal governments, petroleum, pharmaceutical, semiconductor, ship building, state and county governments, telecommunications services, transportation, and utilities. Several of these industries have been benchmarked a number of times to identify performance trends.

The CAPS Research benchmarking data give supply professionals the reference point to evaluate their own organization's performance. As an independent and impartial, not-for-profit research organization, CAPS can collect these data from competing firms. CAPS' researchers aggregate the data and report the average and range for performance data from the largest 10 to 20 firms in an industry. Individual firms and their specific numbers are never identified.

CAPS has established 20 standard benchmarks to enable cross-industry comparisons:[4]

1. Purchase dollars as a percent of sales dollars.
2. Purchase operating expense as a percentage of sales dollars.
3. Purchase operating expense as a percent of purchase spend.
4. Purchase operating expense per purchasing employee.
5. Purchasing employees as a percent of company employees.
6. Purchase spend per purchasing employee.
7. Percent purchase spend managed/controlled by purchasing.
8. Average annual spend on training per purchasing employee.
9. Percent of training time spend for instructor-led training.
10. Percent of training spend for Web and/or computer-based training.
11. Total cost savings as a percent of total savings.
12. Cost avoidance savings as a percent of total savings.
13. Cost reduction savings as a percent of total savings.
14. Percent active suppliers accounting for 80 percent of purchase spend.
15. Percent of purchase spend with diversity suppliers.

[4] CAPS Research, http://www.capsresearch.org/standard, August 2004.

16. Percent of active suppliers who are e-procurement enabled.
17. Percent purchasing spend via e-procurement.
18. Percent of purchase spend via e-auctions.
19. Percent of purchase spend via procurement cards.
20. Percent of purchase spend via strategic alliances.

Conclusion

Research and metrics are two components of a successful supply management process. Without adequate research about purchased items, commodities, suppliers, and the supply process, it is impossible to make optimal decisions that contribute to organizational success. And, without effective measurement systems, it is impossible to validate the success of research and decision making by supply professionals. Therefore, research and measurement initiatives are well worth the investment of resources.

Questions for Review and Discussion

1. How does value analysis differ from value engineering?
2. What are the various subject areas of supply research? Which area do you think would be most productive in (*a*) the short run and (*b*) the long run?
3. In what ways might a firm organize to do supply research? What are the advantages and disadvantages of each? Which would you recommend in a (*a*) small organization, (*b*) a medium-sized organization, and (*c*) a large organization?
4. What questions would be asked in a commodity study? Where would you obtain the information?
5. What is the difference between a supply plan and a supply budget? In which areas should a supply budget be prepared? How would these budgets be established?
6. Why isn't there a standard system for evaluating supply performance that could be used by all types of organizations? How difficult would it be to develop such a standard system?
7. What are the key metrics of supply performance?
8. Are standard costs and budgets useful in the appraisal process? Under what conditions?
9. Why would an organization want to "benchmark" its supply function? How would it do this?
10. What is the difference between performance benchmarking and process benchmarking?

References

CAPS Research Report of Cross-Industry Standard Benchmarks. http://www.capsresearch.org, April 2004.

Carter, Phillip, and Trish Mosconi. *Strategic Measures and Measurement Systems for Purchasing/Supply*. Tempe, AZ: CAPS Research and McKinsey and Company, 2004.

Hartly, Janet L. "Collaborative Value Analysis: Experiences from the Automotive Industry." *Journal of Supply Chain Management*, Fall 2000, pp. 27–32.

Kaufmann, Lutz. "X-BSC—Measuring the Performance of Truly Strategic Supplier Relationships." *PRACTIX,* CAPS Research, vol. 7, March 2004.

Miles, Lawrence D. *Techniques of Value Analysis and Engineering.* 2nd ed. New York; McGraw-Hill, 1972.

Case 13–1

City of Granston[5]

On November 25, Ted Barton, the new purchasing manager at the City of Granston in Canada, was considering a contract extension for two years for the supply of mineral aggregates (rock, sand, and gravel). The contract had to be signed within a week.

CITY OF GRANSTON

The City of Granston had an annual budget of $700 million and employed 9,000 people. There had been a steady population increase over the past two decades. The purchasing department consisted of three support staff, six buyers, and a manager. City budgets were usually adjusted annually to cover the cost of inflation.

THE AGGREGATE INDUSTRY

The city purchased about $3 million worth of aggregates for road construction and repairs and construction projects. The local mineral aggregate sector consisted of three major extracting and processing companies—Lamoulin, Richmond, and Atlantic—and several smaller ones. Lamoulin and Atlantic owned the two dominant concrete production facilities.

The local aggregate industry was near capacity with major construction projects underway and increased demand in export markets.

AGGREGATE PURCHASING

A request for quotation had been issued in 2000 for a three-year agreement for the supply of aggregates, with prices firm for the first three years. If the parties agreed, a two-year option was available, with prices being subject to inflation.

Lamoulin and Richmond were the only two bidders and each received about half of the total contract with each bidder quoting for separate components of the total aggregates contract (see Exhibit 1).

On November 25, both Lamoulin and Richmond sent notice that they were willing to extend the current three-year contract to five years. Both wanted an increase of 2 percent to cover the increased cost of doing business. The suppliers were referring to the Consumer Price Index (CPI) clause in the agreement for price reviews. This clause allowed the supplier an annual price increase based on the change in the CPI. According to the city engineers' department, both suppliers had performed reasonably well during the past three years. Because of a significant slump in the local construction industry, both suppliers had voluntarily lowered their prices by about 3 percent after year one of the contract. However, in the past few months the local economy had shown signs of revival.

EXHIBIT 1
A Selection of Mineral Aggregates Supplied by Lamoulin and Richmond

Description	Original Price	Current Price	New Price Request	City Requirement (metric tons)
Screening*	9.80	9.59	9.78	3,000
Crushed rock*	8.80	8.57	8.74	6,500
Drain rock**	12.20	11.88	12.11	3,000
Tailings**	8.00	7.80	7.95	75,000
Mulch**	7.10	6.98	7.12	250,000

Prices include delivery and are in $Cdn based on annual estimated requirements.
* Lamoulin
** Richmond

[5] This case was prepared by Larry Berglund, C.P.P., MBA, and Collin Ashton, C.P.P., December 2003.

TED BARTON

Ted Barton had become purchasing manager for the City of Granston after having worked in private industry as a supply manager for several decades. He had been selected because the city's administrators wished to integrate supply better into the overall decision processes and to help search for better value for the taxpayer's dollars. Shortly after arriving on his new job, Ted Barton hired a part-time professional to help him develop better metrics for the city's supply function. One of the metrics that concerned Ted was the city's price performance. Thus, he developed a representative basket of 128 city requirements for which the amount used appeared to vary little from year to year. For this basket he asked his assistant to develop a price index, going back three years, starting with a base of 100.0 (see Exhibit 2).

Ted's assistant also developed a list of key cost indicators based on published indices from a variety of sources (see Exhibit 3).

THE DECISION

Ted Barton wondered whether any of the metrics he had recently developed were relevant for his decision on whether to extend the current mineral aggregates contract.

Since a significant number of existing city contracts were also of the multiyear, extendible type, he believed his actions on the aggregate contract might have a bearing on how to deal with other requirements. Having only one week left, he wondered what action to take.

EXHIBIT 2 City of Granston Price Index for a 128-Item Basket of City Requirements

				Current Year		
Year	**3 Years Ago**	**2 Years Ago**	**1 Year Ago**	**Q-1**	**Q-2**	**Q-3**
Cost of supplies (basket of goods)	100.00	.9199	.9446	.9477	.9410	.9614

EXHIBIT 3 Selected List of Key Cost Indicators

					Current Year	
Key Indicators	**3 Years Ago**	**2 Years Ago**	**1 Year Ago**	**Q-1**	**Q-2**	**Q-3**
Business prime rate (%)	7.000	6.875	4.250	4.750	5.00	5.00
CPI	111.4	114.7	116.2	121.9	122.0	122.2
Fats & oils	161.82	165.38	194.44	218.99	221.02	236.98
Raw industrials	258.06	235.55	231.72	258.69	260.01	269.91
Textiles	236.39	230.50	221.41	234.29	241.01	239.83
Diesel fuel	50.36	52.56	54.34	65.04	56.41	58.69
Coarse road salt	57.28	52.91	52.91	52.91	52.91	52.91
Natural gas	4.50	6.08	3.82	6.22	6.00	5.96
Copper (US$ per ton)	1788.00	1578.00	1559.00	1663.00	1641.00	1753.00
Metals subindex	236.06	193.55	178.92	201.50	207.09	218.15

Case 13–2

Industrial Products Corporation (IPC)

Maggie Agnelli, the packaging purchasing manager for IPC, wondered what she should say in tomorrow's meeting with the plant manager of Branco, a major supplier. In the last three quarters, Branco's quality performance rating had shown a steady decline. It was essential for Maggie to get the plant manager's cooperation to avoid future problems.

IPC

IPC, a diversified manufacturing organization offering a wide range of products to both industrial and consumer markets, employed approximately 1,100 people. Sales were $100 million a year, and the company had a long-standing track record of successful business performance.

QUALITY CONTROL

Contributing to the success of IPC was a commitment to strict quality standards in purchasing. Coordination between the supplier and IPC's plant was crucial to avoid production slowdowns. Contact was maintained directly between plant personnel and sales representatives. When a problem in the manufacturing plant arose due to the supplier's product, the appropriate sales representative was immediately notified by fax via a standard form called "Nonconformance Action Report" completed by the plant operator closest to the problem. The sales representative was required to return, by fax, a standard "Feedback Form" to acknowledge the problem and explain how it was to be solved.

Supplier deviations from standard, as reported on the Nonconformance Action Report, were also forwarded to each purchasing manager. The supply assistant compiled these forms, together with information collected on a number of other supplier performance criteria, such as accuracy of the quantity delivered, shipments on time, and accuracy of paperwork (see Exhibit 1). Each quarter, each purchasing manager used the information collected to compute a "Supplier Performance Rating." Suppliers were all rated on the same scoring criteria.

The criteria and scoring system implemented by IPC was developed internally and reflected the key aspects of supplier performance deemed to be important by IPC management. Vendors received a copy of the scoring criteria so that they were fully aware of how they were evaluated. At the end of each quarter, they were advised of their rating. IPC maintained detailed documentation of supplier activity and variance from norms.

The rating criteria included three categories: quality, delivery, and continuous performance, with quality accounting for the largest portion—50 percent of the total rating. Within each category there was a list of items. Each item was scored according to the supplier's provision of that item, on a scale from 0 to 4. Scores were then weighted and totaled. A total performance rating for the quarter was derived by summing categories (see Exhibit 2 for Branco's scoring sheet). The supplier's maximum possible score was 4. An overall rating of 3 was considered the minimum acceptable performance rating.

BRANCO

Maggie had been watching Branco's performance ratings for the last three quarters with some concern. Although the problems incurred each quarter were rectified by Branco, the next quarter brought even more problems. As a result, Branco's performance rating had dropped further each quarter. Finally, in the most recent quarter, Branco's rating dropped below the minimum acceptable standard of 3 (see Exhibits 2 and 3). When Branco's sales representative, Lonnie Crowbak, received the rating, she had called Maggie immediately, and she was just as concerned. They agreed that a meeting was necessary right away, and that IPC's production manager, Bill White, and Branco's plant manager, Joe Kakavalakus, must attend. They agreed to meet at IPC.

Branco was the supplier of packing cartons for IPC's abrasive products. The packing cartons were an odd size and required custom specifications. As a result, it had been necessary for Branco to customize production operations to meet the unique requirements of IPC. Branco, however, had become the only supplier of all custom packing cartons to IPC. As a result, IPC could not source a custom product from a different supplier easily or quickly. Branco delivered on a daily basis, and its yearly sales to IPC amounted to about $280,000. Custom work required a substantial commitment from both parties. The relationship of trust and certainty between IPC and Branco had taken a long time to solidify.

EXHIBIT 1 Supplier Performance Scoring Criteria

Item	Grade	Criteria
Quality		
Item	**Grade**	**Criteria**
Rejected and nonconforming	4	No rejected or nonconforming shipments.
	3	Up to 5% of shipments nonconforming.
	2	>5–10% of shipments nonconforming.
	1	>10–20% of shipments nonconforming.
	0	>20% of shipments nonconforming.
Process capability, data/samples	4	Less than 1% outside control limits and samples/data received for all shipments.
	3	Up to 5% outside limits and 90–99% of shipments have samples/data.
	2	5–10% outside limits and 80–90% of shipments have samples/data.
	1	10–20% outside limits and 70–80% of shipments have samples/data.
	0	More than 20% outside limits and <70% of shipments have samples/data.
Delivery		
Item	**Grade**	**Criteria**
Quantity	4	All correct quantities (within tolerance).
	3	Up to 5% shipments incorrect (within tolerance).
	2	>5–10% shipments incorrect (within tolerance).
	1	>10–20% shipments incorrect (within tolerance).
	0	>20% shipments incorrect (within tolerance).
Time	4	All shipments on time (within tolerance).
	3	Up to 5% of shipments outside tolerance.
	2	>5–10% of shipments outside tolerance.
	1	>10–20% of shipments outside tolerance.
	0	>20% of shipments outside tolerance.
Paperwork	4	No missing lot numbers, packing lists, invoice errors, or other required documentation.
	3	Up to 5% of shipments have errors.
	2	>5–10% of shipments have errors.
	1	>10–20% of shipments have errors.
	0	>20% of shipments have errors.
Shipment condition	4	All shipments received in expected condition.
	3	Up to 5% of shipments have damaged pallets, inadequate packaging, or damaged cartons.
	2	>5–10% of shipments are damaged as above.
	1	>10–20% of shipments are damaged as above.
	0	>20% of shipments are damaged as above.

EXHIBIT 1 *(Concluded)*

Continuous Improvement		
Item	**Grade**	**Criteria**
Corrective action	4	Nonconformance Action Report/Supplier's response and implementation within 30 days.
	3	Nonconformance Action Report/Supplier's response and implementation within 31–60 days.
	2	Nonconformance Action Report/Supplier's response within 30 days.
	1	Nonconformance Action Report/Supplier's response within 31–60 days.
	0	No response within 60 days.
Cost, lead time, lot size reduction	4	Major reduction in unit cost, lead time, and lot size.
	2	Minor reduction in unit cost, lead time, and lot size.
	0	No reduction in unit cost, lead time, and lot size.

EXHIBIT 2 **Scoring Sheet**

Supplier Performance Rating
Branco
For Past 3 Months

		Item		Category		
Category	**Item Description**	**Score**	**Weight**	**Score**	**Weight**	**Total Score**
Quality	Rejected and nonconforming	3	0.65	1.95		
	Process capability, data/samples	2	0.35	0.70		
				2.65	0.50	1.33
Delivery	Quantity	4	0.30	1.20		
	Timely deliveries	4	0.30	1.20		
	Paperwork	4	0.20	0.80		
	Shipment condition	4	0.20	0.80		
				4.00	0.30	1.20
Continuous improvement	Corrective action response	3	0.50	1.50		
	Cost, lead time, lot size reduction	0	0.50	0.00		
				1.50	0.20	0.30
Total						2.83

EXHIBIT 3
Branco's Performance Rating

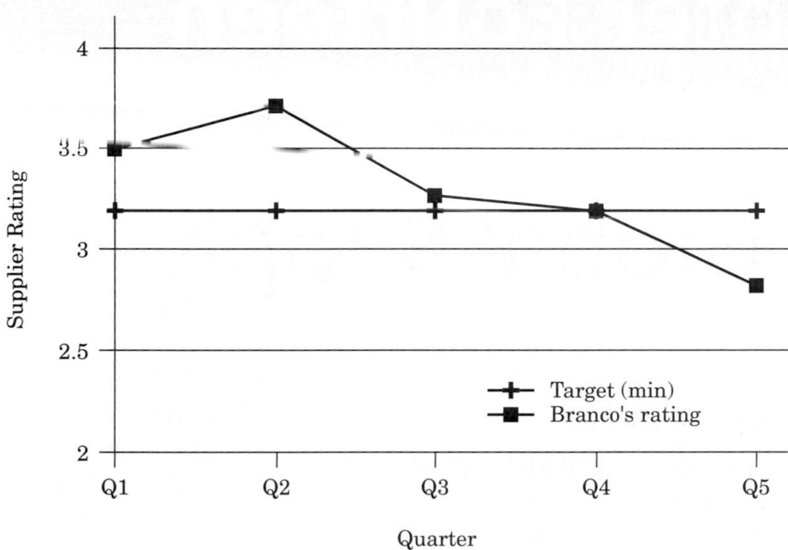

Quality problems were costly for IPC. A number of Branco's orders had included defective cartons due to overlapping flaps. Nonconformance problems such as this were typically not identified until a production run had started and equipment stalls occurred. Production used a fully automated line process, and a stall at one end resulted in a slowdown throughout. Because the defective cartons would not affect the end product to the customer, IPC continued the run in order to meet customer deadlines. However, the last Branco shipment of defective packing cartons resulted in a 30 percent production loss for an entire day's (two shifts) production. At full production, IPC ran 2,000 cartons per hour, with three operators at $18 per hour each.

THE MEETING WITH BRANCO

Over the last few years, Maggie felt things had changed drastically in the industry. At one time, as a purchaser, she might have demanded that the supplier make changes, "or else." This was no longer the case. Maggie reflected, "In such a tight market, you just don't drop suppliers. Relationships are everything."

In the meeting tomorrow morning, Maggie felt it was essential that she impress upon Lonnie and Joe her desire to continue a strong relationship. Yet, she would somehow have to convince Joe that something had to change at his end, without confronting him. Maggie wondered, "What should my agenda be for this meeting? What should I say?"

Chapter Fourteen

Global Supply

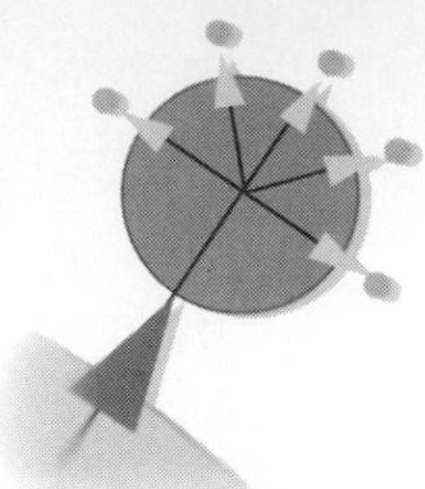

Chapter Outline

Key Questions for the Supply Manager

Should we

- Be more aggressive in sourcing globally?
- Play a more active role in initiating countertrade deals?
- Buy directly from the supplier or through an intermediary?

How can we

- Locate international suppliers?
- Organize to do global supply most effectively?
- Overcome the potential problems faced in supply from international suppliers?

Supply is becoming more global. Since the end of World War II, many different events and forces have relaxed barriers to world trade. Geopolitical events of the past decade, such as the creation of the European Union (EU), the disintegration of the USSR, the reunification of Germany, and the North American Free Trade Agreement (NAFTA), have created major opportunities for the global economy. Furthermore, changes to the global political landscape are continuing at a rapid pace.

In attempting to seize opportunities in the global marketplace, companies are deploying their organizations on a global scale. For supply managers, globalization represents the opportunity to deliver improved value to end customers by developing world-class supply relationships in terms of cost, quality, delivery, and performance. Global supply for many companies is a competitive necessity. Managing international supply networks presents a number of challenges in areas such as source identification and evaluation, international logistics, communications and information systems, and risk management.

THE IMPORTANCE OF GLOBAL SUPPLY

The world has grown a good deal smaller, figuratively, in the last 50 years, with the increased speed of transportation and communication. The Internet has accelerated the trend to global supply, making it easier for source selection and reducing communication problems. A survey by *Purchasing Magazine* found that 63 percent of the purchasing organizations surveyed said their firms sourced some goods offshore. Eighty percent of those that buy globally said that they increased offshore purchases over the previous five years, and 64 percent expected to see a corresponding increase in the coming five years.[1]

The total value of world merchandise imports in 2001 was $6.4 trillion. However, international trade is not restricted to goods alone. World commercial services imports in 2001, such as transportation, construction, communications, computer and information, insurance, and financial services, were $1.4 trillion. As evidence of the growth in world trade since the Second World War, the value of worldwide merchandise trade imports grew by a factor of 95 times between 1948 and 2001.[2]

[1] "Global Sourcing to Grow—But Slowly," *Purchasing,* May 18, 2000, pp. 24–28.

[2] World Trade Organization, *International Trade Statistics 2002*, p. 34.

The total value of U.S. merchandise imports in 2001 was $1.2 trillion. Although Canada and the United States remain important trading partners, there has been a growth in imports from other parts of the world to North America. In 2001, U.S. merchandise imports from Asia and Western Europe represented 36 percent and 17 percent of total imports respectively.

Reasons for Global Purchasing

The reasons for sourcing abroad are many and vary with the specific requirement. However, the underlying, summary reason for using an international supplier is that better value is perceived to be available from that source than from a domestic supplier.

The specific factor that makes the international buy look attractive will vary (technological know-how can shift from one country to another over time, the ability and willingness to control quality can change, and, from time to time, a stronger U.S. dollar makes the price of offshore goods more attractive). There are at least 10 specific reasons that may cause an international supplier to be selected as the preferred source.

1. Unavailability of Items Domestically

The first and oldest reason for international trade has been that domestic sources were not available. For example, cocoa and coffee, certain spices and fruits, chrome, and palladium are available only from certain international sources. And as the comparative economic advantage shifts, some manufactured products—for example, certain office equipment such as desktop computer printers and video equipment—also are available only from international producers. Consequently, for many organizations, global supply has become a necessity.

2. Price

Most studies show that the ability of an offshore supplier to deliver product in the United States or Canada at a lower overall cost than domestic suppliers is a key reason to buy internationally.

While it may seem surprising that an offshore supplier can produce and ship an item several thousand miles at lower cost, there are several reasons why this may be the case for a specific commodity:

A. The *labor costs* in the producing country may be substantially lower than in North America. Certainly this has been the case for many of the producers in the Far East and is a key reason why many U.S. firms have set up manufacturing facilities there. Companies chase low labor costs and move facilities to those countries with the most attractive wage rates. Many companies that moved to South Korea, Hong Kong, Singapore, or Taiwan have now moved to Malaysia, Indonesia, Thailand, China, or the Philippines. A recent study found that average wage rates in Mexico were approximately 10 percent of average wage costs in the United States and approximately 13 percent of average wage costs in Canada. By comparison, the same study found that wage costs in China were less than half of the Mexican labor costs.[3] However, when evaluating labor costs, factors such as productivity and quality also must be taken into account.

[3] Alisa Pride, "Supplier Migration to Emerging Markets," *Ward's Auto World,* April 2004, p. 28.

B. The *exchange rate* may favor buying offshore. When the U.S. dollar gets progressively stronger, as was the case in the late 1990s, it effectively reduces the selling price of products bought from international suppliers. A weakened dollar makes imports more expensive and less attractive.

C. The *equipment and processes* used by the international supplier may be more efficient than those used by domestic suppliers. This may be because their equipment is newer or because they have been putting a greater share of their gross domestic product into capital investment. A good example of this is the steel industry in the Far East.

D. The international supplier may be concentrating on certain *products and pricing* export products at particularly attractive levels to gain volume. While there are many attempts to prevent dumping practices, control of this is complex and has never been particularly effective. Some countries and regions have developed infrastructures and supply networks that support the efficient production of certain goods; for example, integrated circuits, computers, and computer parts in Malaysia; jewelry in Italy; clothes and shoes in China; and wire and cable assemblies in Mexico.

3. Government Pressures

North American firms produce many goods that are sold (exported) around the world. The United States exported $731 billion in 2001, while Canadian exports reached $260 billion.[4] It makes sense to consider the alternatives of buying from suppliers in customer countries; also many multinational firms accept that they have a social responsibility to buy product from suppliers in nations in which they operate plants, as a means of developing those nations. Additionally, many nations insist as a condition of sale of a major product—for example, aircraft—to their country that the seller agree to buy a specified value of goods in that country. These types of arrangements are called *offset agreements,* covered in more detail later in this chapter.

4. Quality

While the quality level of the international sources generally is no higher than from domestic suppliers, on some items it is more consistent. This is due to several factors, such as newer, better capital equipment; better quality control systems; and the offshore supplier's success in motivating its workforce to accept responsibility for doing it right the first time (the zero-defects concept). Also, some North American firms buy internationally to round out their product line, with domestic suppliers furnishing "top-of-the-line" items and international suppliers filling in some of the "low-end" holes.

5. Faster Delivery and Continuity of Supply

Because of limited domestic capacity, in some instances the international supplier can deliver faster than the domestic supplier. The international supplier may even maintain an inventory of products in North America, available for immediate shipment.

6. Better Technical Service

If the international supplier has a well-organized distribution network in North America, better supply of parts, warranty service, and technical advice may be available than from domestic suppliers.

[4] World Trade Organization, *International Trade Statistics 2002,* p. 25.

7. Technology

Increasingly, as domestic and overseas firms specialize, technological know-how in specific lines varies. Particularly in the case of capital equipment, such as for the primary metals industry (steel and aluminum), international suppliers may be more advanced, technologically, than their North American counterparts.

8. Marketing Tool

To sell domestically made products in certain other countries, it may be necessary to agree to purchase specified dollar amounts from suppliers in those countries.

9. Tie-in with Offshore Subsidiaries

Many North American firms operate manufacturing, distribution, or natural resource-based companies in other countries. A conscious decision may be made, particularly in the case of developing countries, to support the local economy by purchasing there for export to North America.

10. Competitive Clout

Competition tends to pressure the domestic supplier to become more efficient, to the long-term benefit of both that supplier and the buyer. Purchasers use imports or the threat of imports as a lever to pressure concessions from domestic suppliers.

POTENTIAL PROBLEM AREAS

While it is not possible in this chapter to give a complete discussion of all the potential problem areas faced in international buying and the methods for minimizing the impact of each, the major ones can be highlighted. The same principles of effective supply discussed throughout this book apply to international supply, but some unique problems arise when dealing across country boundaries. Seventeen potential problem areas will be highlighted. The astute buyer will recognize that he or she must consider the total cost of ownership, and not just the initial purchase price, when evaluating an international source.

1. Source Location and Evaluation

The key to effective supply is, of course, selecting responsive and responsible suppliers. Internationally, this is sometimes difficult because obtaining relevant evaluation data is both expensive and time-consuming. However, the methods of obtaining data on international suppliers essentially are the same as for domestic suppliers (discussed in Chapter 10). In addition to the background data obtained (discussed later in this chapter under "Information Sources for Locating and Evaluating Suppliers"), certainly the best method of obtaining detailed data is an on-site supplier visit. Because a visit to a supplier(s) in another country is expensive and time-consuming, it must be planned in great detail. If the dollars and risk involved are great, the on-site visit is a necessity. Firms doing a great deal of international buying will make frequent visits to overseas sources; for example, in a firm buying millions of dollars' worth of electronics equipment, the responsible supply manager spends a significant percent of his or her time in the Far East visiting and negotiating with potential or actual suppliers.

There are alternatives to personal on-site visits, such as the use of consultants and local third-party purchasing organizations. The Internet has made information on potential sources more readily available, and e-mail represents a cost-effective method of communication.

2. Lead Time and Delivery

Improvements in transportation and communications have reduced the lead time for international purchases. However, there are four areas where the buyer should anticipate additional lead time:

A. Establishing credit for first-time international buyers often involves obtaining a letter of credit.

B. Even with improvements in transportation, the buyer may still experience delays, particularly with inland carriers in the foreign country.

C. Delays in U.S. and Canadian customs are also possible. Proper documentation and customs bonds help expedite shipments through customs. The customs bond allows goods to be released after inspection and lets the buyer pay duties later.

D. The time goods are in port, for both outbound and arrival, also depends on the number of ships in line for unloading and hours of port operations.

Selecting the mode of transport is an important decision in international sourcing because of long supply lines and greater risk of loss or damage. High-value, low-weight items may move by airfreight, and delivery time may be almost as short as from domestic suppliers. But if the purchased item is costly to transport, it should move by ocean shipment, and the lead time may be several weeks. This means that for high-bulk, high-weight, low-value commodities, such as steel, the buying firm must do a much longer-range planning job (which is possible in most firms) and must notify the offshore supplier promptly of any schedule changes. Also, the selection of the transportation carrier must be done with great care. To compensate for transport uncertainty, the buyer may insist that the supplier maintain a safety stock inventory in North America. Some type of performance bond also might be required.

Most large transportation services companies and international freight forwarders have information systems that allow shippers to track and trace shipments. Such information can be useful in inventory planning and can help identify potential problems, such as stockouts or production shortages.

3. Expediting

Because of distance, expediting an offshore firm's production/shipment is more difficult. This places a premium on knowing a supplier's personnel and ensuring that they are responsive. Some firms also arrange to have an expediter on contract in the offshore country or to use personnel from a company-owned subsidiary closer to the supplier to assist with expediting problems.

4. Political and Labor Problems

Depending on the country in which the supplier is located, the risk of supply interruption due to governmental problems—for example, change in government or trade disputes—may be quite high. The buyer must assess the risk and, if it is high, the buyer must establish some system to monitor these concerns so that warning signs of impending problems are flashed in time to devise an alternative solution.

5. Hidden Costs

When comparing an offshore with a domestic source, it is easy to ignore some of the costs in the offshore purchase. The buyer must compare total cost of ownership before opting for an international supplier. The following checklist of cost factors provides some examples of hidden costs.

- Foreign exchange premiums.
- Commissions to customs brokers.
- Terms of payment costs and finance charges: letter of credit fee, translation costs, exchange rate differentials.
- Foreign taxes imposed.
- Import tariffs.
- Extra safety stock/buffer and transit inventory, plus inventory carrying costs due to longer lead times.
- Extra labor for special handling.
- Obsolescence, deterioration, pilferage, and spoilage.
- Additional administrative expenses.
- Packaging and container costs.
- Business travel.
- Fees for freight forwarders, consultants, or inspectors.
- Marine insurance premium.
- Customs documentation charges.
- Transportation costs, including from manufacturer to port, ocean freight, from port to company plant, freight forwarder's charges, port handling charges, warehouse costs.

6. Currency Fluctuations

Should payment be made in the buyer's currency or that of the country in which the purchase is made? If payment is to be made in a short period of time, the currency exchange rate may be less of a problem. However, if payment is not due for several months or if the supply relationship lasts for a long time, the exchange rates could change appreciably, making the price substantially higher or lower than at the time the agreement was originally signed. Most significant world exchange rates float freely, and sometimes change rather rapidly, due to economic, political, and psychological factors. This means that the buyer, when contracting, also must make a forecast of how the exchange rates likely will move between now and the time of payment. In addition, certain countries from time to time impose restrictions and controls on the use of their currency. This requires that the buyer have a good source of financial advice. Probably the most conservative approach is to price in U.S. dollars, for the buyer then knows exactly what the cost will be, but this denies the advantage of a lower price if the dollar increases in exchange value between the time the contract is written and the time when payment is made. Various approaches are possible, such as pricing in the supplier's currency with a contractual limit to the amount of exchange rate fluctuation permitted, up or down. Or the really knowledgeable buyer may protect against an unfavorable rate change by dealing in foreign currency options. It is important that supply cooperate closely with finance to assure the corporation manages its currency risks and cash flows effectively.

7. Payment Methods

The method of payment often differs substantially in international buying than in domestic buying. In some instances, the international supplier may insist on cash with the order or before shipment. Suppliers with whom the buyer has established a long-term relationship may be willing to ship on open account. But the seller may insist that title to goods does not pass until payment is made. The instrument used in this case is a bill of exchange (draft), which the seller draws on the buyer and to which it attaches the shipping document before handing it to its bank for collection. The bank, in turn, sends the documents to a bank in the buyer's country, together with instructions covering when the documents are to be released to the buyer—normally at time of presentation—a sight draft. Or the supplier may insist on a letter of credit, which is drawn by the buyer's bank at the buyer's request, and guarantees that the bank will pay the agreed-on amount when all prescribed conditions, such as satisfactory delivery, have been completed.

8. Quality

It is extremely important that there be a clear understanding between buyer and seller of the quality specifications. Misunderstandings can be quite costly, due to the distances and lead times involved. Also, there could be a problem in interpretation of drawings and specifications. In addition, it is important that both buyer and seller agree on what quality control/acceptance procedures are to be used.

9. Warranties and Claims

In the event of rejection for quality reasons, what are the responsibilities of both parties? Due to distances, return and replacement of items is complex and time-consuming. Are there provisions for the buyer reworking the items? Who pays for rework, and how are the rework costs calculated? Obviously, these areas should be agreed to in advance of the purchase.

10. Tariffs and Duties

A tariff is a schedule of duties (charges) imposed on the value of the good imported (or, in some cases, exported) into a country. While, theoretically, the world is moving to eliminate tariffs through the various World Trade Organization agreements, tariffs still exist. The buyer must know which tariff schedule(s) applies and how the duties are computed. Additionally, the contract should make it clear who pays the duty—buyer or seller. A Certificate of Origin, issued by a proper authority in the exporting country, is the document used to certify the origin of materials or labor in the manufacture of the item. It is used to obtain preferential tariff rates, when available. The United States has adopted the Harmonized Tariff Schedule to provide a uniform, updated international coding system for goods moving in international trade.

The cost of noncompliance with import regulations can be staggering. In a case where containers are marked with incorrect country of origin, the costs can include delayed receipt of goods, charges for freight forwarders or attorneys to get the goods released from customs, remarking, storage, and time to fix the problem. For more serious offenses, fines may apply, legal action may be required, and seizure, and possibly forfeiture, of goods may occur.

11. Administration Costs

Global supply requires additional documentation, mainly for duty and customs, logistics activities, payment, and financial transactions. Even with developments such as electronic funds transfers and Internet-based communications systems, the administrative costs in international buying pose a major problem.

12. Legal Issues

If potential legal problems are a risk in domestic buying, they are several times greater in international buying. If delivery time is critical, a penalty or liquidated-damages clause tied to late delivery may be advisable. Also, a performance bond may be required; or a bank guaranty providing for payment in case of specified nonperformance may be substituted for the performance bond. Litigation is time-consuming and expensive; therefore, agreements to settle international trade disputes by international arbitration are becoming increasingly common.

The U.N. Convention on Contracts for the International Sale of Goods (CISG) went into effect January 1, 1988. The CISG applies only to the sale of goods and does not apply to services. As of 2003, 62 countries, including Canada, Mexico, and the United States, had adopted the CISG. The goal of the CISG is to create a uniform international law for the sale of goods. There are several key differences between the Uniform Commercial Code (UCC) and the CISG, and purchasers should be aware of them. These are:

A. Under the UCC, the terms of a contract may vary in the acceptance from the proposed contract and a contract still may exist. Under the CISG, however, no contract is created if the terms of acceptance differ from the proposed terms.
B. Under the UCC, the statute of fraud requires a written agreement if the value of the goods exceeds $500. Under the CISG there is no dollar limit.
C. Under the UCC, there are implicit warranties, such as warranty of merchantability, and a warranty of fitness for purpose. Under the CISG, there are additional warranties.

Purchasers should consider carefully the laws under which an international contract is governed. If trading with a company in a country where the CISG has been adopted, the CISG governs the contract and the buyer should understand the differences between the CISG and the UCC. CISG allows the parties to "opt out" and agree on other relevant law to govern the contract. However, unless another body of law specifically is stated and agreed upon, the CISG will apply automatically if both nations have adopted the CISG. Likewise, if the other party is from a country that has not adopted the CISG and wants to have its domestic law apply, the U.S. purchaser may try to get agreement on using the CISG.

Other laws affecting international transactions are the Exxon-Florio Amendment to the Omnibus Trade Competitiveness Act, the International Traffic-in-Arms Regulations (ITAR), antiboycott legislation, and the Foreign Corrupt Practices Act.

13. Logistics and Transportation

Logistics presents some of the biggest problems for buyers involved in international sourcing. The trend toward integrated logistics on the domestic side is mirrored by a similar move in global supply. Integrated logistics refers to the coordination of all the logistics functions—the selection of modes of transportation and carriers, inventory management policies, customer service levels, and order management policies. Logistics companies that provide a wider base of services, thereby allowing firms to coordinate logistics functions, should enable more cost-effective and competitive international sourcing.

Many firms outsource their logistics activities to third-party logistics providers. Deregulation and globalization have resulted in a series of mergers and alliances in the third-party logistics industry, as service providers attempt to provide a global presence for their major customers. International freight forwarders are becoming increasingly diversified, offering a number of value-added services, such as payment of freight charges, tracing and expediting shipments, making routing recommendations, issuing export declarations, and preparing certificates of origin. The growth of one-stop service providers is likely to continue and appears to be in congruence with intermodalism (for example, air-sea, rather than all air) and outsourcing.

14. Language

Words mean different things in different cultures. An American word (legitimate or slang) may have a different connotation in the United Kingdom or in South Africa (both English-speaking countries). Consider then the difficulties of communicating with someone who doesn't speak English, when everything must go through a translator and the North American buyer doesn't even know what connotations the words used by the translator have. Because of these language difficulties, some firms insist that the supply manager who is going to have repeated dealings with non-English-speaking suppliers be multilingual or take a language course prior to discussions with foreign suppliers. The buyer still will have to use an interpreter, but the buyer will be a bit more comfortable.

15. Communications

North American purchasers are used to instant communication when dealing with their domestic supply network partners. E-mail, phone, and fax all help make communication fast, inexpensive, and reliable. However, global supply can involve problems with communication. These relate to time zone differences and problems with the communication network itself. When dealing with suppliers in areas such as Asia, purchasers cannot simply pick up the phone and talk with their supplier any time of the day or night. Because of the time differences, some communication must be done in the evening or early hours of the morning. Furthermore, long-distance telephone calls add to the costs of global supply. Poor reliability of communication networks in some regions of the world also may create difficulties in some circumstances.

16. Cultural and Social Customs

Even in various parts of North America, business customs vary from area to area; for example, Boston or New York City compared with Houston or Birmingham. Certainly business/social customs vary even more widely in other countries. Good purchasers do not focus only on the economic transaction but also on the noneconomic needs of their supply network partners.

Furthermore, problems caused by cultural misunderstandings can lead to higher supply chain costs. Therefore, purchasers need to have cross-cultural skills and must adjust to their suppliers' customs if they are to be effective in communicating and negotiating with suppliers.

In general the following guidelines should be followed:[5]

A. Even if English is spoken, speak slowly, use more communication graphics, and avoid the use of metaphors and jargon.

B. Bring an interpreter to all but the most informal meetings. Allow extra time to educate interpreters on issues.

C. Document in writing the main conclusions and decisions.

D. Learn about the country's history and taboos.

E. Do not use first names unless invited to do so.

F. Get cultural advice from professionals or your own company employees, not from supplier representatives in the United States.

G. Expect negotiations to last longer with some cultures as the supplier learns to accept you and your company as a customer.

17. Ethics

Because of perceived problems involving U.S. firms dealing with foreign customers or suppliers, Congress passed the Foreign Corrupt Practices Act (FCPA) in 1977. Basically, this law prohibits U.S. firms from providing or offering payments to officials of foreign governments to obtain special advantages. The FCPA distinguishes between transaction bribes and "variance" or "outright" purchase bribes. The FCPA does allow transaction bribes or facilitating payments ("grease") to persuade foreign officials to perform their normal duties, such as getting a phone installed or processing papers. The types of actions that might trigger an investigation into outright or variable bribes are payments of large commissions, payments to individuals who do not render substantial services, and payments made in cash and labeled miscellaneous. If the North American supply professional has little experience with a particular environment, it is essential that he or she become familiar with the FCPA, the Omnibus Trade Act of 1988, and individual country customs.

INCOTERMS

The shipping terms and responsibilities are more complex in international sourcing than in domestic transportation. The International Chamber of Commerce has created Incoterms (International Commercial Terms) as a uniform set of rules to clarify the costs, risks, and obligations of buyers and sellers in an international commercial transaction. Almost any foreign purchase or sale contains a reference to Incoterms. These rules were first published in 1936 and are modified periodically. The most current version is Incoterms 2000. The 13 Incoterms have been grouped into four different categories:[6]

[5] Dick Locke, *Global Supply Management,* New York: McGraw-Hill, 1996.

[6] Edward G. Hinkelman, *Dictionary of International Trade,* 4th ed., Novato, CA: World Trade Press, 2000.

Group E—Departure

1. EXW: Ex Works (*named place*). The seller/exporter makes the goods available at his or her premises and the buyer assumes all costs and risks from the seller's "named place" of business. The seller does not clear the goods for export and does not load the goods for transport. This arrangement places the greatest responsibility on the buyer, who assumes all risks from the time when the seller has made the goods available.

Group F—Main Carriage Unpaid

2. FAS: Free Alongside Ship (*named port of shipment*). The seller clears the goods for export and places them alongside the vessel for loading. The buyer takes possession at the dock of the port of export.
3. FCA: Free Carrier (*named place*). The seller clears the goods for export and delivers them to the carrier specified by the buyer at the named location, where the buyer takes procession. The "named place" is domestic to the seller and the carrier can be a shipping line, an airline, a trucking firm, a railway, or an individual or firm that undertakes to procure carriage by any of these methods of transport, including intermodal, such as an international freight forwarder. The buyer assumes all risk of loss or damage from the time the goods have been delivered to the carrier.
4. FOB: Free on Board (*named port of shipment*). The seller clears the goods for export and is responsible for the costs and risks of delivering the goods past the rail at the named port of export. Title passes once the goods are passed over the ship's rail. FOB is used only for ocean or inland waterway transport. It should not be confused with the conventional North American term "F.O.B."

Group C—Main Carriage Paid by Seller

5. CFR: Cost and Freight (*named port of destination*). The seller is responsible for clearing the goods for export, delivering the goods past the ship's rail at the port of shipment, and paying the costs to transport the goods to the named port of destination. CFR is used only for ocean or inland waterway transport and the "named port of destination" is domestic to the buyer. The buyer assumes responsibility for risk of loss or damage and additional transportation costs once the goods pass the ship's rail at the port of shipment.
6. CIF: Cost, Insurance, and Freight (*named port of destination*). The seller clears the goods for export, is responsible for delivering the goods past the rail at the port of shipment, pays the costs associated with transport of the goods to the port of destination, and procures and pays for marine insurance in the buyer's name for the shipment. The buyer assumes responsibility for risk of loss or damage once the goods pass the ship's rail at the port of shipment. CIF is used only for ocean or inland waterway transport and the "named port of destination" is domestic to the buyer.
7. CIP: Carriage and Insurance Paid (*named port of destination*). The seller clears the goods for export, delivers them to the carrier, and is responsible for paying for carriage and insurance to the named port of destination. In Incoterms 2000, the seller is also responsible for the costs of unloading, customs clearance, duties, and other costs if included in the cost of carriage, such as in small package delivery. CIP can be used for any form of transport including intermodal and the "named port of destination" is domestic to the buyer, but not necessarily the final delivery point.

8. CPT: Carriage Paid To (*named port of destination*). The seller clears the goods for export and delivers them to the carrier and is responsible for paying carriage to the named port of destination. In Incoterms 2000, the seller is also responsible for the costs of unloading, customs clearance for import, and duties where such costs are included in the cost of carriage, such as small package courier. The buyer is responsible for all additional costs, such as procuring and paying for insurance coverage. CPT can be used for any form of transport including intermodal and the "named port of destination" is domestic to the buyer, but not necessarily the final delivery point.

Group D—Arrival

9. DAF: Delivered at Frontier (*named place*). The seller clears the goods for export and is responsible for making them available to the buyer at the "named place," not unloaded or cleared for import. The buyer is responsible for procuring insurance, unloading, and customs clearance for import and assumes all risks from the time the goods have been delivered to the named point. Frontier can include any frontier, including the frontier of export. DAF can be used for any mode of transport, as long as the final shipment to the "named place" at the frontier is by land.
10. DDP: Delivered Duty Paid (*named place of destination*). The seller clears the goods for export and is responsible for making them available to the buyer at the named place of destination, including customs clearance for import. Therefore, the seller assumes all responsibilities for all costs associated with transportation to the named place of destination, including duties and other costs payable upon import. The buyer is responsible for unloading. DDP can be used for any mode of transport and the buyer assumes all risks from the time the goods have been made available at the "named place of destination."
11. DDU: Delivered Duty Unpaid (*named place of destination*). The seller clears the goods for export and is responsible for making them available to the buyer at the named place of destination. The buyer is responsible for customs clearance for import, duties, transportation costs to the final destination, and any other costs. This term is used when the named place of destination is other than the seaport or airport. The buyer assumes all risks from the time the goods have been made available at the named place of destination.
12. DEQ: Delivered Ex Quay (*named port of destination*). The seller clears the goods for export and is responsible for making them available to the buyer on the quay (wharf) at the named port of destination. The buyer is responsible for import clearance, duties, and other costs upon import, as well as transport to the final destination.
13. DES: Delivered Ex Ship (*named port of destination*). The seller clears the goods for export and is responsible for making them available to the buyer on board the ship at the named port of destination. The buyer is responsible for unloading and clearing the goods for import. The buyer assumes all risks from the time the goods have been made available at the port of destination.

Certain Incoterms apply to only sea transport: FAS, FOB, CFR, CIF, DEQ, and DES. EXW, FCA, CPT, CIP, DAF, DDU, and DDP apply to all modes of transport including intermodal. It is possible, and in some cases desirable, to agree to add wording to the

Incoterms that specifies buyer, seller, and carrier responsibilities. For example, agreeing to DDP terms obligates the seller to pay for import duties, but using the term "DDP VAT Unpaid" means that the seller is not responsible for paying value-added taxes.[7]

Incoterms do not (1) apply to contracts for services, (2) define contractual rights and obligations other than for delivery, (3) specify details of the transfer, transport, and delivery of the goods; (4) determine how title of the goods will be transferred; (5) protect either party from risk of loss; (6) cover the goods before or after delivery; and (7) define the remedies for breach of contract.[8]

In addition, packaging and insurance decisions in international supply are much more complex than in domestic buying situations. Although it is the responsibility of the seller to provide packaging, it is important that the buyer and seller agree on arrangements for packaging in the contract. Although many Incoterms do not obligate either the buyer or the seller to procure insurance, both parties should recognize the risks and make arrangements for suitable coverage.

INFORMATION SOURCES FOR LOCATING AND EVALUATING INTERNATIONAL SUPPLIERS

In international sourcing, the task of locating potential suppliers is more difficult than in domestic source selection. However, with some variation, similar types of information sources are available to the buyer, as follows:

1. The Internet can be used to gain access to Web sites for companies and government organizations. Most large and medium-sized companies have Web sites that describe their main products and services and many governments have extensive Web sites that provide a variety of information, such as trade statistics and assistance for importing and exporting goods and services.

2. A number of government sources are available. The U.S. Department of Commerce can supply current lists of names and addresses of foreign suppliers, by general types of products produced. The district offices, located in most major U.S. cities, can be helpful in obtaining this information. Almost all countries of the world maintain an embassy in Washington, D.C. The major industrial nations (and many of the lesser-developed countries) maintain trade consulates in the United States and Canada (typically in Washington, D.C., or Ottawa, but many also have an office in other major cities, such as New York, Toronto, Miami, New Orleans, Chicago, San Francisco, or Los Angeles). If requested, they will supply names of suppliers and background information, for their role is to promote exports from their country.

3. The chambers of commerce located in major cities in the United States and Canada and around the world will help buyers locate sources. The International Chamber of Commerce has contacts through its country branches around the world and will supply leads to possible sources.

[7] Ibid.

[8] Ibid.

4. Typically, the supply department of a company with experience in international buying is willing to share that information with other buyers, providing they are not direct competitors. The local associations of the Institute for Supply Management (ISM) and the Purchasing Management Association of Canada (PMAC) often can facilitate such an information exchange. The International Federation of Purchasing and Materials Management (IFPMM), made up of member nation associations, maintains a list of correspondents in many foreign countries. These are buyers and supply managers who have agreed to supply to buyers in other nations information on suppliers in their own countries.

5. There are a variety of supply chain partners that can help locate sources. Current domestic suppliers often are in a position to supply information and leads on noncompetitive suppliers and almost all the major banks have an international trade department. In addition to supplying information on currency, payment, documentation procedures, and governmental approval procedures, a bank's international trade department can assist in locating potential sources. Customers also can assist with locating international suppliers. This source of information can be especially useful when the customer also has international operations or markets for its products.

6. Every major industrial country has at least one supplier locator directory, similar to the commonly used *Thomas Register* for North American manufacturers. For example, *Kelly's Directory* publishes supplier locator directories for the United Kingdom as well as many of the countries in Europe, Africa, and Asia. The foreign trade consulate or embassy of any nation should be able refer you to the appropriate directory for their country. Dun & Bradstreet (D&B) also has offices in many countries and can supply a D&B report on many firms.

7. Importers and foreign trade brokers make it their business to keep abreast of developments in the supply base of the countries with which they deal, and they can give the buyer a great deal of useful information.

The evaluation of a specific supplier's capabilities is more difficult than locating the supplier. Two key sources of evaluation information are the shared experiences of other supply people, which usually can be obtained simply by asking, and the supplier visit, which was discussed earlier in this chapter. If a supplier visit is not made, the buyer should at least ask the potential supplier for information such as (1) a list of present and past North American customers; (2) payment procedures required; (3) banking reference; (4) facilities list; (5) memberships in quality, specification-setting associations; and (6) basic business information, such as length of time in business, sales and assets, product lines, and ownership.

GLOBAL SOURCING ORGANIZATIONS

The structure of a global supply organization is influenced by the location of the key suppliers and company operations, and the overall corporate organizational structure. Companies with a decentralized organization structure give business unit and/or local supply staff responsibility for international supply. In a centralized or hybrid structure, global supply activities can be coordinated through several organizational models. One approach is to create regional purchasing offices, such as the approach taken by Unisys. The global supply organization at Unisys has a chief purchasing officer for each of its four regions—the United States; Europe, the Middle East, and Africa; Asia and the Pacific; and Latin America and the Caribbean—each reporting to the corporate vice president of global procurement. Furthermore, the structure in each region was identical. The vice president of global procurement believed that some procurement activities, such as customer sales support, process management, and supplies and services, required close geographic proximity. However, commodity management represented one area where geographic location was not always important. While it was necessary to negotiate local and regional supply agreements for many commodities, responsibility was divided between the European and U.S. commodity purchasing organizations for its global suppliers. Discussions between the corporate vice president of global procurement and the commodity management directors for the United States and Europe led to consensus regarding lead responsibility for global commodities. Such decisions were based on supplier location, previous experience of the U.S. and European purchasing staff with the commodities in question, and staff availability.[9]

Another approach is the creation of a global commodity management organization. This approach makes sense when there are a large number of common requirements across facilities or business units and the supply base is not always located in the same geographic area as the buying company's operations. The global commodity managers are responsible for identifying world-class suppliers for important requirements common to the company's global operations. Meanwhile, local supply managers are allowed to focus on identifying capable local suppliers for requirements unique to their operation. Such was the case at the French electronics and media services company, Thomson (known as the RCA brand in North America), which had its main operations in North America and Europe but relied heavily on suppliers in Asia. Given the large number of common requirements and suppliers, along with the geographical spread of manufacturing and laboratory facilities, the vice president of worldwide sourcing deemed it essential to increase the staffing of global commodity management. Therefore, a number of global commodity coordinators positions were created, each assigned worldwide responsibility for a specific group of common requirements.[10]

A third approach to global sourcing is the creation of international purchasing offices (IPOs). International purchasing offices can be focused on the basis of commodities, such as important raw materials, or on the basis of projects, such as large capital projects. Typically, IPOs are used when the company does not have a presence in the same geographic region where important suppliers are located. The logic of establishing IPOs is that the local presence of supply personnel can provide better access to suppliers and lower total costs. IPOs facilitate activities such as local sourcing and review, supplier development, materials management, quality control, and payment and can employ local personnel thoroughly familiar with the language, culture, and way of doing business in that country or geographic area. Schneider Electric has established a number of IPOs, in countries such as China, India,

[9] Michiel R. Leenders and P. Fraser Johnson, *Major Changes in Supply Chain Responsibilities,* Tempe, AZ: Center for Advanced Purchasing Studies, 2002.

[10] Ibid.

Bulgaria, and South America. They have responsibility for sourcing, research, and market analysis. While the individual Schneider Electric plants work directly with international suppliers once the relationship is established, the IPOs are also available to handle issues that may crop up from time to time.[11]

INTERMEDIARIES

Should purchases be made direct from the supplier or through an intermediary? This depends on factors such as how much specialized international buying knowledge is available in the supply department and the volume and frequency of sourcing expected. Many firms use intermediaries for some or all of their global purchasing. The following list describes some of the options available.

Import brokers and agents. For a fee (usually a percentage of purchase value—and it can be as high as 25 percent), the broker or agent will assist in locating suppliers and handling required documentation. In most situations, title passes directly to the buying organization. The buyer, of course, must make sure the fee is reasonable with regard to the services performed.

Import merchant. The import merchant makes a contract with the buyer and then buys the product in its name from the foreign supplier, takes title, delivers to the place agreed on with the buyer, and then bills the buyer for the agreed-on price. Obviously, the buyer pays a fee (buried in the price paid) for the buying services provided.

Seller's subsidiary. Purchasing from the North American subsidiary of a foreign supplier is a common approach. The subsidiaries provide the benefits of having a better location (right time zone), conducting business in English, and accepting payments in U.S. dollars. They also may provide credit terms.

Sales representatives. Some companies hire sales agents to represent them in various regions of the world. Typically, sales representatives handle low volume/value contracts and are paid a commission by the supplier that is included in the price of the goods.

Trading company. A trading company is typically a large firm that normally handles a wide spectrum of products from one or a limited number of countries. Trading companies are used extensively by Japanese firms to move products into North America. The advantages to the buyer of using a trading company are (1) convenience; (2) efficiency; (3) often lower costs, due to volume; (4) reduced lead times because it often maintains inventory in North America; and (5) greater assurance of the product meeting quality specifications because the trading company inspects in the producing country before shipment. But, as with any supplier, the buyer should check out the trading company carefully.

COUNTERTRADE

Countertrade is a fancy term for a barter agreement, but with some twists. Barter has been around for years and takes place when payment between buyer and seller is made by the

[11] Susan Avery, "Global Purchasing Sharpens Schneider's Competitive Edge," *Purchasing* 131, no, 10, June 6, 2002, pp. 17–20.

exchange of goods rather than cash. U.S. firms, in times of shortage, often swap merchandise; for example, a utility trades fuel oil to another utility in exchange for copper cable, as a matter of expediency. However, the complexities of international trade, particularly with developing countries, have brought some new variations, with supply right in the middle of the action. There are five principal variations of countertrade:

Barter/Swaps

Barter involves the exchange of goods instead of cash. Typically, barter takes place when a country, which is short of hard currency, agrees to exchange its product for another country's product. This normally is a rather clean transaction, for the firms (countries) are exchanging equivalent dollar values. If goods of the same kind, for example, agricultural items or chemicals, are exchanged to save transportation costs, the arrangement is called a *swap.*

In a mixed barter, the seller ships product of a certain value—for example, motors—and agrees to take payment in a combination of cash and product—for example, wheat. It then is up to supply to resell the product for cash or to barter it to someone else. A commodity that changes hands twice is referred to as a *two-corner trade.* If it changes hands three times, it is a *three-corner deal.* Supply often gets involved in situations where working out the particular barters or swaps is both difficult and time-consuming.

Offset Arrangements

Offsets are distinguished by the condition that one part of the countertrade be used to purchase government and/or military-related exports. Under these agreements, in order to make the sale, the selling company agrees to purchase a given percentage of the sales price in the customer country. The negotiation usually starts at 50 percent and then goes up or down from there. Whatever the figure agreed to, it then is up to supply to figure out how it can spend the specified amount for worthwhile goods or products. In some instances, the goods purchased later are resold, putting the supply department largely in the role of a trading company. Such resale occurs when supply cannot locate a supplier of suitable, needed merchandise in the customer country and simply makes a purchase of goods (that hopefully later will be salable) to complete the deal. Even if specific deals are unprofitable, firms engaging in countertrade usually are looking for long-term, meaningful, and mutually advantageous relationships with the other country.

When other countries buy North American–produced merchandise, they often push hard for offsets to gain access to technology, to get U.S. dollars, to increase employment, and/or to help maintain political stability by protecting jobs and domestic producers.

Counterpurchase

Counterpurchase agreements require the initial exporter to buy (or to find a buyer for) a specified value of goods (often stated as a percentage of the value of the original export) from the original importer during a specified time period.

Buyback/Compensation

In buyback agreements, the selling firm agrees to set up a producing plant in the buying country or to sell the country capital equipment and/or technology. The original seller then agrees to buy back a specified amount of what is produced by the plant, equipment, or technology. Buyback agreements can span 10 or more years.

Switch Trade

In switch trades, a third party applies its "credits" to a bilateral clearing arrangement. The credits are used to buy goods and/or services from the company or country in deficit. Usually a broker or trading house handles the switch.

Countertrade is used in situations where a country has a shortage of foreign exchange or a shortage of credit to finance its desired trade flows, wishes to diversify its foreign exchange earnings, or is encouraging the development of the domestic economy by promoting labor-intensive exports. The number of countries participating in countertrade has increased steadily and includes most of the United States' main trading partners, such as Canada, the United Kingdom, and China.

Although the U.S. government generally views countertrade as contrary to an open free-trading system, it does not oppose participation by U.S. companies in countertrade transactions. According to section 309 of the Defense Production Act (as amended in 1992), the secretary of commerce has the responsibility of preparing a report to Congress detailing the impact of offset agreements on the U.S. defense industrial base. Consequently, U.S. firms entering into foreign defense sales contracts must report all offset transactions in excess of $5 million.

The exact value of international countertrade transactions is not known—secrecy surrounding the transactions prevents collection of these data in most situations. However, offset activity reported by the U.S. Department of Commerce found that between 1993 and 2000, U.S. defense contractors reported entering into 345 offset agreements with 32 countries involving export sales of 177 different systems with a total value of $48.6 billion.[12]

While countertrade traditionally was very common in the sale by U.S. firms of armament to foreign nations, its use has been extended into civilian government procurement projects, such as the sale of civilian aircraft, telecommunications, and technology systems. In the competitive global marketplace, the ability to meet countertrade requirements in a cost-effective manner represents a competitive advantage. Supply has a legitimate role in managing countertrade arrangements, and those responsible for negotiating arrangements with customers that involve countertrade should involve supply personnel early in the process in order to provide opportunities for feedback concerning cost implications, the status of the countertrade market, sourcing information, and the availability of suppliers and opportunities for barter.

Unfortunately, supply is not always involved in the decision to engage in countertrade, and becomes involved after the decision has been made, at the stage where potential counterpurchases are being evaluated. Given the risks of countertrade—the possibility of poor-quality goods and services, the development of unprofitable deals, and the acceptance of goods and services that do not match marketing channels—the supply function should be consulted in the proposal evaluation stage.

While in many instances countertrade arrangements may present complex problems to the selling firm's supply department in discharging the countertrade obligations, they may provide the opportunity to develop lower-cost sources of supply in the world marketplace. However, because it has become a "way of life" for many supply professionals, several guidelines are suggested:

[12] U.S. Department of Commerce, *Offsets in Defense Trade, Seventh Report,* July 2003.

1. Decide whether countertrade is a viable alternative. If a company does not have the organization to do the international sourcing required, it should refuse to participate.
2. Build the cost of countertrade into the selling price.
3. Know the country—its government, politics, and regulations.
4. Know the products involved and what's available.
5. Know the countertrade negotiation process—offset percentage, penalties, and time period.

The American Countertrade Association (ACA) is a group whose members include key U.S. manufacturers, exporters, and international trade financiers involved in selling and investing in a variety of industries, including electronics, commodities, telecommunications, power generation, defense, and aeronautics. The purpose of the ACA is to provide a forum to educate and network for the purpose of creating new ways to facilitate trade flows and investments into countries that either have difficulties externalizing hard currency or imposing certain countertrade purchase or offset obligations on vendors.

FOREIGN TRADE ZONES

Foreign trade zones (FTZ): are special commercial and industrial areas in or near ports of entry where foreign and domestic merchandise, including raw materials, components, and finished goods, may be brought in without being subject to payment of customs duties. FTZs are U.S. versions of what are known internationally as free trade zones. Merchandise brought into these zones may be stored, sold, exhibited, repacked, assembled, sorted, graded, cleaned, or otherwise manipulated prior to reexport or entry into the national customs territory. U.S. FTZs are restricted-access sites in or near ports of entry, which are licensed by the Foreign Trade Zone Board and operated under the supervision of the U.S. Customs and Border Protection Service. Zones are operated under public utility principles to create and maintain employment by encouraging operations in the United States that might otherwise have been carried on abroad.[13]

There are two categories of FTZs: general-purpose zones and subzones. General purpose zones handle merchandise for many companies and are typically sponsored by a public agency or corporation, like a port authority. Subzones are special-purpose zones, usually located at manufacturing plants. Subzones are usually preexisting manufacturing sites that operate under the guarantee of a local general-purpose site. There are no legal differences in the types of activities that can be undertaken at zones or subzones. According to government data, subzones accounted for approximately 85 percent of the $204 billion in activity in U.S. FTZs in 2001. In 2001 there were 150 FTZs, with 237 facilities using subzone status.[14]

Each FTZ differs in character depending upon the functions performed in serving the pattern of trade peculiar to that trading area. The six major functions that may be conducted within a zone are:

[13] U.S. Department of Commerce, 64th Annual Report of the Foreign-Trade Zones Board, 2002.

[14] Ibid.

Manufacturing. Manufacturing involving foreign goods can be carried on in the zone area. International goods can be mixed with domestic goods and, when imported, duties are payable only on that part of the product consisting of offshore goods. This activity offers an excellent opportunity for use of foreign trade zones. In some circumstances the final assembled product may qualify for reduced duties, or might have no duties imposed if it has more than 50 percent U.S. content of labor or components. Such merchandise can be classified as "American made" for purposes of export under NAFTA. Besides reduced duties, there is a saving on interest, because duty payments are not due until the merchandise leaves the FTZ and enters the United States.

Transshipment. Goods may be stored, repacked, assembled, or otherwise manipulated while awaiting shipment to another port, without the payment of duty or posting a bond.

Storage. Part or all of the goods may be stored at a zone indefinitely. This is especially important for goods being held for new import quotas or until demand and price increase.

Manipulation. Imported goods may be manipulated, or combined with domestic goods, and then either imported or reexported. Duty is paid only on imported merchandise.

Refunding of duties, taxes, and drawbacks. When imported merchandise that has passed through customs is returned to the zone, the owner immediately may obtain a 99 percent drawback of duties paid. Likewise, when products are transferred from bonded warehouses to foreign trade zones, the bond is canceled and all obligations in regard to duty payment and time limitations are terminated. Also, exporters of domestic goods subject to internal revenue taxes receive a tax refund as soon as such products move into a foreign trade zone.

Exhibition and display. Users of a zone may exhibit and display their wares to customers without bond or duty payments. They can quote firm prices (because they can determine definite duty and tax rates in advance) and provide immediate delivery. Duty and taxes are applicable only to those goods that enter customs territory.

When BMW announced its decision to build a $1.2 billion automotive assembly facility in South Carolina, it applied for FTZ subzone status. As an FTZ subzone, BMW received several benefits. It defers duty payments on imported vehicles and components until the vehicles actually enter the United States; because two-thirds of the plant's production is exported, BMW avoids paying U.S. duties on component parts used on vehicles that are exported; and component parts from overseas suppliers are delivered directly to the assembly facility, supporting JIT delivery arrangements.[15]

If the supply executive has large overseas suppliers or is contemplating importing substantial amounts of dutiable products, savings can be realized on duties or drawbacks, and on the cost of shipping both imported materials to plants in the hinterland and manufactured products back to the same port for export. The functions actually performed in any zone, in the last analysis, depend on the inherent nature of the trading and commercial community and demands made by users of zone facilities.

The principal reason for using an FTZ is to avoid, postpone, or reduce duties on imported goods, making imported goods more competitive in the U.S. marketplace and creating economic benefits for the local community through job creation. The potential disadvantages

[15] Beth M. Schwartz, "FTZ Success," *Transportation and Distribution* 40, no. 7, July 1999, p. 40.

of the FTZ are (1) the additional labor costs and operating and handling costs associated with its use and (2) the uncertainty of its long-term use due to changes in foreign trade agreements that are reducing and eliminating import duties.

Foreign Trade Zones Compared with Bonded Warehouses

Bonded warehouses are utilized for storing goods until duties are paid or goods are otherwise properly released. They are owned by persons approved by the Treasury Department and are under bond or guarantee for the strict observance of the revenue laws of the United States. The purpose of bonded warehousing is to exempt the importer from paying duty on foreign commerce that will be reexported or to delay payment of duties until the owner moves the merchandise into the host country. Goods can be stored for three years. At the end of the period, if duty has not been paid, the government sells the goods at public auction.

All merchandise exported from bonded warehouses must be shipped in the original package unless special permission has been received from the collector of customs. Any manufacturing must be conducted under strict supervision and the resulting items must be reexported.

Maquiladoras

Mexico's maquiladoras are examples of the foreign trade zone concept or industrial parks. Non-Mexicans can own the maquila, or plant, in the maquiladora in order to take advantage of low Mexican labor costs. Parts and supplies enter Mexico duty free, and products exported to the United States are taxed only on the value added in Mexico. There are nearly 4,000 maquiladora facilities currently operating along the U.S.–Mexican border, employing more than 1 million people, a source of $40 billion in Mexican exports.[16]

With NAFTA eliminating North American trade barriers, the future of the maquiladora operations has been called into question. However, in the meantime, maquiladora operations are a critical and successful dimension of Mexico's economy.

TIBs and Duty Drawbacks

A temporary importation bond (TIB) permits certain classes of merchandise to be imported into the United States. These are articles not for sale, such as samples, or articles for sale on approval. A bond is required, usually for an amount equal to twice the estimated duty. While there is a fee for the TIB, the net effect is that no duty is paid on the merchandise, provided it is reexported. The TIB is valid for one year, with two one-year extensions possible. However, if the goods are not exported on time, the penalty can be twice the normal duty, which is why the TIB must be for twice the normal duty.

Duty drawback permits a refund of duties paid on imported materials that are exported later. The buyer enters into a duty drawback contract with the U.S. government, imports the material for manufacture, and pays the normal duty. If the final manufactured or processed product is exported within five years of import, duty drawback can be obtained. There are three main types of duty drawback: direct identification drawback, substitution drawback, and rejected merchandise drawback. Provisions for duty refunds differ slightly under each type.

[16] Lara L. Sowinski, "Maquiladora's: Pending Changes on the Horizon," *World Trade,* September 2000, pp. 88–92.

FREE TRADE AGREEMENTS

In 1994, the North American Free Trade Agreement (NAFTA) took effect for the United States, Canada, and Mexico. Phased in over a 15-year period, NAFTA will eliminate tariffs and nontariff barriers to trade among the three member countries.

Canada and Mexico are the two largest trading partners with the United States and since the introduction of NAFTA, merchandise trade between the NAFTA countries has grown dramatically.

Until tariffs are totally eliminated, buyers must adhere to NAFTA's complicated rules of origin. Goods that are wholly produced in the United States, Canada, or Mexico are classified as "originating goods" and are eligible for preferential reduced tariff rates. Other goods are taxed as if they were from any other country. Filling out and filing the certificate of origin is a major problem for many importers because of inconsistent and product-specific rules and documentation. Purchasers can file an annual blanket certificate if they anticipate buying the same goods more than once a year.

Free trade has also shaped other parts of the world. The euro became the sole currency of the EU member states in 2002, providing a common currency that promised to allow for easier price comparisons and lower foreign currency transaction costs. In May 2004, membership in the EU was expanded by 10 new countries, bringing the total to 25 member states, with a total population of more than 450 million people.[17]

The World Trade Organization (WTO) continues to play an important role in shaping world trade. Following the Uruguay Round of trade negotiations, the WTO was formed on January 1, 1995. It replaced GATT, which had been in existence since 1947, as the international organization overseeing the multilateral trading system. In 2004, the WTO had 147 member countries, which account for more than 90 percent of world trade. Its overriding objective is to help trade flow smoothly, freely, fairly, and predictably. The WTO accomplishes this objective by administering trade agreements, acting as a forum for trade negotiations, handling trade disputes, monitoring national trade policies, assisting developing countries in trade policy issues, and cooperating with other international organizations. While GATT dealt mainly with trade in goods, WTO also has new agreements on trade in services and intellectual property rights.[18]

Conclusion

In our global economy, it is nearly impossible today for most companies to rely on the domestic supply base for 100 percent of purchased goods and services. For many firms, global supply management has become a reality, as they are forced to seek out world-class suppliers to maintain their competitive position. The benefits of global procurement extend beyond simple price and cost advantages. Firms may purchase products and services abroad to gain access to better technology, secure items not available domestically, or purchase better-quality products. While managing an international supply network can represent an important opportunity, it does provide a number of significant challenges. Consequently, the capability of managing global supply chains effectively can be a source of competitive advantage.

[17] The European Union On-Line, http://www.europa.eu.int.

[18] World Trade Organization, http://www.wto.org.

Questions for Review and Discussion

1. What are the factors/forces that have caused the increase in international trade? What changes do you think will occur in the next 10 years?
2. Why have North American firms become actively involved in global purchasing?
3. What do firms see as the principal advantages to be gained when they buy globally?
4. How can the buying firm minimize the problem areas connected with global buying? Which do you feel are most serious?
5. How can the buyer best get a list of potential international sources? Evaluate potential suppliers?
6. What are the pros and cons of buying direct versus using some form of middleman?
7. What are the forms of countertrade and what problems do they cause for the buyer? How can the buyer help make countertrade work?
8. How can the buyer make effective use of foreign trade zones?
9. What advantages are there for purchasers as a result of the North American Free Trade Agreement (NAFTA)? What is a certificate of origin? Why does the buyer need to be concerned with this?
10. What are Incoterms? What factors should be considered when selecting an Incoterm?

References

Avery, Susan, "Global Purchasing Sharpens Schneider's Competitive Edge," *Purchasing* 131, no. 10, 2002, pp. 17–20.

Bendorf, Robi, "Pay Attention to Labor Rates," *Purchasing Today,* August 1999, p. 14.

Forker, Laura B., "Countertrade's Impact on the Supply Function." *International Journal of Purchasing and Materials Management,* Fall 1995, pp. 37–45.

Hinkelman, Edward G., *Dictionary of International Trade,* 4th ed., Novato, CA: World Trade Press, 2000.

Kaufmann, L., and C. Carter, "International Supply Management Systems—The Impact of Price vs. Non-Price Driven Motives in the United States and Germany," *Journal of Supply Chain Management* 38, no. 3, 2002, pp. 4–17.

Larson, Robert K., and Ajay Adhikari, "The Euro: Ready or Not, It's Here!" *Ohio CPA Journal,* January–March 2000, pp. 8–12.

Leenders, Michiel R., and P. Fraser Johnson, *Major Changes in Supply Chain Responsibilities.* Tempe, AZ: Center for Advanced Purchasing Studies, 2002.

Locke, Dick. *Global Supply Management.* New York: McGraw-Hill, 1996.

Trent, R. J., and R. M. Monczka, "International Purchasing and Global Sourcing—What Are the Differences?" *Journal of Supply Chain Management* 39, no. 4, 2003, pp. 26–37.

World Trade Organization, http://www.wto.org, May 2004.

World Trade Organization, *International Trade Statistics 2002.*

Case 14–1

Global Pharmaceuticals Ltd.

Ian Grant was the purchasing agent for the Animal Health Group of Global Pharmaceuticals Ltd. in London, Ontario. In January, he was planning the transfer of production of eight products from the plant in Germany to the London facility. He wondered how he should manage the purchasing transition, particularly the supply of raw materials and packaging for these products.

GLOBAL PHARMACEUTICALS LTD. BACKGROUND

Founded in 1849, Global Pharmaceuticals Ltd. (GPL) was headquartered in New York and had established a worldwide reputation for excellence and innovation. The company employed more than 40,000 persons in 55 countries, and the products were sold in more than 150 nations. Last year, net sales were US $8 billion and net income exceeded US $1 billion, the highest level in company history.

The company was organized into three segments: Health Care, Animal Health, and Consumer Health Care. The Health Care Group marketed prescription drugs, medical implant products and medical devices. This group accounted for 87 percent of company sales. The Animal Health Group produced vaccines and other medicines for dogs, cats, livestock, and poultry. Animal Health's sales were approximately 8 percent of the total. The smallest division, the Consumer Health Care Group (5 percent of total sales), produced over-the-counter products such as suntan lotion, mouthwash, and shaving cream.

The company recently focused on its strategic mission of "discovering, developing, and bringing to market health-care products in an effective manner that fulfill unmet medical needs." A number of operations that either did not meet the company's goals or were not related to health care had therefore been recently sold or closed. A number of businesses that complemented GPL's strategy had also been acquired or were in the negotiation stage.

ANIMAL HEALTH GROUP

The Animal Health Group faced major changes. By the end of January, GPL would have acquired Jones Clarke Animal Health (JCAH), which would push GPL to the number one position in the world in animal health products. GPL had traditionally held the leading position in medicines for large animals, plus a strong presence in Latin America and Japan. JCAH, on the other hand, had leading product lines in companion animal products in North America and in vaccines worldwide, plus superior organizational strength in Europe and Australia. It was planned that the combination of these firms would lead to the creation of a single, integrated unit that would place GPL in a position to satisfy the Animal Health Group vision: "We will be The Driving Force in the animal health industry." Production sites for the joint company of JCAH and GPL numbered 36 in 30 different countries and there were seven research sites.

SUPPLIER APPROVAL PROCESS

In order to manufacture animal health products, GPL required a number of items, such as chemical compounds, syringes, bottles, boxes, and labels. Most of these items were subject to stringent regulatory requirements (content, measurement scale, language, dosage) that varied by country. At the London, Ontario, plant, the purchasing department was responsible for sourcing more than 1,100 raw material and packaging items worth in excess of $11 million (Canadian) per annum. All items had to be purchased from an authorized supplier of GPL. To become an approved supplier, the candidate had to pass a series of tests that could take up to one year to complete. The approximate procedure follows:

1. A copy of the Standard Operating Procedures for the product had to be provided, and these procedures should be accepted by GPL.
2. A Certificate of Analysis of a lot also should be provided, and this certificate had to match the Standard Operating Procedures.
3. Three samples from three different lots should be provided, along with the Certificates of Analysis for each lot.
4. The samples would be chemically tested by GPL, and the results had to match the Certificates provided and be acceptable to GPL.
5. The results would be analyzed and approval had to be received from the following areas: Product Development, Quality Control, and Manufacturing.

6. A small, pilot batch would be run at the GPL plant using the supplies, and the results would then be tested.
7. After the supplier had successfully passed steps 1 to 6 above, then supply would begin. The first three lots were to be fully tested by GPL, and, if accepted, then the supplier would become an Approved Supplier of GPL subject to periodic lot testing.

GERMAN PLANT CLOSURE

It was announced in October last year that its only plant in Germany would close by December of this year. The products produced there would be transferred to the London, Ontario, plant on a phased basis, starting in June and commencing full production a year later. It was planned that the German plant would increase production sufficiently to provide enough inventory to satisfy demand until the London plant could provide adequate supply. The addition of these eight products (see Exhibit 1) to the London portfolio would increase production at that plant by 30 percent. Capacity was not an issue.

By January it was apparent that the German plant would not be able to increase production for sufficient inventory to last the phase-in period due to low productivity rates and morale. Also, the German government would not allow the plant to run on overtime hours. It was clear that the transition to London would have to be achieved even earlier than planned to avoid stockouts.

The approved suppliers for the German plant consisted of both large and small operations that were located all over Europe. A sample of some of the suppliers were:

Name: E. Merk
Location: Karlsruhe, Germany
Size: Approx. 400 employees
Product: Chemicals

Name: R. Knof
Location: Karlsruhe, Germany
Size: Family operation, 3 employees
Product: Printing of barrel of syringes

Name: Union Plastics
Location: St. Didier-En-Valley, France
Size: 100 employees
Product: Syringe barrels and plungers for syringes

Name: Loffler
Location: Freyung, Germany
Size: 410 employees
Product: Syringe barrels and plungers for syringes

As Ian Grant contemplated his moves over the next six months, he wondered how he could ensure that the London plant had all the necessary supplies for production in an efficient and timely manner.

EXHIBIT 1
Global Pharmaceuticals Ltd., Animal Health Products to Be Transferred from Germany to London, ON

Product Name	No. of Formulations	Sizes	No. of Label Languages
Tetratex (injection)	1	1	8
Vetracil (tablets)	2	2	9
Baxotil (Suspension)	1	2	3
Baxotil (Paste for dogs)	1	2	13
Baxotil (Paste for cats)	1	2	13
Federex (Paste)	1	1	1
Vitopax (1% paste)	1	1	2
Vitopax (10% paste)	1	2	2

Case 14–2

Andrew Morton

Andrew Morton, customs and traffic coordinator at the Central Ontario University, in Toronto, had just received a call from Melissa Downing, finance manager at Canadian Marine Lines in Vancouver. It was April 3rd, and Melissa informed Andrew that representatives from Transport Canada had held up a shipping container because a university shipment from Shanghai had not been labeled and documented in accordance with regulations stipulated in the Transportation of Dangerous Goods Act. Andrew was particularly concerned because there were a number of other consignees of goods in the container, and he recognized that he needed to act immediately to resolve the situation.

CENTRAL ONTARIO UNIVERSITY

Central Ontario University was one of Canada's largest universities, with approximately 1,200 faculty and almost 25,000 students. Research was an integral part of the university's mission, and most full-time faculty were engaged actively in research projects.

Andrew Morton was the university's customs and traffic coordinator, which was part of the university's purchasing department. He was responsible for assisting faculty and staff with inbound and outbound transportation arrangements, including domestic shipments, imports, exports, internal equipment moving, and addressing of claims for lost or damaged shipments. The university did not have a central receiving facility for incoming freight, and all shipments were delivered by the carrier directly to the unloading dock of the building indicated on the order. A formal university shipping procedure documented responsibilities of parties involved in each transaction, such as the receiver, recipient, and document matcher.

THE BROMINE PENTAFLUORIDE SHIPMENT

Six months earlier, Peter Goris, a faculty member in the Department of Earth Sciences, placed an order for supply of bromine pentafluoride (BrF_5). Bromine pentafluoride is a colorless to pale yellow liquid chemical that is highly corrosive and reactive. It can be used as an oxidizer and a fluorinating agent in making fluorocarbons. However, breathing bromine pentafluoride fumes can cause kidney, liver, and lung damage.

Peter was conducting advanced research that required bromine pentafluoride of exceptional purity to be used in his experiments. Using the university's low-value purchase order process, which allowed users to deal directly with suppliers for purchases under $1,000, he placed an order for bromine pentafluoride with Shouwu International Trading Company (Shouwu) in Shanghai, China, FOB destination, freight prepaid. Shouwu was selected because they produced the chemical with the purity that Peter required. When Peter placed his order, Shouwu's sales representative, Haiyu Zhao, assured him that the shipment would be sent in compliance with the international maritime law and it would comply with Canadian regulations regarding the transport of dangerous goods.

Andrew first became aware of the shipment on March 15th, when he received a bill of lading from Shouwu, that indicated that shipment was expected to reach the Port of Vancouver in early April. He was concerned that a declaration of dangerous goods did not accompany the bill and the university could be held liable for any incidents once it entered the country. Consequently, Andrew decided to call Melissa Downing at Canadian Marine Lines, who would be handling the shipment in Vancouver. He informed her of the dangerous nature of the shipment, the shipper, the name of the vessel, the bill of lading number, the shipping company in China, and the port of origination. Andrew also prepared a package containing the appropriate shipping labels and documents so that the shipment could be legally transported from Vancouver to the university.

Later that same day, Andrew called his contact at Transport Canada, Sheryl Henderson, to inform her of the situation. Sheryl indicated that Transport Canada's policy was to hold Canadian importers fully liable for any and all violations of transport of dangerous goods regulations, even if the fault lay with the shipper. She expected that customs inspectors would isolate the container when it arrived and that the shipment could be delayed several days.

Peter was also able to get a copy of the invoice that afternoon. He found that the order value was $7,650, and it had been paid in full two months earlier.

Melissa contacted Andrew three days later to report that over a teleconference that morning, Haiyu Zhao had claimed that the shipment was not hazardous but contained only common, nontoxic household chemicals. Andrew now wondered if the shipment had been intentionally misrepresented.

ARRIVAL OF THE SHIPMENT

On April 3rd, Andrew received a telephone message from Melissa Downing that the container with the shipment of bromine pentafluoride had arrived and was being isolated by Canada Customs inspectors. As Andrew had feared, the shipment had been improperly identified on the shipping documents by the shipper as a nonhazardous substance. Melissa indicated that the container had begun incurring demurrage and handling costs, which were $44.90 and $43.00 per day, respectively. Furthermore, it appeared that there were other shipments in the same shipping container, possibly foodstuff and personal items, and there could be claims and other costs associated with holding up these shipments.

Later that afternoon, Andrew received the following e-mail from Melissa:

> Andrew, I just received a call from one of the consignees of goods in the container being held up in Vancouver due to this shipment from China. The company is Kohlpec Canada in Montreal and the contact person is Jason Kohl. Apparently the goods they have in the container are for Wal-Mart, who plans to assess them a late penalty if the shipment is delayed further. Wal-Mart has also threatened to cancel their next order. It is increasingly clear that you may be sued for damages if we can't get this problem resolved. It looks like there are 21 consignees in the container with our goods. Get back to me with how you intend to handle this situation.

Andrew recognized that he had to take steps to remedy the situation quickly. He felt that his earlier dealings with Sheryl Henderson had gone well under the circumstances and that she recognized that he had reacted in a responsible and timely manner.

As Andrew considered what could be done regarding the immediate situation, he also wondered what steps could be taken to avoid similar problems in the future. The director of purchasing, George Kerr, was aware of the situation and had asked Andrew to implement appropriate changes to the university's purchasing and transportation policies by the end of the month.

Chapter Fifteen

Public Supply Management

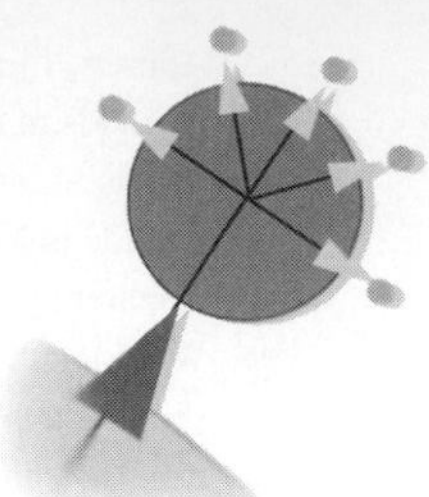

Chapter Outline

Key Questions for the Supply Manager

Should we

- Join a public buying consortium?
- Use a bid process to determine suppliers and prices?
- Incorporate new practices while still upholding our special responsibilities to taxpayers?

How can we

- Use local, small, minority, and women-owned suppliers effectively?
- Deal with outside pressures from our constituents?
- Balance transparency and confidentiality?

Public procurement covers the management of supply in public institutions and agencies as well as publicly owned entities. Taxes represent a major source of the funds expended in public supply. The objectives of sound supply management in the public sector are basically the same as for supply in the private sector: effective contribution to organizational goals and assurance of value for money spent. However, the unique environment in which public sector procurement operates presents special challenges. In every country, the public buyer is subjected to special laws, rules, and regulations and is ever mindful of the politically dictated targets while open to continuous public scrutiny. Public procurement agencies in the industrial world, including the United States, the United Kingdom, Canada, and Australia, share similar supply experiences whether buying pens and paper or NATO-specified equipment. This chapter will identify the major challenges faced by public supply managers and how they deal with them. Due to the size of its governmental spend, American policies and procedures will be highlighted although similar policies and procedures exist in other countries as well.

There are many different types of public agencies and institutions. They include federal, state (or provincial), county, and municipal levels, each with a wide array of subgroups. At the federal level, just imagine the differences between supplying the Department of Agriculture, the State Department, the Federal Reserve Bank, the White House, and the Department of Defense! In the field of education, publicly owned universities, colleges, and schools constitute a large subgroup. In the health sector, publicly owned hospitals and other care-giving institutions as well as research and monitoring bodies represent another major segment of the public spend.

Given that in various countries the percentage that government contributes to the gross domestic product (GDP) ranges anywhere from 25 to 50 percent, it is not difficult to envisage the economic and social impact of public supply. Therefore, the wise and effective spending of taxpayers' dollars ensures that government services benefit those for whom they are intended but also helps build taxpayer confidence and trust in government.

During the 1990s, a number of reform initiatives were undertaken in the United States to streamline government operations to "work better and cost less," with procurement reform representing a significant share of the projected total savings. The 1995 and 1996 congressional debates concerning the need to balance the federal budget in the next seven years showed the continuing interest of the public in more cost-effective government. By 2001, the work had moved from developing new laws and rules to actually implementing procurement reform in contracting offices and changing the behavior and thinking of government contract officers. The transition was from a culture in which purchasing was an audit group checking for compliance to a focus on value for money spent. By 2004 the United States faced a trillion-dollar budget deficit, out-of-control health costs, and a growing defense budget. Effective and efficient supply management in the public sector is more important than ever.

The objectives of governmental supply include (1) assurance of continuity of supply to meet the needs; (2) avoidance of duplication and waste through standardization; (3) maintenance and improvement of quality standards in goods and services purchased; (4) development of a cooperative environment between supply and the agencies and departments served; (5) obtaining of maximum savings through innovative supply and application of value analysis techniques; (6) administration of the supply function with internal efficiency; and (7) purchase at the lowest life cycle cost, consistent with quality, performance, and delivery requirements.

CHARACTERISTICS OF PUBLIC SUPPLY

Unique characteristics of public supply include source of authority, budgetary restrictions, outside pressures, government programs, interest costs, inspection, transportation and logistics, past performance and switching cost, transparency and confidentiality, and specifications.

Source of Authority

The authority of the public buyer is established by law, regulation, or statute, such as federal and state constitutions and laws and municipal ordinances. The public buyer must observe the appropriate legal structure under which purchasing operates; ultimate responsibility is to a legislative body and the voters who elect that body.

When questions of authority or the interpretation of the legal requirements arise, they are referred to the legal officer of the governmental agency (ultimately the attorney general's office in the case of federal or state purchasing). If legislative changes are needed to permit the public buyer to do a more effective buying job, the cooperation of the agency's legal advisor should be sought.

For the federal government, the General Services Administration (GSA) and the Department of Defense are the two main parties responsible for procurement. Since Congress passed a law in 1792 giving the Treasury and War Department the authority and responsibility for government purchases, a series of legislative requirements have focused on government supply. More notable among these were the Federal Acquisition Reform (FAR) Act of 1979 and the Competition in Contracting Act (CICA) of 1984. The Federal Acquisition Streamlining Act (FASA) of 1994 codified the ability of agencies to enter into contracts with multiple firms for the same or similar products, known as multiple award contracts (MAC). The Clinger-Cohen Act of 1996 provided for the use of multiagency contracts and what are known as *governmentwide acquisition contracts* (GWAC), in which one agency may pay an administrative fee to use contracts for information technology products and services operated by another agency. The U.S. federal government, like many of its counterparts in the world, has been anxious to improve both the efficiency and effectiveness of supply by reducing the costs of acquisition and improving value for money spent.

Budgetary Restrictions/Limitations

The use of budgets for planning and control is well known to buyers in both private industry and government. As with any plan, when the environment or assumptions under which the budget was made change, the plan (budget) should be revised. Often the final budget for purchases is approved by a legislative body on a line-item basis, and changes in the budget for each line item must be approved by that legislative body in advance of expenditure. Obtaining such approval may be a time-consuming process, due to the series of steps and public hearings required.

As a result, if the needed funds are not already in the budget, the public buyer may find it impossible to take advantage of spot buys of larger quantities of materials at particularly advantageous prices. This puts a real premium in public buying on the long-term planning and budgeting needed to anticipate requirements and opportunities; this planning often must be done at least 18 months in advance. Additionally, good management is necessary to ensure that last-minute purchases are not made just to obligate funds by an end-of-the-year budget expiration date.

Outside Pressures

The public buyer recognizes that the money spent comes from the taxpayer, and these taxpayers may become vocal in their attempts to influence how their money is spent and with which suppliers. It is not unusual for a given supplier firm to attempt to influence, through the political process, the placement of major dollar purchase contracts. In a sense, this is a type of reciprocity, with the taxpaying supplier firm feeling that since it is providing the tax dollars from which public purchases are made, it should be selected as the supplier from which government buys needed goods and services. It is the rare public buyer who does not, from time to time, receive a telephone call that starts, "You know, our firm pays a substantial amount of taxes, and we feel that we should receive better treatment from governmental purchasing."

Government Programs

In the last decade, there has been increased government support to certain special-interest segments of society. Specific minority member segments are assumed to have been the victims of past unfair, discriminatory actions. The government has deemed that, in the interests of equity, these special-interest segments should receive special consideration in future actions. Through the legislative process, laws have been passed to encourage the redress of these past injustices, and purchasing is one natural area through which funds can be channeled to these special-interest segments. Examples are programs to favor small business firms in the award of purchase contracts, or the support of minority-owned suppliers through special consideration in evaluating supplier capability and the placement of purchases.[1] Some government entities have enacted set-aside programs or price preference programs, requiring that a certain percentage of business be given to targeted groups such as minority/women business enterprise (M/WBE) programs.

Labor Surplus Area Favoritism

The Department of Labor classifies certain cities or areas as ones that have an unusually high unemployment rate or an unusually high number of hard-core disadvantaged persons. Certain government purchasing requirements then are set aside for placement of a given percentage of the total buy with firms in those areas. A small business in a labor surplus area is in a particularly advantageous position to compete for these purchases, although the net effect may be that the government (taxpayer) pays a premium price for purchased requirements.

Buy American Act

Congress passed the Buy American Act ostensibly to make sure that the United States maintains its production capability in several "essential" areas, even though foreign firms are able to produce more efficiently and thus undersell domestic firms on requirements for delivery in the United States. It provides that on certain government requirements the purchase order will be awarded to the domestic firm, providing that its price is not over a given percentage amount (normally 6 percent, or 12 percent if it is a labor surplus area) higher than that offered by the foreign supplier.

Environmentally Preferable Purchases

All federal procurement officials are required by Executive Order 13101 and the Federal Acquisition Regulations (FAR) to assess and give preference to those products and services that are environmentally preferable.[2] The Environmentally Preferable Purchasing Program is a federalwide program to encourage and assist executive agencies in purchasing decisions. Executive Order 13101 defines environmentally preferable as ". . . products or services that have a lesser or reduced effect on human health and the environment when compared with competing products or services that serve the same purpose." Environmentally preferable purchasing is then defined as "incorporating key environmental factors with traditional price and performance considerations in purchasing decisions."[3] The EPA has developed the Environmentally Preferable Purchasing (EPP) database of environmental attribute information for products ranging from appliances to vehicles. The database also includes contract language that has been used by others to obtain products and services considered by the EPA to be environmentally preferable. (See Chapter 11, "Disposal and Investment Recovery," for further discussion of environmental management as it relates to supply management.)

Interest Costs

One of the principal considerations in the industrial firm in determining inventory levels is the interest or opportunity cost of money tied up in inventory. It is often argued that governmental agencies need not consider money costs in their decisions, since the funds are

[1] "Procurement Reform Bill Finally Passes," *Purchasing,* October 6, 1994, p. 19.

[2] Environmentally Preferable Purchasing, Office of Pollution Prevention and Toxics, United States Environmental Protection Agency, http://www.epa.gov/opptintr/epp.

[3] Ibid.

tax dollars. This is spurious reasoning, for (1) government agencies today typically labor under a burden, large or small, of financial indebtedness, either short or long term, and interest cost is a very real cost of operation, and (2) when governmental funds are tied up in purchased inventories, these funds are not available for employment in other productive uses. This effectively means that there is an opportunity cost of funds invested in inventory. The public supply manager may have to take special care to persuade other governmental administrators that inventory investment is expensive, and this cost should be considered in making acquisition/inventory decisions.

Inspection

Governmental agencies (with the military as a notable exception) normally do not have specialized inspection personnel. Yet, incoming inspection is often needed. Steps must be taken to ensure that specifications are met. Depending on the specific purchase: (1) the user can be advised to check delivered items immediately and report any quality variance; (2) the supplier may be asked to supply notarized copies of inspection reports that show the specific tests conducted and the test data that resulted and formed the basis for a decision to ship the items; (3) the buyer may send materials, or samples, out to an independent testing laboratory; (4) the buyer may employ someone to come into the organization to inspect purchased items (for example, the U.S. Department of Agriculture will inspect meat and produce items in most areas at a reasonable charge); (5) the buyer may decide to perform certain simple tests on selected items; or (6) a separate incoming quality control department can be established within the public agency, if a persuasive case can be made, to ensure that specifications are met.

Transportation and Logistics

It is rare for public supply departments to have a traffic or logistics expert or access to such an individual. Yet, materials movement often accounts for a significant part of the total cost of items bought and has increased in importance due to the widened alternatives resulting from transport deregulation (see Chapter 7, "Transportation and Delivery"). As a result of this lack of expertise, the public buyer often specifies FOB destination as the shipping basis, which may not be the most economical, since the buyer loses control over transportation decisions.

A logistics professional might make a major contribution in such areas as classification and routing of shipments, selection of carriers, determination of freight charges, and filing of damage claims. Transportation is one of the areas where many public purchasers are taking a look at outsourcing or contracting out with third-party logistics service companies.

Past Performance and Switching Cost

It is often difficult in public procurement to recognize the past performance of a supplier, particularly if it has been excellent. A simple example will suffice. In a particular school district, Anderson Cleaning did an outstanding job of providing cleaning and maintenance service for school buildings. Anderson lost its multimillion-dollar contract to another supplier that had bid about $1,000 lower. The performance of this second bidder was highly unsatisfactory and caused many complaints. Under the existing procurement bylaws, it was not possible to recognize Anderson's superior performance. Similarly, the cost of switching from one supplier to another was assumed to be nil, a common, but questionable, assumption in public procurement.

Transparency and Confidentiality

The public buyer lives in a "fishbowl." All information on prices submitted by suppliers, and the price finally paid, must be made available to any taxpayer requesting it. Any special arrangements between the buyer and the successful supplier, and the final purchase contract, are public knowledge. Moreover, the public buyer is free to talk and exchange supplier information and prices paid with other public buyers. Thus, keeping information confidential is a challenge.

Importance of Specifications

Since a large part of public acquisition is based on the bidding process, it is vital that specifications for needed items be clear and accurate and written to ensure that multiple suppliers can compete for the business. These specifications take the form of written descriptions, blueprints, drawings, performance requirements, industry standards, or commercial designation (trade or brand name). Unless all potential bidders can be furnished a complete and usable set of specifications, the bidding process will be imperfect. In addition, if a bidder can show that the specifications were not uniform, or were subject to varying interpretations, there is a good chance that legal action can be brought to overturn the purchasing department's contract award, resulting in lengthy and costly delays in contract performance.

The development of good, clean specifications requires considerable time and effort, and some governmental procurement agencies have full-time personnel who work on the preparation and refinement of specifications. Considerable communication between the purchasing agency and the user is necessary to develop clear specifications, and the advantages of standardization between user agencies can be significant.

Both public and private buyers can take advantage of the specification work done by governmental agencies at the local, county, state, or federal level. The federal government, through the General Services Administration, has developed a multitude of specifications for use in federal purchasing, and these are readily available to anyone wishing to use them. The *Index of Federal Specifications, Standards and Commercial Item Descriptions*[4] lists the available specifications three ways: (1) alphabetically, (2) numerically, and (3) by federal supply class (FSC). Each specification or standard is described briefly and the price at which the item can be purchased from the GSA is shown. A similar *Department of Defense Index of Specifications and Standards* lists the unclassified military specifications used by the Defense Department; it is a consolidation of separate indices formerly published by the individual military agencies. It can be purchased from the Superintendent of Documents.

While the work done in preparing these specifications can be of much use to other public buyers, it should be noted that some specifications are more cumbersome than needed. The General Accounting Office has been particularly critical and has advocated using simpler, commercial-type specifications where practical.

[4] The *Index* can be purchased from the General Services Administration, Federal Supply Service Bureau, Specifications Section (3FBP-W), Suite 8100, 470 L'Enfant Plaza, SW, Washington, DC 20407. It is also available at GSA regional offices.

ACQUISITION PROCEDURES

The mandate that the public sector seek maximum competition dictates the procedures used in public buying. The procedure used to purchase a needed good or service is often determined by established dollar thresholds. Typical categories are[5]

1. Small-dollar purchases for items below the threshold for competitive bids or quotes.
2. Request for quotations (RFQ) for items below the threshold for issuing a formal bid solicitation but high enough to require competitive quotations.
3. Invitation for bids (IFB) for items above the threshold to issue formal bid solicitation, normally for a product or contractual (nonprofessional) service.
4. Request for proposal (RFP) for professional services or high-tech needs when formal bid solicitations are required.
5. Emergency purchases for unplanned needs to protect public health or security.
6. Sole-source purchases for a supply, service, or construction item when the purchaser determines in writing there is only one source.
7. Negotiated acquisition, usually part of an RFP or sole-source purchase, or to acquire exempted services such as utilities, power, or landfills.

The Bid Process

Public statutes normally provide that the award of purchase contracts should be made on the basis of open, competitive bidding. This provision seeks to ensure that all qualified suppliers, who are taxpayers or who employ personnel who are taxpayers, have an equal opportunity to compete for the sale of products or services needed in the operation of government. Since the bids received are open to public inspection, it would be difficult for the public buyer to show favoritism to any one supplier. This system tends to put a heavy weight on price as the basis for supplier selection, for it might be difficult for the buyer to defend selecting a supplier whose price is higher than that of the low bidder. Providing a list of criteria for bid evaluations and their weighting along with the invitation to bid allows the buyer to consider factors other than price.

Competitive bidding is time-consuming and requires costly documentation; for this reason, statutes often will specify that informal bids may be used as the basis of award of purchase orders for requirements under a certain dollar amount, for example, $1,000. Also, in the case of items available from a sole source, purchase decisions may be made on the basis of formal negotiation; however, the sole-source supplier situation should be avoided if at all possible, for this is a difficult situation and also costly, in terms of purchasing administrative expense.

When informal quotations are used to buy requirements of relatively low value, all essential steps of formal bidding should be used, except that only a limited number of bids will be solicited, and this can be done by telephone or e-mail requests. The buyer needs accurate records of suppliers requested to give a phone quote and the reason(s) why a particular supplier was selected, in the event that the decision is challenged later. A frequently used practice

[5] *The 2000 Model Procurement Code for State and Local Governments,* American Bar Association, 2000.

is to have a rotation sequence from a list of acceptable suppliers. Chapter 8 contains sections on the use of quotations and negotiation as methods of price determination.

Use of Bid Lists

On the purchase of items that will require repeated purchase actions, a master bid list is compiled. This requires the buyer to specify the characteristics that should be present in any qualified supplier firm, such as size (which relates to ability to provide the needed quantities), financial stability, quality control procedures, finished goods inventory levels (which may determine how quickly items can be obtained), warranty policy, spare parts availability, accessibility of maintenance/repair personnel, and transportation facilities. Then, the purchasing department will conduct whatever type of supplier survey or investigation is required to ensure that a given supplier can meet the minimum level of each important characteristic. If a given supplier is checked out and found to be unsatisfactory, this information should be communicated directly to that supplier so the supplier will know what types of changes would be necessary to compete for future business.

Deletions from the bid list are made in the case of suppliers who receive purchase awards and then do not perform according to the terms of the purchase agreement. Such a decision needs to be substantiated with facts and figures from the purchasing department's supplier performance evaluation system. Obviously, a supplier being dropped from the bid list for cause should be notified of this action and the specific reasons for the action. Another reason for deletion may be the unwillingness of a supplier to submit any bids over an extended period of time. If this were not done, the bid list could become too large and unwieldy. A particularly thorny issue is the supplier who is a sole provider of product or service A who fails to perform on product or service B.

The public buyer generally must be willing to consider any supplier who requests to be put on the bid list, after suitable investigation. However, the competent public buyer should be aggressive in ferreting out new potential supply sources.

Advertising

The bid list, if properly developed and maintained, should provide a large enough group of qualified suppliers to enable the public buyer to obtain competition in the bid process. However, many public purchasing agencies, as a matter of normal operating policy or because they are required by statute or regulation, also advertise upcoming purchase needs in the specified newspapers or electronically on the Internet. The advertisement may simply say that if any given supplier firm wishes to receive a request for bid for a particular requirement, it should contact the purchasing department. The buyer then must determine whether the firm asking to bid meets the minimum supplier qualifications. Advertising ensures that purchasing is not conducted under any veil of secrecy. Under the Free Trade Agreement, public purchasers in North America have to ensure that American, Canadian, and Mexican bidders are aware of bids exceeding a specific amount. Similar requirements have been mandated by the European Community for public sector purchases in the European Union.

Bid Procedures

In a formal bid system, the bidder typically will be sent (1) a complete list of specifications that the supplier must meet (in complicated procurements, the specification package may consist of several pages—several hundred pages, in some instances—and may detail the kinds of quality control procedures the buyer [and supplier] will use to ensure that the goods delivered do, in fact, meet specifications); (2) a list of instructions to the bidder, spelling out how, when, where, and in what form bids must be submitted; (3) general and special legal conditions that must be met by the successful bidder; and (4) a bid form on which the supplier will submit price, discounts, and other required information.

The bidder typically must submit any bid on or before a specified date and hour, as for example, 1 p.m. on March 15. No bids will be accepted after the bid closing; late bids are returned, unopened, to the bidder. Changes are normally not permitted after the formal bid is received, although some agencies do permit the substitution of a new bid for the original, unopened bid, provided it is received before the bid opening date. The place where the bid must be delivered, usually the purchasing department, should be specified, and many public purchasing agencies use a locked container to maintain all sealed bids until the date and hour of the bid opening.

While these bid procedures may appear rather complicated, they do establish an environment in which all qualified suppliers have an equal opportunity.

Use of Bid Bonds and Deposits

Often the bid package requires that any bidder submit a bond at the time of the bid. In some states, this is a legal requirement, particularly in the case of purchased items or construction contracts for large dollar amounts. As an alternative, some public purchasing agencies require that the bid be accompanied by a certified check or money order in a fixed percentage amount of the bid. In the event the bidder selected does not agree to sign the final purchase contract award, or does not perform according to the terms of the bid, this amount is retained by the purchasing agency as liquidated damages for nonperformance. Obviously, the bid bond or bid deposit is an attempt to discourage irresponsible bidders from competing. In high-risk situations, the extra cost of the bid bond, which in some way will be passed back as an extra cost to the buyer, is warranted; in the purchase of standard, stock items available from several sources, the use of a bond is questionable.

Technically, there are three general types of bonds available. Most bidders purchase each, for a dollar premium, from an insurance company, thus effectively transferring some of the risk to the insurance carrier:

1. The *bid (or surety) bond* guarantees that if the order is awarded to a specific bidder, it will accept the purchase contract. If the supplier refuses, the extra costs to the buyer of going to an alternative source are borne by the insurer.
2. The *performance bond* guarantees that the work done will be done according to specifications and in the time specified. If the buyer has to go to another supplier for rework or to get the order completed, purchasing is indemnified for these extra costs.
3. The *payment bond* protects the buyer against liens that might be granted to suppliers of material and labor to the bidder, in the event the bidder does not make proper payment to its suppliers.

In a multiple-year contract or one with high initial costs, the purchaser may want to break the performance bond into periods or stages of completion to avoid having the surety write the bond too high and increase the cost of the contract too much.

Bid Opening

At the hour and date specified in the bid instructions, the buyer or other designated person will open all bids and record the bids on a bidder spreadsheet. In some agencies, the buyer must call out the supplier name and bid, and a clerk records the information, checks the actual bid form for the amount, and then certifies that the information on the spreadsheet is correct. Usually, any interested party who wishes can attend the bid opening and examine any of the bids. Often suppliers who have submitted bids, or ones who have chosen not to bid but who wish to see the bids of other suppliers, will attend the opening. The original bids should be retained for later inspection by any interested party for a specified time period (often 12 months).

Bid Evaluation

Normally, the public purchaser needs an appropriate amount of time after the opening to analyze the bids and prepare a recommended purchase action. If the purchase is a large one, it may require council approval in a municipality or cabinet approval for a federal or state procurement. The first task during bid review is to ensure that all bid requirements have been met and to eliminate those bids that fail to meet this test.

Responsible and Responsive Bidders

One challenge for the public supply manager is the requirement that the contract be awarded to the lowest "responsible" and "responsive" bidder. A *responsible* bidder is a supplier deemed fully capable and willing to perform the work; a *responsive* bidder is one who has submitted a bid that conforms to the invitation for bid. While this sounds reasonable, the public buyer needs to exercise judgment when dealing with suppliers whose ability to perform is marginal. There is a constant need to justify and document all purchaser actions and decisions. Part of the aim of procurement reform is to place the focus on finding the "best value" provider for goods and services.

Competition Concerns

Public purchasers are in a unique position to watch for illegal trade practices by suppliers. Since public purchasers share bid information with other public purchasers they are in a position to detect collusion among suppliers. Such collusion may be evident from artificially high prices, identical prices, unwillingness to bid, the rotation of low bidder among a small group of bidders, the apparent favoring of a particular bidder on a specific requirement area, and so on. Every country has an agency or bureau charged with the investigation of anticompetitive practices and the prosecution of perpetrators. The antitrust division of the U.S. Department of Justice and the Competition Bureau in Canada regularly remind public purchasers to be on the lookout for suspicious practices by suppliers.

Number of Bids

In some public agencies, a purchase award cannot be made unless at least some minimum number of bids (often three) has been received. If the minimum number is not received, the requirement must be rebid, or the buyer must justify that the nature of the requirement is such that it is impossible to obtain bids from more suppliers.

Bid Errors

If the successful, low bidder notifies the buyer after the bid has been submitted, but before the award of the purchase order has been made, that an error has been made, the buyer normally will permit the bid to be withdrawn. However, the buyer makes note of this, since it reflects on the responsibility of the bidder.

A much-more-serious problem arises if the bidder, claiming a bid error, attempts to withdraw the bid *after* it has been awarded. Of course, the use of a bid bond in the bid process is an attempt to protect the buyer if such a problem arises. If no bid bond exists, the buyer must decide on court action to force performance or collect damages or go to the closest other successful bidder (who now may no longer be interested) or go through the bid process again. Legal counsel is normally sought, but if the mistake was mechanical in nature, that is, the figures were added up incorrectly, the courts probably will side with the supplier. However, if it was an error in judgment—for example, the supplier misjudged the rate of escalation in material prices—then the courts generally will not permit relief to the supplier. Also, for the supplier to gain relief in the courts, the supplier must be able to show that once the error was discovered, the buying agency was notified promptly.

Obviously, if the buyer receives a bid that commonsense and knowledge of the market indicates is unrealistic, the bid should be rechecked and the bidder requested to reaffirm that it is a bona fide bid. In the long run, such action likely will be cheaper for the buying agency than if a long and involved legal action ensues, with an uncertain outcome.

Bid Awards

If multiple bid criteria apply and if two or more responsible bidders meet the specifications and conditions, the supplier with the best rating is selected. Any other action the buyer must justify with additional information. If identical low bids are received, and the buyer has no evidence or indication of any collusion or other bid irregularities, then an acceptable way of resolving this issue needs to be found.

The public buyer has no obligation to notify unsuccessful bidders of the award, since the bid opening was a public event and the bid and award documents are retained in the purchasing department and may be viewed, on request, by any interested individual. Courtesy suggests, however, that if an unsuccessful supplier makes a telephone or letter request for information, that information be provided promptly, and the requester invited to come in and examine the file.

MILITARY SUPPLY

The Department of Defense is responsible for military procurement. Issues of national security and future preparedness are additional challenges for military procurement beyond the standard ever-present public supply requirements. Military requirements range from the mundane, such as office supplies, food, and bedding, to development of future aircraft, ship, and land-based vehicles as well as weapons systems. The amount spent for a major development program runs into the billions of dollars and may cover several decades. To deal with the complexities of military acquisitions, military supply officers have a choice of contract types.

Firm-Fixed-Price (FFP) Contract

The price set is not subject to change, under any circumstances. This is the preferred type of contract, but if the delivery date is some months or years away and if there is substantial chance of price escalation, a supplier may feel that there is far too much risk of loss to agree to sell under an FFP contract.

Cost-Plus-Fixed-Fee (CPFF) Contract

In situations where it would be unreasonable to expect a supplier to agree to sell at a firm fixed price, the CPFF contract can be used. This situation might occur if the item is experimental and the specifications are not firm, or if costs in the future cannot be predicted. The buyer agrees to reimburse the supplier for all reasonable costs incurred (under a set of definite policies under which "reasonable" is to be determined) in doing the job or producing the required item, plus a specified dollar amount of profit. A maximum amount may be specified for the cost. This contract type is far superior to the old "cost-plus-percentage" type, which encouraged the supplier to run the costs up as high as possible to increase the base on which the profit is figured. While the supplier bears little risk under the CPFF, since costs will be reimbursed, the supplier's profit percentage declines as the costs increase, giving some incentive to the supplier to control costs.

Cost-No-Fee (CNF) Contract

If the buyer can argue persuasively that there will be enough subsidiary benefits to the supplier from doing a particular job, then the supplier may be willing to do it provided only the costs are reimbursed. For example, the supplier may be willing to do the research and produce some new product if only the costs are returned, because doing the job may give the supplier some new technological or product knowledge, which then may be used to make large profits in some commercial market.

Cost-Plus-Incentive-Fee (CPIF) Contract

In this type of contract, both buyer and seller agree on a target cost figure, a fixed fee, and a formula under which any cost over- or underruns are to be shared. For example, assume the agreed-on target cost is $100,000, the fixed fee is $10,000, and the incentive-sharing formula is 50/50. If actual costs are $120,000, the $20,000 cost overrun would be shared equally between buyer and seller, based on the 50/50 sharing formula, and the seller's profit would be reduced by $10,000, or to zero in this example. On the other hand, if total costs are only $90,000, then the seller's share of the $10,000 cost underrun would be $5,000. Total profit then would be $10,000 + $5,000, or $15,000. This type of contract has the effect of motivating the supplier to be as efficient as possible, since the benefits of greater efficiency (or the penalties of inefficiency) accrue in part, based on the sharing formula, to the supplier.

It is obvious that large dollar amounts can be saved or lost by the military's purchasing decision makers. For example, McDonnell Douglas Corporation was awarded a $6.6 billion defense contract to develop the C-17 cargo plane and to build the first six production aircraft. By August 1991, McDonnell Douglas was one year behind schedule and cost overruns were estimated to be between $1.4 billion and $2.6 billion.[6] Although the C-17s

[6] Rick Wartzman, "McDonnell Douglas Seen Exceeding Cap on C-17 Cost," *The Wall Street Journal,* August 26, 1991, p. A3.

perform well, Congress then initiated a separate offer from Boeing to replace some of the C-17 orders with 747 jumbo jets in an effort to reduce costs. In early 1995, the Air Force estimated that the C-17s "should cost" an average $210 to $220 million. The threat of competition from Boeing has led McDonnell Douglas to offer as much as a 40 percent cut in price on the C-17s.[7]

STATE, LOCAL, AND MUNICIPAL SUPPLY

While purchasing done by state, county, municipal, and other public agencies tends to follow all the basic guidelines of public supply management, some of the unique aspects should be commented on briefly.

Cooperative or Consortium Purchasing

In the last decade or so, the cooperative purchasing approach has received much attention, interest, and use in public purchasing. Two or more public, or not-for-profit, purchasing departments pool their requirements to leverage the combined volume with suppliers. It has been used successfully by local government units, public school districts, and hospitals and is most advantageous for smaller purchasing units. The savings from cooperative purchasing can be significant.

Two basic variations are used in cooperative purchasing: (1) joint buying, where two or more purchasing departments agree to pool their requirements for a particular item and let one of the purchasing departments commit the total purchase quantity to a specific supplier at a specific price, and (2) a formal, contractual arrangement where several individual purchasing departments agree to establish, fund, and use a separate cooperative buying alliance. For example, Premier is a leading health care alliance collectively owned by more than 200 independent hospitals and health care systems in the United States. Together, they operate or are affiliated with nearly 1,500 hospitals and other health care sites. Premier leverages the scale of its owners and affiliates through group purchasing of supplies and services; through greater operational and clinical effectiveness and efficiency in services essential to health care, such as clinical performance improvement, biomedical equipment maintenance, and supply chain management; and by sharing the risk of developing new resources needed in health care, such as electronic commerce capabilities.[8]

Some of the advantages of cooperative buying are (1) lower prices; (2) improved quality, through improved testing and supplier selection; (3) reduced administrative cost; (4) standardization; (5) better records; and (6) greater competition. Among the problems cited as arising from cooperative buying are (1) limited choice of items, which may reduce suitability; (2) longer lead times; (3) more documentation; and (4) inability of small suppliers to compete.

[7] Jeff Cole, "McDonnell Douglas Offers to Cut Price of C-17 Military Planes by Up to 40%," *The Wall Street Journal,* August 1, 1995, p. 1.

[8] Premiere, Inc., http://www.premiereinc.com

In 1981 in Canada, Ron MacDonald spearheaded an initiative to establish Interuniversity Services to purchase the requirements for all universities in the four Atlantic Provinces, which still operates successfully.

Governmentwide and Cooperative Contracts

A common cost-reduction strategy in the private sector is to consolidate volume across business units, divisions, and regions or to bundle goods and services in a manner that gives the buyer more leverage with potential suppliers. Public purchasers at all levels (federal, state/provincial, county, municipality) are increasingly being allowed to consolidate spend across agencies for additional leverage. Some states also work on cooperative agreements with other state procurement offices to work off of their contracts rather than forming a separate one. For example, the State of Arizona Procurement Office identifies cooperative opportunities that are solicitations being conducted by jurisdictions other than the State of Arizona. These solicitations will result in cooperative contracts that may be considered for adoption by Arizona. One such opportunity stated, "The New Mexico State Purchasing Agency (NMSPA) is requesting proposals from computer equipment manufacturers on behalf of the State of New Mexico, the National Association of State Procurement Officials (NASPO) and the Western States Contracting Alliance (WSCA). The purpose of this Request for Proposals (RFP) is to establish master price agreements on a competitive basis with qualified computer equipment manufacturers who shall supply servers and other computer equipment as well as general purpose software, local area network (LAN) hardware, peripherals, maintenance and support services to authorized purchasers nationwide."

Local-Bidder Preference Laws

In many governmental jurisdictions, the applicable law or statute states that, all other things being equal, local bidders must be granted a certain percentage price preference in bidding against nonlocal suppliers. For example, if a local supplier submits a bid that is not over a given percent, for example, 5 percent, higher than nonlocal suppliers, then the local supplier must be awarded the purchase order, assuming all other factors are equal. This is a form of protectionism, similar to that of the Buy American Act. The argument for this is that local suppliers have employees in the local area, and the award of orders to local suppliers provides support for the local economy.

This practice is opposed by most purchasing professionals as being noncompetitive, which means that higher prices are paid for purchases than are necessary. It negates the advantages of economic specialization, and local suppliers, knowing that such a preference is to be applied, will have a tendency to submit a bid that is higher than they otherwise would offer. If one believes in totally fair, open competition, then all suppliers, regardless of location, should be permitted to compete solely on the basis of their ability to provide maximum value for the public funds expended. The National Association of State Purchasing Officials has gone on record as strongly opposing local-preference laws. In a 2003 poll of members of the National Institute of Governmental Purchasing (NIGP), 68 percent of respondents indicated that their agency does not have a local preference ordinance, statute, or law, and that in their opinion such preferences adversely affect competition.

MODEL PROCUREMENT CODE

The Model Procurement Code is a guide and reference for public procurement professionals who are developing or modifying their procurement code based on recognizable standards. Developed by the American Bar Association, it was adopted in 1979 and revised in 1999 to reflect changes in supply management practices. The purpose of the code is to apply sound purchasing practices to state and local purchasing and to ensure that federal funds allocated to these entities are spent in compliance with sound purchasing practices.

The underlying purposes and policies of this Code are:

(a) to simplify, clarify, and modernize the law governing procurement by this [State];
(b) to permit the continued development of procurement policies and practices;
(c) to make as consistent as possible the procurement laws among the various jurisdictions;
(d) to provide for increased public confidence in the procedures followed in public procurement;
(e) to ensure the fair and equitable treatment of all persons who deal with the procurement system of this [State];
(f) to provide increased economy in [State] procurement activities and to maximize to the fullest extent practicable the purchasing value of public funds of the [State];
(g) to foster effective broad-based competition within the free enterprise system;
(h) to provide safeguards for the maintenance of a procurement system of quality and integrity, and
(i) to obtain in a cost-effective and responsive manner the materials, services, and construction required by [State] agencies in order for those agencies to better serve this state's businesses and residents.[9]

The code covers supply organization, source selection and contract formation, specifications, procurement of infrastructure facilities and services, modification and termination of contracts for supplies and services, cost principles, supply management, legal and contractual remedies, intergovernmental relations, assistance to small and disadvantaged businesses, federal assistance or contract procurement requirements, and ethics in public contracting. The American Bar Association later presented a set of recommended, comprehensive, and integrated regulations that a governmental unit could use to implement the code. This document gives the language that could be used in developing a comprehensive policy manual governing a public purchasing operation. They also approved and published a model procurement ordinance for use by smaller units of local government.[10]

The results of the model procurement code–based legislation include (1) changes to competitive bid requirements that allow the purchaser more leeway in analyzing the capabilities of suppliers and room to award to other than the low bidder, (2) the creation of competitive sealed proposals allowing for negotiations and revisions of proposals, (3) suspension and disbarment of suppliers under certain circumstances, and (4) administrative procedures for resolving bid

[9] *The Model Procurement Code for State and Local Governments* (Washington, D.C.: American Bar Association, 2000), http://www.abanet.org.

[10] *The Model Procurement Ordinance for Local Governments* (Washington, D.C.: American Bar Association, August 1982).

protests and claims.[11] As a result of the implementation of model procurement code–based legislation, a body of case law is developing that can be used along with the code in legal disputes. The 2000 revision to the code includes enhancements that (1) allow procurement processes to adapt to the electronic age, (2) extend the benefits of cooperative purchasing of supplies and services among state and local governments, (3) provide flexibility to senior procurement officials to adapt procurement procedures to unusual circumstances with appropriate safeguards and reporting responsibilities, and (4) provide more explicit guidelines on the use of construction delivery methods.[12]

PUBLIC SUPPLY CHANGES

Public supply is changing. Major changes include the use of electronic/Internet-based systems, involvement in services spend, multiyear contracts, privatization, simplified acquisition procedures, and the move to commercial practices.

Use of Electronic/Internet-Based Systems

There is increasing use of automated systems in public supply including e-procurement systems that provide suppliers with easy access to all solicitations; an online means of responding; information on contract awards; and procurement policies, procedures, and forms. Internal customers also use the Internet to post request for information (RFI), request for quotes (RFQ), request for proposals (RFP), and invitation for bids (IFB) and to access information on existing contracts, policies, procedures, and forms. These systems provide greater responsiveness to user needs, decrease the cost of procurement, and may help to obtain superior value by making solicitations more visible and accessible to a wider range of potential suppliers.

Involvement in Services Spend

One of the many changes in private and public sector purchasing is the increase in involvement of purchasing departments in buying services. The 2000 CAPS Research *Cross Industry Comparison* reported that state, county, and municipal purchasing departments spent about 65 percent of the dollars for services.

Multiyear Contracts

The use of multiyear contracts has been adopted extensively in public supply. The larger spend makes it more attractive for suppliers to bid but also reduces the cost of the bid as a percentage of the total contract. It also reduces purchaser time spent on the bidding process for all requirements of the public entity.

Privatization

Outsourcing or privatization, as it is often called in the public sector, is gaining in prominence as the public sector wrestles with the limited availability of funds. Major issues include the termination of public employees, a fair comparison of costs and benefits, and the disposal of taxpayer-owned assets.

[11] Ibid., p. 40.
[12] Ibid.

Simplified Acquisition Procedures

At the federal level, simplified acquisition procedures (SAP) have been adopted to reduce administrative costs; improve opportunities for small, small disadvantaged, and women-owned business concerns to obtain a fair proportion; promote efficiency and economy in contracting; and avoid unnecessary burdens for agencies and contractors. The simplified acquisition thresholds are $100,000 generally and $250,000 inside the United States and $500,000 outside the United States for contingency operations or against terrorist attacks; $5 million for commercial supplies and services and $10 million for contingency operations or terrorist attacks; and $2,500 for micropurchases generally and $2,000 for construction and $15,000 for contingency operations or against terrorist attacks.

Commercial Practices

Procurement reforms in the 1990s led to the adoption and adaptation of many commercial practices to public purchasing. These include payment processes and contract types.

Government Purchase Cards

In 1998, the GSA initiated the GSA SmartPay program. Five credit card services were awarded contracts to provide federal agencies a new way to pay for commercial goods and services as well as travel and fleet-related expenses. The GSA SmartPay contracts, originally effective from November 30, 1998, through November 29, 2003, have five one-year options to renew. The program was adopted to (1) provide flexibility, (2) improve payment processes, (3) streamline the purchasing process, (4) allow agencies to receive performance-based refunds, (5) streamline financial operations and accurately allocate costs, and (6) provide choice of card services.[13] Procurement cards also are used at the state, county, and municipal levels.

Contract Types

At all levels of government purchasing, different contract vehicles are being explored for use. The main concern is to ensure that the type of contracts used do not impede the government's ability to achieve its other goals of fairness and equity to all sizes and types of suppliers. For government purchasers, the social concerns of government cannot be ignored.

Conclusion

Public supply management strives to support effectively the goals of its public entity while assuring value for money spent. There are significant challenges in public procurement, not only because taxpayer funds are spent and political agendas count, but also because the public sector is facing a severe shortage of funds. Thus, like the private sector supply manager, the public supply manager is under increasing pressure to reduce the costs of acquisition while securing better value.

[13] GSA SmartPay, http://www.gsa.gov, December 6, 2004.

Questions for Review and Discussion

1. Which commercial practices would you recommend for adoption by public purchasing to make it more effective? Why? If adopted, would these practices compromise any of the goals of government purchasing?
2. What are the pros and cons of adopting electronic/Internet-based systems in public supply management?
3. Are there any differences between federal purchasing and state and local purchasing?
4. What are the advantages and disadvantages of governmentwide contracts?
5. What are the advantages and disadvantages of local bidder preference laws in state and local purchasing?
6. What are bid bonds and why are they used?
7. How does the bid process in public buying differ from that in industrial buying?
8. What are the major differences between public buying and industrial buying? Which would be easier to do?
9. Under what circumstances should each of the four common military contract types be used?
10. Considering the magnitude and complexity of military purchasing, can it ever really be efficient and cost-effective? What changes should be made in current practices?
11. How can industrial buyers use federal government purchase specifications?
12. Does the Buy American Act promote efficient purchasing? Justify the continuation or repeal of the Act.

References

CAPS Research. *Purchasing Performance Benchmarks for Municipal Governments, 2001.* http://www.capsresearch.org.

CAPS Research. *Purchasing Performance Benchmarks for State/County Governments, 1999.* http://www.capsresearch.org.

Model Procurement Code for State and Local Governments. Washington, D.C.: American Bar Association, 2000.

National Institute for Governmental Purchasing. http://www.nigp.org.

Office of Federal Procurement Policy, Office of Management and Budget, Executive Office of the President. *Best Practices for Collecting and Using Current and Past Performance Information.* May 2000, http://www.arnet.gov/Library/OFPP/BestPractices/pastperformanceguide.htm.

The RFP Report. Surrey, B.C.: Michael Asner Consulting. http://www.rfpadvisor.com.

Small Business Trends in Federal Procurement in the 1990s. U.S. General Accounting Office Report to Congressional Requesters, January 2001.

Survey of State Government Purchasing Practices. 5th ed. Rev. Lexington, KY: National Association of State Procurement Officers, 2003.

Case 15–1

TriCity

On November 20, Elaine Carter, manager of Purchasing and Supply for TriCity, got off the phone frustrated. According to the fleet manager from Environmental Services, an out-of-stock wiper blade had idled an expensive snow-removal truck. Elaine was concerned that the new integrated procurement system was affecting her department's service. How many other orders were not being processed by the new system? She knew that the situation required immediate attention and sat down to think of possible solutions.

TRICITY

TriCity, a Midwestern city of about 330,000, was responsible for an area of 41,110 acres. The city's responsibilities ranged from police services to the management of parks and recreation facilities. The organization of the city's departments is provided in Exhibit 1. Environmental Services represented the highest budget allocation due to the nature of its activities.

Annual budgets defined capital works, money set aside for specific projects like new road construction, and operational expenditures for daily expense needs. Every department was allocated a certain amount of capital works and operational budget yearly. At the end of the year, any unused capital work budget was withdrawn from the departments, whereas unused operational budget was carried forward to the next year.

The city was accountable to the tax-paying public for its expenditures. It was the responsibility of the city's government to ensure efficient and appropriate use of funds.

THE PURCHASING AND SUPPLY DEPARTMENT

Purchasing and Supply was part of the Finance and Administration department of TriCity. It provided purchasing to all departments of the city, excluding the police department. It also provided warehousing services for supplies that were part of the regular materials inventory, such as stationery and maintenance equipment. Essentially, every service within the city departments was a customer of the Purchasing and Supply office. Its mission statement was

> Obtaining the right goods and services when needed at the right price through a fair and competitive process.

THE ORDERING PROCESS

Individual departments initiated the process to purchase goods and services. The request was sent to Purchasing and Supply, who filled the order from the warehouse, or initiated the process of purchasing from third-party suppliers. Supplier selection was restricted to lowest-cost bidder and specifications set by the requesting department. Purchasing and Supply tracked orders to ensure delivery occurred within an acceptable time-frame. Supplier payments were coordinated by the office, too.

The warehouse stocked items that had been purchased in bulk and that were part of operational expenditures. Customers could request an order from inventory, and the Purchasing and Supply staff would ready the items for pickup. It was the responsibility of the end users to ensure that items they used regularly were in stock. Purchasing and Supply would reorder based on request only.

If the order was not in inventory, the office initiated one of the following processes:

Bid	For orders of over $58,000
Formal quote	For orders between $15,000 and $58,000
Informal quote	For orders below $15,000

The format of supplier selection followed a similar process in all cases (lowest bid for customer-defined specifications). Level of approval authority defined which order process would be used.

INTEGRATED PROCUREMENT

A new computer system had been implemented in Purchasing and Supply a month ago. Still in the early stages of implementation, Elaine was faced with several challenges that the new system brought to her department.

Because integrated procurement, as the system was called, was not customized, it limited online ordering to 10 major customers only and relegated the rest to a manual system to order their supplies. The previous system had

EXHIBIT 1 Purchasing and Supply's Customers

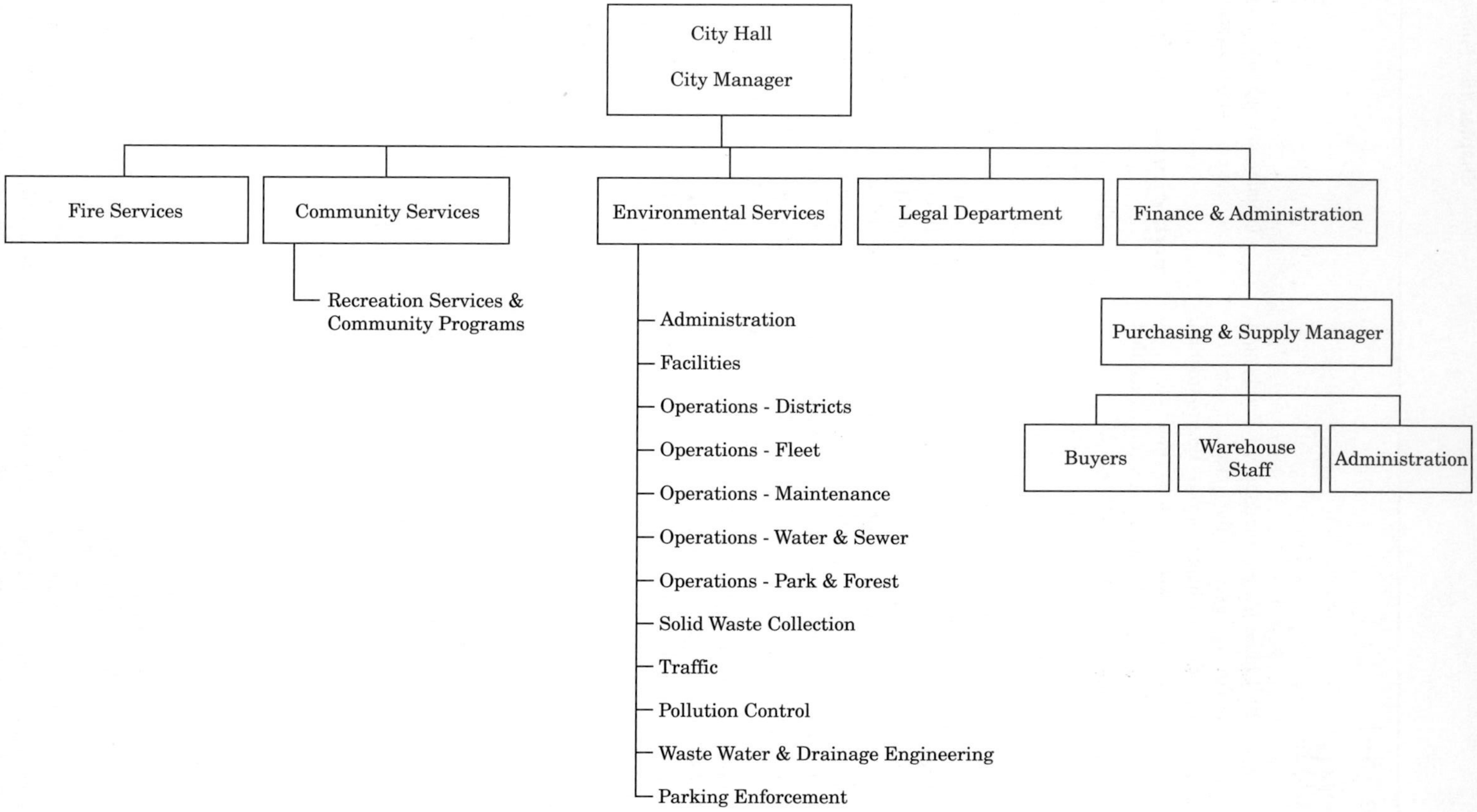

- City Hall / City Manager
  - Fire Services
  - Community Services
    - Recreation Services & Community Programs
  - Environmental Services
    - Administration
    - Facilities
    - Operations - Districts
    - Operations - Fleet
    - Operations - Maintenance
    - Operations - Water & Sewer
    - Operations - Park & Forest
    - Solid Waste Collection
    - Traffic
    - Pollution Control
    - Waste Water & Drainage Engineering
    - Parking Enforcement
  - Legal Department
  - Finance & Administration
    - Purchasing & Supply Manager
      - Buyers
      - Warehouse Staff
      - Administration

allowed all customers online ordering capabilities. The new system provided limited order management information to the customers placing the orders, reducing information on their budget balances. Internally, Elaine found that her staff disliked the data entry requirements of the new system. Whereas the old system allowed for manual input within one screen, the new system required seven screens of input. Most of the staff personnel had been in the department for more than 10 years and were used to the previous system. In their opinion the new system appeared to increase the staff workload, with a lower level of service to the end users.

Integrated procurement was a finance-based system. Because it was not customized to the Purchasing and Supply department, several ordering processes needed revision. For example, for those departments who no longer had online ordering capabilities, faxed requisitions required manual follow-up. Order status checks required telephone contact with the order customer. With resource restrictions ever prevalent in the public sector, Elaine was not sure how to provide adequate staff to handle the increased workload.

However, Elaine also knew that the long-term advantages of the new system were potentially great. The new system integrated previously stand-alone systems. Purchasing, accounts, warehousing, and payroll were some of the main modules of the new system. Integrating these systems allowed superior management control—supplier payments and customer orders could be tracked better, reports on staff productivity were available for the first time, and back orders were filled automatically through the warehouse. Moreover, integrated procurement allowed supplier performance appraisal on a continuous basis. These tools could ultimately help Elaine improve the efficiency of the entire buying process. The new system also provided the initial step towards Internet-enabled business.

IMPACT OF CHANGE

Many of Elaine's customers had not been happy with the new system implemented in her office. They felt they had lost control over some critical parts of the ordering process.

Service issues with major projects could also result in the involvement of elected representatives at City Hall in the process. It was not uncommon for elected representatives to ask about purchasing issues with projects in which they had a particular interest. Therefore, any changes that appeared detrimental to these interests were not looked upon favorably.

Coupled with the external pressures, Elaine had also faced resistance from her staff. During the training on the new system, her staff had voiced concerns about the lower productivity levels. After launch date, new issues arose daily. Elaine had thought the old system could be abandoned soon after the launch of integrated procurement, but she was not sure now.

THE WIPER BLADE STOCKOUT PROBLEM

Elaine reviewed the wiper blade stockout problem. An order entered by the fleet division of Environmental Services, one of the customers who had online access, for a wiper blade had failed to transmit through the new system properly. Because the warehouse had not received a request for the blade, it was not reordered. The fleet manager was claiming that the snow-removal truck that had required the blade could not be used because the blade was out of stock, costing the department idle time.

Elaine wondered what could have caused the order not to be processed. Was it human error in data entry—this *was* a new system? Or were there technical glitches involved? Either way, Elaine had to solve the immediate problem for the fleet department. However, she also was concerned about similar problems arising with other orders. What could she do to prevent this from happening again? What safety measures should she implement?

Case 15–2

Fairview School Board

On Tuesday, April 11th, Peter Lawrence, supply manager for the Fairview School Board, in Oregon, met with Jim Knox, financial supervisor. The board's forecasted operating budget for the following year would be in a deficit and Jim had been asked to make recommendations that would address the problem. During their meeting, Jim proposed eliminating the central distribution center and giving the schools responsibility for managing their own supplies. Peter had to respond to Jim's proposal by the end of the week.

THE SCHOOL BOARD

The Fairview School Board (FSB) was created four years earlier with the amalgamation of four regional school boards into one centralized administrative body. Despite a growing population in the area, the amalgamation was deemed necessary to cut costs through operating synergies. The amalgamated FSB operated approximately 200 schools, employing more than 8,000 full- and part-time staff, in a geographic area covering about 2,000 square miles. Prior to amalgamation, the board for the City of Fairview had been the largest of the four, with approximately 100 schools, while the three others were smaller rural school boards. The current operating budget for the FSB was $525 million.

SUPPLY MANAGEMENT

The supply departments for the three rural boards were eliminated at the time of amalgamation, and the purchasing department at the Fairview City Board was given responsibility for the FSB. Staffing levels were maintained at the pre-amalgamation levels of 12 people.

For a number of years, the supply department had been utilizing technology in order to make it easier for staff to order supplies and to help manage its inventory at the distribution center. At the time of the amalgamation, the three other boards were integrated on its supply system, *supplynet*. The system had been upgraded recently and it helped staff in the supply department manage effectively the large number of orders it processed each day.

Purchases for the FSB, excluding major construction projects, specialized consulting services, and legal and financial charges, were approximately $75 million per year. When a staff member at a school needed to make a purchase, he or she placed an order electronically on the FSB's intranet. The order would be crosschecked against the finance accounts to ensure adequate budget resources to acquire the requested goods or services. The orders were consolidated at the administrative offices and a purchase-order run was executed daily.

THE DISTRIBUTION CENTER

The supply management department maintained a 30,000-square-foot distribution center in the City of Fairview, which served two primary purposes. Inventories were maintained at the warehouse for general supplies, such as office supplies, paper, and janitorial products. These inventories were maintained either because quantity discounts justified bulk purchases or substantial delivery lead times warranted holding safety stock. Inventory levels at the distribution center averaged $1 million, although it fluctuated considerably during the year. Also housed at the distribution center was the board's inventory of educational resource supplies—equipment such as audiovisual material and special teaching supplies—that schools used occasionally and could be loaned on a short- or medium-term basis.

The distribution center also operated the board's delivery system, including interdepartment mail, supplies, educational resources, computer equipment, and audiovisual equipment for repair or loan. In addition, the delivery service handled the removal of surplus equipment and furniture for disposal. Deliveries were made to schools and board offices twice per week, and sometimes more frequently if required. The board owned four delivery vans and one large moving truck.

The distribution center had one supervisor, one clerk, five warehouse staff, and five delivery drivers. Overall, school and administrative staff were satisfied with the current arrangement and the services provided by the distribution center.

JIM KNOX'S PLAN

When Jim Knox met with Peter, he explained that the FSB was forecasting a deficit of $7 million for the coming year and that adjustments to the budget would have to be made in order to address this problem. While early retirement of a number of staff and cuts to various programs would eliminate some of the shortfall, additional reductions were still required. He believed costs could be reduced by allowing schools to handle their own supplies, and proposed that the entire distribution center staff could be laid off, the vehicles and equipment could be sold, and the distribution center permanently closed. Jim argued that closing the distribution center was a more attractive option than making further cuts to the educational programs. He estimated that annual salary costs alone were in the $500,000 range. Reductions in other associated overhead costs, such as rent and utilities, could easily double this number.

Jim asked Peter to consider his idea and get back to him by the end of the week. Peter recognized that he would need to evaluate the implications of this proposal on the FSB before responding. Specifically, he wanted to evaluate the potential costs and benefits of maintaining the distribution center. Furthermore, implementing such a change in operations would have a substantial impact on various stakeholders, such as teachers, school secretaries, and maintenance staff. Peter needed to understand what accommodations could be made to support the needs of various staff if the distribution center was eliminated. Peter also recognized that if he disagreed with Jim's proposal to shut down the distribution center, he would be expected to offer alternative suggestions to help address the budget shortfall.

Chapter Sixteen

Capital Goods

Chapter Outline

Key Questions for the Supply Manager

Should we

- Buy or lease new equipment or buy used equipment?
- Encourage our management to engage in "green" or sustainable building?
- Distinguish between routine and strategic capital acquisitions?

How can we

- Contribute to the acquisition of enterprisewide software?
- Improve the design and development of new equipment?
- Lower total cost of ownership?

Capital assets are long-term assets that are not bought or sold in the regular course of business, have an ongoing effect on the organization's operations, have an expected use of more than one year, involve large sums of money, and generally are depreciated. Assets may be tangible or intangible. Historically, tangible assets (land, buildings, and equipment) have been the primary focus of managerial attention because they were the key drivers of wealth. Today, intangible assets (patents, copyrights, ideas, knowledge, and people) are important generators of wealth. Intangible assets are especially challenging because traditional accounting procedures do not include valuation methods for intangibles.

According to the U.S. Census Bureau, U.S. businesses typically invest between $1 and $1.5 trillion annually in new and used capital goods. In a weak economy, businesses tend to cut back on capital investments and in a strong economy capital expenditures flow again. The impact of such behavior on the sustainability of the organization is one area of concern for supply managers when they evaluate suppliers. Too little investment or inconsistent investment in capital assets may signify serious organizational problems that will affect the supplier's ability to deliver quality goods or services in the long term.

Senior management concentrates on the economic-value-added model, focusing on revenue enhancement, cost reduction, and asset management. Supply managers contribute through a structured sourcing and supply management process.

This chapter addresses the acquisition of capital goods including equipment, hardware and software, and construction.

THE CHALLENGE OF PROCURING CAPITAL ASSETS

The acquisition of capital goods represents a key strategic move for an organization that could affect its competitive advantage for years to come. On the other hand, it could be a routine matter of no great consequence. In capital-intensive industries such as mining or airlines, the acquisition of capital goods represents one of the single largest purchase categories and one of the greatest opportunities for supply to affect topline (revenue) and bottomline growth. The risks associated with the acquisition of capital assets can be high. From the budgeting process to the design of equipment or buildings, determination of location for real estate purchases, and decisions about enterprisewide hardware and software, many factors play into the ultimate success or failure of a capital project. Clearly defined supply objectives that are linked to, and aligned with, organizational strategy and supported by robust supply processes are as important to successful capital acquisition and management as they are to noncapital purchases. Because of the high dollar amount and the long-term consequences of many capital projects, the application of tools and techniques such as enterprisewide spend analysis; standardization of equipment, including hardware, and software; globalization of processes; and cost visibility are important.

The strategy for a specific capital acquisition depends on a number of factors, including the frequency of the purchase, the projected total cost of ownership, the amount and timing of cash flows, and the potential impact of the purchase on business operations. For example, if assets are replaced at regular intervals, it makes sense to form a close working relationship with the supplier and focus on continuous improvement. At the U.S. Postal Service, for example, the mission of the organization is universal service at a reasonable cost in a timely manner. To achieve this mission consistently, large volumes of letters and packages must be sorted accurately and quickly. Therefore, sortation equipment is a strategic capital acquisition for the Postal Service. Because of design requirements and the desire for standardized equipment across the national organization, only a few suppliers are available. The category management team works closely with these suppliers to develop the specification, manage the cost structure, and deliver equipment in a shortened cycle time that delivers consistent quality, operating speed, and lowest total cost of ownership.

For one-time or infrequent high-value purchases, total cost of ownership analysis of the purchase and the total supply chain costs is appropriate. There are many costs beyond purchase price that affect the true "cost to the organization" of any particular buy and especially for capital assets. A generally accepted figure is that the purchase price makes up from 30 to 50 percent of the total cost of ownership (TCO) of a capital purchase. Other factors, such as maintenance and repair costs, operating costs, downtime, and yield, play key roles. Supply personnel must acquire the skills and knowledge necessary to develop total cost of ownership models that estimate and capture costs throughout the supply chain.

NEW TECHNOLOGY—NEW EQUIPMENT

Competitive advantage stems from product or service differentiation or low-cost production. New technology frequently permits an organization to gain competitive advantage on both grounds—different products and services at significantly lower cost. New technology is, therefore, of significant strategic interest to most organizations. And new technology almost always implies new equipment and new processes. It is this strategic dimension of new equipment acquisition that has traditionally been overlooked by purchasing. Intellectual property rights, speed of acquisition, installation and debugging, continuing supplier support for operational performances and upgrades, and development of the next generation of technological advances become prime matters of corporate concern.

For example, in the semiconductor industry, capital equipment purchases normally represent the largest single percentage category of all purchase dollars. At Intel the goal is to tie capital equipment purchasing and equipment service to performance-based contracting.

Thus, the supplier gets paid for uptime and quality output. The more the running time exceeds agreed-to output goals, the greater the rewards for the supplier. Future plans are driven by the need for continuous improvement in cost per wafer and number of wafers per year per machine. Only a few key supplier partners are included in Intel's longer-range technology road maps planning process—looking five years out. Total cost of ownership, not just the cost of the equipment itself, drives future technology decisions. Obviously, the corporate team approach is required to manage this process and exceptionally capable individuals need to represent supply on the corporate team. Not all equipment purchased is as advanced as that described above. There are, however, some basic considerations to procuring new equipment that are ever present.

Equipment purchases involve, in part, engineering and production considerations and, in part, factors largely outside the scope of these functions. From the former standpoint, there are eight commonly recognized reasons for purchase: (1) capacity, (2) economy in operation and maintenance, (3) increased productivity, (4) better quality, (5) dependability in use, (6) savings in time or labor costs, (7) durability, and (8) safety, pollution, and emergency protection. Beyond these engineering questions are those that only the marketing, supply, or financial departments, or general management itself, can answer. Is this a key strategic commitment? Are style changes or other modifications in the present product essential or even desirable? Is the market static, contracting, or expanding? Does the company have the funds with which to buy the machine that theoretically is most desirable, or is it necessary, for financial reasons, to be satisfied with something that is perhaps less efficient but of a lower initial cost? What should be done in a case in which the particular equipment most desirable from an engineering standpoint is obtainable only from a manufacturer who is not thoroughly trustworthy or perhaps is on the verge of bankruptcy? Should we be the first or the last purchaser of this equipment? Such questions are quite as important in the final decision as are the more purely engineering ones. For this reason, it is sound practice to form a cross-functional sourcing team including representatives from engineering, using departments, finance, marketing, and supply to work jointly on major equipment acquisitions.

Equipment Classification

A useful classification of equipment is the division into multipurpose and single purpose. Multipurpose equipment may have a variety of uses, may be used in many industries, tends to have longer technological life, and may have considerable salvage value. Forklift trucks and standard lathes are typical examples. Single-purpose equipment is designed to do one or several operations well, substantially better than a multipurpose piece of equipment could. On the other hand, its specificity limits its potential use, and its usefulness is closely tied to the need for operations it performs. Such special equipment is often limited to one industry and may even be limited to one customer. The purchaser's specifications are important, requiring extensive consultation between the technical personnel of both buyer and supplier. The salvage value of special equipment may be low, with the drawback that the need for the tasks may disappear before the equipment is physically worn out.

Minor or accessory equipment is normally used in an auxiliary capacity and tends to be of much lower dollar value. Its cost may not even be capitalized, and much of it tends to be standardized. Small power packs and motors are typical examples.

Challenges of Equipment Buying

Equipment procurement raises special challenges:

1. Equipment purchases may be of such strategic importance to the organization that factors like secrecy and ability to be first in the marketplace with output from the equipment become prime driving factors. The risk associated with failure, technological or otherwise, also may be high. Supplier selection decisions under these circumstances are key corporate strategic decisions.
2. Equipment buying usually requires that substantial amounts of money be expended for a single purchase. Sometimes the amount calls for a special form of financing, such as a bond issue, leasing, or payment on the installment plan.
3. Because of their comparatively long life, equipment items are likely to be bought less frequently than other types of purchases.
4. The final cost of equipment is more difficult to determine with exactness than, for example, the final cost of raw materials. The initial cost of equipment is only part of the total cost, which involves a whole series of estimates, such as the effects of installation, idle time, obsolescence, maintenance and repair, displaced labor, and even direct operation factors. Some of these items may never be known exactly, even after experience with the particular piece of equipment in question. Moreover, many of the costs, such as insurance, interest, obsolescence, and depreciation, continue even when the equipment is not in actual use. The income to be derived is also problematical, and, thus, even when it is possible to compute approximate costs, it is often difficult to determine how soon they will be offset by revenues. These comments are particularly applicable to nonproduction equipment, such as cranes and hoists.
5. The demand for equipment more than for any other type of industrial good is a derived demand. Therefore, it is particularly difficult to determine the best time to buy pricewise. Only when the need and the justification for the equipment have been established is there a possibility that its actual purchase may be delayed or hastened by price considerations. Since equipment is not commonly bought until needed, it is seldom bought during periods of business recession, although prices for equipment normally are low at such times and many good arguments can be advanced for buying then. Aside from absence of immediate need, manufacturers in periods of slack business tend to watch their assets carefully. Also, labor may be cheaper during recessions, and there is less incentive to substitute machinery for labor. The reverse conditions prevail in times of prosperity.
6. Equipment purchases frequently involve consideration of environmental impact and the wisest method of disposition of the displaced item. Not only may the future disposal of the equipment itself be an environmental issue, but the materials the equipment processes and needs for its operation and maintenance also may have a significant environmental impact. (See Chapter 11, "Disposal and Investment Recovery.")
7. Tax considerations such as depreciation allowances may significantly affect the delivery and transfer of ownership dates.
8. Technology forecasting plays a role in purchasing new equipment. How long before this equipment will be obsolete? Can it be modified subsequently? What kind of technology is likely to replace it? Should we buy now or later? Can we live with the old equipment

a bit longer? The rate of technological obsolescence of equipment is a particularly thorny problem. Equipment, like components, is experiencing shorter life cycles. New technologies permit rapid prototyping such as stereolithography (SLA) and laminated object manufacturing (LOM). Purchasers can specify changes desirable in current equipment and expect rapid modification as well as rapid development of new models. Thus, the risk of technological obsolescence is increasing.

9. Equipment, particularly major installations, may require a significant start-up period during which extra supply support may have to be provided to deal with all kinds of emergencies. The equipment choice may well commit the organization to a series of other decisions of a permanent nature, such as the type of product to be manufactured, training of operators, allocation of space, the method of its production, and the cost of operation.

It is necessary to analyze not only the particular equipment in question but also such elements as plant layout, kind of power used, types of machines used for other operations, and the like. In short, the proposed installation must be considered an integral part of an established process; and its coordination with the existing facilities must be obtained, even though extensive changes may be required to effect economical production.

SOURCING AND SUPPLY ISSUES

While the basic purchasing and supply process discussed in this text applies to capital acquisitions, there are a number of areas that require special consideration. Because capital purchases are typically high-dollar and high-impact purchases, it is critical to focus cross-functional team resources upfront on design, research and development, and the resulting cost structure to ensure the lowest life cycle costs. Effective performance in these early stages greatly reduces risk throughout the remainder of the supply process, including disposition at the end of the asset's useful life, and provides a strong business case during internal budgeting and project approval. These areas are discussed in greater detail in this section.

Design and R&D Considerations

Development and design issues must be addressed when a customer requires new equipment currently not available on the market. If it is a unique application where the equipment is clearly usable only by the one purchaser, the cost of development and design can properly be charged to the one customer. Many defense applications fall into this category. A more complex issue arises when potential benefits might appear to the supplier in terms of additional expertise transferable to other products or services or similar equipment salable to other customers. Who should pay for development and design under these circumstances? What benefits should accrue to the purchaser of the first piece of equipment of the new generation? Should both purchaser and supplier share in the development and design costs and both benefit from future sales to others in the form of patents, royalties, or percentage fees? Furthermore, there are two standard issues in any new equipment product: (1) Who will pay for development and design and how? (2) How will the risk of failure be shared between buyer and supplier? Practices will vary between industries and circumstances. There may be interesting opportunities for purchasers who are capable of assuming the development cost and technological risk factors to reap future rewards from their entrepreneurial role.

Engineering Service

Most sellers of major equipment maintain an intimate and continuing interest in their equipment after it is sold and installed. Two major questions are involved in providing engineering service: Why is the service given and accepted and what is the cost of such service?

Presale Service

Technical sales service is provided by a supplier to a potential or actual purchaser of equipment, to determine the design and specifications of the equipment believed best suited to the particular requirements of the buyer and also to ensure that the equipment functions properly after installation. It is nearly always related to the "individualized buying problem of particular users." There is, however, another side to this question of sales service. For one thing, the prospective buyer may ask for and receive a great deal of presale service and advice without a real intention of buying or knowing full well that the firm providing the service will under no circumstances receive an order. Not only is such a procedure unethical, but the buyer who pursues it will sooner or later find the organization's reputation for fair dealing has suffered seriously. The problem of engineering service is really twofold, with both phases, however, involving cost. The first phase relates to the method followed by the seller in charging for presale service. Such service is clearly a matter of sales promotion, and when no subsequent sale results or when the profit on the sale is insufficient to cover the cost of the service fully, some other means of recovery must be found. One suggestion for meeting this particular problem is that a specific charge, either a flat fee or one computed on the basis of actual cost, be made for presale engineering service, with the recipient of the service paying this charge whether or not a purchase is made subsequently.

Postsale Service

Often equipment is sold with a production guarantee, an additional reason for supervising both the installation and the operation of the equipment. Even after this initial period, the seller may provide for regular inspection to ensure the proper operation of the machine. The prime abuse of postsale services arises from those firms that insist on furnishing and charging for it whether or not the buyer feels a need for it.

Importance of Cost Factors

Once the need for equipment has been determined, one of the first questions to be considered is that of cost. Is the equipment intended for replacement only or to provide additional capacity? What is the installed cost of the equipment? What will the start-up cost be? Will its installation create problems of plant layout? What will be the maintenance and repair costs, and who will provide repair parts and at what cost? Are accessories required, and if so, what will their costs be? What will be the operating costs, including power and labor? What is the number of machine-hours the equipment will be used? Can the user make the machine or must it be bought outside? At what rate is the machine to be depreciated? What financing costs are involved? If, as is usually the case, the equipment is for production, what is the present cost of producing the product compared with obtaining the item from an outside supplier, and of producing the unit with the new equipment?

Life Cycle Costing or Total Cost of Ownership

Life cycle costing (LCC) or total cost of ownership (TCO) is an appropriate decision approach to capital investments. The philosophy behind LCC is relatively simple: The total cost of a piece of equipment goes well beyond the purchase price or even its installed cost. What is really of interest is the total cost of performing the intended function over the lifetime of the task or the piece of equipment. Thus, an initial low purchase price may mask a higher operating cost, perhaps occasioned by higher maintenance and downtime costs, more skilled labor, greater material waste, more energy use, or higher waste processing charges. Since the low bid would favor a low initial machine price, an unfair advantage may accrue to the supplier with possibly the highest life cycle cost equipment. It is the inclusion of every conceivable cost pertaining to the decision that makes the LCC concept easier to grasp theoretically than to practice in real life. Since many of the costs are future ones, possibly even 10 to 15 years hence and of a highly uncertain nature, criticisms of the exactness of LCC are well founded. Fortunately, software programs are available varying from simple accounting programs, which compute costs from project life cycles, to Monte Carlo simulation of the equipment from conception to disposal. The computer allows for testing of sensitivity, and, when necessary, inputs can be changed readily.

LCC is a serious and preferable alternative to emphasizing the low bid. The experience with LCC has shown in a surprising number of instances that the initial purchase price of equipment may be a relatively low percentage of LCC. For example, computers, if purchased, seldom account for over one-third, and most industrial equipment falls into the 20 to 60 percentage range, of LCC. In one TCO study for a multimillion-dollar piece of equipment, 139 different cost elements were identified for the computer simulation of the process.

Considerable skill and knowledge are required to fully utilize LCC or TCO in an organization. Organizations that focus on supply chain or network management also must consider how to spread this concept throughout the chain or network. At SEMATECH, an international organization that supports research and development related to semiconductors, training is provided through a third party to spread TCO concepts throughout the semiconductor supply chain. TCO issues are of equal concern in service organizations where the distinctive competency is information. In these situations, information is made usable and accessible by capital investments in computer hardware and software.

Budgeting Procedures

When the financial budget is set up, it is customary to make provisions for two types of capital expenditures. The first type covers probable expenditures that, although properly chargeable to some capital account, are still too small to be brought directly to the attention of the finance committee or controller. Customarily, some limit is fixed, such as \$2,000 to \$10,000. The second type includes expenditures for larger amounts. The inclusion in the budget normally constitutes neither an authorization to spend that amount of money nor an approval of any specific equipment acquisition. This authorization must be obtained subsequently from the executives concerned, and their specific approval is given only after they have examined carefully a preliminary analysis of the project. A formal appropriation request is called for, giving a detailed description of what is to be bought, estimates of the costs involved, the savings likely to result, the causes that have created the need, the effect of the purchase on the organization as a whole, and whatever other information those initiating the request feel is pertinent. In light of these facts, together with the data regarding other financial requirements of the company and its financial position, a decision is made as to the wisdom of authorizing the particular expenditure under consideration.

Sourcing and Selection

Sourcing and selection of the proper source requires careful consideration in any capital asset purchase. In the purchase of raw materials and supplies, quick and reliable delivery and continuous availability of supply are important reasons for choosing a particular supplier. These characteristics are often not so important in equipment purchases where maintenance and repair costs, operating costs, downtime, and yield often greatly exceed the purchase price. The reliability of the seller and a reasonable price are, of course, important, regardless of what is being bought. But, as contrasted with raw materials, what may be called cooperation in selecting the right type of equipment, the proper installation and common interests in efficient operation—in short, a long-continuing interest in the product after it is sold—becomes very important. So, too, does the availability of repair parts and of repair services throughout the entire life of the machine. Satisfactory past relationships with the equipment supplier weigh heavily in the placing of future orders. The interest of operations, engineering, or technical personnel in capital equipment is such that they usually have a strong supplier preference. For large companies, manufacturing equipment in their own shops has always been an alternative. Some even have subsidiaries specializing in equipment design and manufacture. Where secret processes give a manufacturer a competitive edge, such in-house manufacture is almost essential. In JIT, as identified in Chapter 6, one of the capabilities a JIT adopter is supposed to have is in-house modification of equipment. This is often related to setup time reduction and small-run capability enhancement. In-house equipment design and modification capability clearly is a major asset in assessing supplier technological proficiency.

Legal Issues

Attention also should be directed to the legal questions that arise in connection with equipment buying, including the risk of liability for patent infringement or employee accidents. Equipment sales contracts and purchase agreements are often long and involved, offering many opportunities for legal controversies. Various forms of insurance coverage are used and are often subject to varying interpretations. Purchased machinery must comply fully with the safety regulations of the state, province, or country in which it is operated, and these safety regulations vary greatly in different locations. Federal government OSHA (Occupational Safety and Health Act) requirements have to be followed. The question of consequential damages is a particularly touchy one. Should the seller of a key piece of equipment be responsible for the loss of sales and contribution when the machine fails because of a design or fabrication error? Such losses may be huge for the buyer. In one company, gross revenue of $1 million per day was lost for six months because of the failure of a new piece of equipment costing $800,000! Many equipment acquisitions need careful scrutiny and interpretation by qualified legal counsel.

Disposition of Obsolete or Replaced Equipment

What to do with old or replaced equipment is an interesting question. One procedure is to trade in the old machine on the new, with the supplier making an allowance and assuming the burden of disposal. Barring other considerations, the decision of whether to trade in or not is largely dependent on which will result in the lowest net cost to the purchaser. Since trade-ins are a form of price concession, they may not accurately reflect current market values of the old equipment. In some industries, old equipment may be in perfect operating condition and its disposal may well create unwanted competition. At other times, it may represent a health or environmental hazard, or contain special secret features. Destruction may be a reasonable solution in all these instances.

In large organizations, equipment displaced in one area may be of use in another within the same organization. It is normal practice for supply departments to maintain an online database or circulate lists of items available within the organization before searching for other disposal alternatives. The advantage of an online database is that all business units can post and acquire useable equipment more easily. If a company has global operations, then what has become obsolete equipment for one location may be seen as the latest technology in another. If the equipment can be transported and set up cost-effectively, this may be preferable to buying new equipment. Transfer pricing is usually based on book value and the transportation charges are assumed by the receiving unit or department. Another option is to sell the old equipment to a used equipment dealer. It may be possible to find a direct buyer or to sell the old machine as scrap. Some of these procedures are discussed indirectly in Chapter 11, "Investment Recovery." As in all other situations involving disposal, environmental considerations will impact the disposal method chosen. Disassembly of equipment may be required for proper recycling.

REASONS FOR BUYING USED EQUIPMENT

In our discussion of equipment purchases thus far, it has been assumed that the buyer was acquiring new equipment. An alternative is the purchase of used equipment, which raises special issues. In general, the same rules of evaluation apply as in the case of new equipment. One important difference, however, may be that, ordinarily, manufacturers' services and guarantees do not apply to such purchases. The value of these intangibles is difficult to determine. Many buyers would say that they are more important with used equipment than with new and that their value may be greater than any differential in price.

Fleet management of vehicles requires special attention to the decision of when to replace a vehicle with another. Interesting developments in fleet management include the purchase of vehicles from automobile rental companies (with still relatively low mileage, but a significant amount of new car depreciation knocked off), the use of leasing companies or third-party logistics providers, and driver purchase options.

Some of the reasons for the purchase of used equipment are

1. When price is important, either because the differential between new and used is great or the buyer's funds are scarce.
2. For use in a pilot or experimental plant.
3. For use with a special or temporary order over which the entire cost will be amortized.

4. Where the machine will be idle a substantial amount of time.
5. For use of apprentices.
6. For maintenance departments (not production).
7. For faster delivery when time is essential.
8. When a used machine can be easily modernized for relatively little or is already the latest model.

Sales Contract Terms

Used equipment may be offered with different contract terms:

1. The equipment may be available "as is," and perhaps "where is." A sale "as is" means that the contract carries essentially "no warranty, guarantee, or representation of any kind, expressed or implied, as to the condition of the item offered for sale." "Where is," of course, is self-explanatory.
2. The equipment may be sold with certain specific guarantees, preferably expressed in writing. This practice is found more generally among used equipment dealers, though they sometimes may offer equipment "as is."
3. The equipment may be sold "guaranteed and rebuilt." The equipment is invoiced as such; it has been tested; and it carries a binding guarantee of satisfactory performance for not less than 30 days from the date of shipment.

There are various channels through which used equipment is bought and sold. These include the manufacturer who accepted the used equipment as a trade-in, direct sale to the user, brokers, auctions, and dealers.

LEASING EQUIPMENT

Many manufacturers of capital equipment lease as well as sell their equipment. Leasing advocates point out that leasing involves payments for the use of the assets rather than for the privilege of owning the asset. Short-term rentals are a special form of lease that make a lot of sense when limited use of the equipment is foreseen and the capital and/or maintenance cost of the equipment is significant. Often an operator can be obtained along with the piece of equipment rented. The construction industry is a good example where extensive use is made of short-term rentals. Most lease contracts can be drawn to include an "option to buy" after some stated period. It is important for anyone considering the lease of capital equipment to be sure that the Internal Revenue regulations are understood. Canadian and American government interpretation is similar. The Internal Revenue Service's position on ascertaining the tax status of leases is relevant.

In the absence of compelling factors of contrary implication, the parties will be considered as having intended a purchase and sale rather than a rental if one or more of the following conditions are covered in the agreement:

1. Portions of periodic payments are specifically applicable to any equity to be acquired by the lessee.
2. The lessee will acquire title on payment of a stated amount of rentals.

3. The total amount that the lessee is required to pay for a relatively short period constitutes an inordinately large proportion of the total sum required to be paid to secure transfer of title.
4. The agreed rental payments exceed the current fair-rental values.
5. The property may be acquired under a purchase option that is nominal in relation to the value of the property at the time when the option may be exercised, as determined at the time of entering into the original agreement, or which is a relatively small amount when compared with the total payments that are required to be made.
6. Some portion of periodic payments is specifically designated as interest or is otherwise recognizable as the equivalent of interest.

Unless the lease rental payments can be treated as an expense item for income tax purposes, some of the possible advantages of the equipment lease plan may not be realized.

In the past, some large manufacturers of machines and equipment employing advanced technology preferred to follow a policy of leasing rather than selling their equipment. Government antitrust actions have aimed at giving the user the right to determine whether to lease or purchase. The leasing may be done by the manufacturers of the equipment, by distributors, or by companies organized for the specific purpose of leasing equipment. At times, as in the construction industry, an owner of equipment who has no immediate use for it may lease or rent it to other concerns that may have temporary immediate need for it. An interesting phenomenon with leasing occurs in large organizations, including public agencies. Since lease costs are normally charged to operating instead of capital budgets, department heads may try to acquire equipment through the back door by leasing when the capital budget does not permit purchase. This can easily lead to abuse and some very high rental costs. In one government agency, the rental of recording equipment over a six-month period equaled the purchase cost. Buyers need to be aware of this practice and on the lookout for costly subterfuges involving leasing.

Advantages and Disadvantages of Leasing

The advantages of leasing may be listed as follows:

1. Lease rentals are expenses for income tax purposes.
2. There is a small initial outlay (may actually cost less).
3. Expert service is available.
4. The risk of obsolescence is reduced.
5. It is adaptable to special jobs and seasonal business.
6. A test period is provided before purchase.
7. The burden of investment is shifted to the supplier.

For example, automobile fleet managers frequently prefer leasing when their fleet is spread across the country and when the leasing company has greater purchasing clout and better disposal ability. There are certain equally clear disadvantages, however:

1. The final cost may be high.
2. Surveillance by lessor is entailed.
3. There is less freedom of control and use.

Many leases need to be watched with care since they are one-sided in their terms, placing virtually all the risks on the lessee. For instance, what are the arrangements for replacing equipment when it is obsolete or no longer serviceable? Is the lessee free to buy supplies anywhere? Are the actual charges what they appear to be? Are there onerous limitations on either the maximum or the minimum output or other such operational factors as the number of hours per day or number of shifts the equipment may be used or on using attachments? What limitations, if any, are there to the uses to which the equipment may be put?

Types of Leases

The two main types of leases are the financial and the operational lease. The financial lease may be of the full payout or partial payout variety. In the full payout form, the lessee pays the full purchase price of the equipment plus interest and, if applicable, maintenance, service, recordkeeping, and insurance charges on a regular payment plan. In the partial payout plan, there is a residual value to the equipment at the end of the lease term and the lessee pays for the difference between the original cost and residual value plus interest and charges. The financial lease cost is made up of the lessor's fee, the interest rate, and the depreciation rate of the equipment. The lessor's fee depends on the services offered and may be as low as 0.25 percent of the gross for straight financing without other services. The interest rate will depend on both the cost of money to the lessor and the credit rating of the lessee. The depreciation normally varies with the type of equipment and its use.

The operational lease, in its basic form, is noncancellable, has a fixed term that is substantially less than the life of the equipment, and has a fixed financial commitment that is substantially less than the purchase price of the equipment. Service is the key factor in the operational lease, with the lessor assuming full responsibility for maintenance, obsolescence, insurance, taxes, purchase, and resale of equipment, and so on. The charges for these services must be evaluated by the lessee against other alternatives that may be open.

Categories of Leasing Companies

Careful analysis of how the lessor will profit from the leasing arrangement is vital in obtaining a satisfactory price. Since most leasing companies have standard procedures for calculating leases but are seldom willing to disclose these procedures or the vital figures behind them, it behooves the buyer to search carefully before signing. Since lessors are more likely to disclose competitors' procedures and figures than their own, the search need not be seen as an impossible task. There are four major structures of leasing relationships, each with its special implications (see Figure 16–1).

The Full Service Lessor

Full service lessors are most common in the automotive, office equipment, and industrial equipment fields. The lessor performs all services, purchases the equipment to the buyer's specifications, and has its own source of financing. This type of lessor generally obtains discounts or rebates from the equipment manufacturers that are not disclosed to the lessee. Profits are also obtained on the maintenance and service charges that are included in the lease rate. Care should be taken on long-term leases that contain an escalation provision to allow such escalation only on that portion of the lease on which costs might rise.

FIGURE 16–1
Four Leasing Structural Relationships

The Full Service Lessor

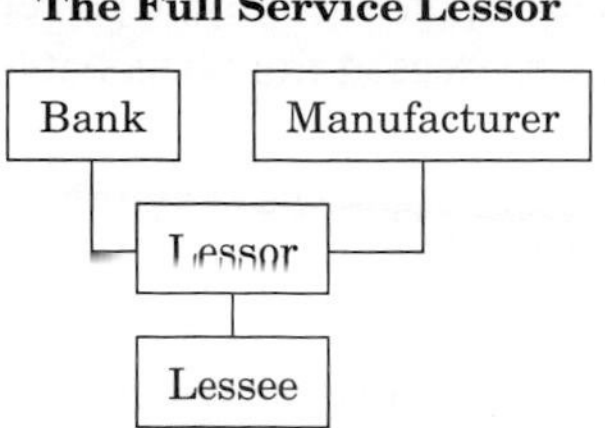

The Finance Lease Company

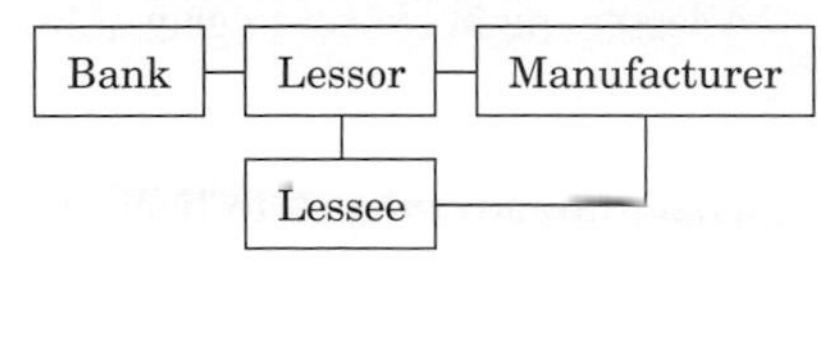

The Captive Leasing Company

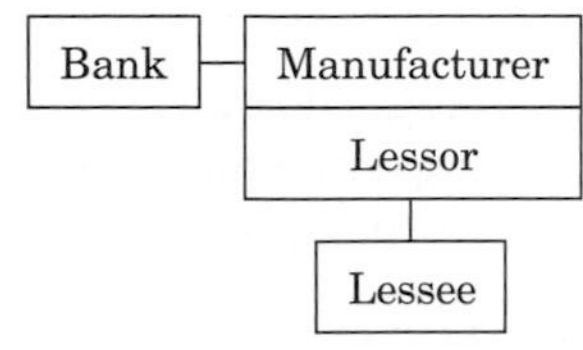

Bank Participation

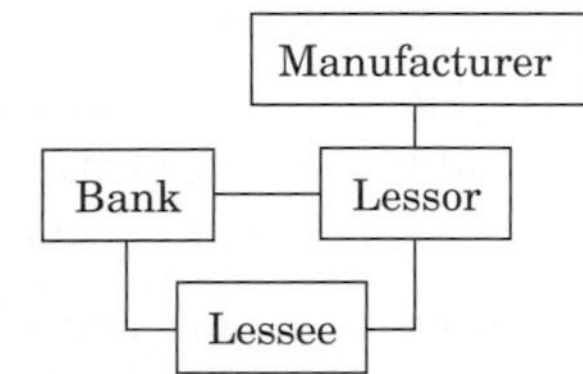

The Finance Lease Company

This type of lessor does not purchase or maintain the equipment, so the lessee deals directly with the equipment manufacturer. The lessor frequently has access to funds at close to the prime rate and is able to make its profit by lending above this. Occasionally, if a relatively short lease is involved, the lessor may wish to profit from the resale value of the equipment and may offer unusually low lending rates. A profitable lessor may benefit from the investment tax credits and depreciation that, to a less profitable lessee, may be meaningless. When a lessee has already reached the limits on its investment tax credits because of large capital expenditures, but the lessor is not yet at the limit, leasing may similarly benefit both.

Captive Leasing

The prime purpose of captive leasing is to encourage the sale and use of the parent's equipment. There are several reasons why the original manufacturer of equipment may choose to lease rather than to sell:

1. To secure either wider distribution or a higher margin.
2. To reduce the credit risk.
3. To sell a full line or to increase the volume of sales of supplies.
4. To control the secondhand market.
5. To stabilize the company's growth through securing distribution in times of recession when sales, especially of new as contrasted with used equipment, are difficult to make.
6. To control servicing.
7. To protect a patent position.

Obviously, a transfer price for the equipment holds between the parent and the lessor. Sometimes a lessor will quote a 2 percent sales tax figure on the rental value, when in reality the lessor may be charged only with a use tax that applies to only 50 percent of the rental value. A lessee might expect to gain at least a 1 percent benefit from negotiation here.

Bank Participation

There are advantages to bank participation in cases where the lessee has a good credit rating. The bank may be willing to finance part of the lease at rates slightly over prime because it is a low-risk and low-nuisance lease. The lessor looks after the purchasing, servicing, and disposal of the equipment, relieving the bank of tasks it normally has little expertise in.

Lessor Evaluation

Quite aside from any weighting of the specific advantages and disadvantages and beyond the actual terms of the lease, any prospective lessee of equipment needs to exercise the utmost care in passing judgment on the lessor. Is the lessor

1. Reasonable and fair in dealing with customers?
2. Devoting as much attention and money to research as alleged?
3. Strong financially?
4. If a sole source, prone to be arbitrary in the periodic adjustment of rental and other fees?

THE ACQUISITION OF TECHNOLOGY

Many organizations spend millions of dollars on information and communications technology, including hardware and software. The potential short- and long-term impact of these purchases on practically every aspect of the organization's business operations makes IT decisions too important to leave to IT alone. While the previous discussion of equipment purchases applies to hardware purchases, there are several other considerations specific to IT purchases.

The technology purchase may be for goods only (hardware), services only (software), or goods and services (hardware and software) bundled together (see Chapter 17, "Services," for a detailed discussion of services purchasing). The experience of many significant technology purchasers shows that the sticker price of the hardware can be one-third or less of the annual costs of supporting the technology and obviously far less of the total costs over the useful life of the equipment (maybe three years for a desktop computer). Therefore, total cost of ownership for technology is a critical piece of analysis. These costs include, in addition to the sticker price, all the costs associated with the maintenance provider, warranty, and training as well as costs to configure, maintain, and update units and train end users and any software and software-related costs.

Hardware such as computers and printers can be purchased or leased. A buy-or-lease assessment should be performed to consider the costs and benefits of each approach. If purchased, one advantage is that the expenses can be depreciated over a period of time. However, the organization also will incur property taxes and the cost to replace obsolete technology every three to four years. By leasing, the organization can defer the tax liability and avoid technology obsolescence but ultimately may pay more in lease prices than the purchase price of the hardware. The supply organization can potentially add value in the early analysis and IT strategy planning if they acquire cost knowledge and use it effectively in total cost modeling, negotiating, and managing the contract. Total cost of ownership is also important when it comes to software purchases. Software TCO is affected by the licensing fee and usage terms, the number of users initially and the cost to add new users, installation costs, training, maintenance and support fees, frequency and number of upgrades, and serial number tracking if required over the useful life of the software (generally two years).

Software is an interesting purchase because it is intellectual property rather than a tangible asset or a service and, in many situations, the costs are capitalized rather than expensed. Capitalization means that costs are depreciated over the life of the software rather than immediately expensed. Since software impacts business operations for years, it makes sense to try to value it as an asset and show its impact on the income statement. The capital budgeting process imposes discipline on IT purchases by requiring IT teams to project costs, benefits, and length of use of capitalized software. It is often difficult, however, to project useful life, and the company runs the risks of having to write off large undepreciated amounts if the software is replaced or scrapped sooner than projected. Intangible assets present challenges to decision makers at all levels and in all functional areas of an organization from senior executives to accountants to IT to supply to users. Strong business partnerships among internal stakeholders and strategic suppliers of intangible assets are increasingly important in a knowledge-based economy.

THE ACQUISITION OF CONSTRUCTION

Construction represents a special class of capital goods. In the first place, land or space needs to be available for construction. Therefore, real estate acquisition may be required with all of the attendant issues of office or plant location involving deeds, access, zoning restrictions, taxes, and availability of services such as water, electricity, telephone, and disposal. Other issues may involve distance from customers, suppliers, and labor and transportation access and costs. Obviously, many of these issues are properly the domain of other functions in the organization. In organizations in a rapid expansion mode, such as fast-food chains, or those with substantial land holdings, a separate real estate or facility management department may manage all real estate acquisition and maintenance. In the construction of buildings for offices, production, warehouses, stores, restaurants, maintenance, hotels, education, or research, the intended use of the facility will be the prime concern in its design. It is possible for larger organizations to maintain an in-house architectural and structural, plumbing, air-conditioning, and electrical engineering staff. Even in these organizations, the possibility of make or buy exists. A core group of specialists on staff may be augmented with outside consulting assistance when demand peaks occur or special expertise is required.

If building in a variety of locations, possibly domestic and international, local expertise familiar with climatic conditions, building codes, and construction contractors may be absolutely necessary. Standardizing building design when feasible also may reduce risks and costs in all subsequent phases of the project and better satisfy the final customer. Most companies in retail, fast-food, and even the semiconductor industry build facilities according to a standard design. It is normal in many construction projects that the cost of the design is a relatively small portion of the total project cost, possibly in the 7 to 12 percent range. Yet, the design itself will be a major determinant of final project cost. Therefore, it is important to examine the question of design acquisition or design management by a set of criteria going well beyond the cost of the design phase itself.

Risks in the Construction Process

Many high-cost risks exist in the traditional construction sequence of project concept, capital request, design, construction bids, contractor selection, and construction. Changes during the construction phase are almost invariably expensive and time-consuming. The capital approval process is often lengthy and, by the time capital is approved, the amount of time available for design, bids, and construction is tight. Rushing through these phases becomes costly and prone to mistakes. The original cost estimate may not be realistic because all details of the design were not yet known, market conditions for construction or labor may have changed, or the project itself may have evolved into a different concept. If construction bids received exceed the original capital request approved, the uncomfortable decision needs to be made whether to start cost cutting or to engage in a lengthy, and possibly futile, attempt to get approval for more funds.

The intent here is not to paint all construction as a messy and problem-filled area. To the contrary, the existence of all of these risks suggests that there is plenty of room for improvement and problem avoidance by sound project management. And, since many of the costs and problems center on the need for outside consultants and contractors, proper supply management is a vital component of successful construction.

Approaches to Construction Acquisition

It is not surprising that a number of approaches have evolved to address the key problem areas in construction. Most attempt to ensure proper quality, on-time delivery, and cost control. Clearly, even if the traditional approach is followed in all the phases of construction, selection of the right consultants and architects, the right contractors and subcontractors with proper coordination and appropriate lead times for all activities will increase the chances of success.

E-construction is the application of Internet tools to the construction project management process. Online tools allow easier, faster, and less costly coordination of numerous separate teams over the life of a project. Centralized communication is the key feature of these e-commerce sites. Large contractors are using e-tools to communicate with partners and subcontractors, buy materials, and bid for jobs. However, e-commerce has not been widely adopted by second- and third-tier suppliers in the construction industry. In these businesses, communication is still done largely by fax, voice mail, and overnight shipping, resulting in a huge loss in potential savings.

An e-commerce provider helps engineering and building professionals manage projects, processes, documents, and teams. Typically, they charge an upfront fee and a monthly maintenance fee. In return, the entire construction team is linked with passwords enabling differing levels of access to information and services related to their project. Through Web collaboration, the most current blueprints and work schedules can be posted, e-mail notifications sent to appropriate parties, and a virtual paper trail created of who viewed what and when, thereby providing a compendium of evidence. Architectural drawings can be viewed online and printed from the user's computer whenever changes are made rather than waiting for them to be commercially printed, packaged, and shipped. After the job is completed, equipment manuals and building specifications can be stored on disks or cartridges.

Project management techniques like the program evaluation review technique (PERT) and critical path method (CPM) can assist greatly. By focusing on the activities on or close to the critical path, they permit proper analysis and planning as well as monitoring. Obviously, purchase lead times for various phases are absolutely critical. The availability of a contingency fund to deal with unexpected problems as they arise also will assist in preventing the project from going off schedule. Incentive clauses or bonuses for early or on-time completion and penalty clauses for lateness also may assist in ensuring on-time completion. In public procurement, the use of bid bonds and performance bonds is intended to ensure contractor commitment and performance.

Some interesting options exist in construction that do not follow the traditional process. For example, one key issue deals with the question of who is the prime contractor. It is possible to perform this task in-house or to use a third party. For those organizations without in-house expertise, this question should not even arise. Another possibility is to go to a turnkey project. The purchaser will specify requirements, probably as a set of performance specifications, and a large contractor or a consulting firm will look after all subsequent phases. This clearly places responsibility for quality, delivery, cost, and performance with one party and allows this party to find its own solutions to specific design or construction challenges. Another option is the request for proposal (RFP) route, rather than having an architect or design engineer produce a specific design. This approach allows the contractors to suggest building materials and a construction design and methodology particularly suited to their own strengths and circumstances. RFPs also may be posted online, bids received electronically, and awards posted after the selection has been made.

The request for quote (RFQ) or request for proposal (RFP) needs to include the unique features of the construction services purchase. These include[1]

Drawings. Include if necessary.

Work changes. Identify when and how changes are determined and accepted and include a requirement for itemized labor and material charges with percentage material mark-up caps.

Acceptance criteria. Clearly identify when acceptance has been made.

Modifications. Acknowledge receipt of modifications to avoid trouble later on. Consider including a document for submitting quotations or proposals for modifications.

Evaluation criteria. Clearly identify the decision criteria for selection; for example, costs, completion date and time frame before project can begin, work schedule, potential subcontractors, expertise of supplier's staff, conformance to buyer's terms and conditions, and past history.

Payment process. Establish the process using referenced American Institute of Architects (AIA) documents.

Insurance and bonds. Establish performance and payment requirements (including figures and reference to AIA documents).

[1] Richard E. Lohmann, "More Than Just Bricks and Mortar," *Purchasing Today,* November 1998, p. 51.

Termination criteria. Establish termination criteria including violation of contract requirements (also covering federal and state laws).

Project schedules. Require the submission of proposed project schedules prior to execution of any work and specifications for any products or materials to be installed. Schedules should include the number of days before project can begin and the number of days for completion.

Site inspection/walk-through. Require information if applicable.

Subcontractors. Require a list.

Liquidated damages. Include in the event of project delays.

Pricing options. List acceptable pricing options.

Statement of work. Clearly define the supplier's responsibility. (See Chapter 17, "Services," for more information on writing a statement of work.)

It is possible and desirable to use value analysis/value engineering techniques during the concept and design steps to ensure that the best value option evolves. Another option is to select a contractor during the concept stage and use the contractor to design and build to a specific performance, cost, and delivery target. Dramatic savings in time and cost may be possible if the right contractor is selected early on.

On-Site Considerations in Construction

If the construction is done on space owned and operated by the buying organization, special contract provisions may be needed to deal with issues such as identification and security; hours of access to the site; noise, dress, and safety regulations; access to food service; recreational, office, production, and other facilities; deliveries; conduct; and cleanliness.

Global engineering, procurement, and construction companies that build large facilities, such as power plants, face special challenges because of the size and costs of the projects as well as the far-flung and often remote locations. Minimizing and managing risk is made more difficult by political and social unrest and the challenges of geography and harsh climates. For example, the design of an offshore oil rig may have to include shields to protect against the currently favored weapons of high seas pirates. Projects in countries where social order is weak and theft is high may require the purchase of special security forces to guard equipment in transit. Remote locations may present a huge challenge if something goes wrong. How does the supply team plan in case a customized piece of equipment with a long lead time ends up at the bottom of the North Sea during a storm?

Developing knowledge management processes and systems to overcome time, distance, and difficult terrain may provide a company a competitive advantage. Capturing and transferring knowledge from one project to another where the dissimilarities may appear to be greater than the similarities is also a source of advantage. In these high-risk and high-stakes projects, engineering, supply, and construction must work together from the design stage to deliver the greatest value to both buyer and supplier. Supply base management and especially early supplier involvement of key suppliers are very important in these projects.

Sustainable Building

Building design, construction techniques, materials, operations and maintenance, and demolition or disassembly have environmental impact on watersheds, habitat, air quality, and community transportation patterns. For example, according to Worldwatch (http://www.worldwatch.org), buildings consume 40 percent of the world's total energy use and 30 percent of raw materials consumption and are responsible for 40 percent of municipal solid waste destined for local landfills. Sustainable building refers to life-cycle costing that considers all the environmental, economic, and social cost factors of a built environment.

The market for green buildings expands as the costs of sustainable buildings decrease, making them more price competitive with conventional buildings. The best motivation for green building is lower total cost of ownership. One of the biggest costs of operating a facility is energy. Building designs that substantially lower energy costs can contribute greatly to lower total cost. Low- and high-tech energy-saving ideas have been incorporated into large construction projects. On the low-tech side, building positioning can maximize sunlight in the winter and awnings can reduce sunlight in the summer to lower both heating and cooling costs. Positioning also can lower the wind's effect on heating costs. Rooftop "chillers" cool water for air-conditioning and save about 35 percent over a conventional building. At Toyota's complex in Torrance, California, a solar energy system generates up to 20 percent of demand. Aside from the hard-dollar cost savings from these energy-saving initiatives, studies show that students learn better in well-lighted facilities, retail stores sell more in stores with skylights, and some employers report lower absenteeism and higher retention in green buildings where they receive fewer complaints about "bad air." The dilemma is how to identify and estimate all cost elements into a total cost model and use those data to drive design and construction decisions.

The 4,000-member Green Building Council's Leadership in Energy and Environmental Design (LEED) program has established industry standards and a scoring system with silver, gold, and platinum ratings based on the "greenness" of a project. A growing number of public purchasers at the federal, state, and local levels require "green" features in buildings that get tax dollars. At the federal level, the General Services Administration (GSA) requires LEED certification on structures that cost $2 million or more.

Supply's Involvement in Construction

In many organizations, construction is largely left to the engineering department, and supply's involvement may be limited to sending out the request for bids, if that. To be meaningfully involved, supply personnel must develop skills and knowledge specific to the construction industry. Moreover, as in all other types of acquisition, early supply involvement in the project is absolutely necessary to capitalize on value analysis, development of performance-driven requests for proposal, and structured analysis of bids and proposals. Throughout the project, supply also can monitor suppliers to increase the speed and breadth of information related to supplier performance, provide early identification of performance problems, decrease the risks from poor-performing companies in the supply chain, and identify opportunities to intervene with a supplier, improve performance, or restructure business to avoid loss or failure.

Since many other functions aside from purchasing and engineering should be involved early in construction planning, the idea of using a cross-functional project team is highly appealing. It is appropriate that the supply function be included in such a team. As with all other purchases, much of the cost and quality are driven in at the need recognition and description stages of the process. Finishing the project at or below budget and on time are two critical success factors in construction. Because of the high risk of missing these targets, construction offers an opportunity for significant cost avoidance, reduction, and savings if the expertise of multiple internal and external stakeholders can be brought together successfully.

Conclusion

Supply managers are concerned with the acquisition of capital assets because they represent significant cash outlays and are often of strategic importance. The shift in importance from tangible assets such as land, buildings, and equipment as wealth builders to knowledge-based assets also increases the challenges and importance of capital asset acquisition and management. Whether tangible or intangible, capital assets represent a significant opportunity to enhance revenue, manage assets, and reduce costs. Meaningful involvement in enterprisewide strategy development and execution requires supply personnel to acquire the appropriate skills and knowledge to build successful internal business partnerships with the more traditional "owners" of capital assets.

Questions for Review and Discussion

1. Why is capital goods acquisition different from the purchase of raw materials?
2. How can a reasonable value be placed on engineering service supplied by a potential supplier of equipment?
3. What are some of the challenges in assessing total cost of ownership of a green building versus a conventional one?
4. How might e-commerce tools be used to reduce, eliminate, or contain construction costs?
5. What could be the advantages of buying on a turnkey basis?
6. How might one dispose of a capital good?
7. Why would anyone prefer to lease instead of buy?
8. Explain how and when equipment purchasing might be strategic?
9. Why are technology acquisitions considered capital purchases?
10. What are the advantages of using a full-service lessor?

References

Isikoff, Brian. "How to Buy Technology," *NAPM InfoEdge* 3, no. 12 (August 1998).

Knod, Edward M., and Richard Schonberger. *Operations Management.* New York: McGraw-Hill/Irwin, 2001.

McConville, John G. *1996 International Construction Costs and Reference Data Yearbook.* New York: John Wiley & Sons, 1996.

Rocky Mountain Institute. http://www.rmi.org.

U.S. Census Bureau. *Current Construction Reports.* http://www.census.gov.

U.S. Green Building Council. http://www.usgbc.org.

Case 16–1

Mark Appleton

In early February, Mark Appleton, senior contracts buyer for Browne and Coulter Engineering (BCE), found himself at odds with Sheila Forker, project engineer, on a small construction project. Mark believed it should be given to the low bidder, but Sheila did not agree.

BCE was a large engineering firm specializing in large, heavy custom-equipment manufacture. It was necessary for one of the current projects in the plant to construct a small testing laboratory with some unusually tight specifications on its soundproofing.

Sheila Forker had asked Mark to request bids for the laboratory's construction and had sent along, as was customary, a list of recommended contractors. On looking over the four contractors engineering recommended, Mark believed BCE would not have much success with them. He, therefore, requested from Sheila Forker, the project engineer, permission to add two more names to the list: Andrews Construction and Moore Brothers.

When the six bids were received, only one of the four contractors engineering had recommended came in with what Mark believed to be a meaningful bid. Foster Construction bid $572,000. The other three companies recommended by Sheila had bids over $650,000, while Moore Brothers bid $604,000 and Andrews Construction bid $404,000. When Mark sent to Sheila his recommendation to go with Andrews, she refused it on the ground that BCE had no experience with Andrews and a "high level of comfort" with Foster. Because Foster had been on engineering's original list of recommended contractors, Sheila insisted this was the logical choice. Given the project's tight deadline Mark knew he had to resolve this issue quickly.

Case 16–2

Casson Construction

On May 20, Robert Casson, vice president of Casson Construction, a general contractor in Portland, Oregon, was considering the performance of the precast concrete subcontractor on a $1.9 million, tightly scheduled, high-profile library renovation. He had just finished writing a letter to Langford Precast advising them of their breach of contract. Robert now wondered what action he should take to ensure the successful completion of the project.

CASSON CONSTRUCTION

Robert Casson for the last two years had been in partnership with his father in the medium-sized general contracting firm, Casson Construction. Currently, the firm had contracts ranging from $100,000 to $5 million under way in a variety of commercial, residential, industrial, and institutional buildings. The firm was known in the local area for quality construction and teamwork. Robert's father described his objective on the library project as "to manage the project to create a partnership between the university, the design consultants, and the contractor in order to produce a building that everyone can look at with pride." He believed that in order for the team members to work together over the course of a project, everyone had to "bend a bit to accomplish something, not trying to point out a weakness and not taking advantage of someone's weakness." He hoped that his sons would continue to manage the business with this philosophy in mind when they took over the firm.

THE COMPETITIVE BID SYSTEM

General contractors bid on new projects in competition with other contracting firms. A general contractor obtained working drawings for a new building from the architect or a local construction association, obtained prices from the various trades required to complete the project (steel, masonry, precast concrete, etc.), and submitted to the university a price for constructing the building. Universities frequently prequalified general contractors to ensure that the contractors who submitted bids had sufficient experience to carry out the work. Once the bids were submitted, the university would select the low bidder, ensure that the bid was in order, and award the firm the project. Occasionally, universities would not prequalify the contractors to open up the field of competition for new entrants on smaller projects.

THE LIBRARY RENOVATION PROJECT

The local university decided not to prequalify the general contractors prior to calling for the submission of bids for the renovation and addition to its Family Law Library. Casson Construction was eager to submit a bid on the project because the job was an opportunity for the firm to take on a large project for a substantial client with the prospect of significant future business.

When the bids were opened on November 10, Robert Casson knew that his firm's bid of $1,886,000 was low by $87,000 in relation to the next lowest bidder's bid. The contract would be a "nosebleed" for his firm and would have to be carefully managed to avoid incurring any additional time on the site that would eat up the firm's slim profit margin.

THE PRECAST SUBCONTRACT

The work contained in the precast subcontract was divided into two categories: precast parking bumpers and architectural precast concrete. The precast parking bumpers were simple in shape and required a low level of finish. The architectural precast, which formed the surrounds for the windows and was incorporated in horizontal bands on the exterior walls of the building, was highly detailed and required several different sections of different lengths and profiles as well as a high degree of finish. During the bid period of the project, Casson Construction requested prices from two local precast concrete suppliers. Of the two, Langford Precast submitted the lower bid and was carried by Casson Construction in their bid price. Once Casson Construction had been awarded the contract by the university, they issued a purchase order on December 4 to Langford Precast. Casson Construction had worked with Langford on other, less complicated jobs and, although they had had a few scheduling problems with Langford, both firms had managed to get the job done.

PROJECT MANAGEMENT

The general contractor was responsible for the overall control of a project, from initial bid to completion, and employed the subcontractors for the specific trades. The individual subtrades on a typical project included everything from site services to the installation of washroom accessories. Casson Construction included a 4 percent fee on the value of subcontractors' work in its bid price for the management and coordination of subcontractors' work. As project manager for the library renovation, Robert Casson scheduled the work of the different subtrades on site and coordinated each subcontractor's work with the other trades.

PROJECT SCHEDULE

The university had dictated in the terms of the contract that the renovation project had to be substantially completed on August 6. Robert knew that the university was serious about the deadline because alternative space could not be arranged if the project was late and the faculty depended on the library to do research. If the project was late, the best that Robert Casson could hope for was that the university would charge his firm $1,000/day minimum for the use of alternative lecture halls. The worst-case scenario was that the university would never again consider a bid from his firm. No monetary value could be ascribed to the loss of the firm's reputation for on-time delivery.

LITIGATION IN THE INDUSTRY

In considering how to handle this situation, Robert could not help himself from thinking about a period of litigation he had just come through. Robert had been in court for $1^1/_2$ weeks the previous month for a case that took place a year earlier on a townhouse project. Robert had taken over the project from another project manager and had opted to throw an excavation subcontractor off the job for breach of contract. The case cost Casson Construction $15,000 before it went to court and $25,000 in court. In the end, the judge ruled that Casson Construction should have nursed the subcontractor along through the job and then back-charged the firm for the delay at the end of the contract.

LANGFORD PRECAST

Robert knew that as of May 20, Langford Precast had very little invested in the library project. Robert could not confirm exactly how much of the architectural precast had been produced in Langford's plant and was concerned that Langford would simply walk off the job if given the opportunity. If Langford abandoned the project, Robert knew it would take him at least five or six more weeks and cost a minimum of $20,000 to get another precast supplier on site. The original order was already five weeks late.

EXHIBIT 1

Letter Dated May 20, from Robert Casson to Mr. Art Langford, President, Langford Precast.

CASSON CONSTRUCTION
May 20
"Registered Mail"
"Copy Hand-Delivered"
Dear Art:

Re: Family Law Library Project
Purchase Order No. 310-6

We have advised your office several times on the importance of meeting the contract schedule.

The project must be substantially complete by August 6.

You were advised by us that your precast was expected to arrive as per our construction schedule during the first two (2) weeks of April.

During a meeting on March 2, you advised both the Architect and me that meeting the schedule date would not be a problem.

You also advised at the aforementioned meeting that the following items, required by the contract documents, would be complied with immediately.

1. Resubmittal of your shop drawings conforming to the Architect's comments made on your initial "revise and resubmit" shop drawing submittal.
2. Submittal of a color and texture sample by March 8. Actual color and texture sample was submitted to the Architect on this site May 6.
3. Submittal of actual precast shapes by March 15. One precast shape was submitted for approval May 6.

In addition, you have indicated verbally to us that your planned production time, for the entire order, is approximately twelve (12) working days.

Well, it is now May 20, and you have not yet delivered a single piece of precast.

We have attempted to be understanding in this situation. We have ignored the several outstanding telephone messages left by both my superintendent and myself. We have offered site dimensions. We have rescheduled other site work around your late delivery.

As of late, you verbally advised me that you would ship May 14. Then you advised me May 17. Then you advised my superintendent May 18. This type of scheduling inconsistency is a nuisance; however, your order is already a minimum five (5) weeks late.

As in the past, we feel it necessary to advise you that your failure to deliver your product is delaying the installation of the stone veneer. The lack of the stone veneer installation is delaying the overall production schedule of the project.

If the project is not substantially complete by August 6, the University will incur costs and will very likely seek to legally recover these costs.

The delay of the project completion will at the very least damage our reputation with this Client. More than likely, the delay will result in litigation between ourselves and the University.

We will have no choice but to litigate with any subtrade or supplier who has substantially delayed the project schedule in order to recover our damages.

Surely, you can appreciate the magnitude of the situation. Our potential losses would far exceed the entire value of your contract.

Please deliver your precast order immediately.

Yours truly,
Robert Casson

As Robert considered his options for managing Langford Precast and completing the project on time, he knew that there were four perspectives he had to consider: his firm's, Langford Precast's, the university's, and the legal eyes that would judge the case on the documentation provided in court if the problem could not be resolved now.

Robert had just finished writing a letter to Art Langford, president of Langford Precast, expressing his serious concerns. (See Exhibit 1.) Although he hoped his letter would spur Langford on to complete the project, he wondered what action to take in case Langford failed to meet its commitment.

Chapter Seventeen

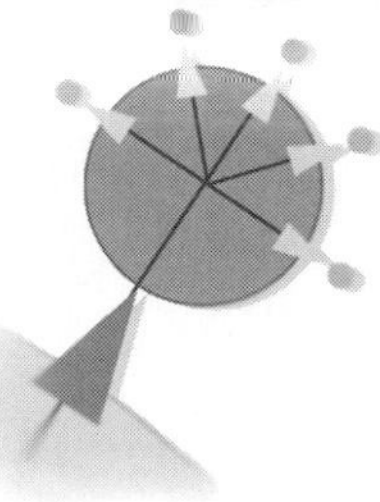

Services

Chapter Outline

Key Questions for the Supply Manager

Should we

- Improve the way we evaluate service suppliers?
- Be concerned with the service purchases that are not handled by the purchasing department?
- Have closer involvement with internal customers?

How can we

- Improve our service make-or-buy decisions?
- Change our service quality assurance?
- Improve the purchase and management of services bundled with goods?
- Work more effectively with the user of the service?

SERVICES

Every organization, whether in the manufacturing sector or the service sector, requires services in the course of its operations. The service sector is growing as a portion of GDP and so is the percent of spend for services. It is not only the sheer dollar volume spent to acquire services but also the impact of these services on organizational success that makes the effective acquisition of services a significant and important challenge.

Services that may be required by any organization are diverse. A brief and far-from-complete listing might include

Advertising
Architectural
Auditing
Banking
Cafeteria/catering
Computer programming
Construction
Consulting
Contract packaging
Courier services
Customs brokerage
Data processing
Demolition
Engineering design
Environmental cleanup
Hazardous waste disposal
Health benefit plans
Household/office moves
Information systems
Inspections
Insurance
Interior decorating/space planning
Janitorial
Landscaping/lawn service
Legal service
Mail services
Maintenance
Medical
Payroll
Photography
Property management
Records management

Recruiting/outplacement	Temporary help
Reproduction/copying	Training
Research & development	Transport of goods
Sales promotion	Trash removal/disposal
Security	Travel (air, hotel, auto rental)
Signage	Utilities (electric, gas, water)
Snow removal	Vending service
Space/storage rental	Workers' compensation insurance
Telephone	

This chapter focuses on the similarities and differences in the process when purchasing a good versus a service and addresses the increasing role of supply in services acquisition.

Significance of Services Spend

A 2003 CAPS benchmarking report, *Managing Your Services Spend in Today's Economy,* reported the breakdown of spend for participating companies as, on average, 44 percent for direct spend, 23 percent for indirect, and 30 percent for services. If the economy were broken into three segments—manufacturing, service, and public—then manufacturing organizations have a higher percent of spend allocated to the purchase of goods than services and public/governmental and service organizations have a much higher percent allocated to services than goods. Service organizations have the highest percent of spend for services.

The magnitude of the dollars spent to acquire services indicates that a professional supply department that attained a reduction of even 5 percent in overall prices paid would have a *major* impact on an organization's profitability. If the focus were placed on lowering total cost of ownership, the contribution from a structured sourcing process and knowledgeable supply managers would be even greater.

What Makes Services Different?

One of the most commonly mentioned special attributes of services deals with the inability to store services because many services are processes (which may or may not be associated with a product). This implies that timing of the delivery has to coincide with the purchaser's specific needs and that the consequences of improper timing may be serious and costly. Service suppliers, trying to accommodate a variety of customers, need to ensure that sufficient capacity is available to satisfy the needs of all. The inability to store services also creates quality assurance difficulties. It may not be possible to inspect a service before its delivery. And, by the time of delivery, it may be too late to do anything about it. Anyone who has ever suffered through a boring speaker or a bad airline flight will attest to that.

The specification and measurement of quality in a service may present significant difficulties. Frequently, services have both tangible and intangible components. In the hospitality industry, the tangible side deals with how well customers' food and drink needs are met. The intangible side deals with the customer's need to be liked, respected, pampered, and treated as a valued client. Such needs are met when service personnel are friendly, courteous, and enthusiastic; when they show they appreciate their customers' patronage; when they are knowledgeable about the products they are selling; when they use sales techniques tactfully and effectively; and when they strive to meet each customer's unique expectations for quality service.

Supply Involvement

Services may be purchased alone or bundled with goods. Other than the purchase of transportation services, which are often bundled with goods, this text has focused primarily on the acquisition of products, raw materials, purchased parts, equipment, and MRO items. In addition to transportation services, these goods also may be bundled with a service such as installation, operator or staff training, technical advice, maintenance, provision of backup capacity or people, troubleshooting, documentation, quality control assistance, inspection, translation, and so on. When services are bundled with goods, almost invariably the product emphasis is primary and the service dimension secondary in the overall purchase decision. Increasingly, the service factor has emerged as a larger portion of total cost of ownership.

Services have typically been acquired by internal users at the local level. While these users possess technical knowledge about the service, they may be inadequately prepared to apply a methodical, structured, and strategic sourcing process to the purchase. Despite the large volume of dollars spent annually to acquire services, the supply group in many organizations has had little involvement in service spend categories such as utilities, insurance, health benefit plans, travel, and so on. There are three possible explanations for this historic lack of supply involvement:

1. The complexity of specifying service needs and analyzing potential service providers means that the user has greater specification expertise than the purchasing department.
2. Buying services involves more of a personal relationship between the service supplier and user. Goods purchasing, on the other hand, is based more on a business relationship between the goods supplier and the purchasing department.
3. Many service industries have only been deregulated for a short time in their history and business practices have been slow to change to meet the changing competitive environment (following tradition).

Strategy Development

Perhaps the most valuable role supply can play is in the development of short- and long-term acquisition strategies for service categories. Supply managers must become business partners with major users and owners of the service category, develop category expertise, acquire market intelligence, and deliver results to persuade the internal user that supply knowledge and expertise are indispensable in the management of the services spend. The need recognition and description stages of the acquisition process offer the greatest opportunity to add value when acquiring services as well as goods. Therefore, supply needs to be involved in these early stages of the process. Without a strong collaborative relationship with internal business partners, the organization will fail to realize the full contribution in managing its services spend.

Process Owner and Manager

In their role as service category managers, supply personnel must be prepared to take the lead in managing the acquisition process. Because of a historical lack of involvement in many organizations, supply personnel may lack the necessary knowledge and skill to fill this role. In the CAPS Research report, *Managing the Services Spend,* respondents reported that their organizations were more competent at sourcing, procuring, and managing goods than services or services bundled with goods. In addition, 70 percent reported that it was more difficult or very difficult to buy services rather than goods. Participants also reported being less confident about their organization's ability to use existing software tools and systems to manage services spend than goods. Clearly, this is a high-potential growth area for both individual supply employees and the supply organization as a whole.

Spend Analysis

Through organizationwide spend analysis, a category or commodity team can better understand who in the organization buys a service category, how much is bought, and for what purpose. This information leads to the ability to standardize services and aggregate demand. This process is similar to the process for analyzing and managing the purchase of goods. It is perhaps more difficult when it involves services because services have often been bought at the local level, and there is a perception, if not reality, that each internal user's service need is somehow unique. The very nature of services, highly personal and often intangible, means that efforts to standardize are complicated by individual user's preferences. For example, organizations in which the annual spend for travel is high will often move to centralize travel to capture cost savings through deals with a travel agent, specific airlines, hotels, and car rental companies. The individual traveler may be dissatisfied with the impact of a new travel policy. A frequent traveler may perceive that his or her willingness to devote a large portion of personal time to company travel is unvalued given the lack of freedom in making travel arrangements. Often the benefits to the organization as a whole are invisible to the individual traveler who only knows that she was not allowed to take the flight she preferred. If supply is going to advocate greater involvement in services acquisition and move to standardize and consolidate services, then they also must develop metrics that capture and communicate the organizationwide results.

E-Sourcing

Some organizations have improved managerial control over the services spend through the use of e-sourcing tools. E-sourcing tools automate any or all of the process including requisition creation and approval, budget checking, purchase order routing to suppliers, order acknowledgment, change orders, receiving, cancellations and returns, and payment. One of the biggest advantages of e-sourcing tools is the improved visibility of information such as who, what, when, where, and from whom services are acquired. Without this information from across the organization it is difficult to manage a particular category of spend. All of the issues and challenges addressed in Chapter 4 come into play when using technology to manage the services spend better. Tools such as e-catalogs, online reverse auctions, buyer–supplier collaboration capability, and spend analytics have enabled information visibility that, if used properly, leads to better decision making and greater control over the services spend.

A FRAMEWORK FOR ANALYZING SERVICES

It is important to recognize that not all services are the same. The variation between services may affect the acquisition perspective. Moreover, as in all other purchases, each service tends to have its own nomenclature, language, tradition, standard practices, technology, and so on, that need to be learned by the supply manager. In the service acquisition process, the following service characteristics must be considered: value, repetitiveness, tangibility, direction, production, nature of demand, nature of delivery, degree of customization, and the skills required for producing the service. Each of these will be discussed in turn.

It is useful to recognize that, ultimately, the goal of effective acquisition of services is to obtain best value. In this sense there is no difference between the acquisition of services and goods. And the best buy in services represents the appropriate trade-off between quality, delivery, quantity, cost, continuity, flexibility, and other relevant factors. Determination of the need and the ability to assess what should be considered best value in any particular service presents the real challenges in the acquisition process.

Value of the Service

One broad cut at services would be to classify them as high, medium, or low value. This could be done in the typical ABC/Pareto analysis or portfolio analysis that looks at both value and risk to acquire. Obviously, from an economic value perspective, greater acquisition attention should be spent on the high-value services. Value in this context is probably best expressed as a combination of money spent on this service in one shot, or over a specific time period such as a year. It also should be recognized that some services may require a very careful acquisition process because of the potential impact they could have on the whole organization. For example, the improper removal of asbestos from a building may make the whole building unusable. A consultant to assist in the long-term strategic planning of the organization may have a very significant, long-term impact.

Degree of Repetitiveness

For the acquisition of repetitive services, it may be possible to develop an acquisition system and specialized expertise within the organization. For example, it would be appropriate to have specialized buying expertise in the acquisition of maintenance and security services. On the other hand, for unique service requirements, special assistance may have to be sought outside of the organization, and the acquisition may be handled on a project basis. Electronic sourcing tools are increasingly used to acquire repetitive services that are easily standardized and low risk to acquire. For example, job descriptions and candidate requirements for some types of temporary labor can be standardized. A hiring manager can use an electronic procurement system to access a designated temporary services agency, submit the standard job requisition, and generate a purchase order at contracted rates. This automated process speeds up the cycle time, reduces purchasing operating costs, and leaves the actual candidate selection to the hiring manager.

Degree of Tangibility

By definition, every service tends to have an intangible dimension, such as the conviviality dimension in the hospitality industry. Even so, some services can be seen as more tangible than others. For example, an architect will produce a drawing or a design that can be examined by others and that ultimately will result in a physical structure. Although the structural features of the physical representation of the design can be examined, the aesthetic features of the design are much more difficult to evaluate and subject to a wide variety of responses.

On the other hand, the advice from a consultant on a new marketing strategy may be almost totally intangible.

The development of standards in any contract for services is obviously difficult. Sometimes it is possible to get around this by using expressions of satisfaction or dissatisfaction by various users or experts as a substitute. For example, how many complaints are received about the cleanliness of the building? Or how many experts believe the software program to be acceptable? It should be recognized that the selection of experts or evaluators in itself represents a statistical quality problem. Some people may be more eager than others to express their opinions, and their views may not be representative of the whole group. Relying solely on complaints may give a biased response.

One way to deal with the acquisition of intangible services is to substitute qualifications for the people or equipment providing the service. For example, the number of personnel in the organization who have appropriate training in the particular discipline, and the capability of the various pieces of equipment, can be specified ahead of time. Similarly, it may be possible to poll a number of clients of the organization to determine their satisfaction with the particular supplier. Unfortunately, many segments of the service sector are plagued by high personnel turnover, and the addition or loss of a few key people can make a significant difference in any one firm.

Direction of the Service

Another aspect of service deals with whether or not it is directed at people. For example, food services are for people; maintenance services may be for buildings or equipment. When services are directed at people, it is important to recognize the special needs of the persons who will be most affected by the service. The ultimate user likely will play a major role in both the specification of the service and the assessment of whether satisfactory quality has, in fact, been delivered. If services directed at people have an important intangible component, assessment may require a period of exposure of both supplier and purchaser personnel to each other to determine compatibility. In babysitting, for example, is it the parents or the children, or both, who determine the selection?

Production of the Service

Services can be produced by people or equipment, or a combination of both. Services of low labor intensity may have a high capital or asset component. Typical examples would include real estate and equipment rentals, computer processing, transportation, and communication services, as well as custom processing of a machine-intensive nature. In the specification stage, understanding the underlying technology or asset base is important. During the acquisition stage, potential suppliers can be assessed on the basis of their asset capacity and availability as well as the state of their technology. The delivery of this kind of service is more likely at the location of the supplier's premises or of its equipment, although hookup may be directly to the purchaser's site. Quality monitoring and evaluation may be process oriented, with emphasis on the performance of the underlying capital asset.

Services with high labor intensity include activities like hand harvesting, installation and maintenance, education, health support, and security, as well as the full range of professional activities like consulting, engineering, accounting, medical, and architectural services. Here the quality of the "people component" is the primary concern.

Services involving largely lower- to medium-skilled people may focus more on cost minimization and efficiency. Services requiring highly skilled individuals may require the purchaser to distinguish between levels of professional skill and may require extensive ongoing communication between requisitioner and supply manager through all phases of the acquisition process.

Nature of the Demand

The demand for a particular service may be continuous, periodic, or discrete. The typical example of a continuous service may be insurance, or a 24-hour, around-the-clock security service. A discrete or one-shot service may be the acquisition of an interior decorator to suggest a new color scheme for an office complex. The continuous service may provide the opportunity to monitor progress and make alterations as information about the quality of service becomes evident. For discrete services, the monitoring capability may have to be shifted to the various stages in the delivery production, if this is possible. The real problem here may be that by the time the service is delivered, it is too late to make significant changes. Periodic service may be regular, such as once a week or once a month, as with regular inspections, or it may vary with need, as in repair services.

Nature of Service Delivery

The nature and place of service delivery may have significant acquisition repercussions. For example, if the delivery of the service occurs on the premises of the purchaser, the contract agreement may have to address a number of provisions. For example, in construction or installation services, questions of security; access; nature of dress; hours of work; applicability of various codes for health, security, and safety; what working days and hours are applicable; and what equipment and materials are to be provided by whom are all issues that need to be addressed as part of the contract.

On the other hand, when the service is provided on the supplier's premises or elsewhere, many of these concerns may not arise, provided the service is not directed at personnel of the purchaser.

Degree of Standardization

It makes a substantial difference whether a service is standard or is customized specifically for the purchaser. Generally speaking, the less the consumer contact, the more standard the service becomes, and, probably, the less the importance of intangibles. Specification of these kinds of services probably is easier because of the standardization and the common nature of the purchase. With many purchasers in the market, standard specifications probably are available. If there are many suppliers, it may be possible to use competitive bidding techniques, expect quantity discounts, and use a standard type of supplier evaluation. Online auctions also may be used to acquire these types of services. One major insurance company bundles windshield repair and replacement claims by locality, posts them daily, and allows prequalified providers to bid by lot. This is a service that combines a good (the windshield) and a service (the installation), and the service is typically provided by a small, local business. The small business owner bids on a lot after deciding the price it wants to charge, and the winning bidder can then smooth out its service delivery. The insurance company reduces the cost of windshield repair and replacement claims.

With highly customized services, the specification process may become more difficult and the options more difficult to understand. The involvement of the end consumers in this specification process then becomes more important. The possibility of trade-offs in various make-or-buy suboptions needs to be explored before final specifications are agreed to. The acquisition process itself may be less definite, since various suppliers may offer substantially different options. Evaluation of supplier performance may have to recognize the purchaser's share of responsibility for quality at the point of delivery.

Skills Required for the Service

The production of a service may require a full range of skills, from unskilled on the one extreme to highly skilled on the other. In services requiring relatively unskilled labor, such as grass cutting and other simple maintenance tasks, price emphasis is likely to be high and ease of entry into (and exit from) the service also may be high. On the other extreme, the acquisition of highly skilled services may focus far more on qualifications of the skilled persons, concern over the specific persons who will be performing the service, and recommendations from other skilled persons and users. Frequently, in highly professional services, the cost of the professional service may be relatively low compared to the benefit expected. For example, a good design may increase sales substantially; a good architect may be able to design a low-cost, but effective structure; and a good consulting recommendation may turn a whole organization around. It often is difficult to deal with this trade-off between the estimated costs for the job and the estimated benefits.

THE ACQUISITION PROCESS FOR SERVICES

Thus far, the discussion has centered primarily on understanding the nature of the service to be acquired. Now, the acquisition process used for services is discussed to highlight several unique dimensions. Four areas of the acquisition process are covered: (1) need recognition and specification; (2) analysis of supply alternatives, including sourcing, pricing, and options; (3) the purchase agreement, including special provisions; and (4) contract administration, including follow-up, quality control, payment, records, and supplier management and evaluation.

Need Recognition and Description

Those in supply must ask some very basic questions regarding any service. Typical questions include: Why is this service necessary? What is important about this service? What represents good value? How is quality defined for the service? How is the service produced? How do we know we received what we expected?

Developing the Statement of Work (SOW)

The statement of work (SOW) is the document that describes the needs of the internal customer, communicates those needs to the supplier, and ultimately becomes the basis of the service contract. The user(s), the buyer, and a key supplier(s) may be involved in its development. Unwritten user expectations either will not be met or end up as an issue during the contract negotiations rather than being part of the proposals prepared by potential

FIGURE 17–1
Sample Scope of Work for a Janitorial Service

Source: Michele B. Knepper and Mark K. Lindsey, "Clean Up Your Act," *Purchasing Today*, March 1999, p. 47.

- Description of premises to be cleaned (including space maps if necessary).
- Specific description of services to be provided; for example, uncarpeted floors shall be wet-mopped, dried, and spray buffed. All wax marks shall be removed from baseboards.
- Frequency of services (nightly, weekly, monthly, quarterly) outlined by area (for example, lobby, kitchen areas, elevators).
- Specification of any materials to be used (such as cleaning agents or polishes) and how they are to be purchased.
- Reports or other required periodic documentation.
- Insurance requirements (for example, automobile liability, commercial general liability, workers' compensation) and liability.

sources. The SOW also provides the buyer with a basis for assessing the supply market to determine the feasibility of a supplier meeting the user's requirements within the established parameters (price/cost, timeframe, quality, etc.). A sample scope of work for a janitorial service is in Figure 17–1.

The characteristics of the particular service to be acquired can be checked against those discussed earlier in this chapter to establish priority and areas of concern. The need for user involvement in need recognition and definition is high in many services because of the user–supplier interface, so common in most services, and the importance of intangible factors. Careful documentation of need requirements, including the necessity for intangibles, is the foundation on which a sound acquisition approach is based. Sound documentation will facilitate supplier search and selection, contract content and administration, and quality control. Where possible, measurable attributes or actions that are part of the service need to be identified and quantified. Also, if the service can be broken down into chronological stages, it will be useful to detail progress due dates. Figure 17–2 is a sample of milestones and deliverables for an employee morale survey.

In many services, it is necessary to document exactly what it is that the supplier will provide, and also what the supply manager and user will do to help the supplier perform as required. Value analysis techniques can and should be applied to service need definition. Early involvement of supply, and sometimes a key supplier(s), with users during need recognition and definition is essential in the appropriate search for value.

FIGURE 17–2
Sample Milestones and Deliverables for Morale Survey

- Overall research design—February 1.
- Questionnaire design—April 1.
- Questionnaire administration—June 1.
- Survey results report—September 1.

The accompanying commitments for the supply organization are

- Overall research design review—January 15.
- Questionnaire approval—March 15.
- Employees available for questionnaire administration—April 1 to June 1.
- Preliminary results report review—August 15.

Analysis of Supply Alternatives

In the acquisition of services, the analysis of supply alternatives includes sourcing, pricing, and source options, as well as make or buy.

Sourcing

In sourcing, it is useful to recognize that many service organizations are relatively small. Therefore, many of the characteristics of small suppliers are likely to be considerations in dealing with service organizations. If the service supplier is small, there also is a high likelihood that it will be a local source. Since many minority- and women-owned businesses are small, services also may represent an opportunity to meet the organization's goals for supplier diversity.

In sourcing, references from other users are particularly useful and should be checked carefully. A typical parallel in consumer buying is the value of a word-of-mouth reference in selecting a restaurant. A typical checklist for rating potential consultants might include factors like reputation, relevant experience, integrity, size, fees, availability, quality and background of personnel, timetable for the work, consulting approach, capability to train and communicate, and even personal chemistry. Each factor would have to be weighted and each consultant rated accordingly. A more detailed discussion of reference checking is in Chapter 10, "Supplier Selection."

Sourcing Methods

There are three main sourcing methods used to acquire services: (1) a master service agreement (MSA), (2) a request for quote (RFQ) or proposal (RFP), and (3) direct sourcing from a sole or single source.

1. *Master service agreement (MSA).* An agreement wherein the supplier(s) provides predetermined services over a specified period of time with total costs not to exceed an amount previously agreed upon. The scope of work for each function or level of service is fully defined and agreed upon before the period of performance starts. Costs are generally fixed for the period of performance and usually have a "not to exceed" value. MSAs are usually awarded for periods of one year or longer.
2. *RF*x. An RFQ is typically issued in situations where the buyer and internal user can clearly and unambiguously describe the need, for example, by using a grade of material, or commonly accepted terminology. In these cases, an RFQ would basically bring the comparison to one of price. When the buyer has a more complex requirement and wants to draw on the supplier's expertise in developing and proposing a solution, an RFP or request for bid (RFB) would be more appropriate than an RFQ. Also, if the buyer is planning to use negotiation as the tool for determining price and terms, then an RFP would be appropriate. If, however, the buyer is planning to use a competitive bid process without the opportunity to negotiate after bid receipt, then an RFB might be more appropriate. Since there are no commonly accepted definitions of these terms, it is important for buyers to communicate clearly to potential suppliers the process that will be followed to analyze and select a supplier(s). Many organizations use different solicitation tools depending on the complexity of the purchase, the dollar value, and the degree of risk they wish the supplier to bear. An electronic quoting tool (e-RF*x* tool) may be used to support and manage the transaction from internal requisitioning to

posting requests; receiving quotes, bids, or proposals; and awarding contracts. Online auctions also are used for services with a clear and unambiguous specification.

3. *Direct sourcing.* Purchasing services from a sole (only one supplier available) or single (decision made to buy from only one supplier) source. The services are typically unique, or are developed for one specific purpose or function. These services are generally sourced initially from suppliers by using RFx-type documents (x = Proposal, Quote) in lieu of purchasing from catalogs or general price lists. Buyers and suppliers generally collaborate on all aspects of the sourcing activity to capture scope, price/costs, delivery terms and conditions, economies, periods of performance, and so forth.

Pricing

Pricing in services may be fixed or variable, by the job or by the hour, day, or week. Prices may be obtained by competitive bid if the size of the contract warrants it; enough competitors are available; and adequate, specific, consistent specifications can be prepared.

Negotiation is another common method for establishing prices and may be the only option in sole-source situations. In services, volume and size leverage count and can be used effectively by the knowledgeable supply manager. Understanding the cost structure of the service will be helpful in revealing negotiation opportunities.

In some situations it may be difficult to estimate the total time required for a given service task, and with professional services it is not unusual to give estimates of professional time required without committing to a specific figure. Most supply managers probably would prefer such contracts to have a "not to exceed limit." Some professionals, such as architects, may quote their fee based on a percentage of the total job cost. But from a purchasing standpoint, this removes the incentive for the architect to seek the best value for the total job.

Total Cost of Ownership

In services, as with goods, total cost of ownership, not price, is the most important calculation and also one of the most difficult. At a minimum, the supply manager should determine the relevant cost elements and estimate the amount to avoid over-weighting price to the long-term detriment of the organization.

Other Terms and Conditions

Besides price, service agreements also may include clauses on confidentiality, discounts, warranties, limitations of liability, and indemnification as well as anything specific or unique to that purchase.

For example, when contracting for consulting services, the contract might include a warranty clause, an independent contractor clause, a work product clause, and a nondisclosure clause.[1]

Warranty clause. Depending on the clarity of functional requirements and the availability of objective criteria for assessing performance, the buyer may be able to negotiate a warranty for the consultant's work. If the work is unacceptable, the clause may require

[1] Sara L. Vinas, "When You Want Renoir Instead of Picasso," *Consulting Services Guide—Supplement to Purchasing Today,* August 1999, p. 5.

the consultant to redo it at no additional charge until it is acceptable. If the functional requirements are vague, it will be more difficult to find a consultant who will agree to this clause.

Independent contractor clause. To protect the buying organization, it is important to meet the IRS requirements for hiring an independent contractor and to include a clause stating that the contractor is independent and therefore responsible for filing his or her own taxes.

Work product clause. This clause will assign the ownership of the work product to the buying organization. While large consulting firms may not be willing to agree to this, many smaller consulting firms will. Even if ownership does not pass to the buying organization, the contract should require documentation of the work product to avoid future problems.

Nondisclosure clause. The contractor should be contractually obligated to keep the buying organization's information confidential. Consultants sell their services to many companies, some of whom may be competitors, and this clause can provide a remedy short of going to court.

Source Options

Requests for proposal are also common in a variety of services where the purchaser believes that supplier ingenuity or skill may reveal options not apparent to the purchaser or user. Proper briefing of potential bidders is still required so that every supplier fully and correctly understands the need to be fulfilled. The difficulty for supply managers with widely varying proposals is one of assessing which is superior. Moreover, the preparation of such a proposal may be expensive and may have to be paid for by the supply manager to ensure proper competition and proposal quality.

Make or Buy in Services

Almost invariably, the question of make or buy is an important one in the acquisition of services. Many services that were once performed in-house are now outsourced or subcontracted out to third parties. Typical examples are security, food service, and maintenance, but also legal, engineering, software development, training, and other professional services traditionally performed in-house. Moreover, particularly with services, the option of partially making or partially buying may be present. For example, in auditing, the preparation of schedules can be left to the inside accountants, or to the outside auditors. An interior decorator may specify colors and furnishings but leave the purchasing to the procurement department and the painting and installation to the internal maintenance staff. On the other hand, the whole task could be purchased on a turnkey basis. The disassembly, repair, cleaning, and reassembly of equipment might be performed in-house, whereas regrinding or recalibration of key parts might be done outside.

An alert supply manager always should be on the lookout for opportunities to substitute low-cost, in-house work for high-cost, outside work. The reverse, of course, also holds true. If inside costs are high and outside costs are low and no other considerations are relevant, it provides much better value to have work done outside. Understanding the full nature of the service and how the various costs are built up for the service is, therefore, an important consideration in assessing the make-or-buy trade-off.

In or after periods of organizational downsizing, it is not unusual to find firms who have let employees go or choose early retirement in a "rehire as a consultant" mode. This way valuable experience can still be accessed, but normally not on a full-time basis or for an extended period of time.

The Purchase Agreement

The purchase agreement for services usually is called a service contract or contract for services. It may be short or long term, a standard or custom document. Services lend themselves to a large variety of contract types, including fixed price, unit price, cost-plus-percentage-fee, cost-plus-fixed-fee, or incentive contracts. Many professional service providers try to use standard contracts agreed to by their professional association. Frequently, the associations even have guidelines as to appropriate fee structures and contracts for a particular kind of work. A purchaser never should feel compelled to accept these contracts as they are.

Most organizations over time develop contract language to suit their own needs and the specific service to be acquired. This tends to result in a wide range of different contracts, each with its own service-specific language. Thus, a security service contract will appear totally different from a contract for corporate maintenance, food service, or marketing consulting. Suppliers in each service area will be anxious to suggest the use of their own contracts. In the case of low-value services, using such a standard contract may be the simplest and least expensive solution. Several types of contracting methods are frequently used in services purchasing. These include service level agreements (SLA), milestone deliverables, time and materials (T&M), volume of service (VoS), and cost and cost plus.

Service level agreement (SLA). A document that details the means, method, organization, and processes along with material requirements.

Milestone deliverables. This contracting method requires that specific activities be completed by a prescribed date, or that supplier(s) prepare and deliver to the buyer documentation that reports on the current status of ongoing projects or activities. The requirements for providing milestone deliverables are generally spelled out in the contract document.

Time & materials (T&M). Acquiring services on the basis of (1) direct labor hours at specified fixed hourly rates that include wages, overhead, general and administrative expenses, and profit and (2) materials at cost, including, if appropriate, material handling costs as part of material costs.

Volume of service (VoS). Generally imbedded in service-level agreements and related contracts, the volume of service refers to the predetermined services that will be provided over a specified period of time. Volume of service agreements may be more project-oriented, wherein the buyer can specify the number of temporary workers needed to satisfy the needs of the project. The scope of work and level of services are usually structured for periods of one year or longer.

Cost and cost plus. These are cost-reimbursement types of contracts that provide for payment of allowable incurred costs, to the extent prescribed in the contract. These contracts establish an estimate of total cost for the purpose of obligating funds and establishing a ceiling that the supplier(s) may not exceed (except at their own risk) without the approval of the buyer. Cost reimbursement type contracts are generally used when a reasonable basis for firm contract pricing may not exist.

Buyer–Service Provider Relationships

Buyer–supplier relationships are just as important with service providers as with sellers of goods. The large dollars spent on services and third-party providers directs attention to longer-term relationships. Buyers may decide to enter into long-term agreements, including partnering arrangements and alliances, with key service providers. Given the importance of people in the service quality equation, working toward more seamless relationships with service providers is a logical approach. Buyers cannot expect suppliers to share risks without also being willing to share rewards. It is important to develop ways to measure productivity gains along with bonus systems or other means of sharing these gains equitably. (See Chapter 19.)

Service Contract Administration

Service contract administration includes follow-up, quality control and supplier performance metrics, payment, records, and other aspects of contract administration.

Follow-Up

Follow-up and expediting in services may require internal as well as supplier checking. Therefore, responsibility for follow-up with the supplier appropriately may be placed in the user department to help ensure user compliance with prior commitments and deadlines, while follow-up on internal commitments may become a joint responsibility for the supply manager as well as the supplier. It is this commonly extensive user interface with supplier personnel during service delivery, and often before, that also affects other aspects of contract administration. For example, if a service is performed onsite, after-hours, security check-in sheets and access systems may be used to verify work patterns or area activity. Periodic site visits and a walk-through of the facility with the supplier's representative may lead to a better understanding of user needs. Some form of benchmarking against other providers also may be useful.

Quality Control and Supplier Performance Metrics

In highly tangible services such as construction, quality control can be geared heavily toward the measurement of the tangible, in ways similar to standard quality assurance and control. Two aspects of service—the intangible and the noninventory—can create special quality measurement difficulties. All aspects of the ability of the actual service provider(s) (people) to consistently perform the service at the desired quality level are vital to the performance evaluation process. Were the supplier's personnel sufficiently courteous when dealing with the purchaser's employees? This may be measured by a survey, or by number of complaints received, but it is important to recognize that any standard, at best, will be imprecise.

Because the nature of many services prevents storage, delivery tends to be instantaneous. In other words, quality control will have to be performed while the service delivery is in progress, or afterward. And it may be difficult to interrupt the process, even if simultaneous quality control is possible. Therefore, the quality risk in services may be relatively high compared to the purchase of products. In cases of quality failure, it may not be possible to return the services for a full refund.

Postservice evaluation is an essential component in effective service acquisition. The same checklist for consultants as used in sourcing, for example, can be used for postservice evaluation. At the very least, an informal evaluation should include two questions:

1. Did your problem or issue get resolved to your satisfaction?
2. Would you rehire this consultant in the future for another problem or issue?

Additional questions regarding conformance to expectations of quality, timeliness, and cost are, of course, appropriate as well as feedback on the professionalism and service orientation of the consultant personnel.

Quality risk avoidance may be achieved by doing business with service suppliers found to be satisfactory in the past, by avoiding repeat business with suppliers who did not do a good job, by careful checking of suppliers beforehand with other users with similar needs, and by careful preservice delivery communications with the supplier and service users to ensure common understanding of requirements and expectations.

A formal service quality evaluation process developed by Parasuraman, Zeithaml, and Berry identifies five quality dimensions:

Reliability: ability to perform the promised service dependably and accurately.

Responsiveness: willingness to help customers and provide prompt service.

Assurance: knowledge and courtesy of employees and their ability to inspire trust and confidence.

Empathy: caring, individualized attention the firm provides its customers.

Tangibles: physical facilities, equipment, and appearance of personnel.[2]

The survey process measures the gap between service expectations along each dimension and the perceptions of actual service performance.

Payment

Payment for services may vary somewhat from payment for goods. Some services require prepayment, such as an eminent speaker; some immediately upon delivery, such as hospitality services; whereas others can be delayed. Small suppliers may find it difficult to offer extended payment terms, and early payment may be used as the inducement for price or other concessions sought by the purchaser. Progress payments are usual for large contracts spread over time, whereas regular payments are appropriate for ongoing services such as building maintenance or food service.

Records and Other Aspects of Contract Administration

As in all purchases, the need for proper records hardly needs to be reinforced for the acquisition of services. Part of the difficulty may be the feedback loop from user to purchasing and the retrievability of information regarding the service performed. Unless care is taken to preserve this information, it may be lost for future reference and consideration.

It is almost inevitable that contract administration for services will encounter the need for changes subsequent to contract signing. Delivery dates, the nature of the service, the quality of the service, the place for delivery, and other aspects may require change. What may seem like an innocuous change to the purchaser may be difficult or expensive for the supplier. For example, a one-week delay in delivery may back the supplier into a serious capacity constraint. This is one reason why big weddings are always planned a long time in advance. The reverse also may happen. A supplier request for change may make life difficult

[2] A. Parasuraman, V. A. Zeithaml, and L. L. Berry, "A Conceptual Model of Service Quality and Its Implications for the Future," *Journal of Marketing,* Fall 1985, pp. 41–50; and "SERVQUAL: A Multiple-Item Scale for Measuring Consumer Perceptions of Service Quality," *Journal of Retailing,* Spring 1988, pp. 12–40. These two references likely were the first presentations of this approach.

for the purchaser. Thus, mechanisms, as well as timely interaction between the appropriate representatives of supplier and buyer, need to be in place to deal with changes as necessary. Changes may be costly and affect budget status and a host of other dimensions. Before changes are agreed to, both purchaser and seller need to assess the impact on their own organizations and the contract changes arising from them, including price. Obviously, if flexibility to change already is foreseen as important before contract signing, this should be addressed as part of the original need description. Then, in the search for a suitable supplier, flexibility becomes a key sourcing criterion, which later is written into the contract.

Developing a Services Sourcing Strategy

It is possible to make a matrix out of the various considerations in service acquisition. A simplified summary is provided in Figure 17–3, highlighting the significant points in service nature and acquisition. This matrix can be used to plan for the key elements in a strategy for the acquisition of a specific service.

OUTSOURCING AND MANAGING THIRD-PARTY SERVICE PROVIDERS

The growth of outsourcing has led to an increase in the need for good decision making processes to determine, first, what should be outsourced, second, how to outsource, and third, how to manage the third-party provider. Many services have been outsourced in the last 15 years, including some purchasing activities. Senior management must decide where the company will gain by developing in-house expertise and where it is better off creating a virtual organization by outsourcing to a third party. Given the difficulty in adequately describing the service required, it is easy to imagine situations where the service provided by the third party falls short of the buying organization's expectations.

For those who look at the purchasing function as a service performed inside one's organization, it is possible to look at the other departments in the organization as the buyers of this service. How differently would the members of the supply department behave if their services actually were bought by the other departments? In a number of organizations, particularly large public and private organizations that operate on a decentralized, divisional basis, it is not at all uncommon to charge central purchasing services to specific divisional or departmental budgets. Neither is it unusual for those internal customers to complain about the size and nature of the charges incurred. Some of the major areas of services outsourcing in the supply management area are supplier-managed inventory programs, transportation services, payment processes (procurement cards, electronic funds transfer), e-auction solutions provider, and so on. When this list is expanded to include all the services that are outsourced for an entire organization, it is apparent that the management of third-party providers is a major challenge for many organizations.

EXPANDING SUPPLY'S INVOLVEMENT

The opportunity to increase profits in an organization through more effective purchasing and supply management probably is greater in the acquisition of services than in goods. Why? A large and growing amount of money is spent to purchase services, and services

FIGURE 17–3 **Summary of Service Characteristics and Acquisition Process Implications**

Service Characteristic	*Acquisition Process*	*Need Recognition, Description*	*Sourcing Alternatives, Pricing, Analysis*	*Agreement, Contract Provisions*	*Contract Administration Follow-up, Q.C. Payment, Records*
Value	High	High attention	Careful Price sensitive Make or buy	Likely negotiated	High attention
	Low	Lesser attention	Low acquisition cost Local source	Standard if possible	Low attention
Repetitiveness	High	Develop standard	Test	Standard longer term	Standardize
	Low	Seek expert assistance	Seek expert assistance	Custom or one shot	Custom
Tangibility	High	Specs important	Pretest, samples	Similar to product purchase	Control for physical characteristics
	Low	References User involvement	Personalities important	Specified persons	User involvement high
Direction of	Equipment	Equipment familiarity	Equipment familiarity	Specified equipment performance	Control process quality
	People	User involvement high	User involvement high	People skills important	Control quality at user interface

Production by	Equipment	Specify equipment capability	Specify equipment capability Control for quality	Specify equipment performance	Conditional on equipment use
	People	Specify people capability	Worry about capacity	Specify availability	User provides quality control
Demand	Continuous	Continuity	Reliability and continuity	Complete coverage	Control quality by sampling
	Discrete	Availability during	Availability during need	Specify delivery need	Control quality at delivery
Delivery	At purchaser	User interface important	User interface important	Access clauses	In-house quality control
	At seller	Good description	Location	Purchase access and progress reports	Concern over service completeness
Customization	High	User specification	Custom capability	Special contract	Quality control very specific and may withhold a large % of payment
	Low	Standard specs	Competitive bid	Standard contract	Standard quality control
Skills	High	User specification	Specify specific persons	Availability of individuals	Professional standards, regulations, user involvement
	Low	Standard specs	Competitive bidding	Standard contract	Minimize user hassle

purchases probably have not received the same amount of attention in the past as the purchase of goods. Services purchases will receive greater attention today, as firms explore more fully all avenues to reduce costs and to increase profits and return on investment.

In most organizations, the supply department has far less involvement in the buying of services than in goods purchasing. If the supply department were to get more involved (and services is a natural for team buying, consisting of internal user and supply), the logical purchasing process it could bring to the team-buying decision process should result in substantial savings. Areas where large dollar savings are possible include advertising, banking, construction, consultants, copying, health benefit plans, insurance, sales promotion, space rental, temporary help, transport of goods, travel, utilities, and workers' compensation insurance. There are three areas of focus in many organizations:

1. Conduct spend analysis to better understand the organizationwide services spend.
2. Standardize and consolidate services spend across the organization for better leverage.
3. Improve supply processes so supply managers can add more value to services acquisition through the application of tools such as total cost of ownership, supply base reduction, supplier partnerships, and automated supply processes.

In many organizations, the effectiveness of services purchasing is not measured and probably could be improved substantially through the discipline provided by a structured sourcing process.

Process Steps

Based on the experience of firms in which their supply department successfully became involved in the buying of advertising; real estate; health benefits; PC/workstations, peripheral hardware, and support/service; and utilities, a CAPS Research report suggested a 10-step process for increasing supply's involvement:

1. Do the people now in the supply department have the skills needed for purchasing services?
2. Do they have the time? Can they make the time?
3. Obtain data on what services are bought, by whom, and dollar amounts.
4. Take one area at a time.
5. Establish the team: the user(s), possibly finance and quality assurance, and supply.
6. Determine if the buying of the service, as now done, satisfies the user and represents effective spending.
7. The supply department should ensure that a logical purchasing process is used to make service purchasing decisions and arrive at the contract or agreement. The actual purchase order then can be handled (written) by the using department, but it is simply a release against the agreement.
8. All parties—user, supplier, and buyer—must agree on the specification.
9. If use of the logical supply process dictates that a change should be made in specification, supplier, price, terms, and so on, the supply department should make sure that the using department and senior management know what change(s) was made and why.

10. If the purchase of a particular service currently is being done by some department other than supply, and it is being measured, and it is being done effectively, then leave it alone. As the saying goes, "If it ain't broke, don't fix it!"[3]

Conclusion

Services are growing rapidly in the economy as a whole. As the percentage of spend that goes to acquire services increases, many senior managers are looking for improved acquisition. Consequently, more and more supply departments are getting involved in the acquisition of services. The purchase of services requires a tremendous amount of cross-functional cooperation and strong internal relationships. The challenge is to couple the internal user's technical and practical knowledge of service providers with the supply manager's sourcing, evaluating, and negotiating expertise. Cross-functional sourcing teams work well in service purchases once the resistance to supply involvement is overcome. Supply must be ready to apply sound purchasing and supply theory and practice to the acquisition of services. Supply professionals must become business partners with internal customers to deliver maximum value from the services spend to the organization.

Questions for Review and Discussion

1. How can supply contribute to cost savings, reduction, and avoidance in services acquisition?
2. Why should it make any difference to the acquisition process whether a service is directed at people or equipment?
3. What are typical quality control difficulties in the acquisition of services?
4. How and where can electronic sourcing tools be used to acquire services?
5. What is a good example of a service high in intangibles and how would that affect the acquisition process?
6. How can one determine what represents good value in a service?
7. How can an organization that allows localized purchase of services consolidate and aggregate service spend?
8. Why are organizations outsourcing more services?
9. Is make or buy a realistic option in the acquisition of services? Why and how?
10. How can cross-functional sourcing teams be used in the purchasing of services?

References

Consulting Services Guide—Supplement to Purchasing Today, August 1999.

Managing Your "Services Spend" in Today's Service Economy. Tempe, AZ: CAPS Research, July 22, 2003.

Parasuraman, V.; A. Zeithaml; and L. L. Berry. "A Conceptual Model of Service Quality and Its Implications for the Future." *Journal of Marketing,* Fall 1985, pp. 41–50.

Parasuraman, V.; A. Zeithaml; and L. L. Berry. "SERVQUAL: A Multiple-Item Scale for Measuring Consumer Perceptions of Service Quality." *Journal of Retailing,* Spring 1988, pp. 12–40.

[3] Harold E. Fearon and William A. Bales, *Purchasing of Nontraditional Goods and Services* (Tempe, AZ: Center for Advanced Purchasing Studies, 1995), p. 10.

Case 17–1

Erica Carson

"We will do it for 10 percent less than what you are paying right now." Erica Carson, purchasing manager at Wesbank, a large western financial institution, had agreed to meet with Art Evans, a sales representative from D. Killoran Inc., a printing supplier from which Wesbank currently was not buying anything. Art Evans' impromptu and unsolicited price quote concerned the printing and mailing of checks from Wesbank.

Wesbank, well known for its active promotional efforts to attract consumer deposits, provided standard personalized consumer checks free of charge. Despite the increasing popularity of Internet banking, the printing of free checks and mailing to customers cost Wesbank $8 million in the past year.

Erica Carson was purchasing manager in charge of all printing for Wesbank and reported directly to the vice president of supply.

It had been Erica's decision to split the printing and mailing of checks equally between two suppliers. During the last five years, both suppliers had provided quick and quality service, a vital concern of the bank. Almost all checks were mailed directly to the consumer's home or business address by the suppliers. Because of the importance of check printing, Erica had requested a special cost analysis study a year ago, with the cooperation of both suppliers. The conclusion of this study had been that both suppliers were receiving an adequate profit margin and were efficient and cost-conscious and that the price structure was fair. Each supplier was on a two-year contract. One supplier's contract had been renewed eight months ago, the other's expired in another four months.

Erica believed that Killoran was underbidding to gain part of the check-printing business. This in turn would give Killoran access to Wesbank's customers' names. Erica suspected that Killoran might then try to pursue these customers more actively than the current two suppliers to sell special "scenic checks" that customers paid for themselves.

Case 17–2

Talbot County School Board

INTRODUCTION

Paul Travers, purchasing manager for the Talbot County School Board, was deciding on his next move. In February, the new owners of the company that serviced photocopiers in Talbot County's 30 schools notified Paul they would be increasing prices by over 50 percent. Paul knew school budgets had already been set and wondered what to do next.

PAUL TRAVERS

Paul had worked as the purchasing manager for the Talbot County School Board for 20 years. He was responsible for all of the purchasing requirements for the county's public schools. These purchases included items such as snow removal, window replacement, and servicing of photocopiers.

Budgets for all schools were typically set early in the year. Budgets were based on existing or new contracts for the services and appropriations that would be necessary for the school in a given year. School boards typically received their funding from municipal and state governments. Because of the funding cuts made at all levels of government, school boards were feeling pressure to cut costs wherever possible, and increasing expenditures once budgets were set was increasingly difficult.

PHOTOCOPIERS IN TALBOT COUNTY'S SCHOOLS

Each school in Talbot County had at least one photocopier. If the photocopier in a school broke down, it required immediate servicing, typically on the same day, as it was the only source the school had for making copies of office and class materials. Over the course of one year, Talbot County's schools collectively made approximately 8 million photocopies. These photocopiers had been purchased by the school board five years ago and required servicing and toner replacement on a regular basis.

SIGMA SERVICING

Paul had dealt with Sigma Servicing, a photocopying service company, for the past six years. The school board never had a written contract with Sigma, but the company had held its prices at 0.9 cent per copy over the length of the relationship and had never indicated any displeasure with the arrangement. The cost per copy included the service charge and the charge for toner necessary over the course of the year, and was paid in advance by the school board.

Last November, Sigma was purchased by an individual who had been in the service business a number of years ago and decided to reenter the market. Upon taking over the company, he began an examination of the existing service arrangements Sigma had with its customers. The new owner discovered that the business with the Talbot County School Board was actually operating at a loss and proceeded to inform Paul in February of his intention to raise prices and seek a new contractual agreement with the school board immediately. Otherwise, Sigma would withdraw its services.

THE NEW DEAL

The new owner of Sigma wanted to change the relationship so that service and toner charges would be applied separately to the school board's photocopiers. The new total price would amount to 1.4 cents per copy, instead of the existing 0.9 cent per copy. Sigma also wanted any new deal to be retroactive to the beginning of the year, so it could recoup its losses.

Paul expected that the new price of 1.4 cents per copy was competitive with that of other companies. However, he requested that Sigma explore some alternative pricing options for the toner charge. As a result, Sigma undertook two studies: one in which generic toner was used instead of the brand the school board currently used and another in which the toner was recycled with the use of a special container. The result of the first study showed that the yield from the generic toner was a disappointing 4,000–5,000 copies per bottle, indicating limited cost-savings opportunities. The second study indicated that the yield was 7,500–10,000 copies per bottle when the toner was recycled, resulting in a potential cost savings of about 0.2 cent per copy.

THE DECISION

Paul was frustrated by developments with Sigma. He had enjoyed a good relationship with the previous owner and was personally proud of the deal he had received during a time of budget cuts. Furthermore, he knew that the negotiations with the new owner would be drawn out and would require a great deal of time in his busy schedule. The negotiations also would be difficult in light of the fact that Sigma felt they had lost money on the previous arrangement, and that schools had already set their budgets for the year.

At this point Paul felt he had several available options. First, he could agree to pay the higher price to Sigma. He was concerned, however, about the budget implications of this alternative. Second, he could ask Sigma to use a recyclable toner, thereby avoiding a portion of the price increase. Third, Paul considered his possibilities of exploring relationships with other vendors.

Paul considered his options and wondered what he should do next. The issue of Sigma's request for a retroactive price increase effective the beginning of the year had to be taken into consideration when making his decision. He knew that he had to respond quickly as the schools required constant servicing and new toner for their photocopiers.

Case 17–3

Hampton Manor

In late November, Mr. John Cameron, director of purchasing and supply for the city of Hampton, was reviewing proposals for the Hampton Manor study. Three consulting groups had responded to a request for proposal (RFP) to study the operation of the city-owned senior citizens' home. Mr. Cameron knew that his recommendations for the selection of a consultant would have to be completed by mid-December.

HAMPTON MANOR

The Hampton Manor was opened about 30 years ago with a bed capacity of 470 for persons requiring nursing care. Staff totaled 235 with nonmanagement personnel unionized under the District Service Workers Union Local 325.

Day-to-day operations of the Manor were the responsibility of the administrator, who reported to Mr. Henry Davis, the city's director of social services. Policy and budget plans were developed by Mr. Davis and his staff in conjunction with Manor administrative staff and the Hampton Manor Committee of Management (HMCM). The HMCM consisted of five aldermen who were appointed or volunteered to fill these positions. The HMCM reported to another aldermanic committee, with broader community service concerns, called the Committee for Community Services. This committee reviewed major expenditures and decisions impacting on community service policy. All major expenditures were then submitted to city council for final approval.

As director of social services, Mr. Davis reported to the city administrator, Mr. J. Peterson, who in turn reported to the mayor.

PURCHASING AND SUPPLY DIVISION (PSD)

The PSD had purchasing and disposal authority for the city's engineering, fire, landfill/sanitation departments, social services division, and city hall building support. The city operated separate purchasing departments in the libraries and the police department. Purchasing authority was granted to the PSD director and buyers by municipal bylaw.

The main objective of the PSD was to respond to the needs of other departments and divisions for goods and services at minimum cost, consistent with desired quality, delivery timing, and reliability. The PSD had expertise in the purchasing of goods and certain services, such as equipment rental, maintenance contracts, and engineering/architectural consulting. However, it had not dealt extensively with management consulting service procurement.

John Cameron became director of PSD two years ago at the age of 35. Prior to this, he was chief buyer and assistant director of purchasing for the city of Forestview, similar in size to Hampton. John reported to the city treasurer, Mr. R. Holbright, and dealt directly with other department and division heads on purchasing matters. He managed a staff of 15, including three buyers.

THE HAMPTON MANOR STUDY

The Hampton Manor had a history of problems related to budgeting and cost control. City council felt that the cost per bed was unnecessarily high, when compared to privately run institutions. Eight months ago, the council directed the city administrator, Mr. Peterson, and the director of social services, Mr. Davis, to prepare a report for submission to the HMCM in early June. The report was to contain

1. An analysis of the comparative costs at Hampton Manor and other state facilities.
2. A review of the feasibility of increasing cost efficiency.
3. A review of the implications of possible alternatives such as
   a. Contract management.
   b. An in-depth operational review and cost-efficiency study carried out by an external agency.

The requested internal report was tabled on June 9. It revealed that costs were approximately 14 percent higher than state averages on a per-bed basis. The report highlighted the difficulties of measuring and controlling costs in the absence of a patient classification system that would enable standard levels of nursing care to be developed. The report recommended an operational review by an outside agency and outlined some general guidelines and objectives.

The council accepted the report's recommendations and directed Messrs. Peterson and Davis to initiate an independent consultant's study of Hampton Manor. This was not a budgeted expense and the approvals of the HMCM, the Committee of Community Services, and city council were necessary prior to letting a consulting contract. Mr. Davis requested the assistance of John Cameron and the PSD in identifying and evaluating potential study participants. John Cameron handled the study personally, since it was beyond the scope of responsibilities and experience of his buyers. He drafted an RFP (see Exhibit 1) and in-state consulting organizations were contacted and a list of consulting companies with relevant experience was developed. Five consulting companies were invited to submit proposals.

Prebid conferences were held in September. The consulting companies sent representatives for preliminary inspections of Hampton Manor and for informal discussions of the scope, terms of reference, and evaluation criteria to be used in the proposal evaluation. Three proposals were submitted by closing, on November 17, with the following costs:

EXHIBIT 1 **Request for Proposal**

You are invited to submit a proposal for the purpose of conducting an administrative and operational review of the Hampton Manor for elder citizens. The review is to include all aspects of operation at the home, including but not restricted to assessment of resident care requirements, review of administration, organizational design, and staffing. The main sections of the home include laundry and housekeeping, nursing and physiotherapy, dietary, special services, property, building maintenance, and administration. The review is to be conducted by examination and analysis of all relevant documentation, physical tour of the facility, and interviews with all levels of staff and administration.

On the basis of the review, you are to develop comprehensive recommendations for introducing improved operating and cost efficiencies for the future operation of the home. All recommendations should offer alternatives, identify savings to be achieved and the related cost in order to implement the recommendations, projected impact on staff and administration and strategies for implementation that are consistent with the city's role as operator of the home, as well as provisions for ensuring the maintenance of the current quality of care.

It is our intent that the cost of the review and subsequent implementation of the recommendations is to be recovered from savings achieved in the operations of the home.

Your Proposal Is to Include the Following Information:

a. Proposed methodology for undertaking the review.
b. Names and qualifications of persons to be involved in the review and development of subsequent recommendations.
c. An estimate of the time required to undertake the review and develop the recommendations.
d. Documentation and references demonstrating your ability to successfully implement recommendations in similar circumstances.
e. Potential cost savings that may be achieved as a result of the review.
f. A copy of any contracts or agreements that are to be entered into as a result of being retained to conduct the review.

It is to be noted that your fee structure including upset limits is to be identified separately, however, but included in the operating cost calculations with the savings shown as a net amount.

Patientcare and Standardcare were both large operators of nursing homes; Clarke-Hamilton was a management consulting firm located 100 miles away.

Proposal	Bid
Patientcare Ltd.	$35,000
Clarke-Hamilton Ltd.	$47,000
Standardcare Ltd.	$77,000

Prior to evaluating the bids, John summarized the proposals as shown in Exhibit 2. As he sat preparing to evaluate the proposals, John wondered what evaluation criteria and weightings he should use, keeping in mind the needs of the social services division and the content of the RFP.

In addition, he knew that his recommendations and justification had to be forwarded to the city administrator by December 15 prior to seeking approval of the various committees of elected officials.

EXHIBIT 2 **Proposals for Hampton Manor**

	Patientcare	Clarke-Hamilton	Standardcare
1. Maintenance	Require liaison person from city administration to assist team. 1. Collect data 2. Review program 3. Conduct interviews 4. Determine and evaluate operational policies 5. Analyze staff and cost 6. Evaluate financial situation 7. Prepare report of funds and recommendations 8. Provide administration and project control 9. Provide assistance with implementation if required • Intend to utilize Department of Health general guidelines for work standards/patient classifications with judgment applied • May not leave Manor with a system to use in the future	Suggest a steering committee be formed from city management and Hampton administration 1. Discuss terms of review with steering committee 2. Examine pertinent documentation 3. Review all sections 4. Conduct interviews and physical tour 5. Identify opportunities for improvement in all sections 6. Develop detailed recommendations 7. Review recommendations with management 8. Prepare and present final report 9. Implement recommendations if required • Work standard/patient classification to remain in place to be utilized by Home staff to maintain standards at minimal ongoing cost	Maintain contact with Hampton Manor management staff 1. Review operating statistics 2. Analyze organizational and operating procedures 3. Review and assess level of service in each section 4. Identify problems and potential improvements 5. Develop staffing schedules for comparison against existing and cost-effectiveness 6. Identify problems in respect to physical environment 7. Provide draft report 8. Assess availability of skills required to implement 9. Prepare final report and recommendation 10. Assist with implementation if required
2. Anticipated reduction and implementation costs	"Patientcare is prepared to estimate that the sum of all proposed operating deficiencies, if implemented, would far exceed the cost of the study and would be at least $350,000."	"The benefits received by our client in terms of reduced operating costs, improved cost-effectiveness, and operations improvement have invariably outweighed the costs of our services. The benefit-to-cost ratio from our assessments has varied from 3 to1 to as much as 30 to 1 or higher."	"With respect to savings, it is difficult to make a definitive statement without having actually completed the study. However, based on previous experience it is expected that savings should be in the order of 8–10 percent of total expenses, which would be approx. $550,000 in the case of Hampton Manor."

3. Experience	• Functional programming and operation at 11 institutions • List of five (5) other consulting projects • All appear large in scope • Manages nursing homes and chronic hospitals • Owns or leases many other facilities	• Operational reviews in 11 institutions—mainly hospitals with three regional centers • Extensive experience in specific areas again, mainly in hospitals • Experience in implementing two different types of work standard/patient classification systems and MIS systems • Extensive management consulting experience	• Appears to have extensive background in similar situations • Extensive list of 15 facilities either completed or in process • Manages Henford Lodge—150-bed restorative care program • Operational review of Martin Nursing Home • Owns or manages 2,400 nursing home beds and units in this state and Florida.
4. References	*Church Nursing Home, Dexter* • could not locate in Dexter or surrounding area *Littlefield Municipal Hospital, Marsland* • Spoke to administration who advised they consulted on construction of an addition to the hospital. Review only of size, layout, and facilities required. No operational or management review undertaken. *Jedd Park Nursing Home Expansion, Detroit* • Could find no home operating under that name in Detroit or surrounding area.	*Department of Community and Social Services* • Firm conducted operational review at Webster Regional Center and they were satisfied with their performance. Although not totally implemented, it appeared that they would meet or surpass their estimated savings. *Webster Regional Center Mgt.* • Talked to administrator who was satisfied with the manner in which they conducted their review. Very professional approach with minimum of disruption.	*Ward Home* • Firm completed operational review and currently involved in implementation. Particular emphasis on restorative care techniques in nursing homes dept. Certain operations being contracted out. Project uncompleted; however, appears they will meet their projected savings of $560,000 * Due to high cost of service, no further references were checked.

	* All other references were either impractical to contact or were facilities currently owned by Patientcare. Our request to visit a home operated locally by them or to review their patient classification system was discouraged.	*Regional Municipality of Gast City Greenfield Home for the Aged* • Firm performed salary review and reclassification of staff • Pleased with performance and methodology used to approach review. Experienced some minor problems with support in implementation.	
5. Review team	All appear to possess qualifications and training related to health care environment (7 individuals)	All appear to possess necessary qualifications and training in health care field (7 individuals)	All appear to possess necessary qualifications and training related to health care environment (6 individuals)
6. Time for review	Approximately six (6) weeks.	Approximately eight (8) weeks.	Commence within ten (10) days; five (5) weeks to complete review.
7. Fee	\$35,000—expenses included	Professional fee \$44,000 Expenses 3,000 \$47,000	Professional fee \$70,000 Expenses 6,000 \$76,000

Chapter Eighteen

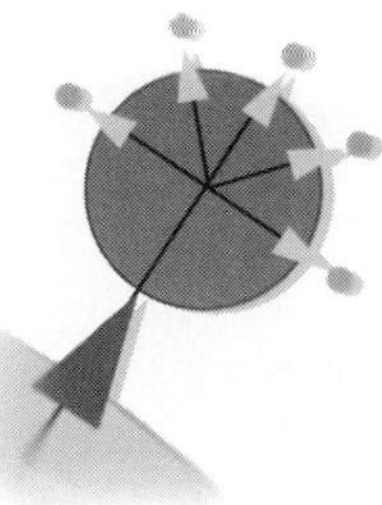

Make or Buy, Insourcing, and Outsourcing

Chapter Outline

Key Questions for the Supply Manager

Should we

- Change the way we currently take make-or-buy decisions?
- Consider insourcing more?
- Outsource more?

How can we

- Improve our ability to find insourcing opportunities?
- Ensure that supply considerations receive full attention in make-or-buy decisions?
- Develop our outsourcing expertise better?

MAKE OR BUY

One of the most critical decisions made in any organization concerns make or buy. When any organization starts its life, a whole series of make-or-buy decisions need to be made and as the organization grows and as it adds or drops products and/or services from its offerings, make-or-buy decisions continue to be made. In this text, the difference between make or buy and insourcing and outsourcing is defined as follows. *Insourcing* refers to reversing a previous buy decision. An organization chooses to bring in-house an activity, product, or service previously purchased outside. *Outsourcing* reverses a previous make decision. Thus, an activity, product, or service previously done in-house will next be purchased. Therefore, for any brand new product or service, make-or-buy decisions need to be made. Later, in view of new internal and external circumstances, these previous make-or-buy decisions are reviewed and some or all may be reversed. Clearly, there is a major role to play for purchasers in make or buy as well as insourcing and outsourcing.

The whole character of the organization is colored by the organization's stance on the make-or-buy decision. It is one of vital importance to an organization's productivity and competitiveness. Managerial thinking on this issue has changed dramatically in the last few years with increased global competition, pressures to reduce costs, downsizing, and focus on the firm's core competencies. The trend is now toward buying or seeking outside suppliers for services or goods that might traditionally have been provided in-house.

Traditionally, the make option tended to be favored by many large organizations, resulting in backward integration and ownership of a large range of manufacturing and subassembly facilities. Major purchases were largely confined to raw materials, which were then processed in-house. New management trends favoring flexibility and focus on corporate strengths, closeness to the customer, and increased emphasis on productivity and competitiveness reinforce the idea of buying outside. It would be unusual if any one organization were superior to competition in all aspects of manufacturing or services. By buying outside from capable suppliers those requirements for which the buying organization has no special manufacturing or service advantage, the management of the buying organization can concentrate better on its main mission. With the world as a marketplace, it is the purchaser's responsibility to search for or develop world-class suppliers suitable for the strategic needs of the buying organization.

A recent North American phenomenon has been the tendency to purchase services outside that were traditionally performed in-house. These include security, food services, and maintenance, but also programming, training, engineering, accounting, legal, research, personnel, information systems, and even contract logistics and purchasing. Thus, a new class of purchases involving services has evolved. (For a detailed description of the purchase of services, see Chapter 17.)

The make-or-buy decision is an interesting one because of its many dimensions. Almost every organization is faced with it continually. For manufacturing companies, the make alternative may be a natural extension of activities already present or an opportunity for diversification. For nonmanufacturing concerns, it is normally a question of services rather than products. Should a hospital have its own laundry, operate its own dietary, security, and maintenance services, or should it purchase these outside? Becoming one's own supplier is an alternative that has not received much attention in this text so far, and yet it is a vital option in every organization's procurement strategy.

What should be the attitude of an organization toward this make-or-buy issue? Many organizations do not have a consciously expressed policy but prefer to decide each issue as it arises. Moreover, it can be difficult to gather meaningful accounting data for economic analysis to support such decisions.

If it were possible to discuss the question in the aggregate for the individual firm, the problem should be formulated in terms of What should our organization's objective be in terms of how much value should be added in-house as a percentage of final product or service cost and in what form? A strong supply group would favor a buy tendency when other factors are not of overriding importance.

For example, one corporation found its supply ability in international markets such a competitive asset that it deliberately divested itself of certain manufacturing facilities common to every competitor in the industry.

Reasons for Make Instead of Buy

There are many reasons that may lead an organization to produce in-house rather than purchase. These include

1. The quantities are too small and/or no supplier is interested or available in providing the goods.
2. Quality requirements may be so exacting or so unusual as to require special processing methods that suppliers cannot be expected to provide.
3. There is greater assurance of supply or a closer coordination of supply with the demand.
4. It is necessary to preserve technological secrets.
5. It helps the organization obtain a lower cost.
6. It allows the organization to take advantage of or avoid idle equipment and/or labor.
7. It ensures steady running of the corporation's own facilities, leaving suppliers to bear the burden of fluctuations in demand.
8. It avoids sole-source dependency.

9. Competitive, political, social, or environmental reasons may force an organization to make even when it might have preferred to buy. When a competitor acquires ownership of a key source of raw material, it may force similar action. Many countries insist that a certain amount of processing of raw materials be done within national boundaries. A company located in a high-unemployment area may decide to make certain items to help alleviate this situation. A company may have to further process certain by-products to make them environmentally acceptable. In each of these instances, cost may not be the overriding concern.
10. The purchase option is too expensive.
11. The distance from the closest available supplier is too great.
12. A significant customer required it.
13. Future market potential for the product or service is expanding rapidly.
14. Forecasts show future shortages in the market or rising prices.
15. Management takes pride in size.

Reasons for Buying Outside

There are many reasons why an organization may prefer to purchase goods or services outside. These include

1. The organization may lack managerial or technical expertise in the production of the items or services in question.
2. The organization lacks production capacity. This may affect relations with other suppliers or customers as well.
3. Frequently, certain suppliers have built such a reputation for themselves that they have been able to build a real preference for their component as part of the finished product. Normally, these are branded items that can be used to make the total piece of equipment more acceptable to the final user. The manufacturers of transportation construction or mining equipment frequently let the customer specify the power plant brand and see this option as advantageous in selling their equipment.
4. The challenges of maintaining long-term technological and economic viability for a noncore activity are too great.
5. A decision to make, once made, is often difficult to reverse. Union pressures and management inertia combine to preserve the status quo. Thus, buying outside is seen as providing greater flexibility.
6. It assures cost accuracy.
7. There are more options in potential sources and substitute items.
8. There may not be sufficient volume to justify in-house production.
9. Future forecasts show great demand or technological uncertainty and the firm is unable or unwilling to undertake the risk of manufacture.
10. A highly capable supplier is available nearby.
11. The organization desires to stay lean.
12. Buying outside may open up markets for the firm's products or services.
13. It provides the organization with the ability to bring a product or service to market faster.

14. A significant customer may demand it.
15. It encourages superior supply management expertise.

The arguments advanced for either side of the make-or-buy question sound similar: better quality, quantity, delivery, price/cost, and service; lower risk; and greater opportunity to contribute to the firm's competitive position and provide greater customer satisfaction. Therefore, each individual make-or-buy decision requires careful analysis of both options. Even in the make decision, there will likely be a significant supply input requirement and there is even a greater one on the buy option. Thus, supply managers are constantly required to provide information, judgments, and expertise to assist the organization in resolving make-or-buy decisions wisely.

The Gray Zone in Make or Buy

Research by Leenders and Nollet[1] suggests that a "gray zone" may exist in make-or-buy situations. There may be a range of options between 100 percent make and 100 percent buy. This middle ground may be particularly useful for testing and learning without having to make the full commitment to make or buy. Particularly in the purchase of services, where no equipment investment is involved, it may be that substantial economies accrue to the organization that can substitute low-cost internal labor for expensive outside staff or low-cost external labor for expensive inside staff.

A good example of a gray zone trade-off in the automotive industry is the supplier who takes over design responsibility for a component from the car manufacturer. In maintenance, some types of servicing can be done by the purchaser of the equipment, other types by the equipment manufacturer.

The gray zone in make or buy may offer valuable opportunities or superior options for both purchaser and supplier.

SUBCONTRACTING

A special class of the make-or-buy spectrum is the area of subcontracting. Common in military and construction procurement, subcontracts can exist only when there are prime contractors who bid out part of the work to other contractors; hence the term *subcontractor*. In its simplest form, a subcontract is a purchase order written with more explicit terms and conditions. Its complexity and management vary in direct proportion to the value and size of the program to be managed. The management of a subcontract may require unique skills and abilities because of the amount and type of correspondence, charts, program reviews, and management reporting that are necessary. Additionally, payment may be handled differently and is usually negotiated along with the actual pricing and terms and conditions of the subcontract.

The use of a subcontract is appropriate when placing orders for work that is difficult to define, will take a long period of time, and will be extremely costly. For example, aerospace companies subcontract many of the larger structural components and avionics.

[1] M. R. Leenders and J. Nollet, "The Gray Zone in Make or Buy," *Journal of Purchasing and Materials Management,* Fall 1984, pp. 10–15.

wings, landing gears, and radar systems are examples of high-cost items that might be purchased on a subcontract. A similar form of subcontracting is often used in the construction industry, where a building contractor might subcontract the electrical or plumbing work.

In the aerospace industry, the subcontract is normally administered by a team that might include a subcontract administrator (SCA), an equipment engineer, a quality assurance representative, a reliability engineer, a material price/cost analyst, a program office representative, and/or an on-site representative.

Managing the subcontract is a complex activity that requires knowledge about performance to date as well as the ability to anticipate actions needed to ensure the desired end results. The SCA must maintain cost, schedule, technical, and configuration control from the beginning to the completion of the task.

Cost control of the subcontract begins with the negotiation of a fair and reasonable cost, proper choice of the contract type, and thoughtfully imposed incentives. Schedule control requires the development of a good master schedule that covers all necessary contract activities realistically. Well-designed written reports and recovery programs, where necessary, are essential. Technical control must ensure that the end product conforms to all the performance parameters of the specifications that were established when the contract was awarded. Configuration control ensures that all changes are documented. Good configuration control is essential to "aftermarket" and spares considerations for the product. Unlike a normal purchase order of minimal complexity, where final closeout may be accomplished by delivery and payment, a major subcontract involves more definite actions to close. These actions vary with the contract type and difficulty of the item/task being procured. Quite often large and complex procurements require a number of changes during the period of performance. These changes result in cost claims that must be settled prior to contract closure. Additionally, any tooling or data supplied to the contractor to support the effort must be returned. All deliverable material, data, and reports must be received and inspected. Each subcontract's requirements will vary in the complexity of the closure requirements; however, in all cases, a subcontract performance summary should be written to provide a basis for evaluation of the supplier for future bidder or supplier selection. Such a report also is necessary in providing information for subsequent claims or renegotiation.

INSOURCING AND OUTSOURCING

Insourcing and outsourcing occur when the decisions are made to reverse past buy-or-make decisions. Just because the decision to buy or make was properly made at the time does not mean it cannot be changed. New circumstances inside the organization, in the market, or in the environment may require the organization to reverse its stance on a previous buy-or-make decision.

If the previous decision to make or buy was improperly made and can be corrected subsequently, this obviously should be done. However, the arguments for constantly reassessing past buy-or-make decisions are particularly strong. Perceived risks may have been minimized or eliminated. New technology may permit processes previously considered impossible. New suppliers may have entered the market or old suppliers may have left. New trade-offs between raw materials and components, such as substitution of steel by plastic, may result in new options. It is this constant change in volumes, prices, capabilities, specifications, suppliers, capacities, regulations, competitors, technology, and managers that requires companies to review their current make-and-buy profile continuously in identifying new strengths, weaknesses, opportunities, and threats (SWOT).

The two questions that need to be addressed on an ongoing basis by a cross functional team including purchasing, operations, accounting, and marketing are (1) which products or services are we currently buying that we should be doing in-house? and (2) which products and services that we are currently doing in-house should we be buying outside?

INSOURCING

Insourcing, the often forgotten twin of outsourcing, deals with past buy decisions that are reversed. Given the demands on procurement managers' time, the likelihood that purchasing will initiate an insourcing initiative is relatively small. Continuing to buy what was purchased before is likely to be standard practice. From a supply perspective there are, however, several reasons why supply might have to trigger an insourcing initiative. The most obvious reason is when an existing source of supply goes out of business or drops a product or service line and no other supplier is available. Assuming the requirement for the product or service continues, the purchaser needs to find an alternate source. Supplier development or the creation of a new supplier who was previously not selling the product or service is one option. The other is to insource. Similarly, a sudden massive increase in price, the purchase of a sole source by a competitor, political events and regulatory changes, or a lack of supply of a key raw material or component required for the manufacture of the purchased product might force supply to consider insourcing. Thus, anything that threatens assurance of supply may provide supply a reason for insourcing. This might be called the necessity argument: "We would prefer not to produce this product or service in-house, but we really don't have any other options."

There are other organizational factors, however, aside from the aforementioned supply considerations that may make insourcing an attractive option. The reasons would be similar to the make arguments provided earlier in this chapter in the make-or-buy discussion. We may have developed a unique process for this product or service. Our quality, delivery, total cost of ownership, or flexibility would be vastly improved. We could provide superior customer service and satisfaction. Insourcing would greatly enhance our competitive ability. This might be called the opportunity argument: "We would prefer to do this in-house because it would give us a strategic competitive advantage."

After the decision to insource has been taken, the smooth transition from outside supply to inside manufacture will require supply's special attention. In the first place, how do we discontinue our dealings with our existing supplier(s)? Can the changeover occur simultaneously with current contract expiries or may penalties have to be paid to terminate existing commitments?

With any insourcing initiatives, there is also a new supply issue in terms of raw materials, components, equipment, energy, and services required to produce the particular requirement just insourced. Therefore, supply's capability to provide the required inputs competently is one of the factors to be considered in any insourcing decision.

OUTSOURCING

Organizations outsource when they decide to buy something they had been making in-house previously. For example, a company whose employees clean the buildings may decide to hire an outside janitorial firm to provide this service. That a huge wave of outsourcing and privatization (in the public sector) has hit almost all organizations during the last decade is evident. In the urge to downsize, "right size," and eliminate headquarters staff, and to focus on value-added activities and core competencies in order to survive and prosper, public and private organizations have outsourced an extremely broad range of functions and activities formerly performed in-house. Some activities, such as janitorial, food, and security services, have been outsourced for many years. Information systems (IS) is one activity that has received much attention recently as a target for outsourcing.

Other popular outsourcing targets are mail rooms, copy centers, and corporate travel departments. Almost no function is immune to outsourcing. Accounts payable, human resources, marketing/sales, finance, administration, logistics, engineering, and even purchasing are examples of functions now outsourced but previously done in-house. An entire function may be outsourced, or some elements of an activity may be outsourced and some kept in-house. For example, some of the elements of information technology may be strategic, some may be critical, and some may lend themselves to lower-cost purchase and management by a third party.[2] Identifying a function as a potential outsourcing target, and then breaking that function into its components, allows the decision makers to determine which activities are strategic or critical and should remain in-house and which can be outsourced.

The growth in outsourcing in the logistics area is attributed to transportation deregulation, the focus on core competencies, reductions in inventories, and enhanced logistics management computer programs. Lean inventories mean there is less room for error in deliveries, especially if the organization is operating in a just-in-time mode. Trucking companies have started adding the logistics aspect to their businesses—changing from merely moving goods from point A to point B, to managing all or a part of all shipments over a longer period of time, typically three years, and replacing the shipper's employees with their own. Logistics companies now have computer-tracking technology that reduces the risk in transportation and allows the logistics company to add more value to the firm than it could if the function were performed in-house. Third-party logistics providers track freight using electronic data interchange technology and a satellite system to tell customers exactly where its drivers are and when the delivery will be made. In a just-in-time environment, where the delivery window may be only 30 minutes, such technology is critical.

For example, Hewlett-Packard turned over its inbound, raw materials warehousing in Vancouver, Washington, to Roadway Logistics.[3] Roadway's 140 employees operate the warehouse 24 hours a day, seven days a week, coordinating the delivery of parts to the warehouse and managing storage. Hewlett-Packard's 250 employees were transferred to other company activities. Hewlett-Packard reports savings of 10 percent in warehousing operating costs.

[2] Mary C. Lacity, Leslie P. Willcocks, and David F. Feeny, "IT Outsourcing: Maximize Flexibility and Control," *Harvard Business Review,* May–June 1995, pp. 86–87.

[3] Jon Bigness, "In Today's Economy, There Is Big Money to Be Made in Logistics," *The Wall Street Journal,* September 6, 1995, p. A1.

The reasons for outsourcing are similar to those advanced for the buy option in make-or-buy decisions earlier in this chapter. There is a key difference, however. Because the organization was previously involved in producing the product or service itself, the question arises: "What happens to the employees and space and equipment previously dedicated to this product or service now outsourced?"

Layoffs often result, and even in cases where the service provider (third party) hires former employees, they are often hired back at lower wages with fewer benefits. Outsourcing is perceived by many unions as efforts to circumvent union contracts. The United Auto Workers union has been particularly active in trying to prevent auto manufacturers from outsourcing parts of their operations. Additional concerns over outsourcing include

- Loss of control.
- Exposure to supplier risks: financial weakness, loss of supplier commitment, slow implementation, promised features or services not available, lack of responsiveness, poor daily quality.
- Unexpected fees or "extra use" charges.
- Difficulty in quantifying economics.
- Conversion costs.
- Supply restraints.
- Attention required by senior management.
- Possibility of being tied to obsolete technology.
- Concerns with long-term flexibility and meeting changing business requirements.

As organizations have gained more experience in making outsourcing decisions and crafting outsourcing contracts, they have become better at applying sourcing and contracting expertise to these decisions. From writing the statement of work or request for proposal to defining the terms and conditions, the success of an outsourcing agreement lies in the details.

OUTSOURCING PURCHASING AND LOGISTICS

The purchasing function has also come under scrutiny in some organizations as a target for outsourcing. For example, when Saturn Corporation streamlined its supply management operations, it determined that supply could add the most value in the management of production materials, and that a distributor could add the most value in the area of nonproduction-related materials.[4] Saturn's purchasing management team supported the idea of outsourcing nonproduction purchasing as a way to minimize the number of suppliers, develop partnering relationships, minimize problems, and reduce the accounts and administrative paperwork. A cross-functional management team drawn from purchasing, manufacturing and product engineering, financial, materials management, and the United Auto Workers evaluated hundreds of potential suppliers before selecting Cameron & Barkley (CAMBAR). CAMBAR, chosen to act as the outside purchasing arm of Saturn Corporation, orders, inventories, delivers, and invoices suppliers. CAMBAR is also responsible for quality control, material warranty, and assistance in supplier selection.

[4] Fred Gardner, "Saturn's Better Idea: Outsource Purchasing," *Electronic Business Buyer,* September 1993, pp. 136–41.

It also agreed to achieve a 5 percent annual cost reduction, which it shares with Saturn, through increased efficiency and organization and supplier price reductions. EDI is used for ordering, receiving, and payment via electronic funds transfer (EFT). Daily requirements are transmitted seven times a day via EDI transmissions, and orders are shipped from the distributor's warehouse, 10 miles from the plant.

In a CAPS study on outsourcing, it was found that there was little outsourcing of typical supply management activities. The activities most likely to be outsourced were inventory monitoring, order placement, and order receiving, with more than 40 percent of respondents expecting increased outsourcing in inventory monitoring and order placement.[5]

Many tasks associated with the logistics function as well as the entire function itself have been heavily outsourced. The tasks typically outsourced include freight auditing, leasing, maintenance and repair, freight brokering, and consulting and training.

Deciding what represents a core competency to an organization is not always an easy task, nor is the decision always the same for a specific function. For example, ownership and management of an in-house fleet of vehicles may be subject to the decision to outsource or maintain in-house. In an organization where the sales force is large, the cars for sales representatives may be seen as an extension of the sales force, and part and parcel of the company's ability to outperform the competition in personal sales. Many of the functions of fleet management may be outsourced—leasing rather than owning vehicles, maintenance, resale of vehicles—but the contact with the drivers may be retained as an in-house function because keeping the drivers (sales force) happy is critical to the success of the organization. In a utility company, the mechanical expertise needed to maintain specialty vehicles may be seen as part of the company's core competency, whereas the maintenance of the automobile fleet may not. The outsourcing decision is a function of many factors, and each organization must assess these factors based on the goals and objectives and long-term strategy of the organization.

PURCHASING'S ROLE IN OUTSOURCING

Research indicates that purchasing has had relatively moderate involvement in the outsourcing decisions made in many organizations. However, given the nature of the decision, purchasing should be heavily involved in outsourcing. Supply managers believe they can add value to the outsourcing decision in the following ways:

- Providing a comprehensive, competitive process.
- Identifying opportunities for outsourcing.
- Aiding in selection of sources.
- Identifying potential relationship issues.
- Developing and negotiating the contract.
- Monitoring and managing the relationship on an ongoing basis.[6]

[5] Lisa M. Ellram and Arnold Maltz, *Outsourcing: Implications for Supply Management* (Tempe, AZ: Center for Advanced Purchasing Studies, 1997), p. 9.

[6] Harold E. Fearon and Michiel R. Leenders, *Purchasing's Organizational Roles and Responsibilities* (Tempe, AZ: Center for Advanced Purchasing Studies/National Association of Purchasing Management, 1995), p. 11.

In terms of purchasing's value proposition, appropriately skilled and knowledgeable supply managers should be able to affect value in the initial exploration of alternatives leading up to an outsourcing decision rather than after the decision has already been made.

The strategic importance of make-or-buy, insourcing, and outsourcing decisions is so high that great care needs to be exercised to make sure these decisions are right. Obviously, appropriate supply input is critical for these decisions as well as supply management subsequently to assure the success of whichever option has been chosen.

Conclusion

Make or buy, insourcing, and outsourcing are key strategic decisions for any organization. That each of these decisions can be reviewed and reversed at a later date, as conditions warrant, adds to the challenge of maintaining an appropriate mix of in-house activities and purchased goods and services. Obviously, effective supply management requires an ongoing active contribution from supply into this continuing assessment process. The more skilled the supply group at exploiting market opportunities and developing competitive sources, the more ready the organization should be to buy outside and outsource.

Questions for Review and Discussion

1. Why should an organization switch from making to buying?
2. What is outsourcing? How might one make the decision to outsource an activity or not?
3. Why is the make-or-buy decision considered strategic?
4. What is the gray zone in make or buy? What are its implications?
5. Why might an organization decide to insource? Can you give an example?
6. What is subcontracting?
7. Why would an organization outsource its logistics? Engineering? Marketing?
8. In the public sector, what name is frequently used for outsourcing? What are some major impediments to outsourcing in the public sector?
9. What role is expected of supply once an insourcing decision has been made?
10. If you were the sole owner of your own company, would you favor the make side or the buy side of the make-or-buy decision? Why?

References

Ellram, Lisa M., and Arnold Maltz. *Outsourcing: Implications for Supply Management.* Tempe, AZ: Center for Advanced Purchasing Studies, 1997.

Gilley, K. M., and A. Rasheed. "Making More of Doing Less: An Analysis of Outsourcing and Its Effect on Firm Performance." *Journal of Management* 26, no. 4 (2000), pp. 763–90.

Lacity, Mary; Leslie P. Willcocks; and David F. Feeny. "IT Outsourcing: Maximize Flexibility and Control." *Harvard Business Review,* May–June 1995.

Mol, Michael J. *Outsourcing, Supplier Relations and Internationalisation: Global Sourcing Strategy as a Chinese Puzzle.* Rotterdam, The Netherlands: Ersamus Research Institute of Management (ERIM), 2001.

Peisch, Richard. "When Outsourcing Goes Awry." *Harvard Business Review,* May–June 1995.

Quinn, J. B. "Strategic Outsourcing: Leveraging Knowledge Capabilities." *Sloan Management Review,* Summer 1999, pp. 9–21.

Takeishi, A. "Bridging Inter- and Intra-firm Boundaries: Management of Supplier Involvement in Automobile Product Development." *Strategic Management Journal* 22, no. 5 (2001), pp. 403–33.

Case 18–1

B&L Inc.

Brian Wilson, materials manager at B&L Inc. in Lancaster, Pennsylvania, was considering a proposal from his purchasing agent to outsource manufacturing for an outrigger bracket. It was the end of April and Mr. Wilson had to evaluate the proposal and make a decision regarding whether to proceed.

B&L INC. BACKGROUND

B&L Inc. manufactured trailers for highway transport trucks. The company comprised three divisions: the Trailer, Sandblast & Paint, and Metal Fabricating Divisions. Each division operated as a separate profit center, but manufacturing operations between each were highly integrated. The Metal Fabricating Division produced most of the component parts of the trailers, the Trailer Division performed the assembly operations, and the Sandblast & Paint Division was responsible for completing the sandblasting and final painting operation. B&L manufactured approximately 40 trailers per year, with about two-thirds produced during the period from November to April.

THE OUTRIGGER BRACKET

The outrigger bracket, part number T-178, was an accessory that could be used to secure oversized containers. The bracket consisted of four component parts welded together, and each trailer sold by B&L had 20 brackets—10 per side.

The Metal Fabricating Division was presently manufacturing the outrigger bracket. The subassembly parts—T-67, T-75, T-69, and T-77—were processed on a burn table, which cut the raw material to size. Although the burn table could work with eight stations, this machine had only been operating with one station. The final assembly operation, T-70, was performed at a manual welding station.

Manufacturing lead time for the outrigger bracket was two weeks. However, the Metal Fabricating Division had been able to coordinate supply and production with assembly operations. Consequently, finished inventory levels of the outrigger bracket were kept to a minimum. B&L's inventory holding costs were 20 percent per annum.

THE OUTSOURCING DECISION

In an effort to reduce costs, the purchasing agent, Alison Beals, who reported to Brian Wilson, solicited quotes from three local companies to supply the outrigger bracket. Mayes Steel Fabricators (Mayes), a current supplier to B&L for other components, offered the lowest bid, with a cost of $108.20, FOB B&L.

Brian met with the controller, Mike Carr, who provided a breakdown of the manufacturing costs for the outrigger bracket. Looking at the spreadsheet, Mike commented: "These are based on estimates of our costs from this year's budget. Looking at the material, labor, and overhead costs, I would estimate that the fixed costs for this part are in the area of about 20 percent. Keep in mind that it costs us about $75 to place an order with our vendors." Exhibit 1 provides B&L's internal cost breakdown and details from the quote from Mayes.

EXHIBIT 1 Manufacturing Costs and Mayes Quote: Outrigger Bracket T-178

Parts	Mayes Steel Fabricators	B&L Manufacturing Costs
T-67	$14.60	$17.92
T-75	21.10	17.92
T-69	18.50	45.20
T-77	13.00	10.37
T-70	41.00	58.69
Total	$108.20	$150.10

Brian expected that B&L would have to arrange for extra storage space if he decided to outsource the outrigger bracket to Mayes, who had quoted delivery lead time of four weeks. Because Mayes was local and had a good track record, Brian didn't expect the need to carry much safety stock, but the order quantity issue still needed to be resolved.

B&L was operating in a competitive environment and Brian had been asked by the division general manager to look for opportunities to reduce costs. As he sat down to review the information, Brian knew that he should make a decision quickly if it was possible to cut costs by outsourcing the outrigger bracket.

CASE 18–2

Rondot Automotive

It was September 28th and Glenn Northcott, purchasing planner at Rondot Automotive in Jackson, Mississippi, was evaluating an important outsourcing opportunity. For the past three months, Glenn had been working on a project that involved evaluating the feasibility of outsourcing the plant's painting requirements, and he had just finished collecting much of the necessary technical and cost information. Glenn had to complete his evaluation in advance of a meeting scheduled with his boss, Terry Gibson, purchasing manager, and the plant manager, Dick Taylor, in one week's time to discuss this matter and to decide what action, if any, needed to be taken next.

RONDOT WORLDWIDE

Rondot Automotive was a wholly owned subsidiary of Rondot Worldwide, a leading global designer and manufacturer of electrical and electronic components. Rondot Worldwide operated in more than 100 countries, employing more than 200,000 people. It was a key player in the information and communications, automation and control, power, transportation, medical, and lighting industries.

Rondot Automotive operated 85 plants in 25 countries. It was known for providing high-quality, innovative products in automotive electronics, electrics, and mechatronics. The Jackson, Mississippi, plant manufactured small motors for a number of applications, including engine cooling, HVAC (heating, ventilation, and cooling), and antilock brake systems. The plant produced approximately 7 million motors per year, which were shipped directly to OEM assembly facilities for customers such as Ford, GM, DaimlerChrysler, Honda, Toyota, and BMW.

Rondot Automotive was facing considerable global competition and significant pressures from its customers for price reductions. As a result, total sales and employment at the Jackson plant had steadily declined over the past five years. The number of employees at the plant had dropped from 1,450 to 600, and plant management was under pressure to lower costs and regain market share.

The purchasing organization at Rondot Automotive was a hybrid structure. The corporate strategic purchasing group operated from the company's head office in Troy, Michigan, and was responsible for negotiating major contracts with suppliers and working on new product development initiatives. Plant-level purchasing organizations reported to the plant managers on a solid-line basis and corporate purchasing on a dotted-line basis. Plant purchasing managers were responsible for materials management, negotiating contracts for local requirements and small-value purchases. The purchasing department at the Jackson plant consisted of four people, including two buyers, a planner (Glenn) and Terry Gibson. Glenn had joined Rondot right out of college the previous year.

OUTSOURCING OPPORTUNITY

A steel housing was manufactured for each of the six different families of motors manufactured at the Jackson plant. The housings were "deep drawn" in large stamping presses in a batch operation. Following stamping, the housings were processed through a zinc phosphate treatment for cleaning and then painted. Quality specifications stipulated that the coating on the housing had to be capable of withstanding 240 hours of salt spray testing.

The cleaning and painting process involved a continuous-flow wet paint system that had been installed in a 20,000-square-foot section of the plant approximately 17 years prior. The system had undergone a number of upgrades and modifications, in part to comply with evolving environmental regulations.

Based on data from the plant controller, Ken Lee, Glenn had learned that the cleaning and painting operations cost 25¢ for each housing. Ken commented to Glenn: "We estimate our costs to include 10¢ in material, 3¢ in labor, and the rest in overhead, including expenses such as taxes, energy, maintenance, and charges from corporate office."

GREVEN E-COATING

Glenn had been approached by an enterprising local vendor several months back, inquiring about Rondot's painting requirements. Cathy Stirling, representing Greven E-Coating Company (Greven), proposed that she prepare samples for each family of housings and provide cost estimates to Glenn. Eager to explore cost savings opportunities, Glenn readily agreed.

Electrocoating, or e-coating, uses a system whereby a DC electrical charge is applied to a metal part immersed in a bath of oppositely charged paint particles. The metal part attracts the paint particles, forming an even film over the entire surface, until the coating reaches the desired thickness. E-coating was generally considered more cost-efficient compared to traditional wet paint systems.

Samples from Greven were sent to Rondot's quality control department for testing and the results seemed encouraging. The tests indicated that parts for five of the six families of housings, representing approximately 60 percent of the Jackson plant's housing volume, could be converted to e-coating using Greven at a cost of $0.15 each. One family of housings failed the tests because of problems with the method of adhering a magnet to the housing. Rondot's assembly process required a magnet to be attached to the top inner portion of each housing using either a cold or hot bonding adhesion process. The use of either method was dependent on product design, and engineering specified the adhesion method used. The one family of housings that used a cold-bond adhesion process had failed the test, while the other five families, which used a hot-bond process, passed the testing process.

As part of the data-gathering process for this project, Glenn also talked to Betty McKinley, from production planning, and John Underwood, in manufacturing engineering. Betty figured that she would need to add another two weeks' worth of inventory if painting operations were to be outsourced. She reminded Glenn to expect to pay 3¢ per part for transportation and packaging.

John was delighted at the prospects of eliminating the paint line, indicating: "In the not-to-distant future, we are going to have to spend some money to upgrade our system or pull the line out completely. These old wet-based systems are less efficient compared to other technologies available today, in terms of both cost and environmental performance."

PREPARING FOR THE MEETING

Glenn was aware that Terry Gibson and Dick Taylor were under significant pressure to reduce costs at the Jackson plant and he felt that outsourcing painting operations represented a good opportunity. However, this was his first major project and Glenn wanted to make sure that he had taken all the necessary issues into account and developed a strong case for his recommendations before his meeting the following week.

CASE 18–3
Huson Manufacturing

Dale Matheson, the new production control manager at Huson Manufacturing in Akron, Ohio, had just been handed his first big assignment. It was May 3rd, and the outsourcing of production from the metal fabrication department four months earlier had resulted in higher costs and problems in plant operations. Morris Phelps, the director of manufacturing, had asked Dale to make correcting the situation his highest priority.

COMPANY BACKGROUND

Huson Manufacturing (Huson) was a leading manufacturer of heat transfer systems, and its products included heating and cooling coils, hydro generator coolers, and transformer oil coolers. The company's mission was "To deliver innovative engineering solutions and quality equipment for industrial heat systems worldwide." Exports to Canada, Mexico, and overseas accounted for approximately 40 percent of total sales, and its products had applications in industries such as steel, petrochemical, pulp and paper, power generation facilities, and the navy.

Heat exchangers, or transfer units, were vital in maintaining the temperatures of operating environments at specified levels. Process fluids (water, oil, etc.) traveled through a set of tubes during which time they were cooled. These fluids then traveled back to the generator or engine and the process began again. An air-cooled fluid cooler consisted of a cooling bundle (tubes), a fan cabinet arranged to create air flow and the proper draft, and a frame or support structure.

Each system was custom designed. The engineering department specified requirements, created a preliminary bill of materials, and, in concert with costing and purchasing, provided the sales department with the relevant information to quote on a contract. Once the contract was secured, the MRP system generated a complete bill of materials, and materials were ordered as needed. Most jobs had delivery requirements of four to six weeks. No finished inventory was stocked; all products were built to order.

THE MANUFACTURING PROCESS

Huson occupied a 120,000-square-foot building, with manufacturing using 100,000 square feet and the remainder being office space. Huson, which had been acquired by a large corporation 10 years previously, operated as a stand-alone profit center and maintained a track record of solid financial performance. An organization chart is provided in Exhibit 1.

The customized nature of Huson's product line required a custom assembly job shop with several departments, each of which produced particular component parts, feeding a final assembly area. Each job moved from work center to work center. The first process involved fitting a liner tube (in which the fluid to be cooled passed) into a base tube. This base tube, made of aluminum, was then pressure bonded to the inner liner tube through a rotary extrusion process that formed spiral fins on the base tube. The depth of the fins and the distance between them determined the amount of air flow across the tubes, and thus the cooling efficiency and power of the unit.

After the tubes were formed, cabinet and end plate fabrication began. The tubes were welded to the cabinet and the end plates. Flanges were then welded to pairs of tubes on the other side of the end plates to create a looped system. The unit was then painted and fans and motors were installed. Finally, the unit was tested for leaks and performance, crated, and shipped to the job site for installation.

Most of the products incorporated proprietary components that were manufactured with equipment designed by the company. The workforce of approximately 100 people was unionized, and relations with the union had been relatively harmonious.

METAL FABRICATING DEPARTMENT

The metal processing department had been equipped with machinery for welding, cutting, forming, and punching metal for use in fabricating enclosures and frames. The machinery in this department was quite large and occupied a 7,500-square-foot area in the plant. Approximately 12 people had been assigned to this department.

Metal fabrication had been a bottleneck. Volatility in demand and wide variation in the level of product customization resulted in the production levels of the department fluctuating significantly. In periods of tight capacity, operators would adjust the production schedule to favor the easier-to-produce parts, creating shortages of the more-difficult-to-produce parts. An additional problem related to product modifications. It was not uncommon for operators from other departments to request minor modifications to fabricated components. However, operators sometimes waited several days for the fabrication department to turn their attention to such requests, potentially delaying customer deliveries and disrupting the overall production schedule.

EXHIBIT 1 **Organization Chart**

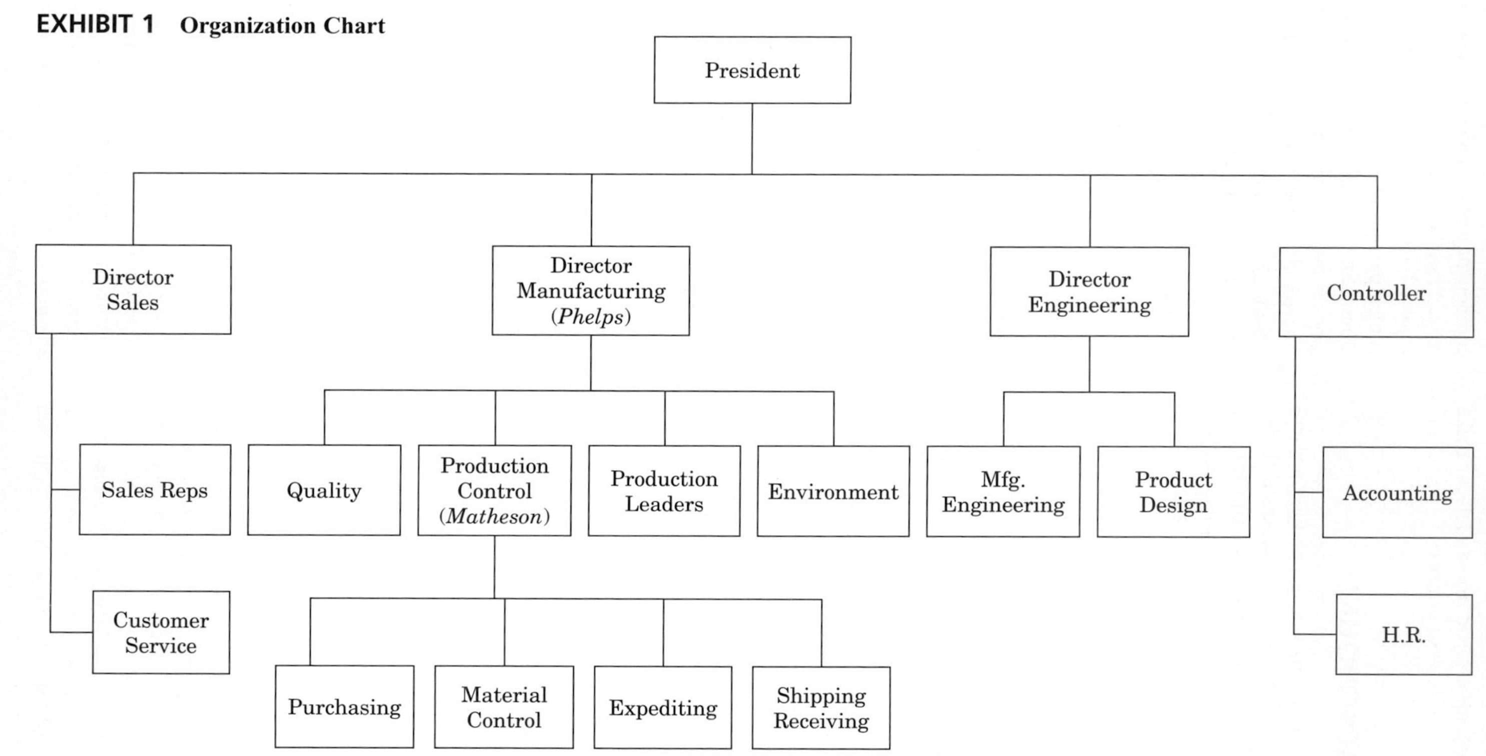

OUTSOURCING HISTORY

In the fall of the previous year, Morris Phelps decided to outsource the metal processing production and instructed Dale's predecessor to implement the decision. The alternative of acquiring additional equipment to handle the peak loads was judged to be uneconomic. It was felt that a supplier whose primary business was metal fabrication would be more cost-effective. Also, Morris believed that the 7,500 square feet of plant space that would be made available could be used for higher value-added production processes.

Huson's ISO 9000 quality procedure required its outside suppliers also be ISO certified, to have qualified welders on staff and be capable of handling all phases of subcontracted work in-house. One supplier met these criteria and was selected to provide the outsourced parts, although no commitment to exclusivity or length of contract was made.

The equipment in the department, most of which was fully depreciated, was sold to the supplier. Operators with sufficient seniority were assigned elsewhere in the plant, and eight people were laid off as a result of the outsourcing. A transition period with gradual phase-in of outsourced parts had been considered but dismissed because modifying the flow of paperwork from the material requirements planning (MRP) system was considered to be too difficult. As a result, on January 5th, the supplier started providing all parts previously produced by the metal processing department.

SUPPLY PROBLEMS

The outsourcing proved to be a greater challenge than anticipated. The supply agreement had been made on the basis of actual material and labor costs plus an agreed markup. Almost immediately, the supplier began receiving a large number of returned parts for modification. Since the required modifications were inconsistent with the engineering drawings provided by Huson, the supplier passed on the cost of the additional work. Material costs were also higher than Huson had expected, as a result of higher production scrap from cutting and punching operations. In addition, it was found that Huson's engineering drawings and bills of materials contained inconsistencies. Parts were ordered for which there were no engineering specifications or for which specifications were incorrect.

For the production control department, the outsourcing proved to be a nightmare. Whereas the MRP system had efficiently generated the production requirements for the metal processing department, the outsourcing arrangement required the generation of purchase orders. Brenda Cowan, purchasing manager, recalled: "We used to handle about 5,000 to 6,000 parts a week. When parts fabrication was outsourced, we immediately went to 12,000 to 14,000 parts. We were all working 70-hour weeks."

Also, each incoming part had its own shipping, receiving, quality inspection, and invoicing paperwork. When a part had to be returned for rework or modification, the paperwork became even more confusing. By March, a purchasing manager and an expeditor were employed full time to keep track of the flow of parts and paper and to expedite orders in order to keep the plant running. As a result, morale in the production control department was at an all-time low. Despite working many extra hours to expedite improperly specified parts, production control was being blamed for the problems. In April, the entire department was relocated from the front offices into office space in the plant. Brenda observed: "This move was explained as a way to give purchasing an opportunity to observe and investigate the problems the plant was experiencing as a result of the parts supply situation. However, we felt like we were being punished."

Continual requests by purchasing for the engineering department to fix incorrect production drawings went unheeded. As a result, relations between the departments deteriorated rapidly. Meanwhile, productivity in other production departments had been affected as well. Parts coming from the supplier had to clear receiving and quality assurance before staging, being sorted into kits, and being transfered to the appropriate production department. Further delays and greater frequency of missing parts were attributed to the extra handling. Also, since operators could no longer take parts requiring even minor modifications over to the metal processing department, parts now had to be returned to the supplier for rework.

NEXT STEPS

Dale knew that the company was committed to substantial sales growth and that production was expected to increase over the next few months. However, much customer goodwill had been lost and several orders had been canceled on account of late delivery as a direct result of problems associated with metal fabrication supply problems. Meanwhile, the union was suggesting that the decision to outsource was a bad one and the company should bring metal fabrication back in-house.

Dale had a meeting scheduled with Morris Phelps the following day to discuss how he proposed to resolve the situation and the immediate action he planned to take. Dale expected that Morris would also ask for his opinion regarding where the company went wrong with the implementation of the outsourcing so as to avoid similar problems in the future.

Chapter Nineteen

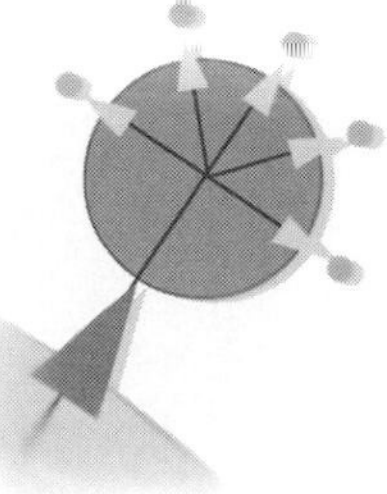

Supplier Relations

Chapter Outline

Key Questions for the Supply Manager

Should we

- Change our stance on multiple sourcing?
- Move to longer-term contracts?
- Do more reverse marketing?

How can we

- Improve our relations with suppliers?
- Involve other functions more effectively in supplier relations?
- Initiate partnerships or alliances with our key suppliers?

The key strategic decisions in supply management center on which supplier to pursue and what kinds of relations to maintain with suppliers. Strategic supply management is founded on the conviction that a significant competitive edge can be gained from the suppliers an organization has developed and its supply systems and supplier relations. Any organization's desire to satisfy its customers and to provide continuing improvement in its customer service is dependent on its suppliers to help it accomplish this goal. (See Figure 19–1.)

Supplier performance has a greater impact on the productivity, quality, and competitiveness of the organization than most managers realize. Recent trends to buy instead of make, to outsource instead of continuing to make, to improve quality, to lower inventories, to integrate supplier and purchaser systems, and to create cooperative relations such as partnerships have underlined the need for outstanding supplier performance.

In the supply chain management perspective, the link between the buying organization and its direct suppliers is obviously one of the two primary external ones. The other link,

FIGURE 19–1
Customer Satisfaction Depends on Supplier Performance

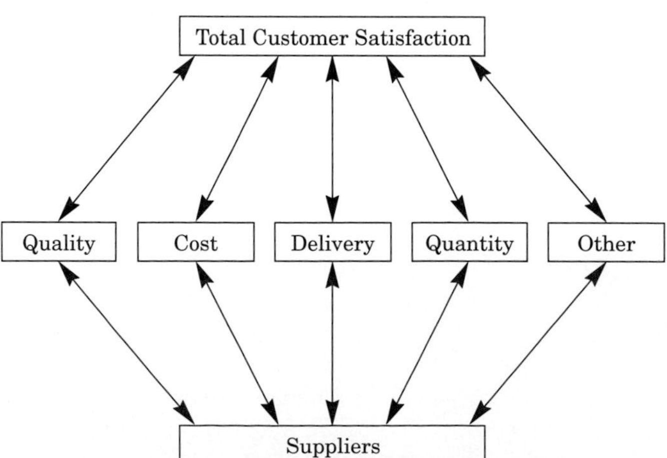

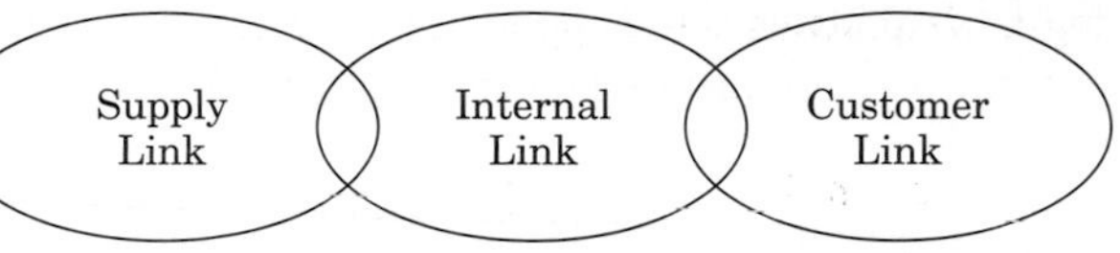

FIGURE 19–2 **Simplified Supply Chain Perspective Showing the Three Core Links**

between the buying organization and its customers, continues the chain on the exit, or distribution, side. The ability of any organization to connect these two external links through its internal organization will, to a large extent, determine the effectiveness of its total supply chain. Figure 19–2 provides a simplified overview of these links. Since, in any chain, the weakest link determines the strength of the whole chain, it is important that the strength of each link be equal and congruent. It is also a relatively simple perspective that greater strength in any one link can create a customer-dominant, internally dominant, or supplier-dominant chain.

In this chapter, the prime objective is to develop a supply link that will provide a short- and long-term strategic competitive advantage.

Depending on the nature of the purchase, whether it is a repeat, a modified repeat, or a new requirement; the size of the dollar amount involved; and the market conditions, the criticality or impact of the supplier choice may vary and the acquisition process and final decision may change. Whereas in the past most buyers felt that the supplier selection decision should be purchasing's domain, today's trend to team procurement recognizes that it is necessary to bring together key organizational resources outside and inside of the supply area to achieve sound supplier choices. Moreover, the trend to fewer suppliers, longer-term contracts, e-procurement, and continuing improvement in quality, delivery, price, and service requires much closer coordination and communication between various people in both the buying and selling organizations. Therefore, improving buyer–seller relationships is a key concern.

Outstanding supplier performance normally requires extensive communication and cooperation between various representatives of the buying organization and the selling organization over a long period of time. In full recognition of this, progressive procurement organizations are pursuing ways and means of limiting their total number of suppliers and maximizing the results from fewer key suppliers. Bringing new suppliers onstream is expensive and is often accompanied by a period of learning and aggravation for both sides. Frequent supplier switching for the sake of a seemingly lower price may not result in obtaining the best long-term value. As quality improvement programs and just-in-time production efforts take hold, proximity of the supplier's premises to those of the purchaser becomes a significant consideration. An imaginative and aggressive supplier development effort, with both existing and new sources, holds high promise as a review of existing suppliers discloses gaps and as new technology evolves into new requirements. System and philosophical compatibility between purchaser and supplier has become more vital as ways and means are found to shorten the time taken from requisition to actual receipt of the order.

These exciting new approaches to supplier choice and relationships between suppliers and purchasers are in stark contrast to the old-fashioned, hard-nosed way of procurement. It used to be reasonably common that suppliers were dropped with little notice when they failed to provide the lowest quote on an annual contract. The ideas of sharing information and assisting suppliers to improve their performance are no longer seen as novel, but more as a necessity for world-class performance.

PURCHASER–SUPPLIER RELATIONS

When one organization supplies another with goods or services, the nature of the relationship between the two organizations is a major influencer of the ultimate value and customer satisfaction achievable. Supply management is, therefore, not simply engaged in the exchange of money for goods and services, but also in the management of the buyer–seller relationship.

In this section, the nature of supplier goodwill is discussed along with the qualifications of good and preferred suppliers, partnerships, strategic alliances, and supply chain management.

Supplier Goodwill

Good sources of supply are one assurance of good quality today, and progressive thinking and planning is a further assurance of improved quality tomorrow. Superior sources of supply, therefore, are an important asset to any organization.

It has long been considered sound marketing policy to develop goodwill on the part of customers toward the seller. This goodwill has been cultivated through the development of trademarks and brands, through extensive advertising, through missionary efforts as well as through regular calls by sales personnel, and through the many other devices that have appealed to the imaginations of marketing managers. These days these efforts are often lumped together under the term *relationship marketing.* Sellers are jealous of this goodwill, considering it one of their major assets. It has real commercial value and is so recognized by courts of law.

Goodwill between a purchasing organization and its suppliers needs to be just as carefully cultivated and just as jealously guarded. When purchasers are as aggressive in their attempts to maintain proper and friendly relations with suppliers as marketing managers are in their relations with customers, congruence in supply chain linkage may be achieved. Since strategic plans are so often based on the assumption that supply sources will be cooperative, it makes sense to ensure that such cooperation will be forthcoming.

Progressive companies have started to measure supplier goodwill on a regular basis using third-party research organizations to conduct surveys. The president of one electronics firm flatly stated: "No company can be world class if it does not measure on a regular basis the satisfaction level of its key suppliers and try to improve constantly on its relations with its suppliers."

One of the interesting outcomes of supplier satisfaction surveys is the general finding that suppliers believe that the best purchasers are those who know more about the supplier's business than the supplier's own employees.

THE PURCHASER–SUPPLIER SATISFACTION MATRIX

One of the major assessments a purchaser must make is whether the current relationship with a supplier is a satisfactory one or not. This relationship is highly complex and different people inside the purchasing organization may have different perceptions of it. In the simplest form, with a new supplier just after a relatively small order has been placed but no deliveries have yet been made, it may consist only of an assessment of the agreement just reached and the buyer's quick impression of the sales representative. For a long-term supplier of major needs, the assessment will be based on past and current performance, personal relationships with a number of personnel in both organizations, and even future expectations. Such assessments may well change as a result of competitive action in the marketplace. What may look like a good price deal today may not look so attractive when information comes to light that a fully competent competitor could have supplied the same materials or services for substantially less.

The matrix in Figure 19–3 provides a simple framework for clarifying the current purchaser–supplier relationship in terms of satisfaction and stability. The assumptions behind it are that

1. Satisfaction with a current supplier relationship can be assessed, whether it is satisfactory or not.
2. An unsatisfied party (seller or purchaser or both) will attempt to move to a more satisfactory situation.

FIGURE 19–3
A Simple Purchaser–Supplier Satisfaction Matrix

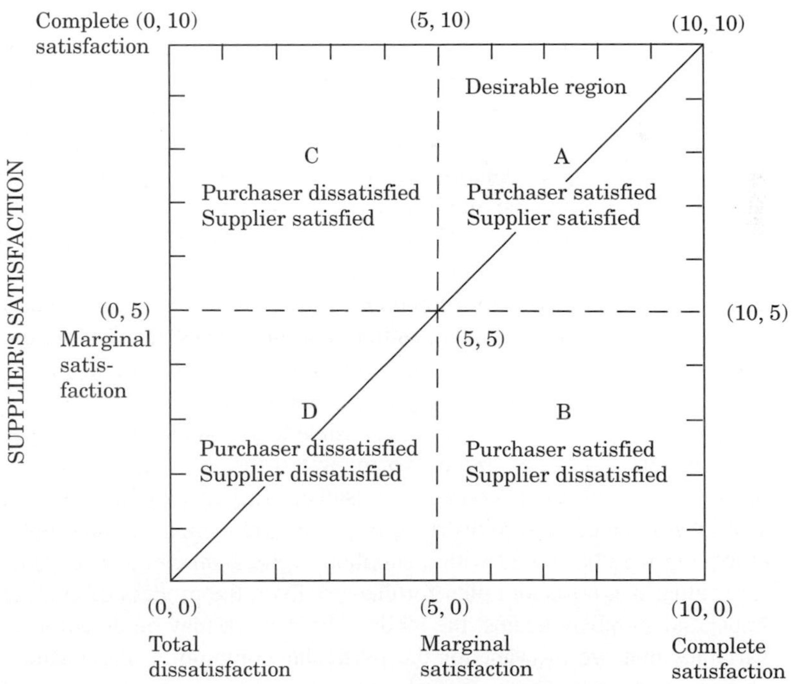

3. Attempts to move may affect the stability of the relationship.
4. Attempts to move may fall in the win–lose, as well as the lose–lose, lose–win, and win–win, categories.
5. Purchaser and seller may well have different perceptions of the same relationship.
6. Many tools and techniques and approaches exist that will assist either party in moving positions and improving stability.

Obviously, any purchaser–supplier relationship could fall into any of the four quadrants in the matrix. However, only quadrant A represents a desirable region in which a reasonably stable relationship can be maintained. In each of the other quadrants, attempts by the purchaser or supplier or both to increase satisfaction may worsen the satisfaction of the other, thereby lowering stability in the relationship. Clearly, quadrant D, with both parties dissatisfied, represents a highly undesirable and unstable relationship.

The diagonal in the diagram may be seen as a "fairness or stability" line. As long as positions move along this line, both purchaser and supplier are at least equally well off. Its end points of (0,0) and (10,10) represent two extremes. The (0,0) position is completely undesirable from either standpoint. The (10,10) position represents a utopian view rarely found in reality. It requires a degree of mutual trust and sharing and respect that is difficult to achieve in our society of "buyer beware" and where competition and the price mechanism are supposed to work freely. However, in some partnerships, a relationship close to the (10,10) state has been developed. Buyers are willing to share risks and information with the seller, and the seller is willing to open the books for buyer inspection. Problems are ironed out in an amicable and mutually acceptable manner and both parties benefit from the relationship.

The middle position of (5,5) should really be considered as a minimum acceptable goal for both sides, and few agreements should be reached by the purchaser without achieving at least this place. Adjustments in positions should, hopefully, travel along the diagonal and toward the (10,10) corner. Substantial departures from the diagonal raise the difficulty that the agreement may be seen as less beneficial to one party than the other, with the possibility of jealousy and the attempt by the less-satisfied party to bring the other down to a more common denominator. The region of greatest stability will, therefore, lie close to the (5,5)–(10,10) portion of the diagonal line.

This model becomes more complex when the perceptions of both parties are considered, with respect to both their own position and the other side's. For example, the purchaser's perception may be that the relationship is in the A region. The supplier's perception may or may not match this view.

From a supply point of view, it is possible to assess the total package of current supplier relationships and to determine how many fall inside the desirable region and how many outside. A significant percentage of unsatisfactory or marginal situations will mean a substantial amount of work to restructure current arrangements. The supply perception of a relationship may be shared with a supplier to check on congruence and as a starting point for mutual diagnosis and plan for change. Even the process of attempting to assess contracts and suppliers against the model's framework may be useful in establishing the key variables that are relevant for the particular commodity under study. Furthermore, the severity of the situation is a good indicator of the need for action and the tools and techniques that might be applied. For example, a purchaser may wish to work harder at a (1,5) than a (5,5) situation of equal dollar value and corporate impact.

Tools and Techniques for Moving Positions

A number of supply management and marketing means may be used to shift positions on the satisfaction chart. The use of some of these will adversely affect the perceptions of the other party, and these might be called "crunch" tools or negative measures. Others are likely to be viewed in less severe terms and might be considered "stroking" methods or positive approaches. For example, crunch tools for the purchaser include

1. Complete severance of purchases without advance notice.
2. Refusal to pay bills.
3. Refusal to accept shipments.
4. Use or threat of legal action.

For the supplier, examples would include

1. Refusal to send shipments as promised.
2. Unilateral price increase without notice.
3. Insistence on unreasonable length of contract, take or pay commitments, onerous escalation clauses, or other unreasonable terms and conditions and use of take it or leave it propositions.

"Stroking" techniques by the purchaser would include

1. Granting of substantial volumes of business, long-run commitments, or 100 percent requirements contracts.
2. Sharing of internal information on forecasts, problems, and opportunities to invite a mutual search for alternatives.
3. Evidence of willingness and ability to work toward changed behavior in the purchasing organization to improve the seller's position.
4. Rapid positive response to requests from suppliers for discussions and adjustments in price, quality, delivery, and service.

On the supplier side, examples could be

1. Willingness and ability to make rapid price, delivery, and quality adjustments in response to purchase requests without a major hassle.
2. Invitation to the purchaser to discuss mutual problems and opportunities.
3. The giving of notice substantially in advance of pending changes in price, lead times, and availability to allow the purchaser maximum time to plan ahead.

It is interesting that "stroking" techniques are more likely to be used in the A region, further strengthening the stability of the relationship, whereas the use of crunch tools may well accomplish short-term objectives but may impair future chances of a desirable stable relationship.

The perception of a relationship is based on both the results obtained and the process by which they have been achieved. For example, a price concession grudgingly granted by a supplier and continually negatively referred to by supplier's personnel may create less satisfaction for the purchaser than one more amicably reached. Crunch methods pleasantly applied may be far more palatable than the same tool used in a hard-nosed way.

For example, an unavoidable price increase can be explained in person by a supplier's sales manager well in advance more palatably than by a circular letter after the increase has been put into effect. A supply manager can visit a supplier's plant to determine ways and means of solving a quality problem and explain that no deliveries can be accepted until the problem is solved, instead of sending back shipment after shipment as unacceptable. The results–process combination puts a heavy emphasis on managerial judgment and capability to accomplish change effectively.

Purchaser–Supplier Relationship Management

The satisfaction–stability matrix underlines the need for extensive communications between both parties in the buying–selling relationship. The whole art of supplier relationship management from a supply perspective is to bring both sides into an effective working relationship. This will require substantial coordination work inside the purchaser's organization to ensure that the people most vitally concerned with a particular supplier's performance are fully involved in the planning and execution of a program leading to the desired long-term relationship. Therefore, the team approach to long-term supplier relations is probably the only reasonable option. In such team acquisition, the buyer or supply manager usually plays the coordination and project manager role.

Without internal cooperation and a congruent strategic internal approach to the improvement of supplier relations, supplier relationship management is impossible. The members of the internal team are the ones who have to deal directly with their appropriate counterparts on the supplier side. The necessity for good management of this interface is obvious. Immediate and concerted action needs to be taken when either side detects problems or sees opportunities. Awareness of the full details of each side's situation, aspirations, strengths, and weaknesses is necessary for any team member to be able to assess the impact of changes, problems, or opportunities on the other side. Simply stated, the seller's and purchaser's personnel need to understand their own and the other organizations very well so that both sides can work on continuing improvement for mutual benefit. Such understanding can come only through exposure, discussion, mutual problem solving, and willingness to investigate every aspect of a meaningful relationship frankly. Given that in many organizations it is difficult for individual employees in different functional areas to work well together toward a common goal, it is easy to appreciate the challenge posed by adding the supplier's organization to this set. It may well be that the development of superior supplier relations will be the most critical challenge for supply managers in the decades ahead.

Moreover, the ability to develop effective working relationships with suppliers will be dependent on supply's ability to develop effective working relationships internally. Thus, supply's status within the organization and the availability of qualified and credible supply personnel will be key determinants of the organization's ability to get the most out of its supplier force.

SUPPLIER RANKING

It is possible to rank suppliers on a scale from unacceptable to exceptional.

Unacceptable Suppliers

Unacceptable suppliers fail to meet operational and strategic needs of the buying organization. Discontinuing business with unacceptable suppliers and substituting better ones is the normal action required. A special case exists where such a discontinuance may create even greater problems for the purchasing organization. A typical example is a sole-supply situation as in the case of a patented or OEM part where the supplier takes undue advantage of its privileged position. Even then, when discontinuance in the short term may not be feasible, in the long term it may be, if the supply organization has diligently worked on finding an appropriate substitute or developing another source of supply. Another exception is a new source of supply that is still learning how to satisfy the purchasing organization's requirements and is assiduously working to achieve significant improvement.

Acceptable Suppliers

Acceptable suppliers meet current operational needs as required by contract. Acceptable suppliers provide a performance that other purchasers could easily match and, hence, acceptable suppliers provide no basis for competitive edge.

Preferred Suppliers

Purchasers have a system or process orientation with preferred suppliers and this integration avoids unnecessary duplication and speeds up transactions, which normally are handled on an electronic basis. Both parties work toward mutual improvements to eliminate nonvalue-adding activities. Preferred suppliers meet all operational and some of the strategic needs of the buying organization. Preferred suppliers react positively to initiatives of the purchaser to improve the current situation.

Exceptional Suppliers

Exceptional suppliers anticipate operational and strategic needs of the purchaser and are capable of meeting and exceeding them. With exceptional suppliers, mutual breakthroughs may be a source of significant competitive advantage. Exceptional suppliers, like exceptional customers, need to be treasured. They can serve as an example of what is possible: an opportunity to experiment with new and different approaches to supply base management and as an early indicator of future supply management and supplier relationship direction and goals.

It requires a substantial amount of work on the part of both the supplier and the purchaser to obtain the big rewards of mutual breakthrough. Patience and persistence are required to sustain the investment in relationship building. The lack of evidence of substantial reward in the earlier stages may be disappointing for those who are interested only in the short haul. A similarity exists in athletic training. World and Olympic records are seldom obtained by those not willing to commit fully beforehand to the intensive training and developmental program.

Leslie Monroe, contract coordinator at Disneyland in Anaheim, California, reports that

> "The innovation that is most common at Disneyland isn't about systems or processes or contracts; the true innovation is in the relationships we are building with key suppliers of goods and services. I need to understand my supplier's business as much as he or she needs to understand mine. We are working together to identify cost savings and value creating opportunities, including alternative products, process changes, or any number of areas that positively impact the bottomline without sacrificing quality, safety, or the environment."[1]

[1] Leslie R. Monroe, "The Relationships We Build," *Purchasing Today,* February 1999, p. 68.

In full recognition that exceptional suppliers are scarce and that substantial investment is required in creating a superior buyer–supplier relationship, a large number of purchasers have started to create partnerships, or strategic alliances. These are a logical evolution arising from supplier rationalization efforts.

PARTNERSHIPS

In the last two decades, a large number of organizations have started to create "partnerships" with their suppliers. The term *partnership* gives lawyers discomfort, because in the legal sense it has certain obligations that are not necessarily part of a standard buyer–seller partnership. Unfortunately, considerable confusion exists regarding the meaning of partnership, and the selling community has further compounded these difficulties by making it part of a standard sales pitch to any customer. To avoid some of this confusion, some purchasers have chosen the term *strategic alliances.*

The interest in buyer–supplier partnerships was fanned in the 1980s by the study of Japanese companies who maintained very close relationships with their suppliers. This was seen as one of the key elements in the achievement of quality, fast delivery, and continuous improvement. Early adopters in North America included companies like Xerox, Honeywell, Polaroid, Motorola, IBM, and the automotive companies, to name just a few. This move into a partnership mode really represents a substantial shift from the traditional buying–selling mode. A summary of some of the key differences is shown in Figure 19–4.

In the late 1990s, buying organizations continued to develop closer relationships or partnerships with suppliers. For example, CompUSA initially formed a partnership with Wallace, a large printing company, to print and replenish forms to 210 retail stores. Next, CompUSA consolidated its requirements for other supplies and purchased them from Wallace at a lower cost. Wallace prints a quarterly catalog of supplies it provides to

FIGURE 19–4
View of Buyer–Supplier Relationship: A Paradigm Shift

Traditional	Partnership
Lowest price	Total cost of ownership
Specification-driven	End customer-driven
Short term, reacts to market	Long term
Trouble avoidance	Opportunity maximization
Purchasing's responsibility	Cross-functional teams and top management involvement
Tactical	Strategic
Little sharing of information on both sides	Both supplier and buyer share short- and long-term plans
	Share risk and opportunity
	Standardization
	Joint ventures
	Share data

CompuUSA as well as some items it replenishes from other suppliers. In the first year, supply expenditures were reduced by 32 percent.[2]

SEMATECH's Partnering Perspective

SEMATECH was originally created through a joint effort of the American electronics industry giants and the American government to assist the electronics industry and its suppliers to be world class. It has evolved into an international consortium through which member companies cooperate precompetitively in key areas of semiconductor technology to accelerate the development of advanced manufacturing technologies needed to build powerful semiconductors.[3] SEMATECH identified quality as the key driver of competitiveness and partnering as the means to achieve quality. Their interpretation of partnering extends to customers, employees, and suppliers. On the supplier side, SEMATECH identified two classes of partnership. Every supplier should be treated as a "basic partner" with mutual respect, honesty, trust, open and frequent communication, and understanding of each other as the minimum guidelines governing the relationship.

SEMATECH identified the need for an "expanded partnership" with selected key suppliers. Expanded partnering builds on basic partnering, is a long-term relationship process, provides focus on mutual strategic and tactical goals, and may include customer/supplier team support to promote mutual success and profitability. Therefore, in addition to basic partnering guidelines, expanded partnering has a long-term view, it must have continuing improvement as an objective, and evidence of it must exist. The partners must have a passion to help each other succeed, place a high priority on the relationship, and include shared risks, opportunities, strategies, and technology road maps. It is expected that most organizations would have a limited number (6 to 20) of expanded partnerships.

An expanded partnership would normally have a top executive assigned to it. This executive would meet at least two to four times per year with his or her counterpart in the selling organization who would monitor internal progress on joint projects and smooth the way for changes necessary for success. In addition, there should be regular monthly meetings planned for buyer–seller representatives and daily and weekly contact on project teams and other activities, involving a substantial number of people from various functions in the buying and selling organizations.

Early Supplier Involvement (ESI)/Early Purchasing Involvement (EPI)

The opportunity to affect value in the acquisition process is significantly greater in the early stages (need recognition and description) than in the later ones. Involving the supplier and the buyer in these early stages can lead to improvements in processes, design, redesign, or value analysis activities. The drive to cut cycle time, improve competitiveness, and reduce cost compels many organizations to include supplier(s) on cross-functional teams. A supplier may participate with the hope of securing the business, or as part of an

[2] Becky S. Moore, "Increased Service," *Purchasing Today,* February 1999, p. 68.

[3] Corporate information, International SEMATECH, http://www.sematech.org, April 17, 2001.

ongoing partnering/alliance relationship. Confidentiality issues often must be dealt with up front, and it must be clear to the supplier(s) if involvement guarantees the business or not.

The benefits from partnering come from intercorporate closeness. The philosophy is similar to design for manufacturability or design for assembly, where internal barriers are removed between design, marketing, manufacturing engineering, quality assurance, procurement, and operations to avoid functional suboptimization. The removal of functional barriers, avoiding "throwing the design over the wall," helps speed the introduction of new designs and achieve significant quality and cost improvements. The same idea extended makes suppliers part of the process—it could be called "design for procurability." Others call it "early supplier involvement" or ESI. Moreover, if suppliers involve their suppliers in the process, the purchasing organization has access to a wide pool of talent all focused on the needs of its customers. When the supplier is making investment decisions, hiring decisions, or new-product or process or system decisions, these can be made keeping the customer-partner's future needs in mind. It is this latent potential for improvement that the partnership tries to tap.

Partnerships may be seen as an alternate solution for the make option in the make-or-buy decision. Similarly, a partnership could be a substitute for vertical integration. A partnership attempts to unlock the benefits from shared information without the disadvantages of ownership.

Partnerships require hard work on both sides to make them effective. They require a tolerance toward mistakes and a real commitment to make the relationship work. The key idea is that each partner might enhance its own competitive position through the knowledge and resources shared by the other.

Partner Selection

From a supplier selection perspective, what is interesting about selecting potential partners is the focus on soft as well as hard factors. All of the traditional hard factors of quality, delivery, cost, environment, safety and continuing improvement, financial and management stability, and technological accomplishment still continue. But, for potential partners, soft factors also become important such as congruence of management values on issues like customer satisfaction, concern for quality, employee involvement, supplier relationships, and personal compatibility between functional counterparts. Vital questions are Can we work well together? Can we respect and trust each other? Do we like each other? Questions like these are not answered easily and quickly. It is, therefore, more likely that potential partners are found among the organization's best current suppliers. (See Figure 19–5.) Developing partnering-type relationships takes time and some organizations may be ill prepared for the amount of time it does take before seeing the desired results.

The Longer Time Perspective

Another interesting question is what happens over a longer period of time. Do benefits continue to accelerate, or does the law of diminishing returns set in? Companies like Honda that have maintained partnering-type relationships with some suppliers since the late 1970s have clearly found a way to continue generating benefits for both parties. Whether all companies can sustain the relationship over the long term probably depends on many variables, including what the original goals of the partnership were, the level of

FIGURE 19–5
Some Indicators of a Successful Partnering Effort

- Formal communication processes
- Commitment to our suppliers' success
- Mutual profitability
- Stable relationships, not dependent on a few personalities
- Consistent and specific feedback on supplier performance
- Realistic expectations
- Employee accountability for ethical business conduct
- Meaningful information sharing
- Guidance to supplier in defining improvement efforts
- Nonadversarial negotiations and decisions based on total cost of ownership

Source: SEMATECH.

commitment of both sides to continuing to develop the relationship, and the specific situation of the companies and industry. Thinking about the longer term at the initial stages of the relationship may help to prevent dissatisfaction in the long run.

Co-location/In-plants

One potential outcome of a partnering effort may be co-location as a supplier in-plant. As organizations look for ways to do more work with fewer people and achieve the productivity and competitiveness goals of the firm, they are increasingly looking to suppliers for expertise and assistance. Having a key supplier locate personnel in a department in the buying organization who can function as buyer, planner, and salesperson can improve buyer–seller communications and processes, absorb work typically done by the firm's employees, and reduce administrative and sales costs.

STRATEGIC ALLIANCES

Strategic alliances in a procurement sense represent special arrangements with key suppliers that make a strategic difference to both buyer and seller. The term *expanded partnership* used by SEMATECH fits this category. Strategic alliance arises from the conviction of both buyer and seller that it is in the interest of both to formalize the relationship beyond the standard buying–selling mode.

Strategic alliances are often technology based and require substantial investment of both buyer and seller to achieve major market breakthroughs. Obviously, as cornerstones of corporate strategy, these alliances are of major concern to top management and reinforce the perspective that suppliers and supplier relationships are of strategic concern to any organization.

In their breakthrough research on problems in alliances, Stuart and McCutcheon identified three "prior conditions scales"—(1) outlook, (2) power, and (3) gains—and two "alliance building process scales": info share and help gap.[4] They found that "to enhance the prospects for success" it is necessary to:

[4] F. Ian Stuart and David McCutcheon, "Problem Sources in Establishing Strategic Supplier Alliances," *International Journal of Purchasing Materials Management,* Winter 1995, pp. 6–8.

1. *Identify supplier firms in which a philosophical match exists* between the two firms' managements on such issues as views toward quality and productivity improvement. Such a fit is possible despite differences in the parties' size and power.
2. *Create an interorganizational task force to establish clear expectations* of the information required for successful problem identification and resolution, the level of technical expertise available from both parties, and how the benefits from such improvements are to be measured and then shared in a mutually agreeable manner.
3. *Slightly exceed the expectations* established in item 2 above.

Concerns about Partnerships

There are serious concerns about the idea of partnerships. Not all purchasers believe that cooperative relationships are better than the competition-based culture upon which most traditional procurement tools and techniques are based. The idea that at least one partner might wish to take advantage of the preferred status and let the commitment and relationship slide is a serious concern. In a technology-driven world, intellectual rights to new technology are extremely valuable and the preservation of secrecy a vital concern. Whether purchasers or suppliers, or either, can be trusted with information that might shape competitive strategy in years to come needs to be weighed carefully.

Similarly, whether cutting off the option to "shop around" is in the best long-term interest of the purchaser will depend on its customer-satisfaction-driven strategies. Clearly, the decision to enter into a partnership mode is an organizational commitment, not just a procurement one, and is of key strategic importance. Often partnerships or strategic alliances involve single or sole sourcing as a particular requirement.

The danger in single sourcing lies in becoming puppets of suppliers. Suppliers know that customers depend on them, and they may charge excessively or let quality or delivery slip, or slow down or stop continuing improvement programs. This is where careful supplier relationship management becomes important. It requires an understanding and identification of value. Value is the ultimate long-term, life-cycle cost and benefit to the user of the product or service acquired. It does not necessarily mean lowest purchase price, or lowest investment in inventory, or fastest delivery time, or lowest delivery cost, or longest life, or highest disposal value, or even the highest attainable quality; it is an optimal amount cutting across all of these. The purchase price frequently is one important part of this total. It is the duty of the supply manager to make sure that the purchase represents exceptional long-term value. Moreover, in the establishment of preferred suppliers or partnerships, it is normal to agree on future quality, delivery, and price goals, in full recognition of learning curve theory and the commitment of both buyer and seller to continuous improvement.

At Alberto Culver, a personal-care products company, partnerships consist of multiyear contracts with key suppliers that include goals for the contract term and a performance-based incentive rebate. A target level for quality and on-time delivery performance is negotiated and performance is measured monthly. The rebate is adjusted accordingly and paid annually. When targets are exceeded, Alberto Culver encourages their supplier partners to return the rebate to their employees as bonuses. The two companies work jointly toward continuous improvement and agree to higher performance targets each year with the ultimate goal of attaining a specific goal by the end of the contract period.[5]

[5] Judy K. Spencer, "Set a Target Level," *Purchasing Today,* February 1999, p. 68.

REVERSE MARKETING/SUPPLIER DEVELOPMENT

In supplier selection, the assumption has so far been made that at least one suitable and willing supplier already exists and that the purchaser's problem is primarily one of determining who is the best supplier. It is possible, however, that no suitable source is available and that the purchaser may have to create a source. Reverse marketing or supplier development implies a degree of aggressive procurement involvement not encountered in supplier selection. For example, it places a purchasing manager in a position where a prospective supplier must be persuaded to accept an order. In this no-choice context, the purchaser does not initiate supplier development as an appropriate technique or tool; it is the only alternative other than making the part in-house.

Reverse marketing/supplier development also has a broader point of view. It defines the need for developing new or existing suppliers as follows: The purchaser is aware that benefits will accrue to both the supplier and the purchaser, benefits of which the supplier may not be aware. These benefits may be limited to the particular order at hand, or they may include more far-reaching aspects, such as technical, financial, and management processes, skills, or quality levels; reduction of marketing effort; use of long-term forecasts or permitting smoother manufacturing levels and a minimum of inventory; and so on.

It is the aggressiveness and initiative by the purchaser that makes the difference (see Figure 19–6). In the normal market context, the purchaser responds to marketing efforts. In reverse marketing, the purchaser, not the marketer, has the initiative and will predetermine prices, terms, and conditions as part of the aggressive role. Taking the initiative requires extensive homework on the part of the purchaser to understand fully the organization's short- and long-term needs, operationally and strategically. Moreover, the purchaser also must understand and assess the supplier's capability to meet these needs so that a win–win proposal can be made. This is why the term *reverse marketing* has been chosen as a synonym for supplier development. Numerous examples show that high payoffs are possible from this purchasing initiative and that suppliers of all sizes may be approached in this fashion.

A further reason for reverse marketing is that there are bound to be deficiencies in the normal industrial marketing–purchasing process in which the marketer traditionally

FIGURE 19–6
Supplier Development Initiative with the Purchaser

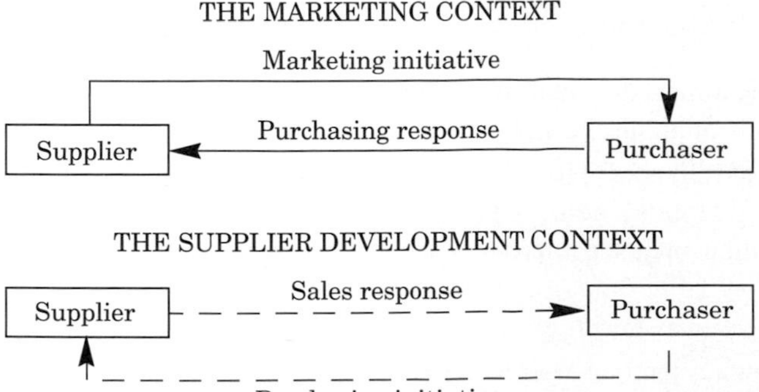

takes the initiative. Even when a supplier and a purchaser have entered into a regular buyer–seller relationship, often neither party is fully aware of all the opportunities for additional business that may exist between them. This might arise because of salesperson and buyer specialization, a lack of aggressiveness by the salesperson, or a lack of inquisitiveness by the purchaser.

If gaps are evident even where an established buyer–seller relationship exists, there must be even greater shortcomings where no such relationship has yet been established. For example, a supplier may be unable to cover its full market because of geography, limited advertising, or lack of coverage by its sales force, distributors, or agents. Most suppliers have lines of products that receive more management attention and sales push than other products also made or sold by the same company. It is always difficult to keep entirely up to date. A time lag may exist between the time of product or service introduction and the time the purchaser finds out about it. By filling these gaps through aggressiveness, the purchaser effectively strengthens this whole process.

One of the most important arguments in favor of reverse marketing not yet mentioned arises from future considerations. If the procurement role is envisaged as encompassing not only the need to fill current requirements but also the need to prepare for the future, reverse marketing is valuable in assuring future sources of supply.

There are at least three outside forces that suggest the increasing necessity for purchaser initiative in the creation of future sources of supply. One of these forces is technological. The increasing rate of development of new products, materials, and processes will tend to make the industrial marketing task even more complex and more open to shortcomings. In addition to this, the stepping-up of international trade will tend to widen supplier horizons and may create a need for purchaser aggressiveness in the development of foreign sources of supply. One of the most demanding and important tasks of management of a subsidiary in an underdeveloped country is the problem of supplier development. Lastly, new management concerns with extracting competitive advantage from the supply chain require purchasers to be more aggressive with suppliers and to develop sources to their expectations.

Honda of America Manufacturing, Inc., offers a good example of a successful supplier development program.[6] Since purchased parts represent about 80 percent of the cost of a finished Honda automobile, suppliers are clearly of strategic importance. Honda works with suppliers in the following ways to develop world-class suppliers:

- Reduce costs through target costing and providing assistance in meeting the targets.
- Improve quality by working together on quality problems, and through the use of quality circles, with a goal of zero defects. No incoming inspection is done at Honda.
- Develop leading-edge technology by linking Honda research and development with suppliers throughout the new-car development process.
- Teach "self-reliance." Honda's goal is to develop suppliers to the point where they no longer need Honda's help, and may, in fact, become teachers in their own organizations and with their own suppliers.

[6] This example is a synopsis of Kevin R. Fitzgerald, "Medal of Excellence: Honda Wins for Superb Supplier Development," *Purchasing,* September 21, 1995, pp. 32–40.

In a CAPS study, *Developing a World-Class Supply Base,* the authors defined supplier development as "a bilateral effort by both the buying and supplying organizations to jointly improve the supplier's performance and/or capabilities in one or more of the following areas: cost, quality, delivery, time-to-market, technology, environmental responsibility, managerial capability and financial viability."[7] The authors continued to describe four major stages in developing a globally aligned supplier network as

1. Identifying, assessing, and rationalizing of the supply base.
2. Problem-solving development.
3. Proactive development.
4. Integrative development.

SUPPLY CHAIN MANAGEMENT

Supply chain management is a systems approach to managing the entire flow of information, materials, and services from raw materials suppliers through factories and warehouses to the end customer. SCM represents a philosophy of doing business that stresses processes and integration.

Channelwide information sharing and monitoring, inventory management, evaluation of costs, and joint planning occur over an extended, and sometimes indefinite, time period. Coordination of efforts occurs across channel members, across management levels, and across functions. Compatible corporate philosophies are essential to achieving the necessary levels of planning and coordination. Because of the difficulty of coordinating across channels, a smaller supply base is desirable to allow for closer integration. Some type of channel leadership also is needed, usually a dominant player in the chain, or, in the future, perhaps a cross-organizational team. Sharing of risks and rewards is also necessary to maintain the appropriate level of commitment to the success of the supply chain as a whole. Operations in the SCM approach are faster than in a traditional system. Electronic data sharing can be used channelwide to reduce cycle times, thereby eliminating some of the uncertainty in the system and reducing the inventory base.

The goals of supply chain management are to reduce uncertainty and risks in the supply chain, thereby positively affecting inventory levels, cycle time, processes, and ultimately end-customer service levels. The focus in SCM is on system optimization. Tools that can assist in systems or supply chain improvements are benchmarking current performance in a particular inventory network, understanding the sources of uncertainty and the impact on upstream and downstream nodes in the supply chain, working to control uncertainty, and planning for changes in policies and procedures that might lead to cost reductions or performance improvements.[8]

Supply chain management makes a lot of sense conceptually. The difficulty is in implementation. As many organizations have found, it is extremely difficult to make

[7] Daniel R. Krause and Robert B. Handfield, *Developing a World-Class Supply Base* (Tempe, AZ: Center for Advanced Purchasing Studies, 1999), p. 8.

[8] Tom Davis, "Effective Supply Chain Management," *Sloan Management Review,* Summer 1993, pp. 36–37.

buyer–supplier partnerships or alliances work well. Extending the concept across a supply channel and encompassing all the aspects of delivering to the end customer is even more difficult. In many cases, the supply chain management concept is a philosophical change in the way business should be done, but many organizations are still struggling to manage processes with one supplier better.

Supply Networks

The term *supply chain* is obviously a misnomer. If we start off with a purchasing organization as a starting point and work into the supply side, the buying organization has a number of suppliers, each of which in turn has its own set of suppliers, and so on. The result is a supply network or a series of chains. This is illustrated in Figure 19–7 for one buying organization and three of its suppliers, tracing through just some of the key requirements generated by the original purchaser (heavier lines indicate a larger volume of business). A supply network can become exceedingly complex very quickly.

The Diminishing Leverage in a Supply Network

Aside from complexity, the diminishing leverage effect of the original purchaser also needs to be emphasized. A number of organizations have attempted to influence the supply management of their first-tier suppliers, for example, by specifying from whom they should acquire certain requirements and, possibly, even at what price. A typical example might be a large food company that directs its copackers to acquire packaging from the same suppliers with whom the large company has extensive contracts at favorable prices. A multidivisional organization might direct its suppliers to acquire certain requirements from another division or subsidiary of the same parent company.

FIGURE 19–7 **The Diminishing Leverage in Supply Chain Management**

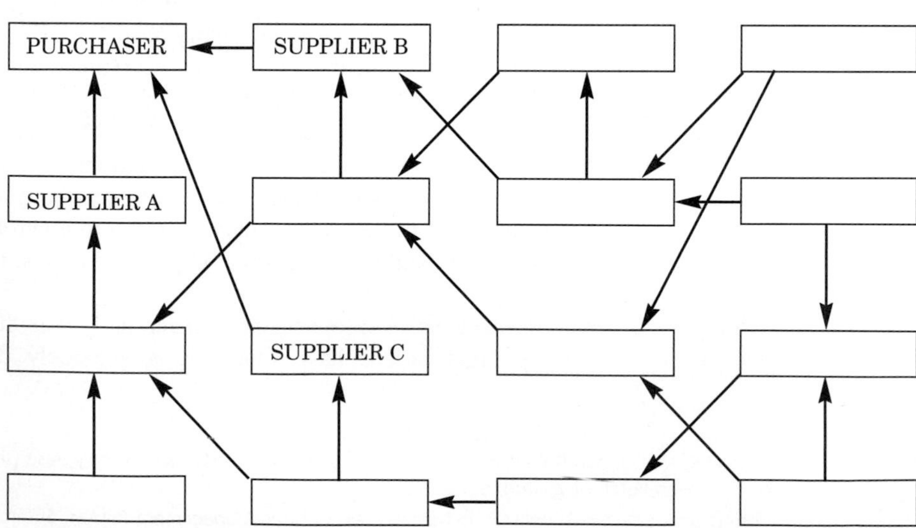

FIGURE 19–8 The Diminishing Leverage in Supply Chain Management

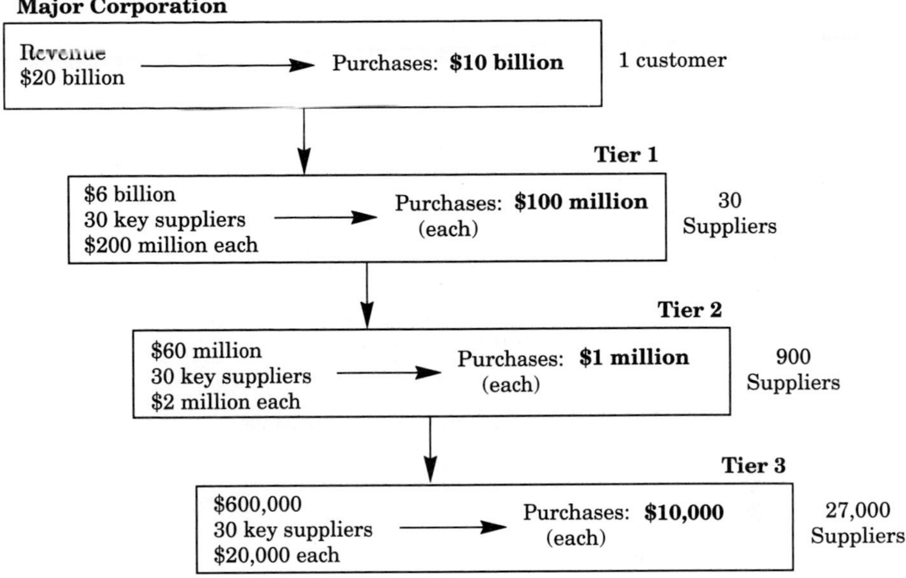

3 Key Assumptions

1. **Purchases 50% of revenue**
2. **30 key suppliers—60% of purchases**
3. **No common suppliers**

Figure 19–8 shows that there is likely to be a substantial diminution of the leverage of the original purchaser as more tiers in the supplier network get involved. Therefore, unless there are overlapping suppliers, in which tier 1, 2, 3, and 4 suppliers all deal with the same supplier at a significant volume level, the clout of the original purchaser has largely dissipated at the third- and fourth-tier levels. This in no way suggests that ignoring supply management strategies or practices of first- and second-tier suppliers is wise and has little potential.

Because transportation and inventories are integral to every supply network, the cumulative effect of multiple transports and storages on timeliness and cost can be very high as a percentage of the acquisition cost of the final customer in the chain or network (see Figure 19–9).

FIGURE 19–9
Supply Chain for a Manufacturer of Consumer Goods Showing Cumulative Effect of Transports and Storages

Conclusion: Each final consumer receives a good that has passed through a minimum of 10 transports and 5 storages.

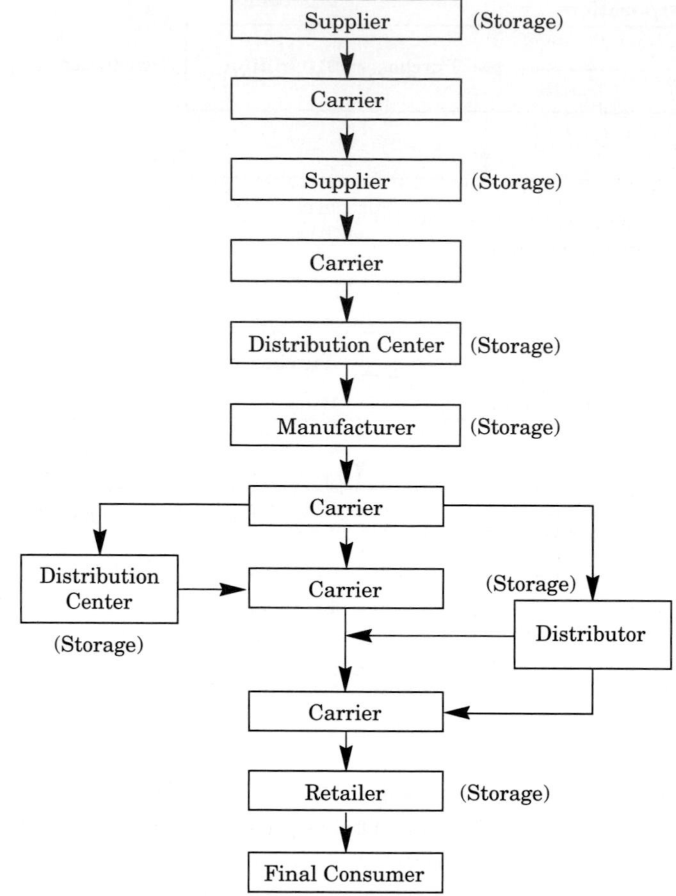

Conclusion

The supplier selection decision has become far more complex as environmental, social, political, and customer satisfaction concerns have been added to the traditional factors of quality, delivery, cost, and service. It is no surprise that approaches like supplier rationalization, preferred suppliers, partnerships, strategic alliances, reverse marketing, and supply chain management have gained prominence. The realization that suppliers and the buyer–supplier relationship can make a strategic difference to an organization's capability of providing continuing improvement in customer satisfaction drives the search for new and better ways of managing the relationships between buyers and sellers.

Questions for Review and Discussion

1. Why are buyer–supplier relationships important?
2. Why create a partnership?
3. What are the characteristics of supply chain management? How can supply managers effectively manage the supply chain?
4. What is reverse marketing and why is it used?
5. What are the advantages of supplier rationalization?
6. What are the goals of early supplier involvement (ESI)? How does ESI fit in with cross-functional teams?
7. What are the risks and rewards of supplier co-location?
8. Might there be anything unique about a strategic alliance?
9. What is the relationship between satisfaction and stability in buyer–supplier relations?
10. How do you know a partnership is not working?

References

Barringer, B. R., and J. S. Harrison. "Walking a Tightrope: Creating Value through Inter-organizational Relationships." *Journal of Management* 26, no. 3 (2000), pp. 367–403.

Bovert, David and Joseph Martha. Value Nets. New York: Wiley, 2000.

Burnes, B., and S. New. "Collaborating in Customer–Supplier Relationships: Strategy, Operations and the Function of Rhetoric." *International Journal of Purchasing and Materials Management* 33, no. 4 (1997), pp. 10–17.

Carter, Phillip L.; Joseph R. Carter; Robert M. Monczka; Thomas H. Slaight; and Andrew J. Swan. *The Future of Purchasing and Supply: A Five- and Ten-Year Forecast.* Tempe, AZ: Center for Advanced Purchasing Studies/National Association of Purchasing Management/A. T. Kearney, 1998.

Dyer, J. H. "Effective Interfirm Collaboration: How Firms Minimize Transaction Costs and Maximize Transaction Value." *Strategic Management Journal* 18, no. 7 (1997), pp. 535–56.

Grandori, A. (ed.). *Interfirm Networks: Organization and Industrial Competitiveness.* London: Routledge, 1999.

Handfield, Robert B.; Daniel R. Krause; Thomas V. Scannell; and Robert M. Monczka. "Avoid the Pitfalls in Supplier Development." *MITSLoan Management Review* 41, no. 2 (Winter 2000).

Krause, Daniel R., and Robert B. Handfield. *Developing a World-Class Supply Base.* Tempe, AZ: Center for Advanced Purchasing Studies, 1999.

Lane, C., and R. Bachmann (eds.). *Trust within and between Organizations: Conceptual Issues and Empirical Applications*. Oxfoxd: Oxford University Press, 1998.

Laseter, T. M. *Balanced Sourcing: Co-operation and Competition in Supplier Relationships*. San Francisco: Jossey-Bass, 1998.

Stuart, F. Ian, and David McCutcheon. "Problem Sources in Establishing Strategic Supplier Alliances." *International Journal of Purchasing and Materials Management*, Winter 1995.

Case 19–1

Plastic Cable Clips

In mid-September Robyn Pemberton, purchasing officer in the laundry division of Fisher & Paykel Limited, located in Auckland, New Zealand, was wondering which procurement option made most sense for the plastic cable clips requirements for the new line of washing machines.

THE LAUNDRY DIVISION

Fisher & Paykel Limited was the largest home appliance manufacturer in New Zealand with sales of its major appliances amounting to $135,000,000 and total sales of $270,000,000 for the fiscal year ending March 31, including $36,000,000 of export sales and royalty income. It comprised eight operating divisions, one of which was the laundry division employing over 500 people to produce washing machines and dryers. Currently, the laundry division produced about 50,000 washing machines, solely for the domestic market.

THE NEW WASHING MACHINE

For the last two years, the laundry division had been developing a new line of automatic washing machines. The planning and development of the new machine was conducted by a seven-person committee of engineers, production, and marketing people as well as a purchasing coordinator.

The new machine, designed entirely by F&P, used electronic controls. It was believed to be technologically advanced by world standards. Its manufacturing process would be highly automated, featuring considerable part rationalization and cost reduction over the old production line. In fact, maintaining costs at the lowest possible level was one of the key priorities of the planning committee.

With good opportunities for export and royalty income, the laundry division hoped to produce between 75,000 and 100,000 new washing machines a year. However, 50,000 machines were planned for the first full year of production. The first production run was scheduled for the beginning of next April.

PLASTIC CABLE CLIPS

The old washing machine used about 20 different plastic cable ties for a total of about 250 ties in each machine. At the moment, the laundry division bought nearly $1,250,000 a year worth of plastic cable ties: about $500,000 from Olson Plastics, a New Zealand manufacturer; $500,000 from Barry Cleaver and Sons, a local agent importing mostly from Japan; $200,000 from G.T. Rollman, another local agent importing from Australia; and at most $50,000 from Plastic Distributing, a relatively new and smaller multisource New Zealand agent.

The ties to be used in the new machine required new specifications because of the automated production process. None of the existing ties suppliers actually had in stock the kind of parts required.

A year earlier, Robyn Pemberton, who was the purchasing coordinator for the new washing machine, managed to convince the planning committee to draw on the technical expertise of Barry Cleaver, the New Zealand agent currently supplying some of the plastic ties. As a result of Barry Cleaver's input, the number of ties required was reduced to half a dozen new parts for a total of about 45 plastic clips to be used in each new machine. Robyn Pemberton made it very clear to Barry Cleaver that all current plastic ties suppliers would be asked to submit quotations as soon as all the specifications on the new clips were finalized and that his involvement would not give him any preferential treatment over the others.

SUPPLIER SELECTION

Because of design changes, the specifications for the new cable clips were not confirmed until early July. Robyn promptly sent letters asking for quotations to the four existing plastic ties suppliers (see Exhibit 1).

OLSON PLASTICS

Olson Plastics, the only New Zealand manufacturer of plastic ties, clips, and rivets, had been supplying F&P for many years. Robyn Pemberton believed that F&P would be among its top five customers. With occasional quality and service problems, Robyn felt the quality of Olson's products was not as high as that of the other ties suppliers. Olson's prices for certain parts were twice as high as prices for imported parts. But deliveries were Robyn's major area of concern with this supplier. Even with a six- to eight-month lead time, deliveries were unreliable and Robyn had to chase every order. She believed Olson had capacity problems although they did not wish to admit it.

EXHIBIT 1
Quotation Request Letter Sample

5 July
Dear Sir,

The following new parts are required, commencing next March. Please advise price, minimum quantity, and delivery details.

Part	Description	Qty/Annum
816549	Clip snap .125M × .5	30,000
816553	Clip snap .250M × .75	30,000
817709	Clip-tie HM FT	60,000
817803	Clip-lock HBX	165,000
817923	Clip-tie HM FT (SS)	650,000
817975	Clip-tie HM RS.2	135,000

Samples would be appreciated when possible.
Awaiting your reply with interest.

Yours faithfully,
FISHER & PAYKEL LIMITED

R.H. Pemberton (Mrs.)
Purchasing Officer
Laundry Division

However, Olson enjoyed government protection in the sense that, under normal circumstances, a New Zealand agent could not import products which could be made domestically.

BARRY CLEAVER AND SONS

Barry Cleaver and Sons, a New Zealand agent for three generations with an excellent reputation, was receiving about $2 million a year worth of orders from F&P. Its prices and service were normally excellent. Delivery was good providing adequate lead time of six to eight months was given. Barry Cleaver was getting F&P plastic parts from Japan and, during seller's markets, would have difficulty obtaining supply because of the relative low importance of its orders.

However, Robyn was concerned about the long-term availability of the imported parts as the agent's license could be revoked if it was proven that a domestic supply alternative existed. F&P was legally free to buy from any agent in New Zealand. It was up to the agent to justify its stance with the Department of Trade and Industry. However, Robyn was well aware of the Department's licensing policy (see Exhibit 2), as she remembered vividly a problem encountered with plastic rivets and a few cable ties in May.

Barry Cleaver had been supplying F&P with Japanese rivets and cable ties until Olson complained to Trade and Industry. As a result, Barry Cleaver not only had to stop importing and start purchasing from Olson at three times the former price, but he was also having a terrible time meeting F&P volume requirements and had to deliver some of the parts on a daily basis. After F&P started noticing that the rivets purchased from Barry Cleaver came in Olson's boxes, Robyn asked Olson for quotes on the rivets, but was subsequently surprised to discover that Olson's prices were dearer than Barry Cleaver's.

G. T. ROLLMAN

G. T. Rollman was a large New Zealand agent importing from Australia. Although the prices were high, the service was excellent and the delivery was good. The average lead time was three to four months but, in urgent situations, it could supply within six weeks by airfreighting the stock.

Robyn Pemberton was also conscious of the advantage of Australian sourcing due to the Closer

EXHIBIT 2
New Zealand Government Standard Licensing Policy[1]

The following policy applies to all item codes except those for which specific policies are set on the following pages.

1. Goods of Types Not Produced in New Zealand
   Licenses will generally be granted to meet reasonable requirements for goods of types not produced in New Zealand.
   Licenses will not be issued under this provision unless it is quite clear that the goods to be imported are not substitutable for domestic alternatives.
   The applicants will need to provide adequate evidence that suitable alternatives are not available from New Zealand manufacturers.
   In considering applications Trade and Industry will assess the extent to which established licensing provisions have been and are being used to import the goods concerned. The aim of this is to ensure that domestic production is not detrimentally affected by the consequential availability of license to import directly competitive goods.
2. All Other Goods
   Licenses may be granted in special circumstances such as:
   - Established trading patterns arising from continuing special licensing provision.
   - Shortfalls in normal domestic supply.
   - Special provision for the requirements of new manufacturers.
   - Applications under general policies and provisions set out in Annex III.

Note: Item Codes which fall under Industry Development Plans are subject to any special import licensing provisions of those plans.

[1] This policy does not apply to Australian-made products.

Economic Relations Agreement between New Zealand and Australia. She knew that a higher New Zealand and Australian content in the new washing machine would permit F&P free or minimum duty access to the Australian market. Although she had to inform the costing department of the country of origin of each part purchased, she did not know at what level some price reduction on a part would offset a duty increase. She had tried to find out more information on this subject but no one had been very explicit. With the labour government in power, a considerable amount of uncertainty existed. All she knew was that the group purchasing department of F&P was pushing for as much New Zealand and Australian content as possible.

PLASTIC DISTRIBUTING

Plastic Distributing was a local agent with annual sales under $1 million that imported plastic products from a number of countries. This young company was eager to obtain orders but offered little technical backup.

In the past, Robyn had given it the odd order, especially when supply was tight. She had asked this agent to quote on the new plastic clips mostly for comparison purposes.

SELECTION DECISION

Quotes started arriving on July 10, with Barry Cleaver's response. But it was not until September 12 that she obtained Olson's prices (see Exhibit 3 for a summary of quotes). In mid-September Robyn called Barry Cleaver and asked for a meeting. Barry Cleaver came with a technical expert to meet with Robyn and her supervisor, John Wardrop. Barry made clear that the recent problem encountered with the supply of rivets and cable ties was in the process of being solved, as they had been able to regain their importing license from Trade and Industry by proving that Olson did not have sufficient capacity to meet the demand. Barry Cleaver assured Robyn and John that he felt there would be no problem to import all the new plastic clips required for the new washing machines.

Robyn was wondering what to do. In light of Deming's philosophy adopted by Fisher & Paykel as a whole, she felt some pressure toward single sourcing. However, she was not convinced of the soundness of single sourcing in

EXHIBIT 3
Summary of Quotes/Prices per 1,000

Part No	Description	Barry Cleaver	Olson	Plastic Dist.	Rollman
816549	Clip snap 1.25M × .5	76.00	54.00	99.95	—
816553	Clip snap .250M × .75	76.00	119.80	99.95	—
817709	Clip-tie HM FT	25.20	36.80	28.26	—
817803	Clip-lock HBX	39.20	61.82	—	134.40
817923	Clip-tie HM FT(SS)	23.06	20.40	28.12	—
817975	Clip-tie HM RS.2	38.40	50.00	63.22	—

the context of this purchase. She was also wondering to what extent Olson Plastics realized what their situation would be once the old washing machine would be phased out, should she choose to go with Barry Cleaver. She was debating whether she should call on Olson for further consultation. In any event, she knew a decision had to be reached quickly in view of the lead time involved, with the first production run scheduled for next April.

Case 19-2

Loren Inc.

On June 15, Brent Miller, raw materials buyer, had to prepare his recommendation for Loren's annual hexonic acid requirements. Four suppliers had submitted substantially different bids for this annual contract to commence August 1. Brent knew his recommendation would involve a variety of policy considerations and wondered what his best option would be.

COMPANY BACKGROUND

Loren (Canada) was the Canadian subsidiary of a larger international chemical company. The company sold both consumer and industrial products and had over the years established an excellent reputation for quality products and marketing effectiveness. This was evidenced by a substantial growth in total sales and financial success. Total Canadian sales were approximately $800 million and after-tax profits were $40 million. Raw material and packaging costs were about 50 percent of sales.

PURCHASING

Brent Miller, a recent graduate of a well-known business school, knew that purchasing was well regarded as a function at Loren. The department was staffed with 12 well-qualified persons, including a number of engineering and business graduates at both the undergraduate and master's levels. The department was headed by a director who reported to the president. It was organized along commodity lines and Brent Miller had recently been appointed raw materials buyer reporting to the manager of the chemicals buying group. The hexonic acid contract would have to be approved by his immediate supervisor and the director of the department.

Brent was aware that several Loren purchasing policies and practices were of particular importance to his current hexonic contract decision. The purchasing department had worked very hard with suppliers over the years to establish a single-bid policy. It was felt that suppliers should quote their best possible offer on their first and only quote and all suppliers should be willing to live with the consequences of their bid. Long-term supplier relations with the best possible long-term opportunities were considered vital to the procurement strategy. Assured supply for all possible types of market conditions was also of prime concern. Multiple sources were usually favored over single sources where this appeared to be reasonable and where no strong long-term price or other disadvantages were expected. Frequent supplier switching would not be normal, although total volumes placed with suppliers might change depending on past performance and new bids. Brent recognized that any major departure from traditional practice would have to be carefully justified. Exhibit 1 shows the four prime objectives of the purchasing department and Exhibit 2 contains excerpts from the company's familiarization brochure for new suppliers.

HEXONIC ACID—RECENT MARKET HISTORY

Loren expected to use approximately 3,000 tons of hexonic acid in the following year. Requirements for the past year amounted to 2,750 tons and had been supplied by Canchem and Alfo at 60 and 40 percent, respectively.

Hexonic acid was a major raw material in a number of Loren products. Its requirements had grown steadily over the years and were expected to remain significant in the years to come. The availability of this material in the marketplace was difficult to predict. The process by which it was produced yielded both hexonic and octonic acids and the market was, therefore, influenced by the demand for either product.

Two years previously there had been major shortages of hexonic acid due to strong European and Japanese demand. Furthermore, capacity expansions had been delayed too long because of depressed prices for hexonic and octonic acid over the previous years. During this period of shortage both of Loren's suppliers, Alfo and Canchem, were caught by the market upsurge. Alfo had just shut down its old Windsor plant and had not yet brought its new Quebec City plant up to design capacity. At the same time, Canchem was in the midst of converting its process to accommodate recent chemical improvements and they, too, found themselves plagued with conversion problems. Both companies were large multiplant companies in Canada and had supplied Loren for many years. The parent companies of both Alfo and Canchem had been faced with too high a demand in the United States to be able to afford any material to help meet the Canadian commitments of their subsidiaries. As a result, both Canadian suppliers were forced to place many of their customers on allocation. However, through considerable efforts both were able to fulfill all of Loren's requirements. The increased prices charged throughout this period fell within the terms of the contracts and were substantially lower than those that would have been incurred if Loren would have had to import offshore material. Quotations on such imports had revealed prices ranging from $1,920 to $2,880 per ton.

The past year was relatively stable with both producers running almost at capacity. Loren again had contracted its requirements with Alfo and Canchem, both of whom continued to perform with the same high quality and service to which Loren had become accustomed over the years.

EXHIBIT 1
Purchasing Objectives

The basic objectives for the Loren purchasing department are:

A) *Assurance of Material Availability.* The major objective of purchasing must be the guarantee of sufficient supply to support production requirements.

B) *Best Value.* Loren recognizes that value is a combination of price, quality, service, . . . and that maximum profitability can only be obtained through the purchase of optimal value on both short- and long-term basis.

C) *An Ethical Reputation.* All dealings must respect all aspects of the law and all business relationships must be founded on a sound ethical approach.

D) *Gathering of Information.* Purchasing involves a constant search for new ideas and improved products in the changing markets. A responsibility also exists to keep the company informed on industry trends including information on material supply and costs.

EXHIBIT 2 Excerpts from Brochure for New Suppliers

The purpose of the information contained herein is to give our suppliers a better understanding of certain policies and practices of Loren. We believe it is important that we understand our suppliers and, in turn, that they understand us. As you know Loren believes in free enterprise and in competition as the mainspring of a free enterprise system. Many of our basic policies stem from a fundamental belief that competition is the fairest means for Loren to purchase the best total value. However, the policies and practices we want to outline here for you relate to Loren business ethics and the ethical treatment of suppliers. In brief, fair dealing means these things to us:

1. We live up to our word. We do not mislead. We believe that misrepresentations, phantom prices, chiseling, etc., have no place in our business.
2. We try to be fair in our demands on a supplier and to avoid unreasonable demands for services; we expect to pay our way when special service is required.
3. We try to settle all claims and disputes on a fair and factual basis.
4. We avoid any form of "favored treatment," such as telling a supplier what to quote to get our business or obtaining business by "meeting" an existing price. In addition, all suppliers that could qualify for our business are given identical information and an equal opportunity to quote on our requirements.
5. We do not betray the confidence of a supplier. We believe that it is unethical to talk about a supplier with competitors. New ideas, methods, products, and prices are kept confidential unless disclosure is permitted by the supplier.
6. We believe in giving prompt and courteous attention to all supplier representatives.
7. We are willing to listen to supplier complaints at any level of the buying organization without prejudice concerning the future placement of business.

We also do not believe in reciprocity or in "tie-ins" which require the purchase of one commodity with another.

We believe that supplier relationships should be conducted so that personal obligations, either actual or implied, do not exist. Consequently, we do not accept gifts and we discourage entertainment from suppliers. Similarly, we try to avoid all situations which involve a conflict of personal interest.

For the past year, Brent's predecessor had recommended a split in the business of 60 percent to Canchem and 40 percent to Alfo based on a number of factors. Important to the decision at the time was the start-up of the new Alfo plant. Alfo's quotation of $1,292 per ton delivered offered a lower price per ton than Canchem's at $1,384 per ton, but it had been uncertain whether the new plant would be able to guarantee more than 40 percent of Loren's hexonic acid requirements. Currently, however, Alfo had brought their plant up to capacity and could certainly supply all of the 3,000 tons required, if called on (see Exhibit 3 for a recent history of hexonic acid purchases).

Brent thought that recently the hexonic acid cycle had turned around. Hexonic acid demand had eased and now it was octonic acid that was in high demand by the booming paint industry. Recent plant expansions by a number of suppliers had been completed. The overall result seemed to be a building of excess hexonic acid inventories. Brent believed this would be reflected in a buyer's market in the coming year and looked forward to aggressive quotes from all potential sources.

MEETINGS WITH HEXONIC ACID SUPPLIERS

An important part of the buyer's job at Loren was to become an expert in the materials purchased. Among other things, this meant keeping an open ear to the market and building strong relationships with suppliers. It was the buyer's responsibility to assure that all information between buyer and seller would be completely confidential. The director of purchasing believed it was important to build a reputation so that suppliers could trust Loren purchasing personnel.

EXHIBIT 3
Hexonic Acid—Purchase History

Period	Total Volume Purchased	Canchem Percent Delivered/Cost	Alfo Percent Delivered/Cost
Three years ago	1,800 tons	50% $828 / ton	50% $828 / ton
Two years ago	2,200 tons	50% $1,176 / ton	50% $1,084 / ton
Last year	2,750 tons	60% $1,384 / ton	40% $1,296 / ton

On May 14, Brent sent out the hexonic acid inquiry to the four suppliers he believed had a chance of quoting competitively on the needs of the Hamilton plant. The two current Canadian suppliers, Alfo and Canchem, were included as well as two American companies. The deadline for bids was June 7, at 4 p.m.

Brent knew that on receipt of the inquiry, supplier sales representatives would be eager to discuss it. Actually, he had two contacts before the inquiry was sent out.

MEETING WITH ALFO

Mr. Baker, sales representative of Alfo, met with Brent on April 20. He said that Alfo had unfilled capacity at its new Quebec City plant and he appeared eager to receive an indication of Loren's future hexonic acid requirements. Mr. Baker informed Brent that he was aware of low-priced hexonic acid on the European market but also made sure to emphasize that it would be uncompetitive in the Canadian market after the cost of duty and freight were added. Brent said it was a published fact that inventories were building in the United States as other hexonic acid users showed signs of easing their demands. The meeting ended with the assurance from Brent that Mr. Baker would again receive an invitation to quote on the next period's business.

PHONE CALL BY MICHIGAN CHEMICAL

Mr. Wallace, sales representative of Michigan Chemical, assured Brent over the telephone on April 30 that his company would be a contender this year. He said that Michigan Chemical would be represented by their Canadian distributor, Carter Chemicals, Ltd., located in Niagara Falls, Ontario. Brent remembered that Michigan Chemical had a good record with Loren (U.S.). According to the U.S. raw materials buying group, Michigan Chemical had supplied close to 99 percent of its commitment in the recent period of shortage. Brent emphasized to Mr. Wallace over the telephone that the present suppliers held the advantage and that he would have to offer better value in order for Loren to swing any business away from them. Brent said at the end of the call that Michigan Chemical would receive an inquiry and that their quote would be seriously considered.

MEETING WITH CANCHEM

On June 3, Mr. Aldert, sales representative for Canchem, personally brought in his company's quotation and presented the terms to Brent with a distinct air of confidence. Mr. Aldert explained that although his delivered price of $1,384 per ton was the same as that which Loren was currently paying for delivered Canchem material, it remained a competitive price. Brent could not help showing his disappointment to Mr. Aldert and he said that he had expected a more aggressive quote. However, he assured Mr. Aldert that every consideration would be given to Canchem once all the quotations were in by the June 7 deadline.

MEETING WITH AMERICAN CHEMICAL INC. (AMCHEM)

On the morning of June 7, two representatives from AMCHEM delivered their hexonic acid quotation and explained its contents to Brent. AMCHEM had recently completed a plant expansion at its Cleveland plant and clearly had the ability to supply many times Loren's total requirements. Brent thought the quote of $1,204 per ton appeared attractive and noted that the price per ton depended on the specific volume allocated to AMCHEM. The price of $1,204 applied to an annual volume to 1,050 tons. For a volume of 2,250 tons per year, the delivered price would be lowered to $1,192.

When the representatives had left, Brent searched the hexonic acid material file for any information about past dealings with AMCHEM. He found that Loren had been supplied with AMCHEM hexonic acid seven years previously. At that time, AMCHEM apparently had quoted a price below Canchem and Alfo and, as a result, had been allocated a portion of the business. This had the result of sparking aggressiveness into the two Canadian suppliers during the next inquiry. Both fought to gain back the tonnage that had been taken away from them. Apparently, neither Canchem nor Alfo had been aware who their competitor was at the time.

Brent also telephoned the purchasing department of Loren (U.S.) in an effort to draw any information about their experience with AMCHEM. Supplier information like this flowed quite freely within the corporation on a need-to-know basis. The U.S. buyer informed Brent that AMCHEM did at one time supply the parent with hexonic acid and that quality and service were excellent. However, he did caution Brent that during the recent period of shortage, AMCHEM did place Loren (U.S.) on allocation and as a result fell short of its commitment by a considerable extent.

MEETING WITH ALFO

Mr. Baker, sales representative of Alfo, presented his company's quote to Brent at 3 p.m., the afternoon of June 7. He explained that the contractual terms and $1,296 delivered price offered were the same as those under the current contract with Alfo. Brent thanked Mr. Baker for his quotation and told him he would be informed in late June when a decision had been made.

QUOTATION BY CARTER CHEMICAL

The quotation from Carter Chemical arrived in the afternoon mail on June 7. The $1,268 per ton FOB destination quote was a pleasant surprise to Brent. He thought that Michigan Chemical had been right when they had said that their distributor would make an aggressive offer. Brent now had received two quotes that offered a better laid-down cost than the two current suppliers.

VISIT OF CANCHEM

At 3:45 p.m. on June 7, Brent received another visit from Mr. Aldert of Canchem, who had apparently been disheartened after his earlier meeting on June 3. He had obviously gone back to his management, for he now had a new quotation prepared. His new quote offered Loren hexonic acid on a three-year contract for $1,192 per ton. With freight included, this price appeared to be equal to the lowest bid that had been received. Brent realized that he had probably inspired Mr. Aldert to resubmit his quotation by the feedback he given him during their June 3 meeting. With this in mind, Brent was wary of accepting this quotation for fear he would be setting a bad precedent. He told Mr. Aldert that he might not be in a position to accept his bid, but would let him know subsequently. The following day Brent discussed the situation with his superior, Mr. Williams. Mr. Williams retraced the steps Brent had gone through. It had been normal practice at Loren to open quotes as they were received. It had also been standard policy not to give suppliers any feedback on their quote until all quotes had been received. Mr. Williams told Brent to think the situation over in his own mind and to make a recommendation on how Canchem's second bid should be treated as part of his hexonic acid contract deliberations.

QUOTE SUMMARY

Brent prepared a quote summary to put all bids on an equal footing (see Exhibit 4). To be able to compare quotes fairly, it was necessary to examine the laid-down cost of each of the four options. Brent realized he did not have much time left and the unusual situation surrounding Canchem's second bid gave him further concern. Mr. Williams was expecting his written analysis and recommendation no later than June 17.

EXHIBIT 4 **Quotation Summary: Hexonic Acid**

		Price			
		Spot	**Contract**		**Terms**
Alfo		$1,296.00 / ton	$1,296.00 / ton		Min. period: 1 year Min. volume: — Price protection: 90 days Notice: 15 days
Canchem	**Bid 1**	$1,384.00 / ton	$1,384.00 / ton		Min. period: 3 years (Bid 2) Min. volume: 1,000 tons
	Bid 2	$1,192.00 / ton	$1,192.00 / ton		Price protection: 30 days Notice: 30 days
American Chemicals			*Min. 1,050 tons*	*Min.2,250 tons*	Min. period: 1 year Min. volume: Stated
		$1,607.72 / ton	$1,204.00 / ton	$1,192.00 / ton	Price protection: Firm Notice: —
Carter Chemicals			*Min. 750 tons*		Min. period: 1 year Min. volume: 750 tons
(Michigan Chemical Material)		$1,268.00 / ton	$1,268.00 / ton		Price protection: 90 days Notice: 15 days

Chapter Twenty

Strategy in Purchasing and Supply Management

Chapter Outline

Key Questions for the Supply Manager

Should we

- Become more concerned about the balance sheet?
- Develop a strategic plan for purchasing and supply management?
- Spend a major part of our time on strategic, rather than operational, issues?

How can we

- Anticipate the professional changes we will face in the next 10 years?
- Ensure supply is included as part of the organization's overall strategy?
- Generate the information needed to do strategic planning?

In strategic supply, the key question is How can supply and the supply chain contribute *effectively* to organizational objectives and strategy? The accompanying question is How can the organizational objectives and strategy properly reflect the contribution and opportunities offered in the supply chain?

A *strategy* is an *action plan* designed to achieve specific *long-term goals and objectives.* The strategy should concentrate on the *key factors necessary* for success and the *major actions* that should be taken now *to ensure the future.* It is the process of determining the relationship of the organization to its *environment,* establishing long-term *objectives,* and achieving the desired relationship(s) through efficient and effective *allocation of resources.*

LEVELS OF STRATEGIC PLANNING

To be successful, an organization must approach strategic planning on three levels:

1. *Corporate.* These are the decisions and plans that answer the questions of *What business are we in?* and *How will we allocate our resources among these businesses?* For example, is a railroad in the business of running trains? Or is its business the movement (creating time and space utility) of things and people?
2. *Unit.* These decisions mold the plans of a particular business unit, as necessary, to contribute to the corporate strategy.
3. *Function.* These plans concern the *how* of each functional area's contribution to the business strategy and involve the allocation of internal resources.

Five CAPS studies done in the 1990s reinforced the notion that linking supply strategy to corporate strategy is essential, but many firms do not yet have mechanisms in place to link the two.[1]

[1]Harold E. Fearon and Michiel R. Leenders, *Purchasing's Organizational Roles and Responsibilities* (Tempe, AZ: Center for Advanced Purchasing Studies, 1995); Robert M. Monczka and Robert J. Trent, *Purchasing and Sourcing Strategy: Trends and Implications* (Tempe, AZ: Center for Advanced Purchasing Studies, 1995); Joseph R. Carter and Ram Narasimhan, *Purchasing and Supply Management: Future Directions and Trends* (Tempe, AZ: Center for Advanced Purchasing Studies, 1995); Phillip L. Carter,

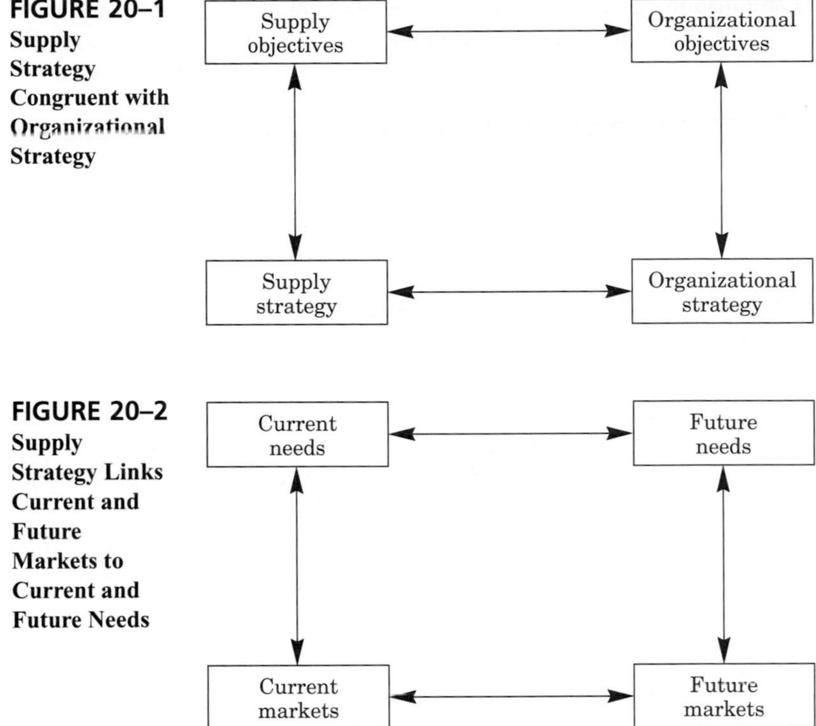

FIGURE 20–1 Supply Strategy Congruent with Organizational Strategy

FIGURE 20–2 Supply Strategy Links Current and Future Markets to Current and Future Needs

Effective contribution connotes more than just a response to a directive from top management. It also implies inputs to the strategic planning process so that organizational objectives and strategies include supply opportunities and problems.

This is graphically shown in Figure 20–1 by the use of double arrows between supply objectives and strategy and organizational objectives and strategy.

A different look at supply strategy is given in Figure 20–2. This shows an effective supply strategy linking both current needs and current markets to future needs and future markets.

One of the significant obstacles to the development of an effective supply strategy lies in the difficulties inherent in translating organizational objectives into supply objectives.

Normally, most organizational objectives can be summarized under four categories: survival, growth, financial, and environmental. Survival is the most basic need of any organization. Growth can be expressed in a variety of ways. For example, growth could be in size of the organization in terms of number of employees or assets or number of operating units, or number of countries in which the organization operates, or in market share. Financial objectives could include total size of budget, surplus or profit, total revenue, return on investment, return on assets, share price, earnings per share or increases in each

Joseph R. Carter, Robert M. Monczka, Thomas H. Slaight, and Andrew J. Swan, *The Future of Purchasing and Supply: A Five- and Ten-Year Forecast* (Tempe, AZ: Center for Advanced Purchasing Studies, 1998); Ulli Arnold, Andrew Cox, Marion Debruyne, Jacques de Rijcke, Thomas Hendrick, Paul Iyongun, Jacques Liouville, and Gyongyi Vorosmarty, *A Multi-Country Study of Strategic Topics in Purchasing and Supply Management* (Tempe, AZ: Center for Advanced Purchasing Studies, June 1999).

of these or any combination. Environmental objectives include not only traditional environmental concerns like clean air, water, and earth but also objectives such as the contribution to and fit with values and ideals of the organization's employees and customers, and the laws and aspirations of the countries in which the organization operates. The notion of good citizenship is embodied in this fourth objective.

Unfortunately, typical supply objectives normally are expressed in a totally different language, such as quality and function, delivery, quantity, price, terms and conditions, service, and so on.

MAJOR CHALLENGES IN SETTING SUPPLY OBJECTIVES AND STRATEGIES

The first major challenge facing the supply manager is the effective interpretation of corporate objectives and supply objectives. For example, given the organization's desire to expand rapidly, is supply assurance more important than obtaining "rock bottom" prices?

The second challenge deals with the choice of the appropriate action plan or strategy to achieve the desired objectives. For example, if supply assurance is vital, is it best accomplished by single or dual sourcing, or by making in-house?

The third challenge deals with the identification and feedback of supply issues to be integrated into organizational objectives and strategies. For example, because a new technology can be accessed early through supply efforts, how can this be exploited?

The development of a supply strategy requires that the supply manager be in tune with the organization's key objectives and strategies and also be capable of recognizing and grasping opportunities. All three challenges require managerial and strategic skills of the highest order, and the difficulties in meeting these challenges should not be minimized.

STRATEGIC PLANNING IN PURCHASING AND SUPPLY MANAGEMENT

Today, firms face the challenge of prospering in the face of highly competitive world markets. The ability to relate effectively to outside environments—social, economic, political, legal, and technological—to anticipate changes, to adjust to changes, and to capitalize on opportunities by formulating and executing strategic plans is a major factor in generating future earnings and is critical to survival. Supply must be forward-looking.

MAJOR SUPPLY STRATEGY AREAS

A supply strategy is a supply action plan designed to permit the achievement of selected goals and objectives. If well developed, the strategy will link the firm to the environment as part of the long-term planning process. An overall supply strategy is made up of substrategies that can be grouped together into six major categories:

1. *Assurance-of-supply strategies.* Designed to ensure that future supply needs are met with emphasis on quality and quantity. Assurance-of-supply strategies must consider

changes in both demand and supply. (Much of the work in purchasing research [see Chapter 13] is focused on providing the relevant information.)

2. *Cost-reduction strategies.* Designed to reduce the laid-down cost of what is acquired, or the total cost of acquisition and use—life-cycle cost. With changes in the environment and technology, alternatives may be available to reduce an organization's overall operating costs through changes in materials, sources, methods, and buyer–supplier relationships.
3. *Supply chain support strategies.* Designed to maximize the likelihood that the considerable knowledge and capabilities of supply chain members are available to the buying organization. For example, better communication systems are needed between buyers and sellers to facilitate the timely notification of changes and to ensure that supply inventories and production goals are consistent with the needs. Supply chain members also need better relations for the communication needed to ensure higher quality and better design.
4. *Environmental-change strategies.* Designed to anticipate and recognize shifts in the total environment (economic, organizational, people, legal, governmental regulations and controls, and systems availability) so it can turn them to the long-term advantage of the buying organization.
5. *Competitive-edge strategies.* Designed to exploit market opportunities and organizational strengths to give the buying organization a significant competitive edge. In the public sector, the term *competitive edge* usually may be interpreted to mean strong performance in achieving program objectives.
6. *Risk-management strategies.* Whereas the various aspects of the previous five types of strategies have been covered earlier in this text, the issue of risk management has not yet been discussed. Therefore, this section will be expanded here, not to imply greater importance, but to assure adequate coverage.

RISK MANAGEMENT

Every business decision involves risk, and supply is no exception. In financial instruments a higher rate of return is supposed to compensate the investor or lender for the higher risk exposure. Risks in the supply chain can be classified into three main categories: (1) the risk of interruption of the flow of goods or services, (2) the risk that the price of the goods or services acquired will change significantly, and (3) reputational risk.

All three risks affect the survival, competitiveness, and bottom line of the organization and may occur simultaneously.

Supply Interruptions and Delays

Every business continuity plan recognizes that supply interruptions and delays may occur. Catastrophic events such as earthquakes, tornadoes, hurricanes, war, floods, or fire may totally disable a vital supplier. Strikes may vary in length, and even short-term interruptions related to weather, accidents on key roads, or any other short-term factor affecting the supply and/or transport of requirements may affect a buying organization's capability to provide good customer service.

A distinction can be drawn between factors beyond the purchaser's or supplier's control, such as weather, and those that deal directly with the supplier's capability of selecting its own suppliers, *managing internally, and its distribution* so as to prevent the potential of physical supply interruption. Careful supplier evaluation before committing to purchase can mitigate against the latter type of supply interruption. In situations of ongoing supply relationships, communication with key suppliers is essential.

Unfortunately, supply interruptions increase costs. If last-minute substitutions need to be made, these are likely to be expensive. Idle labor and equipment, missed customer delivery promises, and scrambling all have increased costs associated with them.

Changes in Prices

Quite different from supply interruptions are those risks directly associated with changes in the price of the good or service purchased. A simple example comes from the commodity markets. Increases in the price of oil affect prices paid for fuel, energy, and those products or services that require oil as a key ingredient or raw material.

A purchaser who has committed to a fixed-price contract may find a competitor able to compete because commodity prices have dropped. Currency exchange rate changes and the threat of shortages or supply interruption also will affect prices, as will arbitrary supplier pricing decisions. Changes in taxation, tolls, fees, duties, and tariffs also will affect cost of ownership.

Given that both supply interruption and price/cost risks directly impact any organization's ability to meet its own goals and execute its strategies, supply chain risks—whether they are on the supply side, internal to the organization, or on the customer side—need to be managed properly.

Reputational Risk

Reputational risk may be even more serious than operational or price risks, because the loss of reputation may be catastrophic for a company. Both legal and ethical supply issues may affect the company's reputation. "You are known by the company you keep" applies not only in one's personal, but also to corporate, life. Thus, the reputation of a company's supply chain members will affect its own image. The internal and external communications decisions and behavior of supply personnel can have both negative and positive impacts. Therefore, the content of the legal issues and ethics (Chapter 12) is highly relevant to reputational risk. Adverse publicity with respect to bribery, kickbacks, improper quality, improper disposal and environmental practices, dealings with unethical suppliers, and so on can be extremely damaging.

Managing Supply Risks

Managing supply risks requires (1) identification and classification of the risks, (2) impact assessment, and (3) a risk strategy.

Given that supply is becoming more and more global and supply networks more complex, risk identification is also becoming more difficult. The preceding discussion identifying supply interruption and price/cost changes as two categories has been highly simplified. Technology, social, political, and environmental factors have not even been mentioned yet. Technology has the potential of interrupting supply through the failure of systems and through obsoleting existing equipment, products, or services, or drastically changing the existing cost/price realities. A purchaser committed to a long-term, fixed-price contract for a particular requirement may find a competitor can gain a significant advantage through a technology-driven, lower-cost substitute. Environmental legislative changes can drastically offset a supplier's capability to deliver at the expected price or to deliver at all.

Because the well-informed supply manager is probably in the best position to identify the various supply risks his or her organization faces, such a risk identification should be a standard requirement of the job, including the estimation of the probability of event occurrence.

Impact assessment requires the ability to assess the consequences of supply interruption and/or price/cost exposure. Correct impact assessment is likely to require the input of others in the organization, such as operations, marketing, accounting, and finance, to name just a few. Assessed potential impact from identified risk may be low, medium, or high.

Combining potential impact assessment with the probability of event exposure creates a table of risks with low probability and low impact on one extreme and high probability with high impact on the other.

Obviously, high-impact, high-probability risks need to be addressed or, better yet, avoided, if at all possible.

Managing supply risks should be started at the supply level, but may escalate to the overall corporate level. Relatively simple actions such as avoiding high-risk suppliers or high-risk geographical locations, dual or triple sourcing, carrying safety stock, hedging, and using longer-term and/or fixed- or declining-price contracts and protective contract clauses have been a standard part of the procurement arsenal for a long time. If most purchasers had their way, they would like to transfer all risk to their suppliers! However, the assumption of risk carries a price tag, and a supplier should be asked to shoulder the risk if it is advantageous to both the supplier and purchaser to do so.

The Corporate Context

Supply risk is only one of the various risks to which any organization is exposed. Traditionally, financial risks have been the responsibility of finance, property insurance part of real estate, and so on. The emergence of a corporate risk management group headed by a risk manager or chief risk officer (CRO) allows companies as a whole to assess their total risk exposure and seek the best ways of managing all risks. A supply manager's decision not to source in a politically unstable country because of his or her fear of supply interruption may also miss an opportunity to source at a highly advantageous price. A corporate perspective might show that the trade-off between a higher price elsewhere and the risk of nonsupply favors the apparently riskier option. Mergers and acquisitions as well as insourcing and outsourcing represent phenomena full of opportunities and risks in which supply input is vital to effective corporate risk resolution. The decision as to how much risk any organization should be willing to bear and whether it should self-insure or seek third-party protection is well beyond the scope of this text. Nevertheless, it is clear that risk management is going to be an area of growing concern for supply managers.

Figure 20–3 is a conceptual flow diagram of the strategic purchasing planning process. It is important to recognize that the planning process normally focuses on *long-run opportunities* and not primarily on immediate problems.

FIGURE 20–3 **Strategic Purchasing Planning Process**

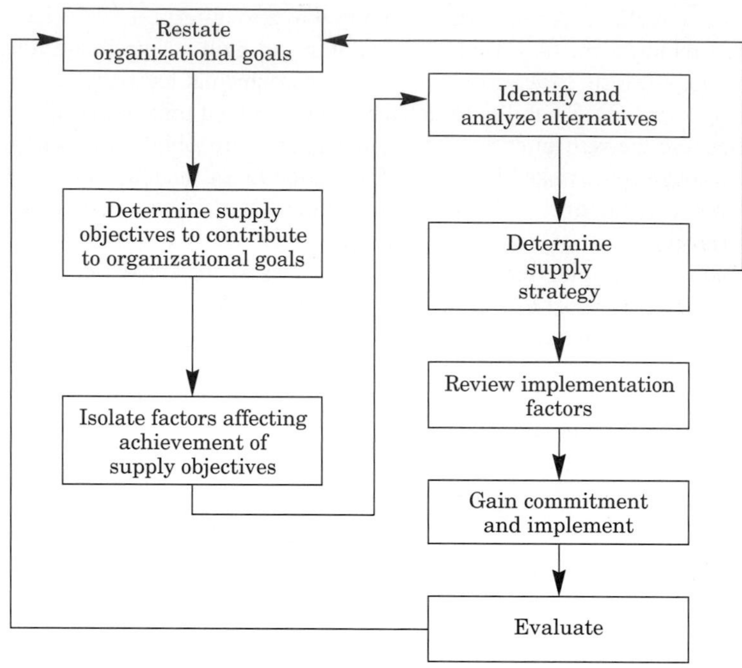

STRATEGIC COMPONENTS

The number of specific strategic opportunities that might be addressed in formulating an overall supply strategy is limited only by the imagination of the supply manager. Any strategy chosen should include a determination of what, quality, how much, who, when, what price, where, how, and why. Each of these will be discussed further. (See Figure 20–4.)

What?

Probably the most fundamental question facing an organization under the "what" category is the issue of make or buy, insourcing, and outsourcing. Presumably, strong acquisition strengths would favor a buy strategy. (See Chapter 18).

Also included under the heading of what is to be acquired is the issue of whether the organization will acquire standard items and materials readily available in the market, as opposed to special, custom-specified requirements. Standard items may be readily acquired in the marketplace, but they may not afford the organization the competitive edge that special requirements might provide.

Quality?

Part of the what question deals with the quality of the items or services to be acquired. Chapter 5 addresses the various trade-offs possible under quality. The intent is to achieve continuous process and product or service improvement.

FIGURE 20–4
Supply Strategy Questions

1. What?
   Make or buy
   Standard versus special
2. Quality?
   Quality versus cost
   Supplier involvement
3. How Much?
   Large versus small quantities (inventory)
4. Who?
   Centralize or decentralize
   Quality of staff
   Top management involvement
5. When?
   Now versus later
   Blank check system
   Forward buy
6. What Price?
   Premium
   Standard
   Lower
   Cost-based
   Market-based
   Lease/make/buy
7. Where?
   Local, regional
   Domestic, international
   Large versus small
   Single versus multiple source
   High versus low supplier turnover
   Supplier relations
   Supplier certification
   Supplier ownership
8. How?
   Systems and procedures
   Computerization
   Negotiations
   Competitive bids
   Fixed bids
   Blanket orders/open orders
   Systems contracting
   Blank check system
   Group buying
   Materials requirements planning
   Long-term contracts
   Ethics
   Aggressive or passive
   Purchasing research
   Value analysis
9. Why?
   Objectives congruent
   Market reasons
   Internal reasons
   1. Outside supply
   2. Inside supply

Supplier Quality Assurance Programs

Many firms have concluded that a more consistent quality of end-product output is absolutely essential to the maintenance of, or growth in, market share. Suppliers must deliver consistent quality materials, parts, and components; this also will effect a marked reduction in production costs and in-house quality control administrative costs. Therefore, a strategy of developing suppliers' knowledge of quality requirements and assisting them in implementation of programs to achieve desired results may be needed. Three of the programs that might be used are

1. Zero defect (ZD) plans. "Do it right the first time" is far more cost-effective than making corrections after the fact.
2. Process quality control programs. These use statistical control charts to monitor various production processes to isolate developing problems and make needed adjustments (corrections) before bad product is produced. The buying firm may need to assist the supplier with the introduction of the needed statistical techniques.
3. Quality certification programs. Here the supplier agrees to perform the agreed-upon quality tests and supply the test data, with the shipment, to the buying firm. If the seller

does the requisite outgoing quality checks and can be depended on to do them correctly, the buying firm then can eliminate its incoming inspection procedures and attendant costs. This approach almost always is a key element in any just-in-time purchasing system, as discussed in the following section.

How Much?

Another major component of any supply strategy deals with the question of how much is to be acquired in total and per delivery. Chapter 6 discussed a number of trade-offs possible under quantity. In JIT and MRP, the trend has been toward smaller quantities to be delivered as needed, as opposed to the former stance of buying large quantities at a time to ensure better prices. Ideally, buyers and suppliers try to identify and eliminate the causes of uncertainty in the supply chain that drive the need for inventory, thus reducing the amount of inventory in the total system. One option available under the how much question may involve the shifting of inventory ownership.

The supplier maintains finished goods inventory because the supplier may be supplying a common item to several customers. The safety stock required to service a group of customers may be much less than the combined total of the safety stocks if the several customers were to manage their own inventories separately. This concept is integral to the successful implementation of systems contracting (discussed in Chapter 3). From a strategic standpoint, supply may wish to analyze its inventory position on all of its major items, with a view to working out an arrangement with key suppliers whereby they agree to maintain the inventory, physically and financially, with delivery as required. Ideally, of course, the intent of both buyer and supplier should be to take inventory out of the system. An area in the buyer's facility may even be placed under the supplier's control.

Dell is one example of a company that has successfully used its supply relationships to create a competitive advantage. Critical to Dell's success is that it carries almost no inventories, either finished products or materials, and everything that Dell buys from its suppliers is immediately assembled into a computer and sold.[2]

Other options are to switch to just-in-time purchasing or to consignment buying. If a supplier can be depended on to deliver needed purchased items, of the agreed-upon quality, in small quantities, and at the specified time, the buying firm can substantially reduce its investment in purchased inventories, enjoy needed continuity of supply, and reduce its receiving and incoming inspection costs. To accomplish this requires a long-term plan and substantial cooperation and understanding between buyer and seller.

In consignment buying, a supplier owns inventory in the buyer's facility, under the buyer's control. The buyer assumes responsibility for accounting for withdrawals of stock from that consignment inventory, payment for quantities used, and notification to the supplier of the need to replenish inventory. Verification of quantities remaining in inventory then would be done jointly, at periodic intervals. This strategy has advantages for both supplier (assured volume) and buyer (reduced inventory investment), and is often used in the distribution industry.

Who?

The whole question of who should do the buying and how to organize the supply function has been addressed in Chapter 2. The key decisions are whether the supply function should be centralized or not, what the quality of staff should be, and to what extent top management

[2] Charles H. Fine, *Clock Speed* (Reading, MA: Perseus Books, 1998).

and other functions will be involved in the total acquisition process. To what extent will teams be used to arrive at supply strategies?

When?

The question of when to buy is tied very closely to the one of how much. The obvious choices are now versus later. The key strategy issue really lies with the question of forward buying and inventory policy. In the area of commodities, the opportunity exists to go into the futures market and use hedging. The organized commodity exchanges present an opportunity to offset transactions in the spot and future markets to avoid some of the risk of substantial price fluctuation as discussed in Chapter 8.

What Price?

It is possible for any organization to follow some specific price strategies. This topic already has been extensively discussed in Chapter 9. Key trade-offs may be whether the organization intends to pursue paying a premium price in return for exceptional service and other commitments from the supplier, a standard price target in line with the rest of the market, or a low price intended to give a cost advantage. Furthermore, the pursuit of a cost-based strategy as opposed to a market-based strategy may require extensive use of tools such as value analysis, cost analysis, and negotiation. For capital assets, the choice of lease or own presents strategic alternatives, as discussed in Chapter 16.

Where?

Several possibilities present themselves under the question of where to buy. Many of these were discussed in Chapter 10 under "Source Selection." Obvious trade-offs include local, regional, domestic, or international sourcing; buying from small versus large suppliers; single versus multiple sourcing; and low versus high supplier turnover, as well as supplier certification and supplier ownership. Lastly, through reverse marketing or supplier development, the purchaser may create rather than select suppliers.

How?

A large array of options exist under the heading of how to buy. These include, but certainly are not limited to, supply chain management integration systems and procedures, choice of technology, e-commerce applications, use of various types of teams, use of negotiations, auctions, competitive bids, blanket orders and open order systems, systems contracting, group buying, long-term contracts, the ethics of acquisition, aggressive or passive buying, the use of purchasing research and value analysis, quality assurance programs, and reduction of the supply base. Most of these have been discussed in Chapters 2 through 10 in this text.

Why?

Every strategy needs to be examined not only for its various optional components, but also for the reason why it should be pursued. The normal reason for a strategy in supply is to make supply objectives congruent with overall organizational objectives and strategies and can be at both an operational and strategic level. Other reasons may include market conditions, both current and future. Furthermore, there may be reasons internal to the organization, both outside of supply and inside supply, to pursue certain strategies. For example, a strong engineering department may afford an opportunity to pursue a strategy based on specially engineered requirements. The availability of excess funds may afford an opportunity to acquire a supplier through backward/vertical integration. The reasons inside supply may be related to the capability and availability of supply personnel. A highly trained and effective supply group can pursue much more aggressive strategies than one less qualified. Other reasons may include the environment. For example, government regulations and controls in product liability and environmental protection may require the pursuit of certain strategies.

What makes supply strategy such an exciting area for exploration is the combination of the multitude of strategic options coupled with the size of potential impact on corporate success. The combination of sound supply expertise with creative thinking and full understanding of corporate objectives and strategies can uncover strategic opportunities of a size and impact not available elsewhere in the organization.

WHAT IS HAPPENING IN PURCHASING AND SUPPLY MANAGEMENT

While the evidence is not conclusive that all the following practices will continue over the coming years, they are under way now. Some have been with us for a considerable period of time, while others are relatively recent.

1. *Nontraditional people in supply management positions.* As organizations continue to rightsize or downsize, many talented managers are available to move out of their current, now-redundant positions into other managerial functions. Some come to supply, in positions where managerial skills and credibility are important.
2. *Technical entry route into purchasing.* In highly technical firms, a requirement for employment in a supply capacity may be a technical educational background; for example, a pharmaceutical manufacturer may require its key supply professionals to have educational credentials in disciplines like biology, medicine, pharmacy, or chemistry.
3. *Emphasis on total quality management and customer satisfaction.* Supply is required to think strategically about its responsibility for, and involvement in, quality management and satisfying the organization's customers. It has to "buy into" responsibility for the quality of output of goods and/or services.
4. *Emphasis on the process used in acquisition, rather than the transactions.* Supply must do the right things, as well as doing things right! Continuous process improvement is a way of life in forward-thinking supply operations.
5. *Purchase of systems and services, as well as products.* To increase value added, more suppliers offer ancillary services, like storage, accounting, disposal, and so on, in addition to production.
6. *Strategic cost management.* Cost management begins with early supply involvement in product design and represents ongoing efforts to analyze cost drivers and target opportunities to reduce total supply chain costs. Such efforts require cross-functional support, supplier involvement, and trained cost management specialists to lead the initiative.
7. *Design engineering, supply, and suppliers capitalizing on their potential synergy.* They recognize their interdependence and develop the communication and coordination to maximize the combined contribution of all.

8. *Reformulation of the supplier base.* The trend to single sourcing, greater use of buyer/supplier alliances and partnerships, and greater sharing of information will continue.
9. *Longer-term contracts.* Many of the agreements for supply of key items will be partnerships/alliances expected to have a life of 5, 10, 15 years, or even longer.
10. *The appropriate use of technology and the Internet.* To simplify and reduce transactions, and speed up communication, transactions between firms and their major suppliers continue to grow. Applications are extended to Web-based fulfillment processes, planning and scheduling, and product development.
11. *Global supply management.* Supply managers need to look globally to identify best possible suppliers. Further reductions and elimination of trade barriers facilitate globalization of supply networks.
12. *MRO items handled by a third-party contractor.* MRO buying involves many transactions, but low average dollars for each. It is difficult for a supply function to add real value in MRO buying other than assuring that an appropriate system for management of MRO requirements is in place. If contracted out, it frees the time of key personnel to concentrate on the high-potential acquisition areas.
13. *Sourcing that includes the complete end product or service and is done proactively.* Sourcing out of items manufactured previously was done as a matter of short-term survival. Due to its dollar potential, firms become proactive in identifying and pursuing both products *and* services—for example, legal, training, internal auditing—that provide a competitive advantage if successfully outsourced.
14. *Closer supplier relationships.* Sourcing out end products shifts technology from the buying firm to the supplying firm. The two firms grow closer together (conceptually).
15. *Teaming.* The complexity of many procurements requires that the analysis and decision making be done by a cross-functional group of key professionals/managers, including a team member from, for example, purchasing, design, engineering, and manufacturing.
16. *Empowerment.* As the ability and skill levels of people in supply increase, organizations delegate increasing amounts of authority to their supply people to make decisions and to improve the supply process. If their creativity can be unleashed, the results could exceed expectations by a wide margin.
17. *Public procurement.* In public procurement, there is greater concern over value for money spent in addition to compliance with policies and procedures.
18. *Consortia.* Requirements of two or more separate organizations in both the public and private sectors are combined to gain price, design, and supply availability benefits of higher volume.
19. *Separation of strategic and tactical supply.* As processes, practices, and strategies change, the roles in supply become differentiated between strategic and operational (tactical).
20. *Greater supply involvement in nontraditional purchases.* Opportunities are recognized where supply expertise can be successfully applied to areas such as insurance, marketing spend, travel, real estate, temporary workforce, and benefit plans.
21. *Environmental supply.* Firms become more proactive to ensure their suppliers conform to environmental regulations and have systems and strategies in place that support sustainable development, and compliance with ISO 14000 standards is becoming more commonplace.

22. *Outsourcing of the procurement process.* The services of an organization's supply department can be bought, in part or in total, from a third-party supplier, just as many firms now outsource their training department and training services. Some firms now outsource their entire MRO buy. This might obtain greater expertise, leverage volume, and/or reduce administrative costs.
23. *Functional lines being blurred or even eliminated.* Experts in disciplines associated in the past with specific functions, such as design, quality assurance, production planning, manufacturing, and supply, work together at each stage in the business process. More of the processes work in parallel rather than in series.
24. *Design for procurability.* The options/alternatives available for the acquisition of materials/services influence the design activity, just as some firms emphasize "design for manufacturability."
25. *Supply chain management.* Supply chain design is a potential source of competitive advantage. Companies need to consider the strategic implications of decisions associated with make or buy and the capabilities of their key suppliers and their suppliers' suppliers. Suppliers network among each other to gain the synergy of their collective design and application expertise, which provide better products and services and result in further reduction in cycle time and cost.
26. *Contracts with multiple suppliers simultaneously to design and build.* Strategic alliance teams are formed with multiple suppliers to ensure low-cost processes, incorporating leading-edge technology with improved design reliability and guaranteed process output. These multiorganization teams work with the business units on design of new or expansion projects and work toward improved reliability and continuous improvement of existing processes.
27. *Expert systems/artificial intelligence.* Expert systems are software applications that contain rules embedded in the program that can make decisions, or can provide decisions/solutions for consideration of the user.
28. *Balance sheet concerns.* There is a growing focus on the balance sheet in addition to the traditional income statement concerns. Thus, insourcing and outsourcing and ownership of capital assets and inventories are more frequent options.
29. *Measurement.* Greater concern over how to measure the actual contribution of supply to organizational goals and strategies requires the development of new and appropriate measures.

Conclusion

The increasing interest in supply strategies and their potential contribution to organizational objectives and strategies is one of the exciting developments in the whole field of supply. Fortunately, as this chapter indicates, the number of strategic options open to any supply manager is almost endless. A significant difficulty may exist in making these strategies congruent with those of the organization as a whole. The long-term perspective required for effective supply strategy development will force supply managers to concentrate more on the future. The coming decade should be a highly rewarding one for those supply managers willing to accept the challenge of realizing the full potential of supply's contribution to organizational success.

Questions for Review and Discussion

1. What role can (should) supply play in determining a firm's strategy in the area of social issues and trends?
2. How can the supply manager determine which cost-reduction strategies to pursue?
3. Can you have a supply strategy in public procurement? Why or why not?
4. Why should a supply manager consider hiring (or obtaining internally) an employee without any supply background?
5. What can supply do to assist in minimizing a firm's risk of product liability lawsuits?
6. What factors have caused the current interest in, and attention to, strategic purchasing and supply planning?
7. What type of data would supply need to contribute to an organization's strategic growth? How might supply obtain such data?
8. How can supply sell itself more effectively internally?
9. What do you believe to be the most difficult obstacles to making a supply function strategic?
10. Why should supply be concerned about the balance sheet?

References

Arnold, Ulli; Andrew Cox; Marion Debruyne; Jacques de Rijcke; Thomas Hendrick; Paul Iyongun; Jacques Liouville; and Gyongyi Vorosmarty. *A Multi-Country Study of Strategic Topics in Purchasing and Supply Management.* Tempe, AZ: Center for Advanced Purchasing Studies, June 1999.

Bowersox, Donald J.; David J. Closs; and Bixby M. Cooper. *Supply Chain Logistics Management*. New York: McGraw-Hill, 2002.

Carter, Joseph R., and Ram Narasimhan. *Purchasing and Supply Management: Future Directions and Trends.* Tempe, AZ: Center for Advanced Purchasing Studies, 1995.

Carter, Phillip L.; Joseph R. Carter; Robert M. Monczka; Thomas H. Slaight; and Andrew J. Swan. *The Future of Purchasing and Supply: A Five- and Ten-Year Forecast.* Tempe, AZ: Center for Advanced Purchasing Studies, 1998.

Cox, Andrew. *Effective Supply Chain Management*. Boston, UK: Earlsgate Press, 2000.

Cox, Andrew, and Peter Hines (eds.). *Advanced Supply Management: The Best Practice Debate.* Boston, UK: Earlsgate Press, 1997.

Cox, Andrew; Joe Sanderson; and Glyn Watson. *Power Regimes Mapping the DNA of Business and Supply Chain Relationships*. Boston, UK: Earlsgate Press, 2000.

Curkovic, Sime; Steven A. Melnyk; Robert B. Handfield; and Roger Calantone. "Investigating the Linkage Between Total Quality Management and Environmentally Responsible Manufacturing." *IEEE Transactions on Engineering Management* 47, no. 4 (November 2000), pp. 444–63.

Delphi Automotive Systems. http://www.delphiautomotive.com, February 2001.

Fearon, Harold E. *Purchasing Organizational Relationships.* Tempe, AZ: Center for Advanced Purchasing Studies, 1988.

Fearon, Harold E., and Michiel R. Leenders. *Purchasing's Organizational Roles and Responsibilities.* Tempe, AZ: Center for Advanced Purchasing Studies, 1995.

Fine, Charles H. *Clock Speed.* Reading, MA: Perseus Books, 1998.

Handfield, Robert B., and Ernest L. Nichols Jr. *Supply Chain Redesign*. Upper Saddle River, NJ: Prentice Hall, 2002.

Heijboer, Govert. *Quantitative Analysis of Strategic and Tactual Purchasing Decisions.* Enschede, NL: Twente University Press, 2003.

Hines, Peter, et al. *Value Stream Management.* Harlow, UK: Prentice Hall, 2000.

Lamming, Richard, and Andrew Cox (eds.). *Strategic Procurement Management: Concepts and Cases*. Boston, UK: Earlsgate Press, 1999.

Leenders, Michiel R., and P. Fraser Johnson. *Major Changes in Supply Chain Responsibilities.* Tempe, AZ: Center for Advanced Purchasing Studies, 2001.

Monczka, Robert M., and Robert J. Trent. *Purchasing and Sourcing Strategy: Trends and Implications.* Tempe, AZ: Center for Advanced Purchasing Studies, 1995.

Nelson, Dave; Rick Mayo; and Patricia Moody. *Powered by Honda.* New York: John Wiley & Sons, 1998.

Reinhardt, Forest L. "Bringing the Environment Down to Earth." *Harvard Business Review,* July–August 1999, pp. 149–57.

Simchi-Levi, David; Philip Kaminsky; and Edith Simchi-Levi. *Designing and Managing the Supply Chain*. New York: McGraw-Hill/Irwin, 2003.

Stock, James R., and Douglas M. Lambert. *Strategic Logistics Management*. 4th ed. New York: McGraw-Hill/Irwin, 2001.

Willcocks, L. P., and M. C. Lacity (eds.). *Strategic Sourcing of Information Systems: Perspectives and Practices*. Chichester, UK: John Wiley, 1998.

Case 20–1

Spartan Heat Exchangers Inc.

On June 10, Rick Coyne, materials manager at Spartan Heat Exchangers Inc. (Spartan), in Springfield, Missouri, received a call from Max Brisco, vice president of manufacturing: "What can the materials department do to facilitate Spartan's new business strategy? I'll need your plan next week."

SPARTAN HEAT EXCHANGERS

Spartan was a leading designer and manufacturer of specialized industrial heat transfer equipment. Its customers operated in a number of industries, such as steel, aluminum smelting, hydro electricity generation, pulp and paper, refining, and petrochemical. The company's primary products included transformer coolers, motor and generator coolers, hydro generator coolers, air-cooled heat exchangers, and transformer oil coolers. Spartan's combination of fin-tube and time-proven heat exchanger designs had gained wide recognition both in North America and internationally.

Sales revenues were $25 million and Spartan operated in a 125,000-square-foot plant. Spartan was owned by Krimmer Industries, a large privately held corporation with more than 10,000 employees worldwide, headquartered in Denver.

Rick Coyne summarized the business strategy of Spartan during the past 10 years: "We were willing to do anything for every customer with respect to their heat transfer requirements. We were willing to do trial and error on the shop floor and provide a customer with his or her own unique heat transfer products." He added, "Our design and manufacturing people derived greatest satisfaction making new customized heat transfer products. Designing and research capabilities gave us the edge in developing and manufacturing any kind of heat transfer product required by the customer. Ten years ago, we were one of the very few companies in our industry offering customized services in design and manufacturing and this strategy made business sense, as the customers were willing to pay a premium for customized products."

MANUFACTURING PROCESS

The customized nature of Spartan's product line was supported by a job shop manufacturing operation with several departments, each of which produced particular component parts, feeding a final assembly area. Each job moved from work center to work center, accompanied by a bill of material and engineering drawing. The first process involved fitting a liner tube (in which the fluid to be cooled passed) into a base tube. This base tube, made of aluminum, was then pressure bonded to the inner liner tube through a rotary extrusion process that formed spiral fins on the base tube. The depth of the fins and the distance between them determined the amount of airflow across the tubes, and thus the cooling efficiency and power of the unit.

After the tubes were formed, cabinet and end plate fabrication began. The tubes were welded to the cabinet and the end plates. Flanges were then welded to pairs of tubes on the other side of the end plates to create a looped system. The unit was then painted and fans and motors were installed. Finally, the unit was tested for leaks and performance, crated, and shipped to the job site for installation.

MATERIALS DEPARTMENT

Spartan's buyers sourced all raw material and components required by manufacturing and were responsible for planning, procurement, and management of inventories. Rick managed an in-house warehouse used for housing the raw material inventories, maintained adequate buffer inventories, and executed purchase contracts with vendors, ensuring specifications were met while achieving the best possible price. Rick's department included two buyers, a material control clerk, an expediter, and two shippers/-receivers.

It was common for Spartan to have multiple vendors for raw material supply, and the materials group used more than 350 vendors for its raw materials, with current lead times ranging from a few days to six weeks. This wide supplier base was necessitated by the customization strategy adopted by the company. Rick noted that approximately 35 percent of Spartan's purchases were for aluminum products, mainly tubes and sheets. On average the plant had $3.5 million worth of inventory, in the form of both raw and work in process. Raw material inventory constituted approximately 40 percent of the total. Rick estimated that Spartan had inventory turns of four times per year, which he believed was comparable to the competition.

Manufacturing operations regularly complained about material shortages and stockouts and regular inventory audits indicated significant discrepancies with inventory records on the company's computer system. Furthermore, a significant amount of stock was written off each year due to obsolescence. Rick suspected that production staff regularly removed stock without proper documentation and that workers frequently deviated from established bills of material.

NEW BUSINESS STRATEGY

Competition in the heat exchanger industry had increased dramatically over the past decade, with much of the new competition coming from Korea and Europe. Korean firms, with their low cost base, competed primarily on price, while European firms focused on standardizing their product lines to a few high-volume products and competed on delivery lead time and price. Spartan's competitors in Europe used assembly-line manufacturing processes, rather than batch or job shop operations.

Senior management viewed the competition from Europe and Korea as an imminent threat. Many of Spartan's customers had recently developed aggressive expectations regarding pricing and delivery lead times and some key customers had decided to opt for standard product design, sacrificing custom design for lower cost and faster delivery.

The changing nature of the industry forced senior management to reexamine their business strategy. As a result, in January, a multidiscipline task force representing engineering, manufacturing, and sales was formed with the mandate to formulate a new five-year business strategy.

The new corporate strategy was finalized in May and reviewed with the management group on June 1st in an all-day staff meeting. The central theme of the new strategy was standardization of all product lines, in terms of both design and manufacturing, reducing variety to three or four basic lines for each product category. The sales department would no longer accept orders for specialized designs. The aim of the new strategy was to reduce the delivery lead time from 14 weeks to 6 weeks and to lower production costs dramatically.

NEW CHALLENGES FOR MATERIAL DEPARTMENT

Max Brisco indicated that he expected the materials group to play a major role in support of the new corporate strategy and needed to know by next week the specifics of Rick's plan. The task force had set a number of ambitious targets. First, customer lead times for finished products were to be reduced to six weeks from the current average of 14 weeks. Second, the new objective for inventory turns was 20 times. Meanwhile, raw material stockouts were to be eliminated. Third, Max believed that product standardization also would provide opportunities to reduce costs for purchased goods. He expected that costs for raw materials and components could be cut by 10 percent over the next 12 months.

Rick fully supported the new direction that the company was taking and saw this as an opportunity to make major changes. He knew that Max would want the specifics of his plan during the meeting in a week's time.

Case 20–2

Sabor Inc.

In mid-April, Ray Soles, vice president of supply chain management at Sabor Inc., had become increasingly concerned about the potential shortage of supply of marconil, a new high-tech raw material for air filtration. Sabor Inc.'s three suppliers, during the last two weeks, had advised Ray Soles to sign long-term contracts and he was trying to assess the advisability of such commitments.

SABOR INC.

Sabor Inc. of Cleveland, Ohio, produced high-quality consumer and industrial air-conditioning and heating units. An extensive network of independent and company-owned installation and sales centers serviced customers throughout the North American market. Total company sales last year totaled $800 million.

AIR FILTRATION AND MARCONIL

Sabor Inc. for decades had sold air humidification and air filtration units along with its prime units in air heating and cooling. Until three years ago, air filtration had accounted for about 7 percent of total corporate sales and had been sold primarily as add-ons to a new air cooling/heating system. However, with the advent of marconil, air filtration had started to increase significantly as a percentage of total sales. Marconil, a new high-tech product developed as part of the U.S. space effort, had a range of unique properties of high interest to a variety of industries. In the case of air filtration, when processed by a Sabor Inc. developed and patented process, marconil could be transformed into a thin, very light, and extremely fine meshlike sponge material capable of filtering extremely small particles.

Given the population's sensitivity to air quality and the increasing number of people with asthma and allergies, the new Sabor filters became popular, not only with new Sabor air system installations but also as retrofits in older air conditioning and heating systems. Moreover, compared to electronic air cleaners that cost about three times as much to install and required monthly cleaning, marconil filters had to be replaced every six months, guaranteeing a continued sales volume of filters for years to come. When combined with an ultraviolet light unit, which killed airborne bacteria, a marconil air cleaning system was considered a huge leap forward in air treatment.

The manufacturing cost of a marconil filter accounted for about 28 percent of its selling price.

AIR FILTRATION SALES

Along with the marconil filtration system introduction three years ago Sabor's marketing department had initiated a significant promotional campaign directed at both the industrial and consumer sectors. Marketing's ability to forecast sales accurately had not been impressive, according to Ray Soles. For the first year, marketing had forecast marconil filter sales at $1 million when in reality they sold $11 million. In the second year, the forecast was for $15 million and actual sales were $29 million, and, in the third year, a forecast of $40 million turned into actual sales of $72 million. The marketing department expected sales growth to level off over the next three years to a rate of 20 percent per year.

MARCONIL SUPPLY

Sabor's first marconil supplier was Bilt Chemical, a long-time supplier of paints and adhesives to Sabor and a large, diversified, innovative chemical producer that held the patent on marconil. Ray Soles did not like the idea of single sourcing and, therefore, when marconil requirements rose significantly in the second year, he brought in a second supplier, Warton Inc., which not only produced the marconil raw materials (under licence from Bilt Chemical), but also manufactured a variety of marconil products in the textile and automotive fields. In the third year, Ray had secured a third supplier, G. K. Specialties, a much smaller company than Bilt Chemical and Warton Inc., which also produced marconil under license for its own applications in aerospace and the military, but which had some excess capacity that it sold on the open market.

All three suppliers sold marconil at identical prices, which had increased over the past three years. Actual volumes purchased by Sabor Inc. from each of the three suppliers were as shown in Exhibit 1. The current price of marconil from all three suppliers was $50.00.

SUPPLIER PROPOSALS FOR LONG-TERM CONTRACTS

During the first two weeks of April, Ray Soles was visited by each of his current three marconil suppliers with Bilt Chemical first. Each warned that a shortage of marconil supply was looming and that unless Ray was willing to sign a long-term contract, they would not be in a position to guarantee supply. However, each proposal was different.

Bilt Chemical proposed a five-year contract with take-or-pay commitments of 25,000 pounds for the current year and 20 percent annual increases in volume for each of the following years. Prices were subject to escalation for energy, raw material, and labor every quarter based on the current $50.00 price per pound.

Warton Inc. proposed a two-year contract for 10,000 pounds each year with similar price provisions to those of Bilt Chemical.

G. K. Specialties suggested an agreement for 12.5 percent of Sabor's annual requirements, which could be dropped at any time by either party, but which proposed a price of $56.00 for the current year, to be adjusted semiannually, thereafter based on inflation, energy, labor, and material.

Although Ray Soles did not know much about the actual manufacturing process for marconil, he had heard that increases in capacity were expensive. He also understood that two of the three component raw materials for marconil were byproducts from industrial processes that were reasonably stable.

Since Ray Soles had been able to buy almost all of Sabor's needs on quarterly, semiannual, or annual contracts, he was not particularly keen on departing from his current supply practice. He had heard some rumors that in a few years a much-lower-cost substitute for marconil might be developed. He suspected that, therefore, his current suppliers were anxious to tie Sabor to a long-term commitment.

APRIL 15

On April 15, the Bilt Chemical sales representative sent an e-mail to Ray Soles requesting a meeting on April 22. The e-mail concluded, "I would like to bring my sales manager so that we may discuss our proposal for the marconil with you. We will not be able to guarantee you supply after August 1, if you are unable to commit."

EXHIBIT 1
Sabor Marconil Purchases and Prices

Company	Capacity (in pounds)	Purchases (in pounds)		
		Year 1	Year 2	Year 3
Bilt Chemical	80,000	5,000	10,000	20,000
Warton Inc.	40,000	0	3,000	8,000
G. K. Specialties	20,000	0		4,000
Prices		$39.00	$42.00	$44.00

Case 20–3

Iowa Elevators

Scott McBride, director of purchasing at Iowa Elevators, was reviewing a consultant's report as he prepared for a meeting with the executive management team scheduled for Wednesday, June 11. Scott had been asked by Walter Lettridge, Iowa Elevator's CEO, to present a five-year plan for the purchasing department at the meeting. In preparation for the meeting, Scott engaged the services of a consulting firm to prepare a report analyzing all expenditures made by the company with outside suppliers over the pervious year. It was now June 3, and Scott knew there was still a lot of work that had to be completed to get ready for the meeting the following week.

IOWA ELEVATORS

Iowa Elevators was one of the largest grain-handling companies in the United States Headquartered in Des Moines, Iowa, the company had annual revenues of $2.3 billion and employed more than 2,500 people. Its two business units were the grain-handling and marketing division and the farm supplies division.

The grain-handling and marketing division operated approximately 300 grain elevators in the midwest. This division represented approximately 75 percent of total company revenues, although total revenues had declined by 20 percent from the previous year due to drought conditions that had affected farm crop production. Over the previous five years, the company had invested heavily in upgrading its elevator system to improve throughput and increase capacity in key regions.

The farm supplies division sold crop-protection products, equipment and supplies, fertilizer, and seed through its network of country elevators and approximately 30 marketing centers. Revenues for this division had doubled over the previous five years as part of a strategy to tap the company's country elevator network to diversify its revenue base.

Iowa Elevators had a past reputation for steady financial performance and profitability. However, the company had seen a steady decline in profitability over the previous three years. In the most recent fiscal year, it experienced a loss of $11 million after taxes and a sharp decline in working capital. Management attributed its disappointing results to lower volumes in its grain-handling and marketing division and increased competition. Despite its rising market share, operating margins at the farm supplies division had remained flat.

Concern over the financial performance of the company led to a decision by the board of directors to make changes to the executive team. In February, Walter Lettridge, a veteran of the grain-handling industry, was brought in as the new president and CEO. Shortly afterward, Jose Sousa joined Iowa Elevators as the new chief financial officer. Both Walter and Jose had worked together at a competitor of Iowa Elevators.

Immediately after joining the company, Walter went to work creating a major cost-cutting initiative, which would include reductions in headcounts, capital expenditure budgets, and overhead expenses. As part of this process, Scott McBride was asked to present a five-year plan to the executive management team, including annual cost reduction targets.

PURCHASING AND SUPPLY MANAGEMENT

Scott supervised a group of 11 people (see Exhibit 1), who were responsible for the acquisition of requirements for head office and some regional sales and administrative offices. Its major purchases were information technology (hardware and software); printing for forms, brochures, and advertising; office supplies; and company automobile leases. The only change in the purchasing organization within the last year had been the addition of a travel coordinator as a result of a contract for air travel and car rentals. The purchasing organization was part of the corporate services organization, which also included the human resources and information technology groups, and reported to the CFO.

Iowa Elevators had a history of decentralized management, with individual divisions held accountable for their own operations and bottom-line performance. As a result, local elevator managers acted autonomously but were responsible for local market share and profitability. In addition, the elevator managers also made decisions concerning the amount and variety of crop-protection products, fertilizer, and seed stock to handle in their retail operation. Purchases for elevator operations were handled locally and monitored based on spending limits set in annual operating budgets.

EXHIBIT 1 Iowa Elevators Purchasing Department

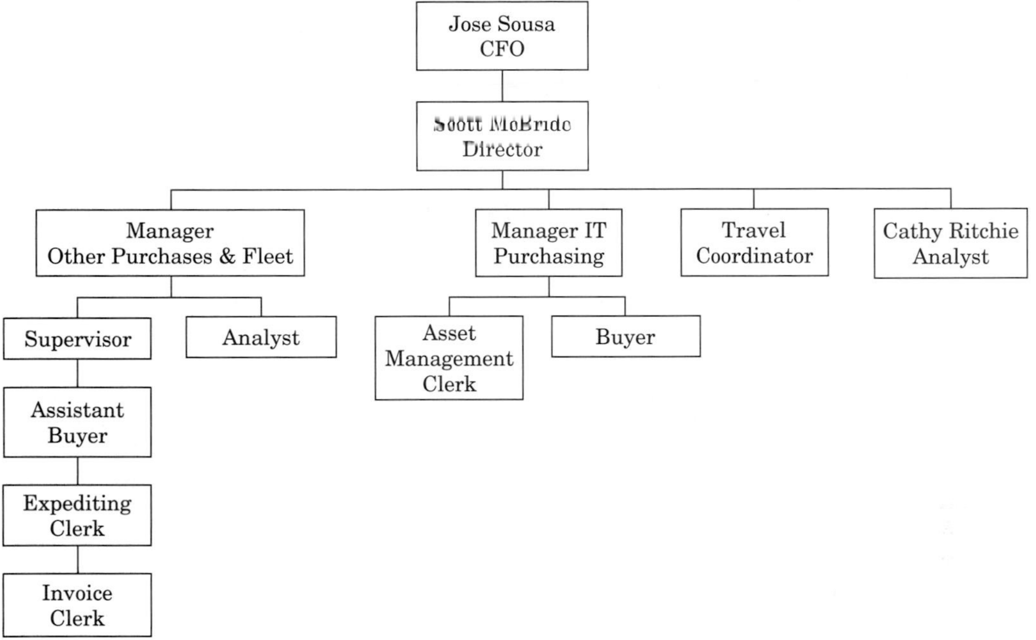

The farm supplies division had a group of four product managers who were responsible for the three main product segments (crop-protection products, equipment and supplies, and fertilizer and seed). These individuals were responsible for supplier selection, product mix, branding, and promotion and assisted elevator and marketing center managers in the areas of promotion, new product development, and inventory planning.

ANALYSIS OF CORPORATE SPEND

In a meeting in early May, Scott was asked by Walter Lettridge and Jose Sousa to present his five-year plan for the purchasing department at an executive management team meeting on June 11. Walter had scheduled time for a number of senior managers to present their plans and ideas aimed at returning the company to profitability. During the meeting, Walter commented to Scott: "I expect purchasing to deliver cost savings and your group needs to play a more significant role in the company. You need to explain what you can deliver and explain how you intend to accomplish your objectives. As far as I am concerned, everything is on the table right now. We need to return the company to profitability and I am not afraid to make some major changes in terms of how we run this business."

Recognizing the need to present a thorough plan, Scott enlisted the support of his analyst, Cathy Ritchie, to help him collect and organize data. The data collection focused on two questions: (1) How much money did Iowa Elevators spend with its outside suppliers? and (2) How much inventory did the company carry? The data collection process had been complicated by the variety of management systems at different levels and at different locations. Scott believed that, if more time had been available, Cathy might have been able to capture more spend and inventory data.

Cathy's analysis identified a total corporate spend of $728 million. Although the company dealt with more than 1,500 suppliers, 20 suppliers accounted for approximately 45 percent of the total spend and the top five represented 35 percent. (The top five suppliers consisted of two railway companies and three suppliers to the farm supplies division for crop protection and fertilizer.) She estimated average annual inventories in the farm supplies division were nearly $120 million with annual purchases of $310 million. A summary of Cathy's key findings is reported in Exhibits 2 and 3.

EXHIBIT 2
Total Purchases by Category ($000)

Spend Category	Annual Spend*
Farm supplies	$ 254,406
Information technology and telecommunications	17,187
Fees, levies, memberships	26,301
Energy	8,602
Financial services and interest expense	24,461
Fleet	4,229
Insurance	5,239
Packaging	10,551
Professional services	7,708
MRO & construction	127,829
Transportation services	208,927
Travel and entertainment	3,557
Other	17,350
Miscellaneous and unclassified	11,926
Total	$ 728,273

* Data for the most recent fiscal year.

EXHIBIT 3
Farm Supplies Division Inventory ($000)

Category	Average Inventory	Annual Purchases
Crop protection products	$ 65,098	$ 124,696
Equipment and supplies	22,388	13,743
Fertilizer	20,938	130,557
Seed	10,389	41,787
Total	$ 118,813	$ 310,783

THE MIS PROPOSAL

Scott was aware that the MIS Group had been asked to make a similar presentation to the executive management team. The MIS director had informed Scott that he would be requesting $10 million in additional spending beyond standard upgrades over the next five years with anticipated cost savings of about $500,000 per year.

PREPARATION FOR THE MEETING

Scott viewed the upcoming meeting as an opportunity to redefine the role of purchasing at Iowa Elevators. His session with executive management was expected to last approximately 90 minutes and he wanted to prepare a five-year plan with specific objectives for each year, including cost reduction targets. In particular, his plan for the coming year had to be very specific and include identifiable projects and initiatives, schedules, project plans, and expected costs and benefits.

As part of his proposal, Scott also wanted to establish a budget and human resource requirements that would be needed to support his recommendations. While he regarded his staff as competent, Scott recognized that he would require new managerial resources if the role of corporate purchasing was to be expanded. Consequently, he also planned on proposing a new organization structure and establishing a headcount plan and budget for the purchasing department.

As Scott reviewed Cathy's report, he began considering where he was going to start and what could be accomplished. His major concern would be resistance from the divisions and field elevator managers, and he wondered what, if anything, could be done to address any organizational resistance to his recommendations.

Case Index

Subject Index

Q